Literacy's Beginnings

Literacy's Beginnings

Supporting Young Readers and Writers

Third Edition

Lea M. McGee
University of Alabama

Donald J. Richgels
Northern Illinois University

Allyn and Bacon
BOSTON LONDON TORONTO SYDNEY TOKYO SINGAPORE

Series Editor: Arnis E. Burvikovs
Vice President, Editor in Chief, Education: Paul A. Smith
Editorial Assistant: Bridget Keane
Marketing Manager: Brad Parkins
Editorial-Production Administrator: Annette Joseph
Editorial-Production Coordinator: Holly Crawford
Editorial-Production Service: Denise Botelho, Colophon
Composition Buyer: Linda Cox
Electronic Composition: Omegatype Typography, Inc.
Manufacturing Buyer: Suzanne Lareau
Cover Designer: Jenny Hart

A Pearson Education Company
160 Gould Street
Needham Heights, MA 02494

Internet: www.abacon.com

Library of Congress Cataloging-in-Publication Data

McGee, Lea M.
Literacy's beginnings : supporting young readers and writers / Lea M. McGee, Donald J. Richgels.—3rd ed.
p. cm.
Includes bibliographical references and index.
ISBN 0-205-29931-8 (alk. paper)
1. Reading (Early childhood)—United States. 2. Language arts (Early childhood)—United States. 3. Literacy—United States.
I. Richgels, Donald J. II. Title.
LB1139.5.R43M33 2000
372.6'0973—dc21 99-40038
CIP

Printed in the United States of America

10 9 8 7 6 5 4 3 2 RRDV 04 03 02 01 00

Photo Credits: pp. 1, 110, 139, 203, 239, 339: Will Hart; p. 31: Laurie Elish-Piper; p. 55: Will Faller; pp. 83, 308: Brian Smith; pp. 171, 275: Donald Richgels

To Richard and Kristen,
and to Mary, Ted, and Carrie

Contents

Preface xv

Chapter 1 ***Understanding Children's Literacy Development*** ***1***

Key Concepts 2
Language Development 2
Schemas and Learning 2
The Relation between Language and Learning 4
Literacy Development 7
A Piagetian Approach 7
A Vygotskian Approach 7
Children's Concepts about Written Language 9
Ted's Delight: Two Children's Reading and Writing 9
Ted's and Carrie's Concepts about Written Language 11
Learning in Social and Cultural Contexts 12
Concepts about Written Language: Functions, Meanings, Forms, and Meaning-Form Links 13
Written and Spoken Language Functions 13
Written and Spoken Language Meanings 15
Semantics in Spoken Language 15
Meaning in Written Language 16
Written Language Forms 16
Syntax in Spoken Language 17
Forms in Written Language 17
Meaning-Form Links 21
Phonological System in Spoken Language 21
Meaning-Form Links, in Written Language 22
Developmental Changes in Children's Reading and Writing 24
Logographic Reading and Writing 24
Alphabetic Reading and Writing 25
Orthographic Reading and Writing 27
Chapter Summary 27
Applying the Information 28
Going Beyond the Text 29
References 29

Chapter 2 ***From Birth to Three Years: Literacy Beginners*** ***31***

Key Concepts 32
What Literacy Beginners Show Us 32

"Let's Read, Daddy": Experiences with Books and Other Familiar Print 32
Concepts about Literacy from Early Book Experiences 33
"Look at All These Raindrops": Experiences with Crayons and Markers 35
Concepts about Literacy from Early Writing Experiences 37
Home Influences on Literacy Learning 39
Booksharing 40
Environmental Print 46
Oral Language Interactions 47
Differences in Home Literacy and Language Interactions 47
Implications for Child Care and Nursery School 48
Developmentally Appropriate Practice 48
Literacy Materials 49
Responding to Children's Literacy Activities 50
Chapter Summary 50
Applying the Information 50
Going Beyond the Text 52
References 52

Chapter 3 ***From Three to Five Years: Novice Readers and Writers*** ***55***

Key Concepts 56
Who Are Novice Readers and Writers? 56
New Insights about Communicating with Written Language 56
Examples of Novices 57
Repertoire of Knowledges 59
Meaning 59
Constructing the Meaning of Environmental Print 59
Constructing Meaning While Listening to Story and Information Book Read Alouds 60
Writing Meaningful Messages 63
Written Language Forms 65
Alphabet Letters 65
Signatures 66
Texts 68
Meaning-Form Links 71
Contextual Dependency 71
Matching Print to Spoken Language: More Than Contextual Dependency 72
Drawing and Writing 72
Phonological Awareness 74
Written Language Functions 75
A Word of Caution 77
Chapter Summary 77

Applying the Information 78
Going Beyond the Text 80
References 80

Chapter 4 From Five to Seven Years: Experimenting Readers and Writers *83*

Key Concepts 84
Who Are Experimenters? 84
Experimenters' New Awareness 84
Examples of Experimenters 86
Experimenting with Meaning 87
Experimenting with Forms 87
Concept of Word 88
Concept of Word Boundaries 89
Texts 89
Experimenting with Meaning-Form Links 94
Sounding Literate 95
Being Precise 98
Using Sound–Letter Relationships 99
Experimenting with Functions of Written Language 104
A Word of Caution 104
Chapter Summary 105
Applying the Information 106
Going Beyond the Text 107
References 107

Chapter 5 From Six to Eight Years: Conventional Readers and Writers *110*

Key Concepts 111
Who Are Conventional Readers and Writers? 111
Examples: Experimenters versus Conventional Readers and Writers 112
Meaning Construction 114
Meaning Making in Reading: Using Strategies 114
Meaning Making in Reading: Constructing Interpretations of Literature 114
Meaning Making in Writing 116
Written Language Forms 117
Concept of Word 118
Story Form 118
Expository Text 122

Meaning-Form Links 128
Spelling 128
Functions 133
The Traditional End Points: Reading and Word Identification, Vocabulary, and Comprehension 133
Chapter Summary 134
Applying the Information 136
Going Beyond the Text 136
References 136

Chapter 6 Literacy-Rich Classrooms *139*

Key Concepts 140
Developmentally Appropriate Practice 140
Characteristics of Literacy-Rich Classrooms 142
Learners 142
The Classroom 142
Literacy Materials 143
Materials 143
The Case for Quality Literature 144
Classroom Literature Collection 144
Physical Arrangement of Classrooms 148
The Case for Library, Writing, and Computer Centers 148
Library Center 148
Writing Center 149
Computer Center 149
Literacy Routines 152
The Case for Classroom Routines 152
Reading Aloud and Telling Stories 153
Independent Reading and Writing 155
Sharing Response-to-Literature Activities 155
Culturally Sensitive and Integrated Curriculum 156
The Case for Culturally Sensitive and Integrated Curriculum 156
Culturally Sensitive Curriculum 157
Literature Theme Units 158
Integrated Content Units 158
Assessment, Instruction, and Grouping 159
The Case for a Variety of Instruction 160
The Case for Multiple Grouping Patterns 161
Instructional Framework 161
Chapter Summary 163
Applying the Information 164
Going Beyond the Text 166
References 166

Chapter 7 Supporting Literacy Learning in Preschools *171*

Key Concepts 172
The Preschool Context 172
What Preschoolers Learn about Literacy 172
The Preschool Setting: Space and Materials 173
Reading and Writing in Mrs. Miller's Preschool Classroom 175
Children at Play 175
The Teacher at Work: Mrs. Miller's Role 177
Preparing for Phonemic Awareness 178
The "I Can Hear" Activity 179
Making Rhymes 181
Preparing for Literary Awareness, Story Concepts, and Concepts of Print 183
Literary Awareness 183
Story Concepts 184
Concepts of Print 184
Preschool Experiences with Book Reading 186
Shared Reading in Miss Leslie's Classroom 187
Miss Leslie's Roles in an Interactive Read Aloud 189
Preschool Experiences with Writing 190
The Preschool Writing Center 191
The Sign-In Procedure 192
Shared Writing 192
Story Writing 193
The Teacher's Role in Writing Activities: Using Written Language Talk 195
Preschool Experiences with Play 196
Dramatic-Play-with-Print Centers 196
Storytelling and Playing 198
The Teacher's Role in Play: Letting Children Take the Lead 199
Another Look: The Teacher's Roles 199
Chapter Summary 200
Applying the Information 200
Going Beyond the Text 201
References 201

Chapter 8 Supporting Literacy Learning in Kindergarten *203*

Key Concepts 204
The Kindergarten Context: What's New Here? 204
What Kindergartners Learn about Literacy 204
The Teacher's Role 205
The Kindergarten Setting: Space and Materials 206

Writing and Reading in Mrs. Poremba's Kindergarten 208
Kindergartners as Researchers 209
The Teacher as Guide: Mrs. Poremba Guides Reading and Discussion 209
Helping Children Attend to Sounds in Words 211
The "What Can You Show Us?" Activity 212
Returning to "Rounding Up the Rhymes" 216
Kindergarten Experiences with Reading 219
Using Classroom Print 219
Shared Reading 220
Shared Reading with Big Books 223
Kindergarten Experiences with Writing 226
Journal Writing 226
The Extended Sign-In Procedure 228
Shared Writing 229
Kindergarten Experiences with Play 232
Dramatic-Play-with-Print Centers 232
Dramatizing Informational Books 234
Another Look: The Teacher's Roles 235
Chapter Summary 236
Applying the Information 237
Going Beyond the Text 237
References 237

Chapter 9 ***Supporting Literacy Learning in First Grade*** ***239***

Key Concepts 240
What's New Here? 240
Learning to Read Conventionally 241
Balanced First Grade Reading and Writing Programs 243
Basal Approaches to First Grade Reading Instruction 244
Reading in Mrs. Walker's First Grade 247
Guided Reading Approach to First Grade Reading 255
Characteristics of Guided Reading 256
Guided Reading Instruction in Mrs. Tran's First Grade 256
Writing Instruction in First Grade 266
Journal Writing 266
Writing Workshop 267
Chapter Summary 272
Applying the Information 273
Going Beyond the Text 273
References 273

Chapter 10 ***Supporting Literacy Learning Beyond First Grade*** ***275***

Key Concepts 276
What's New Here? 276
Increasing Expectations for Traditional Skills and Child-Centered Classrooms 276
New Competence 277
A Balanced Reading and Writing Program 277
Using Writing and Reading Workshop 278
Writing Workshop 278
Reading Workshop 282
Reading and Writing Narratives 283
Core Literature Approach 283
Expanding Comprehension and Interpretation 285
Reading and Writing Poetry 293
Enjoying Poetry 293
Poetic Elements 295
Reading and Writing Informational Text 295
Comprehension of Informational Books 295
Content Units 296
Writing Informational Texts 298
Content Specific Vocabulary 299
Learning Conventions 300
Word Study 301
Spelling Programs 302
Chapter Summary 304
Applying the Information 304
Going Beyond the Text 304
References 305

Chapter 11 ***Diverse Learners*** ***308***

Key Concepts 309
Learners at Risk 309
Using Observations to Modify Instruction 309
Literacy-Intervention Programs for At-Risk Learners 310
At-Risk Revisited 313
Special-Needs Learners 313
Supporting Special-Needs Children's Literacy 313
Avoiding Reductionist Teaching 315
Learners from Diverse Cultural Backgrounds 315
Cultural Influences on Learning 316
Culturally Responsive Instruction 316
Culturally Sensitive Instruction: A Summary 319
Culturally Sensitive Instruction in Multicultural Settings 319

Children from Diverse Language Backgrounds 323
Learners Who Speak Nonmainstream Dialects of English 323
Learners Who Speak English as a Second Language 328
Issues Related to Teaching Children from Diverse Backgrounds 332
Chapter Summary 333
Applying the Information 334
Going Beyond the Text 335
References 335

Chapter 12 Assessment *339*

Key Concepts 340
A Day in Kindergarten 340
A Day in Ms. Orlando's Classroom 340
Ms. Orlando Reflects and Plans 344
Classroom Assessment 345
Portfolio Assessment Is Multidimensional 346
Portfolio Assessment Is Reflective 347
Portfolio Assessment Is Systematic 347
Portfolio Assessment Is Collaborative 349
Assessment Tools 349
Observations 349
Alphabet Recognition Task 350
Concepts-about-Print Task 350
Phonemic Awareness Assessment 351
Emergent Reading Checklist 351
Running Record 351
Retellings 356
Grand Conversations and Response Journals 357
Compositions 360
Using Portfolios 364
Using Portfolios to Make Instructional Decision 364
Using Portfolios to Support Children's Reflections 365
Using Portfolios to Inform Parents 365
Keeping Portfolios Manageable 366
Chapter Summary 367
Applying the Information 367
Going Beyond the Text 370
References 370

Appendix: Children's Literature 373
Author Index 379
Subject Index 387

Preface

POINT OF VIEW

Literacy's Beginnings: Supporting Young Readers and Writers is intended to help preservice and inservice teachers, parents, and other caregivers of young children to be aware of and supportive of children's literacy knowledge as it grows and changes in the years from birth through early elementary school. Our purpose is to provide a guide to the long continuum of literacy growth, from the very beginning years, when children's reading and writing efforts are difficult to recognize, through the early elementary school years, when children begin to receive formal literacy instruction.

We believe that children's literacy learning is developmental, but not in the sense of proceeding in an irreversible, step-by-step progression. No child's discoveries about and experiments with literacy exactly match those of another child. Furthermore, an individual child's literacy behaviors vary in sophistication depending on the task and the situation.

Literacy learning is developmental in a very commonsensical way to anyone who has spent time writing and reading with children. Literacy learning is developmental in the sense that what an individual child knows about writing and reading changes dramatically over time. Not only do young children's constructions of literacy differ from those of adults, but children's present constructions also differ from their own former and future constructions.

We believe that teachers have an important role to play in young children's literacy learning. The subtitle of our book emphasizes the supportive nature of that role. We hope that our descriptions of literacy events involving young children and our suggestions for classroom support will help teachers to be aware of the directions in which children's literacy knowledge can move over the period covered by this book. Such awareness can make easier one of the most difficult tasks in teaching: the close observation of many different children. From a basis of careful observation, teachers can respect what children know and support children's continued learning in ways that make sense to the children.

ORGANIZATION OF THE TEXT

Literacy's Beginnings is grouped into two parts. The theme of Chapters 1 through 5 is that of learners. This part describes the children and how they grow as writers and readers. Chapter 1 is an overview of learning and literacy. We describe critical changes in children's concepts about four areas of written language: meanings, forms, meaning-form links, and functions. The next four chapters elaborate on that picture of development.

The word *literacy* has many connotations in everyday life. To us, being *literate* means being able to find meaning in written symbols. This definition includes much territory left out by everyday definitions of literacy; for example, a pretend reading of a favorite storybook qualifies as a literate act by our definition, but does not usually qualify under the everyday definition. Still, our definition does not include everything that very young children do with books and writing materials.

The terms *beginner, novice, experimenter,* and *conventional reader and writer* also demand clarification. We use them as convenient shorthand for the developments described in Chapters 2 through 5, but we do not mean for them to define rigid, irreversible stages. Indeed, we do not call them stages. A child may exhibit many of the knowledges in the cluster of knowledges that we associate with one of those four terms. Furthermore, a child who usually reads or writes like a novice in some situations and with some tasks will also read or write like an experimenter. The important point is that, over time, children will more often resemble conventional readers and writers.

The second part of *Literacy's Beginnings* concerns *classrooms,* and characteristics of school environments and teacher roles that promote children's development from beginners to conventional readers and writers. Chapter 6 is an overview of the elements included in a literacy-rich classroom. Chapter 7 focuses on preschool, Chapter 8 on kindergarten, Chapter 9 on first grade, and Chapter 10 on second grade and third grade. Chapter 11 describes the literacy needs of diverse learners, and Chapter 12 addresses assessment issues and methods.

This third edition of *Literacy's Beginnings* has several **new features:**

- more information about phonological and phonemic awareness and functional, contextualized ways teachers can promote phonemic awareness
- more attention to the role of computers in young children's explorations of literacy
- a description of the guided reading approach to literacy instruction including interactive writing in first grade
- greater attention to reading and writing of informational texts
- more activities with poetry
- more emphasis on strategy instruction within social-interactive learning groups

Each chapter of *Literacy's Beginnings* again has four sections designed to help readers consolidate and apply what they have learned. First, we list the key concepts used in the chapter. Applying the Information presents a case study on children's interactions with written language similar to the many examples given in the chapter. The reader is asked to apply the chapter's concepts to this example. Going Beyond the Text suggests ways for readers to seek out real-life experiences that will test both the chapter's ideas and the readers' understandings. We ask questions and make suggestions to guide readers' planning and reflecting on those experiences. Finally, References provides a list of all publications cited in the chapter.

THE CHILDREN AND TEACHERS IN THIS BOOK

Literacy's Beginnings is based in part on a growing body of research about emerging literacy and in part on our experiences with young children, including our own children. We incorporate many descriptions of those experiences. We wish to add here two important cautions that we will repeat throughout the text. The first is about children's ages. We usually give the age of the children in our examples in order to fully represent the facts. However, we do not intend for those ages to serve as norms against which to compare other children.

Our second caution is about backgrounds. Many, but not all, of the children in our examples have had numerous and varied home experiences with books and writing materials. Their meaningful interactions with written language are often what one would expect of children from such environments. Children with different backgrounds may exhibit different initial orientations toward written language. However, our involvement with teachers whose children come to preschool or elementary school with different backgrounds has shown us that nearly all children can benefit from the informed observation and child-centered, meaning-oriented support described in this book.

The classroom support chapters of this book are based on our own teaching experiences and on our observations of teachers. Just as we have known and observed many literate young children, so also have we known and observed many very sensitive, intelligent, and effective teachers of young children. All the samples of children's reading and writing in this book are authentic cases from our own research and the research of others cited in the text.

ACKNOWLEDGMENTS

We owe a great deal to the many children whose experiences with written language were the basis for much of this book. We thank them and their parents for cooperating so generously with us—for supporting *us* in the extended "literacy event" of writing this book. We thank the teachers who shared their classroom experiences with us: Mary Jane Everett, Candice Jones, Karen Kurr, Roberta McHardy, Nancy Miller, Terry Morel, Kathy Walker, Leigh Courtney, Karen King, Jackie Zickuhr, Carolyn Vaughn, Monette Reyes, Karla Poremba, Diane Roloff, Cindi Chandler, Laurie Coleman, Richard Lomax, and Michelle Tran.

We owe much to the editors and their assistants at Allyn and Bacon, including Virginia Lanigan, Annette Joseph, and Bridget Keane. We are also grateful to Denise Botelho at Colophon for her careful handling of the manuscript during editing and production. We thank Linda D. Labbo of the University of Georgia for helpful comments and suggestions.

We acknowledge the contributions of our many students. We learned from our discussions with them about literacy's beginnings and from the examples they shared of their interactions with young readers and writers.

Literacy's Beginnings

Chapter 1

Understanding Children's Literacy Development

Key Concepts

concepts
schemas
features
related concepts
personal experiences
tabula rasa
zone of proximal development
scaffolding
meaning-form link
pragmatics
semantics
syntax
phonology
functions
meaning
morpheme
contextualization clues
literary language
forms
graphemes
mock letters
left-to-right organization
top-to-bottom organization
linearity
metalinguistic awareness
concept of word
sound–letter relationships
phonemes
phonological knowledge
phonological awareness
phonemic awareness
grapho-phonic relationships
phonics
orthographics
phonograms
logographic reading and writing
beginners
novices
alphabetic reading and writing
experimenters
conventional readers and writers
orthographic readers and writers

LANGUAGE DEVELOPMENT

How do children begin the process of becoming successful lifelong readers and writers? We begin to answer that question by looking at theories of language development. Piaget (1955) and Vygotsky (1978) examined how children acquire language and the relationship of language to thinking. Each of their theories makes unique contributions to what we understand about young children's literacy development. We use their theories first to explain learning in general and then to explore how learning and language acquisition are related.

Schemas and Learning

An important idea from both Piaget's and Vygotsky's theories is that learning occurs as children acquire new **concepts,** or **schemas.** A concept or schema is a mental structure in which we store all the information we know about people, places, objects, or activities.

Schemas

Consider the concept "pineapple": take a moment to write down everything called to mind by the mention of the word *pineapple.* The word probably brings to most people's minds several **features** of pineapples (that they are fruity, sweet, juicy, hard to eat, spiky, fresh, or canned) and several **related concepts** (Hawaii, fruit salad, fruit cocktail, sharp knife, piña colada, bananas, mangoes, garbage—lots to throw away with fresh pineapples).

The word *pineapple* also may bring to mind actual experiences with pineapples (such as the time you bought a rotten one or the time you did not use the knife you usually use for coring a pineapple—what a disaster!).

The reason that people recall knowledge about features, related concepts, and **personal experiences** associated with the word *pineapple* is that concepts or schemas are organized. That is, as we have personal experiences with pineapples (seeing them at the grocery, eating them, preparing them, and so on), we make mental associations among the word *pineapples,* the concept that word stands for, and the sights, sounds, tastes, smells, and sensations that contributed to our forming that concept. We see that pineapples have spikes at the top, so we automatically make a mental association between the concept "pineapple" and the quality "spiky." We taste that pineapples are sweet, so we automatically make another mental association, this time between the concept "pineapple" and the taste "sweet." Thus, concepts are organized through associations.

We have schemas for many things, including objects, such as "trophy" or "dining room table"; people, such as "president of the United States" or "fashion model"; places, such as "college" or "home"; and activities or events, such as "going to the dentist" or "looking for a job." Thinking and learning depend on these many schemas or concepts. Thinking involves calling to mind information from schemas and using that information to make inferences, predict, draw conclusions, or generalize. For example, suppose we see someone at the grocery store pulling on the green spiky top of a pineapple. We might make an inference that this person is testing the "ripeness" of pineapples.

Similarly, learning involves adding to or changing schemas. Suppose we see, for the first time, someone save the green, spiky-leafed top of a pineapple, root it, and grow it as a houseplant. We might modify our pineapple schema to include the new feature "decorative," and it may become newly connected to such concepts as "houseplant" and "asexual reproduction" (growing a new plant from a leaf, root, or stem of an old plant, rather than from a seed).

Infants and Schemas

Children begin life with few concepts—or even none. Children's minds may be thought of as vacant structures, or empty schemas. There are only empty slots where features can go. This is the **tabula rasa,** or blank slate, notion of the young child's mind. One of Piaget's greatest insights was a suggestion of how children acquire the knowledge to begin filling those slots with features and making connections among schemas. He suggested that the infant's mind is actually far from a blank slate. It is true that young children have no (or very little) knowledge of content or the things (such as pineapples) that will eventually occupy their minds. However, children do have considerable inborn knowledge of processes. They seem to know how to go about acquiring content knowledge, or knowledge of things.

Piaget's idea was that young humans learn through action. They are born with special schemas for how to act and how to respond to their world. These action schemas bring children in contact with reality (things) in ways that produce knowledge of the world. More action produces more knowledge. As children acquire knowledge and continue to act, changes result in the things they are in contact with (for example, milk gets spilled) and changes result in previous knowledge (for example, the schema for milk changed to include the idea that milk does not behave like a cracker—it doesn't keep a shape). The action schemas themselves change as active, problem-solving children evolve more effective strategies for making their way in the world.

Two very important conclusions can be drawn from Piaget's theory of how children learn. One is that children create their own knowledge by forming and reforming concepts in their minds. The second conclusion is that children's state of knowledge—or view of the world—can be very different from one time to the next, and especially different from an adult's.

The point we wish to emphasize is that, because children construct their own knowledge, this knowledge does not come fully developed and is often quite different from that of an adult. Thus, there are differences between how an adult understands concepts and how a child understands concepts. Similarly, a young child's concepts about reading and writing are naturally different from, but no less important than, an adult's concepts about reading and writing.

The Relation between Language and Learning

We have already discussed the importance of action to Piaget's idea of learning. Children's actions may physically change objects in the world. A child may pull or stretch a lump of modeling clay, changing its shape. But then that same action may change the child's concept of modeling clay, adding the feature "stretchy," and it may allow the child to see a connection between modeling clay and bread dough (NOVA, 1985).

But can children change their schema for modeling clay to include the notion that it is stretchy without their hearing or using the word *stretchy?* Can they pretend that modeling clay is bread dough without hearing someone else say, or being able themselves to say, that both are "stretchy"? Another way to put these questions is to ask: How important is it for the child to have the word *stretchy* available as a label for what is experienced in such a situation? Vygotsky stressed the importance of having someone with the child who could supply that language. According to Vygotsky, a mother who says to her child, "Look at that stretchy clay!" plays a vital role in her child's learning about clay. Vygotsky placed a strong emphasis on the social component of cognitive and language development.

Social Basis for Learning

Vygotsky argued that all learning first takes place in a social context. In order to build a new concept, children interact with others who provide feedback for their hypotheses or who help them accomplish a task they could not do on their own. Children's or adults' language is an important part of the social context of learning. Suppose that a child's concept of the letter *W* does not include its conventional orientation (upright). This child may write  and call it *W.* Another child who observes this writing may say, "That's not a *W,* that's an *M.*" This feedback provides the child with a label for the new concept, *M,* and prompts the child to reconsider the concept of *W* by adding an orientation (upright).

Vygotsky believed that children need to be able to talk about a new problem or a new concept in order to understand it and use it. Adults supply language that fits children's needs at a particular stage or in response to a particular problem. Language can be part of a routinized situation. It can label the situation or parts of the situation, or it can help pose a problem or structure a problem-solving task. As the child gradually internalizes the language that was first supplied by an adult, the language and a routine task that helps in solving the problem become the child's own.

An example of a child's internalizing the language of a routine is how the child learns to use the words *all gone.* The parents of a child might repeatedly hide a favorite toy and then say, "All gone!" Then they reveal the toy and say, "Here it is!" This becomes a game for the child. Eventually, the child may play the game without the adult, using the same language, "All gone" and "Here it is."

We can draw two important conclusions from the "all gone" example. First, it suggests that language and cognition really emerge at about the same time. Perhaps using the word *gone* helps children to solve the cognitive problem of object permanence, or perhaps *gone* suddenly acquires a fascination for children who have just solved that problem, making it a word they are very likely to use (Gopnick & Meltzoff, 1986; Meltzoff, 1985).

Second, it suggests that learning is a matter of internalizing the language and actions of others. A young child's ability to play the game of "all gone" alone means that he or she has internalized the actions and language of his or her mother or father. For Vygotsky all learning involves a movement from doing activities in a social situation with the support of a more knowledgeable other to internalizing the language and actions of the more knowledgeable other and being able to use this knowledge alone.

Zone of Proximal Development

Vygotsky spoke of a **zone of proximal development,** which is an opportune area for growth, but one in which children are dependent on help from others. An adult, or perhaps an older child, must give young children advice if they are to succeed within this zone and if eventually, by internalizing that advice, they are to perform independently.

When children are working in their zone of proximal development, they complete some parts of a task, and adults or older children perform the parts of the task that the younger children cannot yet do alone. In this way, young children can accomplish tasks that are too difficult for them to complete on their own. Adults' or older children's talk is an important part of helping young children—it scaffolds the task. **Scaffolding** talk gives advice, directs children's attention, alerts them to the sequence of activities, and provides information for completing the task successfully. Gradually, children internalize this talk and use it to direct their own attention, plan, and control their activities.

Figure 1.1 presents a letter that five-year-old Kristen and her mother wrote together. After Kristen's second day in kindergarten, she announced, "I'm not going to school tomorrow. I don't like being last in line." Apparently, Kristen rode a different bus from any of the other children in her classroom and the teacher called her last to line up for the buses. When Kristen's mother reminded her of all the things she liked to do in school, Kristen replied, "Okay, I'll go [to school], but you tell Mrs. Peters [the teacher] I don't want to be last all the time." Kristen's mother said, "We'll write her a note. You write it and I'll help." Kristen agreed and wrote Mrs. Peter's name as her mother spelled it. Then Kristen said the message she wanted to write ("I always don't want to be the last person in the line"). Her mother said, "The first word is *I*. You can spell that. What letter do you hear?" Kristen wrote the letter *i,* but when her mother began saying the word *always* slowly for Kristen to spell, she refused to spell any more words. So Kristen's mother wrote *always* and then spelled the word *don't* for Kristen to write. She suggested that she write one word and Kristen write one word. As shown in Figure 1.1, the final letter is a combination of Kristen's writing, with invented or incomplete spellings (*t* for *to, b* for *be, Lst* for *last,* and *pwsn* for *person*) as she listened to her mother say each sound in a word, and her mother's writing. Kristen could not have accomplished the task of writing this letter without her mother's scaffolding.

A year and a half later, Kristen ran into the kitchen where her mother was preparing dinner and handed her the note shown in Figure 1.2. This note reads, "I hate when you brought me to Penny's house" (Penny is Kristen's baby-sitter). Kristen had written the note in her room by herself after her mother was late picking her up. This note illustrates the results of scaffolding and working within the zone of proximal development. In kindergarten, Kristen needed her mother's scaffolding to write a letter of protest to her teacher. She needed her mother's support to hear sounds in words, to keep track of what she had written, and to sustain the effort of writing. At the end of first grade, she could write a letter of protest on her own, inventing spellings and reading to keep track of her message as she wrote.

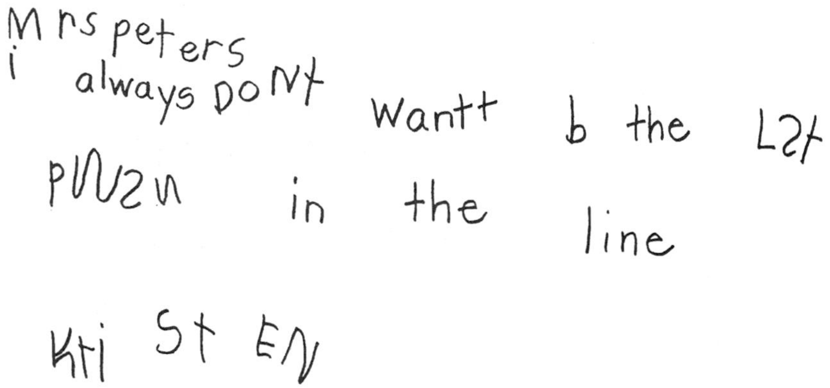
Mrs peters
i always DONt Wantt b the L2t
pWzn in the line
KrI St EN

Figure 1.1 *Kristen's Letter to Her Teacher*

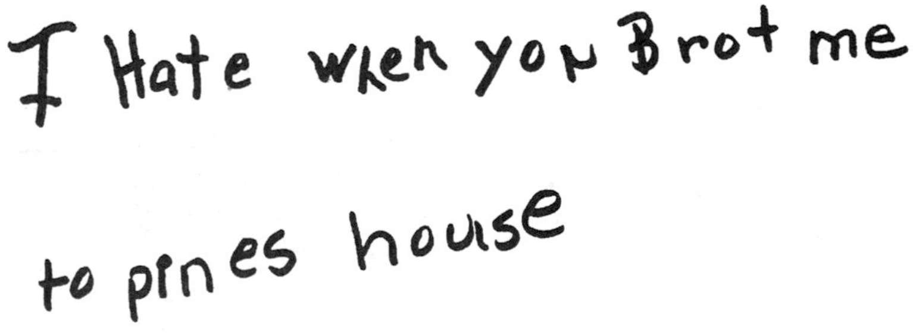
I Hate when you Brot me
to pines house

Figure 1.2 *Kristen's Letter to Her Mother*

LITERACY DEVELOPMENT

Children learn about written language in much the same way in which they learn anything else, including spoken language. They acquire and modify schemas or concepts for various aspects of written language knowledge. They use inborn abilities, and they depend on interactions with others. There are both Piagetian and Vygotskian perspectives on learning written language.

A Piagetian Approach

The Piagetian perspective of literacy development emphasizes stages of development. From this view we would expect that young children's reading and writing behavior at some stages would be very different from adults' reading and writing because it reflects concepts of reading and writing *as the child has constructed them.*

Children's concepts of reading and writing are shaped more by what they accomplished in preceding developmental stages than by their simply imitating adults' behavior or following adults' directions. At an early stage, many children write a word such as Klm vst. This writing reveals that their concept of words might be stated something like this: "Words are a string of letters with spaces between." Of course, words are not strings of randomly selected letters; yet, many preschoolers and kindergartners operate with this concept (Ferreiro & Teberosky, 1982). They may write a string of letters and bring it to their teacher and ask, "What did I write?" They do so because they have a concept of a written word that is very different from an adult's concept. It does not matter that children see adults using letters related to sounds in a particular order. They may actually resent an adult's insistence that they have not spelled a word at all. Adults need not be alarmed about such unconventional concepts. Children eventually develop new, more conventional concepts as they gain experience reading and writing. We explore many of these experiences in the later chapters of this book.

A Vygotskian Approach

The Vygotskian perspective of literacy learning emphasizes social interaction and places less emphasis on predetermined stages of behavior than does a Piagetian view. It focuses instead on the social aspect of young children's literacy behaviors, especially on their intending to communicate with others (Harste, Burke, & Woodward, 1983; Harste, Woodward, & Burke, 1984) and on their using routines to learn about written language (Snow, 1983).

A very young child's unconventional drawing and writing do not always look meaningful. When adults cannot understand what a child intended, they often assume that nothing was intended. However, it is just as important with written language as with spoken language for adults to show children that they know the children intend to convey meanings. One of the best ways of ensuring that this is done is for the child and adult to have routine ways of interacting during literacy events.

We illustrate the importance of expecting children's writing and reading to be meaningful in the following example. Figure 1.3 looks like a meaningless conglomeration of random letters, pictures, and scribbles. It is actually a very meaningful piece; its composition was not at all haphazard.

Figure 1.3 *Cody's Drawing and Writing*

Four-year-old Cody was staying for a few hours with one of her mother's friends. After they had spent time looking at books together, the friend asked Cody if she wanted to write her own book. Cody said she could write her name. She said, "My name is C-O-D-Y" as she wrote the letters CODY (see Figure 1.4). Next, Cody wanted to write an *S*, but said to her friend, "I can't write *S*. Will you write *S* for me?" The friend wrote the large *S* shown in the upper right in Figure 1.3 and then urged Cody to draw a picture for her book. Cody said she would draw herself and proceeded to draw her face, hair, mouth, nose, and eyes (see the face in the upper left in Figure 1.3). When she had finished her drawing, Cody wrote three wavy lines and identified them: "I wrote a bedtime story" (see Figure 1.5). Next, Cody said, "I need a blanket." She scribbled all over the top of her bedtime story (that is, over her wavy lines—making them look like Figure 1.6) and announced, "There is my blanket." Finally, she asked her friend, "How do you spell your name?" Her friend said, "L-E-A." First Cody said "A" and then "E" as she wrote those letters (seen in the bottom right of Figure 1.3). Then she asked, "Now how do you write *L*?" and wrote the backwards *L* in her friend's name shown in Figure 1.3.

Figure 1.4
Cody's Signature

Figure 1.5
Cody's Bedtime Story

Figure 1.6
Cody's Picture of a Blanket

It is probably clear by now that the haphazard-looking drawing in Figure 1.3 is a bedtime story. Because the three wavy lines were so quickly covered up, Cody's friend could not ask her to read the bedtime story, and so we may only guess what it is about. However, this written record of it survives, complete with Cody's name, her friend's name, and a picture of Cody under a blanket.

It is fascinating to note Cody's sophisticated knowledge about written language. She writes names with real letters. Her story is composed of wavy lines that simulate the lines of print on a book's page. This shows that she knows that a story involves a lot more writing than a name does. She strives for unity—the very opposite of haphazardness. She even connected her self-portrait with her bedtime story by putting it under a blanket. It is important to note that all of this would have gone undetected and unsupported if her adult friend had not treated Cody as a writer, communicating the message to Cody that, like the authors of the books they had read together, Cody could write a book. This example provides evidence of the power of the zone of proximal development and the scaffolding of a more knowledgeable other.

CHILDREN'S CONCEPTS ABOUT WRITTEN LANGUAGE

We have shown that children acquire spoken language as they acquire concepts about objects, people, places, and events. Similarly, children acquire literacy as they develop schema for written language. In this part of the chapter, we describe in detail children's concepts about written language. We begin with a case study of Ted and Carrie as they are playing restaurant.

Ted's Delight: Two Children's Reading and Writing

Ted, who is eight years old, and his sister Carrie, who is three years old, were playing in the corner of the living room. They had set up their card table playhouse. Taped on the playhouse was the sign shown in Figure 1.7.

Figure 1.7 *"Ted's Delight" Sign*

Ted and Carrie had collected Carrie's plastic play food and doll dishes and put them behind the playhouse. When their father entered the room, he looked at the sign and said, "Oh, I think I need some lunch." The children asked him to visit their restaurant. He entered the playhouse, and Carrie presented him with a menu (Figure 1.8).

Carrie asked, "May I take your order?" Her father read the menu and said, "I'll take pancakes and coffee." Carrie checked off two items on the menu and took it out to Ted, who was behind the playhouse. He pretended to fix pancakes and pour coffee. Ted brought the dishes into the playhouse to his father, who pretended to eat with much relish. When he had finished he asked, "May I have my check, please?" Carrie picked up a pad of paper and a pencil and wrote a check (Figure 1.9). Her father pretended to pay the check and left the playhouse.

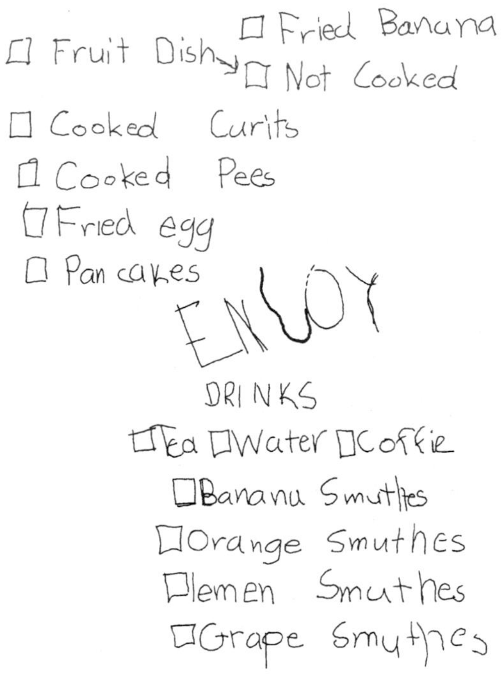

Figure 1.8 *"Ted's Delight" Menu*

Figure 1.9 *Carrie's Check*

Later that evening, the family discussed the restaurant play. Ted said he had made the sign so that the playhouse could be a restaurant. He had asked Carrie if he could use her toy food and dishes. She had wanted to play, too. Ted said that he and Carrie decided to write on the menu the names of the play food they had. In the middle of his writing the menu, Carrie insisted on helping him. "She wrote the letter that looks like a backwards *J* in the middle of the menu," Ted reported. "I had to turn it into the word *Enjoy* to make sense."

Ted's and Carrie's Concepts about Written Language

What do Ted's and Carrie's reading and writing reveal about their concepts of written language? First, both Ted's and Carrie's behaviors indicate that they understand many ways in which written language is used. Carrie knows that a waitperson writes something when a customer orders and when the customer asks for the check. She seems to be learning, just as Ted is, that writing and reading are functional. Ted and Carrie used written language to get their customer into their restaurant (they made a sign), to let their customer know what was available to eat (they made a menu), and to let their customer know how much the meal cost (they wrote a check).

Second, the sign and menu Ted wrote suggest that he is learning about written language meanings. His sign communicated a message to his father: a restaurant is open for business. Ted also knows that the messages communicated in written language should be meaningful given the written language context. Ted knew that the "backwards *J*" that Carrie wrote somehow had to be incorporated into a message that could be communicated on a menu. Random letters on menus do not communicate meaningful messages. Ted made the random letter meaningful by incorporating it into the word *Enjoy*. Carrie also showed that she knows that written language communicates meaning. Even though we cannot read her check, her behavior as she gave it to her father (and her father's reactions to the written check) suggests that her writing communicates a message something like "pay some money for your food."

Third, the sign and menu indicate that Ted is learning about written language forms—what written language looks like. These two writing samples certainly look like a sign and a menu. His menu is written in the form of a list. The content of his menu is organized as a menu is usually organized—drinks and food are grouped and listed separately. Carrie is also learning what at least a few written language forms look like. The writing on her check looks something like the letters *E* and *J*. Even though Carrie's letters are not yet conventional, they signal that she is paying attention to what letters look like. Although Carrie's *E*'s sometimes have too many horizontal lines, she has obviously noticed that horizontal lines are included on letters. And, even though Carrie's *J*'s seem to be backwards, she does include the hook expected on this letter. There is one exception. Carrie put a circle on her letter *E;* most letter *E*'s do not include circles. Figure 1.10 (Carrie's name written as her preschool teacher wrote it) suggests why Carrie may have included the circle on her *E*. Her preschool teacher often used what she called "bubble writing," putting small decorative bubbles on each alphabet letter. Carrie noticed that her preschool teacher wrote circles on her letters, so Carrie may have decided to put the same circles on her own letters.

Finally, Ted's and Carrie's writing demonstrates that they are learning a unique system of written language: the manner in which written language conveys meaning. In English, the way written language conveys meaning is that written words map onto spoken

Figure 1.10 *"Carrie" as Written by Her Preschool Teacher*

words. We call this unique system of written language the **meaning-form link.** In English, the meaning-form link is that written words relate to meaning by being translated into spoken words. Therefore, English is considered an alphabetic language, and learning about sound–letter relationships is an important part of reading and writing. Ted demonstrated his understanding of the alphabetic meaning-form link in his spelling errors. Ted's spelling of *pees* for *peas* shows that he knows that the letters *ee* often take the sound of long *e.*

Carrie's writing demonstrates that she does not yet know sound–letter relationships, the most sophisticated level of the meaning-form link. However, Carrie is using a less sophisticated meaning-form link in her writing. Like many preschoolers, she uses a different concept of meaning-form link. Her concept about how writing can convey meaning is that she writes letters and assumes that a reader, her father, will be able to read her message. We will show that many preschoolers have this concept about the meaning-form link in written language.

Learning in Social and Cultural Contexts

Ted's and Carrie's reading and writing in the "Ted's Delight" case study provides important insights into *how* children acquire written language concepts. Young children are embedded in social environments constructed, in part, by particular family activities and expectations and, in part, by broader cultural and social group memberships (Scollon & Scollon, 1981). These social and cultural contexts support particular kinds of activities, including activities in which reading and writing are used (Taylor, 1983). They allow children to learn and engage in particular kinds of knowledge as a result of engaging in these activities, including learning concepts about the functions, meanings, forms, and meaning-form links of written language (Purcell-Gates, 1995).

Ted and Carrie were engaging in a play activity that was supported by their father and by the social expectations of their mainstream culture. Ted's and Carrie's father entered the play as a highly experienced playmate, extending their "restaurant" dramatic play by enacting all the events that would be expected in a visit to a real restaurant. He scaffolded their play through his words and actions.

Ted's and Carrie's play was also supported by the *expectations* of their family and mainstream culture. Their father and mother are professionals who expect that their children will become proficient readers and writers. Education is valued in their home, and many opportunities are provided for Ted and Carrie to engage in reading and writing. Ted's and Carrie's play revealed some of the experiences that support their literacy acquisition. They have visited many restaurants and participated in reading menus, selecting entrees and drinks, ordering food, and paying for meals.

Concepts about Written Language: Functions, Meanings, Forms, and Meaning-Form Links

Ted and Carrie have learned a great deal about written language, but their knowledge is not unique. As researchers have studied young children in other literacy events, they have discovered that all children—even those who are not traditionally reading and writing—acquire similar concepts, which we have labeled in our case study, "concepts about written language":

functions

meanings

forms

meaning-form links

We selected these labels for describing children's concepts about written language to reflect that children are developing unique concepts about written language systems. However, these concepts are also related to children's acquisition of four linguistic systems of spoken language:

pragmatics

semantics

syntax

phonology

Pragmatics deals with social and cultural contexts of speaking and conveys the function or purpose of speech. **Semantics** is related to the system of meaning, including the meaning of words and their combinations. **Syntax** is related to the order and organization of words in sentences. **Phonology** is the system of approximately forty-four speech sounds that make up all English words.

WRITTEN AND SPOKEN LANGUAGE FUNCTIONS

An important part of learning to read and write involves learning about the **functions** or purposes that written language serves. Children have a head start learning about written language's functions because they already use their spoken language to meet a variety of needs. Children, like the adults around them, use their spoken language in functional ways. Halliday (1975) identified seven functions of spoken language. These functions represent different ways in which we use language. Table 1.1 summarizes Halliday's seven functions of language, using examples from children's spoken language as illustrations of each (Halliday, 1975).

Since children are acquainted with using spoken language for several purposes, it is not surprising that they learn how to use written language to accomplish a variety of goals as

Table 1.1 Halliday's Language Functions

LANGUAGE	FUNCTION	SPOKEN LANGUAGE EXAMPLES	WRITTEN LANGUAGE EXAMPLES
Instrumental	satisfies needs and wants	"I want to watch Big Bird." "I want the colors."	advertisements, bills, reminder notes, sign-up sheet
Regulatory	controls others	"Don't use purple." "Andrew, stop."	traffic signs, policy statements, directions
Interactional	creates interaction with others	"Let's go in the playroom." "Who wants the rest?"	personal letters, notes, personals in the newspaper
Personal	expresses personal thoughts and opinions	"I like Mr. T." "I'm not tired."	editorials, diaries, autobiographies, journals
Heuristic	seeks information	"What does this say?" "What is that?"	letters of request and inquiry, application forms, registration forms
Imaginative	creates imaginary worlds	"You be Judy and I'm Peewee." "This is a big green haystack."	poetry, drama, stories
Informative	communicates information	"Dad's giving a speech tonight." "The flowers opened."	wedding announcements, obituaries, dictionaries, textbooks, reports, telephone books

Adapted from Halliday, 1975.

well. In fact, many of written language's purposes are the same as those of spoken language. Table 1.1 also presents several examples of written language that serve each of Halliday's seven functions.

However, written language also serves unique purposes. We use written language to establish identity or authority. For example, two groups of preschoolers were arguing about the use of a large refrigerator box. One group insisted that the box should be a dollhouse. The other group wanted it to be a fire station. Two boys in the fire station group went to a mother helper and asked her to write the words *fire station.* They copied her writing on a large sheet of paper and taped it to the box. One child pointed to the sign and said, "This is not a house. This is a fire station" (Cochran-Smith, 1984, p. 90).

Written language also has the unique power to make language and thinking permanent and transportable (Stubbs, 1980). We can communicate with others over long distances and share information with people we have never met face-to-face. Because information can be recorded and reread, facts can be accumulated and studied critically. New knowledge is built from a critical analysis of accumulated past knowledge.

WRITTEN AND SPOKEN LANGUAGE MEANINGS

Meaning is at the heart of both spoken and written language (Halliday, 1975). The human experience demands that we communicate messages to one another, and humans are constantly engaged in meaning-making activities whether through face-to-face conversations or through reading and writing. However, meaning is slippery; we must work hard to get and convey it in everyday conversations and in reading and writing. Messages we construct from conversations are never exact; they always differ in some degree from what was actually spoken. All of us have experienced not being understood; we say, "But, that's not what I meant!" Meaning involves more than just capturing the words others say. It involves interpreting messages.

Semantics in Spoken Language

One aspect of semantics, or the system of meaning, is knowing units of meaning. We usually consider the smallest unit of meaning a word; but units of meaning can actually be smaller than a word. Linguists call the smallest unit of meaning a **morpheme.** The word *start* consists of one morpheme, while the word *restart* has two morphemes: *re* and *start. Re* is considered a morpheme because it alters the meaning of the word *start* when it is added to the word. Other morphemes can be added to *start* that will alter meaning by changing the verb tense, such as adding *ed* or *s.* Morphemes can also alter meaning by changing the part of speech, such as when adding *able* to *drink.*

The meaning of words is an important part of the semantic system. We have already discussed how young children begin acquiring word meanings by developing schema or concepts related to words. For example, the meaning of the word *pineapple* may include knowing *spiky, sweet, fruit, yellow, juicy,* and *buy it at the grocery.* We have also stressed that because people have different experiences related to words, they have different meanings associated with them.

Strategies for understanding and conveying meaning in spoken language also apply to written language (Wolf, 1984). Children naturally apply their meaning-making strategies in everyday experiences. When asked what a grocery list might say, a four-year-old will reply, "green beans, bread, coffee." When dictating a letter, five-year-olds say, "I love you." When asked what a traffic sign might say, they reply, "Watch out for children walking." Young children's concepts about meaning are related to their experiences in which different kinds of texts are used. Four-year-olds know the meanings associated with grocery lists because they know the kinds of things found in a grocery store and have shopped with their parents as they read from a grocery list. Young children's concepts about meanings are tied to their awareness of the context in which written language is used and to the variety of written text forms they have observed.

Reading and writing, of course, are only a few of the ways in which we can communicate meanings. We also communicate meanings through facial expression, gesture, dance, art, conversation, and music. For young children, communicating in spoken language and play are very closely related to communicating in written language (Rowe, 1998). Three-year-old Carrie was able to communicate a message through her conventional writing in the context of restaurant dramatic play. Throughout this book are other examples of children's meaning making as they engage in a variety of playful activities.

Meaning in Written Language

However, strategies that are needed to construct meaning in written language are not always needed for spoken language. One difference, paradoxically, is that written language is not exactly talk written down (Cook-Gumperz, 1986). Meaning in spoken language is often conveyed through gestures, facial expressions, and voice intonation, which provide additional **contextualization clues** to meaning. Much spoken language takes place in a context in which the actual objects discussed can be seen, or between people who know a great deal about each other.

Consider a young child saying, "Cookie" to her mother. Without understanding the context—what the mother and child are doing at the time of the utterance—it is difficult to determine the meaning of "cookie." However, suppose we know that it is mid-afternoon, the child has just arisen from a nap, the afternoon routine usually involves a snack, and the child is sitting in her highchair pointing to the cupboard where cookies are kept. Then we know the utterance "cookie" probably means something like, "I'd like my cookie now." In contrast to spoken language, written language does not include contextualization clues such as the context or pointing to objects.

Another difference between spoken and written language is that written language makes more frequent use of unusual words, words that are rarely used in everyday conversation. Words such as *display, exposure, equate, infinite, invariably, literal, luxury, maneuver, participation, provoke,* or *reluctantly* (Cunningham & Stanovich, 1998, p. 10) are found in written stories, newspapers, or textbooks. However, these words are rarely used in daily conversation. Similarly, written language includes **literary language** phrases such as "once upon a time" and "in the previous section," which are not found in everyday spoken language.

Lack of contextualization clues and use of unusual words and literary language are just two examples of the characteristics of written language that require readers and writers to use meaning-making strategies that are not needed by listeners and speakers. As we will show later in the book, reading aloud to young children is a critical pathway to developing the kinds of meaning-making strategies that are necessary for becoming accomplished readers and writers.

WRITTEN LANGUAGE FORMS

We use the label written language **forms** to highlight the visual and spatial components of written language. Written language form knowledge includes awareness of visual symbols, spatial directional properties, and spatially organized formats of texts. For example, in the earlier case study, Carrie was learning the visual shapes of alphabet letters. While her letters are not yet totally conventional, she did show attention to many visual features of letters, such as the vertical and horizontal lines found in the letter *E.* Similarly, Ted demonstrated a sophisticated knowledge of the spatial organization of a specific kind of text, a menu.

He organized words related to drinks below the words organized as entrees. Ted's menu demonstrated a sophisticated awareness of visual and spatial organization.

Syntax in Spoken Language

Learning the visual shapes and spatial organizational properties of text is unique to learning written language. However, learning about order and organization in written language is similar to learning about order and organization in spoken language. Spoken language relies on order and organization at the level of words, sentences, and larger discourse units such as stories, jokes, and gossip. One system of spoken language that relies heavily on order and organization is the syntactic system.

Syntax is the set of rules for how to produce and comprehend sentences in language and draws on order and organization. In some languages, including English, the order of words in sentences is crucial (consider, for example, *The boy kicked the goat* versus *The goat kicked the boy*). In other languages, word order is not important. Instead, word endings are critical for understanding who did what to whom (*Lupus agnum portat,* which means, "The wolf carries the lamb," versus *Lupum agnus portat,* which means, "The lamb carries the wolf").

Forms in Written Language

Readers and writers draw upon syntax to construct and convey meaning. However, they also develop a unique set of knowledge about other forms and organizational structures of written language that are not found in spoken language—the form of alphabet letters (which linguists call **graphemes**), words and word spaces, sentences, and text formats.

Alphabet Letters

One way to find out about children's knowledge of letters and the features which comprise letters is to ask them whether letters are alike or different (Gibson, Gibson, Pick, & Osser, 1962). We might give children the letter *O* and the letter *U* and ask if they are alike or different. (The two letters differ on the feature *closed* versus *open.*) We might show children the letters ∀ and *A*, which differ on the feature *rotated* versus *upright.* Three-year-olds know that the letters *U* and *O* are different, but they do not know that the letters ∀ and *A* are different. They know the feature *closed* versus *open,* but they do not know the feature *rotated* versus *upright.* In contrast, seven-year-olds know that both sets of letters are different, because they know both features.

Children also demonstrate their knowledge of letter features in their writing. Figure 1.11 presents one preschooler's printed letters. This writing does include some conventional or nearly conventional alphabet letter forms (*t, r,* and *M*) as well as many letter-like, but unconventional symbols. These symbols look like alphabet letters because they include many letter features, such as vertical, diagonal, and curved lines (Lavine, 1977). Clay (1975) called letters like these **mock letters.**

Children all over the world construct mock letters, letters that look like the written language children will soon read and write. The features they use in order to write mock letters reveal the unique visual features found in the variety of our world's written languages.

Figure 1.11 *A Preschooler's Printed Letters*

In Figure 1.12, a five-year-old Chinese girl has labeled her picture by writing two symbols that resemble Chinese characters, although neither is a real Chinese character.

Words and Sentences

Children also learn about the features of words. If we wanted to know about children's knowledge of word features, we might ask them to sort cards into two piles, one pile for "words" and one pile for "not words" (Pick, Unze, Brownell, Drozdal, & Hopmann, 1978).

On the cards we would write long and short words and nonwords (such as *keld* or *cafkiton*). Even three-year-olds are willing to perform this task, and they put all the words (and nonwords) with three or more letters in the "word" pile. Thus, their notion of words is that words consist of strings of at least three letters. In contrast, first graders put all the words (including single-letter words, such as *a*, in the word pile, but they reject real words that they cannot read (such as *obese*). Their concept of words is that words may have only one letter but must be readable and meaningful to the reader.

Children also demonstrate their knowledge of word features in their writing (Clay, 1975; Sulzby, 1986). Figure 1.13 presents a letter that five-year-old Zachery wrote to his Aunt Carol.

Figure 1.12 *A Five-Year-Old's Drawing with Mock Chinese Characters*

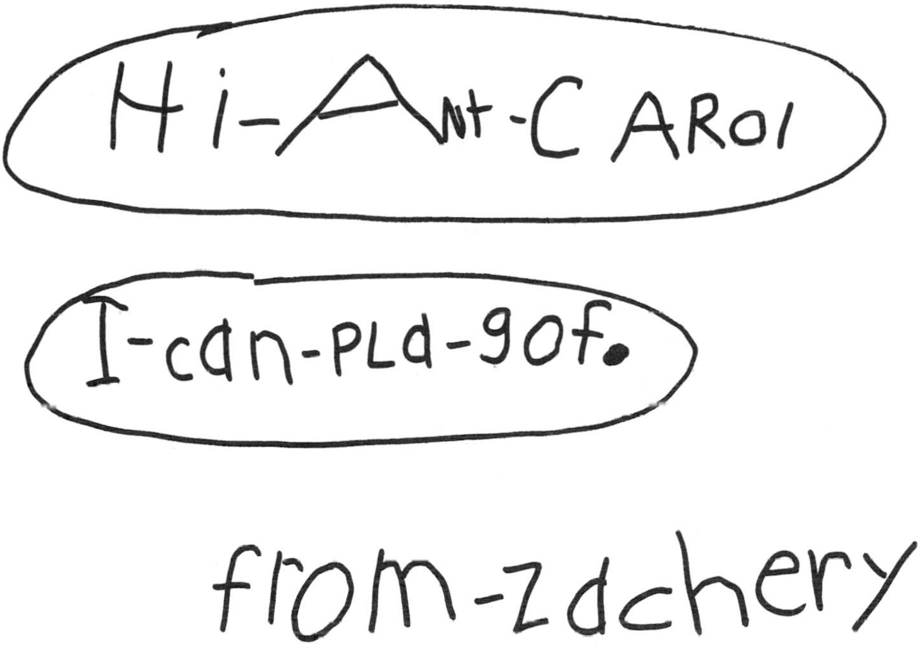

Figure 1.13 *Zachery's Letter to His Aunt Carol*

His writing indicates an awareness of words; he separated each word with a dash. Many young children are unsure that a blank space is enough to mark a word boundary. Instead, they make word spaces very obvious, using dots or dashes or circling words to indicate word spaces to readers. Zachery's writing also demonstrates his strong grasp of the directional principles of written English: he uses **left-to-right** and **top-to-bottom organization.**

This letter also demonstrates Zachery's knowledge of the visual features of two other units of written language: sentences and letter format. Zachery circled each thought unit, which we call sentences, even though he signaled a sentence boundary with the conventional punctuation mark, a period. His writing also shows a sophisticated awareness of how letters are organized. He begins with a greeting ("Hi Aunt Carol") and ends with a closing ("from Zachery").

Text Formats

There are many of kinds of texts, including poems, recipes, maps, newspapers, dictionaries, books, magazine articles, *TV Guides*, and directions. One thing young children learn about these different text forms is how they look. Figure 1.14 presents a preschooler's story. This writing looks like a story—it fills a page with horizontal lines of writing and demonstrates a concept of **linearity.**

Figure 1.15 presents a nine-year-old's letter to her principal. The form of the letter reflects Andrea's concepts about letter form, including a greeting, body, and signature. The content is also organized, with a statement of a problem and solution and with arguments for why the principal should consider the solution.

Figure 1.14 A Preschooler's Story

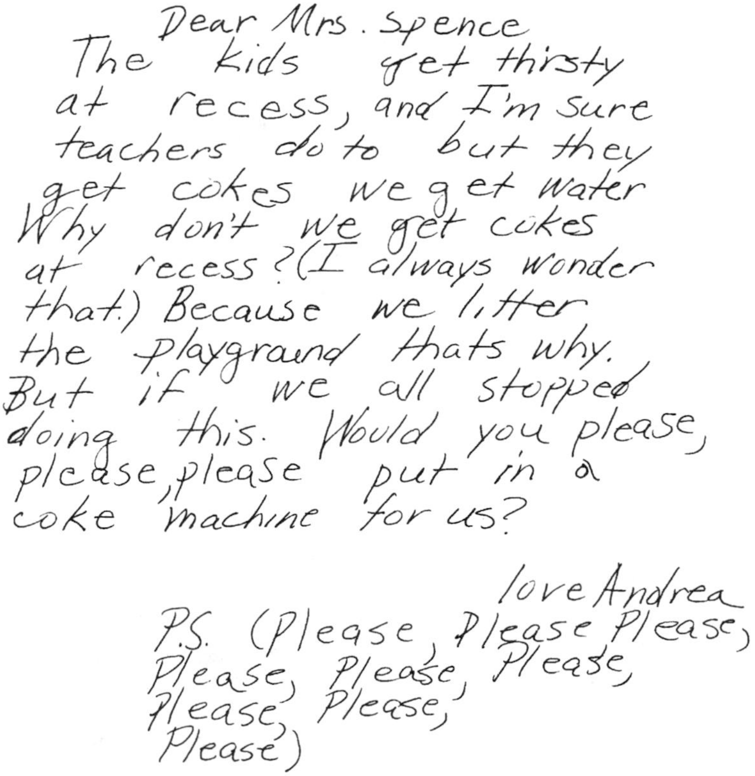

Dear Mrs. spence
The kids get thirsty at recess, and I'm sure teachers do to but they get cokes we get water Why don't we get cokes at recess? (I always wonder that.) Because we litter the playgraund thats why. But if we all stopped doing this. Would you please, please, please put in a coke machine for us?

love Andrea

P.S. (Please, Please Please, Please, Please, Please, Please, Please, Please)

Figure 1.15 A Persuasion Letter

Metalinguistic Awareness of Written Language Units

We have been using words such as *letter, word, sentence,* and *story,* which make it easy to describe written language. They constitute *language about language.* Children's understanding of and ability to use language about language is a particular kind of knowledge called **metalinguistic awareness** (Yaden & Templeton, 1986). Children acquire several aspects of metalinguistic awareness. One aspect is the ability to examine a written language form apart from the meaning associated with the form (Templeton, 1980). For example, the word *dog* can be examined as a written language form—it is composed of three letters with the graphic shape of 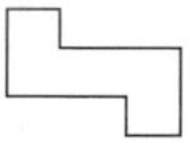 . The word *dog* also has meaning—a hairy, four-legged animal. Young children have difficulty examining form apart from meaning. When asked to name a long word, they might reply "bus." They are likely to say "paper clip" when asked to name a short word. Young children use the meaning of a word to determine whether a word is long or short. Older children who have metalinguistic awareness would use the form of the written word to identify and name long and short words, such as *encyclopedia* and *I.*

The example of saying that "paper clip" is a short word illustrates another aspect of metalinguistic awareness, **concept of word.** A child who gives this answer does not realize either that the question, "What is a short word?" implies that only one word should be given or that *paper clip* is two words. Concept of word has several components, including the ability to identify a single word in a spoken sentence, the ability to identify a single word from a written sentence, and the ability to answer the question, "What is a word?" (Downing & Oliver, 1973–1974).

MEANING-FORM LINKS

We use the term **meaning-form links** to refer to the way in which meaning is connected to written forms. Ted used the conventional meaning-form link in English—he used letters associated with certain sounds (**sound–letter relationships**) so that his written words corresponded to spoken words and the concepts related to those spoken words. He wrote *pees* using *ee* (as in the word *tree*) to represent the sound of long *e.* Despite Ted's unconventional spelling, we are able to construct the expected meaning (the small, round, green vegetables) because we look for correspondences between expected meanings on a restaurant menu and the letters he chose to represent the sounds in the name of the food item peas.

The link between letters in written words and sounds in spoken words is obvious to experienced readers, but it is not always clear to beginning readers and writers. Despite its not being obvious, young children go about finding ways to link meaning with printed forms in a variety of ways. They draw on their knowledge of written language forms and on their phonological knowledge.

Phonological System in Spoken Language

The phonological system refers to the system of spoken sounds in language. Each language uses some of the few hundreds of possible speech sounds of human languages. English, for example, uses approximately forty-four speech sounds, or **phonemes.** Some of English's phonemes are rare: the sound of *i* in *bird* appears in very few other languages. And English does not include some phonemes found in other languages.

Using the phonological system is complex and diverse. **Phonological knowledge** includes abilities to distinguish speech from other kinds of sounds, to distinguish one phoneme from another, to attend to some very slight differences in sounds in some contexts (*zoo* versus *Sue*) but ignore small differences in other contexts (*Sue* pronounced by a child's mother versus *Sue* pronounced by a child's father), to distinguish questions from statements, and so on. For speaking and listening, this kind of phonological knowledge is acquired easily—most preschool and kindergarten children's speech is sufficient for their talking and listening needs, although they will continue to expand their oral language capabilities throughout schooling.

In contrast, **phonological awareness** is necessary for reading and writing. It is a special kind of phonological knowledge that requires the ability to think and talk about these kinds of differences in speech sounds. Children who have phonological awareness notice and identify different sounds units. For example, they can decide if two words rhyme and can clap out syllables in words.

An even more sophisticated level of phonological awareness is called **phonemic awareness.** This is the ability to hear phonemes—for example, to detect if two words begin or end with the same sound. Phonemic awareness is never necessary for speaking or listening. In fact, in everyday speech, phonemes in a word flow together so that it is difficult to say where one phoneme ends and another begins. Nonetheless, because English is an alphabetic language in which alphabet letters correspond to phonemes, acquiring phonemic awareness is important for literacy development (Stahl, Duffy-Hester, & Stahl, 1998; Nation & Hulme, 1997). As we will see later in this book, the ability to segment words in their individual phonemes comes gradually, but is a crucial part of becoming a reader and writer.

Meaning-Form Links in Written Language

In English, words are composed of letters that map on spoken words through a system of sound–letter relationships. These relationships are sometimes referred to as **grapho-phonic relationships.** Each letter in the English alphabet is associated with at least one speech sound; but most letters are associated with many speech sounds. For example, the letter *a* represents many different sounds, such as those found in the words *hat, ape, oral, art,* and *apply.* The study of sound–letter relationships in elementary school is called **phonics.**

Spellings make use of patterns of letters and letter combinations called **orthographics.** For example, we spell the sound associated with long *a* in several ways, including *ay,* such as in *pay; a* consonant silent *e,* such as in *skate; ai,* such as in *paid;* and *eigh,* as in *weigh.* **Phonograms,** or word families, include letter combinations with the same pronunciation. For example, the *at* phonogram is pronounced the same in the words *at, bat, cat, fat, hat, mat, pat, rat, sat,* and *vat.*

Accomplished readers and writers are beyond paying attention to letters and sounds. They focus on the meaning of what they are reading and writing. In contrast, most preschoolers have not yet acquired a concept of the grapho-phonic relationships. However, they do have concepts about meaning-form links (Dyson, 1984). We describe two unconventional ways children attempt to link meaning and form.

Meaning-Form Links through Letter and Scribble Strings

In the case study, Carrie produced a mock letter string. She wrote mock letters without regard for sound–letter relationships. Nonetheless, she expected that her writing would communicate a message. Carrie's father pretended that it indeed was meaningful and paid his bill.

Figure 1.16 presents Johanna's picture and story writing. She read her story, pointing to the print from left to right and then down the side and from right to left across the bottom: "Miss Sharon and Mr. K have a new baby, Emily. I hope we will baby-sit Emily. I love Emily Grace." Johanna's text consists of a string of conventional and mock letters wrapped around the edges of the paper framing her illustration. She does not use sound–letter relationships to connect meaning and form. Instead, Johanna's meaning—her story about a beloved new baby and her desire to be with the baby—is told both through the illustration and by spoken language. Johanna knows that print is important—she pointed to her letters as she read the story. The meaning-form link for Johanna was to write and then compose a related story.

Meaning-Form Links by Matching Print with Spoken Units

An intermediate way that children attempt to link meaning with written language is to match a unit of written language to a unit of spoken language. Sometimes children explore a syllable link between spoken language and written language. For example, Heather memorized the poem "Twinkle, Twinkle Little Star." Her kindergarten teacher wrote the poem on a chart and asked Heather to read it and "point to each word." Heather performed the task by reading and pointing as follows.

Text:	Twinkle	Twinkle	Little	Star		
Heather:	Twink	le	Twink	le		
Text:	How	I	Wonder	What	You	Are
Heather:	Lit	tle	Star	How	I	Won

Heather hesitated and then pointed back at the beginning of the poem:

Text:	Twinkle	Twinkle	Little	Star		
Heather:	Won	der	What	You		
Text:	How	I	Wonder	What	You	Are
Heather:	Are					

Figure 1.16 Johanna's Story

Then Heather stopped, pointed to the remainder of the text, and said, "I don't know what the rest says." Heather used a strategy of linking each written word to a spoken syllable.

Figure 1.17 summarizes the similarities and differences between the four systems of spoken and written language: pragmatics and function, semantics and meaning, syntax and form, and phonology and meaning-form links. As shown in this figure, what children learn as they acquire reading and writing is complex and overlaps with their spoken language development. They acquire these necessary concepts for reading and writing gradually, through many experiences and instructional opportunities.

DEVELOPMENTAL CHANGES IN CHILDREN'S READING AND WRITING

We have shown how children's concepts change as they have more experiences that include reading and writing. Children have many unconventional concepts about words, alphabet letters, and meaning-form links. Yet all children's concepts become increasingly more conventional. Although the journey to becoming a mature reader and writer is long, what happens during the journey is as valid as the end point. Knowing how children's concepts about written language develop is critical for understanding children's reading and writing. Here we discuss major changes in children's concepts about word reading as just one example of their growth toward conventional literacy.

Logographic Reading and Writing

Long before children become conventional readers and writers, they display many behaviors like those of readers and writers. Reexamine Kristen's letter (Figure 1.1), Cody's draw-

Figure 1.17 *Systems of Spoken and Written Language*

SPOKEN LANGUAGE	WRITTEN LANGUAGE
Pragmatics The contextualized purposes spoken language serves	**Functions** The purposes written language serves, including establishing identity, recording information, and accumulating knowledge
Semantics System of meaning, including word meanings; contextualization clues such as gesture, expression, or intonation; morphology	**Meaning** System of meaning, including word meanings, literary language, unusual words; morphology
Syntax The order and organization of words within sentences and spoken	**Form** The order of words within sentences; upper- and lowercase alphabet letters (graphemes); spatial directional principles, including left to right, top to bottom; word spaces; text formats
Phonology System of approximately forty-four speech sounds (phonemes), which make up spoken English	**Meaning-Form Link** Phoneme–grapheme relationships: orthographic spelling patterns, including phonograms

ing and writing (Figure 1.3), Carrie's check (Figure 1.9), and Heather's reading (page 23). These children are not operating with conventional knowledge of written language functions, meanings, forms, and meaning-form links, but they do have considerable understanding of many concepts. For example, young children know that the label on their cereal box reads "Rice Krispies." This is an important accomplishment for preschoolers—they realize that print in the environment communicates meaning.

In addition, preschoolers are willing to reread their favorite books. They may turn the pages and label characters and actions depicted in the illustrations or use the illustrations to retell the story. Sometimes the stories children tell as they reread favorite books match the text nearly verbatim (Sulzby, 1985).

Yet if "Rice Krispies" or the text of a favorite story were printed on a card, preschoolers could not read the words. How, then, can preschoolers read words from familiar environmental print signs or from their favorite storybooks? They do so by assigning meaning to logos and illustrations found in familiar print contexts. This is a visual concept of word reading; it depends on seeing print in familiar environments, such as on the front of a cereal box or on pages in a favorite book. Their reading depends on context.

Similarly, young children's writing reveals a reliance on context for meaning. When Johanna told her story (see Figure 1.16,) she used the context of the illustration in order to construct meaning from her writing. Without being in the context of Johanna's telling of her story, another adult could not read it. Our reading of Johanna's writing is dependent on our being in the context of her story reading. If Johanna were asked to read her story several weeks after writing it, she would likely be unable to reconstruct the story or to retell it in exactly the same way. Researchers have labeled reading and writing that relies on context as **logographic reading and writing** (Ehri, 1991; Juel, 1991).

We think that young readers develop through two stages of logographic reading: what we call beginning literacy and novice reading and writing.

Beginners are very young children who have meaningful experiences with books and writing materials, experiences that lay necessary foundations for later literacy development. The children we call beginners, however, do not find meaning in printed symbols themselves, and they do not make written marks with the intentions of communicating particular messages.

Novices are aware that printed texts communicate messages, and they write with the intention to communicate meaning, although the ways in which they read and write are unconventional. They learn to name and write some letters of the alphabet, and they make texts that have visual features appropriate to their purposes (e.g., a list that looks like a list rather than a sentence or paragraph, even though it may not contain readable words). They read back and assign meanings to their own writing that match their purposes for writing, and they read other texts in ways that depend on visual clues from the immediate environment (e.g., a picture of an ice cream cone on a sign that says "Ice Cream"). They are logographic readers and nonspellers.

Alphabetic Reading and Writing

Children eventually come to recognize that meaning is mapped onto print in systematic ways. Heather's matching of words to syllables while reading "Twinkle, Twinkle Little Star" is the beginning of this understanding. Children who attempt to use sound–letter correspondences in their reading and writing have reached the level called **alphabetic reading and writing** (Ehri, 1991; Juel, 1991).

Children who know at least some alphabet letters come to realize that alphabet letters are associated with certain sounds. When they first acquire this concept, children may perform phonetic cue reading (Ehri, 1991); they read printed words by remembering some sound–letter associations. For example, they may be able to read the word *mom* because they recognize the letter *m* and associate it with the sound /m/.

At this early point in alphabetic reading, knowledge about letters and sounds is not complete. For example, children who can remember *mom* by using the association of the sound /m/ with the letter *m* cannot read the nonsense word *mim;* they cannot yet separate each letter and associate it with a single phoneme. They are not yet able to sound a word phoneme by phoneme (/m/, /i/, and /m/) and then blend the phonemes into the nonsense word *mim.* They might say, "Mom" when reading the word *mim.*

Children operate according to a later version of the alphabetic reading concept when they perform cipher reading (Juel, 1991). At this point, they process words more completely, including being able to segment words phoneme by phoneme. Cipher readers can read nonsense words such as *mim* by decoding or ciphering phoneme by phoneme. This is primarily an auditory concept of word reading. Children read words by segmenting them phoneme by phoneme; they know letters associated with phonemes, and they use the sounds associated with letters to remember words. Similarly, children's writing develops from a gradual ability to use only a few sound–letter relationships in their spelling to being able to capture nearly every phoneme in a word with a letter. This level of writing is alphabetic writing.

We call the reading and writing of children nearing and at the level of alphabetic writing experimenting reading and writing. **Experimenters** use many more conventional tools and strategies than do novices, but most people would not yet mistake them for conventional readers and writers; they are in a transitional period. They use literary language, they can name and form nearly all the letters of the alphabet, they develop an awareness of words, they become inventive spellers, and they read with the support of familiar, predictable text. They are at the beginning of alphabetic reading and spelling.

We use the term *experimenters* deliberately to highlight the transitional stage of these learners. Moving from one concept of word reading to another is a time of transitional knowledge about written language, when children's understandings are about to undergo significant reorganizations, resulting in more conventional literacy behaviors. A possible indicator of such transitional periods is children's "out of sync" reading of their own writing, for example, writing a story using sound–letter correspondences to spell, but using storytelling (rather than reading) to read (Kamberelis & Sulzby, 1988).

Toward the end of alphabetic reading and writing, children move into conventional reading and writing. They can read unfamiliar text on their own and can compose compositions that are read easily by others.

Conventional readers and writers read and write in ways that most people in our literate society recognize as "really" reading and writing. For example, they use a variety of reading strategies, know hundreds of sight words, read texts written in a variety of structures, are aware of audience, monitor their own performances as writers and readers, and spell conventionally. They are fully alphabetic readers and spellers, and they are becoming orthographic readers and writers.

Orthographic Reading and Writing

Orthographic readers and writers have highly sophisticated and complex understandings of written language (Frith, 1985). For example, when reading unfamiliar words, orthographic readers do not resort to letter-by-letter analysis. Rather, they automatically see chunks of letters associated with spelling patterns. This process involves associating familiar spelling patterns with sound segments. For example, the word *night* includes the *ight* spelling pattern, and this pattern is always associated with the sound segment /īt/. With this concept of word reading, children associate more than single sounds with single letters. They automatically notice familiar letter patterns and associate these patterns with sound segments (Adams, 1990).

Consider a word beginning with the letter *d*. When orthographic readers—who have had much experience with English text—see the *d*, their visual perception mechanisms are primed to expect the second letter to be any vowel, including *y*, or one of only two consonants, *r* and *w*, that commonly follow *d* in English spelling. They are not expecting any of the other consonants. In fact, such expectations feed one another, so that readers come to expect high-frequency sequences of letters.

This is mostly a visual concept of word reading. However, it is far different from the visual concept of selective cue or logographic reading. With orthographic reading, children are so familiar with the sequences of letters in written words that they automatically see letters in groups, or clusters.

Orthographic writers know the conventional spellings of hundreds of words and spell unfamiliar words with regular spelling patterns. When orthographic spellers make spelling errors, they reveal knowledge of orthographic patterns much like Ted's misspelling of the word *peas* as *pees*. Orthographic reading and writing appear toward the end of the primary grades in elementary school. However, highly accomplished readers and writers achieve this level of understanding early. Nonetheless, no single accomplishment establishes a child as a novice, an experimenter, or a conventional reader and writer. The boundaries between these identities are fuzzy; children often waver between them. We use them only to help organize and elaborate the vast amount of information we now have about how children's literacy competence changes from birth to the primary grades.

Chapter Summary

Children's learning is dependent on having experiences that lead to the formation of concepts or schemas. Concepts are mental constructions about objects, people, events or activities, and places. Learning is a matter of acquiring new concepts or adding to and changing old concepts. Language is critical for learning when it provides labels for new concepts and when it is used to scaffold children's attempts at difficult tasks.

Children develop special concepts about written language that they use in reading and writing. They develop concepts about the functions of written language, including using reading and writing to label and record.

Their concepts about written language meanings reflect their experiences with different kinds of texts, such as stories, grocery lists, and traffic signs. They create concepts about written language forms, including learning about letter features, words, sentences, texts, and left-to-right organization. They develop understandings about meaning-form links, including unconventional concepts such using letter strings and matching spoken units with written units.

Children's concepts about written language change and grow with their reading and writing experiences. Children begin with unconventional concepts and gradually acquire concepts that lead to conventional reading and writing. They may proceed through logographic, alphabetic, and orthographic reading and writing.

Applying the Information

A case study of a literacy event follows. Read this case study carefully and think about the four domains of written language knowledge. Discuss what each of the children in the case study is learning about written language (1) meanings, (2) forms, (3) meaning-form links, and (4) functions. Figure 1.18 presents drawing and writing composition jointly produced by Kristen and Carrie.

Kristen, a three-year-old preschooler, and Carrie, a six-year-old kindergartner, were playing school together. Carrie began by demonstrating how to draw. She said, "This is me," as she drew the person (1) in the upper right corner of Figure 1.18. Kristen replied, "I can draw you," and she drew the figure (2) at the middle left of Figure 1.18. Carrie pointed out that the person has no hair, so Kristen

Figure 1.18 *Kristen's and Carrie's Drawing and Writing*

drew the figure (3) in the upper left corner. Carrie decided to teach Kristen how to write. She said, "We'll write. Here is a *C*." She wrote the capital *C* (4) on the right side of the figure. Kristen wrote the letter (5) in the top middle of the page and said "I can write *C*, too." Then Carrie wrote the remaining letters in her name, saying the name of each letter as she wrote (6). Kristen wrote similar letters, including an *A*, several *E*'s, and *R*'s scattered around the page. The children finished as Carrie drew a tree and Kristen added dots to the picture.

Going Beyond the Text

Observe a literacy event with at least two children. One way to initiate a literacy event is to prepare for some dramatic play with children. Plan a dramatic play activity that could include reading and writing. For example, plan a restaurant play activity. Bring dramatic props, such as an apron, dishes, and a tablecloth, as well as reading and writing materials, such as large sheets of paper, small pads of paper, crayons or markers, placemats with puzzles, and menus. Suggest to two or three children that they might want to play restaurant and propose that they use the paper and crayons in their play. Observe their actions and talk. Use your observations to find out what the children know about written language meanings, forms, meaning-form links, and functions.

References

ADAMS, M. (1990). *Beginning to read: Thinking and learning about print.* Cambridge: MIT Press.

CLAY, M. M. (1975). *What did I write?* Aukland: Heinemann Educational Books.

COCHRAN-SMITH, M. (1984). *The making of a reader.* Norwood, NJ: Ablex.

COOK-GUMPERZ, J. (Ed.). (1986). *The social construction of literacy.* Cambridge: Cambridge University Press.

CUNNINGHAM, A., & STANOVICH, K. (1998). What reading does for the mind. *American Educator, 22,* 8–15.

DOWNING, J., & OLIVER, P. (1973–1974). The child's conception of a word. *Reading Research Quarterly, 9,* 568–582.

DYSON, A. H. (1984). Emerging alphabetic literacy in school contexts toward defining the gap between school curriculum and child mind. *Written Communication, 1,* 5–55.

EHRI, L. (1991). Development of the ability to read words. In R. Barr, M. Kamil, P. Mosenthal, & P. Pearson (Eds.), *Handbook of reading research* (2nd ed., pp. 395–419). New York: Longman.

FERREIRO, E., & TEBEROSKY, A. (1982). *Literacy before schooling.* Exeter, NH: Heinemann.

FRITH, U. (1985). Beneath the surface of developmental dyslexia. In K. Patterson, J. Marshall, & M. Coltheart (Eds.), *Surface dyslexia* (pp. 301–330). London: Erlbaum.

GIBSON, E. J., GIBSON, J. J., PICK, A. D., & OSSER, H. (1962). A developmental study of discrimination of letter-like forms. *Journal of Comparative Physiological Psychology, 55,* 897–906.

GOPNICK, A., & MELTZOFF, A. Z. (1986). Relations between semantic and cognitive development in the one-word stage: The specificity hypothesis. *Child Development, 57,* 1040–1053.

HALLIDAY, M. A. K. (1975). *Learning how to mean.* New York: Elsevier.

HARSTE, J. C., BURKE, C. L., & WOODWARD, V. A. (1983). *The young child as writer-reader, and informant* (Final NIE Report No. NIE-G-80–0121). Bloomington, IN: Language Education Departments, Indiana University.

HARSTE, J. C., WOODWARD, V. A., & BURKE, C. L. (1984). *Language stories and literacy lessons.* Portsmouth, NH: Heinemann.

JUEL, C. (1991). Beginning reading. In R. Barr, M. Kamil, P. Mosenthal, & P. Pearson (Eds.), *Handbook of reading research* (2nd ed., pp. 759–788). New York: Longman.

KAMBERELIS, G., & SULZBY, E. (1988). Transitional knowledge in emergent literacy. In J. Readence & R. Baldwin (Eds.), *Dialogues in literacy research* (pp. 95–106). Chicago: National Reading Conference.

LAVINE, L. O. (1977). Differentiation of letter-like forms in prereading children. *Developmental Psychology, 13,* 89–94.

MELTZOFF, A. Z. (1985). In *Baby talk* (NOVA transcript No. 1207). Boston: WGBH Transcripts.

NATION, K., & HULME, C. (1997). Phonemic segmentation, not onset-rime segmentation, predicts early reading and spelling skills. *Reading Research Quarterly, 32,* 154–167.

NOVA. (1985). *Baby talk* (NOVA transcript No. 1207). Boston: WGBH Transcripts.

PIAGET, J. (1955). *The language and thought of the child.* Cleveland, OH: World.

PICK, A. D., UNZE M. G., BROWNELL, C. A., DROZDAL, J. G., JR., & HOPMANN, M. R. (1978). Young children's knowledge of word structure. *Child Development, 49,* 669–680.

PURCELL-GATES, V. (1995). *Other people's words: The cycle of low literacy.* Cambridge, MA: Harvard University Press.

ROWE, D. (1998). The literate potentials of book-related dramatic play. *Reading Research Quarterly,* 33, 10–35.

SCOLLON, R., & SCOLLON, S. (1981). *Narrative, literacy, and face in inter-ethnic communication.* Norwood, NJ: Ablex.

SNOW, C. (1983). Literacy and language: Relationships during the preschool years. *Harvard Educational Review, 53,* 165–189.

STAHL, S., DUFFY-HESTER, A., & STAHL, A. (1998). Theory and research into practice: Everything you wanted to know about phonics (but were afraid to ask). *Reading Research Quarterly, 33,* 338–355.

STUBBS, M. (1980). *The sociolinguistics of reading and writing: Language and literacy.* London: Routledge & Kegan Paul.

SULZBY, E. (1985). Children's emergent reading of favorite storybooks: A developmental study. *Reading Research Quarterly, 20,* 458–481.

SULZBY, E. (1986). Children's elicitation and use of metalinguistic knowledge about word during literacy interactions. In D. B. Yaden, Jr., & S. Templeton (Eds.), *Metalinguistic awareness and beginning literacy* (pp. 219–233). Portsmouth, NH: Heinemann.

TAYLOR, D. (1983). *Family literacy.* Exeter, NH: Heinemann.

TEMPLETON, S. (1980). Young children invent words: Developing concepts of "wordness." *The Reading Teacher, 33,* 454–459.

VYGOTSKY, L. S. (1978). *Mind in society. The development of higher psychological processes* (Michael Cole, Trans.). Cambridge: Harvard University Press.

WOLF, D. (1984). Research currents: Learning about language skills from narratives. *Language Arts, 61,* 844–850.

YADEN, D. B., JR., & TEMPLETON, S. (1986). Introduction: Metalinguistic awareness—an etymology. In D. B. Yaden, Jr., & S. Templeton (Eds.), *Metalinguistic awareness and beginning literacy* (pp. 3–10). Portsmouth, NH: Heinemann.

Chapter 2

From Birth to Three Years

Literacy Beginners

Key Concepts

- bookhandling skills
- booksharing routines
- naming game
- motor schemes
- writing and drawing routines
- romancing
- ascribing intentionality
- representational drawings
- meaning-making strategies
- supporting strategies
- decontextualized language
- concept of story
- story grammars
- wordless book
- naming actions
- non-narrative retelling
- environmental print
- nonimmediate talk
- developmentally appropriate practices
- continuum of literacy development
- literacy experiences embedded in culture
- first storybooks

WHAT LITERACY BEGINNERS SHOW US

Many children have literacy experiences very early—as infants or toddlers. While not all infants and toddlers are involved in reading and writing experiences with their families, most preschoolers acquire literacy concepts that form the foundations for their later acquisition of reading and writing.

"Let's Read, Daddy": Experiences with Books and Other Familiar Print

In the example that follows, Kristen shows literate behaviors with books that are common to many literacy beginners. She can turn pages, recognize books by their names, and participate with a parent in booksharing routines. She demonstrates bookhandling skills, such as holding a book right-side-up and turning pages from front to back. At first, she focuses on pictures in books, but then on letters of the alphabet and on the language of books, completing familiar phrases. She reads environmental print, and she talks about characters and actions in familiar books.

Kristen received her first books when she was just a few months old. Many of these were sturdy cardboard books such as *A Goodnight Hug* (Roth, 1986). They were kept in her toy basket along with her rattles. Her mother and father read to her while she sat in their laps. When just a few months old, Kristen began grabbing her books, picking them up, and holding them. Kristen did not look at the pictures in her books; instead, she made insistent attempts to turn the pages.

Some months before her first birthday, Kristen learned to recognize books by their names. Her father would say, "Let's read the Humpty Dumpty book." Kristen would crawl to the book basket and select her "Humpty Dumpty book" (*The Real Mother Goose,* Wright, 1916). She would turn to the page that had the Humpty Dumpty rhyme and sway her body as her father recited the rhyme. Kristen participated in bookreading in other ways as well. She received a copy of *Pat the Bunny* (Kunhardt, 1940) and learned to play peekaboo and wave bye-bye on turning to the appropriate pages.

By her first birthday, Kristen would hold a book right-side-up and turn the pages from front to back. Sometimes she smiled and patted the pictures or turned pages over from one side to the next, intently checking the pictures on each side of the page. Kristen also liked to look at the coupon section of the Sunday paper; she would turn the pages quickly, looking for a familiar animal, such as a dog or cat. Then she would look up at her father and laugh.

A few months after her first birthday, Kristen began to point to things around her, saying "dat?" with a rising intonation. She would also point to and ask "dat?" about animals and people pictured in her books. Her mother or father would obligingly name the animals and people. Kristen's mother often requested that she locate animals or people in her books. She would ask, "Where's the kitten?" and Kristen would point to it. At this time Kristen could say a few words. She would say "bah" and point to the picture of a ball in her book.

When Kristen was about sixteen months old, she began interrupting bookreading by jumping off her father's lap to seek a toy or object in the house. She did this only when she saw certain pictures in her books. Each time Kristen saw a picture of crayons, for example, she would get up and find *her* crayons.

At eighteen months of age, Kristen would sit by herself and look at her books, saying the names of some of the objects in the pictures while pointing at them. Kristen had several ABC books in which she was particularly interested at this time. She noticed the alphabet letters on the endpapers of *Dr. Seuss's ABC Book* (Seuss, 1963a). One day, while she was looking at the letters, her mother sang the ABC song to her and pointed to each letter as she sang. Whenever Kristen read this book, she would turn to the endpapers and repeatedly point at the letters, saying "A-A-A" in her singing voice.

At two years of age, Kristen was able to capture some of the text meaning in her own words. In *Hop on Pop* (Seuss, 1963b), Kristen said, "No. No. No sit" after her mother read, "No, Pat, No. Don't sit on that." As her father read the text of *Goodnight Moon* (Brown, 1947), he would pause for Kristen to fill in part of the rhyme. Kristen began recognizing McDonald's and Burger King signs. She would say "DeDonald's" or "Bugar King" each time she saw the signs. Kristen also pointed to her favorite cereals and cookies in the grocery store, saying "Aisin Ban" and "Oeos."

At three years of age, Kristen participated in book and familiar print reading in many ways. She made comments about characters and actions depicted in her books. Pointing to the picture of the wolf in *Walt Disney's Peter and the Wolf* (Disney Productions, 1974), she said, "He needs to be good." She commented about the predicament of Wully-Wully in *Babar and the Wully-Wully* (de Brunhoff, 1975), saying "He's in the cage" and "He got out" as she pointed to the pictures of Wully-Wully captured and rescued. She asked questions. She asked, "What's that?" as she pointed to one of the characters in the Babar book. She answered questions. Her father asked, "What's she going to do?" referring to the little girl who takes the bear home in *Corduroy* (Freeman, 1968). Kristen replied, "Give him a hug."

Concepts about Literacy from Early Book Experiences

Kristen learned at least five important literacy-related concepts about books and sharing books as a result of her enjoyable book experiences.

1. Books Are Pleasurable

Perhaps one of the most important concepts that children can learn at the beginning of their literacy experiences is that reading is a pleasurable activity. When children are read to beginning early in their lives, they play with books as a preferred and frequent activity (Doake, 1986). Bookreading is one of the closest activities parents and children share. Children nestle in Dad's lap or lean over Mom's arm while they take part in this activity. The special feelings generated from this closeness of parents and children are associated with books. It is no wonder that some children will sit alone and look at books far longer than they will sit with their other toys.

2. Books Are Handled in Particular Ways

In this beginning period, children also learn **bookhandling skills,** ways of handling and looking at books. There are many aspects of bookhandling. Kristen learned how to hold books right-side-up and how to turn pages. She also discovered that books are for viewing and reading and not just for turning pages (Snow & Ninio, 1986).

3. Booksharing Involves Familiar Roles and Language

Toddlers and their parents learn ways of interacting with each other while reading books. They develop **booksharing routines,** that is, familiar, expected actions and language that accompanied their book reading. Kristen learned how to initiate and participate in bookreading sessions. She did not always wait for her bedtime story. Rather, she frequently selected a book and backed into a lap. She clearly signaled that she wanted to share a book. Once her mother or father began sharing a book, Kristen located characters when asked to do so and solicited comments from her mother or father by pointing to something in the picture or making comments and asking questions. She learned to answer questions. Gradually, she learned to listen to more of the story her mother or father was reading. Kristen discovered that, just like her mother and father, she also had certain roles to play in bookreading (Ninio & Bruner, 1978; Taylor & Dorsey-Gaines, 1988).

Booksharing routines make it possible for children to show parents what they are learning. Parents respond by giving children opportunities to use their new abilities and expecting children to use them. This results in an increase in children's roles and a decrease in adults' roles. Kristen and her parents demonstrated this in their playing of a routine known as the **naming game** (Ninio & Burner, 1978). As described earlier, it began with Kristen's mother's pointing to and naming pictured animals, people, and objects; it progressed through Kristen's and her mother's "dat?" and "Where's the kitten?" questions; and it ended with Kristen's pointing to and labeling pictures on her own.

4. Pictures in Books Are Symbols

Another aspect of literacy learning involves discovering that the shapes and colors in pictures represent things—pictures are symbols for objects and actions. Kristen showed that she had discovered this when she found her crayons after she saw a picture of crayons in a favorite book. She was discovering not only that pictures are interesting to look at, but also that they are representations of real things. Children learn that pictures in books are not things; rather, they represent things (Snow & Ninio, 1986). Kristen learned that she was not patting real objects when she patted the pictures in her books; they were only symbols for real things that she could pat.

5. Books and Print Communicate Meaning

A crucial outcome of children's early experiences with books and other kinds of print is that they learn that books and other print materials communicate meaning—they tell a message. Kristen learned to look through catalogs so that she could talk with her mother about familiar animals or objects. She learned that her storybooks showed pictures of familiar objects and events.

Learning to "mean" (Halliday, 1975), to understand what others say and do, is involved in nearly every activity, not only in literacy activities. It is the great undertaking of life—we constantly try to understand the messages that bombard us and to send messages to others. We use many cues to help us understand others and to help others understand us. We use the situation we are in and its clues to meaning (characteristics of the location or people's clothing), as well as spoken language and its clues to meaning (words, stress, and intonation). Because our society is a literate one, another powerful set of clues to meaning is written language. Written language, too, is used along with situation (getting out a checkbook at the grocery store), with spoken language ("That will be $81.47"), and with written symbols (81.47 printed on the computer display of the cash register).

Children learn to use these cues, including the written language cues, to make meaning. We are not implying that infants look at print and try to read it like an adult does. However, when an adult reads print aloud, tells a story, or talks about pictures in a magazine, infants and toddlers try to make sense of what is going on. They attempt to understand the situation, the talk they hear, and the visual symbols they see.

"Look at All These Raindrops": Experiences with Crayons and Markers

In the following example, Kristen shows literate behaviors with writing and drawing materials that are common to many literacy beginners. She demonstrates increasing control of her writing and drawing. She makes quick back-and-forth marks, then round-and-round lines and dots, then jagged lines and single straight lines, and finally, controlled circular shapes. She progresses from attending to the drawing of others, to after-the-fact identification of her writing and drawing products, and finally, to telling what she'll make before drawing.

Kristen received crayons as a Christmas present when she was fifteen months old. Her first attempts at drawing were rapid back-and-forth swipes at paper (see Figure 2.1). She would quickly make a few marks and push the paper on the floor, indicating that she wanted another sheet of paper. Kristen would try to write whenever her mother or father were writing. When she was twenty-one months old, Kristen began making round-and-round lines and dots. Her mother and father began drawing to entertain her. They drew people, houses, flowers, cats, dogs, and other familiar objects.

When Kristen was two years old, she began making jagged lines and single straight lines. She often labeled her pictures "dots." At that time, Kristen often commanded that her

Figure 2.1 Back-and-Forth Lines

Figure 2.2 Circular Shapes

parents draw "a little girl," "a little boy," or any other object she could think of. She also asked them to write "Kristen," "Mommy," "Daddy," and the names of all the people she knew.

At twenty-seven months of age, Kristen made concentrated efforts to control her marks. She would slowly draw a continuous line all around the edges of her paper. It seemed as if she were pushing the crayon around the paper and watching its progress. She began making circular shapes of just a single line or a few lines (see Figure 2.2). One day she drew several loopy scribbles, filling a page. Her mother asked her, "What did you write?" and Kristen replied, "ABCs." This was a rare occurrence. At this time, Kristen did not often choose to use her markers or crayons to draw. Rather, she insisted that her mother or father draw or write. She also frequently refused to answer when her mother asked, "What did you draw?"

Once, when Kristen was two and a half years old, her mother began drawing a face. She stopped after drawing the shape of the head, and she asked Kristen to point to where the eyes, nose, mouth, and hair should go. Kristen pointed to where each feature belonged. Her mother coaxed her to draw some eyes. Kristen tried to put eyes on the face, but became frustrated. She announced, "I can't draw that." One morning, Kristen's mother convinced her to draw by saying, "Just do some lines and dots and circles." Kristen selected a blue marker and made several quick line strokes down her page (see Figure 2.3). After making several of these marks, she cried, "Look at the rain." She made several more marks, saying, "More rain. Look at the rain, Mommy." Then she began making dots, saying, "Look at all these raindrops."

A few days later, Kristen was encouraged to make a picture for her aunt. She made a single line down her page and said "B" (see Figure 2.4). She made another line and said "C." She continued making lines and naming letters. As she gave her picture to her aunt, she said, "Look at the ABCs."

By the time Kristen was three years old she was drawing people (see Figure 2.5). She would draw a circle, add two lines for arms, two lines for legs, and some dots for eyes. After drawing the person in Figure 2.5, Kristen said, "This is a picture of Daddy."

Figure 2.3 *"Rain" and "Raindrops"*

Figure 2.4 *"ABCs"*

Figure 2.5 *"This is a picture of Daddy"*

Concepts about Literacy from Early Writing Experiences

As a part of these rich experiences interacting with her parents and with crayons, markers, and other writing materials, Kristen learned at least five concepts about drawing and writing.

1. Drawing and Writing Are Pleasurable

Children enjoy drawing and writing. Adult observers sense children's intense concentration as they hold tightly to both markers and paper and watch intently the shapes they create

(Taylor & Dorsey-Gaines, 1988). Kristen often chose drawing and writing over other activities. For her, getting a new box of crayons or a set of markers was an important occasion, followed by hours of pleasurable drawing and writing.

2. Movements Are Controlled

Children learn motor "schemes" for drawing shapes and lines (Gardner, 1980). **Motor schemes** allow children to control their movements so they can make intentional shapes and lines. In order to be able to put circles and dots on a page where they intend them to go, children must learn how to control their movements. Kristen showed that she was learning to control her movements when she intently watched the progress of her crayons as she drew. As with Kristen, most children first develop motor schemes for making back-and-forth marks, round-and-round lines, dots, and jagged lines. Later, they make circlelike shapes and single lines (Gardner, 1980). Eventually, children learn to make as many as twenty basic scribbles, which become the building blocks of art and writing (Kellogg, 1969).

3. Writing and Drawing Involve Familiar Roles and Language

Toddlers and their parents develop **writing and drawing routines** similar to the book-sharing routines described earlier. Young children draw both to engage their parents' attention and to engage other children in play. Kristen quickly learned many routines that initiated drawing and writing as social interactions. She would say to her friends, "Let's make ABCs," or to her father, "Let's draw. You draw. Draw a little girl." When her father suggested that she draw (because he suspected she needed a new activity), Kristen replied, "No, you draw." Kristen, like other young children with willing parents, engaged in "command-a-picture" or "command-a-word" routines (Lass, 1982). In these routines, children name a word, letter, or object, and parents write or draw it.

4. Drawing and Writing Can Be Named

Children learn to label their lines and shapes. Gardner (1980) reported that he often drew things for his son. One time, he drew a bird and, while drawing, talked about birds. Later, his son drew round-and-round lines, which did not resemble a bird in the least, and called his picture "bird." Gardner called this **romancing.** Many children romance both drawings and writing. They draw with no apparent intention to create something specific or meaningful, and when they finish, they label their creation, as Gardner's son did. Kristen romanced writing "the ABCs" (Figure 2.4). Such drawings are not really representational drawings or symbols because they do not objectively resemble the object labeled. However, romancing pictures and drawings—not planning what a written mark will be or even intending it to be meaningful, but rather labeling it or assigning meaning to it after the mark is completed—is a step in the direction of creating symbols in representational drawing. Children are led in this direction when their parents treat even their unintentional drawings as if they were intentionally representational. They beckon children, "Tell me about your picture." This is an example of **ascribing intentionality,** when parents act as if what children do is intentional. Ascribing intentionality moves children onward toward representational drawing.

5. Drawings Are Symbols

Sometime between the ages of two and five, children begin to plan their drawings, and these drawings begin to resemble recognizable objects. When children's drawings begin to look to an objective viewer like what children label them, they are called **representational drawings.** The drawings become recognizable symbols. Children learn that their drawings can not only be named, but also become representations of things. Kristen demonstrated the beginning of this knowledge as she drew her "rain" picture. She drew lines and noticed that they looked like rain. Then she made dots that she called "raindrops." Kristen learned that she could not only make lines and dots, but also make "rain" and "raindrops." She used her lines and dots as symbols.

Children's early representational drawings or symbols depict humans. Most children's early representational drawings of people consist of a circle with two vertical lines reaching downward. These drawings are called tadpoles (see Kristen's drawing of her father in Figure 2.5).

Kristen's story provides one example of a young child's early literacy concepts. Yet we could ask whether all young children have experiences like Kristen's and whether they all learn the kinds of concepts that she learned. We could also ask *how* Kristen acquired so many literacy concepts at such an early age. Obviously, one of the important variables in Kristen's learning was the nature of the interactions she had with her parents as they shared books and wrote together. In the next section, we discuss further how children acquire literacy concepts and describe the influence of home experiences in supporting young children's literacy learning.

HOME INFLUENCES ON LITERACY LEARNING

Literacy learning begins in the home. Children's first experiences with literacy are mediated by the ways in which parents and other caregivers use reading and writing in their lives (Purcell-Gates, 1996). There are two critical components at work here for children's learning: first, children's interactions with others create contexts for learning (see Chapter 1 and the discussion of Vygotsky's zone of proximal development); and second, literacy is embedded in everyday living activities. Parents help socialize their young children into the activities that are expected in everyday living, including reading and writing. Kristen's mother and father valued literacy, and reading and writing were an important part of every day of their professional and personal lives. Therefore, they included Kristen in these activities and had every expectation that Kristen would learn to read and write and eventually participate in the same kinds of literacy activities.

One way in which parents invite very young children to participate in literacy activities is to read storybooks aloud. In fact, one of the best predictors of children's reading achievement in school is the number of hours they were read to as preschoolers (Wells, 1986). We also know that preschoolers who interacted more with their parents as they read aloud have larger vocabularies and better story understanding as five-year-olds than do children who contributed less during storybook readings (Dickinson & Tabors, 1991; Whitehurst et al., 1988). Clearly, reading aloud with young children is an important vehicle through which they acquire literacy concepts.

Booksharing

We relate the interactions between three children and their parents as they shared books together. These interactions demonstrate the strategies used by parents and other caregivers to support young children's construction of meaning. They also show how children's abilities to construct meaning expand as a result of participating in booksharing interactions.

The three children play increasingly sophisticated roles in conversations with their parents about books they are reading. The youngest, Kristen, participates in interactive labeling; she labels a picture and anticipates and observes her mother's confirmation. Elizabeth, who is older than Kristen, participates in parent-initiated questioning and answering about picture elements that her mother considers central to plot development; her mother asks, Elizabeth answers, and her mother comments about the answers. Both Kristen and Elizabeth are in charge of the bookreading; they turn the pages. The oldest, Jon-Marc, is in charge in a different way. He initiates the questioning about both pictures and text; he asks, his father answers, and then Jon-Marc comments on the answers.

Kristen and Her Mother Share *Billy Goats Gruff*

Figure 2.6 presents a portion of the dialogue between Kristen and her mother as they shared *Billy Goats Gruff* (Hellard, 1986). Kristen was seventeen months old at the time of this interaction. The dialogue demonstrates that Kristen already knew much about meaning construction; she labeled objects (saying "tee" as she pointed to a picture of a tree) and sought confirmation of her label (she repeated "tee" each time, looking at her mother as if for confirmation of her meaning and label). Kristen also monitored her meaning; she observed her mother's reaction to her label.

Kristen's mother used several strategies to encourage Kristen to participate actively in the booksharing interaction and to expand on what Kristen could currently do. She allowed

Figure 2.6 *Kristen and Her Mother Share* Billy Goats Gruff *(Hellard, 1986)*

Bracket indicates portions of the dialogue that occurred simultaneously.

Kristen: (brings *Billy Goats Gruff* to her mother, sits on her mother's lap, holds book, and turns book with cover facing up)

Mother: Three billy goats gruff. (points to each goat on the cover) Look, a little one. (points to a small goat) A middle-size—

[K: (opens book and turns two pages, gazes at picture, and points to a picture of a tree) tee (looks up at her mother)

M: Yes, it's a tree.

K: (points to another tree) tee (looks up at mother again)

M: Hm, um.

K: (points to another tree) tee.

M: (points to picture of troll, puts her arm around Kristen, and shakes them both) (changes voice to deeper tone) Look at the Trollllll. I'm going to eat you up.

K: (laughs, turns page)

Kristen to take charge of the reading by turning pages, even when doing so interrupted the reading. She provided feedback to Kristen's labels ("Yes, it's a tree") and helped Kristen focus on the more important narrative elements of the story. She hugged and shook Kristen and used her voice to attract Kristen's attention to a character, the troll.

It is noteworthy that none of the story text was read in this bookreading episode. Kristen's mother knew that Kristen found her talk, not her reading of the text, most meaningful. Although Kristen contributed very little language in the interaction, she was actively participating. She turned pages, used gestures and movements, gazed at her mother, and said words. Kristen's mother did not want to teach her that booksharing demands sitting still and being quiet. The interaction between Kristen and her mother was anything but quiet.

Elizabeth and Her Mother Share *Where's Spot?*

A portion of the interaction between Elizabeth (twenty-six months) and her mother as they shared *Where's Spot?* (Hill, 1980) is presented in Figure 2.7. In this interaction, Elizabeth followed both the story and the story text much more closely than Kristen did. In addition, Elizabeth contributed more language to the reading episode. However, her mother still contributed the majority of talk.

***Figure 2.7** Elizabeth and Her Mother Share* Where's Spot? *(Hill, 1980)*

Paraphrased text is underlined. Brackets indicate portions of the dialogue that occurred simultaneously.

[Mother: We are looking for Spot. Let's turn the page. He's a little tiny puppy. Can you see if you can find him <u>behind the door.</u> Is he there?

[E: (turns to next page)

M: No?—What's inside the clock? Is he in there?

E: He's in there.

M: That's a snake. That's not a little dog.

E: Let me read it.

M: Okay.

E: It's a snake.

[M: Turn the page. Where's Spot? Let's see if we can find the puppy. Is he—

[E: (turns back to look at snake again)

M: Let's see what's behind the next page. We need to find Spot. Is he in there? (points to piano)

E: There's a doggy there (points to Mother Dog, Sally)

M: He's looking for another doggy. Spot's not there.

E: There? (points to Sally on next page)

M: Yes. That's a doggy. He's looking for another doggy, a puppy. Is there a puppy <u>in the piano</u>?

E: No.

Elizabeth used many of the same meaning-making strategies that Kristen used. She took charge of the interaction by turning the pages and making comments. She labeled objects in the pictures ("There's a doggy there") and answered her mother's questions.

Elizabeth's mother used many strategies for expanding and supporting Elizabeth's participation in this booksharing event. First, she featured an important narrative element (action and character motivation) by telling Elizabeth that the mother dog was looking for her puppy. She continually used this as a context for helping Elizabeth understand why the dog was looking behind doors and under beds. She matched her reading style to Elizabeth's ability to participate in the booksharing (as did Kristen's mother) by interweaving her talk with reading the text (Altwerger, Diehl-Faxon, & Dockstader-Anderson, 1985). The story text seemed to be included as part of a conversation she was having with her daughter about the story. She helped Elizabeth find meaning from the words of the text by using her explanations and expansions on the story as a support for meaning construction. In addition, she asked Elizabeth questions that called for labeling ("What's inside the clock?") and provided feedback to her daughter's answers (correcting Elizabeth when she mistook the mother dog for the puppy).

Jon-Marc and His Father Share *The Story of Ferdinand*

Figure 2.8 presents part of a booksharing interaction between Jon-Marc, a three-year-old, and his father. Jon-Marc listened carefully and looked intently at each illustration as his father read *The Story of Ferdinand* (Leaf, 1936). He interrupted his father at times to ask questions and make comments. He asked not only about the meaning of words, but also about reasons for story events and actions. He asked, "Why (did they have to take Ferdinand

Figure 2.8 *Jon-Marc and His Father Share* The Story of Ferdinand *(Leaf, 1936)*

Text is presented in all capital letters.

Illustration:	Ferdinand in a small cart going over the mountain. A bull ring is the background.
Father:	SO THEY HAD TO TAKE FERDINAND HOME.
Jon-Marc:	Why?
Father:	Because he wouldn't fight. He just wouldn't fight. He didn't like to fight. He just wanted to smell the flowers. (Note, this is a paraphrase of the text that had just been read on the previous pages.)
Jon-Marc:	Is that why they wanted to . . . to . . . to fight in the drid?
Father:	In Madrid? Yeah, they wanted . . . they wanted him to fight in Madrid. Madrid's the name of a city. They wanted him to fight the matador. But he didn't. He just wanted to go home and smell the flowers.
Jon-Marc:	And . . . and . . . and love her mother cow?
Father:	Yeah, and . . . and love his mother.
Jon-Marc:	Where's her mother cow?
Father:	Well, she's back in the book a little bit.

home)?" He listened carefully to his father's explanations and asked clarifying questions ("Is that why they wanted to fight in the drid?").

Another strategy Jon-Marc used to make meaning was to apply his understanding of events in the real world to make inferences about story events. Jon-Marc asked if Ferdinand would (go home) "And . . . and . . . and love her mother cow?" This question reveals that Jon-Marc used inferences to predict story events (after going home, Ferdinand would love his mother). It also illustrates that he used his own life as a frame of reference for understanding the story. Jon-Marc probably went home to love his mother, so he inferred that Ferdinand would be going home to love his mother.

Jon-Marc's father, like Kristen's and Elizabeth's mothers, was skillful at adapting the booksharing event to Jon-Marc's abilities. He knew that Jon-Marc was able to sit and listen to long stretches of text. Jon-Marc's father expanded on information from the text and related to Jon-Marc's concerns (he explained that Madrid is a city), and he provided more adult models of language ("And love his mother"). He drew attention to information in the text as a way of helping Jon-Marc understand the story. He repeated information from the story text to answer Jon-Marc's question and, therefore, made explicit the causal relations among events in the story ("They wanted him to fight the matador. But he didn't. He just wanted to go home and smell the flowers.") All of his talk was contingent on Jon-Marc's talk; that is, it was in response to Jon-Marc's questions and comments.

Meaning Making in Booksharing

Table 2.1 presents a summary of the strategies that these three children used to construct meaning as their parents shared books with them. They used these *processes*, or strategies, to understand or construct meaning from the stories read aloud to them. These **meaning-making strategies** become part of the booksharing routines that we described earlier in the chapter. Children know that they play certain roles during booksharing, and these roles enable them to construct meaning.

As shown in Table 2.1, one meaning-making strategy that children use is to label objects. They learn that they can talk about things and actions in pictures by naming them (Snow & Ninio, 1986). Later, they can talk about things by describing them and comparing them to other experiences or people. A second meaning-making strategy is to ask questions

Table 2.1 *Meaning-Making Strategies and Supporting Strategies*

CHILDREN'S MEANING-MAKING STRATEGIES	PARENTS' SUPPORTING STRATEGIES
label objects	provide labels
ask questions	adjust reading style
connect story to life	raise cognitive level
make inferences	give feedback and extend
use parents' talk	draw attention to narrative elements
pay attention to narrative elements	follow children's lead
	up the ante

(about word meanings, characters, actions, character motivations, and causal relationships between events). Children actively seek more information (Yaden & McGee, 1984; Yaden, Smolkin, & Conlon, 1989), sometimes as a way of monitoring their understanding of the pictures and story. Children also connect their lives to the story (Snow & Ninio, 1986). They draw on their "scripts" of daily activities—their knowledge of what goes on, for example, at bedtime (McCartney & Nelson, 1981)—to make sense of descriptions of these activities. Children make inferences about actions, motivations, and relationships. They make explicit what is implied in the story text. They incorporate and expand on information provided by their parents. At first, young children listen to their parents' talk about the story as a way of constructing meaning. Later, they use the words of the text read aloud to construct meaning. Finally, children pay attention to salient narrative elements, such as characters, actions, relationships between events, and character motivation. They learn to use what they know about stories to better understand and remember stories.

Table 2.1 also presents a summary of the strategies that the parents used to support and stretch their children's participation in meaning making. These **supporting strategies** encourage children to participate, provide information, and expand on their parents' contributions. It is as if parents demand that children help coconstruct the meaning of the story as they read and talk together.

As shown in Table 2.1, parents provide labels for objects and characters, adjust their reading style to their children's ability to participate, ask questions that require children to label objects, and draw attention to important narrative elements. An important strategy that parents use is to raise the cognitive level of talk by commenting on and asking about character motivations and logical relations. These questions and comments require children to analyze characters, make predictions based on understandings of character motivations, and make inferences. Parents also provide feedback to their children as they expand on and extend their children's comments. Parents allow their children to take the lead in booksharing interactions. Early on, parents permit children to turn pages and identify topics of discussion. Later, parents follow their children's leads by making comments and asking questions contingent on the content of the children's talk. Finally, parents up the ante by encouraging children to participate in ever more cognitively demanding ways and to take on more and more of the meaning making independently.

Obviously, children learn a great deal from these rich interactions, and their learning is related to their future success as readers in school (Dickinson & Tabors, 1991; Wells, 1986). That is, children not only learn strategies or processes for making meaning as they interact with books, but also learn concepts about the nature of stories and the language in books. They learn the special kind of language related to written stories and other text, decontextualized language (Dickinson & Smith, 1994). **Decontextualized language** is language in which all the information must be conveyed in the words or language itself. Unlike conversation, in which much meaning can be conveyed by looking at the same object or events or carefully watching facial expressions or listening to tone, decontextualized language must convey meaning linguistically in the words that are spoken or read. Young children also learn that stories have certain narrative or literary elements and qualities that are particularly important in the process of constructing meaning. We call the knowledge that children acquire of narrative elements and how they work in stories the **concept of story.**

e story, as when Kristen
ted if a child had a prim-
own in Table 2.2.
children have poorly de-
d concept of story when
uestions she asked Eliza-
n of Spot's being lost.
oncept of story improves.
han one-year-old Kristen
did they have to take Fer-
out the reaction (just love

l than is retelling a story.
more difficult task. Even
llings. Four-year-old Ben
he Forest (Figure 2.9). His
es. This is typical of liter-
of illustrations or **naming**
cts or actions in the illus-

ading. Ben is a four-year-
be in the next chapter. His
rkle, 1976) demonstrates
e boundaries of beginner,
describe in this book, de-
uenced by the fact that he
as reading to a stranger.

es in addition to sharing
s read lists, clip coupons,
r help older children with
willingness and ability of
the amount of knowledge
include more frequent lit-
d writing letters or lists)
Casbergue, 1992; Purcell-

---

d. The people. Crying. Bear.

---

w it changes, we need to describe an
eat deal about stories. In its simplest
rium followed by a disruption of that
ion, and an action aimed at repairing
ment of the initial equilibrium (Leon-

stories have a basic structure to create
dyke, 1977). Story grammars are de-
es and how that content is organized.
ry (based on Stein & Glenn, 1979).
the same concept or schema of a story
is very important in learning to con-
ut what their concept of story might
Smith, 1977). Children gradually ac-
e an adult's story schema (Applebee,
rs and settings, that some action trig-
performs actions to try to achieve the
aining (or not obtaining) the goal.
ow they understand stories, retell fa-
bout stories. For example, when tod-
nly objects in pictures (Sulzby, 1985).

PLE *A SMART DOG*

---

his grandson Jim, and their sheepdog Shep

ountain side

orning, while Jim was watching the sheep,
Shep and set out to look for wild berries.
ped on the wet grass and broke his leg.

send Shep for help.

l his scarf around Shep's neck and sent
he sheep.

w the scarf around Shep's neck, he knew
was in trouble. He left Shep to watch the
lowed Shep's tracks in the dewy grass to-
Grandpa lay. Soon he heard Grandpa's
elped his grandfather back to their house
uld call a doctor.

Jim were glad that they had such a smart

The objects they label may have little or nothing to do with t
labeled the tree in *Billy Goats Gruff.* This situation would be expe
itive concept of story with little understanding of the elements s

Concept of story can play a role in booksharing even wher
veloped story grammars. Adults can use their own well-develop
making choices of what to feature during booksharing. In the
beth about *Where's Spot?,* Elizabeth's mother featured the proble

As children have more experiences with booksharing, their
Three-year-old Jon-Marc has a more developed concept of story
or two-year-old Elizabeth. He asked about the problem ("Why [
dinand home]?") in *The Story of Ferdinand,* and he speculated ab
her mother cow).

Asking questions during a story reading is easier for a chil
Knowledge of story grammar is less likely to appear in the latte
four-year-olds may act like literacy beginners in storybook ret
displayed little or no concept of story in his retelling of *Deep in*
retelling of this **wordless book** consists largely of labeling pictu
acy beginners. Their retellings typically consist of labeling parts
actions found in pictures. They do not attempt to relate the obj
trations to one another, and, therefore, they do not tell a story.

Concept of story is just one factor in children's emergent r
old who often reads and writes like the literacy novices we descri
beginner-like, **non-narrative retelling** of *Deep in the Forest* (T
that children's performances may vary back and forth across th
novice, experimenter, and conventional reader and writer that w
pending on the situation. Ben, for example, may have been infl
had only shared the book a few times with his mother, and he w

Environmental Print

Children observe and participate in a variety of other activit
books. Children are included in shopping trips for which parer
or write checks. They observe as parents write reminder notes
homework. The number of literacy events in the home and the
parents to include their children in these activities are related to
that young children have about literacy. Children whose homes
eracy events (such as parents' reading magazines and books a
know more about how reading and writing are used (Burns &
Gates, 1996).

Figure 2.9 *Ben's Emergent Reading of* Deep in the Forest *(Turkle, 1976)*

Bear. Bear. Bench. Oh oh. He's eating it. Broke chair. Jumping on the b
She found him. She chased that bear. Find his mother.

Environmental print items play an important part in the beginning literacy experiences of toddlers and two-year-olds. As children eat breakfast, they see a box of Rice Krispies and they hear talk about eating the Rice Krispies. They observe and listen in the grocery store as their parents look for Rice Krispies. As children acquire language, they learn to talk about "Rice Krispies" just as they learn to talk about "ball" or "baby" or "car." Just as children learn that things in pictures have names and can be labeled, they learn that things like cereal boxes and cookie packages can be named as well.

Many toddlers and two-year-olds do not notice or pay much attention to the print on their cereal boxes or cookie packages; nonetheless, the print is there. The print on the packages becomes part of what children know about those objects. Later, children will recognize just the print and stylized picture or logo without the object's being there.

Oral Language Interactions

Snow (1991) and Heath (1984; 1989) argue that certain oral language interactions are more like the language found in books and other texts than are other oral language interactions. Some language interactions require that children sustain a topic (talk for extended times about one topic without the support of another speaker), focus on **nonimmediate** events or objects (talk about things that the speaker cannot see at the time of talking), and make clear relationships between ideas and events (use logical reasoning, including making talk contingent on or connected to a previous speaker's talk). We describe such talk as decontextualized language (Beals & DeTemple, 1993; Heath, 1986). These language interactions are connected not only to language found in books, but also to some language events in schools.

Some children have many opportunities to observe adults as they use decontextualized language to recount events of the day, plan for future events, give explanations, or tell stories. Similarly, some parents encourage their children to participate in such language activities and support their children's attempts by asking questions, providing prompts, and expanding on children's comments (Beals, 1993). These experiences may be quite important for children's later literacy success. Children who are experienced in using decontextualized language are likely to be more successful in school language and literacy activities (Beals & DeTemple, 1993; Heath, 1984).

Differences in Home Literacy and Language Interactions

We can now return to the questions of whether all children learn the same concepts about literacy that Kristen learned and whether her literacy experiences are like those of most young children. We have shown that there are many ways in which literacy is supported in the home long before children go to school—in the ways in which parents and other caregivers interact with children as they share books, draw and write, read environmental print, and engage children in certain oral language routines. Any of these experiences has the potential of helping children become better readers and writers later, when they enter school.

By and large we know that middle class, mainstream families are likely to engage their children in many of these language and literacy activities. But, of course, families differ from one another, and the inclinations of children differ as well. Therefore, even children in the same family do not have exactly the same literacy and language experiences.

It is especially difficult to make generalizations about early literacy and language experiences across social class and ethnic lines. Some researchers have found infrequent uses of reading and writing in low-income homes (Purcell-Gates, 1996), although variations within these families also point to difficulties in generalizing across families. Some researchers have shown that the ways in which parents share books with children differ (Heath, 1984), and sometimes parents have difficulty reading with their young children (Edwards, 1989). Other researchers have documented rich and frequent literacy experiences in low-income families (Taylor & Dorsey-Gaines, 1988).

Some researchers have found differences in the ways in which parents in Mexican American and Chinese American families include their children in decontextualized language experiences (Heath, 1986; Pease-Alvarez, 1991). Heath (1989) argues that in many cultural groups children are not expected to use certain language patterns. It is safe to say that not all children come to school with experiences or concepts like Kristen's and that teachers should expect and celebrate the richness these differences bring to the language mix of the classroom. The next section of the chapter describes how teachers can enhance even very young children's literacy learning in child care and nursery school settings.

IMPLICATIONS FOR CHILD CARE AND NURSERY SCHOOL

Soon after they are born, many children spend many of their waking hours in the care of adults at child care centers and nursery schools. We do not believe that infants, toddlers, and two-year-olds ought to have structured literacy activities. However, teachers in these situations can take advantage of what we know about how parents support literacy learning to provide appropriate opportunities for young children to explore literacy.

Developmentally Appropriate Practice

In a joint position statement, adopted in 1998, the International Reading Association (IRA) and the National Association for the Education of Young Children (NAEYC) describe **developmentally appropriate practices** for young children's learning to read and write (IRA and NAEYC, 1998). We support this statement and encourage all teachers of young children to read and follow the recommendations it contains. IRA and NAEYC begin by recognizing the importance of literacy learning to success in school and in later life and by identifying children's first eight years of life as crucial to their literacy learning. They describe a **continuum of literacy development** with guideposts along that continuum for preschool, kindergarten, first grade, second grade, and third grade. They describe children's abilities and suggest what teachers and families can do to support children's movement from awareness, through experimenting, to reading and writing, even ultimately reading independently and critically.

Understanding of such a continuum is essential to developmentally appropriate practice. Good teachers challenge children, but they also provide sufficient support so that children can meet those challenges. The continuum is not a rigid sequence; each child's progress along it is unique.

IRA and NAEYC warn that "[r]ecognizing the early beginnings of literacy acquisition too often has resulted in use of inappropriate teaching practices suited to older children or adults perhaps but ineffective with children in preschool, kindergarten, and the early grades" (p. 197). This does not, however, mean that teachers have no role to play in young children's literacy development. Not teaching as one would to older children or adults does not mean not teaching at all. "[T]he ability to read does not develop naturally, without careful planning and instruction. Children need regular and active interactions with print. Specific abilities required for reading and writing come from immediate experiences with oral *and* written language" (p. 198). This book is devoted to describing the provision of such interactions and experiences.

IRA and NAEYC emphasize that language and **literacy experiences** are **embedded in culture,** and that in present day American schools the cultural context is one of diversity. They recommend not only appropriate teaching practices, but also public policies necessary to the providing of all children with such teaching in preschool through the early elementary grades.

Literacy Materials

Reading aloud to preschoolers is "[t]he single most important activity for building [the] understandings and skills essential for reading success" (IRA & NAEYC, 1998, p. 198). Children need functional, personally motivated, truly communicative experiences with reading and writing. "Classrooms filled with print, language and literacy play, storybook reading, and writing allow children to experience the joy and power associated with reading and writing while mastering basic concepts about print that research has shown are strong predictors of achievement" (IRA & NAEYC, 1998, p. 203).

Teachers can provide literacy materials even for very young children. Books should be in easy-to-reach locations. We recommend that nursery schools and child care centers have at least one book nook set up in an out-of-the-way place in each room (Schickedanz, 1986). Some teachers of toddlers prefer to keep books in large baskets, which they can bring out during booksharing time. Paper, crayons, and markers should be available on a daily basis. Toddlers and two-year-olds enjoy trying out new kinds of pencils, markers, and crayons. They also enjoy using new colors and writing on new textures.

Environmental print items can be used in a housekeeping center, or they can be brought in as part of other activities. One teacher of toddlers kept a bag of familiar environmental print items (such as a McDonald's bag, cereal boxes, and candy wrappers) to use during talk time. Talk time is a special time during the day when she invites one child at a time to sit on her lap in a rocking chair and talk with her. The environmental print items are one of the things the children might select to talk about.

Teachers need to be sensitive to the kinds of books that are most appropriate for the children they work with. Infants enjoy board books because the pages are easier to turn and the books are more durable. Experts on children's literature also recommend Mother Goose and rhyme books for infants and toddlers (Huck, Hepler, & Hickman, 1993).

Concept books capitalize on toddlers' growing language abilities (Huck, Hepler, & Hickman, 1993). They encourage children to label pictures. Simple ABC and counting books with few objects per page are especially appropriate for naming. Older toddlers and two-year-olds can be introduced to **first storybooks** (Friedberg, 1989), many of which, such as *The Runaway Bunny* (Brown, 1942) and *The Gingerbread Boy* (Galdone, 1975), include repetition or patterns. The Appendix presents a list of suggested storybooks for toddlers and two-year-olds.

Responding to Children's Literacy Activities

We believe children should see teachers read and write and that they should be invited to read and write daily. Exemplary nursery school teachers read aloud to small groups of children. Two-year-olds sometimes enjoy sharing books in groups of two or three children. This number of children allows teachers to sit close to the children just as parents do in one-on-one booksharing. Teachers can use the same strategies and routines in sharing books with children that parents use. Effective teachers are very willing to share favorite books again and again. They are more likely to talk about the story than to read the text. They invite children to participate by asking questions and making comments. Effective teachers use gestures and intonation to enrich the story meaning, and they tell how pictures and story actions are related to children's real-life experiences.

Chapter Summary

Very young children begin their literacy learning when they interact with their parents and other caring adults as they share books or other kinds of print items. Young children who have opportunities to draw and to talk about their drawing are also on their way to knowing about literacy. Infants, toddlers, and two-year-olds are not yet literate (as we describe *literate* in the preface of this book), but they do have many literacy behaviors and they do know something about literacy. They find reading and writing activities pleasurable, and they have bookhandling skills and participate in booksharing routines. Young children gain control over their arms, hands, and fingers as they develop motor schemes for creating shapes they have in mind. They know that the shapes they draw and the pictures they view can be named, are symbols or representations of reality, and communicate meaning.

Young children's home experiences have a powerful influence on their literacy learning. Children acquire literacy concepts through booksharing, through other literacy activities (including interactions with environmental print and drawing), and in decontextualized oral language routines.

As children share books with their parents and other caregivers, they acquire meaning-making strategies and a concept of story. Parents support children's meaning-making through storybook reading that is responsive and interactive. They also support children as they interact with environmental print. They respond to their children's drawings in ways that signal that these drawings are meaningful (ascribe intentionality). Finally, they invite children to participate in decontextualized oral language experiences, including giving explanations and telling stories.

Teachers can also play an important role in young children's literacy learning. They can make literacy materials available, offer literacy experiences, and respond to children's literacy attempts. Figure 2.10 presents a summary of what literacy beginners know about written language meanings, forms, meaning-form links, and functions.

Applying the Information

Complete the following case study. Discuss Steven's literacy knowledge and behaviors. Also discuss the role Steven's baby-sitter plays in Steven's learning.

When Steven was nineteen months old, he retold *Bears in the Night* (Berenstain & Berenstain, 1971). He turned the book so that the cover faced him right-side-up. He turned

Figure 2.10 *Summary: What Literacy Beginners Know about Written Language*

Meaning

- know booksharing routines
- learn meaning-making strategies
- use decontextualized language
- develop concepts about stories
- use decontextualized language

Forms

- develop motor schemes
- recognize the alphabet as a special set of written signs

Meaning-Form Links

- make symbols

Functions

- draw and share books as pleasurable activities
- use books and drawing to gain the attention of others

past the first page (title page) quickly. Figure 2.11 presents Steven's retelling.

When Steven was twenty-five months old, he enjoyed drawing with his baby-sitter. She would encourage him to get his crayons, and he would color while she folded clothes or cleaned. He often made nonsense sounds as he colored. His sitter would talk to him as she worked. She would imitate his sounds and he would imitate hers. Sometimes Steven would sing songs he knew as he colored. Figure 2.12 presents one of Steven's pictures. He said, "This is a car."

Figure 2.11 *Steven Retells* Bears in the Night *(Berenstain & Berenstain, 1971)*

Story: Bears investigate a sound in the night by creeping out of bed, down a tree, and up a hill.

Steven:	(points to moon) moon (points to lantern) i-eet	TEXT: IN BED Illustration: Seven bears in bed. Open window with a crescent moon. A lantern hangs on the wall.
	(turns page, points to moon) moon (points to lantern) i-eet	TEXT: OUT OF BED Illustration: One bear out of bed, otherwise similar to previous page.
	(turns several pages rapidly, gazes at picture for several seconds)	TEXT: UP SPOOK HILL Illustration: Bear going up hill with lantern in hand. Moon in sky. Owl at the top of hill.
	(turns page) shakes head, points at owl OOOOOOOOOOO	Illustration: The word "WHOOOOO," an owl, and four frightened bears jumping up.

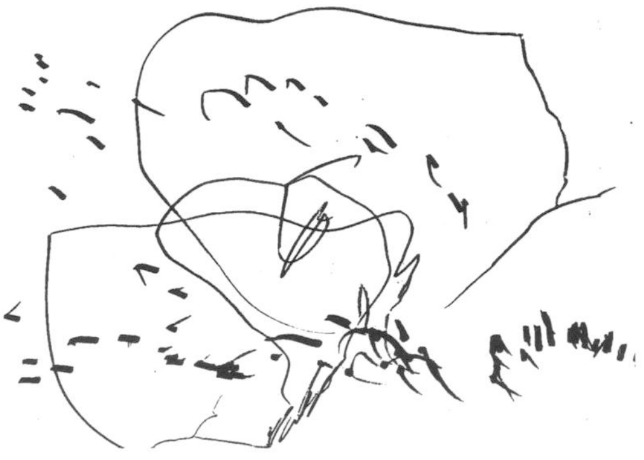

Figure 2.12 *Steven's Drawing*

Going Beyond the Text

Visit a child care center and take note of the literacy materials and activities in the infant, toddler, and two-year-old rooms. What books are available? How often and how do caregivers read with children? How frequently do children draw? Take at least three books to share with a small group of toddlers or two-year-olds. Describe their booksharing strategies. Join the children as they draw. Describe their drawing behaviors and make inferences about their literacy knowledge. Interview at least one caregiver. What does he or she believe about reading and writing for infants, toddlers, and two-year-olds?

References

ALTWERGER, B., DIEHL-FAXON, J., & DOCKSTADER-ANDERSON, K. (1985). Read aloud events as meaning construction. *Language Arts, 62,* 476–484.

APPLEBEE, A. N. (1978). *The child's concept of story.* Chicago: University of Chicago Press.

BEALS, D. (1993). Explanatory talk in low-income families' mealtime conversations. *Applied Psychololinguistics, 14,* 489–513.

BEALS, D., & DETEMPLE, J. (1993). Home contributions to early language and literacy development. In D. Leu & C. Kinzer (Eds.), *Examining central issues in literacy research, theory, and practice* (pp. 207–215). Chicago: National Reading Conference.

BERENSTAIN, S., & BERENSTAIN, J. (1971). *Bears in the night.* New York: Random House.

BOTVIN, G. J., & SUTTON-SMITH, B. (1977). The development of structural complexity in children's fantasy narratives. *Developmental Psychology, 13,* 377–388.

BROWN, M. W. (1942). *The runaway bunny.* New York: Harper and Row.

BROWN, M. W. (1947). *Goodnight moon.* New York: Harper and Row.

DE BRUNHOFF, L. (1975). *Babar and the Wully-Wully.* New York: Random House.

BURNS, M., & CASBERGUE, R. (1992). Parent-child interaction in a letter-writing context. *Journal of Reading Behavior, 24,* 289–312.

DICKINSON, D., & SMITH, M. (1994). Long-term effects of preschool teachers' book readings on low-income children's vocabulary and story comprehension. *Reading Research Quarterly, 29,* 105–122.

DICKINSON, D., & TABORS, P. (1991). Early literacy: Linkages between home, school, and literacy achievement at age five. *Journal of Research in Childhood Education, 6,* 30–46.

DISNEY (WALT) PRODUCTIONS. (1974). *Walt Disney's Peter and the wolf.* New York: Random House.

DOAKE, D. B. (1986). Learning to read: It starts in the home. In D. R. Tovey & J. E. Kerber (Eds.), *Roles in literacy learning* (pp. 2–9). Newark, DE: International Reading Association.

EDWARDS, P. (1989). Supporting lower SES mothers' attempts to provide scaffolding for book reading. In J. Allen & J. Mason (Eds.), *Risk makers, risk takers, risk breakers: Reducing the risks for young literacy learners* (pp. 222–250). Portsmouth, NH: Heinemann.

FREEMAN, D. (1968). *Corduroy.* New York: Viking.

FRIEDBERG, J. (1989). Helping today's toddlers become tomorrow's readers. *Young Children, 44,* 13–16.

GALDONE, P. (1975). *The gingerbread boy.* New York: Clarion Books,

GARDNER, H. (1980). *Artful scribbles.* New York: Basic Books.

HALLIDAY, M. A. K. (1975). *Learning how to mean: Explorations in the function of language.* London: Edward Arnold.

HEATH, S. B., with THOMAS, C. (1984). The achievement of preschool literacy for mother and child. In H. Goelman, A. Oberg, & F. Smith (Eds.), *Awakening to literacy* (pp. 51–72). Exeter, NH: Heinemann.

HEATH, S. (1986). Sociocultural contexts of language development. In California State Department of Education (Ed.), *Beyond language: Social and cultural factors in schooling languages* (pp. 143–186). Los Angeles: California State University, Los Angeles.

HEATH, S. (1989). The learner as cultural member. In M. Rice & R. Schiefelbusch (Eds.), *The teachability of language* (pp. 333–350). Baltimore, MD: Paul H. Brookes.

HELLARD, S. (1986). *Billy goats gruff.* New York: Putnam.

HILL, E. (1980). *Where's Spot?* New York: Putnam.

HUCK, C., HEPLER, S., & HICKMAN, J. (1993). *Children's literature in the elementary school* (5th ed.). Orlando: Harcourt Brace.

INTERNATIONAL READING ASSOCIATION & NATIONAL ASSOCIATION FOR THE EDUCATION OF YOUNG CHILDREN (1998). Learning to read and write: Developmentally appropriate practices for young children. *The Reading Teacher, 52,* 193–216.

KELLOGG, R. (1969). *Analyzing children's art.* Palo Alto, CA: National Press Books.

KUNHARDT, D. (1940). *Pat the bunny.* New York: Western Publishing.

LASS, B. (1982). Portrait of my son as an early reader. *The Reading Teacher, 36,* 20–28.

LEAF, M. (1936). *The story of Ferdinand.* New York: Viking.

LEONDAR, B. (1977). Hatching plots: Genesis of story making. In D. Perkins & B. Leondar (Eds.), *The arts and cognition* (pp. 172–191). Baltimore, MD: Johns Hopkins.

MANDLER, L., & JOHNSON, N. (1977). Remembrance of things parsed: Story structure and recall. *Cognitive Psychology, 9,* 11–51.

MCCARTNEY, K. A., & NELSON, K. (1981). Children's use of scripts in story recall. *Discourse Processes, 4,* 59–70.

NINIO, A., & BRUNER, J. (1978). Antecedents of the achievements of labeling. *Journal of Child Language, 5,* 1–15.

PEASE-ALVAREZ, L. (1991). Home and school contexts for language development: The experience of two Mexican-American pre-schoolers. In M. McGroarty & C. Faltis (Eds.), *Language in school and society: Policy and pedagogy* (pp. 487–509). Berlin: Mouton de Gruyter.

PURCELL-GATES, V. (1996). Stories, coupons, and the "TV Guide": Relationships between home literacy experiences and emergent literacy knowledge. *Reading Research Quarterly, 31,* 406–428.

ROTH, H. (1986). *A goodnight hug.* New York: Grosset & Dunlap.

SCHICKEDANZ, J. A. (1986). *More than the ABCs.* Washington, DC: National Association for the Education of Young Children.

SEUSS, DR. (THEODORE GEISEL) (1963a). *Dr. Seuss's ABC Book.* New York: Random House.

SEUSS, DR. (THEODORE GEISEL) (1963b). *Hop on pop.* New York: Random House.

SNOW, C. (1991). The theoretical basis for relationships between language and literacy in development. *Journal of Research in Childhood Education, 6,* 5–10.

SNOW, C. E. (1983). Literacy and language: Relationships during the preschool years. *Harvard Educational Review, 53,* 165–189.

SNOW, C. E., & NINIO, A. (1986). The contracts of literacy: What children learn from learning to read books. In W. H. Teale & E. Sulzby (Eds.), *Emergent literacy: Writing and reading* (pp. 116–138). Exeter, NH: Heinemann.

STEIN, N., & GLENN, C. (1979). An analysis of story comprehension in elementary children. In R. Freedle (Ed.), *Advances in discourse processes: (Vol 2). New directions in discourse processing* (pp. 53–120). Norwood, NJ: Ablex.

SULZBY, E. (1985). Children's emergent reading of favorite storybooks: A developmental study. *Reading Research Quarterly, 20,* 458–481.

TAYLOR, D., & DORSEY-GAINES, C. (1988). *Growing up literate: Learning from inner-city families.* Portsmouth, NH: Heinemann.

THORNDYKE, P. (1977). Cognitive structures in comprehension and memory of narrative discourse. *Cognitive Psychology, 9,* 77–110.

TURKLE, B. (1976). *Deep in the forest.* New York: Dutton Children's Books.

WELLS, G. (1986). *The meaning makers.* Portsmouth, NH: Heinemann.

WHITEHURST, G., FALCO, F., LONIGAN, C., FISCHEL, J., DEBARYSHE, B., VALDEZ-MENBCHACA, M., & CAULFIELD, M. (1988). Accelerating language development through picture book reading. *Developmental Psychology, 24,* 552–559.

WRIGHT, B. F. (ILLUSTRATOR) (1916). *The real Mother Goose.* New York: Rand McNally.

YADEN, D. B., JR., & MCGEE, L. M. (1984). Reading as a meaning-seeking activity: What children's questions reveal. In J. Niles (Ed.), *Thirty-third yearbook of the National Reading Conference* (pp. 101–109). Rochester, NY: National Reading Conference.

YADEN, D., SMOLKIN, L., & CONLON, A. (1989). Preschoolers' questions about pictures, print convention, and story text during reading aloud at home. *Reading Research Quarterly, 24,* 188–214.

Chapter 3

From Three to Five Years

Novice Readers and Writers

Key Concepts

novice reader
novice writer
intention to communicate
repertoire of literacy knowledges
environmental print
contextualized written language
literal meaning
inferential meaning
evaluative meaning
storybook reading styles
amount of participation
levels of cognitive engagement
intentionally meaningful messages
writinglike scribbles
letterlike forms
letter strings
features of letters
concept of letters
mock letters
concepts about signatures
text forms
text features
concept of story
story-as-a-whole
sequence
causal relationships
pretend readings
emergent readings
organization of informational books
contextual dependency
sign concept
phonological awareness
phonemic awareness
phonemes
phonics

WHO ARE NOVICE READERS AND WRITERS?

In this chapter, we examine the literacy learning of many preschoolers, kindergartners, and even some first graders whom we call **novice readers and writers.** Our choice of words to describe these children's reading and writing is intentional: in everyday usage, the words *novice* and *beginner* are nearly synonymous. Our decision to use the word *novice* in this chapter and the word *beginner* in Chapter 2 signifies that although we describe a change in literacy behaviors, we recognize that there are overlaps and interactions between our two concepts of beginning literacy and novicelike literacy.

Learning about written language is a gradual process. Children's literacy development is a matter of their taking small steps and making minor adjustments in their hypotheses. Children form new hypotheses in response to the discovered inadequacies of past strategies. Thus, it is not possible to identify a single criterion of novice literacy. A child may act like a literacy beginner in one literacy event and like a novice reader or writer in another event. Still, careful observers will notice that in some literacy events children begin using written language in ways that signal new insights about literacy. In this chapter, we will describe the many indications that children have constructed new understandings about literacy.

New Insights about Communicating with Written Language

Preschoolers sometimes use written language in ways that differ from those beginners use. They go beyond labeling their written marks as beginners do (in Chapter 2 Kristen called her written lines and shapes "ABCs"). *Novices intentionally create written symbols that they use to communicate a message.*

Figure 3.1 shows Thomas's writing. He gave his writing to his mother and said, "I have a message for you." His mother asked, "What does it say?" and Thomas replied, "um, um, I love you." Thomas's writing is unconventional; in fact, it does not even have letters, just round-and-round scribblelike lines. However, Thomas intended his writing to be read, and he knew that his mother would find it meaningful.

Novice readers and writers also signal their new insight that written language communicates meaning when they construct meaning from the printed words and logos found on environmental print. They may recognize "Raisin Bran," "McDonald's," and "Coca-Cola" on the familiar cereal box, fast-food restaurant sign, and drink can. However, novices go beyond simple recognition of meaning in familiar items or contexts that happen to include printed symbols and words. *Novices react to the meaning communicated in printed signs and labels even when they are not located on the items they represent or in the context in which they are usually found.* They construct meaning from the symbol of the printed words and logos. They recognize the Raisin Bran and McDonald's logos even when the actual object (the box of cereal) is not present or when the familiar context (the restaurant building) is not available.

Examples of Novices

Three literacy events involving Quentin, Kristen, and Courtney are described next. These children have had many experiences sharing books with their parents and nursery school teachers.

Quentin is three and a half years old. He frequently draws with his older sister as she does her homework. Sometimes she draws pictures and writes words or letters at Quentin's request. One day, while his sister was doing her spelling homework, Quentin drew a large circle with one line radiating down from it. He pointed to this primitive *Q* and said "Quentin." Later, when his mother was checking his sister's spelling words, he gave her his paper and said, "I wrote mine."

Kristen is thirty-two months old. One day, while she was riding in the car with her mother, she said, "Pizza man." Her mother looked and finally spotted a Domino's pizza sign. This sign consists of two domino shapes in red, white, and blue and the word *Domino's*. Kristen's family frequently has a Domino's pizza delivered to their home. Kristen had never been to a Domino's pizza place because Domino's only delivers pizzas—it is not a restaurant.

Figure 3.1 *Thomas's Message*

Courtney is twenty-nine months old. When her mother signs birthday cards or makes lists, she gives Courtney paper and pens or crayons and suggests that Courtney write, too. One day, as her mother was writing a letter to accompany a birthday card, Courtney said, "I write 'Happy Birthday to you' " (see Figure 3.2). Courtney's mother suggested that they send her letter, too.

Quentin's, Kristen's, and Courtney's behaviors and talk indicate that they intend for their written symbols to communicate messages and that they recognize that messages can be communicated in written symbols. What is significant about these events is that Quentin, Kristen, and Courtney constructed meaning from *written symbols that they constructed or noticed on their own.*

Kristen constructed the meaning "pizza man" from a printed sign and logo without the clues of an actual pizza, a delivery man, or a familiar location associated with eating pizza. Her behavior indicated a new understanding that printed symbols communicate messages. She knew that written marks in environmental print are significant. Quentin constructed the meaning "Quentin" by printing something like a letter Q, and Courtney constructed the meaning "Happy birthday to you" by writing round-and-round and jagged lines. Their behavior, too, indicated their awareness that printed symbols communicate messages. It is significant that the messages Quentin and Courtney constructed were part of a larger activity involving writing to communicate. Quentin joined his sister as she practiced her spelling words, and Courtney joined her mother as she wrote a birthday message.

Are they reading and writing? This important question has been the center of controversy for the past few years. Traditionalists define *reading* as the ability to identify words printed in isolation or in simple stories. Similarly, they define *writing* as the ability to write identifiable words in isolation or in simple stories. After careful observation of children such as Quentin, Kristen, and Courtney, some educators have argued that we need a new definition of reading and writing (Baghban, 1984; Goodman, 1980; Harste, Woodward, & Burke, 1984).

We believe that *children are novice readers when they intend to get meaning from written symbols,* even when those symbols are highly familiar signs, labels, and logos. Kristen did not say that the Domino's pizza sign said "Domino's"; rather, she indicated that it meant "pizza man." Obviously, Kristen was not reading the words on a sign as a conventional reader would; nevertheless, she constructed meaning from the sign. Even when signs and labels appear in situational context, novice readers frequently respond to the written symbols rather than merely to the context. Three weeks after Kristen identified the pizza sign,

Figure 3.2 *"Happy Birthday to You"*

she asked, "What does that *name say?*" about a familiar sign on a Baskin Robbins ice cream store. For months Kristen had said, "I want ice cream," as she passed the store. Because a picture of an ice cream cone is prominently displayed on the front of the store, we might conclude that Kristen was merely interpreting a picture (of an ice cream cone) or recognizing a familiar context (an ice cream store) when she said, "I want *ice cream.*" However, Kristen's later request that her mother tell her what the *name said* demonstrated her awareness of the written sign and its power to communicate.

We believe that *children are novice writers when they* **intend to communicate** *meaning with written marks.* Quentin communicated meaning when he made his printed symbol *Q.* It is important to notice that Quentin's writing was not yet conventional; he did not write his full name, *Quentin,* nor did he form the letter *Q* perfectly. Still, he intended to write something that was meaningful—a symbol for his name. Courtney communicated meaning when she made her jagged and round-and-round lines. She did not include any letters or words in her writing at all, but she intended her writing to convey the message "Happy birthday to you."

Repertoire of Knowledges

Some researchers have noted that children seem to display a **repertoire of literacy knowledges** as they engage in different kinds of literacy activities (Dyson, 1991; Sulzby, 1985). That is, when performing one kind of literacy task, children might display one level of literacy knowledge, and when performing another task, they might display another level of literacy knowledge. We have observed many children who display different kinds of literacy knowledges in different literacy events. At the time Kristen's mother noted her new awareness of printed symbols in some environmental signs, she also noted that Kristen was not responding to all environmental signs, nor was she using her written marks to communicate messages. After Courtney wrote her birthday message, she spent several months writing lines and shapes that she labeled as letters or words but that she did not intend to be messages.

We believe that children draw on a variety of understandings about literacy as they participate in literacy events. Although we use the terms *literacy beginner* and *novice reader and writer* (and later *experimenting reader and writer* and *conventional reader and writer*) as useful devices for describing children's literacy behaviors and understandings, we do not intend these words be used as labels for young children. Rather, we believe that our descriptions of beginning literacy and novice reading and writing will provide teachers with useful guides for carefully observing what children do with reading and writing in specific literacy events.

MEANING

Novice readers and writers learn to construct meaning from an ever-increasing variety of texts, including menus, *TV Guides,* telephone books, grocery lists, coupons, and, especially, stories. Novice writers make meaning by creating an increasing variety of written symbols.

Constructing the Meaning of Environmental Print

By the age of two-and-a-half or three, many young children find some **environmental print** symbols meaningful (Goodman & Altwerger, 1981; Hiebert, 1978). Most young children learn to recognize McDonald's, Coke, and Burger King at remarkably early ages. Other young children may point to the word *Crest* on a tube of toothpaste and say "toothpaste" or might point to the word *Cheerios* on a cereal box and say "cereal." Novice readers are not reading the words on environmental print. Unlike beginners, however, they are paying attention to the print on environmental print objects. While beginners respond to such objects as wholes, which include print, novices focus on the print; they point to it. They know that the print is an important part of the object, that somehow it conveys meanings appropriate to the object. They know the kinds of meanings usually associated with the objects and actions signaled by the environmental print item.

Children's first experiences with environmental print also occur in contexts that make the meaning of the printed symbol obvious (Laminack, 1990). A McDonald's sign is located in front of the place where children get hamburgers. The McDonald's logo is on the bag that holds the hamburgers and on the paper in which the hamburger is wrapped. This kind of print is **contextualized written language.** It appears in a context or situation that usually helps cue the meaning; it is similar to contextualized oral language. Children naturally apply their oral-language strategy of paying attention to the context as a way of constructing meaning from environmental print.

Eventually, children no longer need the actual physical context to signal meaning. When children are familiar with printed symbols such as the McDonald's logo, the context of the building or hamburger is not necessary to cue its meaning. Children find the printed symbol itself meaningful. They operate with the knowledge that written language symbols communicate meaning. Many children begin to ask "What does that say?" about environmental signs. They know that the signs they see communicate some message that might be interesting to learn about.

For example, a few months after Kristen read the Domino's Pizza sign she said, "Look, Mom, Barbie." Her mother had received an advertisement for ordering magazines. The advertisement included a page of perforated stickers on which the magazine titles were printed. One of the magazines was *The Barbie Magazine,* and the word *Barbie* was printed on the sticker in pink stylized letters just as it appears on the doll box. There was no picture of a Barbie doll on the sticker, and the sticker with *Barbie* written on it was more than halfway down a page of nearly a hundred stickers. Kristen recognized the word *Barbie* without the clues of a toy store, a doll, or even a picture of a doll.

Children expect meaning from many kinds of print items in addition to environmental print. For example, four-year-old Takesha was asked to read a handwritten grocery list. She said, "Green beans, coffee, and bread." She also offered to read a telephone book and said, "Takesha, 75983." Although Takesha did not really read the grocery list or the telephone book, she knew the meanings associated with these kinds of print and used this knowledge to read.

Constructing Meaning While Listening to Story and Information Book Read Alouds

In order to construct the meaning of a story being read to them, children must listen to the words of the story. Of course, most books for children include pictures that provide salient contextual cues for understanding the stories. Eventually, however, children must learn to rely only on the text and not on picture context to construct meaning from stories that they read. These strategies are particularly important for later success in reading (Dickinson & Smith, 1994; Dickinson & Snow, 1987).

Most children's early experiences with constructing story meanings take place as they share stories with a parent or other adult. These sessions are highly personalized; they capitalize on children's experiences with particular stories. In Chapter 2 we saw that such personalized booksharing is a context for literacy beginners' learning bookhandling skills, engaging in routines such as the "naming game" (Ninio & Bruner, 1978), and interacting with adults in meaning construction, especially about the pictures in books.

As children approach school age—preschool or kindergarten—their storybook experiences will be in many-to-one situations. Teachers are likely to share books with groups of children rather than with one child at a time. In group story-sharing situations, children are not as close to the pictures as they are in one-to-one story-sharing situations. Thus they have to rely more on the teacher's reading of the words of the text to construct story meaning than on extensive viewing of pictures.

Effective preschool and kindergarten teachers are skilled in capturing each child's attention as they share books with small groups of children (Cochran-Smith, 1984). Still, young children must learn to pay attention not only to what the teacher is doing and saying (showing pictures, asking questions, making comments, and reading text), but also to what their classmates are doing and saying.

In the example that follows, Mrs. Jones's students show literate behaviors with books that are common to many literacy novices. They can construct a complete understanding of the literary meaning of a story read to them (unlike Kristen's and Elizabeth's sampling of story, and especially picture, elements in Chapter 2). They make some inferences, going beyond the literal meanings in the story, and they make predictions. They frequently connect story elements with their world knowledge and personal experience, as we saw Jon-Marc beginning to do in Chapter 2. Finally, benefitting from group bookreading sessions, they respond to their peers' responses, building collective as well as individual story meanings.

Children's Meaning-Making Strategies

Mrs. Jones is a preschool teacher who is skillful in sharing books with her class of four-year-olds. Figure 3.3 presents a portion of the interaction among nine four-year-olds and Mrs. Jones as she shared *There's a Nightmare in My Closet* (Mayer, 1968).

The children's comments and questions demonstrate that they understood much of the **literal meaning** of the story. Obviously, the children understood that there was a nightmare in the closet; they knew that the character needed protection. Their comments and questions demonstrate that they also made many inferences about implied meanings in the story. They made inferences about motivations for the character's actions (he shut the door "Cause he doesn't want the nightmare to come out"); about the character's traits ("He's a scaredy cat"); and about reasons for the character's feelings (he was afraid "cause the wind blow"). The children also made predictions about upcoming story events. Just before Mrs. Jones turned to the last page of the story, which contains an illustration of a second nightmare peeking out of the closet, one child predicted, "There's gonna be another one."

In addition to making inferences and predictions about sequence and causal relations, the children projected themselves into the story ("My momma take the light off, I'm not

***Figure 3.3** A Portion of the Interaction as Mrs. Jones and her Pre-kindergartners Share* There's a Nightmare in My Closet *(Mayer, 1968)*

Brackets indicate portions of the dialogue that occurred simultaneously.

Mrs. J:	(shows cover of book, invites children to talk about nightmares, reads title and author, and reads first page of text stating the character's belief that a nightmare once lived inside his bedroom closet)
Child 1:	He got toys and a gun on his bed.
Mrs. J:	Umm, I wonder why?
Child 2:	So he can protect him.
Mrs. J:	Protect him. Umm. (reads text about closing the door to the closet)
Child 1:	Cause he's scared.
[Child 3:	He's a scaredy cat.
Child 1:	My momma take the light off, I'm not scared.]
Child 4:	He might lock it.
Mrs. J:	Why would he lock it?
Child 4:	Cause he doesn't want the nightmare to come out.
Mrs. J:	(reads text about character being afraid to even look in the closet)
Child 1:	Cause the wind blow.
Mrs. J:	The wind blows?
[Child 3:	Yeah, the curtain's out.
Child 2:	It's blowing.]
Mrs. J:	It must have been a dark, windy night. (continues reading text, making comments, and asking questions)
Children:	(continue making comments and asking questions)
Mrs. J:	(reads text about character deciding to get rid of the nightmare)
Child 1:	I guess he ain't cause that's not a real gun.
Mrs. J:	(turns page to illustration of the nightmare coming out of the closet and walking toward the boy in the bed)
[Child 1:	There he is.
Child 5:	Why he's awake?]
Mrs. J:	Well what did it say? He was going to try to get rid of his nightmare, so he stayed awake waiting for his nightmare.

scared"). They also evaluated the story meaning based on their knowledge of the real world ("I guess he ain't [getting rid of the nightmare] cause that's not a real gun.")

In addition, the children paid attention to each other's comments. When one child commented about an action of the character ("Cause he's scared"), another one agreed ("He's a scaredy cat"). Similarly, when one child noted that "the wind blow," another child added, "Yeah, the curtain's out."

This short story interaction illustrates that four-year-olds in group story-sharing can construct many kinds of meanings (Martinez, 1983). They understand what the author says—the literal meaning. They understand what the author implies—**inferential meaning.** They make judgments about what the author says—**evaluative meaning.**

Teachers' Role in Meaning Making

Several researchers have examined the ways in which teachers share storybooks with young children and have argued that some **storybook reading styles** are more effective than others. (Dickinson & Smith, 1994; Martinez & Teale, 1993; McGill-Franzen & Lanford, 1994). First, effective storybook readers provide a large **amount of** children's **participation.** Teachers expect children to do a great deal of talking during the storybook reading. They ask questions to encourage children's comments, and when children make comments, these teachers extend and clarify them.

Some teachers encourage most talk during their reading of the story. Like Mrs. Jones (in Figure 3.3) they ask children questions, make comments, and invite predictions throughout the reading of the story. Other teachers encourage talk before and after reading the story but usually read the story with little talk.

Effective storybook readers demand high **levels of cognitive engagement.** Teachers expect children to make inferences about a character's motivations or to discuss the causal relations among events. They expect children to talk about the meanings of words, predict outcomes, or recall the important events of a story.

Writing Meaningful Messages

In Chapter 2 we saw that even literacy beginners gain increasing control of pens, crayons, markers, and pencils, and they come to intentionally represent meanings with their drawings. Literacy novices go beyond these beginnings by writing **intentionally meaningful messages,** not just with pictures, but also with **writinglike scribbles, letterlike forms,** and **letter strings.** This writing sometimes serves as labels for their drawings. Novices have a new interest in participating in the sending of the message and not just in the activity of writing. Much of novice writers' message making is a part of playful activity. They imitate their parents' or siblings' sending messages in their dramatic play. One day, when Giti and her mother had returned from having a snack at the Big Wheel Restaurant, Giti walked around with a pencil and paper and stood in front of her mother with the pencil held over the pad just as she had seen the waitress at the restaurant do. She said, "You want?" Her mother dictated "Hot dog," and Giti wrote a jagged line. Then her mother said "French fries," and Giti wrote again. After several minutes of this game, Giti said "Ready?" just as her mother had when she was ready to leave the restaurant (Baghban, 1984, pp. 61–62). Giti's behaviors indicated her intention to write something meaningful. She wrote the food orders that her mother dictated. The "words" she wrote ("French fries" and "hot dog") reflected Giti's growing awareness of the content expected in a written food order.

Children's interest in producing written messages can also be initiated through school experiences. Two-year-old Natalie made the zigzag lines in Figure 3.4. She wrote left-to-right zigzags with her right hand and right-to-left zigzags with her left hand. After her first zigzag, she said, "I did it! That's my name. I'll spell your name." Then she made another

Figure 3.4 *Natalie's Name Writing*

zigzag and said, "That's your name, Daddy." For others she said, "That's Mary's," and "Don's is easy," and, "That's your name, Mommy." We asked Natalie where she learned to write. She said, "I do it at school," referring to her day care center.

Similarly, Vang's kindergarten teacher provides many real-life experiences, such as flying kites, finding caterpillars, and visiting the zoo (Abramson, Seda, & Johnson, 1990). She believes that these experiences are particularly important for the learning of her children, whose first languages include Hmong, Spanish, Laotian, and Cambodian. Several days after visiting the zoo, Vang drew a picture of an elephant and wrote what appears in Figure 3.5a, saying "elephant." Then he drew a picture of a second, smaller elephant and discussed it with his teacher (Abramson, Seda, & Johnson, 1990, p. 69)

Vang: Teacher, look it. I made baby. Baby el-fant.

Teacher: A baby elephant. Oh, that's great. Can you write "baby elephant"?

Vang: Sure!

Vang wrote what appears in Figure 3.5b. Vang knows that writing can be used to label drawings. The meaning he constructed ("elephant" and "baby elephant") is highly dependent both on his picture and on the teacher's suggestion.

Much of children's meaning making in writing depends on their experiences with meaningful uses of reading and writing. Giti would not have used writing to create a food order if she had not observed orders for food being written. Natalie would not have taken

Figure 3.5a *"Elephant"*

Figure 3.5b *"Baby Elephant"*

From Abramson, S., Seda, I., & Johnson, C. (1990). Literacy development in a multilingual kindergarten classroom. *Childhood Education, 67,* 68–72. Reprinted by permission of the authors and the Association for Childhood Education International, 11501 Georgia Ave., Ste. 315, Wheaton, MD. Copyright © 1991 by the Association.

up name writing if she had not associated writing at school with classmates' names and then been encouraged by her parents. Vang would not have created a message in his journal if he had not had a highly meaningful trip to the zoo or observed his classmates' daily journal writing and his teacher's responses to those written messages.

WRITTEN LANGUAGE FORMS

While they are developing new insights about written language meanings, novices also demonstrate new awarenesses about written language forms. This is a new area of written language knowledge, one not developed by literacy beginners. It reflects novices' newfound focus on print. They notice the print on environmental print items and in books, they acquire notions of how print looks and how it is organized, and they begin to display those notions in their own writing. In particular, they acquire a great deal of knowledge about alphabet letters, names, and text.

Alphabet Letters

Novices demonstrate in many ways their understanding of the importance of letters of the alphabet, that letters are fundamental units of written language, that they play a basic role in the way written language works. Novices do not yet know what that role is (to represent the fundamental units of spoken language, sounds). They just know that it is something important. Novices recognize the uniqueness of letters among other visual graphics; they associate letters with people, places, and objects; they name and write some letters; and they write letterlike forms, using knowledge of **features of letters.**

Before they learn to name any alphabet letters or to write recognizable letter formations, children discover a great deal about alphabet letters and written language. One thing young children learn is that alphabet letters are a special category of visual graphics that can be named. Lass (1982) reported that her son began calling each of the letters in his alphabet books or in environmental print signs *B* or *D* when he was still a toddler. It seemed as if Jed had learned to recognize the special category we call letters. He called all the visual graphics (letters) in his category *B* or *D.*

A second thing that children learn about alphabet letters before they can name them is that alphabet letters are associated with important people, places, or objects. For example, Giti noticed the letter *M* in the word *K-Mart* and called it "McDonald's." She also noticed the letter *Z* on one of her blocks and said, "Look, like in zoo." (Baghban, 1984, pp. 29–30). Notice that Giti did not call the letters *M* or *Z* by their names. Rather, she associated their unique shapes with two meaningful places where she had seen those shapes. This unadult-like **concept of letters** is typical of novices. They do not think of letters as units of written language that are parts of words and related to sounds; rather, they think of letters as belonging to or symbolizing something meaningful.

Anders told his mother that the letter *a* in *Safeway* was "one of mine" (Goodman, 1980, p. 28). Santiago said about the letter *S*, "That's Santiago's." When asked, "Does it say 'Santiago'?" he replied, "No, it's Santiago's" (Ferreiro, 1986, p. 19). Dexter said, "*N* spell my grandmama." His grandmother's name was Hele*n* (Dyson, 1984, p. 262). These children's comments about letters show that they did not have the same concepts about letters that more accomplished readers have. Santiago did not think of *S* as a letter, as representing the sound of the letter *S*, or even as part of his name. Instead, he thought of the letter *S* as belonging to him.

As preschoolers, some children learn the names of many letters and acquire the ability to write several recognizable alphabet letters. By the age of three, some children can name as many as ten alphabet letters (Hiebert, 1981; Lomax & McGee, 1987). By age four, some children can write some recognizable letters, especially those in their names (Hildreth, 1936). It takes some time even for these early letter learners to acquire the names of all the alphabet letters. Even precocious youngsters who become accomplished readers and writers prior to entering kindergarten take about six months to learn all the letter names (Anbar, 1986; Lass, 1982). Children may take as long as two or three years to perfect writing their names (Hildreth, 1936). In this area, as in all literacy learning, there is wide variation in the age at which children acquire certain knowledges (Morgan, 1987). Many children entering kindergarten do not recognize any alphabet letters and cannot write their names.

As children learn to name alphabet letters and to write recognizable letter formations, they also acquire other kinds of knowledge about letters and written language. One of these is knowledge about letter features, the special lines and shapes that make up letters. For example, the letter *T* is made up of a horizontal and a vertical line; the letter *O* is made up of an enclosed, continuous curved line; and the letter *N* is made up of two vertical lines and a diagonal line. Children must learn to pay attention to letter features in order to distinguish between letters (for example, between the letters *w* and *v* or *l* and *i*).

Children show that they pay attention to letter features in their writing. Figure 3.6 presents Carrie's writing, which consists of both mock letters and conventional letters. As we described in Chapter 1, **mock letters** are letterlike shapes with many of the same features of conventional alphabet letters. In Figure 3.6 Carrie wrote a conventional letter *O* and the mock letters resembling *T* and *E*. These mock letters have several of the conventional letter features of these letters, but they also have some unconventional features (the small circles at the bottom of the letters and the extra horizontal line in the mock letter *E*).

Signatures

Just as children learn to name and write alphabet letters and acquire concepts about what alphabet letters are, they also learn to write their names and acquire concepts about what written names are. Children's ability to write recognizable signatures develops in an iden-

Figure 3.6 *Carrie's Writing*

From McGee, L., & Richgels, D. (1989). "K is Kristen's": Learning the alphabet from a child's perspective. *The Reading Teacher, 43*, p. 211.

tifiable pattern (Hildreth, 1936). Their ability depends on their growing motor control, awareness of letter features, and knowledge of letters as discrete units. Figure 3.7 presents Robert's name-writing attempts over a nine-month period while he was in a prekindergarten program for four-year-olds. The first example of his signature, produced in early September, was a jagged line. Like Robert's early signatures, many children's initial attempts at writing their names contain no letters at all; they are frequently a single line or shape. Such signatures may reflect that children are relatively unaware that the letters in their names are discrete units.

As children gain practice writing their names and begin to notice written language in environmental print or in their parents' writing, they start to produce a number of discrete, letterlike symbols as a part of their signatures. In the second example of Robert's signature, produced in October, there are five letterlike shapes. These shapes do not include many letter features. In contrast, in the third example of Robert's signature, produced in December, there are again five shapes, but they include many letter features. This signature has a recognizable *R* and *o*. Eventually, children include more conventional formations for all the letters in their signatures. They begin to place the letters in order and to include every letter, although at first the letters are likely to be scattered around the page or in scrambled order.

The fourth example of Robert's signature, produced in February, includes a symbol for each letter of his name; the letters are recognizable, but not conventionally formed. The

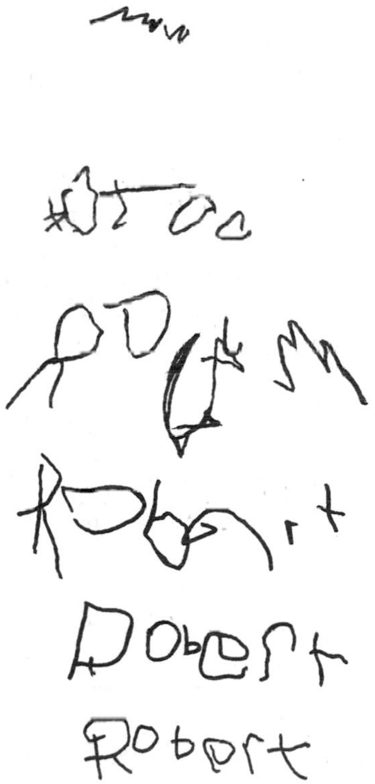

Figure 3.7 *Robert's Signatures*

letters are in order and written linearly. The fifth and sixth examples, produced in March and May, show his growing control over writing. The letters are conventionally formed, and by May, the writing indicates Robert's growing control over letter size and proportion.

As children learn to recognize and write their names, their **concepts about signatures** are quite different from those of adults. Ferreiro (1986) described Mariana, who claimed that she could write her name. She wrote five capital letters (*PSQIA*) as she said "Mariana" several times. When asked, "What does it say here?" about the letters *PS*, she replied, "Two Mariana." When asked, "What does it say here?" about the letters *QIA*, she replied, "Three Mariana" (Ferreiro, 1986, p. 37). Her answers reflect that Mariana believed each letter she wrote would say her name.

Mariana's comments about her name illustrate that children do not conceive of signatures as words composed of letters that represent sounds. Their ideas about signatures are interwoven with their concepts of alphabet letters.

Texts

Novice readers and writers learn a great deal about different kinds of writing, and they use this knowledge to create a variety of texts, especially story texts. Novices come to know a variety of text forms that are used in special contexts and for particular functions. They become aware of and use text features (such as "Dear ______ " at the beginning of a letter). And their concept of story and concept of informational book organization develop (Duke & Hays, 1998).

Novice writers produce many different **text forms.** Carrie wrote a restaurant check (Chapter 1, Figure 1.9) and Courtney wrote a birthday message (Figure 3.2). Later in this chapter we will describe Johanna's birthday list (see Figure 3.11) and Jeremy's "Book of Poems." Much of these texts was included in their talk as they wrote and in the contexts in which the texts were produced. When we look only at Courtney's writing, it does not appear to be a text. It is only apparent that it is a text when we pay attention to her talk, to her actions (she put her writing in an envelope), and to the context (she and her mother were writing birthday cards). It is interesting to note that function plays an important role in novices' creation of texts. Courtney created a birthday message as she participated in the functional activity of sending birthday greetings.

Sometimes the forms found in children's writing signal their growing awareness of the different features of texts. Figure 3.8 presents two pieces of Christopher's writing. Although Christopher composed both of his pieces using a combination of mock letters and conventional alphabet letters, the two compositions look quite different. One composition was written in the home center when Christopher decided to go grocery shopping with two friends. Christopher said, "I need candy, milk, bread, and cereal." The other composition was written at the writing center. Christopher later read this story to the teacher: "My dad went fishing but he didn't catch any fish. I caught a big fish."

It is easy to distinguish Christopher's grocery list from his story both by the meaning he assigned to his writing and by how each piece of writing looks. The story includes two main characters (Dad and Christopher) and contrasting event descriptions of those characters (Dad couldn't catch any fish; Christopher caught a big fish), whereas the grocery list includes four food items (candy, milk, bread, and cereal). The story is composed of three horizontal lines of text with an illustration; the list is composed of a vertical line of text. These features of Christopher's writing indicate his growing awareness of **text features.**

Figure 3.8 *A Story and a Grocery List*

Christopher's story and grocery list demonstrate that he had the growing awareness of the kinds of content found in different texts and how that content should be organized that is particular to novice readers and writers. We have called this kind of knowledge about stories **concept of story,** or story schema (see Chapter 2). In Chapter 2 we saw that literacy beginners have a limited concept of story. At best, like Jon-Marc in Chapter 2, they may begin to ask questions about stories based on a notion of how a story works (Figure 2.8). Novices' questions are even more guided by such considerations. In addition, they begin to use knowledge of typical story elements in their dictating of stories and in their retelling of the narratives of favorite storybooks.

Novice readers' and writers' concepts about stories grow as they gain experience with more complex stories. One of the most important ways in which novices' concepts of stories change is that they begin to understand **story-as-a-whole.** Novices learn two important organizational structures that can be used to link events together in stories: **sequence** and **causal relationships.** Novices learn that events in stories occur in sequence and that some events in stories cause other events to occur. They discover that the event of a character's falling down while skating is related to the event of scraping a knee—falling down caused the character's knee to become scraped. Children's concept of story influences many aspects of their literacy behaviors. Children draw on their concept of story as they listen to stories read aloud and construct the stories' meanings. They know to focus on the main characters and their characteristics, including motivations and problems. They know that the events in a story will be related to one another in a specific order. Increasingly, their questions during storybook reading reveal their attention to these elements (see Figure 3.3).

Children's concept of story also influences their creation of text in imaginary play (Wolf & Heath, 1992). They demonstrate their awareness of literary language and their ability to enter a story's world. Three-year-old Nat did this when he called his cereal "porridge" and said, "We are the three bears. My chair's broken" (Voss, 1988, p. 275). Three-year-old Kristen was "cooking" on her play stove after she and her mother had shared *Three Little Kittens* (Galdone, 1986). As she slipped on her hot-pad mitten, she said, "Oh, Mother dear, Mother dear. My mitten, my mitten here. Hey, Mommy, you be the mother."

Children also draw on their concept of story as they compose stories. Christopher included main characters and contrasting events in his fishing story (Figure 3.8). As children

Figure 3.9 *Johanna's Emergent Reading of* The Very Hungry Caterpillar *(Carle, 1969)*

Once upon a time there was a little egg on a leaf. It popped and out came a little caterpillar. One day he was hungry and he ate one apple. He was still hungry. At Sunday he had two pears. He was still hungry. At Saturday he ate three pineapples and he was still hungry. Then he ate four strawberries. He was still hungry so he ate a chocolate piece of cake, a piece of pear, some sausages, and then he was fat. He made a cocoon and he pushed his way out. And he became a beautiful butterfly. That's the story.

play, draw, write, and sing, they weave characters and events in and out of their familiar story settings (King & McKenzie, 1988). They create their own stories not only by making up characters and events, but also by mixing in characters and events from familiar stories.

Novices also use their concept of story when they attempt to retell stories (Hough, Nurss, & Wood, 1987). A special kind of retelling is when children look at favorite picture books—ones they have shared many times with their parents or teacher—and attempt to reread them on their own. These retellings or rereadings are called **pretend readings** (Pappas, 1993) or **emergent readings** (Sulzby, 1985). The pretend readings of literacy beginners, like Ben in Chapter 2 (see Figure 2.9), do not tell a story. The pretend readings of novices do tell a story.

Figure 3.9 presents Johanna's emergent reading of *The Very Hungry Caterpillar* (Carle, 1969). Johanna's mother had to read this book to her dozens of times. Johanna's emergent reading retells the events of the story in a sequence and includes some of the language found in the text (notice the use of past tense and the repetition of the phrase "he was still hungry"). Nonetheless, it is important not to dismiss Johanna's reading as mere memorization. She is displaying important literacy knowledge, such as concept of story and literary language, that she will use in many other literacy contexts now and in the future.

Johanna's concept of story and knowledge of literary language developed, in part, from the frequent pleasurable experiences of booksharing with her mother that preceded this emergent reading. Importantly, another result of such experiences is a positive attitude toward reading, including Johanna's conception of her own performance as reading. And, though not conventional, it *is* reading; it is an intentional recreation of the meaning of the text.

During the preschool and kindergarten years, children listen to more than just stories. They enjoy poems, songs, and informational books. Just as they gain a growing awareness of the characteristics of storybooks and the organizational patterns in stories, children learn **how informational books are organized.** (Duke & Hays, 1998; Pappas & Pettegrew, 1998). From listening to informational books read aloud, children learn that these books tell about classes of things, such as trucks or squirrels or tunnels (Pappas, 1993). Unlike stories, which tell about a particular squirrel (the main character) and his problem, an informational book tells about squirrels in general, what they are like (a description of their characteristics), and what they do (a discussion about their behaviors).

Children's concepts about informational texts also influence their emergent readings, retellings, and compositions of such texts. For example, Jean, a kindergartner, began her retelling of the storybook *The Owl and the Woodpecker* (Wildsmith, 1971), "Once in the forest there was a woodpecker" (Pappas, 1991, p. 455). This sounds like the way a story starts, with a setting and the introduction of a particular woodpecker. The actual text of the book does the same thing. It begins, "Once upon a time in a forest, far away, there lived a Woodpecker." In her retelling of *Squirrels* (Wildsmith, 1974), an information book, however, the same kindergartner used quite different language. She began, "Squirrels are very easy to find cause they have furry bodies and nice furry bodies and some nice furry ears which they stick up" (Pappas, 1991, p. 456). Here Jean is describing squirrels in general. The actual text does that, too. It begins, "It is easy to recognize a squirrel. He is a furry, small animal with a long, bushy tail, two strong back legs, two small front paws, two large tufted ears which stick up, and two big front teeth." The rest of Jean's retellings of these two books show that "she is just as successful in reenacting the information book as she is the story" (Pappas, 1991, p. 450).

MEANING-FORM LINKS

Novice readers and writers find print in the environment meaningful, engage in emergent readings, and communicate messages in their writing. They link meaning with form in their reading and writing by using context and talk. Whether in their scribbles (see Figures 3.1, 3.2, and 3.4), their letterlike forms (see Figure 3.6), or their letter strings (see Figures 3.5a and 3.5b), novices intentionally represent meanings. The link between such writing and novices' intended meanings is context. Only when others share that context, by observing or participating in the activities and language surrounding a novice's writing, are they able to recognize the novice writer's intention to communicate and retrieve his or her intended meanings from the writings, that is, read them. Similarly, when novices read, context determines what sorts of links they can make between the written forms they observe, whether in books or environmental print, and the meanings they can construct.

This dependence on context does not mean that novices are unaware of the importance of print. They know it is important, but they are mistaken about how it works. They think it is enough to make scribbles, letterlike forms, or letter strings that look to them like print. They have not yet grasped the alphabetic principle—that letters must systematically represent sounds.

As their literacy knowledge develops, novices eventually move beyond such dependence on context. They begin to appreciate that print must somehow match up with speech.

Contextual Dependency

Contextual dependency means that written forms convey meaning through the context of their use or through children's talk about their writing. Thomas's message (Figure 3.1), Courtney's birthday card (Figure 3.2), Vang's journal entry (Figure 3.5), and Christopher's story and grocery list (Figure 3.8) have a common characteristic: the use of contextual dependency to link written form to meaning. If we took the children's writing out of the context in which it was written and did not know what the children said about their writing, we would not be able to determine the messages that the child writers intended to communicate. We can only know the messages that novice writers convey when we know the context in which they wrote and when we listen to what they say about their writing. Clay (1975) called children's dependency on context to link meaning and form the **sign concept.** The sign concept is evident when children use the context of play to construct meaning in their writing and reading.

Matching Print to Spoken Language: More Than Contextual Dependency

Although novice readers and writers depend primarily on the context in which their writing is produced and in which written symbols are found to link meaning and form, some use more than context to link meaning and form. Many researchers have explored children's concepts about the links between meaning and print (Dyson, 1982, 1985; Ferreiro & Teberosky, 1982; Sulzby, 1985). They have found that not all children have the same concepts about the relations between meaning and form, that their concepts about the relations between meaning and form change as children gain experience using written language, and that children's knowledge of meaning-form links is very complex (Ferreiro, 1986).

We will describe two children's responses to a writing task which illustrate their knowledge of links between meaning and form in their writing. The task involves asking children to write a story and then read it (Sulzby, 1985).

Figure 3.10 presents John's writing and story ("I have a dog. He is big. He is my best friend."). As John read the story, he swept his finger from left to right across each line of text as he said each sentence. He demonstrated contextual dependency in making meaning from his own writing. But, in addition, John noticed that printed text must be matched somehow to the oral message; he matched a line of text with a spoken sentence. Although not yet conventional, this matching of the text with the oral message is a precursor to a later, more-developed kind of meaning-form linking, that is, matching one spoken sound (or phoneme) with one letter (or grapheme).

Figure 3.11 presents Johanna's writing and story. She did not write an actual story, but instead wrote a list of things she wanted for her birthday. Although her list is composed entirely of jagged lines, correlating what Johanna said with her jagged lines reveals that Johanna often matched one continuous jagged line with one spoken word. Johanna realized that the written forms she wrote should correspond with the spoken meaning she intended.

Drawing and Writing

Most novices' written texts include both drawing and writing. Dyson (1982, pp. 365–366) found that children combined drawing and writing in several ways in their texts.

Lorena's text is presented in Figure 3.12. She said, "This is a dresser," as she pointed to her drawing, and, "This is dresser, too," as she pointed to her writing. Her text shows that some children use both drawing and writing to communicate the same meaning. Lorena used her writing to label her drawing.

I have a dog.

He is big.

He is my best friend.

Figure 3.10 *John's Story*

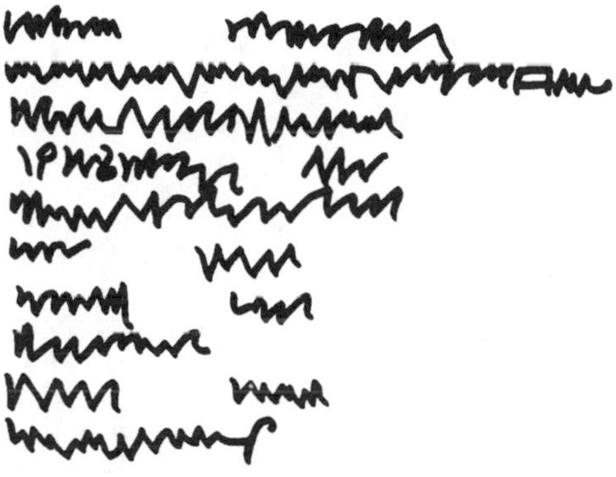

hula hoop
Wishbow kids with a bed
more Mapletown animals
Prince Strongheart
horse for Prince Strongheart
a baby
baby bottles
bonnet
baby clothes
slide

Figure 3.11 *Johanna's Birthday List*

Given that children so often include drawings with writing and that they read pictures in the same ways in which they read print, researchers have wondered whether children differentiate between the two symbolic systems, drawing and writing. We might suspect that they do not differentiate between drawing and writing. However, the relation between drawing and writing is complex. Some researchers have noticed that the lines and shapes that children call pictures are different from the lines and shapes that they call writing (DeFord, 1980; Harste, Burke, & Woodward, 1981). This observation suggests that children notice differences between drawings and writing and that their own drawing and writing reflect these differences. Figure 3.13 presents three-year-old Ryan Patrick's drawing and writing. Careful observation of Ryan Patrick's product suggests that he differentiates between drawing and writing, even though the drawing is not representational and the writing is not conventional.

There are three important characteristics of children's use of drawing and writing. First, it is clear that children's drawings are an important part of their written communications, and teachers can use them to encourage children's writing. Second, the talk that

Figure 3.12 *Lorena's Text*

Figure 3.13 *Ryan Patrick's Drawing and Writing*

surrounds both drawing and writing is crucial for understanding what children intend to communicate. Third, the talk provides useful information for finding out what children know about written language and how they learn to link meaning and written forms.

Phonological Awareness

Although novice readers and writers do not make the connection between sounds and letters, they do learn something important about oral language that, at a later time, will help them discover sound–letter relations. Novice readers and writers learn to pay attention to the sounds in oral language.

The sound system of language includes sounds in words, such as the /p/ at the beginning of *pin* and the middle of *happy,* but it also includes the qualities of sounds, such as pitch and stress and pause, which contribute to the melody of language. **Phonological awareness** comprises awareness of all of these things.

Phonemic awareness is a special kind of phonological awareness. It is conscious attention to **phonemes,** which are the units of sound from which words are built. The word *conscious* is extremely important here. Although difficult to observe in infants, even they have *un*conscious perception of phonemes (Eimas devised an intriguing method for proving this in infants as young as 4 weeks old; see, for example, Eimas, Sigueland, Jusczyk, & Vigorito, 1971). By their third birthdays, however, it is easy to see that children surely know, albeit unconsciously, what phonemes are, because by that age, most children are fluent speakers and listeners. Like all speakers and listeners, they must know one phoneme from another, for it is the combination and especially the contrasting of phonemes that make words happen. For example, in English, the phonemes /k/, /ă/, and /p/ are combined to make the word *cap,* and the /p/ and /b/ phonemes are contrasted when distinguishing the words *cap* and *cab.*

This combining and contrasting of phonemes in speech, however, is unconscious, both for children and adults. They know phonemes without needing to know that they know them. It is only in written language, with its extra layer of symbolization, in which letters stand for phonemes, that knowledge of phonemes must rise to the level of consciousness. Phonemic awareness is the *conscious* knowing that you know the sound units of language. And phonemic awareness is essential to learning how to read and write (see Adams, 1990, for an extensive review of research establishing this).

This book will include many examples of children's and teachers' using phonological awareness, phonemic awareness, and phonics. **Phonics** is a body of knowledge about how to use phonemic awareness and knowledge of the alphabet to encode and decode words. Children use phonics when they spell inventively (we will describe invented spelling in Chapter 4) and when they sound out words they encounter in books or in environmental print. Parents and teachers use phonics when they direct children's attention to sound–letter relationships in words children want to spell or read. Teachers use phonics when they plan and deliver explicit instruction in sound–letter relationships.

Because of the big role of phonemic awareness and phonics in literacy learning and teaching, a very important question is to what degree success depends on explicit instruction about them. The answer depends on many factors, including—at the time instruction is contemplated—the nature of children's previous experiences with print and their existing levels of understanding of phonemes and phonics. We have seen that novices have not yet developed phonemic awareness. That is a mark of the experimenting with literacy that we describe in the next chapter.

However, phonological awareness is germane to novices' literacy development. (Remember, phonemic awareness is only one kind of phonological awareness.) Novices are capable of other kinds of phonological awareness that are equally important to their successful development as readers and writers. For example, some novice readers and writers show that they have some phonological awareness because they make up rhyming words.

The ability of novice readers and writers to create rhyming words emerges from their earlier experiences with nursery rhymes and other books with language play. The rhythm created in nursery rhymes highlights and segments speech sounds in a way that conversation does not (Geller, 1983). The syllables *PE ter PE ter PUMP kin EAT er* are naturally separated by the stress in the rhyme. This natural play with language sounds invites children to enjoy the music of language. Children who have listened to nursery rhymes and other books with language play soon begin to play with speech sounds themselves. While four-year-old James was playing with blocks in his preschool room, he muttered "James, Fames, Wames" to himself. James was demonstrating phonological awareness. This ability will serve him later when he begins to notice that certain letters appear at the same time that certain sounds of language are heard.

WRITTEN LANGUAGE FUNCTIONS

One characteristic of young children is that they want to do whatever they see someone else doing. If Dad is sweeping the porch, his son wants a broom to sweep, too. We find these actions charming, but they are more than that. This willingness, even insistence, on joining in family activities forms a strong foundation for literacy learning. When Dad writes checks to pay bills, his son will want a pen and paper so that he can join in the activity of writing. Later, his son will want to join in the activity of writing checks to pay bills. Children not only observe adults' reading and writing, but also participate in using written language, especially in their play (Jacob, 1984, p. 81).

Many children from literacy-rich homes go beyond using literacy in their play. They use literacy as themes for play. One day Jeremy announced that he was going to make a book (Gundlach, McLane, Scott, & McNamee, 1985, p. 13). His father suggested that he use some index cards and write his book on the typewriter. After Jeremy had finished typing his cards, he and his father stapled the cards together to make the book. When his father asked him what was in his book, Jeremy replied, "A surprise" (p. 13). The next day, Jeremy's father invited him to listen to a radio program of children reading their poetry. After the program, Jeremy asked his mother and father to come into the living room to listen to him read his "Book of Poems." He opened the book he had made the previous day and said, "Page 1." Then he recited a poem that he knew. As he read "Page 2," he could not seem to remember any more poems, so he made up rhyming words and used singsong intonation. His mother and father applauded his reading.

Unlike Jeremy, who uses literacy as a way of playing and gaining the attention of his parents, Tom uses literacy in more functional ways. When Tom was four, he became angry because his mother would not buy him a new toy. His mother said that she would be paid in three weeks and that Tom could have a toy then. Tom asked how many days were in three weeks and went to his room. He made the calendar (a portion of which is presented in Figure 3.14) with a number for each of the twenty-one days remaining until he could get a new toy. Every day as his father read him a story at bedtime, Tom crossed off a day on his calendar, and on the twenty-first day, his mother bought him his new toy.

Children learn what to do with written language as they function within families and communities that use written language in particular ways. In most families, reading and writing are used as a part of daily living. Children in these families participate in these activities as well as observe them (Taylor, 1983; Taylor & Dorsey-Gaines, 1988). Many of the writing and reading examples presented in this chapter reflect the kinds of reading and writing found in many homes: writing birthday messages, reading menus and giving orders

Figure 3.14 *Tom's Calendar*

at a restaurant, writing and reading grocery lists, marking calendars to remember important events, and locating numbers in a telephone book.

Written language functions in different ways in different communities (Heath, 1983; Schieffelin & Cochran-Smith, 1984). In some communities, print serves the practical functions of paying bills, providing information about guarantees, and affirming religious beliefs. In other communities, print is used for recreation and entertainment as well; people are likely to read for pleasure. Print serves even wider functions in other communities; it provides a means of critically analyzing political, economic, or social issues. Children growing up in these different communities have different concepts of the functions served by reading and writing (Purcell-Gates, 1996; Schieffelin & Cochran-Smith, 1984).

A WORD OF CAUTION

We add two cautions to our discussion of novice readers and writers. First, we have noted the ages of several of the children we described as novice readers and writers. We believe that many children become novice readers and writers around the ages of two or three. However, children may display knowledge like that of novice readers and writers in one literacy event and knowledge like that of literacy beginners in other events. Many children display novice reading and writing literacy knowledge throughout their preschool years. Many kindergartners and first graders seem to operate with novice reading and writing knowledge. We caution that not all three-, four-, or five-year-olds will be novice readers or writers and that novice reading and writing often does not end at age five.

Second, much of the knowledge we have of young preschoolers' literacy derives from research involving middle class families. The ages at which many of these youngsters display novice reading and writing may be deceptive; these children have had early and frequent experiences of the kind that would be expected to support early literacy learning. When preschoolers who have not had many literacy experiences gain access to those experiences, they quickly acquire literacy concepts (Morgan, 1987).

However, we have been careful in this chapter to include many examples of novice reading and writing from children who do not come from middle-class backgrounds. Vang (Figure 3.5) did not speak any English when he began kindergarten. Gradually, he acquired English, and his writing and talking about writing seemed to be an important vehicle for his learning of English. John's and Lorena's writing was collected from a preschool program for at-risk young children. All these children had parents and teachers who surrounded them with literacy and provided numerous opportunities for children to participate in reading and writing activities (much like those we describe in Chapters 6 and 7).

Chapter Summary

Novice readers and writers approach reading and writing in unconventional but systematic ways. They expect written language to be meaningful, and the meanings they associate with particular kinds of texts (such as environmental print, grocery lists, stories, and telephone books) reflect their growing awareness of the language associated with these texts. Novice readers and writers find environmental print meaningful. The contextualized nature of this type of print initially supports children's meaning-making efforts, but novice readers respond to environmental print even when it is not in contexts that clue its meaning. Novice readers make strides in understanding the decontextualized print in stories that are read aloud to them. They learn to construct stories-as-wholes. They learn that stories are more than individual pictures, that stories are formed by a causally related series of events. They learn to make inferences and evaluations about characters and events.

Novice writers often intend to communicate a meaning in their writing, and the meaning they communicate reflects how they expect to use their written products (as a birthday card or a story). Novice readers and writers gradually begin to learn names for alphabet letters and to form conventional letters and signatures. Their concepts of letters and signatures differ from those of adults. Their learning to write many kinds of texts reflects knowledge of text features, and their talk about texts reveals an awareness of the content associated with different kinds of texts. In particular, novice readers and writers develop more complex understandings of the content, language, and organization of stories and informational books.

Novices rely on stylized print and pictures to read the logos in environmental print, and they depend on the context of their writing and talk to assign meanings to their writing. They use reading and writing for a variety of purposes, including playing, interacting with others, and conducting the business of daily living in their families and communities. The kinds of reading and writing activities in which children participate may vary, and what children learn about written language functions may differ accordingly.

Figure 3.15 provides a summary of the concepts presented in this chapter. It is important to keep in mind that a concept may appear in more than one section of the figure. For example, children's concept of story is an important part of their knowledge of written language forms. However, concept of story is also an important part of novice readers' and writers' knowledge about written language meanings. They use their concept of story as they construct meanings of the stories read aloud to them and as they compose the content of their own stories. Children's reading and writing ultimately reflect the interdependence of meaning, form, and function.

Applying the Information

Two literacy events follow. The first event involves Maryanne's reading a word she found on one of her toys. The second event concerns Jeffrey's writing a card to his friend Temp. Discuss what each of these events shows about Maryanne's and Jeffrey's understandings of written language meanings, forms, meaning-form links, and functions.

Four-year-old Maryanne was in her room getting dressed for school. She had been trying to get her mother's attention, but her mother was busy dressing and did not respond. Maryanne noticed a toy cradle lying on the floor (see Figure 3.16). Maryanne looked at the cradle, then slowly moved her hand from left to right across the two words *Baby Bear* on the cradle and said, "Bear. Look, Mom, come here, I can read this. Bear." She picked up her toy baby bear, placed it over the picture of the baby bear on the cradle, and said, "See, bear. Mom, look."

Jeffrey was playing with his writing box. He answered his toy telephone and had an imaginary conversation with a friend he had recently visited. "Hi, Temp. This is Jeffrey. Do you want to come play with me? Okay. See you later."

Figure 3.15 Summary: What Novice Readers and Writers Know about Written Language

Meaning Making

- know printed text communicates messages
- intend to communicate meaning in writing
- assign meaning to environmental print
- assign meaning to a variety of texts by applying knowledge of the content and language used in those texts
- apply concept of story in constructing the meaning of stories read aloud, retelling stories, and emergent reading of stories
- construct literal meaning
- construct inferential meaning
- construct evaluative meaning

Forms

- recognize alphabet letters as a special set of graphic symbols
- learn alphabet letter names and formations
- learn letter features (and may write mock letters)
- write own signature
- use a variety of text features to construct different kinds of texts
- use concept of story to compose story content, especially using sequence and causality
- use concept of story in emergent readings in which stories are formed (rather than labeling pictures)

Meaning-Form Links

- use contextual dependency
- differentiate pictures from print (but sometimes think pictures are read)
- pay attention to print (and sometimes know that print is read)
- go beyond contextual dependency by matching segments of the printed text with segments of the spoken text (sometimes matching lines to spoken sentences, segments of text to spoken words, or letters to syllables)
- develop the beginnings of phonological awareness (by constructing rhyming words)

Functions

- use writing to label pictures
- use writing to create an imaginary story world
- use reading and writing in play
- use reading and writing to interact with others
- use reading and writing across time to regulate the behavior of self and others
- use reading and writing as part of family and community activities (such as to complete daily-living routines)

Figure 3.16 Bear Cradle

He hung up the phone and looked at his mother. He said, "Temp is sick and needs me to make a card for him." Jeffrey took a sheet of paper from his writing box and cut the paper into two pieces. He cut a rounded shape out of the top center of the larger piece of paper and said, "This is going to be the envelope."

Then he took the smaller paper and wrote four lines of mock cursive. His mother asked, "What does the card say?" Jeffrey ran his finger across each line of text as he read, "I love," "you, Temp," "from," "Jeffrey." Then Jeffrey asked, "How do you spell *Temp?*" He wrote the letters as his mother spelled it for him. Jeffrey's card and envelope are shown in Figure 3.17.

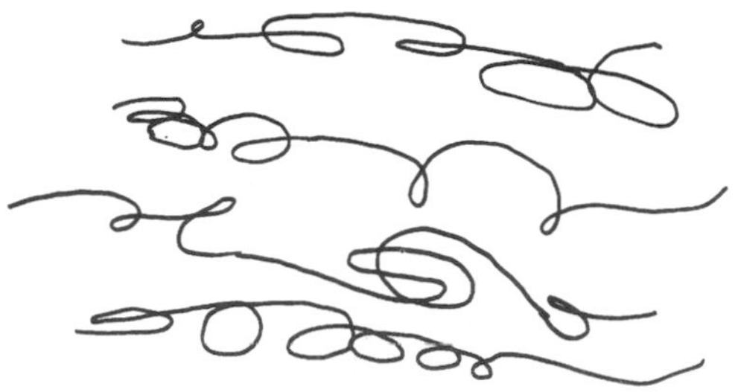

Figure 3.17a *Jeffrey's Card*

Figure 3.17b *Jeffrey's Envelope*

Going Beyond the Text

Arrange to visit with a family that has a preschooler, or visit a preschool or kindergarten. Take a book and be prepared to tape-record your interaction as you share the story with the preschooler or kindergartner. Take some paper and markers or crayons and invite the child to draw and write about the story. Record what the child says while drawing and writing. Ask the child to write his or her name and everything else he or she can. Invite the child to read what he or she has written. Describe the child's knowledge of written language meanings, forms, meaning-form links, and functions.

References

ABRAMSON, S., SEDA, I., & JOHNSON, C. (1990). Literacy development in a multilingual kindergarten classroom. *Childhood Education, 67,* 68–72.

ADAMS, M. J. (1990). *Beginning to read.* Cambridge, MA: M. I. T. Press.

ANBAR, A. (1986). Reading acquisition of preschool children without systematic instruction. *Early Childhood Research Quarterly, 1,* 69–83.

BAGHBAN, M. (1984). *Our daughter learns to read and write.* Newark, DE: International Reading Association.

CARLE, E. (1969). *The very hungry caterpillar.* New York: Philomel.

CLAY, M. M. (1975). *What did I write?* Auckland: Heinemann.

COCHRAN-SMITH, M. (1984). *The making of a reader.* Norwood, NJ: Ablex.

DEFORD, D. E. (1980). Young children and their writing. *Theory into Practice, 19,* 157–162.

DICKINSON, D., & SMITH, M. (1994). Long-term effects of preschool teachers' book readings on low income children's vocabulary and story comprehension. *Reading Research Quarterly, 29,* 104–122.

DICKINSON, D. K., & SNOW, C. E. (1987). Interrelationships among prereading skills in kindergartners from two social classes. *Early Childhood Research Quarterly, 2,* 1–25.

DUKE, N. K., & HAYS, J. (1998). "Can I say 'Once upon a time'?": Kindergarten children developing knowledge of informational book language. *Early Childhood Research Quarterly, 13,* 295–318.

DYSON, A. H. (1982). The emergence of visible language: Interrelationships between drawing and early writing. *Visible Language, 16,* 360–381.

DYSON, A. H. (1984). Emerging alphabetic literacy in school contexts: Toward defining the gap between school curriculum and child mind. *Written Communication, 1,* 5–55.

DYSON, A. H. (1985). Individual differences in emerging writing. In M. Farr (Ed.), *Advance in writing research: Vol. 1. Children's early writing development* (pp. 59–125). Norwood, NJ: Ablex.

DYSON, A. (1991). Viewpoints: The word and the world—reconceptualizing written language development, or do rainbows mean a lot to little girls? *Research in the Teaching of English, 25,* 97–123.

EIMAS, P. D., SIQUELAND, E. R., JUSCZYK, P., & VIGORITO, J. (1971). Speech perception in infants. *Science, 171,* 303–306.

FERREIRO, E. (1986). The interplay between information and assimilation in beginning literacy. In W. H. Teale & E. Sulzby (Eds.), *Emergent literacy: Writing and reading* (pp. 15–49). Norwood, NJ: Ablex.

FERREIRO, E., & TEBEROSKY, A. (1982). *Literacy before schooling.* Exeter, NH: Heinemann.

GALDONE, P. (1986). *Three little kittens.* New York: Clarion.

GELLER, L. G. (1983). Children's rhymes and literacy learning: Making connections. *Language Arts, 60,* 184–193.

GENISHI, C., & DYSON, A. H. (1984). *Language assessment in the early years.* Norwood, NJ: Ablex.

GOODMAN, Y. (1980). The roots of literacy. In M. Douglass (Ed.), *Claremont reading conference, 44th Yearbook* (pp. 1–32). Claremont, CA: Claremont Graduate School.

GOODMAN, Y., & ALTWERGER, B. (1981). *Print awareness in preschool children: A study of the development of literacy in preschool children* (Occasional Paper No. 4). Tucson: Arizona Center for Research and Development, College of Education, University of Arizona.

GUNDLACH, R., MCLANE, J. B., SCOTT, F. M., & MCNAMEE, G. D. (1985). The social foundations of children's early writing development. In M. Farr (Ed.), *Advances in writing research: Vol. 1. Children's early writing development* (pp. 1–58). Norwood, NJ: Ablex.

HARSTE, J. C., BURKE, C. L., & WOODWARD, V. A. (1981). *Children, their language and world: Initial encounters with print* (Final Report NIE-G-79-0132). Bloomington, IN: Indiana University, Language Education Department.

HARSTE, J. C., WOODWARD, V. A., & BURKE, C. L. (1984). *Language stories and literacy lessons.* Portsmouth, NH: Heinemann.

HEATH, S. B. (1983). *Ways with words: Language, life, and work in communities and classrooms.* New York: Cambridge University Press.

HIEBERT, E. H. (1978). Preschool children's understanding of written language. *Child Development, 49,* 1231–1234.

HIEBERT, E. H. (1981). Developmental patterns and interrelationships of preschool children's point awareness. *Reading Research Quarterly, 16,* 236–260.

HILDRETH, G. (1936). Developmental sequences in name writing. *Child Development, 7,* 291–302.

HOUGH, R. A., NURSS, J. R., & WOOD, D. (1987). Tell me a story: Making opportunities for elaborated language in early childhood classrooms. *Young Children, 43,* 6–12.

JACOB, E. (1984). Learning literacy through play: Puerto Rican kindergarten children. *Research in the Teaching of English, 17,* 73–83.

KING, M. L., MCKENZIE, M. G. (1988). Research currents: Literary discourse from a child's point of view. *Language Arts, 65,* 304–314.

LAMINACK, L. (1990). "Possibilities, Daddy, I think it says possibilities": A father's journal of the emergence of literacy. *The Reading Teacher, 43,* 536–540.

LASS, B. (1982). Portrait of my son as an early reader. *The Reading Teacher, 36,* 20–28.

LOMAX, R. G., & MCGEE, L. M. (1987). Young children's concepts about print and reading: Toward a model of word reading acquisition. *Reading Research Quarterly, 22,* 219–256.

MARTINEZ, M. (1983). Exploring young children's comprehension during story time talk. *Language Arts, 60,* 202–209.

MARTINEZ, M., & TEALE, W. (1993). Teacher storybook reading style: A comparison of six teachers. *Research in the Teaching of English, 27,* 175–199.

MAYER, M. (1968). *There's a nightmare in my closet.* New York: Dial.

MCGEE, L., & RICHGELS, D. (1989). "K is Kristen's": Learning the alphabet from a child's perspective. *The Reading Teacher, 43,* 216–225.

MCGILL-FRANZEN, A., & LANFORD, C. (1994). Exposing the edge of the preschool curriculum: Teachers' talk about text and children's literary understandings. *Language Arts, 71,* 264–273.

MORGAN, A. L. (1987). The development of written language awareness in Black preschool children. *Journal of Reading Behavior, 19,* 49–67.

NINIO, A., & BRUNER, J. (1978). Antecedents of the achievement of labeling. *Journal of Child Language, 5,* 1–15.

PAPPAS, C. C. (1991). Fostering full access to literacy by including informational books. *Language Arts, 68,* 449–462.

PAPPAS, C. (1993). Is narrative "primary"? Some insights from kindergartners' pretend readings of stories and information books. *Journal of Reading Behavior, 25,* 97–129.

PAPPAS, C. C., & PETTEGREW, B. S. (1998). The role of genre in the psycholinguistic guessing game of reading. *Language Arts, 75,* 36–44.

PURCELL-GATES, V. (1996). Stories, coupons, and the "TV Guide": Relationships between home literacy experiences and emergent literacy knowledge. *Reading Research Quarterly, 31,* 406–428.

SCHIEFFELIN, B. B., & COCHRAN-SMITH, M. (1984). Learning to read culturally: Literacy before schooling. In H. Goelman, A. Oberg, & F. Smith (Eds.), *Awakening to literacy* (pp. 3–23). Exeter, NH: Heinemann.

SULZBY, E. (1985). Kindergartners as readers and writers. In M. Farr (Ed.), *Advances in writing research: Vol 1. Children's early writing development* (pp. 127–199). Norwood, NJ: Ablex.

TAYLOR, D. (1983). *Family literacy.* Exeter, NH: Heinemann.

TAYLOR, D., & DORSEY-GAINES, C. (1988). *Growing up literate: Learning from inner-city families.* Portsmouth, NH: Heinemann.

VOSS, M. M. (1988). "Make way for applesauce": The literate world of a three year old. *Language Arts, 65,* 272–278.

WILDSMITH, B. (1971). *The owl and the woodpecker.* Oxford: Oxford University Press.

WILDSMITH, B. (1974). *Squirrels.* Oxford: Oxford University Press.

WOLF, S. A., & HEATH, S. B. (1992). *The braid of literature: Children's worlds of reading.* Cambridge, MA: Harvard University Press.

Chapter 4

From Five to Seven Years

Experimenting Readers and Writers

Key Concepts

- experimenters
- alphabetic writing system
- phonics
- breaking into print
- word-by-word speech-to-print matching
- literary syntax
- metalinguistic awareness
- concept of word
- invented spelling
- concept of word boundaries
- informed refusal
- mock cursive
- stringing letters together
- composing by dictation
- alliteration
- composing by copying
- composing by spelling
- print-bound reading and writing
- tracking print
- alphabetic reading
- sounding literate
- scale of emergent readings
- parallel reading
- written language–like talk
- dialogue markers
- being precise
- finger-point reading
- voice-to-print match
- sight words
- phoneme
- phonemic awareness
- relating letters to sounds
- manner of articulation
- identity of sound
- letter name strategy
- affrication
- stages of invented spelling
- non-spelling
- early invented spelling
- purely phonetic spelling
- onset
- rime
- phonetic cue reading

WHO ARE EXPERIMENTERS?

Learning about written language is a gradual process, and it is not possible to identify absolute milestones. There is no single, great accomplishment that divides beginners and novices from the **experimenters** described in this chapter. A child may act like an experimenter one day and then go back to the ways of a novice for a while. A child may experiment in storyreading, but not yet in spelling. Good observers notice a combination of changes that together suggest that a child is dealing with written language in a new, experimental manner.

Experimenters' New Awareness

One of the most important changes in children as they become experimenters takes place in their *attitude*. Over a period of time, a careful observer can notice a new attitude that might be described as being more aware, thoughtful, tentative, and testing. Experimenters are aware that certain conventions are related to reading and writing. They know that readers and writers attend to print as they read and write, and that print governs what is read and written. But young experimenters know that they cannot do what conventional readers do; they have not yet worked out the puzzle of what exactly readers and writers are doing. However, *experimenters work hard at trying to figure out the conventions that enable conventional reading and writing.* They focus on trying to produce conventional readings of texts and conventionally written texts. In doing so, they work at understanding how the written language system works.

By experimenting with a variety of hypotheses about how written language works, how someone really reads or writes, experimenters eventually (and gradually) come to discover an important insight about conventional reading and writing—that readers read words and that words are composed of letters related to the sounds in spoken words. That is, experimenters eventually discover that the English written language system is an **alphabetic writing system.** They discover the principle of **phonics**—that letters in written words relate to sounds in spoken words.

As we shall see, experimenters' understanding about the relationships between sounds and letters is not the conventional understanding that more accomplished readers and writers hold. Experimenters only gradually become aware of the conventions related to written words and how the letters in words relate to the sounds in spoken words. Yet it is this gradual understanding about words and sound–letter relationships that moves experimenters from emergent reading and writing to the beginnings of conventional reading and writing. Experimenters also acquire new understandings about written language meaning or functions, which are discussed later in the chapter. What is most important about experimenters, though, is what happens with forms and meaning-form links. Experimenters are **breaking into print;** their reading and writing attempts are influenced by print.

Compared with novices, experimenters have taken an important step closer to what adults do with print. They actually attempt to decipher the print rather than depend on memorization or pretend reading. Because early experimenters are aware of the shortcomings of such attempts, they are especially prone to frustration and feelings of inadequacy. They are likely to say, "I can't read" or "I don't want to write." Experimenters need understanding, support, and patience.

Experimenters may need adults' encouragement even when they do not finish a task. For example, they may work hard at how to represent the sounds in a single word of a longer message they wish to write, or they may work hard at reading a favorite storybook by concentrating on a single page, its pictures and print, and their memory of what adults have read on that page.

An important distinction between experimenters and more conventional readers and writers is that *experimenters usually concentrate on only one aspect of conventional reading and writing at a time.* Experimenters may want to write a conventional list (for example, when sending a birthday wish list to a grandparent) and refuse to invent spellings. Or, experimenters may look at a storybook page and laboriously try to puzzle out how to read individual words using sound–letter knowledge and ignoring the powerful meaning-making strategies they have been using for years.

The important thing to remember is that experimenters are trying out many pieces of the literacy puzzle and are experimenting with each one. It is an exciting process for both the children and those who support them (Hilliker, 1988; Matthews, 1988). In this process, they gain important literacy knowledge that will be used later when they will be better able to put the pieces together.

Examples of Experimenters

Here are two examples of experimenters:

> Three-year-old Sophie listens to her uncle read a storybook. She directs his reading, "Read that. . . . Read that." She always points first to the left-hand page and then to the right-hand page. When they finish the book, Sophie begins pointing to individual words on a page and again says, "Read that. . . . Read that," this time for each word she points to. This pointing proceeds right to left, word by word, until Sophie's uncle has identified every word in a line.
>
> Five-year-old Ted has been sent to his room for misbehaving. He either does not remember or does not understand why he was sent there. With pencil and paper, he writes the message shown in Figure 4.1. He dashes out of his room, tosses this written query or protest on the floor before his mother, and runs back into his room.

Sophie knows left-to-right directionality for pages. More important, although she does not know left-to-right directionality for word reading, her careful pointing to words shows that she is able to identify word boundaries. She has a concept of written word. She explores the power of written words, the combinations of letters bordered by spaces, to evoke particular spoken words from a reader. Compared with novices, who may point to whole lines of text as representations of anything from a sentence to a word, Sophie has a much more precise, **word-by-word understanding of how speech matches print.**

Ted's writing is a record not only of his query or protest, but also of his analysis of English words and their component sounds. He knows that he does not know the adult way to spell. At the time he wrote his protest, he often consulted an authority. However, when he was left to his own devices, he knew that he could get his words on paper if he thought about letter names and sounds in words. Compared with novices, who do not know about phonics, Ted has a very mature understanding of how writing works. Although his spelling

Figure 4.1 *Ted's Protest: "Mom, why are you punishing me? Ted"*

is not conventional, he systematically pairs letters with sounds. His invented spellings show his knowledge of the alphabetic principle.

Ted's message contains other examples of experimenter traits. He does not always use sound–letter relations to spell. He has learned in school how to read and spell the word *you* conventionally. Unlike novices, experimenters often have school-gained literacy knowledge. They must integrate this with literacy knowledge that they are gaining concurrently from home literacy experiences and that they gained earlier in their lives as preschoolers and literacy novices.

Ted's message shows an intensity that is often characteristic of experimenters. He sometimes worked intensely, especially when a message was as important to him as this one was. Ted's query appears unfinished; he wrote nothing for the word *me.* It is unlikely that he knowingly wrote an incomplete message; perhaps the effort required for this writing task distracted him so much that he did not realize he had omitted a word.

EXPERIMENTING WITH MEANING

The meaning making of experimenters is only slightly more complex than that of novices. Novices and experimenters share a basic orientation toward written language that is one of novices' greatest achievements. Both write in order to communicate a message, and both engage in interactive storybook reading using sophisticated strategies for constructing meaning. Experimenters continue to use the meaning-making strategies they devised as novices (Yaden, 1988).

For example, experimenters are likely to have a fully developed concept of story or story schema (see Chapter 2). They use their concept of story both to make sense of stories that are read aloud to them and as they compose their own stories. Later in this chapter we will describe experimenters' new attention to the literary properties of stories and informational texts. They have learned that written stories and informational books have certain language forms and word orders not found in spoken language. Experimenters are likely to use literary word order, or **literary syntax,** when composing and recalling stories, for example, "Away we went to grandmother's house."

The most striking new achievements of experimenters are related to their greater control over form and meaning-form links. However, in the face of their students' striking achievements with form and meaning-form links, teachers should not lose sight of the important fact that children do not experiment with form in a vacuum. Solving problems of form is not an exercise for its own sake. The meaning making learned as novices is the basis of all that experimenters do.

EXPERIMENTING WITH FORMS

Experimenters go beyond novices' exploring of alphabet letter forms. They have considerable knowledge about letters; they can name most letters, write most letters with conventional formations, and recite the alphabet. Experimenters also have **metalinguistic awareness** of letters; they can talk and think about the names and properties of letters ("Your *M* is upside down. I know how to make a *W* and a *M.*"). Experimenters show their **concept of word** in reading and writing. They make a variety of texts using a variety of writing strategies.

Concept of Word

A fully developed concept of written words includes knowledge that words are composed of combinations of letters; that words have boundaries, spaces; and that words have particular letters related to the sounds in spoken words (Roberts, 1992). Experimenters acquire bits and pieces of this concept as they move forward in learning to read and write. They may invent words in their writing for others to read or ask about words others have written. As they read, they may work at recognizing combinations of letters and word boundaries, yet not understand that letters in words have a particular relationship to sounds in spoken words. As they write, they may segment words at syllable boundaries or spell words using sound–letter relationships.

One way children show their interest in words is by inventing words when they write. Figure 4.2 shows some writing that Kathy produced one day as she sat by herself in her room. When her mother asked her to read her writing, she replied, "It's just words." Notice that Kathy's writing is much like a novice's—we could not know the meaning Kathy intended to communicate unless we listened to Kathy read her writing (and, in this case, Kathy did not seem to intend to communicate a message).

Three aspects of Kathy's word inventing are typical of experimenters. First, she is experimenting with letter combinations to produce writing that she calls words. Second, she is experimenting with using spaces between letter combinations to signal boundaries between her words (we will discuss more about children's concepts of word boundaries later in this chapter). Third, Kathy seems to be paying attention to only one aspect of written language, words and how they look, and ignoring other aspects of written language, such as meaning.

Another way experimenters signal their interest in words is by asking questions about words. One day, Carrie's father was silently reading a typewritten letter. Carrie climbed into

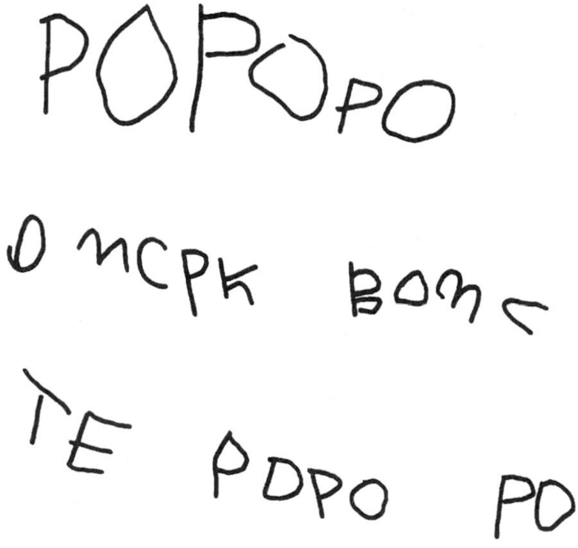

Figure 4.2 *Kathy's Invented Words*

his lap, pointed to a word in the letter that began with the letter *C*, and asked what it was. When told that the word was *concern*, she replied, "Oh. It has a *C* like my name." Carrie had noted that the word *concern* was something like her name. Both were composites of letters and both began with a *C*. Carrie then asked, "What's that word?" about several other words in the letter.

Children also signal their attention to words by attempting to write words in which some of the letters in the word capture some of the sounds in spoken words (we call this **invented spelling** and devote considerable attention to this topic later in the chapter). For example, Bissex's son Paul wrote VRMAT for *Vermont* (1980, p. 22). What is important about many invented spellings is that readers can read words by attending to their spellings and that the writer must have attended to words (or some segmented portion of spoken language) in order to spell.

Concept of Word Boundaries

As children become aware that words in spoken and written language can be segmented, they develop a **concept of word boundaries.** In conventional writing, we use spaces to show boundaries between individually printed words. Experimenters begin to respond to individual words in environmental print and in books, and they experiment with ways to show the boundaries between words in their own writing. In the example at the beginning of this chapter, Sophie pointed to and asked about individual words in the storybook her uncle read to her. Kathy (see Figure 4.2) used spaces between her invented words, but Paul used dots between words, for example: PAULZ•HOS•PLANF•ELD•VRMAT (Paul's house, Plainfield, Vermont) (Bissex, 1980, p. 22). His dot between PLANF and ELD also shows his awareness of syllables within words; another time he wrote TAL.A.FON for *telephone* (Bissex, 1980, p. 23). A child's writing the Spanish word *estaba* as *es taba* provides another example of segmenting written words at syllable boundaries (Edelsky, 1982, p. 216).

Other children circle words, put them in vertical arrangements, or even separate them with carefully drawn and blackened squares (Harste, Burke, & Woodward, 1983; Temple, Nathan, Burris, & Temple, 1988). In Chapter 1, we described the writing of a boy named Zachery; he distinguished one word from another by inserting dashes between words. When Carrie was three years old, her eight-year-old brother, Ted, wanted her to separate the words of a letter she was writing (she had asked for his help with spelling). He advised her to use a vertical arrangement, apparently thinking that it would be easiest for her (see Figure 4.3). When Carrie began experimenting by herself with the concept of word and how to show it, she chose to circle words (see Figure 4.4). She seemed to have a very physical sense of wordness and explained that the little bump on the top of each circle was a handle "for if somebody wants to pick the letters up."

Texts

Another question of form that young children try to answer during the experimenting stage is, "How do whole written language products look?" They are concerned not only with such components of written language products as words and collections of words, but also with the overall organizational features of different kinds of writing.

Figure 4.3 *Carrie's Letter to Keely, Tom, and Holly*

Figure 4.4 *Carrie's Letter to Jade*

Even novices are aware of several text formats when they play with writing in different contexts for various purposes. Chapter 3 included several examples of novices' greeting cards, lists, and stories. Experimenters continue to be interested in a variety of text forms.

The texts that experimenters create usually look more conventional than those produced by novices. Experimenters generate a greater variety of texts as well. There are several reasons for the differences between these two types of writers. Experimenters are more likely to ask for an adult's assistance in constructing their messages because they are aware that they cannot yet produce a readable message on their own. Experimenters also continue to have exposure to a wide variety of texts. Carrie explained that she made the chart shown in Figure 4.5 to keep track of when her parents were nice to her; just at this time, they had made a similar chart to encourage her good table manners (see Figure 4.6).

Figure 4.7 presents a letter that Carrie wrote to her grandfather when he was in the hospital. Her family frequently wrote and received letters, and Carrie was well aware that her grandfather would read her letter (on Carrie's next visit to her grandparents after her grandfather's return from the hospital, she saw her letter displayed on their refrigerator).

Carrie's letter looks very conventional. It has conventionally spelled words and appropriate punctuation. The sophisticated format of this letter resulted from Carrie's father's spelling words, showing her the space bar before writing a new word, and pushing the return button for each new line. This letter illustrates the experimenter's attention to the specific kinds of language related to certain types of texts. The letter includes such conventions as starting with "Dear _______ " and ending with "Love, _______ ," which Carrie probably learned from having letters read to her.

Like novices, experimenters are interested in writing stories and other kinds of literary texts, such as poems. They write in a variety of ways.

Although it sounds paradoxical (because even novices are willing to write stories), we would expect some experimenters to refuse initially to write a story. Those who refuse are comparing easy writing tasks that they can do well, such as writing their names, with the more difficult task of writing a story, and they are saying in effect, "I can't do *that!*" This

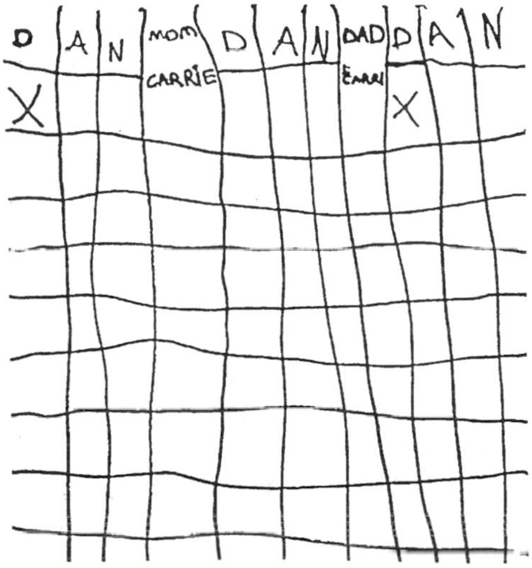

Figure 4.5 *Carrie's Chart*

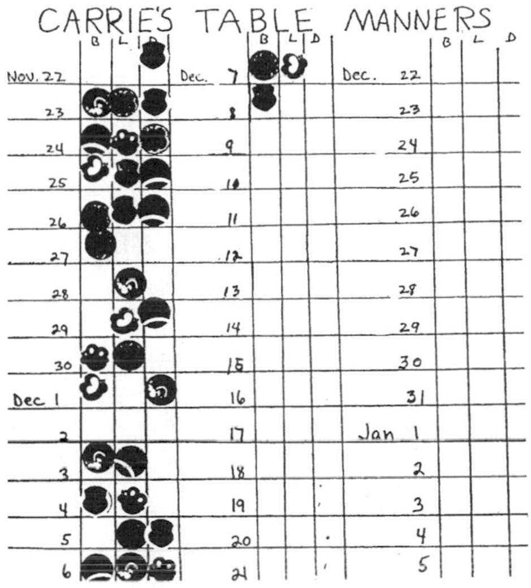

Figure 4.6 *Good Manners Chart*

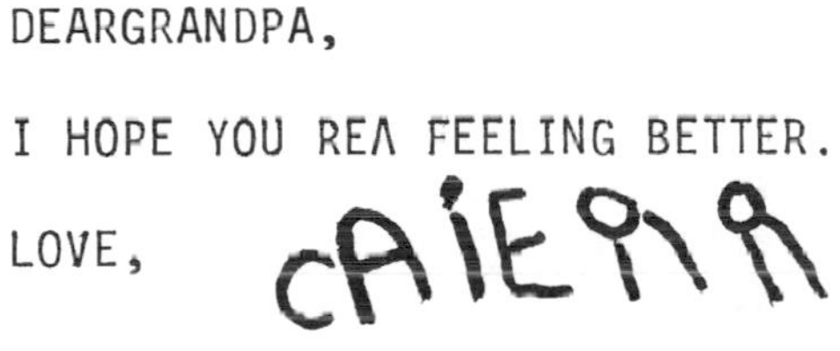

Figure 4.7 *Carrie's Letter to Her Grandfather*

kind of refusal implies some knowledge of what *that* entails. It is not the outright refusal of a beginner. It is an **informed refusal.** These experimenters know that there are requirements for storywriting, and they feel unable to satisfy those requirements (Sulzby, 1985b).

Informed refusal is typical of the experimenters' characteristic of being aware of what they do not know. It is not that experimenters do not know what a story is; even novices have begun to develop a concept of story. Rather, experimenters know that stories have many more words than they could hope to write on their own.

Eventually, most experimenters can be encouraged to try writing a story, especially if they know that adults will be satisfied with less than a complete story. Then they will take up paper and pencil with the intention of writing a story. This behavior is an example of experimenters' new awareness that we described at the beginning of this chapter.

Experimenters often compose by writing in **mock cursive** or by **stringing letters together** and telling a story as they write. Figure 4.8 presents a story Marianne wrote about seeing a zebra at the zoo.

Figure 4.8 *Marianne's Story*

Figure 4.9 shows another way experimenters **compose—by dictaction.** This is a story that four-year-old Carrie told to her mother during lunch, knowing that her mother would write it down on the blank pages of a little book for Carrie to illustrate. The story has some unity in that it is about events in the day of a single character (a chip). There is some temporal ordering of those events (school in the morning, lunch, Mother's arrival, and Mother's lunch), but only a few events are necessarily connected.

The most revealing thing about this early story, which was only the second story that Carrie had dictated to someone else, is that so much of it was tied to Carrie's immediate experience. The main character was a chip; Carrie was eating chips for lunch. This made a novel character, but there was no follow-up, nothing to suggest how the life of a chip would be different from Carrie's own. After the school episode, which reflected Carrie's own nursery school experience, she depended on immediately available props to invent additional events. She included the deck and the apple tree as soon as she noticed them outside the window. The story ended with what Carrie actually wanted her mother to do with her after lunch (play and read a story).

Figure 4.9 *Carrie's Dictated Story*

The Chip Goes to School

A chip went to school. When he was at school, he thought, "Oh dear, maybe I need to go home." Then the teacher ringed her bell and said, "It's time to go home." Then he goes home. He looks out the window and sees his friend. He sits on his deck and thinks a little bit. He climbs on his tree and picks some apples. He eats his lunch. He washes his dishes. He sees his mommy driving her car in the garage. He goes in the dining room with his mother, Mrs. Chip. She holds him in her lap. Then they go in the living room and play. The mother has her lunch. Then they read a story. The end.

Children sometimes dictate literary texts other than stories. Jeffrey dictated a poem to his mother as he ran back and forth across his patio.

The Running Poem
Bubble gun boppers,
Candy heart sneakers,
Sparky love.
Buster slimers,
Booger man,
Barbecue pit.
Blue ribbons win.
The end.

While the content of Jeffrey's poem relates to what he was doing (running) and seeing (his sneakers, the barbecue pit, and the family dog, Sparky), it also shows Jeffrey's understandings of the conventions of poetry forms. His poem consisted of phrases rather than sentences, and he used **alliteration**—five lines of his poem started with words beginning with the sound /b/. It is interesting that Jeffrey ended his poem with "The end," which is the formulaic ending for a story rather than a poem. Still, his poem demonstrates Jeffrey's experimentation with the specific language forms associated with poetry.

Experimenters also **compose by copying.** Figure 4.10 presents a story that Joel copied from his book *Bears in the Night* (Berenstain & Berenstain, 1971). His story provides several indications of a young child's experimenting. First, he wrote the words in the story in a column instead of in a line, indicating his attention to words. Second, he labored a long time producing his story. He copied each word letter by letter, and writing the entire story took forty minutes (we show only part of his writing, which covered several pages). This demonstrates experimenters' willingness to concentrate on literacy tasks and devote considerable energy to their constructions. Joel's story illustrates his experimentation with how words from stories are made.

Figure 4.10 *Joel's Copied Story*

As shown in Figure 4.11, children may **compose by spelling.** Ashley drew a picture and then asked her mother to help her spell. Her mother insisted, "If you write it, I'll be able to read it." Ashley said very slowly, "Nora," and wrote the letter *N;* then she said "flies," and wrote the letter *F;* and last she said "kites," and wrote the letter *k.* She wrote ASH and said, "That is my nickname, and here is my real name," (she wrote ASHLEY). Ashley's story was very primitive—she introduced a character and told one thing the character does. However, she listened to the spoken words she wanted to write and captured the initial sound of each word in her spelling. Notice that her arrangement of letters was not linear, written in left-to-right order; rather, it seems that Ashley let go of her more sophisticated knowledge about story meanings and the linearity concept in the effort of listening to sounds as she was spelling. This is a good example of experimenters' inability to control all aspects of written language as they experiment with a small part of the written language puzzle.

It is important to keep in mind that experimenters use some of the same conventions as more conventional readers and writers. We tend to think of children at this stage as not yet being very knowledgeable about written language. Even when we are accepting and supportive, what usually catches our attention in children's experimental products are their mistakes. However, there is much that is correct in their products, even by conventional standards.

EXPERIMENTING WITH MEANING-FORM LINKS

Discovering the essentials of how meanings and forms are linked in an alphabetic writing system is the main work of experimenters. It is the achievement that most clearly sets them apart from novices and puts them on the path to conventional reading and writing. In

Figure 4.11 *"Nora Flies Kites"*

Chapter 3, we saw that novices' ways of linking form and meaning often are limited by their dependence on context, and that novices lack understanding of sound–letter relations. Experimenters' attention to print is much more purposeful than is novices'. Not only do they know that print is important, but begin to discover how it works—that the alphabetic principle is at the core of the relation between print and meaning. Their reading and writing are no longer context bound; rather, they become **print bound.** Experimenters progress from merely retelling storybooks, using the vocabulary and language patterns in the texts, to **tracking the print** as they retell. They may even become completely governed by the text, as when they limit their retellings to reading isolated words that are in their small but growing word-recognition repertoires.

In their writing, experimenters develop two important kinds of awareness: awareness that their written messages are permanent and stable (they and others can return to them to retrieve their meanings) and awareness of phonemes, the units of sound from which words are built and to which letters are systematically matched. They move from writing by dictating stories, using booklike language, to writing with invented spelling.

Experimenters' writing and reading discoveries interact. For example, phonemic awareness practiced and enhanced during invented spelling is put to use in **alphabetic reading.**

Sounding Literate

One method that children use to link meaning and form might be stated: "Use special words and special combinations of words when you write or read. Everyday conversational talk will not do." Acquiring this special talk is related to experimentation with text forms, such as stories and poems. Examples of special talk include children's use of "Once upon a time" and their use of past tense in stories they tell or write.

Experimenting readers use **sounding literate** when they pretend to read favorite books (Cox, Fang, & Otto, 1997). Recall from Chapter 3 that early emergent reading consists of labeling parts of the illustrations or actions of the characters or telling a story that matches the illustrations. The stories that novices tell in their emergent readings usually do not closely match the words in the text. In contrast, experimenters' emergent readings of favorite storybooks not only closely resemble the words in the text, but also are influenced by print. At first, of course, experimenters do not watch print while they read. However, experimenters' emergent readings include much of the language of the text and, therefore, sound literate. Eventually, experimenters' emergent rereadings are exact, word-for-word readings of the text, and these readings are carefully matched to the text on the page.

Figure 4.12 presents a developmental **scale of emergent readings** of favorite storybooks (Sulzby, 1985a). A major step is the transition from story retellings that are like oral language to retellings that are like written language. The intonation of written language–like retellings is different from the intonation of conversational speech. By slowing their rate of speech and using stress expressively, children sound as if they are reading. Even though the wording may not be verbatim, a written language–like retelling may use some unusual expressions from the text; it often includes the more formal, more complex sentence structure that the child has come to expect from books (Sulzby, 1985a).

An example of an experimenter's emergent reading is provided by Carrie. Four-year-old Carrie had often listened to her parents and older brother read *The Three Bears* (1952).

Figure 4.12 *Emergent Reading Scale*

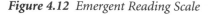

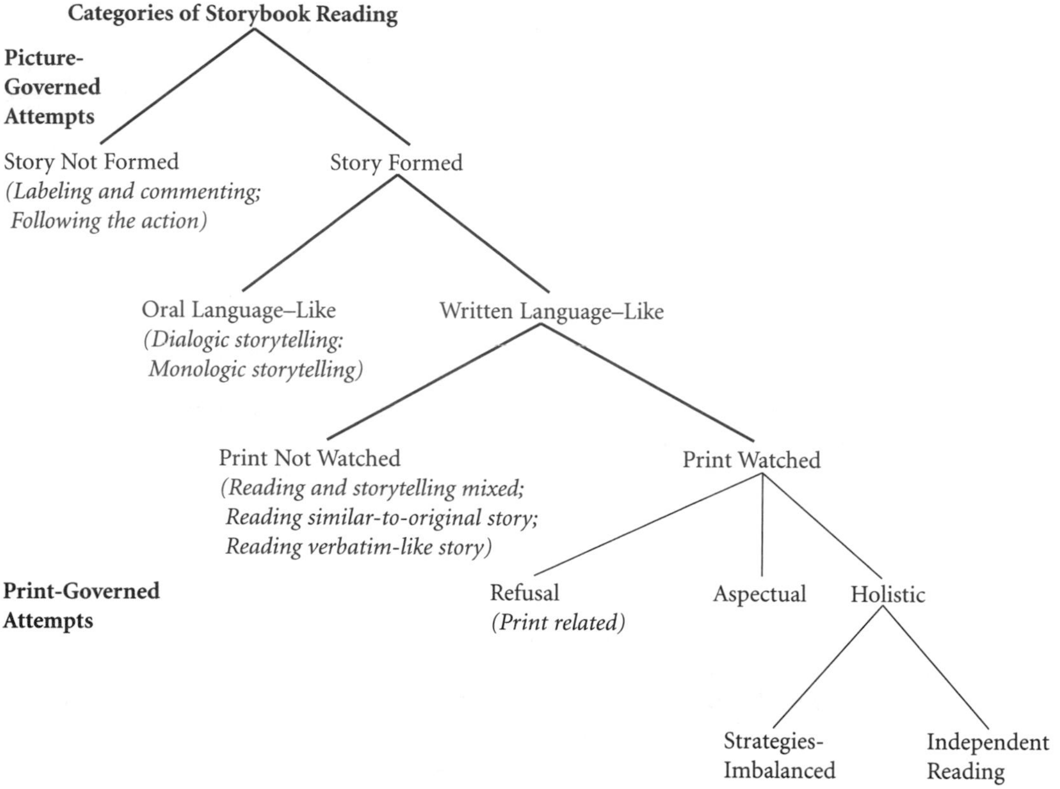

Note: This figure includes independent reading attempts only: the child is making the reading attempts without dependence upon turn-taking reading or interrogation by the adult.

From Sulzby, E. (1985). Children's emergent reading of favorite storybooks: A developmental study. *Reading Research Quarterly, 20,* p. 464. Reprinted with permission of Elizabeth Sulzby and the International Reading Association. All rights reserved.

It was one of her favorite books. When Carrie read the entire story of Goldilocks and the three bears to her father, she included elements unique to her book's version. Figure 4.13 presents a portion of Carrie's emergent reading of *The Three Bears,* in which she included descriptions of Papa Bear's repairing the roof, Mama Bear's watering flowers, and Baby Bear's doing tricks on the lawn. Although her book had illustrations of the three bears doing just those things, an important quality in Carrie's reading of the story is that she did not merely give a present-tense description of those pictures. The one time when she did just describe a picture ("The bird's just watching!"), she shifted out of a story-reading mode into a conversational mode. As she talked about a part of the illustration that she found charming, she used varied and faster intonation, in contrast to the steady, even voice and past tense of her reading.

Carrie's reading used language that was peculiar to the text of her very familiar book. She recreated the book's odd description of Papa Bear's behavior. Both the book and Carrie described him not as repairing the roof or fixing the roof, but as pounding nails in the roof!

Figure 4.13 *Carrie's Emergent Reading*

TEXT	READING
. . .	. . .
(From second and third pages. The illustration shows Mama Bear and Baby Bear in the foreground. She is watering tulips. He and a rabbit are doing handstands while a little bird watches. In the background Papa Bear is on the ladder repairing the roof of their house.)	(In an even voice, at a steady pace, until the end, when her voice rises)
Papa Bear pounded nails in the roof. Mama Bear watered the flowers. Baby Bear did tricks on the lawn.	"And Papa nailed the roof. Mama—Mama watered the flowers. And Baby Bear did tricks on the lawn."
	(Short pause. Laughter. Then in higher pitch, with rising and falling intonation, and faster pace)
	"The bird's just watching!"
. . .	. . .
(From twenty-first page)	(In a very high-pitched voice)
"Someone has broken my tiny chair all to pieces!"	"'And she's broken it all to pieces!'"
. . .	. . .

Throughout Carrie's emergent reading of *The Three Bears*, she clearly indicated who was talking, at first with dialogue markers, such as "Papa said" and "Mama said," and later by using a loud, deep voice for Papa Bear, a high voice for Mama Bear, and a very high voice for Baby Bear.

In other ways as well Carrie's emergent reading was a **parallel reading** of, but not a perfect replication of, the text. She frequently used the book's verb tenses in her recreation of the characters' speech. For example, in the second excerpt shown in Figure 4.13, she did not have Baby Bear say—as a four-year-old might—that someone "broke" his chair; rather, she repeated the book's *has broken* in her "she's *broken*." Her reading also included the book's attempt at a happy ending, with the three bears calling to Goldilocks as she ran away, "Come back! We want to be friends!"

Experimenting writers also use special **written language–like talk** in their dictated stories (Sulzby, 1985b) and in the stories they write on their own. Recall the story Marianne wrote using letter strings (see Figure 4.8). She read that story as follows:

> Once upon a time I went to the zoo and saw a zebra. Then I yelled, "Yeah," because I never saw a zebra before. He licked me on the hand. Then I said, "Mom and Dad, look. Sister, look." Then we went home. The end.

What is noteworthy about Marianne's story is her use of specialized language found only in written stories and not in spoken language. In everyday speech Marianne would not call her sister "Sister." She likely would not use the **dialogue markers** "I yelled" and "I said" in such a careful, repetitive-yet-varied way. She also would not have included the formulaic literary language used to open and close stories—"Once upon a time" and "The end." Marianne shows that she is experimenting with the special kinds of language forms unique to written stories.

Experimenters know that dictating a story is different than telling a story. They are aware that they are authors. They do not speak in order to communicate with or to entertain their scribe. Instead, they communicate with unknown, nonpresent future readers. Recall Carrie's dictated story (see Figure 4.9). Although it may lack sophistication in story format, it does show an experimenter's attention to the literary language and forms found in written stories. Like Marianne, Carrie used dialogue markers. The characters' thoughts and words are made explicit by using "he thought" and "the teacher . . . said."

Being Precise

A second way in which children link meaning and form might be stated: "Be precise about which words you (or your scribe) write and about which words you read back from your writing (or from someone else's). Only the words that the author formulated while writing may be read when the author or someone else reads what was written." In other words, reading is different than telling.

Being precise in reading begins as experimenting readers track print in order to capture the story text nearly verbatim. They not only have learned the language of the text (as when they sound literate), but also can match the text language to the exact page of the storybook. Thus, being precise leads to another kind of matching, finger-point reading. **Finger-point reading** is when children say a word from the story while pointing to a word in the printed text (Ehri & Sweet, 1991; Morris, 1993); it is also called **voice-to-print match.** At first, finger-point reading may not be completely accurate. Children may match a spoken syllable with a written word, for example. Eventually (as their concepts of spoken and written words and their perceptions of word boundaries mature), children begin to match each spoken word with a written word as they pretend read. Children who are accurate finger-point readers are not yet conventionally reading, but they are watching the print and coordinating what they say with the printed text.

Sometimes children's preoccupation with precision is so great that they will not attempt to read parts of a story that they have not memorized. Later, when they are able to identify words rather than rely on memorization, some children are similarly preoccupied—they become "glued to print" (Chall, 1983, p. 18). Sometimes, unlike mature readers (Goodman, 1967), children are so concerned with correct word identification that they neglect to attend to the meaning of text.

This kind of precision is part of the later stages of the emergent reading scale. Children's performances at this stage should not be dismissed as "just memorization." Their effort to retrieve the actual story shows a new sophistication about how written language works.

An identifying characteristic of experimenters is that they can be aware that they do not know all there is to know about writing and reading. When they are able actually to read print, they will refuse to use their previous strategies, such as pretend reading ("print-related refusals"; Sulzby, 1985b, p. 470); they will read only when there is print they know ("aspectual reading"; Sulzby, 1985b, p. 470). An aspectual reader recited "Grandma," "the," "and," "the a," "and" (Sulzby, 1985a, pp. 471–472) page after page because those were the only words of which she was sure. She could identify them wherever she saw them. Words that a child can identify on sight, without using any sounding out or context strategies, are called **sight words.** The final step on the emergent reading scale heralds a still higher level of knowledge and marks the beginning of conventional reading and writing.

Children may also demonstrate precision in writing. They reveal this by the way they attempt to reread their own writing. Figure 4.14 presents a Father's Day card that four-year-old Brooke composed. On the front of her card she drew a bird and some flowers. On the inside she wrote nine letters: *R, A, Y, g, P, G, O, G,* and *I.* Afterward, she read her writing to her mother, pointing to the first five letters one at a time: "I/ love/ you/ dad/ dy." Then she paused for a few moments and pointed at the remaining four letters one at a time, reading, "ver/ y/ much/ too." Brooke is being precise by carefully matching each letter of her writing with a segment of her spoken message (in this case, a syllable).

Using Sound–Letter Relationships

Experimenters also link meaning with written form through the use of sound–letter relationships in their spellings and emergent readings. Preschool experimenters may gain this knowledge from experiences with text and feedback from supportive adults. For example, a child whose parent frequently reads a book of nursery rhymes may notice that both *Jack* and *Jill* start with the letter *J* and that both words and the letter's name start with the /j/ sound. When the child comments about this and the parent acknowledges and confirms this, the child is gaining phonics knowledge. School-age experimenters may gain and consolidate such knowledge from both indirect (Dahl, Scharer, Lawson, & Grogan, 1999) and explicit (McIntyre & Freppon, 1994) phonics instruction.

We have provided some examples of children who invent spellings—children who look for systematic relationships between sounds and letters. For example, Ted spelled *why* with a *y* and *punishing* as PNShAn (see Figure 4.1), and Ashley spelled *Nora* with an *N* (see Figure 4.11). It may appear that experimenters are using the relationships between sounds and letters just as more conventional readers and writers do, but this is not always the case.

In order to spell, writers need a system: they need a rather precise, analytic understanding of the relationship between spoken and written language; they need the ability to examine words one sound unit at a time; and they need an awareness of some kind of relationship between spoken sounds and letters. What this means is that young writers must first be able to segment their spoken message into its component parts—words. Then spellers must further segment words into smaller parts—eventually, into phonemes. A

Figure 4.14 *Brooke's Father's Day Card*

phoneme is a unit of sound (e.g., /t/, /ă/, /n/, /ĭ/, /θ/, and /ŋ/) that can contrast with another unit of sound when such units are combined to make words (e.g., *tan* vs. *tin, tin* vs. *thin, thin* vs. *thing*). In conventional spelling, phonemes are associated with single letters—such as *t, a, n,*—or with letter combinations—such as *th* or *ng*. Hence teachers call /t/ the "T sound" or /θ/ the "T-H sound."

Early inventive spellers do not usually pronounce single phonemes one at a time; this is a later-developing ability. Instead, they may pronounce a multisyllable word one syllable at a time. Even in these cases, however, their spelling efforts begin with paying attention to part of that syllable, often the first part, that is, the first phoneme. Then spellers must decide which letter to use to represent that phoneme. This is a long and complicated process that involves a great deal of conscious attention.

The process of attending to phonemes is part of the phonological awareness we described in Chapter 3. Phonological awareness includes attention to all aspects of the sounds of a language. One of those aspects is phonemes. Paying attention to phonemes, **phonemic awareness,** is most developed when a person can segment a word into each and every one of its phonemes, for example, segmenting the word *tan* into /t/, /ă/ and /n/. This most developed kind of phonemic awareness only gradually emerges.

Kristen's first spellings provide a case in point. She announced that she could spell and looked around the room for things to spell. She said, "I can spell phone," and repeated the word to herself, saying it slowly, stretching out the initial /f/ sound, "Ph ph ph phone, phone. I know—it's spelled *V*." Then she looked around again and said, "I can spell window, too." Again she slowly repeated the word, stretching out the initial /w/ sound, "W w w window. Window is *Y*."

Kristen's spellings are not conventional, but they have the characteristics of true spelling; they are systematic, and they demonstrate phonemic awareness. Using only one letter to spell each word is consistent with not pronouncing each phoneme of a word one at a time. She pronounced a whole word and paid attention to the first phoneme in that word. She was not doing the complete phoneme-by-phoneme analysis that demonstrates the most developed form of phonemic awareness, but her attention to each word was at the level of the phoneme.

Once children can segment smaller-than-a-word sound units, they must also have a way to **relate letters to the sounds** they segment. While attending to the phonemes at the beginnings of *phone* and *window,* Kristen used two clues for choosing an appropriate letter for spelling: manner of articulation and identity of sound. **Manner of articulation** is the placement of the mouth, tongue, and teeth when speaking. Kristen noticed that her upper teeth were biting down on her lower lip both when she started to say the word *phone* and when she started to say the name of the letter *V*. Kristen also may have used manner of articulation to spell *window.* In order to say the sounds at the beginning of the word *window* and at the beginning of the name of the letter *Y*, a speaker's lips are rounded into a distinctive *O* shape.

Manner of articulation provides a way to spell not only consonant sounds (as in Kristen's spellings of *phone* and *window*), but also some of the most difficult sounds to spell, the short vowel sounds. Say the short *e* sound and then the letter name *E.* Now say the short *e* sound and the name of the letter *A*. While the manner of articulation for the short *e* and the letter name *A* are not exactly the same, they are closer than the manner of articulation of the short *e* and the letter name *E*. Therefore, children sometimes use the letter *a* to spell the sound of short *e.*

With *window* and *Y*, there is another possible explanation of Kristen's spelling. She may have used **identity of sound.** Both *window* and the name of the letter *Y* start with /w/ (the letter name *Y* is made up of two phonemes /w/ and /ī/). Spellers can use the phonemes in the letter names and associate them with the phonemes in the spoken words they wish to spell. Ashley did this when she linked the phoneme /k/ in the letter name *K* with the phoneme /k/ in the word *kite* (see Figure 4.11). We might also expect a young speller to associate the phoneme /ch/ in the letter name *H* with the phoneme /ch/ in the word *chain*, as in the invented spelling HAN.

Ted's spelling of the word *why* with a *Y* shows another way of linking letters and sounds—using the name of the letter to represent a sound segment in a word that sounds like the letter's name. This is called the **letter name strategy.** Spelling the word *eyes* with IZ and the word *knee* with NE are two additional examples of using the letter name strategy (Wilde, 1992, p. 39).

Sometimes children link letters with sounds by hearing sounds in spoken words that are ignored in standard spellings (and, therefore, that many adults forget are even there). Both standard spelling and invented spelling are abstract—they both ignore some sounds in words. But the standard system and invented spelling do not ignore the same things. Standard spelling ignores the affrication in *tr* and *dr* blends. **Affrication** is the burst of air that occurs in the pronunciation of these blends. That sound is not represented in conventional spellings of words that begin with the *tr* and *dr* blends. Yet that same burst of air *is* spelled with a *j* or a *ch* in other contexts, such as in *juice* and *chain.* Read (1971) found that inventive spellers repeatedly chose to represent that burst of air in the *dr* and *tr* blends. Children spelled the affrication in *try* with a *ch* (CHRIE) and in dragon with a *j* (JRAGIN). On the other hand, invented spelling ignores nasals before consonants (NUBRS for *numbers,* AD for *and,* PLAT for *plant,* and GOWEG for *going*), while standard spelling represents them.

Read's (1971) work has influenced both classroom practice (e.g., Chomsky, 1971; Lancaster, Nelson, & Morris, 1982; Paul, 1976; Sowers, 1988; Timberlake, 1995) and research (Richgels, 1995; Rubin & Eberhardt, 1996; Tangel & Blachman, 1995; Vukelich & Edwards, 1988). One finding from this research is that **inventive spellers progress through stages** that culminate with conventional spelling (Gentry, 1982; Morris, 1981). This finding is reassuring to skeptical parents and teachers, and it is also not surprising. We have just described what inventive spellers know as a system; their spellings are not haphazard. The fact that their spelling system is not the conventional one adults use is not as important as the fact that it *is* a system. Inventive spellers know what spelling is supposed to accomplish. They must only progress to knowing how to accomplish it in the conventional systematic way rather than in their invented systematic way.

Table 4.1 describes three stages in that progression. These stages are intended to clarify the direction of change in children's spelling development. Children often show spelling behaviors from more than one stage in a single piece of writing. What is important is that over time their spellings resemble later stages more than earlier stages.

Table 4.1 is based on similar schemes described by Gentry (1982) and Morris (1981), who derived their stages from Read's (1975) and Henderson and Beers's (1980) work. The three stages are labeled non-spelling (because it is random, not systematic), early invented spelling, and purely phonetic spelling.

The first stage, **non-spelling,** is what novices do. They write mock cursive or letter strings to stand for messages (contextually dependent writing). This activity reflects

Table 4.1 Stages of Invented Spelling

Non-Spelling

Some alphabet knowledge

No sound–letter knowledge

Random stringing together of letters of the alphabet

No concept of word

Example: YHZOT for *hair*

Early Invented Spelling

Nearly complete alphabet knowledge

Use of manner of articulation

Knowledge that sounds can be associated with letters

Letter name strategy

Frequent omission of vowels (especially non–long vowel sounds for which a letter name strategy does not work)

Encoding of only some parts of a word

Emergence of concept of word (some segmentation of word strings at word boundaries)

Examples: K for *kite,* BD for *bird,* SWM for *swim*

Purely Phonetic Spelling

Based strictly on sound–letter correspondences

Use of manner of articulation for some short vowels; some conventional short vowel spellings

Encoding of all or nearly all parts of a word, including vowels

Letter name strategy for long vowels

Omission of unheard vowels and nasals before consonants

Segmentation of letter strings at most word boundaries

Examples: KRI for *cry,* BRD for *bird,* BREJ for *bridge,* PLAT for *plant*

Stages are based on Gentry (1982) and Morris (1981). Examples of early invented spelling and purely phonetic spelling are from research conducted by the authors.

novices' fixation with letters. This stage is primarily characterized by a lack of awareness of sound–letter correspondences. Non-spellers choose letters randomly. Because they seem to believe in some power of the letters themselves to communicate, non-spellers can also be characterized as lacking a concept of word. Individual letters in their writing are not even representative of beginning sounds in the words of their intended messages.

The second and third stages, **early invented spelling** and **purely phonetic spelling,** represent the kinds of spellings that we expect from experimenters. In these two stages experimenters use letters to make words based on analyses of sound units in words and knowledge of sound–letter correspondences. They progress from only partial (initial or initial and final sounds) to nearly complete encoding of word sounds, and from representing only consonant sounds to representing consonants and vowels.

A proven way to help children notice more than one phoneme in a word is to help them segment syllables into two parts: (1) the first phoneme if it is a consonant (this is called the **onset,** e.g., /b/ in *bat*), and (2) the rest of the syllable (this is called the **rime,** e.g., /ăt/ in *bat*). With practice, children progress from spelling just the onset to spelling part of and then all of the rime.

At the end of this experimenting time, they may begin to incorporate some English spelling conventions for frequently occurring word parts (such as *-ed*). However, the primary characteristic of experimenters is spelling without regard for standard conventions. Instead, they systematically use sound–letter correspondences.

Children's growth in spelling does not stop at the end of the purely phonetic stage of spelling development. In Chapter 5 we will describe two more stages of invented spelling that are beyond what experimenters do.

Children's awareness of systematic (but unconventional) relations between letters and spoken language influences their reading. Children's reading of environmental print, storybooks, and their own writing gradually reflects their awareness of written words and the relationships between letters in words and sounds in spoken language. For example, one day a young child noticed something different about an environmental print sign that she had been reading for quite some time as *Emporium,* . . . "a San Francisco department store whose stylized spelling is dominated by a very large initial *E.* On one of this child's frequent visits to the store, she looked at its name and commented in surprise, 'Mom! That doesn't say Emporium (i.e., *mporium*). That says *E-porium!*' " (Ehri, 1991, p. 411).

Another example of the influence of children's awareness of sound–letter knowledge on their reading occurred when Jeffrey looked at a word book (an alphabet picture book that had several pictures on a page depicting objects and actions associated with a particular letter). He was looking at the *F* page when he called out to his mother, "Do you want to hear me read this page?" Jeffrey's mother knew that he could not really read, but she was willing to be an audience as he pretended to read this favorite book. Jeffrey pointed to the word *fence* and said "fence." He pointed to each of the words *fruit tree, flag, funny face,* and *four fish* and said the appropriate word or phrase. Then he paused as he scanned the picture of a farmer driving a tractor. The words accompanying this picture were *front wheels* and *fertilizer.* Finally Jeffrey said, "I'm looking for the word *tractor* because this is a tractor. But I can't find it. All of these words have *F*'s. But tractor shouldn't be *F.* Where is it, Mom? Can you find the word for 'tractor'?"

These examples demonstrate children's attention to letters and their sounds. In the case of *Emporium,* the child was applying a letter name strategy (*m-porium*); and in the case of *tractor,* Jeffrey knew that the word *tractor* did not begin with the phoneme associated with he letter *F.*

The ability to use some sound–letter relationships to read and remember words marks the beginning of alphabetic reading (Ehri, 1991). Children who are early inventive spellers can demonstrate the beginnings of alphabetic reading in their guesses about environmental print and as they monitor their emergent readings of favorite storybooks.

Jules used invented spelling to spell *bear* (BAR), *duck* (DAC), and *caterpillar* (CAURPELR). When he was shown any of the words with the letters scrambled, he made an attempt to sound out the new words (Barnhart, 1988). Using some sound–letter knowledge in this way, to figure out new words, is **phonetic cue reading** (Ehri, 1991), and it contributes to remembering the words. Phonetic cue readers, for example, might learn to recognize the words *tub*, *dog*, and *fat* because the associations between the letters and sounds (most likely the beginning and ending consonants) help them remember the words. Children whose spelling is at the later early invented spelling stage or purely phonetic stage can be phonetic cue readers; they are more likely to learn to read some words by sight if they know some of the letter–sound relationships in the words (Richgels, 1995).

EXPERIMENTING WITH FUNCTIONS OF WRITTEN LANGUAGE

We have presented much information about children's experimentation with the functions of written language. Young experimenters continue what they began as novices. They continue to use written language to communicate for a variety of purposes. Experimenters do, however, cover some new ground in the domain of written language functions. They read and write with the two new purposes of learning to read and write and of preserving specific messages.

In this chapter are many examples of experimenters' devoting considerable energy to reading and writing, to *experimenting* with how written language works. Unlike literacy beginners and novices, they are aware of the work involved in becoming literate. Sometimes this means that the experimenter chooses to focus on a small, concentrated part of the whole process of reading and writing. Especially when adults support and encourage such self-assigned work (Clay, 1975), experimenters come to know that learning to read and write is one of the goals of reading and writing. They learn by doing, even when the doing is at times painstaking. Their appearing to work hard is the result of the careful analysis, the concentrated thinking, and the reasoned trying out that is the essence of experimentation and invention. If it is true that what they are doing at this stage is inventing literacy for themselves (Goodman, 1980), then it is no wonder that such hard work is involved.

We have seen that experimenters, unlike novices, understand that written messages, whether their own or others', are stable and permanent. Ted (see Figure 4.1), Carrie (see Figures 4.3 and 4.4), and Joel (see Figure 4.10) knew that by writing a protest, a thank you, or a story, they rendered their messages retrievable. Ted wanted his parents to notice his protest; Carrie wanted her relatives to know of her thanks; Joel wanted to have as his own copy of *Bears in the Night* (Berenstain & Berenstain, 1971). All three children could achieve those goals by writing. All three had accomplished the most significant function-related conceptual change of the experimental stage, the discovery that written language can preserve a writer's message exactly. This is known as the message concept (Clay, 1975).

A WORD OF CAUTION

We began this chapter by characterizing experimenters as children who are aware that there is a system to learn, but who do not know what that system is. Throughout the chapter we have described the variety of concepts that children must grasp in order to puzzle out the system, to become what others would judge conventional readers and writers. Children gradually come to have many behaviors and understandings that we call conventional. The understandings that experimenters have about written language are unconventional in many ways (for example, their using manner of articulation to link letters and sounds or their counting syllables or phrases as words). Yet, their reading and writing also have signs of much that is conventional (for example, their using knowledge of literary syntax to compose stories and their using sound–letter knowledge to monitor their reading).

We hope that this chapter does not lead readers to two misconceptions. The first has to do with ages. Ages are not the important part of any description of children as experimenters. The children in our examples have been various ages. We have provided their ages only to accurately present the facts in some of our real-life examples. The ages of these children do not set norms against which to compare other children. Many children come to kindergarten and even to first grade not acting as experimenters. We have no reason to believe that they will fail to learn to read or write, or even that they will fall behind. Of much greater value than age is the behavior that can be observed in a literacy event; what the child knows or learns in the event; and how adults support that behavior, knowledge, and discovery. From this information, teachers can gain insights that will guide instruction.

The second misconception has to do with identification of children as experimenters. Identification is not important for its own sake. It does not really matter whether Carrie or Paul or any other child is called an experimenter. What matters is that teachers know in which literacy behaviors children are willing and able to engage. Then teachers will understand and support children in the provision of resources, in actions, and in talk. We know that some children's literacy behaviors fall in some manner—however imprecisely—within the broad territory described as the experimenter's. We hope that when teachers recognize such children, they will know how to support the children's continued development as writers and readers.

Chapter Summary

Experimenters are aware that there is a system of written language that they only partly understand. Still, they are up to the adventure of exploring the unknown territory. They respond to adults' encouragement with deliberate, focused episodes of reading and writing.

The meaning making that experimenters do is similar to what they did as novices. They continue writing in order to present a message, and they continue using sophisticated strategies for interacting with books.

Some of the most striking new achievements of experimenters are related to their greater control over form and meaning-form links. They make letters of the alphabet that are recognizable according to conventional standards. They acquire a concept of spoken and written words, and they devise means for showing word boundaries in their writing. In addition to knowing what physical arrangements are appropriate for different text forms, they know what special language is appropriate.

Experimenters' reading and writing are print governed. They achieve phonemic awareness and use it in alphabetic reading and invented spelling. They carefully analyze speech sounds in almost any word they want to write, and match those sounds with letters. Experimenters also show new knowledge of meaning-form links by using special written language–like talk in literacy events. Often they are aware that written language is more precise than spoken language and that what readers say depends on what writers write.

As with novices, written language serves a variety of functions for experimenters. A new purpose for their reading and writing is simply to experiment.

A summary of what experimenters know about written language meanings, forms, meaning-form links, and functions is presented in Figure 4.15.

Figure 4.15 *Summary: What Experimenting Readers and Writers Know about Written Language Meanings, Forms, Meaning-Form Links, and Functions*

Meaning Making

assign meaning to text by applying knowledge of specialized literary language (such as literary syntax, alliteration, and letter-writing conventions)

Forms

know nearly all alphabet letter names and formations

have metalinguistic awareness of letters

develop concepts of spoken words

develop concepts of written words

develop concepts of word boundaries

use specialized literary knowledge to construct a wide variety of texts

use a variety of strategies to produce conventional texts (including copying, asking for spellings, dictating, and spelling)

Meaning-Form Links

sound literate when assigning meaning to storybooks and compositions

are precise when assigning meaning to storybooks and compositions

develop phonemic awareness

use manner of articulation to associate sounds and letters in spellings

use letter names to associate sounds and letters in spellings

use identity of sounds to associate sounds and letters in spellings

spell at the levels of early and purely phonetic spelling

use knowledge of sound–letter relationships to monitor emergent reading

use finger-point reading (demonstrating voice-to-print matching)

can use phonetic or alphabetic cues to learn some sight words

Function

read and write to experiment with written language

understand that written language is precise (develop the message concept)

Applying the Information

Two literacy events follow. The first event involves four-year-old Maria and her mother, and the second concerns a story written by five-year-old Ben. Discuss what these events show about Maria's and Ben's understandings of written language meanings, forms, meaning-form links, and functions.

Maria wrote OPMN (see Figure 4.16) on a piece of paper and asked her mother, "What does this word say?" Her mother answered, "It

Figure 4.16 Maria's Words

isn't really a word. I guess it says /o-p-m-un/" sounding out the nonsense word slowly and pointing to each letter as she said the sounds. Next Maria wrote ON (one of the few words she knows how to spell conventionally). When she asked her mother to read the word her mother said, "You know what that says." Maria said "on." Maria wrote OrNMP and OrMO and then asked her mother to read these words. Her mother again slowly sounded out the words and pointed to the letters. Finally, Maria wrote NO and said, "Mom, I know how to read this word. No."

Ben complained that he had nothing to do. His mother suggested that he write a story. He had never written one before, but to his mother's surprise, he took up the challenge. He returned in a few minutes with these three lines of letters.

> WNSAPNATMTEWDKDRWOTOTNTE
> BOSAD HEDKD
> FEH

He read them as, "Once upon a time the woodcutter went out in the boat and he did catch fish." Ben's mother understood why Ben ended the story as he did. Ben had been unsuccessful on a recent fishing excursion.

Going Beyond the Text

Visit a kindergarten classroom. Join the children who are writing. Notice what their writing activities are. What experimenting behaviors do you observe? What text forms are the children using? How many of them are spellers? Begin your own writing activity (writing a letter, a story, a list of some kind, a reminder to yourself, or a poem). Talk about it with the children. How many of them take up your activity and attempt similar pieces? Does the character of their writing change from what it was for their own activities? Is there more or less invented spelling, more or less word writing, more or less scribbling?

Ask the teacher if children have favorite storybooks. If so, invite children to read their favorites to you. How do they interpret that invitation? If they would rather you read to them, how willing are they to supply parts of the reading? What parts do they know best? What parts do they like best?

References

BARNHART, J. (1988). The relationship between graphic forms and the child's underlying conceptualization of writing. In J. Readence & R. Baldwin (Eds.) *Dialogues in Literacy Research* (pp. 297–306). Chicago: National Reading Center.

BERENSTAIN, S., & BERENSTAIN, J. (1971). *Bears in the night.* New York: Random House.

BISSEX, G. L. (1980). *GNYS AT WRK. A child learns to write and read.* Cambridge: Harvard University Press.

CHALL, J. S. (1983). *Stages of reading development.* New York: McGraw-Hill.

CHOMSKY, C. (1971). Invented spelling in the open classroom. *Word, 27,* 499–518.

CLAY, M. M. (1975). *What did I write? Beginning writing behavior.* Exeter, NH: Heinemann.

COX, B., FANG, Z., & OTTO, B. (1997). Preschoolers' developing ownership of the literate register. *Reading Research Quarterly, 32,* 34–53.

DAHL, K., SCHARER, P., LAWSON, L., & GROGAN, P. (1999). Phonics instruction and student achievement in whole language first grade classrooms. *Reading Research Quarterly 34,* 312–341.

EDELSKY, C. (1982). Writing in a bilingual program: The relation of L1 and L2 texts. *TESOL Quarterly, 16,* 211.

EHRI, L. (1991). Development of the ability to read words. In R. Barr, M. Kamil, P. Mosenthal, & P. Pearson (Eds.), *Handbook of reading research* (2nd ed., pp. 395–419). New York: Longman.

EHRI, L., & SWEET, J. (1991). Finger point reading of memorized text: What enables beginners to process the print? *Reading Research Quarterly, 26,* 442–462.

GENTRY, J. R. (1982). An analysis of developmental spelling in GNYS AT WRK. *The Reading Teacher, 36,* 192–200.

GOODMAN, K. (1967). Reading: A psycholinguistic guessing game. *Journal of the Reading Specialist, 4,* 126–135.

GOODMAN, Y. M. (1980). The roots of literacy. In M. P. Douglas (Ed.), *Claremont Reading Conference, 44th Yearbook* (pp. 1–32). Claremont, CA: Claremont Reading Conference.

HARSTE, J. C., BURKE, C. L., & WOODWARD, V. A. (1983). *Young child as writer-reader, and informant* (Final Report Project NIE-G-80–0121). Bloomington, IN: Language Education Departments, Indiana University.

HENDERSON, E. H., & BEERS, J. W. (Eds.). (1980). *Developmental and cognitive aspects of learning to spell.* Newark, DE: International Reading Association.

HILLIKER, J. (1988). Labeling to beginning narrative: Four kindergarten children learn to write. In T. Newkirk & N. Atwell (Eds.), *Understanding writing: Ways of observing, learning, and teaching* (2nd ed., pp. 14–22). Portsmouth, NH: Heinemann.

LANCASTER, W., NELSON, L., & MORRIS, D. (1982). Invented spellings in Room 112: A writing program for low-reading second graders. *The Reading Teacher, 35,* 906–911.

MATTHEWS, K. (1988). A child composes. In T. Newkirk & N. Atwell (Eds.), *Understanding writing: Ways of observing, learning, and teaching* (2nd ed., pp. 9–13). Portsmouth, NH: Heinemann.

MCINTYRE, E., & FREPPON, P. A. (1994). A comparison of children's development of alphabetic knowledge in a skills-based and a whole language classroom. *Research in the Teaching of English, 28,* 391–417.

MORRIS, D. (1981). Concept of word: A developmental phenomenon in the beginning reading and writing processes. *Language Arts,* 58, 659–668.

MORRIS, D. (1993). The relationship between children's concept of word in text and phoneme awareness in learning to read: A longitudinal study. *Research in the Teaching of English, 27,* 133–154.

PAUL, R. (1976). Invented spelling in kindergarten. *Young Children, 31,* 195–200.

READ, C. (1971). Pre-school children's knowledge of English phonology. *Harvard Educational Review, 41,* 1–34.

READ, C. (1975). *Children's categorizations of speech sounds in English.* Urbana, IL: National Council of Teachers of English.

RICHGELS, D. (1995). Invented spelling ability and printed word learning in kindergarten. *Reading Research Quarterly, 30,* 96–109.

ROBERTS, B. (1992). The evolution of the young child's concept of word as a unit of spoken and written language. *Reading Research Quarterly, 27,* 124–139.

RUBIN, H., & EBERHARDT, N. C. (1996). Facilitating invented spelling through language analysis instruction: An integrated model. *Reading and Writing: An Interdisciplinary Journal, 8,* 27–43.

SOWERS, S. (1988). Six questions teachers ask about invented spelling. In T. Newkirk & N. Atwell (Eds.), *Understanding writing: Ways of observing, learning, and teaching* (2nd ed., pp. 130–141). Portsmouth, NH: Heinemann.

SULZBY, E. (1985a). Children's emergent reading of favorite storybooks: A developmental study. *Reading Research Quarterly, 20,* 458–481.

SULZBY, E. (1985b). Kindergartners as writers and readers. In M. Farr (Ed.), *Advances in writing research: Vol 1. Children's early writing development* (pp. 127–199). Norwood, NJ: Ablex.

TANGEL, D. M., & BLACHMAN, B. A. (1995). Effect of phoneme awareness instruction on the invented spelling of first-grade children: A one-year follow-up. *Journal of Reading Behavior, 27,* 153–185.

TEMPLE, C., NATHAN, R., BURRIS, N., & TEMPLE, F. (1988). The beginnings of writing (2nd ed.). Boston: Allyn and Bacon.

THE THREE BEARS. (1952). Racine, WI: Western.

TIMBERLAKE, P. (1995). Christopher Robin, Owl, Eeyore, and Nvntd Splling. *Young Children, 50,* 66–67.

VUKELICH, C., & EDWARDS, N. (1988). The role of context and as-written orthography in kindergartners' word recognition. In J. E. Readence & R. S. Baldwin (Eds.), *Dialogues in literacy research* (Thirty-seventh yearbook of the National Reading Conference) (pp. 85–93). Chicago: National Reading Conference.

WILDE, S. (1992). *You kan red this! Spelling and punctuation for whole language classrooms,* K–6. Portsmouth, NH: Heinemann.

YADEN, D. (1988). Understanding stories through repeated read-alouds. *The Reading Teacher, 41,* 556–560.

Chapter 5

From Six to Eight Years

Conventional Readers and Writers

Key Concepts

cue systems
monitor
strategy
predict
confirm
visualize
summarize
metacognitive awareness
fix-up strategies
interpretation
transaction
symbol
theme
referential dimension
morpheme
all-about story
setting
characters
plot
episodes
conflict
climax
point of view
style
mood
theme
expositions
consistency
ordered relationships
hierarchical relationships
label exposition
main idea–detail exposition
ordered paragraphs
ordered expositions
discovery strategies
performance strategies
prior knowledge
word families
early orthographic spellings
phonograms
decoding by analogy
orthographic readers and writers
later orthographic spellers
polysyllabic words
meaning-based spelling
word identification
vocabulary
comprehension

WHO ARE CONVENTIONAL READERS AND WRITERS?

Learning about reading and writing is a gradual process. It is not possible to identify the exact moment when a child becomes a reader or writer in a conventional sense. At first, children's reading or writing may seem more like experimenting than "really" reading or writing. As children move on to this next stage, they begin in some reading or writing events to orchestrate and control many of the understandings that they worked on as experimenters.

At first, children have only an intuitive understanding of reading strategies. They use a few dozen sight words to read texts that have simple language structures and familiar words from their spoken vocabularies. Young writers rely on invented spellings and a few known spellings to compose text with relatively simple text forms. Eventually, children acquire a variety of reading strategies and thousands of sight words, which they use to read text with complex structures and unfamiliar vocabulary and concepts. They use writing processes and knowledge of many conventional spellings to compose complex texts of different genres for a variety of purposes and audiences. They are conventional writers and readers.

Readers' and writers' accomplishments are partly the result of the formal reading and writing instruction that usually begins in first grade and continues through the primary grades. But their accomplishments are also the result of their discoveries, inventions, and experiments with literacy, described earlier.

The hallmark of conventional reading and writing is the ability to *orchestrate many different components of written language while maintaining a focus on meaning*. Reading is no longer a matter of remembering stories. Instead, readers recognize printed words and use their sense of the special literary syntax of stories, their concepts of stories, their knowledge of the world, and their understandings of sound–letter relationships to read fluently. Writing is no longer merely inventing spellings word-by-word, but instead involves a variety of drafting and revising strategies.

Examples: Experimenters versus Conventional Readers and Writers

In the following examples, two children are operating with understandings characteristic of experimenters and two with understandings more characteristic of conventional readers and writers. Decide which children are experimenters and which are readers and writers.

> Near the beginning of his first grade year, Graham's teacher shows his class the cover of a storybook, *Cookie's Week* (Ward, 1988). Graham tries to read the first word of the title. " 'Coke' is part of it," he says.
>
> A first grader is reading with his teacher. He says, "Up, up, up can, I mean came, little spider, to see what he can, could, see." The teacher points to the word *came* and says, "I like how you changed *can* to *came*. Why couldn't that word be *can*?" Ryan replies, "Because up, up, up *can* little spider doesn't sound right." Then his teacher remarked, "You also made another good self-correction when you said 'to see what he *could* see.' How did you know to change that?" Ryan answers, "Because if it was *can*, I would see an *n* and there is no *n*, so it has to be a word with a *d* and *could* is the word with a *d* that sounds right" (Lyons, 1991, p. 214).
>
> Tuñg decides to write a good-bye letter to a frequent visitor to his first grade classroom. His letter appears in Figure 5.1.
>
> Michael and his classmates are making a book about planets. They have read the repetitive book *Brown Bear, Brown Bear, What Do You See?* (Martin, 1967) and are using its pattern to write about the planets. Michael writes in his book:
>
> Sun Sun
> WutDOYouC (What do you see?)
> IC Mercury (I see Mercury)
> LokNAtMe (Looking at me)
> Mercury Mercury
> WutDOYouCICVenus (What do you see? I see Venus)
> LokN atme (Looking at me)

Graham and Michael are experimenters. Their reading and writing demonstrates that the majority of their attention was on only one or two components or **cue systems** of written language. Graham focused exclusively on using sound–letter relationships to identify words. He knew that he had only partially sounded out the first word of the title, which

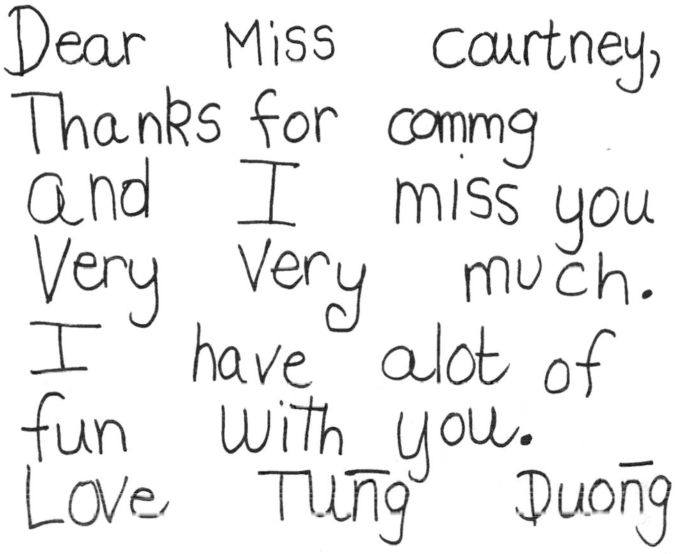
Dear Miss courtney,
Thanks for comng
and I miss you
Very Very much.
I have alot of
fun With you.
Love Tun̄g Duon̄g

Figure 5.1 *Tun̄g's Letter*

indicates that he was not looking beyond that to see if "Coke" would make sense with the other parts as a plausible title for the story whose cover illustration was before him.

Similarly, Michael focused on using sound–letter relationships to spell his words, although he can spell some words conventionally. His writing shows that even though he segments spoken words to spell, he rarely uses spaces to mark word boundaries. In addition, his understanding of the relationship between spoken sounds and letters is not entirely conventional (he uses the letter name *C* for the word *see*).

In contrast to Michael and Graham, Tun̄g and Ryan are conventional readers and writers. Tun̄g's writing uses mostly conventional spellings, formulaic letter-writing language ("Dear ______ " and "Love"), and conventional word spaces and punctuation. These accomplishments reflect his ability to orchestrate knowledge about a variety of written language forms. Tun̄g is a writer in a conventional sense; he orchestrates knowledge about written language meanings, forms, meaning-form links, and functions.

Ryan's reading marks him as a conventional reader as well. Ryan reads words by sight and monitors the meaning of what he reads (he realizes that the sentence "Up, up, up can little spider" does not make sense and does not sound like language). Ryan also pays attention to the print. He monitors what he says to make sure that it matches with the print. Ryan orchestrates meaning, form, meaning-form links, and function.

What conventional readers do is more complete than what novices and experimenters do. We do not mean that the children we call conventional readers and writers have finished with their literacy learning, nor that beginners, novices, and experimenters do not accomplish a great deal. We do mean that conventional readers and writers are better at putting together the pieces of the literacy puzzle. Unlike experimenters, they combine all of their literacy knowledge into single literacy events.

MEANING CONSTRUCTION

As conventional readers and writers who have mastered literacy skills, the children described in this chapter are able to transfer their earlier meaning-making strategies to what they do on their own with books and paper and pencils. In other words, they are able to construct meaning from what they read by themselves (What did the author intend?) and in what they write for someone else (How can I convey for others what I intend?). They are even more aware than are novices and experimenters that written language is a communication process.

Meaning Making in Reading: Using Strategies

We have shown that readers focus on meaning while orchestrating a variety of cue systems. One of the first and most important methods that children use to orchestrate all these possible sources of information during reading is to **monitor** whether what they are reading makes sense (is meaningful), sounds like language (has acceptable syntax), and looks right (has the sequences of letters that they expect after much experience with texts). Monitoring while reading is a **strategy** for keeping reading flowing smoothly while making sure that reading makes sense and is consistent with the printed text. Children show that they are monitoring by rereading a portion of the text when what they have read does not make sense or by rereading to correct a word that does not match with the text.

Eventually readers are able to use several different reading strategies to help them understand or comprehend what they read (Paris, Wasik, & Turner, 1991). For example, readers pause to **predict** what will happen, and as they read they look for information to **confirm** or disconfirm their predictions. They **visualize** scenes in stories and **summarize** to themselves what has happened so far. Sometimes readers remember events in their own lives or people they know that are like the events and characters in stories, or they think about characters from other stories.

At first, readers use simple strategies of rereading, sounding out words, and skipping confusing parts of stories. Even these simple strategies may be used deliberately by beginning readers (Freppon, 1991). This conscious use of strategies is called **metacognitive awareness.** Later children develop **fix-up strategies** for fixing up problems they notice while reading (Brown, 1980). Readers may reread a portion of a story when they realize that something does not make sense or that they have missed one of the elements of story form that they know to expect. They may skip a word they do not know if they are aware that they are still able to understand the story. Sophisticated readers may adjust their pace or change their level of engagement, looking for main ideas and a developing gist, or noting finer details. They may skim, look for repeated key words, use titles and headings, use past knowledge of the topic and of how similar texts like the ones they are reading are typically organized, pay closer attention to the exact wording of the text, reread sections, and use pictures and other graphics.

Meaning Making in Reading: Constructing Interpretations of Literature

An important hallmark of readers is that they go beyond understanding a story—they build interpretations of a story. An **interpretation** is an attempt to understand the story at a more abstract level, using the story to understand the self or the world (Many, 1991). As they read a story, readers construct their own personal understandings and, sometimes, interpretations of that text, partly based on their unique background experiences. This unique interaction between the text and the reader is called a **transaction** (Rosenblatt, 1978). Transactions also take place for children who listen to stories read aloud.

An important way in which young children build interpretations of literature is to participate in group discussions of books in which children share personal responses to what they read and listen to others' responses. Such experiences lead readers to insightful interpretations of stories, of which they may not have been aware before the group discussion (McGee, 1992; 1998).

Figure 5.2 presents part of a class discussion about *Rosie's Walk* (Hutchins, 1968). In this story, a hen, Rosie, goes for a walk around the farmyard. A fox follows her and tries to capture her, but each time ends up missing her. The teacher initiates the conversation by asking, "Did Rosie know the fox was following her?" One class member argues that Rosie knew the fox was behind her (line 1), but another classmate disagrees (line 4—"she didn't know") and even offers evidence from the text to support the argument ("The string on Rosie's foot. She just stepped . . . and the stuff fell on the fox"). Still another classmate reasserts the original argument and offers textual evidence (line 12—"cause her eyes are always going straight ahead").

Figure 5.2 *Discussion of* Rosie's Walk *(Hutchins, 1968)*

1 C: Yeah, I think she (the hen) knew some of the time (that the fox was behind her). Like when the mice, cause like the mice jumped and the fox fell in the hay.

2 C: Yeah, she knew, she knew.

3 T: She knew?

4 C: Well, the string on Rosie's foot. She just stepped and she didn't know then, and the stuff fell on the fox.

5 T: Yeah.

6 C: She knew, she knew all the time, but she was just keeping on going, she wouldn't even turn around, she just kept on walking like it was a trap.

7 T: It was a trap?

8 C: Yeah, and the fox got tricked cause he's so stupid.

9 T: You say the fox is stupid?

10 C: The fox is stupid cause he got stinged by all the bees and he had to run away and everything was wrong. He was always getting in trouble.

11 C: Yeah, the poor fox.

12 C: I think she knew but she didn't turn cause her eyes are always going straight ahead and then she just keeps going.

13 C: And everytime the fox, he gets in a trap and she never gets scared or anything.

From McGee, L. (1992). An exploration of meaning construction in first graders' grand conversations. C. Kinzer & D. Leu (Eds.), *Literacy research, theory, and practice: views from many perspectives*, p. 185. Reprinted with permission of the National Reading Conference.

This discussion shows how conventional readers are able to take the perspective of others and draw on evidence to support their own perspectives. More important, the children are moving toward an interpretation of the story (line 13): "And everytime the fox, he gets in a trap and she never gets scared or anything."

In the following discussion about *Hey, Al* (Yorinks, 1986), children demonstrate their perception of two highly abstract literary elements: symbol and theme. A **symbol** is an event, object, person, or activity that represents two meanings—a literal meaning and an abstract meaning. A **theme** is the abstract statement about life or humanity that is reflected in a story or poem. The story of *Hey, Al* tells of a janitor who is dissatisfied with his life and is enticed by a strange bird to fly to a paradise. On reaching paradise, Al begins to turn into a bird, but he flies home before he completely loses his identity. Figure 5.3 presents a portion of a class discussion of *Hey, Al.*

In this discussion Annie made one theme explicit (line 1) when she said, "He (Al) would be better as a janitor instead of up there. *Never talk to strangers.*" "Never talk to strangers" is an abstract statement of theme (more than likely called to mind by the familiar admonition). She also noticed a symbol when she said (line 6), "They painted it yellow *like the place.* He was happy at the end." She noticed that the yellow color that Al painted his room when he returned from the false paradise represented both his initial happy experience at the island ("like the place") and his newfound happiness and contentment with his own life on his return ("He was happy at the end"). Children's concepts about theme and symbols and their ability to articulate them develop gradually through the primary grades (Lehr, 1988).

Meaning Making in Writing

Conventional writers draw on many strategies for writing. Rachel wrote the story presented in Figure 5.4 when she was in second grade. Several elements of this story are noteworthy. Although Rachel uses knowledge of everyday activities (such as hide-and-go-seek) and

Figure 5.3 *First Graders Talk about* Hey, Al *(Yorinks, 1986)*

1	Annie:	I think he (Al) would be better as a janitor instead of up there. Never talk to strangers.
2	Ryan:	If he stayed up there, he would really be a bird and we don't know if he could change back again and his whole body would be a bird.
3	John:	He loves his house.
4	T:	How do you know?
5	John:	Because he was happy to be back and the dog came back and they painted it.
6	Annie:	They painted it yellow like the place. He was happy at the end.
7	Chris:	Yea, and he got a new shirt like it wasn't the shirt from, like he was a janitor again, but he's got a nicer shirt and he looks happy.
8	Alice:	Eddy is smiling. Yeah. The story has a happy ending.

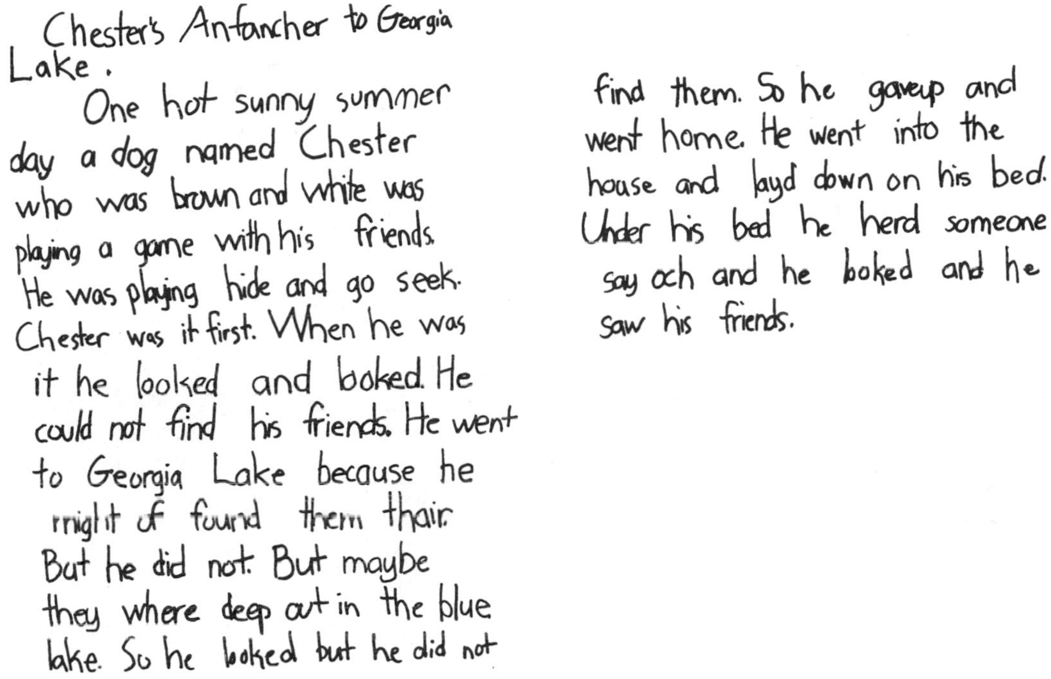
Chester's Anfancher to Georgia Lake.
One hot sunny summer day a dog named Chester who was brown and white was playing a game with his friends. He was playing hide and go seek. Chester was it first. When he was it he looked and loked. He could not find his friends. He went to Georgia Lake because he might of found them thair. But he did not. But maybe they where deep out in the blue lake. So he loked but he did not find them. So he gaveup and went home. He went into the house and layd down on his bed. Under his bed he herd someone say och and he loked and he saw his friends.

Figure 5.4 *Chester's Adventure to Georgia Lake*

familiar others (such as her friends) in her compositions, she clearly uses these elements to construct a believable and consistent, but imaginary, story-world. Unlike experimenters such as Jeffrey (see Chapter 4 for his dictated poem), conventional writers are able to go beyond the personal and immediate—what is happening or just recently happened—to the abstract—what has not yet happened or might never really happen. The relation of the writer with the subject matter (from immediate to abstract) is called the **referential dimension** of writing (Moffett, 1968).

Rachel's writing is also noteworthy for the rich use of descriptive detail and its unity of meaning. Chester, the dog, is brown and white; Lake George is deep blue. Her story is unified throughout by the problem of not being able to locate friends in a game of hide-and-seek.

WRITTEN LANGUAGE FORMS

As they become conventional readers and writers, children refine much of what they learned as experimenters about the form of written language. First, as they learn how to identify a growing number of words, they may pay close attention to identifying individual words in their reading. Chall (1983) calls this being "glued to print" (p. 18). Because of their close attention to the written text, they gain knowledge of the fine points of form at the word level in English writing. Children's writing begins to show their achievement of a fully conventional concept of word. Second, they start to use narrative form in their writing. Most children already know a great deal about narrative form, and they use it to tell stories. During this period, they begin to use it as well to write stories on their own. Third, their knowledge of a different category of text form, *exposition,* grows, and they begin to develop strategies for reading and writing expository texts.

Concept of Word

Conventional readers and writers know how to show word boundaries and use punctuation. An experimenter's dots and squares between words or circles around words give way to spaces between words. Periods and even commas, question marks, and exclamation marks appear in their writing.

Conventional readers and writers learn how morphemes work in written language. The **morpheme** is the smallest unit of meaning in a language. Conventional readers and writers learn that morphemes may be written as individual words, such as the articles *a, an,* and *the,* or they may be written as word parts, such as *-ed, -ing,* and *-s.* At age six and a half, Paul Bissex used *A* as a morpheme that is part of a word (in *awake* and *asleep*) and as a morpheme that is a separate word (the article in *a owl*). He wrote, "I AM AWACK AT NITE ASLEP IN THE DAY/ BUT I AM NOT A OWL" (Bissex, 1980, p. 57).

Story Form

Children eventually write complex story compositions, but early on their compositions hardly qualify as stories. They rely on talking to fill out their compositions, or they write more descriptive pieces called all-about stories.

Early Story-Writing Strategies and Texts

Observations of young writers reveal that they sometimes have trouble remembering what they want their stories to say when they are attending to the difficulties of writing (Calkins, 1986). Young writers solve this problem by drawing and talking. If they first draw pictures of their stories, they are able to return later to the pictures for reminders of how their stories should go.

Young authors' stories often barely qualify as stories (Calkins, 1986). Beginning writers seem to avoid the story form altogether. That is, they do not use in their writing all the story structure knowledge that they exhibit during storytelling. Many first written "stories" are not stories; rather, they are "all I know about something" pieces. They are more like inventories of information—and misinformation. Figure 5.5 shows an **all-about story** written by a first grader.

A typical all-about piece lacks story form, a precise sequence of events, and a real end. It may be a book composed of several pages, each with a picture and a caption that tells about some part of the subject the child has chosen. The captions may contain pronouns that refer to earlier mentions of the subject. Except for such pronoun usage, however, most pages could stand on their own; they have no direct link with what went before or what comes after.

Story Writing

Eventually, conventional writers become skilled at doing all that is entailed in writing complex stories, that is, stories that reflect a very developed concept of story and sophisticated

Figure 5.5 All-About Book

literary knowledge. Writers in the primary grades only begin this long process of learning to compose coherent, engaging, and insightful stories. Still, we can lay out what we might expect to find in the very advanced stories that conventional writers in these grades might compose.

Literary elements in stories. We would expect well-written stories to include many of the literary elements already discussed, such as point of view and theme. And although we would never presume that young children would be able to write stories containing all the literary elements we expect in well-written stories (few adults can craft stories using all the elements we will describe), we can expect them to write stories that have some of these elements. After all, young readers explore many of these elements in their story discussions (see Figures 5.2 and 5.3), and children dictate stories that include some of these elements. We will first describe literary elements found in high-quality stories. Then we will present two stories composed by young writers and discuss the literary elements found in these stories.

All stories have seven major literary elements: setting, character, plot, point of view, style, mood, and theme (Lukens, 1995). These elements are summarized in Table 5.1. The **setting** introduces the location, time period, and weather in which the story takes place, and reveals mood and character. For example, characters who are put in harsh settings (such as a desert or a lonely island) are often revealed as resourceful, hardworking, and independent. The setting is sometimes used as an antagonist to introduce conflict to the story.

Table 5.1 Literary Elements of Narratives

ELEMENT	COMPONENTS	PURPOSE
setting	time place weather	reveals mood; reveals character; and introduces conflict
character	thoughts actions appearance words (dialogue)	reveals motives and traits; must be believable and consistent
plot	problem conflict climax resolution	must be logical and consistent; introduces tension; and propels story forward
point of view	first person third omniscient third limited omniscient objective	positions reader in story-world
style	imagery figurative language word choice	reveals author's voice
mood		sets emotional tone
theme		provides consistency for story at the abstract level

For example, a character may have to travel through a snowstorm (an antagonistic setting) in order to get to school.

There are two kinds of **characters** in stories: main characters and supporting characters. The main characters are at the center of the action of the story, and supporting characters serve as helpers to the main characters. Characters are not always people (they can be animals or objects that are animated), but main characters must have human traits—we must come to know them as people. Characters are revealed through their thoughts, actions, words, and appearance. We must be able to see a character in action and hear what a character says and thinks.

A critical component of stories is the plot. The **plot** includes **episodes,** each with a problem and obstacles. The last episode in a story includes the climax and resolution of the story. The main character does not usually solve the problem simply or easily, but encounters difficulties or obstacles along the way that create **conflict.** A critical moment comes when the problem is solved (the **climax**) and the story is resolved (often happily in literature for children). Conflict is an important part of stories, because it produces tension (we do not know how the story will end, although we hope all will go well) and propels the story forward.

Point of view is the perspective from which the story is told. Sometimes the story is told by a narrator who allows the reader to know the thoughts of all the characters. At other times, the narrator is a character, and we know only his or her thoughts. At other times, the narrator is an objective observer; in this case, the narrator tells only what an observer might see or hear and never reveals the thoughts of any characters. Point of view is particularly important, because it positions the reader inside or outside the story. When point of view allows readers inside the story, they know all the characters' thoughts and feelings.

Style is the way the author uses language, including use of imagery (descriptions that appeal to the senses, such as sight, sound, or touch), word choice, and figurative language (such as the use of simile or metaphor). Each author uses language in unique ways to describe setting and character and to uncover the plot.

Mood is the emotional tone of a story (humorous, somber, lighthearted, mysterious, frightening). **Theme** is the abstract statement about life or humanity revealed by the story as a whole. Through theme, stories achieve a consistency at an abstract level.

Children's Narrative Writing

What kinds of literary elements might we expect to find in primary schoolchildren's compositions? Return to Rachel's story presented in Figure 5.4. It includes a main character, Chester, the brown and white dog. It also includes Chester's friends (who act as playful antagonists in the game of hide-and-seek and the story). Rachel implied one of Chester's character traits: he is persistent (he looked and looked for his hidden friends). Tension arises naturally from the conflict of searching; the friends are very difficult to find! The story is told consistently from the third-person point of view with a narrator speaking directly to the reader about how clever Chester was for searching for his friends at Lake George. Rachel's literary style includes the use of repetition (looked and looked). The mood is playful, beginning with the title ("Chester's Adventure to Georgia Lake") and continuing through to the climax when "och" reveals Chester's friends hiding under his bed.

Figure 5.6 presents another story written by a primary-grade student. Although the story sometimes loses sequence, it has several characters who act in a consistent manner, as we would expect (a cat chases a chick). The author tells us about the characters by revealing their feelings (the cat is hungry, and the chick is afraid) and by showing us what they say ("Peep, peep" and "Meow"). The story has a problem (the cat is trying to eat the chick) and actions to solve the problem (the mother bites the cat, and the chick hides).

Figure 5.6 *"Peep Peep" Story*

Yo tengo un pollito. El pollito hace—¡pio, pio!—. El pollito se va a jugar y viene. Tiene hambre. El pollito hace—¡pio, pio!—. El gato lo persigue. La madre lo pica y el gato hace—¡miau!— . . . Por eso la gallina y mi pollito dice la gallina y el pollito estaba escondido. Tenía miedo que el gato lo agarrará.

(I have a chick. The chick says, "Peep, peep." The chick goes out to play and comes [back]. He's hungry. The chick says, "Peep, peep." The cat chases him. The mother bites him and the cat goes, "Meow." . . . Therefore the hen and my chick say the hen and the chick was hidden. He was afraid the cat will catch him.)

Edelsky, C. (1986). *Writing in a Bilingual Program,* p. 91. Reprinted with permission from Ablex Publishing Corporation.

From these two stories, we can conclude that children do use many literary elements of narratives in their stories, but not necessarily all elements, nor are the elements always well developed. We understand that primary schoolchildren's stories may lack plot complexity and descriptive detail. We might expect that young conventional writers' stories would gradually acquire overall story consistency, believability, and detail, but much of this development occurs after the primary grades.

Expository Text

Not all texts are stories. Some texts inform or explain, rather than relate a story; these are called **expositions.** Much nonfiction takes this form. We expect conventional writers eventually to compose informative, engaging, and accurate expositions. Of course, readers and writers in the primary grades only begin the process of learning to compose highly structured informational texts and to read and remember ideas from informational books. We will first describe the forms of well-structured expository texts and then present what we know about young children's expository writing next.

Expository Text Structure

There are three important components in highly organized informational material: consistency, ordered relationships, and hierarchical relationships (Newkirk, 1987). For a text to have **consistency,** all its ideas must be related to one another. The all-about story about butterflies presented in Figure 5.5 is consistent: all of the ideas in the text are related to butterflies and feelings about butterflies. However, this text does not have ordered relationships.

Ordered relationships are ideas that are related in some order. For example, two ideas might be related because one idea is an example of or illustrates another idea. Causes and effects, problems and solutions, comparisons, or sequences are all ideas that are ordered—they are related to one another in specific ways. A third grader wrote the following composition about doing chores in order to receive an allowance. In this composition, each sentence is not only consistent with the topic, but also related to the preceding sentence through sequence or cause–effect relationships.

> My mother wants me to set the table because that is my job. First, I get out the silverware and then the glasses and last the butter. When I set the table all week, I get my allowance.

The last component of expository text structures is **hierarchical relationships.** Most expository texts are complex and can be broken into one or more main topics, which, in turn, can be broken down into subtopics, forming a hierarchy. The relationships among the main topics and between the subtopics and the main topic in expositions are also ordered or related. An example of an expository text with hierarchical relationships, ordered relationships, and consistency is presented in Figure 5.7.

This composition presents information about the problems and solutions of staying safe while staying in a hotel. All information in the composition is consistently related to the problem of safety in hotels. Three solutions to the problem are presented: knowing the location of stairwells, following safe procedures in case of a fire, and being careful about security. At the highest level of organization or hierarchy, the three main solutions (location of stairwells, safe fire procedures, and personal safety) are each related to the problem.

Figure 5.7 *Hotel Safety: An Exposition*

Hotel Safety

Each year hundreds of vacations are cut short because travelers are victims of hotel room burglary or suffer injury from hotel fires. Most travel-related burglaries and injuries can be avoided by learning simple rules of hotel safety.

One hotel safety rule is knowing the location of all stairwells in the hotel. In cases of emergency, the safest exit is down the stairs and out nearby emergency exits. Therefore, travelers should take note of the location of all stairwells upon checking in. Hotels post maps in each room which show the location of all stairwells. Travelers should note all stairwell locations in case the path to the nearest stairwell is blocked.

Knowing procedures to follow in case of a fire alarm is another hotel safety must. As soon as a fire alarm sounds, travelers should first feel the door. If the door does not feel hot, they can quickly exit the building through the nearest stairwell. If the door feels hot, travelers should soak a bath towel and stuff it beneath the door to prevent smoke from entering the room. They should turn off the air conditioner or heater to prevent smoke from entering. Travelers should stay low in the room until rescue arrives.

A final hotel safety rule is to be security conscious. Travelers should keep room doors locked at all times and use the deadbolt at night. They should identify anyone seeking entrance to the room, report suspicious loiterers to the front desk, and keep keys secure at all times.

In addition, the ideas presented within each solution paragraph are related to one another through the ordered relationships of sequence and causation. Therefore, this composition includes topic consistency, ordered relationships, and hierarchical organization.

Children's Expository Writing

As beginning writers, young children explore many ways of presenting information in their compositions (Casbergue, 1998; Langer, 1986; Newkirk, 1987), including writing labels and lists, main-idea paragraphs, ordered paragraphs, and ordered expositions.

Label expositions. Figure 5.8 presents one of the simplest ways that young children organize their expositions—by labeling information in a picture or diagram using words or short sentences following the pattern "This is a ______." Ted's Halloween composition (Figure 5.8) is an example of an early **label exposition.** It resembles all-about stories in that it lacks a precise expository form and precise relationships among ideas other than implied consistency (all about Halloween or all about butterflies—see Figure 5.5). Ted's Halloween exposition in Figure 5.8 consists of a collection of labels for a Halloween picture. This exposition has implied consistency (all the labels are related to the topic of Halloween), but it lacks ordered or hierarchical relationships.

Main idea–detail expositions. Some early expository compositions go beyond labels by being more obviously topic consistent. However, these compositions still lack ordered relationships among ideas; the ideas in main idea expositions are not related to one another beyond being consistently related to a topic. Figure 5.9 presents a **main idea–detail exposition**

***Figure 5.8** Ted's Collection of Halloween Labels*

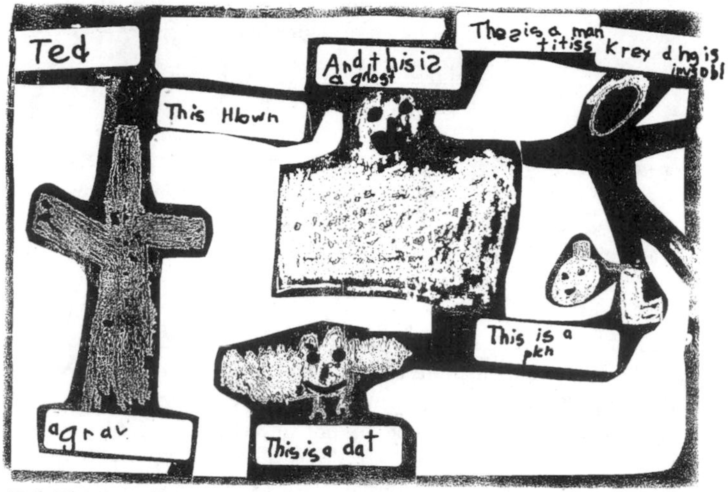

Ted. This is Halloween. And this is a ghost. This is a man. It is gray because he is invisible. A grave. This is a bat. This is a pumpkin.

***Figure 5.9** Ted's Attribute List*

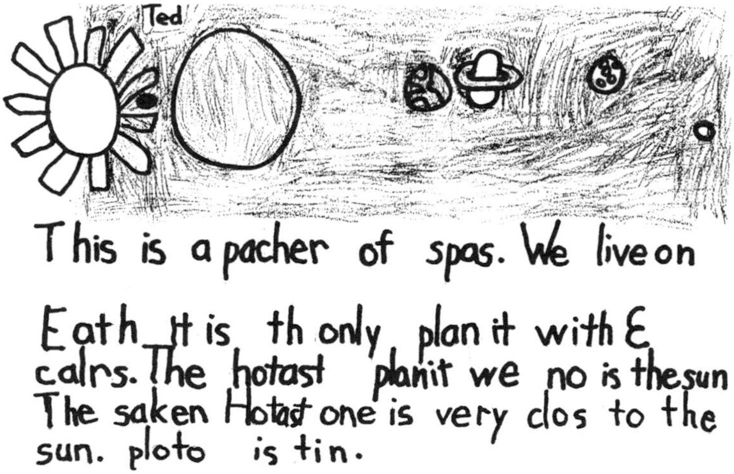

This is a picture of space. We live on Earth. It is the only planet with 3 colors. The hottest planet we know is the sun. The second hottest one is very close to the sun. Pluto is tiny.

describing the solar system. All the ideas in the composition are related to the topic, the solar system, but they are not related to each other, with the exception of two. The idea "the hottest planet we know is the sun" is related to the idea "the second hottest one is very close to the sun" by the relationship of comparison.

Most main idea–detail expositions could be compared with lists; that is, these compositions relate information about a topic that could simply be listed; the order of ideas is not important. However, list making in label and main idea–detail expositions is an important signal that young children are attending to the unique features of written language.

List making is a decidedly written-language activity. It is true that many children have experiences with lists at an early age, just as they have experiences with stories. They see their parents write lists (Heath, 1983), and they are willing to try to read lists (McGee, Lomax, & Head, 1988), but they do not tell lists as they tell stories. If the expression we just used, "tell lists," sounds wrong, there is a good reason. Listing has a different function from "storying." Listing allows the list maker not only to search memory, but also to sort and categorize in a way "that is almost impossible in speech" (Newkirk, 1987, p. 132).

"The child who writes a list is not writing down talk; he or she is doing something which talk cannot do" (Newkirk, 1987, p. 141). Thus, children who learn expository text structure are not just learning to write what they could previously tell quite well. They are learning a new, exclusively written language form, with an appropriate written language function.

Making lists may actually provide a bridge between using simpler forms of organizing ideas in an exposition and using more complex forms of organization. Figure 5.10 presents a third grader's list of daily activities. It uses a sophisticated, top-level organization which labels the two parts of the list ("Time" and "Thing"), and each idea in the list goes beyond being merely related to the topic by using time sequence. Thus, this composition uses ordered relationships.

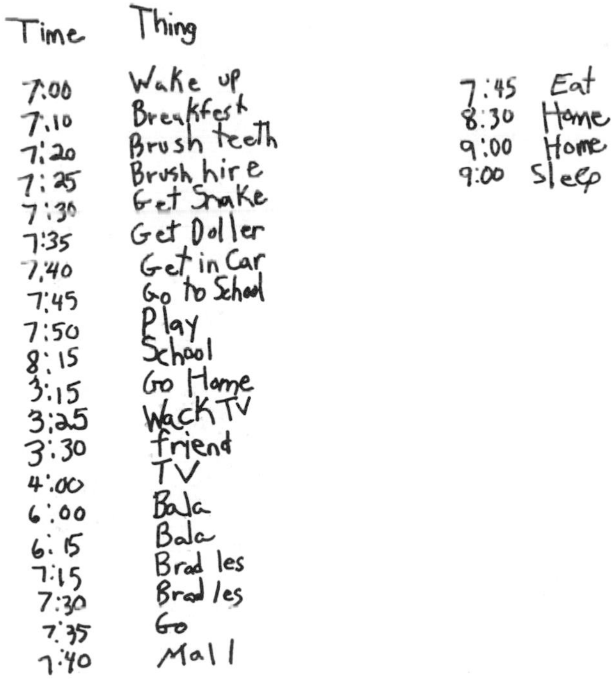
Time Thing
7:00 Wake up
7:10 Breakfest
7:20 Brush teeth
7:25 Brush hire
7:30 Get Snake
7:35 Get Doller
7:40 Get in Car
7:45 Go to School
7:50 Play
8:15 School
3:15 Go Home
3:25 Wack TV
3:30 friend
4:00 TV
6:00 Bala
6:15 Bala
7:15 Brad les
7:30 Brad les
7:35 Go
7:40 Mall
7:45 Eat
8:30 Home
9:00 Home
9:00 Sleep

Figure 5.10 A Third Grader's List of Daily Activities

Ordered paragraphs. Eventually young writers compose **ordered paragraphs,** in which the ideas are not only related to a topic (are consistent), but also related to one another through sequence, cause and effect, or compare and contrast ordered relationships. Ordered paragraphs contain at least three statements that are related to a single topic and that are logically connected or related to each other (Newkirk, 1987). Writing ordered paragraphs means that writers have begun learning various ways to connect ideas logically.

An elementary-school student wrote the paragraph shown in Figure 5.11. This student is beginning to understand how to use cause-and-effect logic to organize ideas in writing, but this paragraph barely qualifies as an ordered paragraph. The first idea, "the dinosaurs died," is causally related to the subsequent idea, "because of a comet that landed on the earth." But this line of reasoning does not reach a conclusion until farther into the paragraph: "The comet blocked the sun," "there was a lot of radiation," "and that killed the dinosaurs." These ideas are not only consistent, but also causally related.

Ordered expositions. The most organized expository text structure consists of **ordered expositions,** in which ideas are not only consistent and related, but also hierarchical (the main topic is broken down into subtopics). Few primary-school-age students achieve this organization in their expository writing (Newkirk, 1987), perhaps because one of the last steps in learning exposition is knowing that, to present a topic well, one must find the best way to organize its content. Choosing the best organization depends on having a repertoire of expository text structures available, such as compare–contrast and cause and effect. This knowledge is also part of learning a subject thoroughly. A complete understanding of crocodiles requires knowing how crocodiles are both different from and similar to alligators. A report about crocodiles and alligators could be well organized using a compare–contrast text structure. Similarly, a complete understanding of the age of glaciers requires knowing what

Figure 5.11 *An Initial Ordered Paragraph*

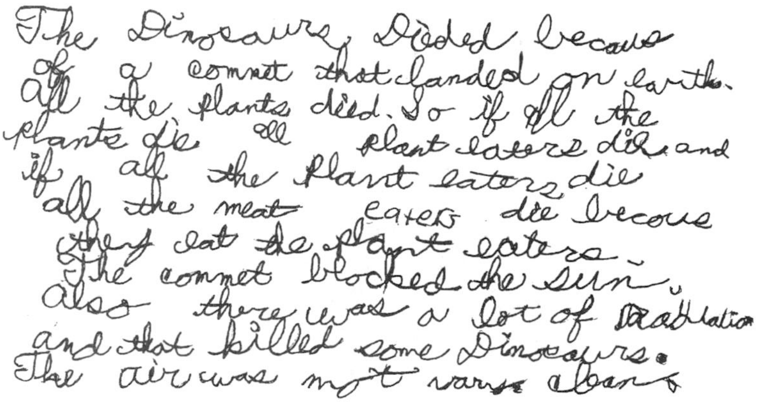

The dinosaurs died because of a comet that landed on earth. All the plants died. So if all the plants die, all plant eaters die, and if all the plant eaters die, all the meat eaters die because they eat the plant eaters. The comet blocked the sun. Also there was a lot of radiation and that killed some dinosaurs. The air was not very clean.

effects the glaciers had on plant and animal life and on the topography of the continents. A report about glaciers could be well organized using a cause-and-effect text structure. Bruner (1960) called this "the mastery of the structure of the subject matter" (p. 18). Most accomplished readers and writers are only beginning to acquire this sophisticated knowledge.

Mixing Narrative and Exposition Forms

Some young children's expository reports have a strong narrative thread. It is not, as some (e.g., Moffett, 1968) have argued, that children must make do with the narrative form because they are ignorant of any other; rather, children are using what they know in order to take their early steps toward a new form. In some cases, we can see a strong interplay between listing and storying.

However, mixed narrative and exposition compositions serve a different purpose from story writing; they are written primarily to convey or to preserve information rather than to create an imaginary world. In order to serve the function of preserving information, children draw on many of the shared conventions of the narrative and expository forms.

Children recognize that narrative and expository texts share similar literary elements, although they are used differently in narratives and expositions. For example, both kinds of text may include the element of "character," such as a particular penguin like Tacky in the book *Tacky the Penguin* (Lester, 1988) in the case of narrative form, or a specific, but unnamed penguin, such as the penguin described in *See How They Grow: Penguin* (Fletcher, 1993) in the case of exposition. Thus, although "character" is dealt with differently in a narrative (a specific and named character) and in an exposition (generalized character or characters), the two text forms clearly share the element of "character."

Writers of informational text draw on many other narrative elements, including dialogue, setting, sequence, causal relations, conflict, and tension. Therefore, it is not surprising that children's compositions include a mixture of narrative and expository elements. Figure 5.12 presents Ted's report of his sighting of Halley's comet. He blended two kinds of expository form: description ("It looked like a big fuzzy blob with a big fuzzy tail," "It was a very bright object, and I couldn't see the tail") and comparison–contrast ("I had seen many pictures of the comet, but this one looked different," "When I got to look through the telescope,

Figure 5.12 *Ted's Narrative Report about Viewing Halley's Comet*

The Comet

In the middle of the night my dad woke me up. It reminded me of when my mom had my baby sister. I thought we were going to have another baby. But Dad said, "Do you want to see the comet?" so I got up, changed my clothes and got in the car with Dad. It was 4:00 a.m. when we left. It took us about a half an hour to get there. We came to an open field and before we got our binoculars out, somebody told us that the baseball field had a better view of the comet. So we went there in our car. It took us about one minute. There was a big group of people looking through binoculars because the people with the telescopes had not come yet. Dad asked one of the people where the comet was. The person told him, "Look for one short pole and one long pole. It would be above the long pole." So he took out his binoculars and looked for the comet, and then he saw it. He let me see. I had seen many pictures of the comet, but this one looked different. But my dad told me it was Halley's Comet. It looked like a big fuzzy blob with a big fuzzy tail.

the comet did not look at all like it did in the binoculars," "when it last came, it was higher in the sky and brighter"). He also used such narrative elements as time sequence and dialogue.

MEANING-FORM LINKS

Young experimenters with written language already know a great deal about meaning-form links (see Chapter 4). They try to sound literate and be precise. Their invented spellings show an awareness of sound–letter correspondences and an ability to use that awareness to put words in writing.

An important difference between experimenters and conventional readers and writers is that the latter group uses more literacy strategies. We can better understand this change if we first distinguish between two kinds of literacy strategies. **Discovery strategies** are strategies for finding out how reading and writing work. "Pay attention to such salient features of literacy experiences as letters, letters' names, and sounds in words" is a discovery strategy that leads to experimenters' becoming inventive spellers, and thus to their knowing one way in which spelling works. **Performance strategies** are strategies for successfully accomplishing an act of reading or writing. Although "Be precise" and "Sound literate" are experimenters' performance strategies, most other strategies that experimenters use are discovery strategies. For conventional readers and writers, however, performance strategies dominate.

Many performance strategies involve knowledge that children already have—**prior knowledge.** Prior knowledge can be knowing the content of reading or writing—facts and concepts related to the subject matter. Prior knowledge also can be knowing reading and writing processes, such as knowing how to spell words, how to sound out words, how to organize a report, or what to include in a story. An increase in the latter kind of prior knowledge, which is usually learned in elementary school, contributes significantly to most children's becoming conventional readers and writers.

Spelling

Conventional writers learn new spelling strategies, especially visual ones, that contribute to conventional spelling. As experimenters, they may have spelled the word *weight* as *yt* or *wt* (in the early invented spelling stage) or as *wat* (at the purely phonetic stage). As conventional spellers, we may expect that they spell the word as *wayt* or even *wate* before finally spelling it conventionally. We have seen that experimenters' spellings are influenced merely by sound. Purely phonetic spellers capture each phoneme in a word and assign at least one letter to that sound. Therefore, purely phonetic spellings are often more accurate phonetically than are conventional spellings (Wilde, 1992).

The end of the purely phonetic spelling often overlaps with the beginning of conventional reading and writing. Many early conventional writers use a mixture of known spellings and purely phonetic spellings. However, the hallmark of conventional writing is beginning to use new, more visual strategies for spelling. Conventional writers' spellings are influenced by four visual factors: (1) knowledge of the standardized spellings of certain morphemes (*jumped* is spelled with an *ed* even though it sounds like *jumpt*); (2) an expectation of certain letters in certain contexts (for example, the *ight* sequence in *sight, might,* and *fight*)—the similar words that give rise to the expectation described in this second factor are called **word families;** (3) knowledge of spelling patterns for long vowel and other vowel pairs (*meat* is spelled with *ea*, while *meet* is spelled with *ee*), consonant doubling (*stopping* includes the doubled *p*), and adding affixes (*re*start and place*ment*), and (4) awareness of meaning-related similarities (for example, *reverence* is spelled with *ence* rather than *unce* or *ince*, because of its relationship with *revere*).

The learning of spelling regularities based on meaning-related similarities, standardized spelling of morphemes, and word families is best seen as another step in the developmental invented spelling behavior described in Chapter 4. Although invented spelling is an important hallmark of the young experimenter, it is not merely a passing phase to be put aside or forgotten either by students, as they become conventional readers and writers, or by their teachers (Gentry, 1982). Conventional writers' early drafts continue to include invented spellings.

We now turn to three additional stages of developmental spelling: early orthographic spelling, later orthographic spelling, and meaning-based spelling (Bear, Invernizzi, Templeton, & Johnston, 1996). These stages are presented in Table 5.2 (and follow the three stages described in Table 4.1 in Chapter 4). These last three stages of spelling continue considerably beyond the primary years of schooling; however, we would expect many second and third graders to use spellings reflective of at least early orthographic spelling.

Early Orthographic Spelling

Early orthographic spellings emerge while children are also using purely phonetic spellings. Gradually children move from merely writing a letter for each sound that they hear to knowing spelling patterns involving more than one letter. For example, children begin to spell

***Table 5.2** Early Orthographic, Late Orthographic, and Meaning-Based Spelling*

Early Orthographic Spelling

Going beyond one-to-one encoding of sounds with letters

- includes preconsonantal nasals (jump)
- uses long vowel patterns (not necessarily conventional; *grate* for great, *tee* for tea)
- consistent use of constant blends and digraphs (*ship, whip, blow*)
- consistent use of morphemes *ing, ed, s* (*runs, walked, drinking*)

Later Orthographic Spelling

Using orthographic patterns beyond the syllable level

- spells long vowel patterns conventionally
- uses consonant doubling at syllable junctures (*rattle, riddle*)
- uses morphological patterns (*inches, flies, giving, clapping, libraries, relaxes*)
- uses affixes (*motion, agreement, happily, mountain, restart*)
- uses confusable affixes (*adventure, enclosure, procedure, insecure, pasture, rancher*)

Meaning-Based Spelling

- uses usual affixes related to meaning (competition to relate to compete)

Based on Bear, Invernizzi, Templeton, & Johnston, 1996.

words conventionally that include letters which are nearly or completely silent (such as the *m* in *jump* or the *l* in *walk*). They learn spelling patterns for long vowels and consistently spell the morphemes *ed* or *s* conventionally, despite differences in their pronunciation in words.

Learning to read some some words conventionally and read words by sight may actually propel young writers into the orthographic stage of spelling. For example, as children learn to read the words *map, cap, tap, clap, flap,* and *lap,* they have many opportunities to notice that the /ap/ rime in these words is consistently spelled with the letters *ap.* The letters that members of word families have in common (their rime), such as *ap,* are called **phonograms** (Adams, 1990). Learning some words from a word family allows children to apply phonograms intuitively to both read and spell additional words in the same family. This practice is called spelling or reading by analogy, or **decoding by analogy** (Ehri & Robbins, 1992). Readers who notice word-family patterns and who use analogies to read unknown words are called **orthographic readers and writers** (Ehri, 1991).

During the early orthographic stage of development, conventional readers and writers spell many words conventionally and others unconventionally. Rachel's story in Figure 5.4 includes nearly all conventionally spelled words with just a few developmental spellings (*Anfancher* for *adventure, thair* for *there, layd* for *laid,* and *herd* for *heard*). As shown in Rachel's developmental spellings, unconventionally spelled words at this stage often include letter sequences more typical of conventional spellings than of earlier invented spellings. Children still spell many words unconventionally, but they realize that English spelling is more complex than simply matching single letters with single sounds. For instance, they learn that every syllable must contain a vowel, so they spell *jar* as JAR rather than as JR. A related discovery is that letters often work in combination. Thus, they spell *tail* as TAILL or TALLE (using *A* in combination with *I* or *E* to spell the long *a* sound) rather than as TAL.

Another new understanding is that some sounds are represented in more than one way. The letter combinations *ai, ae,* and even *eigh,* for example, can be used to spell the long *a* sound, and it is sometimes difficult to know which is correct in a given word.

Children learn about letters that seem to have no sound, or that are difficult to hear. In the earlier stages of invented spelling, they simply omitted such letters. Again, context is important; it can help them to know when to include those letters, and it can explain why a letter's sound is sometimes hard to hear. The letters *m* and *n,* for example, belong in the obvious places, such as at the beginning of *map* and the end of *fun* and even in the middle of *pencil* and *hamster,* but they must also sometimes be included before a consonant that takes over so quickly that the *m* or *n* sound is eclipsed, as in *pant* and *lamp.*

Finally, children learn that meaning and visual configuration are important in spelling. The regular past-tense morpheme, for example, is always spelled with the same two letters, *ed.* Even though there is no single pronunciation for *ed* (compare *wanted, played,* and *walked*), conventional readers and writers know that it is simply a convenient visual sign that means "past." It is used to spell the past tense of *all* regular English verbs and it never sounds like the *ed* in *red.*

Early Orthographic Spellers

Figure 5.13 presents a first grader's end-of-the-year composition, and Figure 5.14 presents a second grader's to-do list. Each of these writers uses both conventional spellings and spellings that we would expect from children as they make the transition from purely phonemic to early orthographic spelling. As shown in Figure 5.13, short vowels are consistently

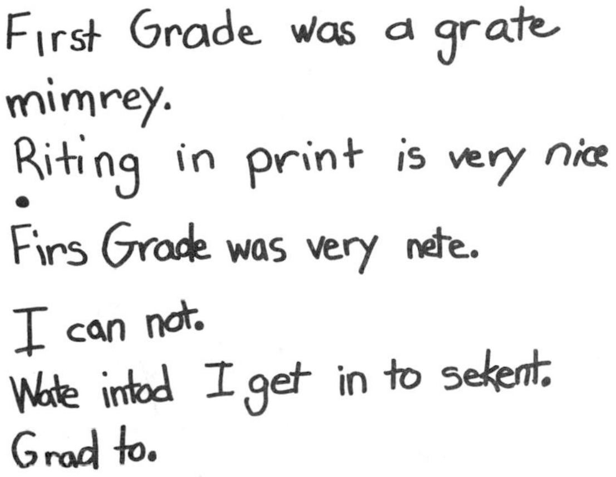

First Grade was a grate
mimrey.
Riting in print is very nice
.
Firs Grade was very nete.
I can not.
Wate intod I get in to sekent.
Grad to.

Figure 5.13 *A First Grader's End-of-the-Year Composition*

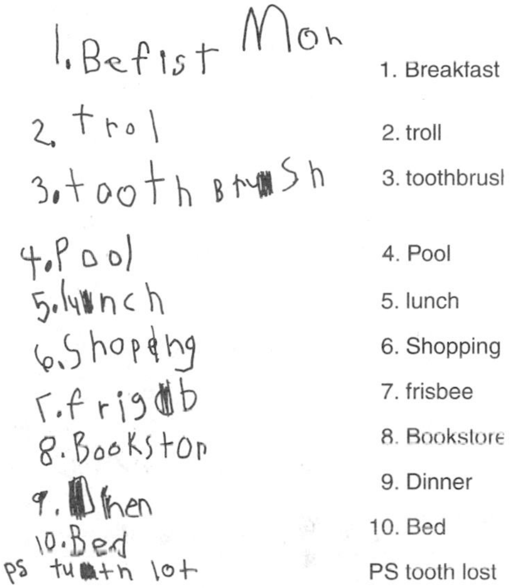

Figure 5.14 *A Second Grader's To-Do List*

spelled as we would expect, as in *in, print, can, not, get,* and *sekent.* Also, blends and digraphs are nearly consistently spelled, as shown in *first,* gr*ate,* pr*int,* and *sekent* (only leaving off the *t* in *firs*). These are patterns of spelling we expect in purely phonemic spelling. However, this writer also uses some spellings we would expect in early orthographic spelling. The writer uses, but confuses, long vowel patterns as seen in *grate* (*great*), *nete* (*neat*), and *intool* (*until*).

In the composition presented in Figure 5.14, most short vowels are spelled conventionally, as in *lunch, shoping* (*shopping*), *frisb* (*frisbee*), *diner* (*dinner*), *bed* and *lot* (*lost*). However, blends are spelled conventionally in some words, such as in tr*ol* (*troll*), *bookstor* (*bookstore*) and fr*isb* (*frisbee*), but not conventionally in other words, such as *befist* (br*eakfast*) and *lot* (*lost*). Digraphs are nearly consistently used as in *tooth*br*us*h, *lun*ch, and *tuth* (*tooth*). The only vowel pattern used by this speller is *oo,* as in *pool, and toothbrush* (but not *tuth*). What these writers lack is exactly what later orthographic spellers learn: conventional long vowel patterns, consonant doubling at syllable junctures, and morphological rules for adding suffixes, such as doubling the consonant before adding *ing* or dropping the *y* before adding *ies.*

Later Orthographic and Meaning-Based Spelling

Later orthographic spellers go beyond learning spelling patterns within single-syllable words; they pay attention to spelling patterns in **polysyllabic words,** or words with more than one syllable. Figure 5.14 presented several polysyllabic spellings, including *toothbrush, shoping* (*shopping*), *frisb* (*frisbee*), *bookstor* (*bookstore*), and *diner* (*dinner*). A later orthographic speller would have used consonant doubling at the syllable juncture, such as in the word *dinner,* and when adding the morpheme *ing* to some words, such as in *shopping.* Figure 5.15 presents a journal entry with an example of a later orthographic spelling: doubling the *ff* in *offis* (*office*). The spelling of *offis* in the composition presented in Figure 5.15 demonstrates an important spelling insight. That is, the writer has captured a generalization that can be used in many English words.

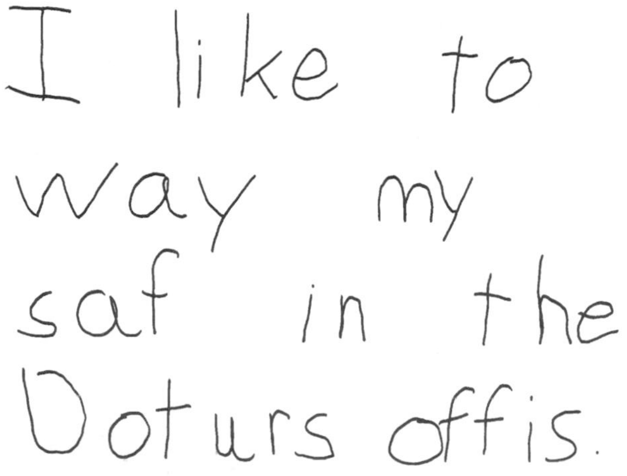

Figure 5.15 *Doctor's Office*

Because we learn spelling generalizations, we do not have to memorize the spelling of each word. Hence most people, even most third graders, can spell a large number of words correctly. They can spell many more words than the twenty words per week presented for study in their spelling books.

Although there are many glaring irregularities in English spelling, there are also many spelling regularities which help us learn spelling generalizations. Two useful strategies for learning spelling regularities are to notice the possible ways of spelling a sound and to pay attention to the contexts in which different spellings of the same sound can occur. For example, one spelling regularity is that the *f* sound (/f/) is spelled only four ways in English: *f, ff, ph,* and *gh.* It is true that there is no apparent reason for spelling /f/ at the end of *laugh* and *half* differently. Still, there is some regularity in how the letters for the *f* sound are used: /f/ is never spelled with *gh* or with *ff* at the *beginning* of an English word; and *ph* is used only with a special class of words, such as those that are built from *phon-* (meaning "sound") and *-graph* (meaning "write"), with the exception of the word *elephant.* So, knowing the spelling regularity of the *f* sound suggests that the spellings of /f/ in *telephone,* or even *phone,* and *phonics* and *geography* and *paragraph* are to be expected; but that spellings such as *phunny* or *ghunny* or even *ffunny* are not to be expected.

Children's errors reveal their growing awareness that certain spellings can only occur in certain words and in certain parts of words. A child's writing *laff* (for *laugh*) is consistent with our observations about the usual context of *ff* (at the end of words), and so it is less wrong than writing *ghish* for *fish. Laff* is not as great a violation of our expectations as is *ghish. Laff* is wrong in a way that shows that a child is learning about English spelling conventions. Expectations about where alternative spellings of the same sound occur are automatic with mature readers and spellers. Still, acquiring such expectations is a big job and an important one for children. It is a significant part of their becoming conventional writers and readers.

The last stage of developmental spelling, **meaning-based spelling,** is usually beyond primary-grade spellers. In this stage, spellers learn that sound–letter correspondence is not always the most important consideration. *Competition,* for example, is spelled with an *e* because its meaning-based relation to the word *compete* is more important than the sound–

letter correspondence that might suggest the incorrect spelling, *computition* (Bear, Invernizzi, Templeton, & Johnston, 1996, p. 27).

FUNCTIONS

Nowhere are both the continuities and the changes involved in children's becoming conventional readers and writers more evident than in their learning more about the functions of written language. Children continue to read and write for their own purposes, but they also learn another set of purposes for reading and writing—school-related purposes. In schools, reading and writing often entail considering the purposes the teacher has set, the special purposes the textbook authors have for writing, and the unique criteria by which classmates will judge one's writing.

In classrooms, students do not always read and write because they need to enter imaginary worlds, to gain information about their own expanding real world, to discover for themselves how written language works, or to create a permanent record of their ideas and wants. They have a new purpose for reading and writing: completing assignments and satisfying their teachers.

Successful elementary schoolteachers make sure that the assignments they give are congruent with children's own urges to write and read. They support children's ideas of the purposes of reading and writing. Children's reading and writing must continue to serve their own purposes, even when teachers make use of them for instruction.

However, conventional readers and writers have a keener awareness of audience than do experimenters. They have a more constant and pervasive realization that literacy involves creating meaning with someone else in mind, whether it is the author whose book they are reading, the intended reader of their writing, or the listener to whom they are reading. They understand that such meaning making is the single most important element of reading and writing.

All of these factors can contribute to the creative hum of a classroom in which children still proceed from their own purposes, but in which teachers create more specifically reading-directed and writing-directed institutions than they do in preschools. These institutions can include explicit lessons, the writing workshop, the conference, the reading workshop, the author's chair, assignments, rules and expectations, and assessment (all of which we describe later).

THE TRADITIONAL END POINTS: READING AND WORD IDENTIFICATION, VOCABULARY, AND COMPREHENSION

We have not used traditional terms to describe what children learn about reading during the early elementary grades. Reading educators traditionally describe the *what* of reading learning in terms of **word identification** skills, **vocabulary** knowledge, and **comprehension** ability. Those terms emphasize the view that, in order to become readers, children must do three things. They must learn to identify new words they encounter in print by sounding them out using phonics knowledge, by recognizing known word parts, and by using the context in which the words occur. They must know the meanings of, and know related words for, many of the words that they encounter in their reading. They must be able to understand what they read (for example, by knowing how the complex sentences that they are likely to encounter are constructed and by knowing how main ideas in a passage are supported by details). We agree with this description of what able readers must do. The following discussion is intended to show that the terms we have used cover the same ground and that they were used for sound reasons.

Although the descriptions *word identification, vocabulary,* and *comprehension* sound very unlike what was used in this chapter, there are similarities. The phenomena defined by the traditional perspective are not entirely different from the writing and reading processes described from our psycho-sociolinguistic perspective. The difference is in emphasis. The traditional terms emphasize an end point. Our terms emphasize development. By using the same categories and terms in this chapter that were used in the first four chapters of this book (*meaning making, forms, meaning-form links,* and *functions*), we have tried to call attention to the *origins* of conventional reading and writing, not just what they are. Our terms assume a long period of development in which children truly are readers and writers even though "the person on the street" would not think so. This is a period in which children derive important literacy knowledge, which is the basis for their eventual conventional reading and writing, especially when we acknowledge their accomplishments along the way.

By the end of the period described in this chapter, children are conventional readers and writers, and the traditional terms of description work quite well. We can demonstrate this by casting two of the descriptions given in this chapter in traditional terms. The recasting for the sake of demonstration involves what we have called meaning making; we could have called one end point of development of meaning-form knowledge *phonics.* However, this term ignores invented spelling behaviors that first appeared during the experimental period described in Chapter 4. We emphasize that children experiment with sound–letter correspondences long before they are conventional readers or writers. They use phonics in writing as well as in reading; in fact, they use phonics in writing even *before* they use it in reading.

This is neither a matter of semantics nor an effort to confuse our readers who come to this book with a traditional perspective. By maintaining the categories and terms we have used throughout this book, we show the importance of respecting children's early developing knowledges and allowing children to use them in their own ways for their own purposes. Invented spelling provides just one example. Letting children experiment early with invented spelling and talking with them about their spellings may eliminate the need for many isolated phonics lessons later, in the primary grades. If so, the same end point is achieved: children are able to use phonics knowledge efficiently for the word-identification and spelling purposes that make sense to conventional readers and writers.

Chapter Summary

Conventional readers and writers achieve a new independence in their reading and writing, but they are never alone. They are aware of the author who wrote what they read and of the audience that will read what they write. Thus, they show a keen awareness that written language is a communication process.

Conventional readers and writers are able to maintain several processes and to juggle several communication strategies in extended episodes of writing or reading. They are aware of how well or how poorly the juggling act is going; they have fix-up strategies for when it goes poorly.

Conventional readers' meaning making extends to being able to make interpretations and understand abstract literary elements, including point of view, symbol, and theme. They know the fine points of form at the word level in English; they have a conventional concept of word. They acquire sophisticated awareness of story form that comprises knowledge about setting, characters, plot, point of view, style, mood, and theme.

These children also gain a greater knowledge of text structure than they had as experimenters, especially knowledge of expository text structure.

Conventional readers and writers have many new performance strategies. They build on their previous understandings of what spelling is all about by adding multiple strategies for representing words in print, some using their earlier knowledge of sound–letter correspondences, and some using visual, contextual, and semantic information in new ways.

Conventional readers and writers have new, school-related purposes for reading and writing. Written language can make them participating members of a literate classroom community and can facilitate a more intense or intimate interaction between authors and audiences than was possible before they reached this stage of reading and writing.

Figure 5.16 summarizes what conventional readers and writers know about written language meanings, forms, meaning-form links, and functions.

Figure 5.16 *Summary: What Conventional Readers and Writers Know about Written Language Meanings, Forms, Meaning-Form Links, and Functions*

Meaning Making

- use metacognitive strategies to focus on meaning while reading, including monitoring that reading makes sense
- use strategies for generating ideas during composing, including knowing the expectations of audience
- interpret literature and move toward interpretations at the abstract level, including point of view, theme, and symbol
- use knowledge of abstract literary elements and style to compose stories and other literary texts

Forms

- have fully developed concept of word
- understand morphemes
- develop an ever-increasing stock of sight words
- know conventional spellings of an ever-increasing stock of words
- use knowledge of literary elements in narratives to compose stories that include settings, characters, and some plot elements and that signal growing control over point of view, mood, and style
- develop knowledge of how exposition is organized, using consistency, ordered relationships, and hierarchical relationships to produce gradually more organized expository text compositions

Meaning-Form Links

- develop conventional spelling ability, including learning alternative spelling patterns, phonograms, and morphemes
- use orthographic concepts to spell and to decode words in reading (decoding by analogy)

Functions

- read and write to meet a variety of personal needs
- read and write to join the classroom literate community

Applying the Information

In the following literacy event, a first grader writes a story and shares it with his classmates. Discuss what this event shows about understandings of written language meanings, forms, meaning-form links, and functions.

Figure 5.17 displays Zachary's "whale story." He wrote this as a first draft on six sheets of paper. Later, he read his story aloud to his classmates as part of an author's circle (a gathering of students who listen to others read their compositions, give compliments, and ask questions): "Made and illustrated by Zachary. To my mom and dad. Once upon a time there were two whales. They liked to play. One day when the whales were playing, a hammerhead came along. They fought for a time. Finally it was finished and the whales won. And they lived happily ever after."

After Zachary read his composition, his classmates asked him several questions, including "What kind of whales are they?" "Where do they live—what ocean?" and "How did they win the fight?" After listening to his classmates' questions, Zachary announced, "I am going to change my story by saying they lived in the Atlantic Ocean and they won the fight because they were bigger than the hammerhead and used their tails to defeat him."

Going Beyond the Text

Visit a third grade classroom. Observe the class during a time devoted to reading or writing. Try to identify two children whose behaviors suggest conventional reading or writing. Interview them. How aware are they of their own literacy knowledge and processes? Ask them what they do when they begin a new writing piece. How do they know when a piece is going well? What do they do to make a piece better? Ask how they choose a book to read for enjoyment. What is leisure reading like when it is going well? What makes them see what the author imagined when he or she wrote the book? How do they begin a reading assignment for social studies or science class? What do they do to be sure that they are learning from it what their teacher expects? Ask them if they would be willing to show you something they have written lately. Ask if they would read part of a book or tell about part of a book they are reading.

Do your interview subjects talk easily about reading and writing? Are they aware of what they know about literacy? Are they aware of audience in both reading and writing?

References

ADAMS, M. (1990). *Beginning to read: Thinking and learning about print.* Cambridge: MIT Press.

BEAR, D. R., INVERNIZZI, M., TEMPLETON, S., & JOHNSTON, F. (1996). *Words their way: Word study for phonics, vocabulary, and spelling instruction.* Upper Saddle River, NJ: Prentice-Hall.

BISSEX, G. L. (1980). *GNYS AT WRK: A child learns to write and read.* Cambridge: Harvard University Press.

BLUME, J. (1974). *The pain and the great one.* New York: Bradbury.

BROWN, A. (1980). Metacognitive development and reading. In R. J. Spiro, B. C. Bruce, & W. F. Brewer (Eds.), *Theoretical issues in reading comprehension* (pp. 453–481). Hillsdale, NJ: Erlbaum.

BRUNER, J. (1960). *The process of education.* Cambridge: Harvard University Press.

CALKINS, L. M. (1986). *The art of teaching writing.* Portsmouth, NH: Heinemann.

CASBERGUE, R. M. (1998). How do we foster young children's writing development? In S. B. Neuman

Figure 5.17 *Zachary's "Whale Story"*

& K. A. Roskos (Eds.), *Children achieving: best practices in early literacy* (pp. 198–222). Newark, DE: International Reading Association.

CHALL, J. S. (1983). *Stages of reading development.* New York: McGraw-Hill.

EDELSKY, C. (1986). *Writing in a bilingual program: Habia una vez.* Norwood, NJ: Ablex.

EHRI, L. (1991). Development of the ability to read words. In R. Barr, M. Kamil, P. Mosenthal, & P. Pearson (Eds.), *Handbook of reading research.* (2nd ed., pp. 395–419). New York: Longman.

EHRI, L., & ROBBINS, C. (1992). Beginners need some decoding skills to read words by analogy. *Reading Research Quarterly, 27,* 12–26.

FLETCHER, N. (1993). *See how they grow: Penguin.* New York: Dorling Kindersley.

FREPPON, P. (1991). Children's concepts of the nature and purpose of reading in different instructional settings. *Journal of Reading Behavior, 23,* 139–163.

GENTRY, J. (1982). An analysis of developmental spelling in GNYS AT WRK. *The Reading Teacher, 36,* 192–200.

HEATH, S. B. (1983). *Ways with words: Language, life, and work in communities and classrooms.* New York: Cambridge University Press.

HUTCHINS, P. (1968). *Rosie's walk.* New York: Scholastic.

LANGER, J. A. (1986). *Children reading and writing: Structures and strategies.* Norwood, NJ: Ablex.

LEHR, S. (1988). The child's developing sense of theme as a response to literature. *Reading Research Quarterly 23,* 337–357.

LESTER, H. (1988). *Tacky the penguin.* Boston: Houghton Mifflin.

LUKENS, R. (1995). *A critical handbook of children's literature* (5th ed.). Glenview, IL: Scott, Foresman/Little, Brown.

LYONS, C. (1991). Helping a learning-disabled child enter the literate world. In D. DeFord, C. Lyons, & G. Pinnell (Eds.), *Bridges to literacy: Learning from reading recovery* (pp. 205–216). Portsmouth, NH: Heinemann.

MANY, J. (1991). The effects of stance and age level on children's literary responses. *Journal of Reading Behavior, 23,* 61–85.

MARTIN, B. (1967). *Brown bear, brown bear, what do you see?* New York: Holt, Rinehart and Winston.

MCGEE, L. (1998). How do we teach literature to young children? In S. B. Neuman & K. A. Roskos (Eds.), *Children achieving: Best practices in early literacy* (pp. 172–179). Newark, DE: International Reading Association.

MCGEE, L. (1992). An exploration of meaning construction in first graders' grand conversations. In C. Kinzer & D. Leu (Eds.), *Literacy research, theory, and practice: Views from many perspectives* (pp. 177–186). Chicago: National Reading Conference.

MCGEE, L., LOMAX, R., & HEAD, M. (1988). Young children's written language knowledge: What environmental and functional print reading reveals. *Journal of Reading Behavior, 20,* 99–118.

MOFFETT, J. (1968). *Teaching the universe of discourse.* Boston: Houghton Mifflin.

NEWKIRK, T. (1987). The non-narrative writing of young children. *Research in the Teaching of English, 21,* 121–144.

PARIS, S., WASIK, B., & TURNER, J. (1991). The development of strategic readers. In R. Barr, M. Kamil, P. Mosenthal, & P. Pearson (Eds.), *Handbook of reading research* (2nd ed., pp. 609–640). New York: Longman.

ROSENBLATT, L. (1978). *The reader, the text, the poem: The transactional theory of the literary work.* Carbondale: Southern Illinois University Press.

WARD, C. (1988). *Cookie's Week.* New York: Putnam.

WILDE, S. (1992). *You kan red this: Spelling and punctuation for whole language classrooms, K–6.* Portsmouth, NH: Heinemann.

YORINKS, A. (1986). *Hey, Al.* New York: Farrar, Straus and Giroux.

Chapter 6

Literacy-Rich Classrooms

Key Concepts

developmentally appropriate
literacy-rich classrooms
big books
picture books
chapter books
genres
traditional literature
fables
folktales
myths
legends
fantasy
realistic fiction
historical fiction
biographies
autobiographies
informational books
poetry
wordless picture books
predictable books
alphabet books
reference materials
visual dictionaries
children's magazines
library center
writing center
computer centers
Writing to Read lab
storytelling props
SSR (sustained silent reading)
response-to-literature activities
response journal
curriculum
culturally relevant topics
curriculum integration
integrated language arts
culturally relevant topics
curriculum integration
integrated language arts
multicultural literature
culturally authentic literature
literature theme units
integrated content units
assessment
kid watching
homogenous reading abilities
reading aloud
shared reading
guided reading
reading workshop or literature circles
cooperative groups or partner reading
independent reading
shared writing or language experience
interactive writing
writing workshop
independent writing

DEVELOPMENTALLY APPROPRIATE PRACTICE

Early childhood professional organizations have taken an active role in defining the kinds of classroom environments, learning activities, and instruction that best support young children's learning. Early childhood professionals argue that the early childhood years, from birth through eight years of age, are crucial for all aspects of children's development: physical, emotional, social, cognitive, and aesthetic. Quality early-childhood education provides opportunities for children to grow in all these areas. Literacy learning is only one part of children's growth and development.

A joint position statement by the International Reading Association (IRA) and the National Association for the Education of Young Children (NAEYC) on developmentally appropriate practices in literacy instruction for young children outlines ambitious goals for young children's literacy development (National Association for the Education of Young Children, 1998). These goals are reflected in later chapters in this book (see Chapters 7 through 10). According to this statement, the goals and expectations for young children's literacy accomplishments should be **developmentally appropriate;** that is, they should be challenging but achievable with adult support. Young children's literacy learning is a result of children's discovery of concepts and understandings and their social interaction with engaging and knowledgeable readers and writers (such as parents, caregivers, and teachers). Developmentally appropriate literacy practices celebrate the current level of children's understandings about literacy, but provide strong instructional support for children taking the next step. Instructional support occurs not just in primary-grade classrooms, where formal reading and writing instruction is expected. It also occurs in day care, preschool, and kindergarten classrooms.

We wish to stress that developmentally appropriate classrooms do support and encourage children's literacy learning. This is true whether the classroom is for three-year-olds or for eight-year-olds. Unfortunately, developmentally appropriate practice has sometimes wrongly been interpreted as meaning that "reading and writing are 'academic skills' that do not belong in a child-centered early childhood program" (McGill-Franzen, 1992, p. 57). In addition, many literacy activities that occur in early-childhood classrooms are not appropriate for young children's developmental levels or learning styles.

However, it is clear that many young children have numerous experiences with reading and writing long before they come to school and that these experiences are important for their later success as readers and writers (see, for example, Chapter 2). Therefore, experiences with reading and writing *are* appropriate for young children (McGill-Franzen, 1992).

Developmentally appropriate literacy practice is strongly dependent on (1) continuous assessment of children's current levels of understandings and (2) knowledge of the expected continuum of development. Being able to provide instruction that is challenging, but achievable, implies that teachers must constantly assess where children are in the long continuum of literacy learning and plan instruction accordingly. The previous chapters in this book were intended to provide teachers with the kind of knowledge they need in order to assess children's current understandings about literacy and to predict where children might be headed. Later chapters are designed to provide suggestions for instruction that can be tailored to meet the learning needs of children with diverse literacy understandings.

Developmentally appropriate practice is similar to a child-centered early-childhood program. Teachers who use developmentally appropriate practice recognize that children's growth and development can naturally be described in predictable sequences (remember the changes in literacy knowledge discussed in Chapters 2 through 5), but that children also have individual patterns of growth and home experiences that have an impact on what they know and how they learn. Developmentally appropriate practice acknowledges that not all children learn in the same way or need the same experiences at the same time.

A wide range of individual variation in literacy learning is to be expected at all levels from birth through age eight due to differing literacy experiences and expectations. Effective teachers recognize that children will have many different levels of understanding about reading and writing. They will expect that some children may not advance through a sequence of literacy achievements in quite the same way as other children. Therefore, single instructional strategies or sets of materials with lock-step sequences of instruction will not be appropriate to meet the needs of the wide range of children teachers can expect in preschool, kindergarten, or primary-grade classrooms (Snow, Burns, & Griffin, 1998). Instead, teachers will embrace a wide range of literacy instructional practices embedded within literacy-rich classroom environments.

CHARACTERISTICS OF LITERACY-RICH CLASSROOMS

Literacy-rich classrooms provide child-centered, developmentally appropriate support for children's literacy learning. All children, whether they have many or few home literacy experiences, whether they speak English or another language at home, and whether or not they have special learning needs, thrive in such classrooms.

Learners

As a result of being in literacy-rich classrooms, children are reflective, motivated readers and writers who use literacy to learn more about themselves and the world in which they live. This use of literacy begins before the elementary years. For example, four-year-olds who listen to their teacher read about the differences between tortoises and turtles to help identify the animal that one of them brought to school are reflective, motivated readers who use reading to find out more about their world.

Being reflective means that children are thinkers; they construct meaning for themselves and can use the thinking of others to modify their meaning. Reflective readers construct personal understandings from informational books, poems, and stories. Their initial understandings are usually tentative and unfocused. Sharing such undeveloped understandings requires great risk taking. However, reflective readers and writers use their first tentative understandings to build more fully developed and complex knowledge. They often modify their understandings given additional information from books or from talking with their friends or teachers. Similarly, reflective writers compose personally meaningful stories and poems, but also take into account the needs and interests of their audience. Constructing and sharing personal meanings with others both honors the voice of children and creates a "rich broth of meaning" (Oldfather, 1993, p. 676). This concept of literacy emphasizes the social nature of learning.

Being motivated means that children are self-directed and self-motivated (Oldfather, 1993). Many children, especially in the primary grades, are expected to participate in reading and writing activities because the teacher tells them to, but motived learners also participate in many activities because they choose to. Motivating activities have three characteristics: they allow children some choices in materials and experiences, provide challenges but call on strategies previously modeled by the teacher, and require social collaboration (Morrow & Gambrell, 1998).

The Classroom

The goal of all literacy instruction is not merely to produce children who are capable readers and writers (although that is certainly an admirable goal), but also to encourage and support children as they use reading and writing to achieve their own worthwhile personal and social goals. To achieve this aim, teachers must make careful decisions about materials, physical layout of the classroom, classroom routines, curriculum, instruction, grouping, and assessment.

Drawing from research, we argue that literacy-rich classrooms have seven characteristics: (1) an abundance of children's literature and other high-quality literacy materials; (2) physical arrangements that encourage a wide range of reading and writing; (3) daily literacy routines, including read alouds, independent reading and writing, and sharing; (4) a culturally sensitive curriculum, which integrates the language arts and content study; (5) continuous assessment, which guides instruction; (6) a variety of instructional practices; and (7) a variety of grouping patterns. An overview of the characteristics of a literacy-rich classroom is presented in Figure 6.1.

LITERACY MATERIALS

Materials

It makes sense that children who have access to quality literature will be highly motived readers and discerning writers. A good book inspires wonder, curiosity, deep thinking, emotional involvement, and aesthetic pleasure as well as provides models of memorable language.

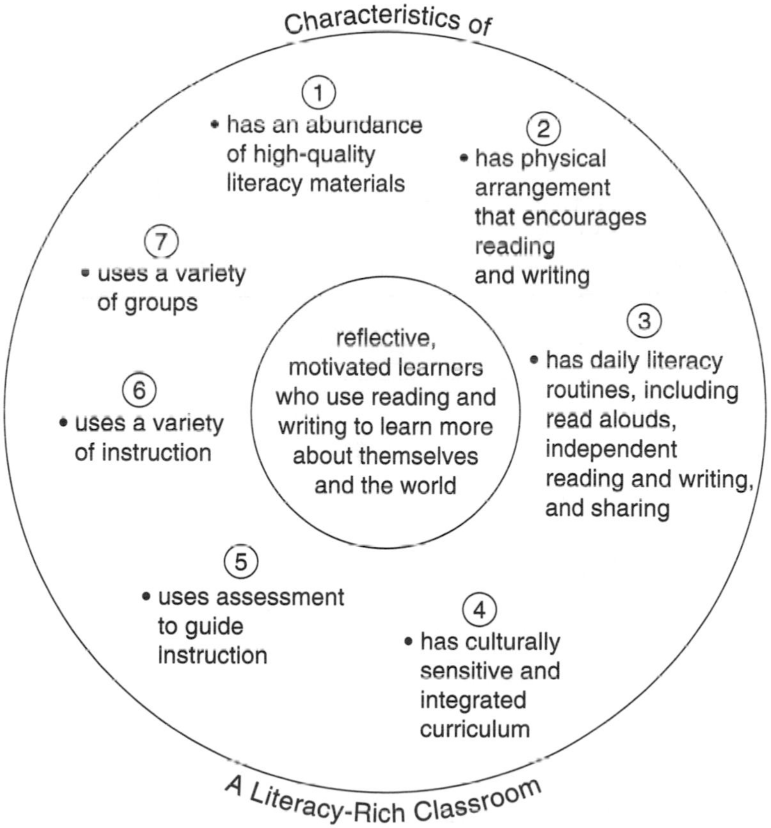

Figure 6.1 *Seven Characteristics of Literacy-Rich Classrooms*

The Case for Quality Literature

Research confirms that the amount of experience children have with literature correlates with their language development (Chomsky, 1972), reading achievement (Feitelson, Kita, & Goldstein, 1986), and quality of writing (Dressell, 1990). Children who are exposed to quality literature are more likely to learn to love literature and to include reading quality books as an important part of their lives (Hickman, 1979). They are more willing to sustain their involvement with a book through writing, doing projects, and participating in discussions (Eeds & Wells, 1989). Research has also shown that children whose classrooms have a large number of books in a high-quality library center choose to read more often (Morrow & Weinstein, 1982, 1986) and have higher reading achievement (Morrow, 1992).

One of the first decisions that a teacher faces is the selection of literacy materials. Teachers are responsible for using their local resources to locate and evaluate materials for their literacy programs. Teachers should gather (1) a large classroom literature collection, (2) a collection of reference materials, (3) children's magazines, and (4) a variety of writing materials.

Classroom Literature Collection

Teachers in literacy-rich classrooms know a great deal about children's literature. They are aware of literary elements, are familiar with many authors and illustrators, and keep up with recent publications (Tomlinson & Lynch Brown, 1996; Temple, Martinez, Yokota & Naylor, 1998). They select books on topics of interest to children and that represent a range of difficulty levels.

Teachers choose books in picture book and chapter book format (collections for preschoolers may contain only picture books, but as children get older, they enjoy chapter books as well). Teachers may also include quality **big books** in their classrooms. **Picture books,** such as *Where the Wild Things Are* (Sendak, 1963), *Allison* (Say, 1997), and *The Wall* (Bunting, 1990), present stories or information through both the words of the text and the illustrations. **Chapter books,** such as *Sarah, Plain and Tall* (MacLachlan, 1985), *Ramona Quimby, Age 8* (Cleary, 1981), and *Dominic* (Steig, 1972), present stories or information primarily through text (although some chapter books, especially informational books, may have illustrations).

The process of locating a sufficient number of quality books can be daunting. Experts recommend that the number of books in a high-quality classroom collection should be eight to ten times the number of children (Fractor, Woodruff, Martinez, & Teale, 1993). Teachers can borrow books from local and school libraries, use bonus points from book clubs to obtain free books, and collect inexpensive books from book clubs and bookstores that offer educational discounts. (The Appendix provides lists of suggested literature for a classroom library.)

Genres of Literature

Literature is generally classified into several broad categories, or **genres,** including traditional literature, fantasy, realistic fiction, historical fiction, biography and autobiography, informational books, and poetry. The classroom literature collection in literacy-rich classrooms includes many books from each of these genres.

Traditional literature has its roots in the oral storytelling tradition of long ago, which still exists today. Familiar stories such as *Goldilocks and the Three Bears* (Cauley, 1981) and *Little Red Riding Hood* (Hyman, 1983) are traditional tales once told by storytellers or family members that have been captured anew by modern illustrators. Traditional stories are found in every culture in the world, and the classroom library collection in a literacy-rich classroom should include many of these multicultural stories. Tales such as *The Brocaded Slipper and Other Vietnamese Tales* (Vuong, 1982) from Vietnam, *The King and the Tortoise* (Mollel, 1993) from Africa, and *Elfwyn's Saga* (Wisniewski, 1990) from Iceland allow children to find out about a wide variety of cultures and literary traditions.

Fables usually have animal characters and an explicitly stated moral. Most children enjoy the familiar fable of *The Town Mouse and the Country Mouse* (Cauley, 1984). Fables can be found in the folk literature of many different countries.

Folktales are usually short, have flat characters (all good, evil, or tricky), and have a happy ending, with good triumphing over evil. Some folktales include animal characters, for instance, *The Three Little Pigs* (Galdone, 1970) and *The Elephants's Wrestling Match* (Sierra, 1992). They may include motifs such as magic or transformations, as in *Frog Prince* (Grimm & Grimm, 1989), or a trickster, as in *Anansi the Spider: A Tale from the Ashanti,* (McDermott, 1972).

Myths were created to explain natural occurrences, such as the seasons, constellations, or the creation of life. They include heroes or heroines who have superhuman and magical abilities. **Legends** are similar to myths, but are thought to be based on true stories that grew to exaggerated proportions. Legends contain heroes or heroines who have fantastic powers. Examples of myths and legends include *The Story of Jumping Mouse* (Steptoe, 1984), *The Fire Children: A West African Creation Tale* (Maddern, 1993)

Fantasy includes elements that could not really happen, such as fantastic characters or fantastic settings. There are many fine examples of fantasies for young children in both picture book and chapter book format. Cassie Louise Lightfoot, a young African American girl, takes a fantastic flight above her apartment's roof to marvel at the sparkling beauty of the George Washington Bridge and makes wishes for the good fortune of her family in *Tar Beach* (Ringgold, 1991). *Bunnicula* (Howe & Howe, 1979) is the amusing story of a rabbit who is mistaken for Dracula by the family dog.

Realistic fiction refers to stories about things that could plausibly happen in true life. The characters, setting, and events are realistic and believable. Some realistic fiction presents the humorous side of life, such as Judy Blume's hilarious tale, *The Pain and the Great One* (1974). Other realistic stories help children understand everyday problems, such as dealing with a stepparent, being homesick and lonely, or overcoming prejudice. For example, Alex and his stepfather both learn to respect each other more in *Like Jake and Me* (Jukes, 1984), and a homeless boy manages to keep his hope for a brighter future despite having to live at the airport in *Fly Away Home* (Bunting, 1991).

Historical fiction is set in the past and accurately reflects the time period in which it is set. Often historical fiction is intended to reflect truths about our own society or the universal conflicts that all of us must face, for example, having to overcome fear or learning the value of family relationships. *Dakota Dugout* (Turner, 1985) relates the story of a young woman's first sod house on the prairie, but comments on the values of simple things. *When Jessie Came Across the Sea* (Hest, 1997) tells the story of a young Jewish immigrant girl who earns money sewing lace to pay for her Grandmother's passage to the United States.

Biographies and **autobiographies** are stories about the lives of everyday or famous people. Written accurately and authentically, these texts often include photographs, letters, diaries, newspaper articles, and legal documents to provide supporting evidence. Biographies have been written about sports figures, such as *Teammates* (Golenbock, 1990); bullfighters, such as *El Chino* (Say, 1990); and presidents, such as *The Joke's on George* (Tunnell, 1993).

An autobiography is the life story of its author. Many famous children's authors have written autobiographies, which can be shared with children. Examples include *Bill Peet: An Autobiography* (Peet, 1989) and *The Art Lesson* (de Paola, 1989).

Informational books are books that provide realistic, accurate, and authentic information. Quality informational books avoid stereotyping, present more than one side of issues, have logical organizations, and arouse curiosity. Some examples of quality informational books are *Sugaring Time* (Lasky, 1983), which details the steps of making maple syrup, and *Water* (Canizares & Chanko, 1998), which describes a variety of liquid and solid forms of water; both books are suitable for very young children.

Joanna Cole (1986; 1987; 1989; 1990) has written a series of *Magic School Bus* books, which are very popular with young children. In these stories, set in a classroom, a wacky teacher, Ms. Frizzle, takes the children on fantastic field trips. Howker (1997) uses a similar technique to describe a wolf pack in *Walk with a Wolf.*

Poetry is text that contains condensed language, special lining, and imagery. Poetry often includes elements of rhythm and sound, such as rhyming, alliteration, and repetition. Poetry may capture a single moment in time or allow readers to see everyday events and objects in a new light. It appeals to the senses and calls to mind strong emotions. Some anthologies, or collections, of poems that appeal to young children are *Sing a Song of Popcorn: Every Child's Book of Poems* (de Regniers, Moore, White, & Carr, 1988) and *The Random House Book of Poetry for Children* (Prelutsky, 1983). Other books of poetry include poems written by a single author, such as *Brown Angels* (Myers, 1993), a series of poems inspired by turn-of-the-century photographs of African American children.

Special Picture Book Genres

In addition to the genres just discussed, there are several additional types of picture books. These books are especially enjoyable for young children, and they have great potential for encouraging children's exploration of literature. Teachers should include several wordless picture books, predictable books, and alphabet books in their classroom libraries.

Wordless picture books portray a story through illustrations only. They appeal to a range of ages, even to adults (Abrahamson, 1981). *Pancakes for Breakfast* (dePaola, 1978) is a favorite of both preschoolers and older children. It illustrates the efforts of a little old woman as she makes pancakes. Young children enjoy the wordless book *Sunshine* (Ormerod, 1981), which illustrates the actions of a young girl who dresses herself while her parents oversleep. Second and third graders enjoy *Deep in the Woods* (Turkle, 1976), especially when they discover its play on the Goldilocks story.

Predictable books contain repeated dialogue or events. For example, the character Gingerbread Boy in the book *The Gingerbread Boy* (Galdone, 1975) repeats actions—he runs past a series of characters who chase him. He also repeats dialogue—each time he runs past a character, he taunts, "I've run away from a little old woman. I've run away from a little old man. And I can run away from you, I can." Predictable books are especially useful for helping children learn to read their first printed words (Bridge, 1986).

Alphabet books use the sequence of the alphabet to organize information or a story. They appeal to both very young and older children. In some alphabet books, a single picture represents the sound associated with an alphabet letter. In *Eating the Alphabet* (Ehlert, 1989), one or two fruits or vegetables are pictured and named for each letter of the alphabet. Other alphabet books tell stories, such as the story of growing, picking, and selling apples in *Applebet* (Watson, 1982). Still other alphabet books present information about a single topic. For example, Jerry Pallotta has written several alphabet books about a variety of topics, including insects, frogs, and reptiles (e.g., *The Yucky Reptile Alphabet Book,* 1986). Still other alphabet books are puzzles for readers to solve. Chris Van Allsburg's *The Z was Zapped* (1987) invites readers to guess what happens to letters by closely examining the illustrations (such as "the *B* was badly bitten," unpaged).

Audiovisual Materials

Audiovisual materials are an important part of the classroom literacy program. Teachers can borrow copies of audiotapes, films, filmstrips, and videotapes of children's literature from local or school libraries. In addition, children enjoy learning more about favorite authors and illustrators through videotaped and audiotaped interviews. School librarians are especially helpful in locating these materials. Teachers may contact the following publishing companies for more information: Houghton Mifflin, 2 Park Street, Boston, MA 02108; Pied Piper, PO Box 320, Verdugo City, CA 91046; Weston Woods, Weston, CT 06883.

Reference Materials and Magazines

Reference materials include dictionaries, thesauri, atlases, and encyclopedias and are intended to provide information about word meanings, concepts, geography, and other familiar topics. Today, many reference materials are published with detailed photographs and drawings so that even very young children enjoy looking at the illustrations in these materials. Publishers have also made available reference materials at a variety of difficulty levels. For example, very young children find picture dictionaries and encyclopedias intriguing. Two examples appropriate for young children are *My First Dictionary* (Roof, 1993) and *My First Encyclopedia* (Roof, 1993). Older children enjoy locating and reading information in *The Random House Children's Encyclopedia* (1992), a single-volume text loaded with diagrams, photographs, and drawings about common topics of study in the primary grades. A specialized dictionary that appeals to primary school-age children is *The Dictionary of Nature* (Burnie, 1994).

A new kind of dictionary, the visual dictionary, seems especially attractive to young children. **Visual dictionaries** rely on illustrations to define words. *The Macmillan Visual Dictionary* (actually intended for adults) defines words by presenting labeled drawings. For example, it includes a drawing of a bird in which more than twenty body parts, such as *pin feather,* are labeled. Other visual dictionaries are written for elementary schoolchildren and focus on single topics. Such dictionaries include *The Visual Dictionary of the Universe, The Visual Dictionary of the Earth,* and *The Visual Dictionary of the Human Body* (all published by Dorling Kindersley, 1993).

Many publishers produce highly useful informational books that children may use as references to locate information about topics of study. Noteworthy are the information series such as *Eyewitness Books* (published by Knopf) and *Eyewitness Science Books* (published by

Dorling Kindersley). These books present detailed photographs, drawings, diagrams, and information about a variety of life science topics. Although the text of these books is often too difficult for many primary schoolchildren to read independently, the illustrations are informative and can heighten children's curiosity about scientific concepts.

Children's magazines are an important functional print item included in literacy-rich classrooms. They provide stimulating information on a variety of topics in both social studies and science, and they prompt children to experiment with new ideas in art or writing. Many teachers have found that having two or three copies of a magazine encourages children to read together or collaborate on a research project.

PHYSICAL ARRANGEMENT OF CLASSROOMS

Teachers arrange classrooms so that there are spaces for whole-class and small-group gatherings and so that invitations for reading and writing abound. Many early-childhood classrooms, especially those for preschoolers, are center based, and the centers are arranged to encourage the functional use of reading and writing. All literacy-rich classrooms include a library, a writing center, and a computer center. Teachers arrange these spaces so that materials are organized and easily accessible.

The Case for Library, Writing, and Computer Centers

Research confirms that the arrangement of space in the classroom library and writing center also affects children's reading and writing. Children spend more time reading in classrooms with well-designed library centers (Morrow, 1997; Morrow & Weinstein, 1982, 1986). They generate and test hypotheses about written language and develop self-monitoring strategies in classrooms with well-designed writing centers (Rowe, 1994).

Computers also are an important component of the literacy-rich classroom. Research has shown that introducing computers into the classroom allows children to develop literacy concepts through play (Labbo, 1996). Computers increase social interaction among children as they share ideas and compose jointly (Bruce, Michaels, & Watson-Gregeo, 1985). Computers also encourage expanded explorations and new insights about literacy through multiple kinds of symbol making. For example, children may produce multimedia texts that include icons, drawn scribbles or illustrations, and word-processed text (Labbo, 1996). As a part of this multimedia composition process, children learn that constructing meaning involves manipulation of not just alphabet letters, but also a variety of other symbols. The physical arrangement of a computer center, type of software available, and incorporation of the computer into the overall literacy program affect the amount and quality of interactions that children have with the computer (Labbo & Ash, 1998).

Library Center

All classrooms have a **library center,** which houses a large part of the classroom literature collection. To provide a pleasant space for reading, listening to stories on audiotape, and talking about books, teachers

Place the center label in a prominent location.

Use bookshelves, hanging mobiles, or screens to partition the space from the remainder of the classroom.

Provide space for four to six children.

Arrange pillows, small rugs, or other comfortable seating.

Organize the books (using last name of author or genre).

Display several books with their covers facing outward.

Display props for telling stories, such as three stuffed bears, a doll, and the book for retelling *Goldilocks and the Three Bears.*

Arrange a display of books and objects on a special topic, such as an author, genre, or content topic (Fractor, Woodruff, Martinez, & Teale, 1993; Morrow & Weinstein, 1986).

In addition to spaces for reading books, the classroom library may also have a space for listening to stories on audiotape (or a listening center may be established in a nearby location). A listening center includes several audiotapes of stories that are either commercially available or made by parents or other volunteers. Each tape is accompanied by at least one copy of the story. Tapes and books can be kept in plastic bags and stored in plastic bins or hung on special display racks. Figure 6.2 shows a classroom library and listening center.

Writing Center

The **writing center** serves a variety of purposes. For preschoolers it is an important place for groups of children and their teacher to gather, talk, write, and learn. For older primary schoolchildren, the center is used for small groups of children to meet to revise or edit their writing (see the explanation of writing processes presented in Chapter 10). It may also become a publishing center.

To create a writing center, teachers arrange a large table and several chairs of comfortable height for children. The table is large enough to accommodate several children and to include displays of greeting cards, messages, signs, and special words that encourage children to write. Shelves or a rolling cart for storing writing materials are nearby. Writing materials are labeled and easily accessible on the shelves. The materials are changed frequently so that children can explore a variety of writing implements and surfaces. Table 6.1 presents a list of materials that may be included in a writing center.

Computer Center

Computer centers are most effective when they are more centrally placed in the classroom to encourage creative and imaginative interactions rather than relegated to a back corner (Labbo & Ash, 1998). Children often consider computers a site for play; and playing on the computer, just like other kinds of dramatic play, can lead to important literacy insights (Labbo, 1996). For example, children may want to bring stuffed animals, informational books, storybooks, and other artifacts to the computer center to support their interactions with the computer. Therefore, computers should be placed on large tables that can hold a

Figure 6.2 *Classroom Library and Listening Center*

variety of objects in addition to the computer. For example, when viewing a talking book, children might want to bring a stuffed version of the main character or the print copy of the book with them to the computer.

The computer center should include displays of books, posters, or computer-generated products that will encourage children to engage in creative activities. A "Helpful Hint" poster about basic computer operations also should be displayed. Pictures of icons, examples of illustrations using the "paint brush" and "pencil," or illustrations from children's computer explorations may stimulate further imaginative computer-generated products. Children may also be encouraged to use the computer to enrich dramatic play. For example, when children are playing in a "bank," they can use the computer to generate checks or bank books. Children would enjoy creating imaginative menus for use in a "restaurant" dramatic play center.

Two broad types of software should be available for use in the computer center: expressive and receptive (Labbo & Ash, 1998). Expressive software includes programs that allow children to discover insights about literacy concepts as they create text and graphics (Labbo & Ash, 1998). Programs such as *Kidpix, KidWords 2,* and *Kidwriter Golden Edition*

Table 6.1 *Materials for a Writing Center*

A variety of writing tools, including
pencils or pens with interesting shapes or fancy toppers such as feathers or objects
markers such as highlighters, smelly markers, or markers that change colors
alphabet stamps, tiles, cookie cutters, sponge letters, magnetic letters, felt letters
crayons, chalk
A variety of writing surfaces, including
clipboards, small white boards, chalk boards
lined and unlined paper in a variety of shapes and colors
a variety of writing pads, including Post-It notes, spiral notebooks, to-do lists
sand tray
A variety of bookbinding materials, including
a camera to take photos for "all about the author" page
stapled books of four to eight pages
computers with word-processing programs and other publishing programs
A variety of reference materials, including
a photo book of all the children with their first and last names
special words on index cards (such as seasonal or theme vocabulary)
pictionaries, dictionaries, visual dictionaries
handwriting chart

encourage children's active exploration of a variety of symbols, including drawing, painting, assembling images and pictures, and printing text. Receptive software allows children to learn new concepts and share literature through computer automation and graphics, including automated storybook programs. Table 6.2 presents a list of software that might be included in a computer center.

Many schools already make extensive use of computers in their literacy program through the *Writing to Read* program (Labbo, Murray, & Phillips, 1996). This program is delivered in an IBM computer lab in which children rotate through five "stations": a computer station where children are taught sound–letter relationships; a work journal station where children use paper-and-pencil work sheets to practice saying and writing words, using the sound–letter relationships they were taught at the computer station; a writing–typing station where children may copy words or stories by hand or on an electronic typewriter or computer; tape library stations where children listen to stories that stress the sound–letter relationships being taught; and a make words station where children play games to reinforce their knowledge of sound–letter relationships.

While the ***Writing to Read lab*** may be successful with some children, with alterations it can be a powerful support for all young children's literacy learning. First, the computer sound–letter learning activities should be embedded in a more meaningful experience provided by a theme that extends over a week or two. For example, if the computer sound–letter lessons focus on the words *cat, dog,* and *fish* for teaching consonants and short vowel sounds, the

Table 6.2 Software for a Computer Center

A to Zapp by Sunburst Software
The Art Lesson by MECC
Bailey's Book House by Edmark
Chica Chica Boom Boom by Davidson
Curious George Learns the Alphabet by H. A. Rey by Queue, Inc.
Kid Phonics by Davidson
Kidpix by Broderbund
KidWords 2 by Davidson
Living Books by Broderbund (including *Dr. Seuss's ABC, Green Eggs and Ham, Just Grandma and Me,* and *Stellaluna*)
Mixed Up Mother Goose Delux by Davidson
Reading Blaster Journal by Davidson
Tales from Long Ago and Far Away by Queue
Storybook Theater by Learningways, Inc.
Wiggleworks by Scholastic Beginning Literacy Skills

theme might be "Caring For and Enjoying Pets" (Labbo, Murray, & Phillips, 1997, p. 317). Children can gather together when they first arrive at the lab to listen to their teacher read a story or informational book aloud that is related to the theme. Storytelling, drama, and **storytelling props** (all described later in this chapter) encourage children's active participation. Second, children should be encouraged to experiment with word processors for drawing and writing responses to literature, stories, or other texts rather than copying words. Finally, stories for listening should come from literature and can be selected to focus on the theme.

LITERACY ROUTINES

Teachers in literacy-rich classrooms read aloud or tell stories daily and set aside time for children to read and write independently. Children have frequent opportunities to share their writing and engage in activities that extend their responses to literature (Hoffman, Roser, & Battle, 1993). Response-to-literature activities include retelling, drama, writing, talking, and other creative activities.

The Case for Classroom Routines

There is ample evidence that daily reading and writing experiences are crucial for children's literacy development. Children whose teachers read aloud or tell stories to them on a daily basis are highly motivated readers with extensive vocabularies and effective comprehension strategies (Dickinson & Smith, 1994; Feitelson, Kita, & Goldstein, 1986; Morrow & Weinstein, 1982, 1986). Similarly, the more time children spend reading independently, the better their vocabularies, understanding of spelling principles, and comprehension (Adams, 1990; Anderson, Hiebert, Scott, & Wilkinson, 1985).

Research has shown that the amount of independent reading in which children engage has a major impact on their vocabulary knowledge. By fifth grade, the average student reads independently less than five minutes *a day* (Anderson, Wilson, & Fielding, 1988). This yields only 282,000 words read per year. In contrast, a student who reads independently an hour a day, reads over 4,300,000 words per year. Increasing the amount of children's independent reading is a critical component of every reading program.

Sharing experiences about reading and writing is also a critical component of supporting literacy development. Children who talk together about a book, write responses to literature, and share writing with classmates construct interpretations of literature, use higher levels of thinking, and write better quality compositions (Barone, 1990; Eeds & Wells, 1989; Five, 1986; Kelly, 1990).

Reading Aloud and Telling Stories

Teachers share literature with children by reading stories, telling stories, or showing films and filmstrips about quality literature. Teachers plan carefully before sharing literature with children. They keep in mind the age and interests of the children as they select books to read aloud. Books selected for reading have illustrations that are large enough for a group of children to see (Glazer, 1981). Teachers preview books carefully to become familiar with story texts and illustrations and to develop purposes for sharing (we will describe more what these purposes might be in later chapters).

Frequently, teachers tell stories using special **storytelling props** (Cliatt & Shaw, 1988; Ross, 1980). Among the many kinds of literature props that teachers can use to tell a story are objects, clothesline props, flannel board props, puppets, and masks. *Object props* are objects that represent certain characters and actions. Object props for the story *Where the Wild Things Are* (Sendak, 1963) might include a teddy bear (to represent Max sent to bed with no supper), an oar (to represent his travels to the land where the Wild Things Are), and a crown (to represent Max's becoming King of the Wild Things).

Clothesline props include pictures drawn to represent important events in the story. These pictures are clothespinned to a clothesline stretched across the classroom as a story is read or told. Clothesline prop pictures that could be used to tell the story *Where the Wild Things Are* are shown in Figure 6.3.

Figure 6.3 *Clothesline Props*

Puppets make perfect props for storytelling. Finger puppets can be made by drawing characters on paper and carefully cutting them out to include special tabs for fastening around the finger. Stick puppets can be made by coloring characters on stiff paper, cutting them out, and attaching them to soda straws. Figure 6.4 presents a finger puppet and stick puppet that could be used in retelling *Where the Wild Things Are.*

Flannel board props can be made from Velcro, felt, yarn, lace, or other sewing notions. Figure 6.5 shows flannel board props that can be used in telling *Where the Wild Things Are.* Figure 6.6 presents a mask that could also be used in telling this story.

Children have many creative ideas for constructing their own story-retelling props. First graders used a green pipe cleaner for the hungry caterpillar and punched holes in con-

Figure 6.4 *Finger and Stick Puppets*

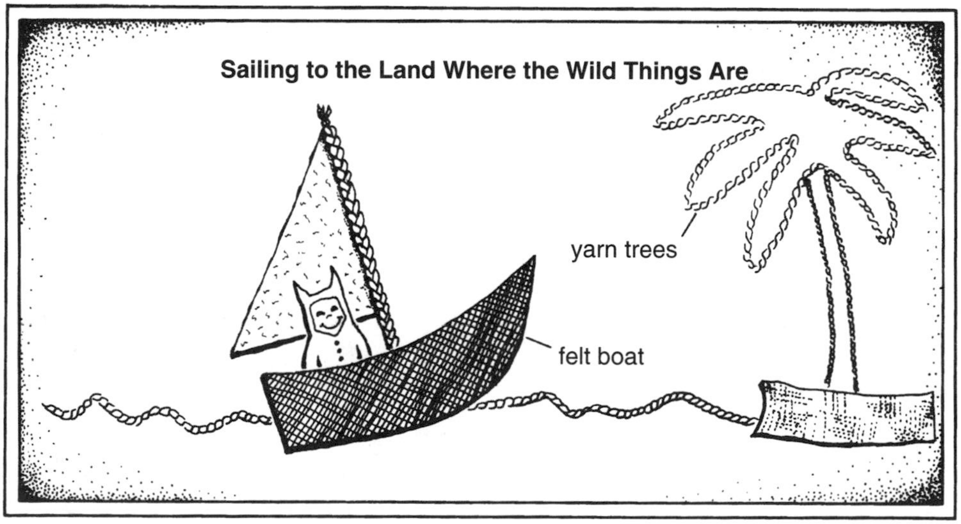

Figure 6.5 *Flannel Board Props*

Figure 6.6 *Mask of a "Wild Thing"*

struction paper food cutouts to retell *The Very Hungry Caterpillar.* As they retold the story, they slipped each food cutout onto the green pipe-cleaner caterpillar. Third graders worked together to decide the number and content of pictures needed to retell *Nine-in-One. Grr! Grr!* (Xiong, 1989) on a story clothesline. They retold the story collaboratively—each illustrator hung his or her picture on the clothesline and retold that portion of the story.

Independent Reading and Writing

Teachers provide children with plenty of time to browse through and read books of their choice and to write on self-selected topics. Some classrooms and entire schools promote daily reading by using **SSR (sustained silent reading).** During this time, everyone in the classroom (even the teacher) or school (including the principal and other school personnel) reads silently for a specified period of time (usually ten to twenty minutes). However, with so many schools adopting a literature-based reading program, time for self-selected reading is usually a part of reading instruction (we discuss more about shared reading and reading workshops—both of which include daily reading of self-selected texts—in later chapters).

One way to establish a daily writing activity is to have children write in a journal (Hipple, 1985; Kintisch, 1986). Each child in the classroom is given his or her own journal. Journals may simply be small books made by stapling paper together, or they may be more elaborate books that children or adults have bound. A special time each day is set aside to write in journals. Children are allowed to write anything they wish.

Sharing Response-to-Literature Activities

Response-to-literature activities encourage children's emotional and intellectual involvement with literature. These activities can serve many purposes, including helping children explore the language of stories, the themes of literature, the media of illustrations, and the connections between literature experiences and life experiences. Response activities can support children's imaginative, creative, social, moral, intellectual, and language development (Glazer, 1981). Examples of activities include laughing, writing, drawing, retelling, commenting, questioning, rereading, modeling in clay, pantomiming, dramatizing, dancing, singing, cooking, and painting (Hickman, 1981). Teachers in literacy-rich classrooms plan a variety of these activities from which children can choose and provide time for children to engage in them.

Through sharing response-to-literature activities, children's understandings of literature are expanded and enriched. One way children respond to literature is by writing in a **response journal.** Primary school-age children's written responses often consist of retellings, evaluations, and related personal experiences (Dekker, 1991). Figure 6.7 presents an entry from a first grader's response journal. Vivian responded to *Hey, Al* (Yorinks, 1986) by describing how Al felt when the bird came into his bathroom.

CULTURALLY SENSITIVE AND INTEGRATED CURRICULUM

Curriculum is what children learn related to the disciplines of language arts and literature, social studies, science, mathematics, art, music, health, and physical education. Recent research and theory regarding the literacy curriculum suggest that children learn better when the curriculum is integrated across the language arts and across disciplines and when it is culturally sensitive.

The Case for Culturally Sensitive Integrated Curriculum

All children belong to cultural groups that shape their attitudes, beliefs, and ways of making meaning with written language in some way (Heath, 1983). When children perceive of a writing task or a text as having content that reaffirms their cultural identities, they are more likely to become engaged in the task and to construct personal meaning (Ferdman, 1990). **Culturally relevant topics,** topics that children perceive as culturally affirming, are an important avenue to learning and literacy development (Au, 1993; 1998).

Figure 6.7 *Vivian's Response to* Hey, Al *(Yorinks, 1986)*

Curriculum integration—teaching broad topics that cover areas in more than one discipline—improves teaching and learning (Dewey, 1933; Vars, 1991). One way of integrating the curriculum is to capitalize on the "interrelationships of the language processes—reading, writing, speaking, and listening" (Routman, 1991, p. 272). **Integrated language arts** activities are those in which children talk, listen, read, and write. For example, writing a poem often includes talking to others about possible topics for writing, listening to others as they talk about topics or read their poems, and reading one's own composition.

Recent recommendations for curriculum development strongly support curriculum integration across content topics (Hughes, 1991). Children learn concepts and ideas related to a topic that cuts across more than one content, for example, incorporating earth science, geography, and math. This kind of instruction allows children to see connections among facts and theories, provides a focus for selecting instructional activities, provides for coherence of activities, allows children to study topics in depth, and promotes positive attitudes (Lipson, Valencia, Wixson, & Peters, 1993).

Culturally Sensitive Curriculum

The curriculum in literacy-rich classrooms reflects sensitivity for children's cultures in both its content (what is taught and what children are expected to read and write) and its instruction (how concepts are taught). In most classrooms, one or more students have recently arrived in the United States and speak a language other than English at home. Many classrooms include children from a variety of cultural and language backgrounds. Regardless of the mixture of children in a particular classroom, all children need exposure to literature that presents nonstereotyped information about a wide variety of cultural groups.

A culturally sensitive curriculum eliminates the artificial dichotomies created when studying "other" cultures; it includes examples from many cultures as a part of all learning experiences. That is, the content that children study and the material they read naturally present many different cultures. Teachers are careful to include many examples of multicultural literature in all their literature theme units and content units. **Multicultural literature** consists of

> fiction with characters who are from cultural groups that have been underrepresented in children's books: African-Americans, Asian-Americans, Hispanic-Americans, Native Americans, and Americans from religious minorities;
>
> fiction that takes us to other nations and introduces readers to the cultures of people residing outside of the United States; and
>
> information books, including biographies, that focus on African-Americans, Asian-Americans, Hispanic-Americans, Native Americans, Americans from religious minorities, and people living outside the United States. (Zarillo, 1994, pp. 2–3)

The best in multicultural literature presents culturally authentic information (Bishop, 1992). **Culturally authentic literature** portrays people and the values, customs, and beliefs of a cultural group in ways recognized by members of that group as valid and authentic. Most culturally authentic literature is written or illustrated by members of the cultural group. The Appendix provides a list of multicultural literature including culturally authentic literature.

An important part of a culturally sensitive curriculum is consideration of the language of instruction. Children learn best in their home language. However, many teachers are unable to provide instruction in children's home languages. They may not be qualified speakers of the language, or there may be children with several different home languages in one classroom. Teachers should always be sensitive to children's natural tendency to use home language to communicate complex ideas. Chapter 11 provides more information about teaching children whose home language is not English.

Literature Theme Units

Teachers can integrate activities across the language arts by using literature themes as a focus for curriculum development. **Literature theme units** are units of instruction focused on learning about authors or illustrators, genres, themes, or a single book.

As a part of literature theme units, children engage in activities that include talking, listening, reading, and writing. For example, in a kindergarten literature theme unit comparing versions of "The Gingerbread Boy" story (Tompkins & McGee, 1993), the teacher could read five versions of the story aloud to the class, including

Arno, E. (1985). *The gingerbread man.* New York: Scholastic (this book is also available in big book format).

Brown, M. (1972). *The bun: A tale from Russia.* New York: Harcourt Brace Jovanovich.

Cauley, L. (1988). *The pancake boy.* New York: Putnam.

Galdone, P. (1975). *The gingerbread boy.* New York: Seabury.

Sawyer, R. (1953). *Journey Cake, Ho!* New York: Viking.

Figure 6.8 presents a web of talking, listening, reading, and writing activities that could be included in this literature theme unit.

Integrated Content Units

Integrated content units use themes to plan instruction. Units of instruction are organized around a broad theme that includes learning concepts across more than one content area, active inquiry activities, and activities incorporating all the language arts.

For example, a teacher may use the theme of "growing" as a focus for learning experiences for a group of first graders. This theme explores physical changes that occur as a part of growth in plants, animals, and humans; measurement; and the literary theme "growing up." As a part of the activities included in the theme, the teacher may read aloud folktales in which plants grow to enormous sizes (such as *The Enormous Turnip,* retold by Kathy Parkinson, 1986), stories that contrast children at different ages (such as *Stevie,* by John Steptoe, 1969), poems about childhood activities at different ages (*I Want to Be,* by Thylias Moss, 1993), and informational books about growing up (such as *Pueblo Boy: Growing Up in Two Worlds,* by Marcia Keegan, 1991). The teacher may guide the children in dramatizing the stories, and children may create storytelling props to use in retelling the folktales.

Figure 6.8 *Integrated Language Arts Activities for "The Gingerbread Boy" Literature Theme*

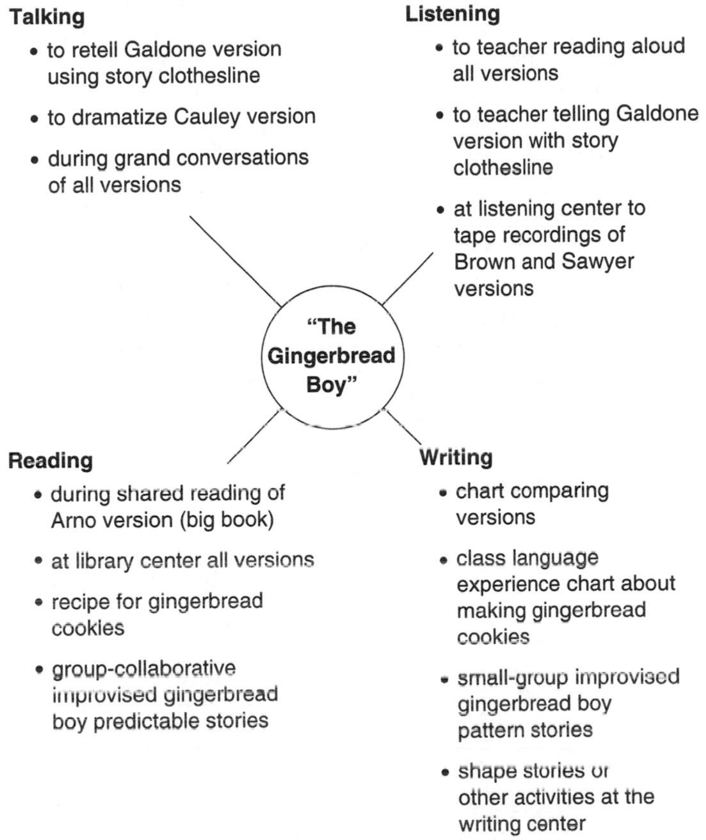
Talking
• to retell Galdone version using story clothesline
• to dramatize Cauley version
• during grand conversations of all versions
Listening
• to teacher reading aloud all versions
• to teacher telling Galdone version with story clothesline
• at listening center to tape recordings of Brown and Sawyer versions
"The Gingerbread Boy"
Reading
• during shared reading of Arno version (big book)
• at library center all versions
• recipe for gingerbread cookies
• group-collaborative improvised gingerbread boy predictable stories
Writing
• chart comparing versions
• class language experience chart about making gingerbread cookies
• small-group improvised gingerbread boy pattern stories
• shape stories or other activities at the writing center

The teacher may also read informational books about the growth of plants and animals (such as *How a Seed Grows,* by Helen Jordan, 1992, and several books from the *See How They Grow* series published by Dorling Kindersley (1992), including *See How They Grow: Butterfly, See How They Grow: Frog,* and *See How They Grow: Mouse*).

ASSESSMENT, INSTRUCTION, AND GROUPING

We have stressed the social nature of becoming literate: children expand their understanding of literacy concepts as they interact with others. They learn from each other in a variety of activities in the classroom, such as sitting together at a computer to construct graphics or a story. They also learn from their teacher as she or he talks with them about the story they are composing. Children learn from the multiple models and demonstrations offered in a literacy-rich, talk-filled classroom. However, children also learn from instruction that is thoughtfully planned and based on careful assessment of their current level of literacy accomplishments.

Assessment bridges the gap between the specific concepts that an individual child currently uses in reading and writing and instruction that is aimed at enhancing that child's current level of knowledge. In order to know what to teach next, teachers carefully watch what children do as they are reading and writing. **Kid watching** involves direct and informal observation of children as they are using reading and writing in play, reading or writing independently, or working in a cooperative group to accomplish an assigned task (Goodman, 1978).

Good assessment cannot be separated from teaching. While teachers are teaching, they are also assessing. Research confirms that children's literacy learning is enhanced when teachers draw from informed observation during teaching to provide feedback on children's reading and writing (DeFord, Pinnell, Lyons, & Place, 1990) and to plan instruction (McCormick, 1994). A critical component of assessment is determining not just what kind of feedback and instruction individual children need, but how to deliver instruction and provide opportunities for practice.

The Case for a Variety of Instruction

Teachers use a variety of instructional approaches in a literacy-rich classroom in order to meet the needs of their diverse learners. They use instructional talk, modeling, and planned direct instruction.

Talk is an important component in children's literacy learning (Genishi, McCarrier, & Nussbaum, 1988; Linfors, 1988). As children talk together about their compositions, they help each other read, construct ideas, spell, use correct grammar, and clarify information (Kamii & Randazzo, 1985; Rowe, 1994). When children talk with their teachers while they are reading and writing, they learn to use reading strategies (DeFord, Pinnell, Lyons, & Place, 1990). Teachers' talk helps children compose, revise, and edit (Calkins, 1986; Graves, 1983).

Most researchers conclude that talk surrounding literacy activities extends children's literacy understandings because it helps situate them in their zone of proximal development (Vygotsky, 1978; see Chapter 1 for a discussion of the zone of proximal development and its influence on literacy learning). Chapters 7 through 10 provide multiple examples of children learning from a teacher's careful modeling and demonstration of reading and writing strategies.

Research also shows that children learn from direct, planned instruction based on assessment of children's current level of literacy accomplishments. Children's comprehension is enhanced when teachers help students "construct understandings about: (a) the content of the text itself; (b) strategies that aid in interpreting the text; and (c) the nature of the reading process itself" (Dole, Duffy, Roehler, & Pearson, 1991, p. 252). Planned instruction also influences the development of reading skills, especially the ability to decode or "sound out" words. Teachers who provide coaching at the moment of need (such as when a child is struggling to identify or spell a word) and who provide direct, planned instruction in using letter patterns to unlock unknown words have a significant impact on children's reading abilities (Dahl, Scharer, Lawson, & Grogan, in press; Foorman, Francis, Fletcher, Schatschneider, & Mehta, 1998). Chapters 7 through 10 provide many examples of direct and planned instruction that extends children's reading and writing achievement.

The Case for Multiple Grouping Patterns

Children learn in whole-class groups, small groups, partner or other cooperative tasks, or individual assignments. Children's learning can be fostered through any grouping pattern and experts recommend that teachers use all four grouping patterns (Hiebert & Colt, 1989). Whole-class group activities foster a sense of community; small groups provide more natural one-on-one language interactions; and independent activities allow children to pursue personal interests (Berghoff & Egawa, 1991). However, the way in which children are selected for groups is an important factor in their literacy learning. In elementary schools, there is a long history of using reading ability as a criterion for selecting children for reading group membership (Barr & Dreeben, 1991). Traditionally, children grouped for reading had similar, or **homogeneous, reading abilities.** Unfortunately, research has shown that children in low-ability groups receive a different kind of reading instruction from that given children in high-ability groups (Allington, 1983). Children in lower achieving groups typically get instruction with a stronger focus on reading words, while children in higher achieving groups get instruction with a stronger focus on comprehension. Therefore, some experts have recommended that children not be grouped by ability for reading instruction.

However, when children begin formal reading instruction, it is critical that they spend some time reading challenging, but readable text (Clay, 1991). The text that children read as a part of this kind of instruction should be carefully matched with their level of achievement. Therefore, it is likely that children will spend some time reading with other children of similar reading ability in order to maximize the effectiveness of instruction with appropriate text. Because teachers will be working with small groups of children on a variety of reading levels, it is critical that teachers achieve a balance of instructional focus for all children: instruction that focuses on children's developing a variety of strategies for reading words accurately and fluently and instruction that focuses on helping children acquire a variety of strategies for constructing meaning (McIntyre & Pressley, 1996). It is also critical that children have experiences working in a variety of grouping patterns. Teachers need a framework for instruction that provides children with opportunities to learn in whole-class groups, in small groups with children on a variety of achievement levels, with partners, and alone. They also need a framework that balances teacher-initiated instruction, in which teachers guide, lead, and provide explicit instruction, with child-responsive activities, in which children initiate, guide, and participate in reading and writing experiences (Baumann & Ivey, 1997).

Instructional Framework

The instructional framework we provide here allows children many opportunities to observe teachers as they model reading and writing. It also makes provisions for children to engage in reading and writing guided by the teacher and independently (Fountas & Pinnell, 1996; Pinnell & Fountas, 1998). We provide a brief overview of these activities here, and they appear throughout Chapters 7 through 10.

Reading

We have already discussed a critical daily routine: **reading aloud** to children. In read alouds, teachers share books on a range of topics, capture children's attention, and engage them in deep thinking about books (Dickinson, Hao, & He, 1995). Read-aloud books should be challenging stories or informational books that provide multiple opportunities to talk about word meaning, puzzle over character's motivations, or discover new concepts (McGee, 1998). Reading aloud provides opportunities to acquire new vocabulary, extend understandings about the world and oneself, and develop an awareness of story and text structures.

Teachers provide demonstrations of reading in **shared reading** of big books or large charts of poems or songs. During shared reading, teachers and children read in unison from the enlarged text of the big book or chart. Texts selected for shared reading are usually familiar, predictable tales, poems, or chants. Teachers may focus children's attention on particular aspects of print during short instructional activities using the big book or chart. They may have children locate words that begin with a specific letter or match words on cards to words in the text. Because shared reading uses enlarged text, the activity can be used with the whole class or a small group. Through repeated reading of the text, children can take on the role of reader by pointing to the text, finding repeated words, or locating words with targeted letters. Because shared reading provides opportunities to develop children's alphabet knowledge, concepts about print, and understanding of the alphabetic code, it is a frequent activity in preschool and kindergarten classrooms.

Guided reading occurs in small groups as children begin to attend to print and make the transition from experimenting to conventional reading. As a part of guided reading lessons, children are expected to learn to read some words by sight and employ other reading strategies to figure out unknown words and construct meaning. Guided reading may begin in kindergarten as teachers observe children operating with knowledge much as we described as experimenting reading in Chapter 4. Guided reading is a critical component of beginning reading instruction and expanding reading in the first grade and beyond. Children are placed in guided reading groups based on current levels of reading achievement. Texts for guided reading lessons are carefully selected from sets of leveled texts so they provide challenging, but readable texts. As a part of guided reading lessons, teachers may provide planned, direct instruction in reading strategies.

As an alternative to guided reading, conventional readers beyond the very beginning stages may engage in **reading workshop or literature circles,** in which children choose books to read either alone or in small groups. As part of the workshop, the teacher presents short lessons about reading strategies, and children meet with the teacher to talk about the book selection. They may extend their reading by selecting a response such as putting on a puppet show, making illustrations, or writing in a response journal. Reading workshop and literature circles extend children's reading development through wide reading of a variety of literature and deep discussion.

Children may read as part of **cooperative groups or partner reading.** In cooperative learning groups, children teach each other content information, guide each other in learning new strategies, and complete joint projects (Slavin, 1986). As a part of the cooperative group process, children may acquire new literacy skills, apply reading strategies, and extend reading interests. Reading with a partner is often a way that children engage in reading practice which allows them to consolidate new strategies and skills learned during instruction.

Finally, children engage in daily **independent reading.** Very young children may browse through familiar storybooks or other texts of interest. In kindergarten, children may also reread small versions of familiar big books or charts and poems posted around the room. In the first grade and beyond, children can reread texts from guided reading selections or other texts at their level of independent reading. They continue to enjoy browsing through informational and storybooks beyond their independent reading level. Extensive amounts of independent reading extend children's vocabulary and build fluency.

Writing

Teachers write for children during **shared writing or language experience.** As children dictate a message during language experience, teachers write it on a chart or an individual picture or in a journal. Groups of children may create a shared language chart after an experience such as visiting a turkey farm. As teachers write, they may demonstrate writing one word at a time and making obvious spaces between words, and they may comment on alphabet letters. Teachers invite children to share in the writing process by asking them to suggest which letters should be used to write the beginning or ending of a word or to reread the message already written. Like shared reading, shared writing and language experience extend children's concepts about print, alphabet knowledge, and awareness of the alphabetic code in a highly supportive context.

Children take on more of the role of writer during **interactive writing.** In this activity, the teacher helps a small group of children compose a short message they will write together. Teachers share the pen with children by inviting them to listen to the beginning, middle, and end sound in words and to write the letters they hear. Teachers may write parts of words while children write other parts. Sometimes children write a whole word. Interactive writing allows teachers to demonstrate how to spell words by stretching out a word's pronunciation, listening for sounds in sequence, and rereading to cross-check spellings with pronunciations. Children extend their writing strategies as they interact with each other and the teacher in this supportive context.

Children write on their own as a part of **writing workshop.** Teachers provide short lessons on composing or spelling strategies, and children write about self-selected topics or topics suggested by the teacher. They receive feedback about their compositions from other children or their teacher during editing conferences. Children's writing develops as a result of the short instructional lessons and the feedback from conferences and through extended writing practice. As a part of writing workshop, children may engage in daily **independent writing.** Writing in journals is another way teachers encourage daily independent writing. Extended amounts of independent writing afford practice for skills and strategies learned in other contexts.

Chapter Summary

Early childhood professional organizations stress the importance of all aspects of children's development. Children's literacy learning should be embedded within child-centered early-childhood programs with developmentally appropriate practices. Exemplary early-childhood programs are found in literacy-rich classrooms where children are reflective, motivated readers and writers who use literacy to learn about their world.

To create literacy-rich classrooms, teachers select quality classroom literature collections that include traditional literature, fantasy, realistic fiction, historical fiction, biography, informational books, poetry, wordless picture books, predictable books, and alphabet books. They select reference materials, audiovisual materials, children's magazines, and writing materials.

Teachers infuse reading and writing materials throughout the room to encourage functional use of literacy. They set up a classroom library center, a writing center, and computer center.

Teachers establish three daily routines using reading and writing. Teachers read or tell stories, poems, or informational books daily; they set aside time for children to read and write on topics of their choice; and they plan activities in which children share their writing and responses to literature.

The curriculum is organized around literature content units that include talking, listening, reading, and writing activities. All units include multicultural literature.

Teachers provide instruction in a variety of settings as they demonstrate reading and writing, guide interactive discussions, and provide direct teaching through modeling. They form a variety of groups, including whole-class gatherings, small groups, and partners, and they set aside time for children to work alone. Groups usually incorporate children with a variety of different ability levels who are encouraged to work cooperatively. Teachers assess children's literacy learning and use information from their assessments, in part, to guide decisions about instruction.

Applying the Information

A description of Mrs. E's kindergarten classroom and literacy activities follows. Use the seven characteristics of a literacy-rich classroom to think about the literacy environment in Mrs. E's classroom. Discuss how Mrs. E's classroom illustrates each of the seven characteristics. What suggestions might you make about room arrangement and instruction?

Mrs. E has twenty-two kindergartners in a relatively small room. Nearly all of the children who attend this school receive free lunch (their families fall below the poverty limit established by the federal government). A map of the classroom is presented in Figure 6.9. This map illustrates that Mrs. E's room is equipped with twenty-four desks and two tables. The entire room is carpeted.

Each morning Mrs. E reads at least one selection of children's literature to the entire class. The children gather around her on the rug in the large-group area. Next, Mrs. E has experience time. During this time, she might demonstrate a science experiment, have a guest speaker, or read nonfiction. Each of these daily experiences is related to a topic of study. For example, one unit of study focused on insects. A man who keeps bees visited the classroom and brought his equipment to the class. The children kept ants in an ant farm. Mrs. E read many books that had insects as characters as well as informational books about insects.

After experience time, the children usually dictate and read accounts of what they learned that day or dictate retellings of favorite stories or charts. Sometimes Mrs. E prepares her own accounts of the previous day's experience for the children to read with her.

Next, Mrs. E holds a five- to ten-minute lesson or discussion designed to motivate the children to write. During the insect unit, children were encouraged to write poems, stories, and predictable stories about insects. One of the lessons Mrs. E taught was to show the children a poster she had made about the letters *b* and *c*. On the poster were several pictures of objects with names beginning with these letters (*boat, bat, beaver, cat, candy, cookie*). Mrs. E reminded the children that as they listened to words they wanted to write, they might

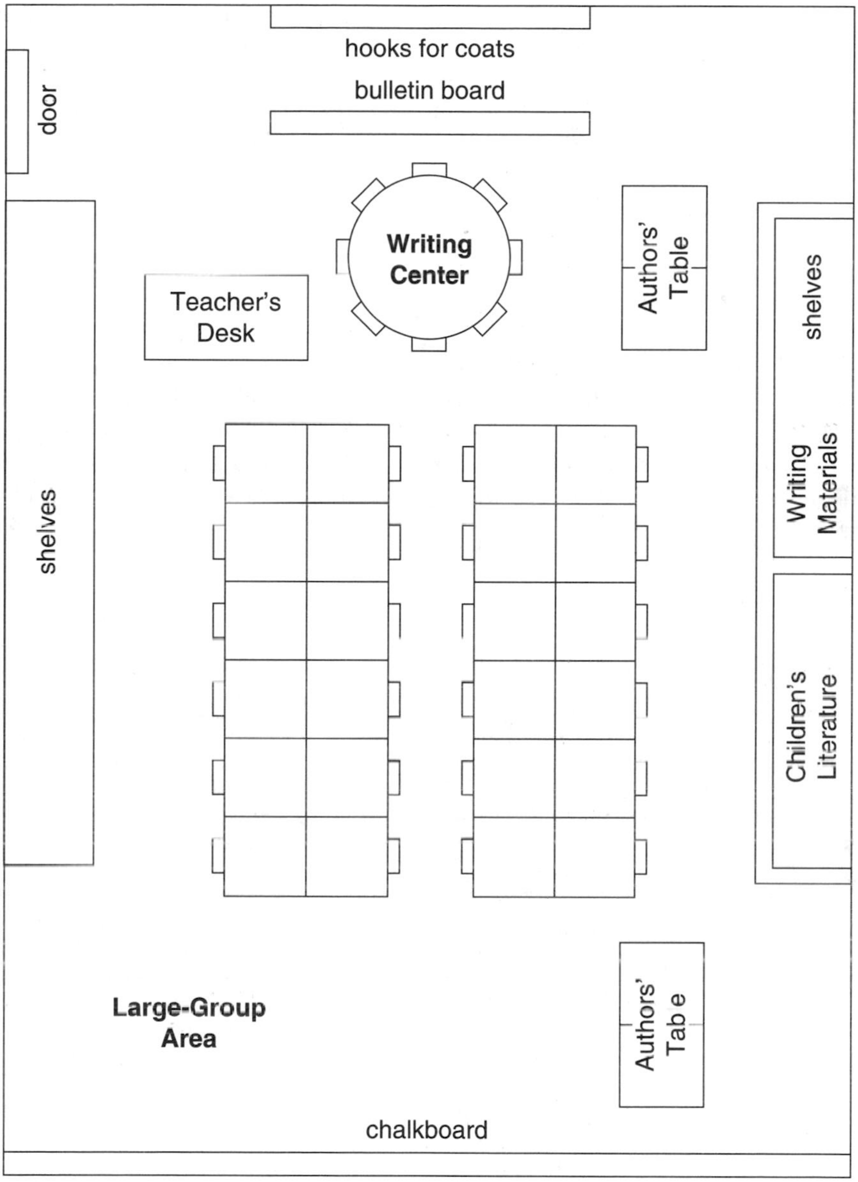

Figure 6.9 Mrs. E's Classroom

hear some sounds like those in the words *boat* or *cat*. They could use the letters *b* and *c*.

After the lesson, the children write at their desks. Mrs. E circulates around the room, asking questions, making comments, and answering children's questions. As the children finish their writing, they read their writing to each other, select books from the library center, or read child-authored poems, stories, and books that are kept on the authors' tables.

Last, Mrs. E holds author's chair. (A special chair is placed in the group area on the rug for a child to sit in as he or she reads his or her writing.) Many children have opportunities to read their writing. The children know that they may choose to "talk about their writing" or "read what they wrote." They feel very comfortable as the other children make comments and offer praise. Mrs. E always comments on some aspect of the content of the writing, "I didn't know there were ants called carpenters. We will need to read more about them. Will you help me find out about them?"

Going Beyond the Text

Visit a preschool or elementary school classroom and observe literacy instruction and activities. Look carefully at the literacy materials that are available in the room. Note how often children interact with these literacy materials. Observe the children and their teacher as they interact during literacy instruction and as the children work on literacy projects. Use the seven characteristics of literacy-rich classrooms as a guide for discussing your observations.

References

ABRAHAMSON, R. F. (1981). An update on wordless picture books with an annotated bibliography. *The Reading Teacher, 34,* 417–421.

ADAMS, M. (1990). *Beginning to read: Thinking and learning about print.* Cambridge: MIT Press.

ALLINGTON, R. (1983). The reading instruction provided readers of differing ability. *Elementary School Journal, 83,* 255–265.

ANDERSON, R. C., HIEBERT, E. H., SCOTT, J. A., & WILKINSON, I. A. G. (1985). *Becoming a nation of readers: The report of the commission on reading.* Washington, D.C.: The National Institute of Education.

ANDERSON, R. C., WILSON, P. T., & FIELDING, L. G. (1988). Growth in reading and how children spend their time outside of school. *Reading Research Quarterly, 23,* 285–303.

AU, K. (1993). *Literacy instruction in multicultural settings.* New York: Harcourt Brace Jovanovich.

AU, K. (1998). Constructivist approaches, phonics, and the literacy learning of students of diverse backgrounds. In T. Shanahan & F. Rodrigues-Brown (Eds.), *47th Yearbook of the National Reading Conference* (pp. 1–21). Chicago, IL: National Reading Conference.

BARONE, D. (1990). The written response of young children: Beyond comprehension. *The New Advocate, 3,* 49–56.

BARR, R., & DREEBEN, R. (1991). Grouping students for reading instruction. In R. Barr, M. Kamil, P. Mosenthal, & P. Pearson (Eds.), *Handbook of reading research, vol. 2* (pp. 885–910). White Plains, NY: Longman.

BAUMANN, J. F., & IVEY, G. (1997). Delicate balances: Striving for curriculum and instructional equilibrium in a second-grade, literature/strategy-based classroom. *Reading Research Quarterly, 32,* 224–275.

BERGHOFF, B., & EGAWA, K. (1991). No more "rocks": Grouping to give students control of their learning. *The Reading Teacher, 44,* 536–541.

BISHOP, R. (1992). Multicultural literature for children: Making informed choices. In V. Harris (Ed.), *Teaching multicultural literature in grades K–8.* (pp. 37–53). Norwood, MA: Christopher-Gordon.

BLUME, J. (1974). *The pain and the great one.* New York: Bradbury.

BRIDGE, C. (1986). Predictable books for beginning readers and writers. In M. R. Sampson (Ed.), *The pursuit of literacy: Early reading and writing* (pp. 81–96). Dubuque, IA: Kendall/Hunt.

BRUCE, B., MICHAELS, S., & WATSON-GREGEO, K. (1985). How computers can change the writing process. *Language Arts, 62,* 143–149.

BUNTING, E. (1990). *The wall.* New York: Clarion.

BUNTING, E. (1991). *Fly away home.* New York: Clarion.

BURNIE, D. (1994). *The dictionary of nature.* London: Dorling Kindersley.

CALKINS, L. M. (1986). *The art of teaching writing.* Portsmouth, NH: Heinemann.

CANIZARES, S., & CHANKO, P. (1998). *Water.* New York: Scholastic.
CARLE, E. (1970). *The very hungry caterpillar.* New York: Viking.
CAULEY, L. (1981). *Goldilocks and the three bears.* New York: Putnam.
CAULEY, L. (1984). *The town mouse and the country mouse.* New York: Putnam.
CAZDEN, C. (1988). *Classroom discourse.* Portsmouth, NH: Heinemann.
CHOMSKY, C. (1972). Stages in language development and reading exposure. *Harvard Educational Review, 42,* 1–33.
CLAY, M. M. (1991). *Becoming literate: The construction of inner control.* Portsmouth, NH: Heinemann.
CLEARY, B. (1981). *Ramona Quimby, age 8.* New York: Morrow.
CLIATT, M., & SHAW, J. (1988). The storytime exchange: Ways to enhance it. *Childhood Education, 64,* 293–298.
COLE, J. (1986). *The magic school bus at the waterworks.* New York: Scholastic.
COLE, J. (1987). *The magic school bus inside the earth.* New York: Scholastic.
COLE, J. (1989). *The magic school bus inside the human body.* New York: Scholastic.
COLE, J. (1990). *The magic school bus lost in the solar system.* New York: Scholastic.
COONEY, B. (1982). *Miss Rumphius.* New York: Viking.
DAHL, K. L., SCHARER, P. L., LAWSON, L. L., & GROGAN, P. R. (in press). Phonics instruction and student achievement in whole language first grade classrooms. *Reading Research Quarterly.*
DEFORD, D., PINNELL, G., LYONS, C., & PLACE, Q. (1990). *Report of the follow-up study, Columbus Reading Recovery program 1988–1989* (Report Vol. 11). Columbus: The Ohio State University.
DE PAOLA, T. (1978). *Pancakes for breakfast.* New York: Harcourt Brace Jovanovich.
DE PAOLA, T. (1989). *The art lesson.* New York: Putnam.
DEKKER, M. (1991). Books, reading, and response: A teacher-researcher tells a story. *The New Advocate, 4,* 37–46.
DE REGNIERS, B., MOORE, E., WHITE, M., & CARR, J. (Compilers). (1988). *Sing a song of popcorn: Every child's book of poems.* New York: Scholastic.
DEWEY, J. (1933). *How we think* (rev. ed.). Boston: Heath.
DIAMOND, B. J., & MOORE, M. A. (1995). *Multicultural literacy: Mirroring the reality of the classroom.* White Plains, NY: Longman.
DICKINSON, D., & SMITH, M. (1994). Long-term effects of preschool teachers' book readings on low-income children's vocabulary and story comprehension. *Reading Research Quarterly, 29,* 104–122.
DICKINSON, D.., HAO, Z., & HE, W. (1995). Pedagogical and classroom factors related to how teachers read to 3- and-4-year-old children. In K. A. Hinchman, C. K. Kinzer, & D. J. Leu (Eds), *Perspectives on literacy research and practice* (pp. 212–221). Chicago: National Reading Conference.
DOLE, J., DUFFY, G., ROEHLER, L., & PEARSON, D. (1991). Moving from the old to the new: Research on reading comprehension instruction. *Review and Educational Research, 61,* 239–264.
DRESSEL, J. (1990). The effects of listening to and discussing different qualities of children's literature on the narrative writing of fifth graders. *Research in the Teaching of English, 24,* 397–414.
EEDS, M., & WELLS, D. (1989). Grand conversations: An exploration of meaning construction in literature study groups. *Research in the Teaching of English, 23,* 4–29.
EHLERT, L. (1989). *Eating the alphabet.* New York: Harcourt Brace Jovanovich.
FEITELSON, D., KITA, B., & GOLDSTEIN, Z. (1986). The effects of listening to series stories on first graders' comprehension and use of language. *Research in the Teaching of English, 20,* 336–356.
FERDMAN, B. (1990). Literacy and cultural identity. *Harvard Educational Review, 60,* 181–204.
FIVE, C. (1986). Fifth graders respond to a changed reading program. *Harvard Educational Review, 56,* 395–405.
FOORMAN, B., FRANCIS, D., FLETCHER, J., SCHATSCHNEIDER, C., & MEHTA, P. (1998). The role of instruction in learning to read: Preventing reading failure in at-risk children. *Journal of Educational Psychology, 90,* 1–15.
FOUNTAS, I. C., & PINNELL, G. S. (1996). *Guided reading: Good first teaching for all children.* Portsmouth, NH: Heinemann.
FRACTOR, J., WOODRUFF, M., MARTINEZ, M., & TEALE, W. (1993). Let's not miss opportunities to promote voluntary reading: Classroom libraries in elementary school. *The Reading Teacher, 46,* 476–484.
GALDONE, P. (1970). *The three little pigs.* New York: Seabury.
GALDONE, P. (1975). *The gingerbread boy.* New York: Clarion.
GENISHI, C., MCCARRIER, A., & NUSSBAUM, N. R. (1988). Research currents: Classroom interaction as teaching and learning. *Language Arts, 65,* 182–191.

GLAZER, J. I. (1981). *Literature for young children.* Columbus, OH: Merrill.
GOLENBOCK, P. (1990). *Teammates.* San Diego: Harcourt Brace Jovanovich.
GOODMAN, Y. M. (1978). Kid watching: An alternative to testing. *National Elementary Principals Journals, 57,* 41–45.
GRAVES, D. H. (1983). Teacher intervention in children's writing: A response to Myra Barrs. *Language Arts, 10,* 841–846.
GRIMM, J., & GRIMM, W. (1989). *Frog prince.* New York: North-South.
HARRIS, V. J. (1992). *Teaching multicultural literature in grades K–8.* Norwood, MA: Christopher-Gordon.
HEATH, S. B. (1983). *Ways with words: Language, life, and work in communities and classrooms.* New York: Cambridge University Press.
HEST, A. (1997). *When Jessie came across the sea.* Cambridge, MA: Candlewick Press.
HICKMAN, J. (1979). *Response to literature in a school environment. Doctoral dissertation,* The Ohio State University, Columbus, OH.
HICKMAN, J. (1981). A new perspective on response to literature: Research in an elementary school setting. *Research in the Teaching of English, 15,* 343–354.
HIEBERT, E., & COLT, J. (1989). Patterns of literature-based reading instruction. *The Reading Teacher, 43,* 14–20.
HIPPLE, M. L. (1985). Journal writing in kindergarten. *Language Arts, 62,* 255–261.
HODGES, M. (1984). *Saint George and the dragon.* Boston: Little, Brown.
HOFFMAN, J., ROSER, N., & BATTLE, J. (1993). Reading aloud in classrooms: From the modal toward a "model." *The Reading Teacher, 46,* 496–503.
HOWE, D., & HOWE, J. (1979). *Bunnicula: A rabbit tale of mystery.* New York: Atheneum.
HOWKER, J. (1997). *Walk with a wolf.* Cambridge, MA: Candlewick Press.
HUGHES, M. (1991). *Curriculum integration in the primary grades: A framework for excellence.* Alexandria, VA: Association of Supervision and Curriculum Development.
HUTCHINS, P. (1968). *Rosie's walk.* New York: Macmillan.
HYMAN, T. (1983). *Little red riding hood.* New York: Holiday House.
JORDAN, H. (1992). *How a seed grows.* New York: HarperCollins.
JUKES, M. (1984). *Like Jake and me.* New York: Knopf.
KAMII, C., & RANDAZZO, M. (1985). Social interaction and invented spelling. *Language Arts, 62,* 124–133.
KEEGAN, M. (1991). *Pueblo boy: Growing up in two worlds.* New York: Dutton.
KELLY, P. (1990). Guiding young students' response to literature. *The Reading Teacher, 44,* 464–470.
KINTISCH, L. S. (1986). Journal writing: Stages of development. *The Reading Teacher, 40,* 168–172.
LABBO, L. D. (1996). A semiotic analysis of young children's symbol making in a classroom computer center. *Reading Research Quarterly, 31,* 356–382.
LABBO, L. D., MURRAY, B. A., & PHILLIPS, M. (1996). Writing to read: From inheritance to innovation and invitation. *The Reading Teacher, 49,* 314–321.
LABBO, L. D., & ASH, G. E. (1998). What is the role of computer-related technology in early literacy? In S. Neuman & K. Roskos (Eds.), *Children achieving: Best practices in beginning literacy* (pp. 180–197). Newark, DE: International Reading Association.
LASKY, K. (1983). *Sugaring time.* New York: Macmillan.
LINFORS, J. W. (1988). From "talking together" to "being together in talk." *Language Arts, 65,* 135–141.
LIPSON, M., VALENCIA, S., WIXSON, K., & PETERS, C. (1993). Integration and thematic teaching: Integration to improve teaching and learning. *Language Arts, 70,* 252–263.
LYNCH-BROWN, C., & TOMLINSON, C. M. (1996). *Essentials of children's literature* (2nd ed.). Boston: Allyn and Bacon.
LYNCH-BROWN, C., & TOMLINSON, C. (1998). *The essentials of children's literature* (3rd ed.). Boston: Allyn and Bacon.
MACLACHLAN, P. (1985). *Sarah, plain and tall.* New York: Harper and Row.
The Macmillan visual dictionary. (1992). New York: Macmillan.
MADDERN, E. (1993). *The fire children: A West African creation tale.* New York: Dial.
MARTIN, B., JR. (1983). *Brown bear, brown bear, what do you see?* New York: Holt, Rinehart and Winston.
MCCORMICK, S. (1994). A nonreader becomes a reader: A case study of literacy acquisition by a severely disabled reader. *Reading Research Quarterly, 29,* 156–176.
MCDERMOTT, G. (1972). *Anansi the spider: A tale from the Ashanti.* New York: Henry Holt.
MCGEE, L. M. (1998). How do we teach literature to young children? In S. Neuman & K. Roskos (Eds.), *Children achieving: Best practices in beginning literacy* (pp. 162–179). Newark, DE: International Reading Association.

MCGILL-FRANZEN, A. (1992). Early literacy: What does "developmentally appropriate" mean? *The Reading Teacher, 46,* 56–58.

MCINTYRE, E., & PRESSLEY, M. (1996). *Balanced instruction: Strategies and skills in whole language.* Norwood, MA: Christopher-Gordon.

MEHAN, H. (1979). *Learning lessons.* Cambridge: Harvard University Press.

MOLLEL, T. M. (1993). *The king and the tortoise.* New York: Clarion.

MORRIS, D. (December, 1998). *Preventing reading failure in the primary grades.* Presented at the National Reading Conference, Austin, TX, December 1998.

MORROW, L. (1992). The impact of a literature-based program on literacy achievement, use of literature, and attitudes of children from minority backgrounds. *Reading Research Quarterly, 27,* 250–275.

MORROW, L. (1997). *The literacy center: Contexts for reading and writing.* York, ME: Stenhouse.

MORROW, L., & GAMBRELL, L. B. (1998). How do we motivate children toward independent reading and writing? In S. Neuman & K. Roskos (Eds.), *Children achieving: Best practices in beginning literacy* (pp. 144–161). Newark, DE: International Reading Association.

MORROW, L. M., & WEINSTEIN, C. S. (1982). Increasing children's use of literature through program and physical design changes. *The Elementary School Journal, 83,* 131–137.

MORROW, L. M., & WEINSTEIN, C. S. (1986). Encouraging voluntary reading: The impact of a literature program on children's use of library centers. *Reading Research Quarterly, 21,* 330–346.

MOSS, T. (1993). *I want to be.* New York: Dial.

MYERS, W. D. (1993). *Brown angels.* Walter Dean Myers.

National Association for the Education of Young Children. (1998). Learning to read and write: Developmentally appropriate practices for young children. *Young Children, 53,* 30–46.

OLDFATHER, P. (1993). What students say about motivating experiences in a whole language classroom. *The Reading Teacher, 46,* 672–681.

ORMEROD, J. (1981). *Sunshine.* New York: Lothrop.

PALLOTTA, J. (1986). *The yucky reptile alphabet book.* Watertown, MA: Ivory Tower.

PARKINSON, K. (1986). *The enormous turnip.* Niles, IL: Albert Whitman.

PEET, B. (1989). *Bill Peet: An autobiography.* Boston: Houghton Mifflin.

PINNELL, G. S., & FOUNTAS, I. C. (1998). *Word matters: Teaching phonics and spelling in the reading/writing classroom.* Portsmouth, NH: Heinemann.

PRELUTSKY, J. (1983). *The Random House book of poetry for children.* New York: Random House.

The Random House children's encyclopedia (rev. ed.). (1992). New York: Random House.

RHODES, L. K. (1981). I can read! Predictable books as resources for reading and writing. *The Reading Teacher, 34,* 511–518.

RINGGOLD, F. (1991). *Tar beach.* New York: Crown.

ROOF, B. (1993). *My first dictionary.* London: Dorling Kindersley.

ROOF, B. (1993). *My first encyclopedia.* London: Dorling Kindersley.

ROSS, R. R. (1980). *Storyteller.* (2nd ed.). Columbus, OH: Merrill.

ROUTMAN, R. (1991). *Invitations: Changing as teachers and learners K–12.* Portsmouth, NH: Heinemann.

ROWE, D. (1994). *Preschoolers as authors: Literacy learning in the social world.* Cresskill, NJ: Hampton Press.

SAY, A. (1990). *El Chino.* Boston: Houghton Mifflin.

SAY, A. (1997). *Allison.* Boston: Houghton Mifflin.

SENDAK, M. (1962). *Chicken soup with rice.* New York: Harper and Row.

SENDAK, M. (1963). *Where the wild things are.* New York: Harper and Row.

SIERRA, J. (1992). *The elephant's wrestling match.* Toronto: McClelland and Stewart.

SLAVIN, R. (1986). *Using student team learning* (3rd ed.). Baltimore: Johns Hopkins University, Center for Research on Elementary and Middle Schools.

SNOW, C., BURNS, S., & GRIFFIN, P. (Eds). (1998). *Preventing reading difficulties in young children.* Washington, D.C.: National Academy Press.

STEIG, W. (1972). *Dominic.* New York: Farrar, Straus and Giroux.

STEPTOE, J. (1969). *Stevie.* New York: Harper and Row.

STEPTOE, J. (1984). *The story of jumping mouse.* New York: Mulberry.

TAYLOR, M. D. (1976). *Roll of thunder, hear my cry.* New York: Penguin Books.

TEMPLE, C., MARTINEZ, M., YOKOTA, J., & NAYLOR, A. (1998). *Children's books in children's hands: An introduction to their literature.* Boston: Allyn and Bacon.

TOMLINSON, C. M., & LYNCH-BROWN, C. (1996). *Essentials of children's literature* (2nd ed.). Boston: Allyn and Bacon.

TOMPKINS, G., & MCGEE, L. (1993). *Teaching reading with literature: Case studies to action plans.* New York: Merrill/Macmillan.

TUNNELL, M. O. (1993). *The joke's on George.* New York: Tambourine.
TURKLE, B. (1976). *Deep in the forest.* New York: Dutton.
TURNER, A. (1985). *Dakota dugout.* New York: Aladdin.
TURNER, J. C. (1995). The influence of classroom contexts on young children's motivation for literacy. *Reading Research Quarterly, 30,* 410–441.
VAN ALLSBURG, C. (1987). *The Z was zapped.* Boston: Houghton Mifflin.
VARS, G. (1991). Integrated curriculum in historical perspective. *Educational Leadership, 49,* 14–15.
VUONG, L. (1982). *The brocaded slipper and other Vietnamese tales.* New York: Addison-Wesley.
VYGOTSKY, L. S. (1978). *Mind in society. The development of higher psychological processes.* Cambridge: Harvard University Press.
WATSON, C. (1982). *Applebet.* New York: Farrar, Straus and Giroux.
WISNIEWSKI, D. (1990). *Elfwyn's saga.* New York: Lothrop, Lee and Shepherd.
XIONG, B. (1989). *Nine-in-one. Grr! Grr!.* San Francisco: Children's Book Press.
YORINKS, A. (1986). *Hey, Al.* New York: Farrar, Straus and Giroux.
ZARRILLO, J. (1994). *Multicultural literature, multicultural teaching: Units for the elementary grades.* New York: Harcourt Brace Jovanovich.

Chapter 7

Supporting Literacy Learning in Preschools

Key Concepts

"I can read" bags
environmental print puzzles
letter game
onset
rime
"I can hear" activity
word play books
name displays
metalinguistic awareness
calendar routine
rhyming games
"Rounding Up the Rhymes" activity
pocket chart
segmenting phonemes
literary awareness
booksharing techniques
concept-about-story activities
concepts of print
big books
interactive read alouds
clothesline props
literary prop boxes
shared writing activity
sign-in procedure
pattern stories
story extensions
pattern writing
list making
written language talk
dramatic-play-with-print centers
text and toy sets
story telling and playing activity

THE PRESCHOOL CONTEXT

Every classroom is a context for the interaction of two powerful currents: what children bring to the classroom, and what teachers, parents, school administrators, school boards, and taxpayers expect of schools. A significant part of any teacher's effective support of language and literacy learning is to plan for this inevitable interaction. In one way, the children's contribution remains the same: no matter at what grade level, from preschool through the primary grades, children present teachers with all or nearly all of the array of literacy knowledges described in Chapters 3 through 5. That is, although the relative proportions represented by each group vary depending on their home and previous school experiences, it is likely that some children in any classroom will be novices, some experimenters, and some conventional readers and writers. The expectations for what children ought to learn, however, change significantly from preschool, to kindergarten, to first grade, and beyond. Society, teachers, school systems, and parents have quite definite and unique expectations about the outcomes of literacy instruction for each level.

What Preschoolers Learn about Literacy

The joint statement of the International Reading Association and the National Association of Educators of Young Children (1998) describes developmentally appropriate literacy expectations for preschoolers, including children's enjoyment of storybook read alouds and discussions, their identifying signs and labels, their playing rhyming games, their having partial alphabet and sound–letter knowledge, and their using some alphabet letters or mock letters to write meaningful words and phrases. We would add that preschoolers can be expected to retell favorite storybooks and informational books; write pretend messages as part of dramatic play; make rhymes in response to language play books and other texts, such as lists and poems; and conventionally form some alphabet letters in their pretend play writing, writing center work, or name writing.

The teacher's role in this is demanding, for even at the preschool level, children's knowledge and their terms for engagement are quite varied. The IRA and NAEYC description of this role includes that teachers "share books with children, including Big Books, and model reading behaviors; talk about letters by name and sounds; establish a literacy-rich environment; reread favorite stories; engage children in language games; promote literacy-related play activities; [and] encourage children to experiment with writing" (1998, p. 200). The IRA and NAEYC also suggest that parents and other family members engage preschool children in talk about names of things and about experiences and ideas that are important to their children; read and reread books, especially those with predictable texts; take their children to the library regularly; and provide writing and drawing materials. Preschool teachers, however, cannot expect that all families will provide such literacy experiences. Then the teacher's role assumes even greater importance.

Without frequent opportunities to engage in literacy events in preschool, children whose homes offer few such opportunities are at a disadvantage in kindergarten and the primary grades. They will be less successful at learning to read and write in those grades than their peers whose homes offer many literacy opportunities.

This point is worth repeating. It is crucial that children with few experiences with written language in their homes have especially rich preschool experiences. Preschool teachers must provide demonstrations of reading and writing (which we show later in this chapter in Mrs. Miller's and Miss Leslie's classrooms). They must also engage children in reading and writing activities and become especially attentive and sensitive audiences to children's efforts. In the following sections we describe a preschool setting that surrounds children with print and encourages their reading and writing.

The Preschool Setting: Space and Materials

One of the teacher's roles in preschool is to arrange spaces and select materials that will engage children's active exploration of their environment through construction and play. This environment naturally encourages language and literacy development when children talk and play together and when reading and writing materials are an important part of these activities.

Figure 7.1 presents our design of a well-appointed and well-arranged preschool classroom with many traditional centers. The block center has bin and shelf storage spaces for large cardboard blocks, large wooden blocks, smaller wooden blocks, and durable model cars and trucks. It includes a workbench for play with pegs and hammer and wrench. On the bulletin board are posters of city skylines and their distinctive buildings (e.g., the Chicago lakefront with the skyscrapers of The Loop in the background), other distinctive buildings (e.g., Frank Lloyd Wright's Falling Water, a cantilever-constructed house over a waterfall, and the Eiffel Tower), and vehicles (e.g., ocean liners on a travel-agency poster and truck and car posters from a car dealership). These posters contain the print that is part of the poster (e.g., "Chicago," "Cruise the Caribbean") as well as taped-on labels (e.g., "skyscraper," "ship"). On the workbench are hardware-store advertising flyers and a do-it-yourself carpentry book. There are two large, empty pasteboard boxes. There is a large area for playing with blocks.

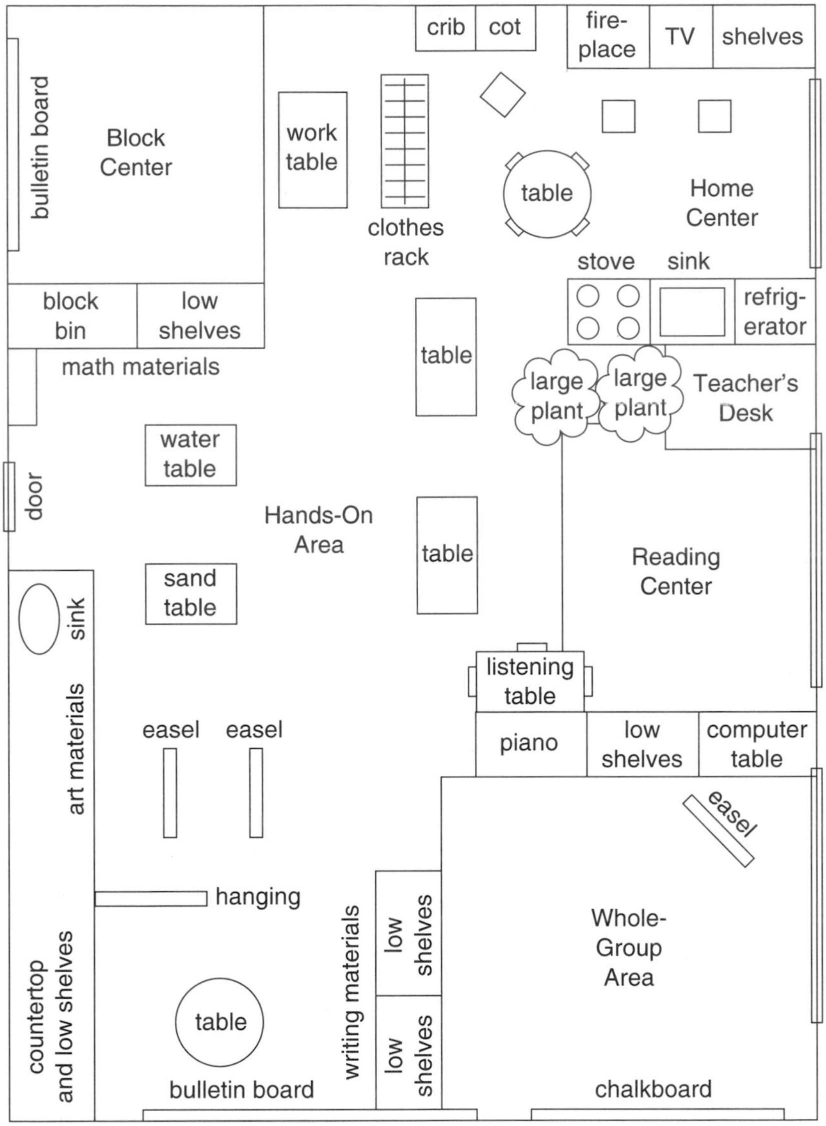

Figure 7.1 *A Preschool Classroom*

The home center includes a cardboard fireplace with chairs around it, a cardboard television (such as furniture stores use in their entertainment-center displays), shelves, a kitchen set with a small table and four chairs, a small cot, a doll crib, and a doll high chair. The bookcase is stocked with magazines, including *TV Guide,* newspapers, a phone book, a few adult books, and a few children's picture books. The kitchen is stocked with plastic food, empty food containers (e.g., cereal boxes, a plastic ketchup bottle, a cottage cheese container), and several illustrated cookbooks, including *My First Cookbook* (Wilkes, 1989). Over the crib is a *Sesame Street* poster picturing Bert and Ernie and displaying their names.

Between the home and block centers is a clothing rack to serve dramatic play in the home and block centers. In both play centers, there are several small, spiral-bound, vertical-flip notebooks, small clipboards with paper, and pencils. In the home center, a waiter or waitress may use these props during restaurant play to take an order, or a mommy or a daddy may use them to take a telephone message or to make a grocery list; in the block center, astronauts may use these items for a countdown checklist.

In the hands-on area are a sand table, a water table, and the art center. There are a sink and storage for supplies, including water toys and plastic aprons, and storage for and places to use children's individual collections of environmental print items, math manipulatives (e.g., Unifix cubes), musical instruments, puzzles, Legos™, clay, and science manipulatives (e.g., magnets). There is display space for content centers. All items and storage places are labeled. There is a travel poster of a beach near the sand table and one of Niagara Falls near the water table. The musical instruments are stored near the piano and an easel; sometimes the easel displays the lyrics to a song the children are learning, written on a large piece of posterboard. There are small easels for painting near the art supplies, tables for using many of the manipulatives, and a large, open area for group singing activities and for other large-group activities, such as story performances.

The reading and writing centers are on the opposite side of the room from the play centers. These contain writing materials, a computer, books (including pattern books, movable books, alphabet books, and big books), and space to use them, as described in Chapter 6. A large, round table at the edge of the writing center is the location for children's signing in at the beginning of their day and for checking out and checking in books from the classroom library.

READING AND WRITING IN MRS. MILLER'S PRESCHOOL CLASSROOM

The space and materials just described lay the foundation for providing many opportunities for children to interact with print. When such opportunities abound, children will choose experiences that naturally support their literacy development as well as their growing emotionally, socially, and in other areas of learning, such as science, social studies, and math. In this section we describe children as they interact in a classroom rich with print. A guiding principle of infusing the classroom with print is that the print must remain functional. The focus of the reading and writing in the case study that follows is on children's reading and writing print, not learning to read specific words or learning isolated print skills.

Mrs. Miller teaches in a program for at-risk four-year-olds. She arranges her classroom so that print is included in every center, and she provides large blocks of time for children to play in the centers. First we describe the children as they play in Mrs. Miller's centers, and then we describe how Mrs. Miller interacts with the children as they play.

Children at Play

Mrs. Miller's classroom has many centers, including book, McDonald's, writing, games, art, science and math discovery, and home centers. By midmorning, children are working and playing at nearly every center. Two children are on the rug in the book center. They are looking at several books together, commenting about the pictures and talking about the stories. Then they take paper bags labeled with their names and "I can read" from a storage shelf for manipulatives. They look at the coupons, paper bags, and fronts cut from food boxes that they have taken from their **"I can read" bags.** One child gets a doll from the home center, puts it in her lap, and points to each of the items. She reads to her doll by saying a word or two for each item.

Four children are at a McDonald's center. The center is made from a puppet theater to which Mrs. Miller has attached a sign and menu. Inside the theater are empty containers for hamburgers and French fries. Two children are behind the counter in the center. Both have on hats worn by employees at McDonald's. One child is writing on an order pad, and the other is pretending to put a McDLT™ in a container. Two children are standing in front of the counter. One is dressed in a hat and heels from the home center. She is "Mama." She asks "Baby" what he wants to eat and then orders. The child taking orders announces, "That will be ten dollars." "Mama" looks in her purse for money and pays her bill.

Two children are at the writing center. A number of menus and placemats from local restaurants are displayed at the center. Also displayed are several menus composed by children. Some menus have pictures cut from magazines; some have children's mock letters or mock cursive writing; some have words children have copied from menus or newspapers; and others were written and drawn by parent volunteers. One of the menus on display was composed by Mrs. Miller. It is titled "Miller's Meals" and consists of a drawing of people eating, cutout pictures of food from the food section of the newspaper, and words. One of the children at the center is drawing and writing a menu. She announces, "I'm going to have ice cream," and draws a picture of a double dip cone. The other child comments, "I like ice cream, too. Maybe I'd better write *ice cream.* People might want ice cream on their cake."

Two children are in the games center. They play for several minutes with Legos™ and other small manipulative toys in the center. Then they remove two **environmental print puzzles** from the game shelf. The puzzles consist of boxes of brownie and cake mixes. Inside each box are pieces cut from the fronts of identical boxes. The children spread the cut-up puzzle pieces on the table. They put the puzzles together by looking at the pieces and then placing them on top of the boxes where they match. They talk together as they complete the puzzles, "I like chocolate. I could eat a whole box of these."

Two other children come to the games center and sit on the floor to play the **letter game.** A large *L* is painted on the front of a pasteboard box and a *K* on another. Attached to one of the boxes is a plastic bag containing several *L*'s and *K*'s that have been cut from construction paper and laminated. The two children play the letter game by sorting the letters and placing them inside the large pasteboard boxes. As they sort the letters, they say, "I'll be the *L* and you be the *K*. I know whose letter *K* is—Kelita's."

Tammy and Jonathan are painting at easels in the art center. Two index cards are clothespinned to the top of each easel; one card is on top of the other. Tammy's and Jonathan's names are on the top index cards on their easels. When they finish painting, they will unclip their name cards and take them to the bulletin board in the whole-group area where a small poster reads "I painted today." They will clip their name cards to the poster. When their name cards are removed from the easels, the two bottom cards will tell who can paint next.

One child is in the science and math discovery center. Included in this center is a graph divided into two segments, "No TV Last Night" and "TV Last Night." The first title is accompanied by a picture of a TV with a big *X* over it. The second title is accompanied by a picture of a TV. Under each title some squares of paper have been pasted. Many squares have children's names written on them. Most of the squares are pasted under the "TV Last Night" title. Jermain writes his name on a square of paper and pastes it under the "TV Last Night" title. Displayed on the bulletin board in the center is a graph that the children completed the day before. Under this chart are two sentences: "Two children saw no TV Monday night. Ten children saw TV Monday night."

Three children are in the home center. Two children decide to cook a meal for their babies, using empty food containers and plastic food in the center. One child says, "I think I'll cook some chicken. Let me look up a good recipe." She opens a cookbook on one of the shelves in the center and begins looking through the pages. Another child is sitting in a rocking chair, looking at magazines. Nearby, Mrs. Miller steps into a telephone booth made from a large box. She looks up a number in the telephone book (class telephone book with each child's name and telephone number). She says, "Ring. Ring. Is Melody home?" The child in the rocking chair says, "I'll get that," and answers a toy phone in the center. She says, "Melody is not here. Can I take a message?" She writes on a tablet near the phone and then says, "I'll give her the message. Bye-bye."

The Teacher at Work: Mrs. Miller's Role

These examples from Mrs. Miller's classroom clearly show that her students can make meanings with and understand the functions of many kinds of print. They are able to do so because she situates the print so as to maintain its original purpose and accepts her children's reading and writing even when it is unconventional. We saw her students making meanings consistent with the original functions of print when they read coupons to their dolls, used McDonald's wrappers and newspaper food advertising in restaurant play, and consulted a cookbook in their kitchen play.

Most of Mrs. Miller's children's reading and writing is not conventional. Two of the orders written as part of the McDonald's play are presented in Figure 7.2. The children said as they wrote, "Two McDLT's and a Coke" and "Three cheeseburgers and a chocolate shake." The telephone message for Melody that was taken in the home center is presented in Figure 7.3. These examples of children's reading and writing demonstrate that novice readers

Figure 7.2 *McDonald's Orders*

Figure 7.3 *Telephone Message*

and writers intend to communicate meaning even when their efforts are unconventional. Mrs. Miller accepts these efforts and treats them as meaningful reading and writing.

Mrs. Miller uses the writing of words from environmental print as an opportunity to focus on written language form. As part of their unit on foods, Mrs. Miller's class reads many menus and placemats. These are put in the writing center to stimulate children's writing. Mrs. Miller uses group time to compose environmental and functional print, such as the menu "Miller's Meals." As Mrs. Miller writes, she names letters and points out features of written language, such as specific letters, long or short words, or words that are repeated. She invites children to find letters they know.

Mrs. Miller frequently sits in the writing center so that she can call attention to written language features in the children's writing. In one activity, Mrs. Miller encouraged some children to dictate a "Trash Can Book." The children pasted environmental print items into books made from paper cut in the shape of trash cans. Serita made three pages in her book. She dictated, "I saved Rice Krispies from the trash. I saved Cabbage Patch from the trash. I saved potato chips from the trash." Mrs. Miller drew attention to the words *Rice Krispies, Cabbage Patch,* and *potato chips* written on the environmental print and in the words that she wrote in the book. She asked Serita to talk about how the words were alike and different in the two contexts. She invited Serita to find all the letters that were the same and name the letters she knew. Seeing familiar and meaningful words in more than one context helps children begin to move beyond context-dependent reading and writing (Hiebert, 1986). As children focus on form within the meaningful context of the environment, they begin to make connections between written forms (letters and words) and spoken forms (sounds and meaning).

We have seen that Mrs. Miller made and capitalized on opportunities to support preschoolers' literacy engagements. She planned specific activities and ways of interacting with children so that they would expand their knowledge about writing language forms and meaning-form links.

Effective teachers realize that children need support in moving from merely attending to the meaning of familiar print to attending to written language forms and how forms link with meanings. In the following sections, we describe how teachers can support preschoolers' taking their first steps toward acquiring phonological awareness, literary awareness, story concepts, and concepts about print.

PREPARING FOR PHONEMIC AWARENESS

Phonemic awareness, that is, conscious attention to individual sounds (phonemes) in words, is essential to learning to read and write (Adams, 1990; Share, 1995). Fully developed phonemic awareness, the sort of awareness that allows children to use the alphabetic principle in reading and writing, entails phoneme-by-phoneme segmentation of words. Most preschoolers do not achieve this level of awareness. However, preschoolers can develop other sorts of phonological awareness that are first steps toward this fully developed phonemic awareness; they can attend to sounds in words in other ways than by phoneme-by-phoneme analysis. Preschoolers can attend to chunks of sound in syllables and words and recognize and make rhyming words. Research (Goswami & Bryant, 1990; Treiman, 1985; Treiman & Zukowski, 1996) has shown that especially helpful chunks of sound in syllables are the onset and the rime. The **onset** is the sound or sounds before the vowel in a syllable; the **rime** is the rest of the syllable. For example, in *plan*, the onset is /pl/ and the rime is /ăn/. Some words or syllables (for example, the word *out*) have no onset because they begin with a vowel. In this section, we describe ways teachers can help preschoolers to take these first steps toward phonemic awareness.

The "I Can Hear" Activity

One of children's best sources of information about word and syllable parts is their teachers' causal talk about those parts. We do not advocate that preschool teachers deliver self-contained lessons about hearing onsets, rimes, and phonemes. We do suggest that preschool teachers frequently take opportunities to model phonological awareness by talking about sounds in words in a matter-of-fact, informal way. Teachers can say, "This is the Grinch. **I can hear** the /gr/ part in *grinch*—/gr/, /gr/—and I can hear the /ĭnch/ part—/ĭnch/, /ĭnch/." If this were among the first times a teacher made such a comment, this is all that needs saying or doing; the teacher can go on reading *How the Grinch Stole Christmas!* (Seuss, 1957). The teacher might also point to the word *Grinch* on the cover of the book. If it were a later instance of making such a comment, the teacher might also identify some or all of the letters that spell the /gr/ and /ĭnch/ parts of *Grinch*. In any case, these statements are just passing comments; the main activity is reading and enjoying a good storybook.

Storybooks, especially when shared as big books, readily provide a context for such "I can hear" teacher talk. **Word play books** are also particularly useful for this. These books are specially designed to highlight sounds in words. *Charlie Parker Played Be Bop* (Raschka, 1992), for example, is a picture book that contains a bit of a story line—about Charlie Parker's cat waiting for him to come home. But its power to captivate listeners is in its rhythm and rhyme, its made-up words, and its imaginative illustrations. Readers and listeners of any age can enjoy its use of the sounds and accents in the made-up words to recreate the feel of be bop music. Preschool teachers can also use it (after more than one reading just for fun) to heighten awareness of sounds in words. After reading the single line of text displayed across two facing pages, "Boppitty, bibbitty, **bop. BANG!**", a preschool teacher might say, "I can hear /b/ in those words!" and repeat all four words, emphasizing their initial *b* sound. Another page has four lines of text, each composed of a different multisyllable word repeated three times, followed by the first syllable of the word. Teachers can turn this into a syllable-segmentation game. Children suggest several multisyllable words, and they make a "Charlie Parker Be Bop" stanza out of them. *Elephant, tambourine, pencil, dinosaur* becomes

Elephant, elephant, elephant, el,

Tambourine, tambourine, tambourine, tam,

Pencil, pencil, pencil, pen,

Dinosaur, dinosaur, dinosaur, di!

The Appendix lists other word play books.

Case studies of the literacy learning of preschoolers have shown that children begin to learn the names of letters in meaningful environmental print words and in familiar persons' names (Baghban, 1984; Lass, 1982). This finding suggests that the familiar words in environmental print and the names of children in the classroom may be the most powerful resources for helping children learn about units of sound and the letters associated with them. Preschool teachers can find "I can hear" opportunities in special mentions of children's names, in calendar work, and in reading of special displayed texts, such as lists and poems written on chart paper.

Many preschool classrooms include multiple **displays of children's names,** for example, as part of group-forming, attendance-taking, helper-naming routines. We saw that Mrs. Miller's students used their names in print to keep track of turns at the painting easels, to construct a graph about television viewing, and to compose a class telephone book.

Teachers can make "I can hear" statements using these displays of children's names. If Miguel is chosen as helper for the day, the teacher can say, "I can hear Miguel's /mmmm/." Or she may say, "I can hear /mmmm/ at the beginning of *Miguel.*" In a later instance of Miguel's being helper, the teacher might ask, "What sound do you hear at the beginning of *Miguel?*" Still later, the teacher might withhold display of Miguel's name card until she gets a response to "The name of today's helper starts with /mmm/. Who could it be?"

Although with preschoolers, such talk is appropriately focused on sounds, they are also seeing the letters in the printed name. Eventually, "I can hear" comments and related questions can also be about sound–letter correspondences. Still, the purpose is exposure to, not mastery of, such correspondences. The teacher might say, "I can hear Miguel's *M*—/mmmm/" or "I can hear the *M* for /mmmm/ at the beginning of *Miguel*" or (withholding the name card) "I can hear /mmm/ at the beginning of *Miguel.* What letter do you think you will see at the beginning of his name?" Or the teacher might show and say, "Here's the /mmm/ part, and here's the '-iguel' part."

The teacher talk in these examples serves two important purposes. It demonstrates for children that words are composed of sounds, and it introduces children to talking *about* words. In their spoken language experiences, they use sounds in words. That is how they end up with different images, depending on whether a friend says, "My dad has a new van," or says, "My dad has a new fan." But they do this automatically, without consciously thinking about it. Later in their literacy development, when they learn to read the word *van,* they will need conscious awareness of its three phonemes, /v/, /ă/, and /n/ (this is called phonemic awareness), and conscious knowledge of the letters that stand for those phonemes (this is called phonics knowledge or knowledge of sound–letter correspondences). They will also need to be able to talk about and understand others' talk about words. They will need to know that *van* is a word, and that it has a beginning, a middle, and an end. This is called **metalinguistic awareness** (Chaney, 1994; Yaden & Templeton, 1986). "I can hear" talk, such as the comments described above, helps children to develop phonemic awareness and metalinguistic awareness.

Discussion of the **calendar** is a **routine** in many preschool classrooms. This presents another opportunity for teachers' informal, matter-of-fact "I can hear" talk. They might say, "I can hear /mmmm/ in *March.* That's just like the /mmmm/ I hear in *Monday* and in *Miguel.*" Often children notice the replication of the syllable *-day* in *Sunday, Monday, Tuesday, Wednesday, Thursday, Friday, Saturday,* and in the word *today.* Teachers can confirm this by pointing to the printed sentence, *Today is Monday,* and saying, "I can hear 'day' in *today,* and I can hear 'day' in *Monday.*" They can point to and say, "Here's the 'day' part in *today,* and here's the 'day' part in *Monday.*"

Part of the environmental print in most preschool classrooms is specially displayed texts, such as lists composed as a record of a discussion, or poems displayed at an easel for a shared reading. The primary purpose of these texts is to convey their message ("This is what we talked about," "This poem tells me that . . . "). A secondary purpose of such displays is to create opportunities for "I can hear" talk. A list of pets composed during a discussion that is part of a unit about animals, for example, might include names of children's pets (Ralph, Rusty, Joey, Flipper) and kinds of animals that are often pets (kitty, dog, goldfish, cat, puppy, gerbil). While writing and rereading such a list, the teacher can include "I can hear" talk. She might say, "I can hear /rrr/ in *Ralph* and *Rusty*" or "I can hear /g/ at the end of *dog*—/g/—and at the beginning of /g/—*goldfish*."

Poems, when they use rhyme, are excellent contexts for talk about rhyming words, onsets, and rimes. Figure 7.4 shows a poem written by one of the authors of this book to provide an enjoyable, wintertime experience with long *O* words. When copying the poem on chart paper for sharing with students at the easel, the teacher can use format and underlining to highlight the rhyming *-old* words. The teacher might say, as part of the shared reading, "I can hear rhymes: *cold, told, sold, hold.*" At a later rereading, she might say, "I can hear /ōld/ in *cold,* and I can hear /ōld/ in *told,*" and so on. Still later, she might say and show, "I can hear /s/ in *sold*. Here's the /s/ part. And I can hear /ōld/ in *sold*. Here's the /ōld/ part."

Making Rhymes

A next step, following teacher's "I can hear" talk about rhyming words, is to invite children to make rhymes, to involve them in **rhyming games.** From "I can hear rhymes," teachers can proceed to "Let's make rhymes." Teachers cannot expect most preschoolers to master making rhymes, which requires complex manipulation of sounds, but they can provide examples that make rhyming fun.

Many of the same contexts for "I can hear" are suitable for rhyming games. For example, children who discover the repeated *-day* in calendar words *today, Sunday, Monday, Tuesday, Wednesday, Thursday, Friday,* and *Saturday* are prepared to make rhymes from *day*. The teacher might say, "I can make a rhyme: *day*—*pay!*" She might add other *-ay* words or say, "I can hear /ā/ in *day,* and I can hear /ā/ in *pay*." She might even write the rhyming words and point to and say, "Here's the /ā/ part."

Figure 7.4 *"I Don't Like the Cold"*

I Don't Like the *Cold*

I *told* you I don't like the *cold*!

I'm not *sold* on *cold*—

I *told* you **so**!

Take this **snow** and **go**!

I *told* you **so**!

I'll *hold* out for sun and hot—
not *cold* and **snow**!

I *told* you **so**!

Rhyming games include inviting children to repeat rhymes the teacher has made and to make their own rhymes. However, because of the difficulty of making rhymes, preschool teachers can expect students to give responses that involve sound similarities but are not rhymes. Teachers' responses can be accepting, while distinguishing among "rhymes with," "sounds like," "sounds the same at the beginning," and "sounds the same at the end." If a student offers *dinosaur* as a rhyme for *day,* the teacher might respond, "*Dinosaur* and *day* sound the same at the beginning. *Pay* and *day* are rhymes. Can you say, 'Pay—day?' "

Professional literature for teachers includes many activities—even entire programs—to promote phonemic awareness. Preschool teachers can use many of these as long as they remember that the objective is not mastery, not fully developed phonemic awareness. Most children will not achieve that until kindergarten or first grade. Often, preschool teachers must adapt these activities, usually by abbreviating them, keeping in mind the sorts of understandings we ascribe to literacy novices (see Chapter 3).

Cunningham (1998), for example, describes an activity she calls **"Rounding Up the Rhymes."** This activity is meant as a follow-up to a reading of a book, story, or poem containing many rhymes. Cunningham emphasizes the importance of first reading the text, maybe even more than one time, for meaning and enjoyment. Then the book is somewhat familiar to the children, and they can be invited, with the reading of each page or two, to chime in and to try to "hear the rhymes they are saying" (p. 90). As the children identify rhyming words, the teacher writes them on index cards and displays them in a **pocket chart.** This is usually enough for one day's rereading of the text. Cunningham suggests limiting such activities to fifteen to twenty minutes and to no more than seven sets of rhyming words.

The next step of "Rounding Up the Rhymes" is another day's rereading of the text, with children again chiming in. This time, when they identify a set of rhyming words, they and the teacher find them in the **pocket chart.** Now Cunningham suggests further work involving analysis of spelling patterns, using knowledge of letter names, vowel letters, and onsets and rimes. This is beyond what most preschoolers can do. For preschoolers, "Rounding Up the Rhymes" must be abbreviated. Rather than doing spelling-pattern analysis, the teacher might use some of the same talk we suggested for the activities described above, such as pointing and saying, "Yes, here's the *mouse* and *house* words you heard. And here's the 'ouse' part in *mouse,* and here's the 'ouse' part in *house.* They both have 'ouse,' don't they?"

We wish to emphasize the importance of enjoyable, informal experiences in preschoolers' preparing for phonemic awareness, especially experiences with rhymes. We have described games and matter-of-fact, informal "I can hear" talk that is inserted in other activities, such as booksharing or calendar time. We suggest that among the best preparations for phonemic awareness that preschool teachers can provide is reading a lot of rhyming texts, including nursery rhymes, Dr. Seuss books, and other poems.

Rhyming activities with preschoolers require patience. Rhyming ability is a building block of phonemic awareness. One reason rhyming is difficult and complex is that it involves segmenting and substituting beginning phonemes. Word reading also involves **segmenting phonemes,** so that letters can be associated with them. Even if preschoolers only gain experience hearing rhymes, they are preparing for someday reading and writing words using sound–letter correspondences.

For some children, mastery of rhyming will come only *after* they know how to read and write, because the relationship works in both directions. Rhyming lays part of the foundation for reading and writing, but knowing how to read and write—being able to see letters and word parts and know what they stand for—consolidates rhyming ability.

PREPARING FOR LITERARY AWARENESS, STORY CONCEPTS, AND CONCEPTS OF PRINT

Phonemic awareness is a very important contributor to success in reading and writing. It is, however, by no means the only such contributor. In this section, we describe ways preschool teachers can lay other foundations for literacy, including literary awareness, story concepts, and concepts of print.

Literary Awareness

Literary awareness is at the other end of the spectrum of literacy prerequisites from phonemic awareness. Phonemic awareness is conscious attention to the very smallest units of language, the sound units with which words are built. Literary awareness operates at the level of whole texts. It involves conscious attention to some of the biggest contributors to effective communication with written language, such as character and plot development in a well-crafted story. As with phonemic awareness, fully developed literary awareness is beyond most preschoolers, but skillful teachers will help preschoolers to take the first steps toward such awareness, mostly through well-planned gesturing and commenting during booksharing. Teachers can ask questions and make comments that help children identify settings, characters, and characters' motivations. They can help children predict events and think about causes and effects during booksharing.

Teachers can use gestures to help children understand stories. They can point to characters and objects in illustrations as they talk about them or read related text. Teachers can use their voices to help children understand stories. They can look at the children frequently and use facial expressions to heighten interest in stories. Table 7.1 summarizes these booksharing techniques, which are an extension of techniques presented in Chapter 2. Teachers can fine-tune their **booksharing techniques** by tape-recording and analyzing a booksharing event with their children. They can use the suggestions presented in this chapter and in Table 7.1 as a guide for self-reflection about booksharing.

Effective teachers adapt their booksharing techniques to meet the needs of their children. Some young novice readers and writers have had few booksharing experiences. For these children, teachers spend more time telling the story and talking about the illustrations than reading the story text. Other novices have had extensive booksharing experiences; therefore, their teachers spend more time reading and commenting on the story's text. Although all teachers want to take time to comment on and discuss the language of stories, they do not need to simplify text language as they read books to children. Fox (1985) found that even three-year-olds tolerate uncertainty about the meaning of unfamiliar words in stories they particularly enjoy. As they learn the meanings of words through repeated booksharing opportunities, children begin to use the language of stories as they retell the stories, tell original stories, and later, write stories (Fox, 1985; McConaghy, 1985).

Table 7.1 Guidelines for Booksharing

The Teacher:

Interweaves text reading with asking questions and making comments.

Asks children questions about characters and objects in pictures.

Asks children to predict.

Asks questions that help children identify with characters and actions in the story ("What would YOU do . . . ").

Makes comments about characters and actions in pictures and story.

Explains text words and concepts.

Makes comments about relations between the story and real life.

Predicts actions and outcomes.

Makes statements about personal reactions to the story.

Uses gestures.

Points to objects and characters in pictures.

Varies voice to indicate character dialogue.

Answers children's questions.

Acknowledges children's comments by commenting or further questioning.

Extends children's questions and comments by providing additional information.

Story Concepts

We saw in Chapter 3 that even novices begin to understand how stories work. Preschool teachers can support their students' developing more complete and more sophisticated concepts of story. They can plan special **concept-about-story activities** (Tompkins, 1998; McGee & Tompkins, 1981). These activities are designed to help children learn five important concepts about stories, such as that all characters in stories have problems and do many things to try to solve their problems. (These concepts are presented in Figure 7.5.) Activities to help children learn about story problems include having them retell stories using props or having them predict different ways in which a character might solve a problem. Figure 7.5 also lists concept-about-story activities, including dramatizing, retelling, drawing, and painting.

Concepts of Print

Another kind of awareness that is crucial to learning to read and write is awareness of how texts work, for example, that they have lines of print that are read from left to right, top to bottom, and that books are read from front to back. These understandings are called **concepts of print.** Novice readers and writers begin to acquire concepts of print when they notice particular letters (e.g., the first letter of names) and details or style of illustrations (Kiefer, 1988). They refine their concepts of words, letters, and story texts through increased experience with books. One of the easiest ways preschool teachers can demonstrate concepts of print is to read from big books (Holdaway, 1979).

Figure 7.5 *Activities for Developing Concepts about Stories*

STORY CONCEPT	EXAMPLE ACTIVITIES
1. Characters are the animals and people in the story.	a. Have children draw, paint, or make characters in clay. b. Make a three-page book by having children draw and dictate what a character looks like, does, and says. c. Make a book of "Story Characters I Know." Have children draw and dictate characters' names.
2. Stories take place in different places, times, and types of weather, called settings (Lukens, 1986).	a. Have children identify different places characters go in the story. b. Have children identify changes in weather in the story. c. Have children decide whether settings are real or make-believe. d. Make a list of "Story Places I Have Visited."
3. Characters in stories have problems; they do many things to try to solve their problems.	a. Compose a "Problem Book" by listing the problems of story characters and children's characters. b. Act out the story using story props. c. Have children suggest other methods of solving the character's problem. d. Use a story line to retell the story. e. Use a flannel board to tell the story. f. Play a guessing game in which the teacher describes a problem and children guess the name of the character.
4. Some events in stories happen over and over and some words in stories are said again and again (Tompkins & McGee, 1989).	a. Use story line to retell the story, emphasizing repeating words. b. Act out story, emphasizing repeating events and words. c. Make a list of repeated events. d. Make a big book of the story. e. Compose a story using the structure but adding new content (Tompkins & McGee, 1989).

(continued)

Big books are enlarged copies—approximately twenty inches by thirty inches—of literature selections. Many publishing companies now sell big book versions of some of their popular books. Both the illustrations and the print are large. As they read aloud to children, teachers can naturally draw attention to the print and demonstrate concepts about print as they underline text (Combs, 1987; Fayden, 1997; Heald-Taylor, 1987). Because a group of children can easily see the printed text, they can talk about letters and words. As they

Figure 7.5 *(continued)*

STORY CONCEPT	EXAMPLE ACTIVITIES
5. Stories have a beginning that tells about characters, a middle that tells what characters do to solve problems, and an ending that tells the problem's solution (Tompkins, 1998)	a. Make a four-page booklet with one page each for title, beginning, middle, and end; children should draw pictures and dictate the story. b. Make a "The End" book. Children can dictate endings to favorite stories. c. Use three shoe boxes to make a story train as shown here. Make pictures of the events in the beginning, middle, and end of the story. Have children put pictures in the train and tell about the story.

Adapted from McGee, L. M., & Tompkins, G. E. (1981). The videotape answer to independent reading comprehension activities. *The Reading Teacher, 34,* 430–431. Reprinted with permission of the International Reading Association.

hear the text and see the text, children also notice the link between the text and what teachers read.

Written language is complex. Knowledge of meaning making, written language forms, meaning-form links, and written language functions involves many kinds of awareness at many levels of writing, from how sounds work within words to how lines of text and pages of books work in storybooks, from how letters correspond with sounds to how characters and events interact in narrative plots. When preschool teachers make opportunities for effective teacher talk, their students can take important first steps toward phonemic awareness, literary awareness, story concepts, and concepts of print. In the sections that follow, we show how preschool teachers and students do this in their book reading, their writing, and their play.

PRESCHOOL EXPERIENCES WITH BOOK READING

In this section, we discuss opportunities for children's literacy learning that are centered on group reading activities. We begin by describing how Miss Leslie reads books aloud to her three- and four-year-olds and encourages them to participate in response-to-literature activities. A guiding principle of sharing books with children in preschool is that effective booksharing encourages interactions between the reader and his or her listeners, including listeners' individual responses to what is read. This case study illustrates the importance of going beyond merely reading aloud to children.

Shared Reading in Miss Leslie's Classroom

Miss Leslie teaches in a private preschool with an emphasis on academic learning. She is careful to meet those expectations while maintaining a child-centered approach. One way in which she balances these two needs is through **interactive read alouds** (see Chapter 6). The interaction comes from children's being expected to answer questions, make comments, and predict outcomes. Miss Leslie plans questions that help children use analytic talk and call for high levels of cognition. She also plans response-to-literature activities to extend the read aloud experience.

Miss Leslie and six three-year-olds are gathered for storytime on the rug in their classroom. The children are sitting in a square area bordered by tape on the rug. As she announces storytime, Miss Leslie points to a sign entitled "Storytime" that has a picture of a mother reading to two children. On the sign are clothespinned cards with the names of the children who are to come to storytime: Cory, Echo, Leah, Paul, Laura, and Evan. Miss Leslie points to the name on the chart as she calls each child and reminds the child to come to the rug for storytime. As the children approach the rug, she begins to sing one of the children's favorite songs, "Twinkle, Twinkle Little Star."

After she and the children are settled on the rug, Miss Leslie holds up the book *The Little Rabbit Who Wanted Red Wings* (Bailey, 1987). She reads the title, pointing to each word. She reminds the children that she has read this book to them before. The book is about a little rabbit who is not happy with himself and wishes he had what other animals have. The children ask questions and make comments during the booksharing. Miss Leslie reads the text, talks about the illustrations, and asks questions. Figure 7.6 presents a segment of their interactive read aloud.

Figure 7.6 *Miss Leslie and Three-Year-Olds Share* The Little Rabbit Who Wanted Red Wings *(Bailey, 1987)*

Text is presented in all capital letters. Brackets indicate portions of the dialogue that occurred simultaneously.

The illustration depicts a porcupine who is wearing glasses standing under a tree. Little Rabbit is sitting in a large hole in the tree looking at the porcupine.

Miss L: Now who does Little Rabbit see? (points to porcupine)

[Child 1: um um its . . .

Child 2: Mr. Beaver.

Child 3: Mr. Porcupine.]

[Miss L: It does look a little like a beaver. This is Mr. Porcupine.

Child 2: (reaches up and touches the picture of the porcupine) Ouch.]

Miss L: Ooh, I wouldn't want to touch that.

(continued)

Figure 7.6 *(continued)*

Child 1: Me either.

Child 4: Oh, oh.

Miss L: His bristles would stick me. They would stick like a needle.

Child 3: Not me.

Child 2: He sticks you? If you touch him like this? (puts her finger on the picture of the porcupine and pulls it off as if she were stuck)

Miss L: Yes, he might. Those bristles are special. Now I wonder what Little Rabbit likes about Mr. Porcupine?

Child 5: Glasses. (porcupine has on glasses)

Child 1: Needles.

Child 2: I wouldn't want to touch Porcupine.

Miss L: I wouldn't want to touch him either. But what about Little Rabbit? What do you think *he* thinks about those bristles? What do you think Little Rabbit likes?

Child 3: um, um.

Child 4: Glasses.

Child 1: Needles.

Miss L: Do you think *he* wants those bristles? or maybe those glasses? (Laughs, and smiles at Child 1)

Child 1: Yeah.

Miss L: What would *you* like to have like Mr. Porcupine?

Child 2: I want glasses.

Child 5: Bristles.

Child 1: I want needles.

Miss L: Let's see. (looks at book) WHEN MR. PORCUPINE PASSED BY, THE LITTLE RABBIT WOULD SAY TO HIS MOMMY (looks at children as if inviting them to join in), "MOMMY, I WISH I HAD (looks back at print) A BACK FULL OF BRISTLES LIKE MR. PORCUPINE'S."

Child 1: Mommy, I want those needles.

Child 5: I wish I had those bristles.

Child 4: I want some bristles.

Child 2: Mommy, . . .

Then Miss Leslie takes a paper bag from beneath her chair. She tells the children that it contains pictures of each of the animals Little Rabbit met in the story. She asks the children to guess what they are. As the children guess, she pulls out a construction-paper picture of the animal and asks, "What did Little Rabbit like about this animal?" She clothespins each animal picture to a clothesline hung a few feet off the floor behind her chair. She tells the children they might want to use the **clothesline props** to retell the story to a friend during center time. She also suggests that they might want to draw pictures and write about the animals or Little Rabbit in the writing center. She shows the children paper cut in the shape of a rabbit's head and tells them that the rabbit-shaped paper will be in the writing center for them to use during center time. All the children are then free to select center activities.

Some children go to the block center. One goes to the home center to join three four-year-olds who have been playing there during storytime. The other three children sit down with the animal props on the clothesline. They take the construction-paper animals and clip each one on the line. As they do this, they talk about the story.

Miss Leslie goes to the writing center and announces that she is going to write. Echo and Cory join her, along with three of the four-year-olds who were not participants in storytime. She says, "I think I'll draw a picture about Little Rabbit. I want to draw his red wings." The children comment on what they might draw, "I'm going to do Mrs. Puddleduck" and "I like trucks." As the children draw and talk, Miss Leslie comments that she is going to write. "I think I'll write that Little Rabbit didn't like the red wings." Cory says, "I'm gonna write, too. I'll write about her feet." Echo says, "I don't want to write." Miss Leslie and the children continue to talk about their pictures and writing. Then Miss Leslie invites the children to read their stories and talk about their pictures.

Miss Leslie's Roles in an Interactive Read Aloud

This example from Miss Leslie's preschool classroom shows that her children were active participants in the construction of the meaning of the story *The Little Rabbit Who Wanted Red Wings.* One of Miss Leslie's goals for booksharing is to enhance children's meaning-making strategies, and she uses several techniques for creating such meaning-making opportunities. The first is her skillful interaction with children during reading aloud.

Miss Leslie encourages booksharing interactions. She uses a variety of booksharing techniques to help her children understand the story and to encourage their interactions. She encourages children to identify characters (she asks, "Now who does Little Rabbit see?" while pointing to the porcupine in the illustration) and to make predictions ("Now I wonder what Little Rabbit likes about Mr. Porcupine?"). She also encourages children to participate by accepting and extending their comments and questions (when Leah touched the picture of the porcupine and said "Ouch," Miss Leslie commented, "Ooh, I wouldn't want to touch that. His bristles would stick me. They would stick like a needle."). She uses questions that are intended to help children identify with story characters ("What would you like to have like Mr. Porcupine?"). She provides information that will help children understand words used in the story. (Miss Leslie commented that the porcupine's bristles "would stick like a *needle*" to clarify the meaning of the word *bristles* used in the story text.) She also recognizes all of the children's responses—even when they deviate from the story text. Miss Leslie acknowledged the prediction that Little Rabbit wanted Mr. Porcupine's glasses even though that was not a part of the story.

Miss Leslie adjusts to the needs of children. Another reason that her three-year-old listeners were such able meaning makers is that she knows that the best group-reading opportunities for preschoolers are often activities for well-chosen small groups rather than large groups. She has found that the six children she calls together comment more about stories when they are in smaller groups. She included two children in this group whose oral language was more mature than that of the other children. Miss Leslie believes that children learn much from interacting with other children whose abilities are slightly more mature than their own.

In addition to planning activities that she believes fit the needs of children, Miss Leslie also allows the children in her preschool class freedom of choice. She knows that children have individual preferences for and responses to books and activities. She knows which books her children enjoy, and she reads them frequently. When she discovers that she has selected a book that is uninteresting to the children (they wiggle right off the rug), she does not insist that they sit still and listen. Rather, she substitutes an old favorite and tries another book the following day. Children are allowed free choice of center activities. Note that this freedom means that a small-group reading activity can lead quite naturally to individual writing activities. Miss Leslie entices children to join in activities that they may be reluctant to select on their own. She encourages some children to write by going to the writing center herself and offering an open invitation to the children to join her there. She welcomes children who were not in the story-sharing group to the writing center.

Miss Leslie plans response-to-literature activities that extend children's opportunities for meaning making. For example, she encouraged children to use her clothesline props to retell the story during center time, and she provided special rabbit-shaped paper in the writing center to encourage children to write their own stories. Another response-to-literature activity involves special literature props in boxes to stimulate children's dramatic response to literature through play. These **literary prop boxes** include props designed to encourage children's becoming characters from favorite stories. In the *Little Rabbit Who Wanted Red Wings* literary prop box, Miss Leslie gathered several pairs of rabbit ears (made from headbands and construction paper), acorns, glasses, several pairs of rubber boots, a mirror, a pair of red wings (made from construction paper attached to an old vest), several head scarves, a toothbrush, a bowl and spoon, and two fur vests. She placed an extra copy of the book in the prop box along with the other props. Children are encouraged to use the props to act out the story or create their own stories.

PRESCHOOL EXPERIENCES WITH WRITING

In this section we describe preschool writing opportunities and what novice readers and writers can learn from them. A guiding principle of using writing to support literacy learning in the preschool classroom is to use it in a variety of ways. Thus, teachers plan for a variety of kinds of writing and allow children choices about their writing, such as what to write about or even whether to write at all.

Some writing activities are more controlled by the teacher and others are controlled by the child. In group activities, the teacher writes for children as he or she records what several children say as a part of a **shared writing activity.** In shared writing, teachers have more control over writing. Children have a chance to contribute to the composition, but the topic and purpose of the writing activity are usually decided by the teacher. Some activities involve the teacher's recording what a single child says, such as when the teacher records a message about a picture that the child has drawn. Children in these activities have more control over writing, especially when they decide the topic and purpose of their drawing and writing.

Some activities involve children's writing. When children visit the writing center to write a note to a classmate, they initiate the writing and they choose the topic. Other activities originate in children's play. As children play house, they may decide to write a phone message. Children have most control over writing when they write for purposes of their own and on topics of their choice. It is important for children to have writing experiences over which they are more in control so that they can try out their written language knowledge.

The children in Miss Leslie's and Mrs. Miller's classrooms write as a part of many classroom activities, including writing to take orders at a McDonald's center and writing telephone messages. They write graphs in the math center and make menus as part of a food unit. They also write in the writing center, composing "Trash Can Books" and stories about "Little Bunny." We describe three preschool writing opportunities from Miss Leslie's and Mrs. Miller's classrooms: the writing center, sign-in procedure, and shared writing. In addition, we describe story writing by a preschooler in the classroom of another teacher, Ms. Reyes.

The Preschool Writing Center

Miss Leslie and Mrs. Miller created many literacy opportunities in their writing centers. They correlated many of their group activities with extending activities in the writing centers. For example, Miss Leslie put special-shaped paper in the writing center that correlated with a story she had read aloud, and Mrs. Miller wrote a menu in a group meeting and then encouraged children to write their own menus later in the writing center. Teachers plan many activities for writing centers.

Making greeting cards is always a favorite writing activity; holidays present numerous opportunities for children to write cards (Beardsley & Mareck-Zeman, 1987). Literature is another important stimulus for writing; teachers can record children's retellings of stories. Children enjoy writing on paper cut into shapes suggested by characters or themes of literature. Another favorite writing activity is for children to compose their own print items, such as menus, grocery lists, catalogs, and *TV Guides*.

Mrs. Miller knows the importance of interacting with children during writing center activities. She introduces new writing center activities during group time and follows a routine as she interacts with the children in the center. In December, Mrs. Miller plans several activities related to writing letters to Santa. First, she plans a whole-group activity in which she writes a letter to Santa, using suggestions from the children. She places stationery cut from green construction paper and envelopes in the writing center. She also displays words such as *Santa, Dear,* and *Love.* Then she places a "Santa Letter" sign-up sheet in the writing center; this is a piece of paper with "I will write to Santa today" written at the top and space for four children to sign at the bottom. The children know to sign up as they enter the classroom in the morning if they want to have Mrs. Miller record their letters to Santa. We believe that preschoolers should not be required to go to the writing center to complete a particular project. Rather, they should be invited, encouraged, and enticed to go to writing centers and other writing activities.

Teachers who know what motivates and interests young children in their classrooms can create opportunities that will entice many seemingly reluctant readers and writers to participate in activities that lead to reading and writing. Such children may visit a writing center to use the typewriter or letter stamps or to engage in fingerpainting or pudding-writing activities. They may be willing to tell an adult or teacher about a picture that they have drawn, especially if that person is genuinely interested in the drawing. However, teachers must always be able to accept "no" and wait for children to be ready. We saw writing opportunities like these in Mrs. Miller's and Miss Leslie's classrooms.

The Sign-In Procedure

Novice readers and writers who realize that written marks can communicate messages are ready for the **sign-in procedure.** In this procedure, each child writes his or her name each day on an attendance sign-in sheet (Harste, Burke, & Woodward, 1981). This procedure is functional; it should actually serve as the attendance record of the classroom. With young three-year-olds, the procedure may consist of having children place a card with their name on it in a box or on a chart. Later, they may place their name card and a slip of paper (the same size as the name card) on which they have written their names in the attendance box. Eventually, children will sign in by writing their signatures on an attendance sheet. Naturally, three- and four-year-olds' signatures will not be conventional when they first begin the sign-in procedure (recall Robert's early signatures presented in Figure 3.7 in Chapter 3). However, by signing in daily, children gradually refine their signatures into readable names.

Mrs. Miller uses the sign-in procedure for two reasons. First, many of the children who come to her classroom have had few writing experiences prior to beginning preschool. Many children do not have crayons and paper in their homes. Before she began the sign-in procedure, few children voluntarily visited the writing center. The sign-in procedure gave the children an opportunity to write each day. As they became comfortable with that very brief writing experience, they gained confidence and began visiting the writing center for more lengthy writing experiences. The children also observed that their writing was useful; Mrs. Miller used the sign-in list to comment on children's absences.

Shared Writing

Having children draw or write in response to literature is another way to help them share their thoughts about what they read. Writing (or telling) **pattern stories** is an excellent response activity that connects reading and writing. These are sometimes called **story extensions.** Pattern stories are stories composed by children using the repetitive pattern found in pattern books as a guide. For example, *A Dark Dark Tale* (Brown, 1981) tells the story of entering a scary house, going slowly up the stairs, and looking inside a shadowy cupboard only to find a mouse. It includes the repetitive pattern, "In the dark, dark ______ , there was a dark, dark ______ ." (See the Appendix for a list of other pattern books.)

A group of four-year-olds retold the story using their school as the setting:

> Once there was a dark, dark school.
> In the dark, dark school there was a dark, dark hall.
> Down the dark, dark hall was a dark, dark classroom.
> In the dark, dark classroom there was a dark, dark cubbie.
> In the dark, dark cubbie there was a SPIDER!

Children can dictate their pattern stories for teachers to write on chart paper or as teacher-made big books.

Mrs. Miller and her children used a pattern to create their "Trash Can Books." They used the pattern "I saved the ________ from the trash can." Patterns for writing can be integrated into any unit or theme. Mrs. Miller's children used the pattern "I hate ________ , but ________ is my favorite food," as another part of their unit on foods.

It is important to keep in mind that the purpose of using **pattern writing** is to help children become more fluent and creative, rather than to make them conform to an expected pattern (Wason-Ellam, 1988). Often the most creative contribution to a pattern-writing activity is a response that breaks the pattern.

List writing is another form of shared writing, using group dictation with small children. **List making** is effective with young children because each child can contribute several times. Lists can be made quickly, since it only takes a few seconds to write a word in the list. Miss Leslie and Mrs. Miller regularly write lists with their children as part of book-sharing and environmental print reading. Miss Leslie wrote several lists with her children related to the book *The Little Rabbit Who Wanted Red Wings.* The children dictated a list of animals included in the book, a list of animal features they would like to have, and a list of wishes. Figure 7.7 presents several books and examples of lists that can be written before or after their sharing.

Sometimes young children have difficulty knowing what to say when they are asked to add to a list. Some children may show their confusion by repeating what someone else dictated. We suggest that teachers write what each child contributes even when he or she repeats someone else's responses. Repeated responses provide children with opportunities for paying attention to written language forms. As the teacher and children read and reread their list, they will discover that some words are repeated and that the repeated words look the same.

Story Writing

One of the authors of this book was a frequent visitor to Ms. Reyes's preschool classroom. At one visit, he thanked four-year-old Caitie for reading a book to him during his previous

Figure 7.7 *Making Lists with Literature*

LITERATURE SELECTION	SUGGESTIONS FOR LISTS
Brown, M. (1947). *Goodnight moon.* Harper and Row.	**1.** Things in the green room **2.** Things in my room **3.** Before I go to bed, I
Carle, E. (1974). *The very hungry caterpillar.* New York: Philomel.	**1.** Things the caterpillar ate **2.** I was so hungry I ate
Goss, J., & Harste, J. (1981). *It didn't frighten me.* School Book Fairs.	**1.** Outside my window was **2.** I'm not afraid of **3.** Fantastic Creatures
Pienkowski, J. (1980). *Dinnertime.* Los Angeles: Price/Stern/Sloan.	**1.** Animals having dinner **2.** Things for dinner
Viorst, J. (1977). *Alexander and the terrible, horrible, no good, very bad day.* New York: Atheneum.	**1.** Alexander's bad things **2.** Our bad things **3.** Wonderful, marvelous, good things

visit and asked her if she would like to write a story this time. Caitie begins by reminding him that she does not know how to read.

Caitie: I don't know how to read.

Mr. Richgels: Well, you know how to do your own kind of reading, though—

Caitie: Yeah.

Mr. Richgels: —because you did that with me the last time I was here.

Caitie: Yeah. . . .

Mr. Richgels: Even if it's your own way that's okay . . . I know that you don't write the same way that grownups do but that's okay.

With this assurance, Caitie remembers a well-known story that she can use as a prompt for her writing. One of Caitie's favorite books is a read-along book and tape, Walt Disney Productions' *The Story of Robin Hood* (Disney Productions, 1973). Her parents reported that Caitie had listened to the audiotape and followed along in the twenty-four-page picture book many times at home. Caitie begins writing her Robin Hood story by taking up a crayon and drawing the main characters, Maid Marian and Robin Hood, the two large figures with raised arms at the center and left of center in Figure 7.8. She explains as she writes, "That's Maid Marian. . . . I'm going to draw Robin Hood much taller than Maid Marian. . . . Tail, arms."

Like all the characters in Caitie's Disney book, Robin Hood and Maid Marian are animal cartoon characters. They have tails because they are foxes, and Caitie is attentive to this detail as she writes/draws.

As she draws the figure with a big head and small arms to the right of Robin Hood, Caitie explains, "Little John's a bear." Then Caitie draws the spiral-like shape and the figure

Figure 7.8 *Caitie's Robin Hood Story*

next to it at the top of Figure 7.8 and explains, "Here's Skippy's coin. The Sheriff of Nottingham took it. . . . Now I have to draw Robin Hood . . . his bow and arrow."

At one point, Caitie's talk changes from describing her drawing to speaking in character. She says in a deep voice, imitating Robin Hood, "Here, Skippy—take my bow and arrow, and here's my hat. It's a little big, Skippy, but you'll grow into it."

Again, Caitie is faithful to the version of the story of Robin Hood in her favorite book. In that version, Skippy, a little rabbit friend of Robin Hood's, is the victim of the sheriff's men. They take his birthday-present penny; Robin compensates by giving Skippy his bow and arrow and hat. Robin's words on page seven are exactly as Caitie told them, except that she added the second *Skippy,* after "It's a little big."

When she finishes drawing parts of her story, Caitie begins writing the letterlike forms at the bottom of Figure 7.8. These begin under the large figure of Robin Hood and continue to the left edge of the page. She is finished with her story, but not with her writing.

So far, Caitie has used crayon, but now she picks up a pencil and announces a new project. She says, "I'm going to write my name." She writes the recognizable letters above Skippy's coin, now writing from left to right. She wrote the *C* while she was saying, "I'm going to write my name." Now she says other letter names from *Caitie* as if spelling her name, "A-I-T-I-T." But she is not finished with this different kind of writing. She says, "Now I'm going to draw my phone number." She writes her phone number with the recognizable numerals at the right-hand edge of her paper, naming each as she writes it. The last four numbers are 3100; she says, "Three, one, zero, zero. One zero, two zero."

Whether because she realizes she has left out a digit or for some other reason, Caitie decides to write her phone number again, lower and to the left of her first effort. She says, "I need to draw a little better." Now she writes all seven digits of her phone number, the first three left to right and the last four under them, right to left, again naming each as she writes it.

The Teacher's Role in Writing Activities: Using Written Language Talk

Children learn much about written language from the kinds of comments that teachers make. Sometimes these are comments of encouragement, as when Mr. Richgels told Caitie, "Even if it's your own way, that's okay." Other times, they are comments about literacy processes. For example, we have already described teachers' "I can hear" comments that prepare preschoolers for phonemic awareness. Effective teachers use **written language talk** to support students' learning about all aspects of written language: meaning making, forms, meaning-form links, and functions. Their careful observation of children in literacy events guides their decisions about what kinds of written language talk might be most useful.

As Mrs. Miller wrote her letter to Santa with her children, her written language talk helped them learn about written language forms. She told the children she would begin her letter by writing "Dear Santa Claus." At the end of her letter, she wrote, "Love, Mrs. Miller." She explained that letters always begin with the word *Dear* and often end with the word *Love.* From this written language talk, the children learned about the text form of a letter.

As Mrs. Miller wrote her Santa letter, her written language talk helped the children learn about meanings. She explained that the letter would start with a sentence about her good behavior in the last year. She reminded the children that Santa would want to know that in order to bring what she wanted for Christmas. Through her talk about meaning, the children learned about the kinds of language found in letters. They also learned the kinds of information appropriate to include in a letter to Santa.

As Mrs. Miller wrote, her written language talk helped the children learn about meaning-form links. She said each word as she wrote it. As she read her letter, she underlined the text with her hands. The children had many opportunities to connect what they heard Mrs. Miller read with the print she was highlighting. Mrs. Miller's talk about letters provided children with information for discovering sound–letter relationships. Some of the children in her class had begun making some of these discoveries. When Mrs. Miller was writing that she wanted a new sewing machine, Serita commented, "I know what letter sewing has, an *S*." Mrs. Miller knew that Serita only made these sound–letter comments about *S* words. Still, Serita was beginning to display some sound–letter relationship awareness. We will talk more about this knowledge in Chapters 8 and 9.

As Mrs. Miller talked about taking the letter to the post office and mailing it, her written language talk helped the children learn about function. She reminded the children that Santa could keep her letter to remember what she wanted for Christmas. She commented that it was a good thing that Santa would have her letter because he would be getting many, many requests for gifts. She did not want him to forget what she wanted.

Children use written language talk as they watch their teacher write and as they write. Mrs. Miller encourages children to use this kind of talk and always takes time to respond to a child who makes a written language comment. She knows that children's comments provide information about written language that all the children can use to learn about reading and writing.

PRESCHOOL EXPERIENCES WITH PLAY

Play is the most important learning activity in the preschool classroom, and we have already shown many instances of children's reading and writing in their play. We described play with print in Mrs. Miller's McDonald's center and dramatic-play responses to literature facilitated by Miss Leslie's literary prop boxes. A guiding principle of play as a literacy-learning opportunity is that it must remain the child's endeavor. We have emphasized that teachers must play an active, involved role in providing literacy support in preschool classrooms. Their role in children's play, however, must also be subtle (Neuman & Roskos, 1997). Teachers can facilitate play; they can influence it; they can even enter children's play; but they must never intrude on it. The difference between the last two items is that entering is on the children's terms, intruding is breaking the spell that children have cast with their play. In this section, we describe two active, but nonintrusive, ways in which preschool teachers can ensure that literacy-learning opportunities are part of the play in their classrooms. They are Mrs. Miller's dramatic-play-with-print centers (e.g., Neuman & Roskos, 1990) and story telling and playing (e.g., Paley, 1990).

Dramatic-Play-with-Print Centers

We have described a well-appointed preschool classroom as filled with print. This description extends to the play centers, where posters, labels, and notebooks take their places with blocks, toy trucks, dress-up clothing, and plastic food. Teachers can plan **dramatic-play-**

with-print centers around themes and activities that are familiar to children and that have the potential for pretend reading and writing (Neuman & Roskos, 1997). For example, children are familiar with having their hair cut. From their experience visiting hair salons or barbershops, children are likely to have seen customers reading magazines in the waiting area and stylists writing bills and appointments. Therefore, teachers can easily capitalize on children's knowledge by setting up a hair salon–barbershop dramatic-play center enriched with literacy materials such as magazines, pads of paper, small cards, and a large appointment book. To arrange dramatic-play centers enriched with print, teachers

- Select play themes that are familiar to children and have literacy potential.
- Separate the center from the classroom with movable furniture, such as bookcases, screens, or tables.
- Label the center with a sign posted prominently at children's eye level.
- Select dramatic-play props related to play themes, for example, empty food boxes, a toy cash register, plastic bags for a grocery story or plastic food, trays, and wrapping paper for a fast-food restaurant.
- Select literacy props related to play themes, for example, coupons and pads of paper for the grocery store and an appointment book, appointment cards, patient's chart, and prescription slips for the doctor's office.
- Arrange the materials within the space to suggest a realistic setting related to the play theme (Newman & Roskos, 1990).

Teachers sometimes play with children in dramatic-play centers and model new and more complex ways in which reading and writing can be used (Morrow & Rand, 1991). For example, a teacher in a hair-salon play center may comment, "I'll write you a card so that you can remember your next appointment," as she writes a child's name and date on a small card.

Teachers can make a variety of dramatic-play-with-print centers (Roskos, 1988; Schickedanz, 1986). Figure 7.9 describes dramatic-play-and-print props that can be used to create three such centers. If classrooms are not large enough to permit a dramatic-play-with-print center, teachers can place the props in boxes. Children can take the boxes and set up their play in any open space in a classroom.

Mrs. Miller carefully prepares her children for these centers. On the day that she introduces a center, she uses whole-group time to orient the children to the center. They discuss what happens, for example, at McDonald's. She shows the children the dramatic-play-and-print props, and they discuss how the props might be used. Mrs. Miller and two or three children role-play with the center props. Several children have opportunities to play with Mrs. Miller. Later, while the children play in the center during center time, Mrs. Miller occasionally joins in. She realizes that children will think of many ingenious ways to use props in their dramatic play and that they should have plenty of opportunities to create their own unique imaginary worlds. However, she also knows that she can help expand the children's language and increase the complexity of their play by playing along with them (Neuman & Roskos, 1993).

Dramatic-play-with-print centers bring literacy into play activities. **Text and toy sets** bring play into the reading center (Rowe, 1998). Teachers display realistic, small-scale toys

Figure 7.9 *Dramatic-Play-with-Print Centers*

	DRAMATIC PROPS	PRINT PROPS
Shopping Mall Center	1. standing racks for drying clothes 2. hangers and play clothes (hang on racks) 3. cash registers 4. hats, purses, wallets 5. play baby strollers 6. dolls	1. checkbooks and play money 2. signs, such as names of departments, sale signs 3. sales slips 4. pads to write shopping lists 5. tags to make price tags 6. paper bags with store logos 7. credit cards 8. credit application forms
Drugstore Center	1. boxes for counters 2. cash register 3. empty bottles, boxes of various sizes for medicine 4. play shopping carts	1. magazines and books 2. play money 3. checkbooks 4. prescriptions 5. paper bags for prescriptions 6. labels for prescription bottles
Beauty and Barber Shop Center	1. chairs 2. towels 3. play barber kit with scissors, combs 4. telephone 5. hair clips, curlers 6. empty bottles of cologne	1. appointment book 2. checkbooks and play money 3. magazines for waiting area 4. bills

and other props in the book center along with related books. Children help with finding related toys and props, and they talk about connections between their play with these items and the stories or information books with which they are displayed. Children reenact scenes from the books.

Storytelling and Playing

In several compelling narratives about her years as a preschool teacher, Vivian Paley (1981, 1984, 1986, 1988, 1990, 1995) describes a method for combining storytelling and play. In the **storytelling and playing activity,** she plays the role of scribe. She writes the stories that children dictate, and then the children perform these stories as informal drama. As children tell their stories, other children are the audience; they are free to make comments or ask questions. These interactions influence children's storytelling, and Paley accepts revisions to stories as they occur. "In storytelling, as in play, the social interactions we call interruptions usually improve the narrative" (1990, p. 23).

Paley invites children to dictate their stories as they arrive for their school day. She sits where she is accessible to all the children. As children tell their stories, Paley repeats each dictated sentence as she writes it down. She wants the storyteller to be able to correct her if she makes a mistake or to revise if a new idea comes to mind. She questions any part of the story that she is not certain she has gotten correctly. "The child knows the story will soon be acted out and the actors will need clear directions. The story must make sense to everyone: actors, audience, and narrator" (1990, p. 22). During the day she talks about the stories, always looking for and voicing connections. "Throughout the day I may refer to similarities between a child's story and other stories, books, or events, though I try to avoid doing this while the story is being dictated. I don't wish to impose undue influence on the course of the story" (1990, p. 22).

Acting out the stories at the end of the school day is equally social and open to change. Paley says, "If in the press of a busy day I am tempted to shorten the process by only reading the [dictated] stories aloud and skipping the dramatizations, the children object. They say, 'But we haven't *done* the story!' " (1990, p. 25). To play out the story, Paley reads the dictation, and the storyteller and selected classmates dramatize it. Children are free to comment on the dramatizing, and their comments often result in revision in the dramatization. "Intuitively the children perceive that stories belong in the category of play, freewheeling scripts that always benefit from spontaneous improvisations" (1990, p. 25).

The Teacher's Role in Play: Letting Children Take the Lead

The roles of a teacher in children's literacy-related play are to create opportunities and then to follow the children's lead. They will show when an opportunity exists to emphasize meaning making, forms, meaning-form links, or functions of written language. When children tell about a picture while pretending to read from a magazine in the waiting area of the beauty parlor and barbershop center, they show that they know written language is about making meanings. When Mrs. Miller's students examine the broadcast script, weather maps, and computer printouts of weather information that the weatherperson brings to their class, they learn about an important aspect of form, that written language comes in many formats. When Matthew says two very different and very appropriate things for his two very different-looking pieces of writing ("Your eyes look good. Your throat is red," for his doctor's chart, and "Take these pills ten times," for his prescription), he demonstrates knowledge of meaning-form links. When Melody takes a phone message, she shows an understanding of an important function of writing, that it preserves a message for later reading by someone not now present.

Paley describes the literacy-related benefits of story telling and playing in broader terms. About a three-year-old's first story, Paley writes, "She has contributed to the literature and culture of a previously unknown group of children. Now she is known, and soon she will know others through their stories, those revealed in play and those made permanent on paper. The stories are literature; the play is life" (1990, pp. 18–19).

ANOTHER LOOK: THE TEACHER'S ROLES

We have presented descriptions of preschoolers and their teachers as they are engaged in language and literacy activities. The children had multiple opportunities to learn, and the teachers used subtle instruction to support that learning. Preschool teachers *infuse the environment with print,* as Mrs. Miller did in her classroom. They *invite children to interact with print,* as Mr. Richgels did when he invited Caitie to write a story and as Vivian Paley did when she invited children to tell and dramatize their stories. They *demonstrate reading and writing by participating in literacy events,* as Mrs. Miller did when she joined in play in the home center. She pretended to phone someone, and one of the children took a message about the call. Miss Leslie sat in the writing center and said, "I'm going to write. I think I'll draw a picture of Little Rabbit. I want to draw his red wings."

Preschool teachers *model reading and writing strategies,* as Miss Leslie did when she read big books with her children and as Mrs. Miller did when she wrote a letter to Santa with her children. They *plan group activities involving reading and writing,* as Miss Leslie did during booksharing and Mrs. Miller did in composing a menu with her children. They *plan individual activities involving reading and writing,* as Miss Leslie did when she prepared storytelling props for the book she used in booksharing and as Mrs. Miller did when she organized graphing activities in the math center. Finally, *they become audiences for children's reading and writing,* as Mr. Richgels did when he listened as Caitie composed and read a story.

Chapter Summary

Preschoolers can be expected to achieve much written language competence. They enjoy storybook read alouds and discussions, identify signs and labels, play rhyming games, have partial alphabet and sound–letter knowledge, and use some alphabet letters or mock letters to write meaningful words and phrases, including their names. They retell favorite storybooks and informational books and write pretend messages as part of dramatic play. Although most preschoolers do not develop full phonemic awareness, teachers help them to take first steps through enjoyable, informal phonological awareness activities, such as "I can hear" and rhyming games.

Preschoolers acquire concepts about written language when their classrooms are filled with print and when teachers model how to use that print in play. Mrs. Miller's classroom included many games and dramatic-play opportunities in which children used print in entertaining and functional ways.

Well planned interactive read alouds and response-to-literature activities support preschoolers' developing literary awareness, story concepts, and concepts of print. Miss Leslie demonstrated effective booksharing techniques, including making comments and using gestures and voice to interpret stories as she read aloud. She was especially skillful at getting children to participate in booksharing. She provided story concept activities and literary prop boxes.

Effective preschool teachers use written language talk to demonstrate how print guides their meaning making and to encourage children's own meaning-making efforts. In shared writing activities, including pattern writing and list writing, preschoolers learn from their teachers' modeling about written language meanings, forms, meaning-form links, and functions. Finally, preschoolers learn much from play, including play in dramatic-play-with-print centers and in story telling and playing activities.

Applying the Information

We suggest two activities for applying the information presented in this chapter. First, make a list of the seven characteristics of literacy-rich classrooms presented in Chapter 6. Then reread this chapter and locate classroom activities from Miss Leslie's and Mrs. Miller's classrooms that are examples of these characteristics. Discuss these examples with your classmates.

Second, make a list of all the literacy learning activities mentioned in this chapter, including teacher activities of infusing, inviting, demonstrating, modeling, and acting as an audience. List all the group activities described (booksharing, reading and making big books, shared writing, writing lists, and story concept activities) and individual activities (response-to-literature activities, prop boxes, sign-in procedure, card making, dramatic-play-with-print centers, print puzzles, letter games, "I can read" bags, graph making, and story telling and playing). For each of these activities, describe what children learn about written language meanings, forms, meaning-form links, or functions. For example, as children participated in booksharing with Miss Leslie, they had opportunities for meaning making by answering questions and retelling the story with storytelling props. As children wrote "Trash Can Books" with Mrs. Miller, they focused on the form of written language. They compared words in environmental print and printed forms and they named letters. Discuss your list with classmates.

Going Beyond the Text

Visit a preschool classroom and observe several literacy activities. Take note of the interactions among children as they participate in literacy experiences. Also note the teacher's talk with children in those experiences. Make a list of the kinds of literacy materials available in the classroom. Talk with the teacher about the kinds of literacy activities he or she plans. Compare these materials, interactions, and activities with those found in Ms. Reyes's, Miss Leslie's, and Mrs. Miller's preschool classrooms.

References

ADAMS, M. J. (1990). *Beginning to read.* Cambridge: M.I.T. Press.

BAGHBAN, M. (1984). *Our daughter learns to read and write.* Newark, DE: International Reading Association.

BAILEY, C. (1987). *The little rabbit who wanted red wings.* New York: Platt and Munk.

BEARDSLEY, L. V., & MARECK-ZEMAN, M. (1987). Making connections: Facilitating literacy in young children. *Childhood Education, 63,* 159–166.

BROWN, R. (1981). *A dark, dark tale.* New York: Dial.

CHANEY, C. (1994). Language development, metalinguistic awareness, and emergent literacy skills of three-year-old children in relation to social class. *Applied Psycholinguistics, 15,* 371–394.

COMBS, M. (1987). Modeling the reading process with enlarged texts. *The Reading Teacher, 40,* 422–426.

CUNNINGHAM, P. (1998). Looking for patterns: Phonics activities that help children notice how words work. In C. Weaver (Ed.), *Practicing what we know: Informed reading instruction* (pp. 87–110). Urbana, IL: National Council of Teachers of English.

DISNEY PRODUCTIONS (1973). *Walt Disney Productions' story of Robin Hood.* Burbank, CA: Disney.

FAYDEN, T. (1997). What is the effect of shared reading on rural Native American and Hispanic kindergarten children? *Reading Improvement, 34,* 22–30.

FOX, C. (1985). The book that talks. *Language Arts, 62,* 374–384.

GOSWAMI, U., & BRYANT, P. (1990). *Phonological skills and learning to read.* Hillsdale, NJ: Erlbaum.

HARSTE, J. C., BURKE, C. L., & WOODWARD, V. A. (1981). *Children, their language and world: Initial encounters with print* (Final Report NIE-G-79-0132). Bloomington: Indiana University, Language Education Department.

HEALD-TAYLOR, G. (1987). How to use predictable books for K–2 language arts instruction. *The Reading Teacher, 40,* 656–661.

HIEBERT, E. H. (1986). Using environmental print in beginning reading instruction. In M. R. Sampson (Ed.), *The pursuit of literacy: Early reading and writing* (pp. 73–80). Dubuque, IA: Kendall/Hunt.

HOLDAWAY, D. (1979). *Foundations of literacy.* Sydney, Australia: Ashton Scholastic.

INTERNATIONAL READING ASSOCIATION & NATIONAL ASSOCIATION FOR THE EDUCATION OF YOUNG CHILDREN. (1998). Learning to read and write: Developmentally appropriate practices for young children. *The Reading Teacher, 52,* 193–216.

KIEFER, B. (1988). Picture books as contexts for literary, aesthetic, and real world understandings. *Language Arts, 65,* 260–271.

LASS, B. (1982). Portrait of my son as an early reader. *The Reading Teacher, 36,* 20–28.

LUKENS, R. L. (1986). *A critical handbook of children's literature* (3rd ed.). Glenview, IL: Scott, Foresman.

MCCONAGHY, J. (1985). Once upon a time and me. *Language Arts, 62,* 349–354.

MCGEE, L. M., & TOMPKINS, G. E. (1981). The videotape answer to independent reading comprehension activities. *The Reading Teacher, 34,* 427–433.

MORROW, L. M., & RAND, M. (1991). Promoting literacy during play by designing early childhood classroom environments. *The Reading Teacher, 44,* 396–402.

NEUMAN, S. B., & ROSKOS, K. (1990). Play, print, and purpose: Enriching play environments for literacy development. *The Reading Teacher, 44,* 214–221.

NEUMAN, S., & ROSKOS, K. (1993). Access to print for children of poverty: Differential effects of adult mediation and literacy-enriched play settings on environmental and functional print tasks. *American Educational Research Journal, 30,* 95–122.

NEUMAN, S. B., & ROSKOS, K. (1997). Literacy knowledge in practice: Contexts of participation for young writers and readers. *Reading Research Quarterly, 32,* 10–32.

PALEY, V. G. (1981). *Wally's stories: Conversations in the kindergarten.* Cambridge: Harvard University Press.

PALEY, V. G. (1984). *Boys and girls: Superheroes in the doll corner.* Chicago: University of Chicago Press.

PALEY, V. G. (1986). *Mollie is three: Growing up in school.* Chicago: University of Chicago Press.

PALEY, V. G. (1988). *Bad guys don't have birthdays: Fantasy play at four.* Chicago: University of Chicago Press.

PALEY, V. G. (1990). *The boy who would be a helicopter: The uses of storytelling in the classroom.* Cambridge: Harvard University Press.

PALEY, V. G. (1995). *Kwaanza and me: A teacher's story.* Cambridge: Harvard University Press.

RASCHKA, C. (1992). *Charlie Parker played be bop.* New York: Orchard.

ROSKOS, K. (1988). Literacy at work in play. *The Reading Teacher, 41,* 562–566.

ROWE, D. W. (1998). The literate potentials of book-related dramatic play. *Reading Research Quarterly, 33,* 10–35.

SCHICKEDANZ, J. A. (1986). *More than the ABCs.* Washington, D.C.: National Association for the Education of Young Children.

SEUSS, DR. (1957). *How the Grinch stole Christmas!* New York: Random House.

SHARE, D. (1995). Phonological recoding and self-teaching: *Sine qua non* of reading acquisition. *Cognition, 55,* 151–218.

TOMPKINS, G. (1998). *Language arts: Content and teaching strategies* (4th ed.). Upper Saddle River, NJ: Merrill.

TOMPKINS, G. E., & MCGEE, L. M. (1989). Teaching repetition as a story structure. In D. M. Glynn (Ed.), *Children's comprehension of text* (pp. 59–78). Newark, DE: International Reading Association.

TREIMAN, R. (1985). Onsets and rimes as units of spoken syllables: Evidence from children. *Journal of Experimental Child Psychology, 39,* 161–181.

TREIMAN, R., & ZUKOWSKI, A. (1996). Children's sensitivity to syllables, onsets, rimes, and phonemes. *Journal of Experimental Child Psychology, 61,* 193–215.

WASON-ELLAM, L. (1988). Using literary patterns: Who's in control of the authorship? *Language Arts, 65,* 291–301.

WILKES, A. (1989). *My first cookbook.* New York: Alfred A. Knopf.

YADEN, D. B. JR., & TEMPLETON, S. (1986). Introduction: Metalinguistic awareness—An etymology. In D. B. Yaden, Jr., & S. Templeton (Eds.), *Metalinguistic awareness and beginning literacy: Conceptualizing what it means to read and write* (pp. 3–10). Portsmouth, NH: Heinemann.

Chapter **8**

Supporting Literacy Learning in Kindergarten

Key Concepts

explicit focus on print
academic agenda
sign-in sheet
kindergarten-style research
alphabetic reading
invented spelling
fully developed phonemic awareness
direct instruction
functional and contextualized experiences with written language
"What Can You Show Us?" activity
preparation
previewing
student demonstrations
applications
word frames
phoneme segmentation
phoneme deletion
"Rounding Up the Rhymes" activity
spelling patterns
vowels
reading-new-words activity
writing-new-words activity
say-it-and-move-it activity
Elkonin boxes
classroom print
specials schedule
birthday chart
shared reading
choral reading
text reconstruction
pointer reading
journals
extended sign-in procedure
writing the room
shared writing
interactive writing
language experience approach
Words for Today activity
dramatic-play-with-print centers
sign making
dramatizing information from nonfiction

THE KINDERGARTEN CONTEXT: WHAT'S NEW HERE?

In this and the next two chapters, we discuss the context for instruction and learning in terms of how it is different from that presented in the preceding classroom chapters. In this case, we distinguish between the preschool context discussed in Chapter 7 and the unique kindergarten context.

In the last twenty-five years, there has been a shift toward a more academic kindergarten experience. No longer is kindergarten viewed as merely a socialization for school, a year to get used to how to behave for teachers and with other children. Many children have already been away from home and in the organized, long-time company of large numbers of their age cohort for several years before coming to kindergarten. Kindergarteners are expected to recognize and write numerals, count, and understand the number line. The academic agenda also includes knowledge in a variety of mandated social studies and science curriculum units (e.g., the neighborhood or the life cycle). Expectations about literacy learning in kindergarten also have changed.

What Kindergartners Learn about Literacy

The greatest change from preschool to kindergarten is that kindergartners approach written language with an **explicit focus on print.** The International Reading Association and the National Association of Educators of Young Children, in their joint statement about developmentally appropriate literacy expectations (1998), suggest that kindergartners can recognize and begin to write alphabet letters, match spoken and written words, know rhyming words and beginning sounds in words, know sound–letter correspondences, understand concepts of print, and begin to write some high-frequency words. All of these expectations involve an attention to print and a mastery of knowledge of forms and meaning-form links that are not expected of preschoolers (see Chapter 7). In addition, the IRA-NCTE joint statement suggests that kindergartners can "enjoy being read to and themselves retell simple narratives or informational texts [and] use descriptive language to explain and explore" (p. 200). We would elaborate on these suggestions and add to this list by describing kindergartners' abilities to write their first and last names; identify initial and final sounds in spoken words; know sounds associated with many letters, especially consonants; use sound–letter correspondences in invented spellings; and participate in read alouds with increasingly complex comments and answers to teachers' questions.

The Teacher's Role

The constraints inherent in this new academic kindergarten context often are not limited to content. Frequently, kindergarten teachers feel less independence than in the past, in terms of not only what they teach, but also how they teach it. Teachers' manuals and children's practice booklets and work sheets accompany mandated curricula in many kindergartens.

We feel that it is possible for kindergarten teachers who are knowledgeable about the characteristics of young children as they emerge into literacy to turn this academic expectation to their advantage. Furthermore, we believe that it is possible and desirable for kindergarten teachers to maintain the child-centered approach that has always been part of their outlook, even while addressing the new **academic agenda.** Kindergarten teachers can still be attentive to and responsive to individual children's interests and abilities; they can still be flexible.

Teachers can be flexible by presenting models of conventional reading and writing, but expecting kindergartners to respond in unique ways. For example, a teacher may model a handwriting method and give children many opportunities to write (in a sign-in routine, at a dramatic play with-print center, or at a writing center), but not require conformity to that handwriting model or drill and practice in that method. A kindergarten teacher may offer shared reading experiences in big book stories or chart-paper poems, opportunities for individual children to tell the class what they know on a big book page or on a poster at the easel, and follow-up experiences with little books and individual reading and writing activities, but not require learning all the words in the big book or poem as sight words.

Most important of all is for kindergarten teachers to provide models (theirs and children's) and to provide children with opportunities for the unique kind of exploration that we have argued is characteristic of experimenters. Then children will show what they know, what they are working on, and what scaffolding they can benefit from. When teachers let the children shape the task, children can achieve goals that will surprise even the most academically oriented parents and administrators.

The IRA and the NAEYC (1998) suggest that the kindergarten teacher's role is to

> encourage children to talk about reading and writing experiences; provide many opportunities for children to explore and identify sound-symbol relationships in meaningful

contexts; help children to segment spoken words into individual sounds and blend the sounds into whole words (for example, by slowly writing a word and saying its sound); frequently read interesting and conceptually rich stories to children; provide daily opportunities for children to write; help children build a sight vocabulary; [and] create a literacy-rich environment for children to engage independently in reading and writing." (p. 200)

In Chapter 6, we shared our vision of a literacy-rich environment. In the following section, we specify characteristics of that environment in kindergarten.

The Kindergarten Setting: Space and Materials

As with all teachers, an important part of being a kindergarten teacher is arranging the classroom and gathering materials. Figure 8.1 presents our design for a well-appointed and well-arranged kindergarten classroom. One whole-group area in this classroom is the large, open, carpeted area in front of a bulletin board. Teachers often use an area like this when they conduct opening-of-the-day activities, such as their calendar activity.

In our exemplary classroom, the bulletin board holds a Helpers' Tree on which the names of each day's two helpers are displayed (on apple-shaped cutouts taken from an apple basket containing every child's name); a tooth graph (on which the names of children who lose teeth are written); a calendar; a specials schedule and hook for displaying a sign that tells each day's special class (gym, music, art, or library story); and a weather chart with yes and no options for reporting whether it is sunny, cloudy, windy, rainy, or snowy.

A pocket chart hangs from a nearby stand. This large vinyl chart has several horizontal pockets running the width of it in which words on cards can be placed to make sentences or lines from poems. Also near to the carpeted whole-group area is a piano for music activities and an easel used for displaying big books, chart paper, and an erasable marker board.

This classroom has a second whole-group area where children can sit at tables near the chalkboard. There are five centers in the classroom: blocks and make-believe play, home and restaurant, computing, writing, and reading. In addition, children play in the large-group center when it is not being used for group activities. Play props are stored in bins and low cupboards in these centers and in the home center's kitchen furniture.

The writing center looks much like the one in the preschool classrooms described in Chapter 7. There is a large, round table where children are able to see others' work and to share their own work. There is also a smaller table with a typewriter and space for one or two children to write without interruption or distraction. On low shelves, there are many kinds of writing tools and paper; picture dictionaries; several letter-stamp sets and ink pads; several laminated cards, each showing the alphabet in uppercase and lowercase letters; and a file box filled with words that children have written on cards and saved for future reference, some of which are illustrated. On the countertop above the shelves are pigeonhole mailboxes, one for each child. They hold unfinished writing and letters to kindergartners from classmates or the teacher.

In the reading center, children's books stand on low, deep shelves and lie on low cupboard tops, where they are easily accessible. These include story and informational picture books, often chosen to complement a unit of study; class-made books (such as a book of

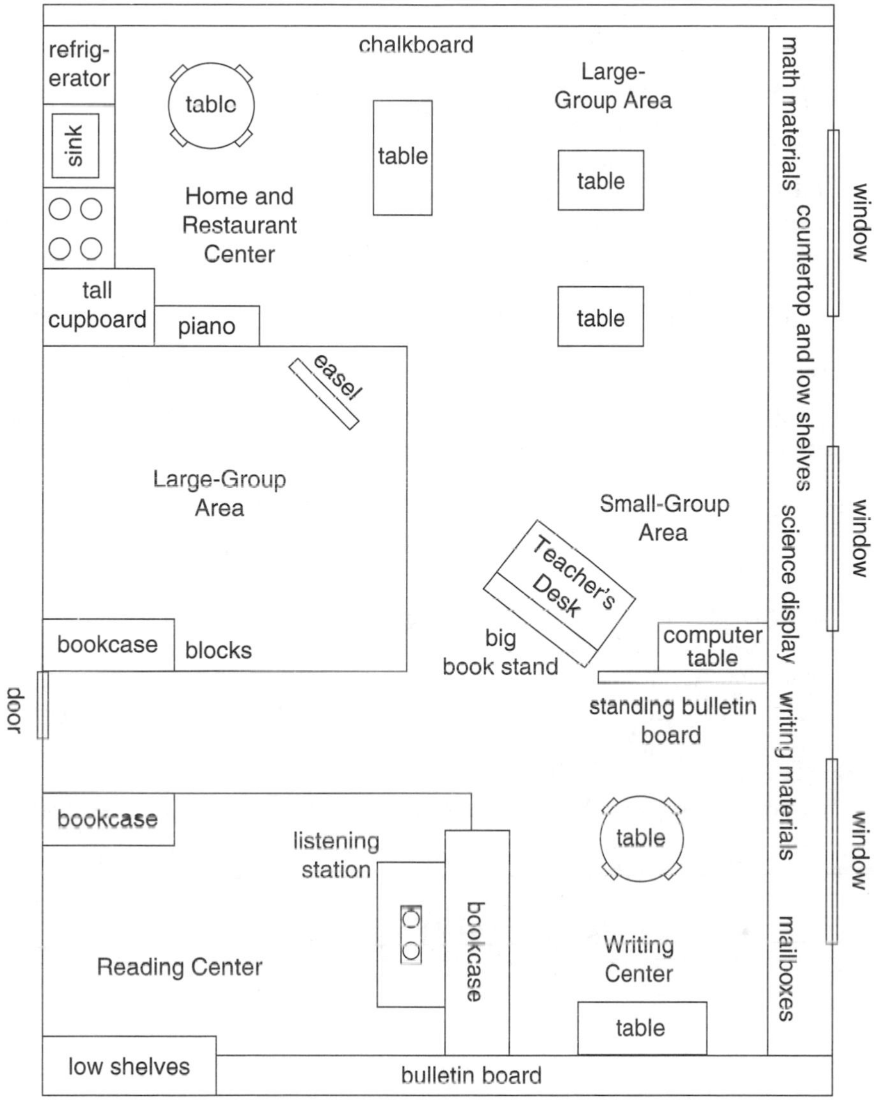

Figure 8.1 *A Kindergarten Classroom*

bear stories written from children's dictation on bear-shaped pages during a bear unit); big books that the class has read; and multiple standard-sized copies of some of the big books. There are soft cushions on which the children can make themselves comfortable when they read. The cushions can be stacked out of the way when the reading center is used for a small-group area. The listening station is set up on a small table in the reading center, with chairs for four children to use a tape player with headsets.

WRITING AND READING IN MRS. POREMBA'S KINDERGARTEN

The space and materials just described provide the setting for kindergarten teachers to support literacy development in a flexible, child-centered way. This flexibility and response to individual children is critical—a kindergarten class is likely to include some children from each of the descriptions given in Chapters 3 through 5—some novices, some experimenters, and some conventional readers and writers. In the examples from Mrs. Poremba's classroom that follow, some children are learning to recognize alphabet letters, whereas others can read words and notice spelling patterns. Still others can read poems independently. Mrs. Poremba plans activities that allow all children to show what they know.

As kindergartners arrive in Mrs. Poremba's room on February 24, they sign in and write their answers to a question written at the top of their **sign-in sheets:** "Can a dinosaur jump?" (see Figure 8.2). They have not seen these words together in a question before. In sign-in groups of four, they determine what the question is:

Bill: "Do dinosaurs jump?"

Josh: No—It says, "*Can* a dinosaur jump?"

and they debate the answer ("Yes!," "No!," "I say yes!," "The answer is no!," "Yes they can!").

Then Mrs. Poremba leads the class through a copying of the question on the chalk board. She writes the sentence as the children dictate. She comments and asks about the number of words she will write ("Did you say, 'Can—a—dinosaur—jump?' Those four words?"), spacing between words ("Now I need to scoot over and leave a space"), word parts (about the second syllable of *dinosaur,* "There's that *no* word in there"), sound–letter correspondences (about the third letter in *jump,* "And an *m*—Jummm—I hear the *m* in that"),

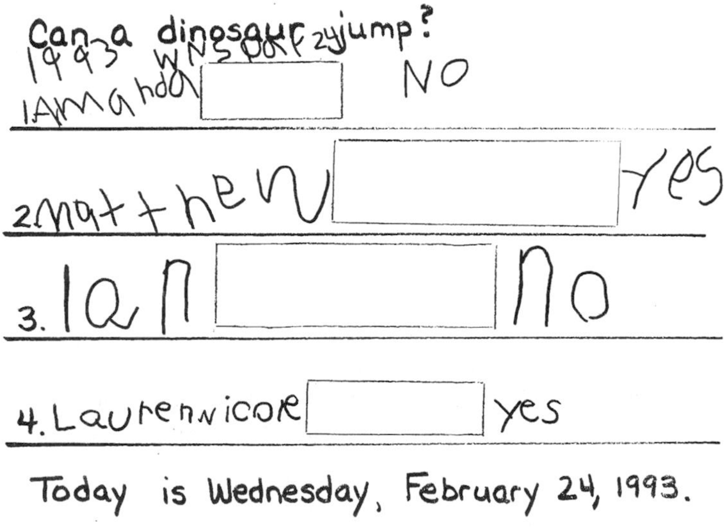

Figure 8.2 *A Sign-In Sheet with Sign-In Question (Last Names Masked)*

and punctuation (after Bill directs her to end with a question mark, she asks him to explain and he says, "It's asking, it's asking, it's asking you a question!").

As Mrs. Poremba collects the children's sign-in sheets, she comments about their writing:

Mrs. Poremba: Oh, Matt, Matt's seen some jumping dinosaurs in books. Good for you. Ian says no. . . . Derek, great that you are writing your last name. Good for you. Derek says no . . .

Kindergartners as Researchers

Later, as the children gather on the floor in the large-group area, Mrs. Poremba begins a discussion about dinosaurs that will lead into what she calls **kindergarten-style research.**

Mrs. Poremba: I have a question for you. On the sign-in sheet today, it asked you a question. Bill said it was an asking question. It needed to know something. It said, "Can a dinosaur jump?" Some of you said yes and some of you said no. What could we do, what could we do to find out more information about that?

Two children: Look in a book!

Mrs. Poremba: What is it called when you're, when you're trying to get more information, you need to learn something, and you decide to do things like look in books to find answers? What did we call that?

One child: Research.

Mrs. Poremba: Research! That's right! Kindergarten-style research. . . . I need some kindergartners to do some kindergarten-style research. We need to know if dinosaurs can jump.

Mrs. Poremba has already introduced several books about dinosaurs. Some are narratives and some are informational books. Some are from her own collection, some from the school library, and some from the children, who have been invited to bring dinosaur books from home to support the dinosaur unit. The children know these books can be found on a book cart in the reading center, and they know how to work in pairs on a learning task. All the children volunteer to do kindergarten-style research about the question, "Can a dinosaur jump?" Soon they are working in pairs all about the room.

Bill: I found one! I found one jumping!

Another child: Some could jump.

Another child: I found one that's jumping!

Another child: Oh, there's one jumping!

Another child: That one's *not* jumping.

The Teacher as Guide: Mrs. Poremba Guides Reading and Discussion

As they work, Mrs. Poremba moves from group to group and talks with children about their discoveries.

Mrs. Poremba: What do you think helps that dinosaur to be able to jump?

She asks one group about the difference between the fictional and nonfictional dinosaur books in the classroom library.

Mrs. Poremba: If you needed to know the truth, which one helps you the most?

One child: The *real* books!

And with another group:

Mrs. Poremba: Very interesting! You might want to save this for us, Samantha. Would you just hang on to that picture—because we need to talk about that.

After several minutes of kindergarten-style research, Mrs. Poremba rings a bell.

Mrs. Poremba: We need to gather as a team over on the carpet.

After a period of sharing, some kindergartners still are not convinced by their classmates' pictorial evidence of jumping.

Mikey: . . . they can't be jumping, I don't think, because like one foot's up, the other foot's down.

Matt and Dan: Well, Mike . . . *about* to jump.

Mrs. Poremba: Matt and Dan think they are getting, they are just about ready to jump. Any ideas on what might help these dinosaurs here, this, this kind of dinosaur to be a jumper? Ian, what do you think—could this be a jumper?

Ian: I think they're jumping.

Mrs. Poremba: Any ideas about that? Derek?

Derek: . . . could be jumping . . . possible . . . or could not be, too. Could just be walking or running.

Mrs. Poremba: So you're not convinced yet. Is anybody convinced about this? Dan?

Dan: I know why, I know, I know why they don't think he's jumping. 'Cause he's not in the air yet.

After much discussion:

Mrs. Poremba: Okay. I think we've done a good amount of research. And I think we've got some good ideas on, on whether dinosaurs could jump or can't jump. Now if you saw on your sign-in sheet "Can a dinosaur jump?" now that you've done some research and you've gotten some ideas, how would you answer that question now?

Several children: Yes.

One child: Well, actually, I think yes.

Several other children:	No.
Bill:	Some dinosaurs can jump, some can't.
Mrs. Poremba:	. . . Bill, you made an interesting comment. . . . (to the whole class) How would you feel about that for today?

This case study contains many examples of literacy and content learning in kindergarten. Mrs. Poremba continually emphasizes the meaning-making nature of reading and writing.

Signing in tells who is present, but it also involves children in reading and debate about a question relevant to a current topic of study. A special book collection reflects students' current interest in dinosaurs, but it also serves as an authentic source of information for kindergarten-style research. Mrs. Poremba emphasizes written language forms in her discussion of the number of words in the question and the spaces between words. She emphasizes meaning-form links when she expects children to be able to spell *yes* and *no* and when she discusses sound–letter correspondences, such as the letter *m* for the third sound in *jump.* Mrs. Poremba emphasizes the functions of written language when she acknowledges children's *yeses* and *nos* on the sign-in sheets as a record of their opinions and when she provides an organic, noncontrived reason for using books in kindergarten-style research.

Mrs. Poremba is especially skillful at helping children think for themselves. Her crafting of questions such as, "Can a dinosaur jump?" and using the kindergarten-style research activity illustrate her role as a facilitator of thinking. Because of these questions, children formulate hypotheses and test them through their research and thinking. Children know that it's okay to have differences of opinion and that marshalling evidence for an idea is an important part of what they do in research. Children formulate hypotheses not only about the content they are learning, but also about written language. Children read the sign-in sheet carefully and make hypotheses about what it says. They work together to explore the print and to test their hypotheses about what it says.

In three of the remaining sections of this chapter, we describe how kindergarten teachers can support students' learning about meaning making, forms, meaning-form links, and functions of written language in their reading, writing, and play. First, however, we devote a section of this chapter to kindergartners' most important work in the area of meaning-form links—their gaining phonemic awareness and knowledge of sound–letter correspondences.

HELPING CHILDREN ATTEND TO SOUNDS IN WORDS

Learning to read and write requires conscious recognition of the individual sounds in words (Adams, 1990; Share, 1995). When children can segment phonemes in words, they can begin to associate letters with those phonemes and thus perform **alphabetic reading** and **invented spelling,** both phonics-guided processes. In Chapters 3 and 7, we saw that **fully developed phonemic awareness** is beyond the ability of most novices, and therefore of most preschoolers. These achievements, however, are a mark of being a literacy experimenter (see Chapter 4). In this section, we describe ways kindergarten teachers can support their students' becoming experimenters and making these achievements.

The "What Can You Show Us?" Activity

Kindergarten teachers must go beyond the matter-of-fact modeling of phonological awareness that we described, for example, in the "I can hear" teacher talk (see Chapter 7). They must take the additional step of frequently and explicitly focusing children's attention on print. Explicitness does not mean, however, that kindergarten teachers must engage in the sort of **direct instruction** of phonemic awareness that uses heavily scripted lessons and focuses on isolated sounds and words (e.g., Lindamood & Lindamood, 1969; McGuinness & McGuinness, 1998).

Our work with children and teachers shows us that many kindergartners are capable of acquiring phonemic awareness from **functional and contextualized experiences with written language** (McGee & Purcell-Gates, 1997). Functional experiences are those that serve a real purpose in the everyday home and classroom lives of children. Contextualized experiences are those that use whole texts. The immediate focus may be on words, and letters and sounds within those words, but those words are found, for example, in the text of a big book the class is reading, in a poem they are rereading with the goal of eventually doing a choral reading, or in a list of facts generated from a discussion of a social studies or science topic of study.

The fact that some kindergartners may need additional help in the form of direct instruction does not justify depriving them of functional, contextualized literacy experiences. Those experiences benefit all children in ways besides their promoting phonemic awareness. They also, for example, demonstrate the functions of written language, foster the message concept, and provide enjoyment of literature. And functional, contextualized literacy experiences provide a context for practice, application, and strengthening of phonemic awareness skills that some children may need to acquire in other, direct-instruction activities.

Nor does the fact that some kindergartners need additional help in the form of scripted, direct instruction justify subjecting all children to such instruction. Much of direct instruction is so divorced from actual reading and writing of authentic texts for real purposes as to be counterproductive for those students who already have phoemic awareness, or are on their way to acquiring it in other, more functional and contextualized ways.

One way of providing functional, contextualized support for acquiring phonemic awareness is the **"What Can You Show Us?" activity** (Richgels, Poremba, & McGee, 1996). The four elements of this activity are preparation, previewing, student demonstrations, and applications.

Preparation involves the teacher's choosing or composing and displaying a text that is relevant to ongoing events or units of study. Figure 8.3 shows a letter Mrs. Poremba wrote as a pretend message from Uncle Wally. He and Aunt Edith are large, floppy, stuffed dolls who reside in the reading center. The letter was written on chart paper and displayed on the classroom easel.

Previewing is the creating of an opportunity for students to look at the text before working with it as a group. As children enter her room at the beginning of a day when there is a new poem or letter on the easel, Mrs. Poremba invites them to begin looking at the chart: "You might want to visit the easel during your sign-in time today. There is a new poem there for you."

Student demonstrations are the core of "What Can You Show Us?" Before she reads the displayed test, Mrs. Poremba invites children to come to the chart and point out some-

Dear Kindergarteners,
It is fall!
Fall is apple time.
We picked an apple
on a tree.
Yum! Yum!
Love,
Uncle Wally

Figure 8.3 *A Letter from Uncle Wally*

thing they know. Children take turns stepping up to the easel and talking about a variety of letters or words or even trying to read the poem on their own. The other children are appreciative of whatever their fellow students can teach them about the text.

In October, Erin participates in the "What Can You Show Us?" activity by reading a word in a chart-paper letter from the class's imaginary Uncle Wally (see Figure 8.3). Richgels, Poremba, and McGee describe the benefits of student demonstrations:

> This gives children the opportunity to engage with the text based on their current interests and abilities. Children may identify letters or words, or even try to read the text on their own. The teacher learns about students' interests and abilities, and the children come to appreciate what their fellow students can teach them about the text. The teacher is observer, helper, and commentator. It is very important for him or her to hold back and let students do the teaching, and to make positive, affirming comments about whatever students demonstrate. (p. 635)

With the applications step, the teacher extends and applies what students have done in their demonstrations. **Applications** occur during what is now the teacher's first reading of the text (remember that the teacher has not yet read the text when students do their demonstrations), during later rereadings, and during reading of related texts. Richgels, Poremba, and McGee (1996) include an example of applications using such a related text, the label print on a can of chicken with rice soup, which Mrs. Poremba and her students discussed after a shared reading of Maurice Sendak's poem *Chicken Soup With Rice* (Sendak, 1991). The authors summarize,

> The children read words and phrases by using letter names, letter sounds, co-occurrence of words in the two texts, and context clues. Again, they learned from one another as well as

> from their teacher. Poremba performed an active, though not imposing, role. She had intended to highlight the word *chicken* and the *S* sound–letter correspondence during her sharing a favorite poem and a related piece of environmental print, but . . . it was a child who first identified the word *chicken* and . . . the children went beyond the *S* sound–letter correspondence in their exploration of meaning-form links. (p. 641)

The following examples are from "What Can You Show Us?" lessons in Mrs. Poremba's class, using Uncle Wally's letter (see Figure 8.3), a similar letter from Aunt Edith, and two poems. In October, Erin is at the easel doing a student demonstration with Uncle Wally's letter. She points to the word *is.*

Mrs. Poremba: You're pointing to that *i-s,* Erin. Tell us about it.

Erin: It's *is!*

Mrs. Poremba: That's the word *is?* (Erin nods, and Mrs. Poremba points to the word and reads.) "Is."

Mrs. Poremba calls on Eric to come to the easel. Unlike Erin's focus on the whole word *is,* Eric's focus is on a letter that he recognizes.

Mrs. Poremba: (to the class) Watch Eric.

Eric: There's a *Y* for Freddy (pointing to the first letter in *Yum*).

Mrs. Poremba: Oooh. There's a *Y* for Freddy. What do you mean "a *Y* for Freddy"? Does Freddy have a *Y* somewhere in his name?

Eric: Yeah, and he has an *F* (pointing to the first letter in *Fall*).

Ten days later, the class reads another letter, this time from imaginary Aunt Edith. Now Mayra, who speaks almost no English at this point in the school year (Spanish is her first language), shares what she knows about letters.

Mrs. Poremba: Mayra has something she would like to teach you. . . .

Mayra: A *W* (pointing).

Mrs. Poremba: A *W!* (pointing to the same *W* that Mayra had pointed to).

Mayra: *W.*

Mrs. Poremba: That's a *W.* Thank you, Mayra, for showing us the *W.* Thank you.

Mayra bows and makes the American Sign Language sign for "Thank you" that Mrs. Poremba has taught the class (Bornstein, Saulnier, & Hamilton, 1983; Children's Television Workshop, 1985; Rankin, 1991; Riekehof, 1978). Then Eric shows what he learned from Mayra.

Eric: (pointing from his place on the floor to another *W* in Aunt Edith's letter) "And there's another *W!*"

In February, when children are invited to show what they know about a new poem, Freddy makes a connection with a familiar word. He uses one of Mrs. Poremba's **word**

frames (window-shaped cutouts with handles that can be placed around a word to isolate it from the other words in a text) to show the word *Little.*

Freddy: It starts like—(He goes to the wall and points to the word *Library* in the "Library Story" sign posted there for that day's special class.)

Jason: *Library* has the same two letters.

Another child: And *Lisa* (his sister's name.)

Mrs. Poremba: Okay now, Freddy, you touch the *L* and the *i* right there and I'll get the *L* and the *i* right here. Freddy, that's very interesting. What about the rest of the word, Freddy?

Freddy: No.

Mrs. Poremba: . . . Freddy noticed the *L* and the *i* at the beginning of that word—the same thing as in *Library.* Freddy, that was important.

Freddy's and his classmate's recognition of the beginning similarities in *Little, Library,* and *Lisa* is indeed important. Mrs. Poremba's affirmation of student demonstrations includes explicit talk about letters and sounds. Her talk appropriately goes beyond the "I can hear" talk we suggested for preschool teachers (see Chapter 7). While preschoolers typically cannot achieve full phoneme awareness and sound–letter correspondence knowledge, kindergartners usually are capable of such achievements. Reenforcing their focus on print can result in their associating letters with sounds and doing the sort of **phoneme segmentation** and **phoneme deletion** required for explicit work with onsets and rimes. Children's work with phonemes and teachers' supportive talk in such contexts *is* the stuff of phonics. Note the phonics learning and phonics instruction in the remaining examples of "What Can You Show Us?" in Mrs. Poremba's classroom.

Later in February, Ian reads the word *Lincoln* in a poem about that president.

Mrs. Poremba: How do you know that says *Lincoln?*

Ian: *L* (pointing to the *L*).

Mrs. Poremba: So the *L* in the beginning of the word helped you to read it to be *Lincoln.*

In March, during the applications step of "What Can You Show Us?" with a poem about leprechauns, Lauren uses a word frame to show that she can read *old* in the words *gold* and *told.*

Mrs. Poremba: Lauren, what did you want to show us?

Lauren: There's the word *old* (putting her frame around the *old* part of *gold*).

Mrs. Poremba: She found the word *old* inside of—(Lauren moves her frame to *old* in *told*) oh!

Lauren: And there.

Mrs. Poremba: Look, there's *told,* but if you cover up the *t,* you just have the *old* part left. And there's *gold;* cover up the *g* and *old* is left. Isn't that interesting?

Another child: Old—gold!

Then Lauren shows the *an* part in *man.*

Lauren:	An!
Mrs. Poremba:	Oh and you saw the *an* word inside of *man.* Thank you, Lauren!

Returning to "Rounding Up the Rhymes"

In Chapter 7, we suggested abbreviating phoneme awareness activities for preschoolers, omitting this sort of explicit talk about letters and sounds, and about phonemes, onsets, and rimes. Now, with kindergartners, this explicit talk can be restored; many phoneme awareness activities described in professional literature for teachers can be used in their entirety. **"Rounding Up the Rhymes"** (Cunningham, 1998) is a contextualized activity that promotes awareness of beginning phonemes and rhyming words. With preschoolers, we suggested using the first steps of "Round Up the Rhymes": the children's listening to a text and chiming in when they hear rhymes, and the teacher's writing those words on cards for display in a pocket chart (see Chapter 7). With kindergartners, teachers can continue with the next steps, which involve analysis of spelling patterns, using knowledge of letter names, vowel letters, and onsets and rimes. Cunningham reminds teachers that these later steps will probably occur on a later day from the first identification of the rhyming words, because each lesson should not exceed twenty minutes. After another reading of the text, with children again chiming in with the rhymes and finding them on the cards in the pocket chart, the teacher says, "Now we know that all these words rhyme. Our job today is to look very closely and see which ones have the same spelling pattern" (p. 91). Part of using this step of "Rounding Up the Rhymes" is helping children to understand words such as **spelling pattern** and **vowel.** With frequent use of "Rounding Up the Rhymes," children begin to remember that the vowels are *a, e, i, o,* and *u,* and that the spelling pattern is the part of the word from the first vowel to the end.

The teacher picks up a pair of rhyming word cards from the pocket chart, explains or reminds the children what *spelling pattern* and *vowel* mean, and invites children to identify the letters in the spelling pattern in the rhyming words, for example, *o-l-d* in *gold* and *told.* Then the teacher underlines the *-old* part of each word, and the teacher and children decide that *gold* and *told* have the same spelling pattern and rhyme. "We emphasize that we can *hear* the rhyme and *see* the spelling pattern" (p. 91). Then the teacher replaces those word cards and moves on to another pair of rhyming words from the pocket chart. If some rhyming pairs have different spelling patterns (e.g., *snow* and *go*), they are discarded. Finally, when the teacher and students have underlined spelling patterns in several pairs of rhyming words, they move to an application activity that involves using the word card words to read and write additional words. For the **reading-new-words** part, the teacher writes words that rhyme with and have the same spelling pattern as the words of an already displayed pair (e.g., *sold* and *fold* to go with *gold* and *told*), elicits the children's telling what letters to underline in the new words, displays them in the pocket chart under the original pair of words, and helps the children to read the new words using the spelling pattern.

For the **writing-new-words** part, the teacher mentions a word the children might want to write and gives an example of a sentence in which it might be needed. For example, if one of the already displayed rhyme pairs is *dog* and *log,* the teacher might say, "What if you wanted to write *fog,* like in 'I saw *fog* on the way to school today'?" Then the teacher leads the children through a reading of all the rhyme pairs in the pocket chart, adding *fog* after each, until they find the pair that rhymes with *fog:* "*gold, told, fog; man, can, fog; dog, log, fog!*" When they notice that *fog* rhymes with *dog* and *log,* the children can use the underlined spelling pattern in the two displayed words to help the teacher to spell the new word on a word card for display.

Like "What Can You Show Us?," "Rounding Up the Rhymes" is suitable for groups of children who have varying abilities. It

> has something for everyone. Struggling readers and writers whose phonemic awareness is limited learn what rhymes are and how to distinguish rhymes from beginning sounds. Other children whose phonemic awareness is more developed may learn spelling patterns and also that words that rhyme often share the same spelling pattern. Our most advanced readers and writers become proficient at the strategy of using words they know to decode and spell unknown words. This proficiency shows in their increased reading fluency and in the more sophisticated nature of the invented spellings in their writing. (Cunningham, 1998, p. 93)

Kindergarten teachers can extend other preschool activities we suggested in Chapter 7. They can add more explicit teacher and student talk about letters, sounds, and word parts. For preschoolers, we gave an example of a "Charlie Parker Be Bop" stanza patterned on the text of a page from the word play picture book *Charlie Parker Played Be Bop* (Raschka, 1992):

> Elephant, elephant, elephant, el,
>
> Tambourine, tambourine, tambourine, tam,
>
> Pencil, pencil, pencil, pen,
>
> Dinosaur, dinosaur, dinosaur, di!

Preschoolers enjoy inventing such stanzas. For them, the game—and the phonological awareness benefits—is in the hearing and the repeating of the stanzas.

Kindergarten teachers might extend this activity by writing the stanza on chart paper and using that displayed text for explicit talk about the spellings of the words and word parts. For example, with the last line of the above stanza, the teacher identifies the letters as he writes the first *dinosaur* word, invites the children to repeat the letters as he writes and spells aloud *dinosaur* the second time, and then has the children tell him how to spell *dinosaur* as he writes it the third time. Then he reads what they have, "Dinosaur, dinosaur, dinosaur," and says, "Now we have to write just the *di* part." He moves his hand below the last *dinosaur* word they have written as he stretches out his reading of it, "Diiiii-noooooo-ssssaurrr. Which is the *di* part?" He might have to underline the *di* part in the first three words. Then the children tell him how to spell *di.*

The examples we have given so far—"What Can You Show Us?," "Rounding Up the Rhymes," and "Charlie Parker Be Bop" stanzas—are functional and contextualized activities. They include explicit teacher and student talk about sounds, letters, and word parts that will help most kindergartners to achieve phonemic awareness, alphabetic reading, and invented spelling. They involve all participants in enjoyable, meaningful experiences with written language.

Some children may benefit from additional more direct instruction. Many phonemic awareness training methods are adopted from research tasks. Some involve children's clapping or other rhythmic activity to coincide with spoken words or syllables (e.g., Lundberg, Frost, & Petersen, 1988). Some involve **say-it-and-move-it activities,** in which children move poker chips or other such tokens as they pronounce syllables or individual phonemes in words (Elkonin, 1973).

Yopp (1992) describes several singing activities, peformed to the tunes of traditional children's songs, that help children to isolate, blend, or substitute sounds in words. She suggests first using these as strictly oral activities, especially with preschoolers or beginning kindergartners, who may lack alphabet knowledge and for whom the use of written letters may be a distraction from the intended work with sounds. Then, as children learn alphabet letters—often during the kindergarten year—written words or letters may be used.

Ball and Blachman (1991) concluded that their study of phonemic awareness training in kindergarten "supports the notion that phoneme segmentation training that closely resembles the task of early reading may have more immediate effects on reading . . . than instruciton that does not make this connection explicit. . . . It may be . . . that the most pedagogically sound method of phoneme awareness training is one that eventually makes explicit the complete letter-to-sound mappings in segmented words" (p. 64). They suggest using blank tokens for say-it-and-move-it phoneme awareness activities and then introducing tokens with letters written on them as children learn to identify the letters.

Griffith and Olson (1992) describe a say-it-and-move-it activity borrowed from Clay (1985) that can be changed in a similar way as children learn the alphabet. Students are given a picture, below which are **Elkonin boxes,** that is, boxes arranged in a horizontal matrix, one box for each phoneme in the pictured word. As the teacher slowly pronounces the word, the children move tokens into the boxes. She says "mmmmmmmaaaaaaannnnnn" for *man,* for example. The children move a token into the first box while she is pronouncing the phoneme /m/, move another token into the second box while she is pronouncing the phoneme /ă/, and, finally, move a third token into the third box while she is pronouncing the phoneme /n/. As children learn the alphabet, rather than moving tokens into boxes, they can write letters in the boxes.

We suggest that whenever teachers use these direct-instruction activities, which use isolated words and rather prescribed sequences of teacher talk and student behavior, they keep in mind ways to reestablish connections to children's classroom and home lives and to whole texts—in other words, ways to make them more functional and contextualized. The words used for Elkonin box work, for example, can come from a displayed big book text or chart-paper poem, and after doing the Elkonin box work, the teacher and students can return to that text and highlight the words there. Or the Elkonin box words may be used in a subsequent piece of writing that is meaningful to the children, such as a class letter to parents that tells about a current unit of study. The letter is composed on chart paper, reproduced by word processor on the classroom computer, and taken home the same day.

The activities that we have described in this section are only a part of the kindergarten literacy agenda. There are other contexts for supporting kindergartners' learning about phonics besides those described. In addition, there is much more besides phonics-related knowledge that kindergartners must achieve. In the sections that follow, we describe experimenters' learning about meaning making, forms, meaning-form links, and functions of written language in additional kindergarten reading, writing, and play contexts.

KINDERGARTEN EXPERIENCES WITH READING

We return to Mrs. Poremba's classroom to describe additional kindergarten reading experiences. These include classroom print reading and shared reading of big books and other enlarged texts.

Using Classroom Print

The exemplary kindergarten setting is filled with print. An important part of the teacher's role in this classroom is to invite children's responses to that print that reveal their current understandings about written language. This practice allows the teacher always to validate those understandings and at times to give children support for expanding those understandings.

A guiding principle of using **classroom print** is that it is always appropriate if presented to children in a supportive way. Teachers ask, "What can you read here?" and then accept the child's interpretation of that task. Some children will identify the object on which the print is found. When asked to read a toothpaste box, they may reply "toothpaste." Teachers celebrate their reading, saying, "Yes, it is a *toothpaste* box and it says *toothpaste* right here" (pointing to the appropriate word). Other children may identify letters (replying, "C-R-E-S-T"). Teachers celebrate this reading by saying, "Yes, you're right, and it says *Crest.*" Still other children may identify words (replying, "Crest"), and others may read connected text (replying, "Tartar control Crest"). In each case, teachers recognize children's reading as valid.

Mrs. Poremba includes classroom print in a variety of ways in her units and activities. During a unit about taking care of the environment, children were examining bottles, cans, and other packaging that Mrs. Poremba had collected in a recycling bin. She had told the class about using the recycle symbol, a triangular shape formed from three interlocking arrows with a number in the center, to determine which numbered items their trash collectors would accept for recycling. Jason noticed a similar symbol on an empty cottage cheese carton. This was a symbol used by the dairy to indicate a real dairy product, an oval formed from two interlocking curves with the word *REAL* printed in the center. It was very similar in appearance to the recycle symbol. Jason asked, "Does this mean anything?" He knew that this symbol should have meaning, that it did not appear on packaging randomly—in effect, that it was readable.

Some classroom print in Mrs. Poremba's room is presented in a more organized manner. Several charts provide information that children use frequently. Two examples are a specials schedule and a birthday poster.

On the **specials schedule** are the words "Today we have:". Underneath are a hook and an envelope. The envelope contains four laminated signs, one each for art, music, gym, and library story, to hang on the hook. On the envelope is the word *Specials.* Each sign has a word telling the special class and a picture: a gym shoe for gym, a paintbrush for art, a musical note for music, and a book for library story. In early October, Mrs. Poremba posted a specials schedule beneath the specials envelope. Information is organized in this schedule by column, color, and picture. Across the top is the word *Specials.* Heading the left column is the word *Morning;* heading the right column is the word *Afternoon.* Each column has five cells, one for each day; in each is the name of the day of the week, the name of the special class that day, the time of the class, and the same picture symbol for that class as on the special signs. The day names are color coded: pink for Monday, yellow for Tuesday, green for Wednesday, blue for Thursday, and orange for Friday.

As part of beginning-of-the day activities, one of the two helpers posts the specials sign for that day. For a time after introducing the specials schedule, Mrs. Poremba directed the helper's attention to the appropriate column, cell, and picture. By the middle of the year, children knew the schedule, and helpers seldom needed to consult it, but if they forgot what day it was, Mrs. Poremba said, "You can look at the schedule. Today is Tuesday," and, if necessary, "That's in a yellow rectangle."

The specials schedule is a resource for self-scheduled practice using informational print. In October, Jeff and Tara were reading the specials schedule together during free-choice time. Tara pointed to the appropriate columns and cells on the schedule and said, "On Tuesday we have library; on Tuesday, they have gym, the afternoon class. On Wednesday we have gym and they have library story."

Near the door in Mrs. Poremba's room is a laminated **birthday chart.** It organizes important information, the children's birthdays, using pictures for the months (e.g., a pumpkin for October). With erasable marker, so she can use it again next year, Mrs. Poremba has written each student's name and birthday on the appropriate month's picture. When lined up at the door to go home at the end of the morning, children often read the birthday chart, especially as they became better at reading one another's names.

On May 19, Mayra suggested that her classmate Deborah write the word *June,* because "One more month is my birthday." Deborah twice consulted the birthday chart in order to make a complete, correct spelling of *June.* When she read what she had written, Mayra said, "June 16!" Deborah said she would check the chart and again returned to the birthday chart, now not as a spelling guide, but as a source of information to verify Mayra's birthday. She added a *16* to her record of Mayra's birthdate so that it read *jUNe 16.*

Mrs. Poremba's students' experiences with classroom print are opportunities to learn much about written language. Her kindergartners learn that classroom print provides models of how to form letters and spell words for their own writing. Deborah demonstrated this when she copied the word *June* from the birthday chart. They know that environmental print has meaning, as Jason showed when he asked about the meaning of the *REAL* symbol on a cottage cheese container. They know that reading informational print sometimes requires knowing how content is organized. Jeff and Tara, for example, used the columns and rows to locate information on the specials schedule.

Shared Reading

An important way in which kindergartners learn from each other is through planned group-literacy experiences. In this section we describe **shared reading** (Holdaway, 1979). With this technique, teachers read aloud from charts or big books (with large-sized print so that children can look at the print as teachers read). Then the children and the teacher read together (the shared reading portion of the activity). Finally, children read with a partner or alone.

Shared reading guides children's learning about print so that they gradually learn more conventional concepts. They can develop concepts about print, such as the concept of a written word, directionality (left-to-right orientation), and knowledge of sound–letter relationships and spelling patterns in word families. Some children learn to read some words by sight. Shared reading also demonstrates meaning-making strategies, such as predicting, connecting with real experiences, and making inferences. Mrs. Poremba frequently uses the shared reading technique with a poem that she has written on chart paper and displayed on the easel.

Step One: Orienting Children to Print

Before Mrs. Poremba reads a new poem to them, she orients the children to print. She has already emphasized the poem's line-by-line structure by printing the poem on the chart in two colors of ink, alternating colors for each new line. Mrs. Poremba always invites children to study a new chart-paper text on their own before the class gathers to read it as a group.

During a whole-class time, Mrs. Poremba continues to orient children to the text of a poem. She points out the names of the author and illustrator. When the author is unknown, Mrs. Poremba discusses what "Author Unknown" means. At this point in shared reading, Mrs. Poremba may do the student demonstrations step of "What Can You Show Us?" Earlier in this chapter, we saw examples of Ian's and Lauren's demonstrations of what they knew in the texts of a poem about Abraham Lincoln and a poem about leprechauns.

Step Two: Teacher Reading

The teacher reading portion of shared reading ensures that students attend to meaning. As teachers read, they invite children's comments and questions and model using meaning-making strategies. Mrs. Poremba maintains the interactive talk of the orienting-children-to-print portion of shared reading as she reads a poem, a story, or other text aloud to the class and as she and the children read together. When she reads, she stops to comment about character or plot, to invite predictions, to remark about illustrations, and to accept and acknowledge students' comments and questions. Sometimes she points out a familiar or an unusual word; comments about punctuation, especially a question mark or an exclamation point; or reminds the class of a student's earlier observation during their orientation talk.

Step Three: Teacher and Children Reading Together

In shared reading in kindergarten, poems, letters, stories, and informational books are read many times. Sometimes, when a poem has become familiar enough, Mrs. Poremba's class reads it aloud together, while she directs with a pointer on the chart-paper text. She knows that it is important for children to look at the print during this reading. Before such a **choral reading,** she says, "Where will you look to find the first word of the poem?" and makes sure children are looking there.

Step Four: Response Activities

The final step of shared reading involves response activities with the text. The purpose of these activities is for children to attend to print on their own without the support of a teacher. In kindergarten, many of these activities take place in pairs or small groups; some are done by individuals.

A pocket chart provides opportunities for response activities that focus on print. After reading a poem about November, Mrs. Poremba wrote the poem on long strips of posterboard, one strip for each line of the poem. She placed these strips in the pocket chart, one strip per pocket, and the class read the poem one line at a time. Then she invited students to step up to the pocket chart, choose a line of the poem, read it, and remove that strip from the chart. When all the strips were removed, Mrs. Poremba returned them to the pocket chart and repeated the activity until every student had had a turn choosing and reading a line of the poem.

On another day, this opportunity to attend to print with a now familiar poem was extended through a **text reconstruction** activity. Mrs. Poremba assigned students to small groups. Each group had all the words of the poem on separate word cards and a large piece of lined posterboard. Their job was to work together to reconstruct the poem by placing the word cards onto the lines on the posterboard.

The pocket chart with the poem displayed on strips was still available as a model for students who wanted one during their text reconstruction. As some children worked in their small groups to reproduce the poem, they used the model from the pocket chart to match words. Some children were able to locate words using picture clues, such as a drawing of blades of grass on the word card for *grass* in the line "No green grass."

As an individual activity with the November poem, Mrs. Poremba's students made their own books, each page of which contained a line from the poem and a pop-up illustration. Because they had listened to Mrs. Poremba read the poem, had read the poem together, and had done a small-group activity with the poem, all the children could read their November poem books when they took them home.

Another individual response activity, **pointer reading,** provides opportunities for the student to focus on print and for the teacher to assess the student's print-related knowledge. An example of pointer reading occurred in May after Mrs. Poremba's class had observed the three-week-long process of chicken eggs' incubating and hatching in their room. A chart-paper poem/song used during this unit began, "Cluck Cluck Red Hen" and followed the pattern of "Baa Baa Black Sheep." During free-choice time, Zack was singing this song while visiting the brooder box that contained the class's newly hatched chicks. Mrs. Poremba noticed this and invited Zack to the easel. She pointed out that he was singing what was written on the chart paper, which the class had read together many times. She invited him to point with a pointer as he read the text. She watched and listened, nodding as he read, even when his pointing did not always match his reading. Her role was audience, not instructor; she did not correct him. When he finished reading, both Mrs. Poremba and Zack were smiling broadly. She said, "You did it! Very nice, Zack!"

Zack's reading attracted Alyssa, Tara, and Elise, each of whom took a turn pointing to and reading the poem. These three varied in the accuracy of their pointing, with only Elise pointing perfectly; all three had an appreciative, fully attentive audience in Mrs. Poremba.

Even when Zack's, Alyssa's, or Tara's pointing sometimes digressed from their reciting or singing of the poem, they were able to recover, that is, to find a place in the poem where they could identify a word with confidence and proceed. Their self-correcting using sight words or beginning sound–letter correspondences demonstrated significant growth from what they were able to do in individual reading activities at the beginning of the year. Their confidence and the number of reading strategies now in their repertoires made pointing and reading a chart-paper poem a viable free choice for them in May. Mrs. Poremba was aware of this when she seized the opportunity presented by Zack's singing to the chicks and by the girls' interest in what Zack was doing at the easel.

Shared Reading with Big Books

Big books (see Chapter 6) are excellent texts for shared reading. Big books can be effective in extending kindergartners' literacy knowledge, especially in helping them to appreciate written language forms, to understand the relations between what a reader says and what is written in a book, and to become increasingly influenced by a book's text in their pretend reading. Big books make text especially accessible to children who are taking these steps (Martinez & Teale, 1988; Trachtenburg & Ferruggia, 1989).

Early in the year Mrs. Poremba reads the big book *Bears, Bears Everywhere* (Connelly, undated). This is a pattern book with the title repeated on every page, followed by a three-word phrase, the last word of which rhymes with *where*. Mrs. Poremba's orienting the children to *Bears, Bears Everywhere* demonstrates that a picture book's illustrations are as important as the text. She helps children to use both illustrations and text to answer questions about the book. One of these questions concerns a topic the class has been exploring. They have already made a large poster from index cards on which were written facts about bears dictated by the children. Also, Mrs. Poremba had asked parents to write bear stories their children dictated at home and send the stories to school. When Mrs. Poremba read these to the class, she always asked if they were real or pretend stories. Now, with *Bears, Bears Everywhere,* she asks the same question, and the answer can be found in the cover illustration of bears that are behaving more like humans than like bears.

Mrs. Poremba: I want you to look at the cover of the book and get your ideas for what this book is about.

Children: (loudly and all together) Bears!

Mrs. Poremba: Turn and tell a friend.

Children: (whispering to one another) Bears. Bears.

Mrs. Poremba: I have a thinking question for you right now. . . . I want you to think about whether this book will be about pretend bears or real facts about real bears. Don't say it, just think.

After a short pause, many children answer.

Mrs. Poremba: Can you turn and share your idea with a friend?

Children whisper their predictions to one another, but some loud *no*s and *yes*es can be heard as children disagree with one another. One child suggests that the illustration might be showing real bears who are in the circus.

Mrs. Poremba: Now there's an idea—I hadn't thought of that. Why don't we read and then we'll get more ideas about whether these are real bears or pretend bears, bear facts, or pretend things about bears.

Now Mrs. Poremba shifts the focus to the print on the cover of the book. She helps the children to concentrate on where to begin reading, how to spell the first sound in *bears,* and how a written word looks (by counting words in the title).

Mrs. Poremba: Where could I look to find the name of the story?

Children: B! B!

Mrs. Poremba: What do you mean *B?*

Child: The title page.

Mrs. Poremba: Well that's one place to look.

Child: The cover.

Mrs. Poremba: The cover? Okay . . . and I noticed that some of you said the letter *B* because that's the very first letter in the word (pointing) *Bears.* Here's another one (pointing to the *B* at the beginning of the second word *Bears*). This story is called (pointing) *Bears, Bears Everywhere!*

Child: Bears, bears everywhere?

Mrs. Poremba: I'll read it again—first of all, how about if we count the words in the title, so we know how many words there are. (with some children reading and counting along) "Bears"—one. "Bears"—there's two. "Everywhere"—three words in the title.

Child: No, how about that top one (referring to writing above the title)!

Mrs. Poremba: Up here it says "CTP Big Book"—that's the name of the store, or the company, I should say, that printed this book.

Child: There's some down there.

Mrs. Poremba: Down here it says, "Author, Luella Connelly"—she wrote the words—and . . . the other words here say, "Illustrator Neena (hesitating) Chawla Koeller."

Child: That's hard.

Mrs. Poremba: That's a lot—she's the person who did the pictures. She's the illustrator.

Child: Two people worked on it!

Mrs. Poremba: (confirming) Two people worked together to make this book.

Child: Teamwork!

Mrs. Poremba: (confirming) Teamwork, teamwork—that's a very good idea!

During her first reading of the big book *Bears, Bears Everywhere,* Mrs. Poremba points out where to look when reading; contrasts the spellings of two similar words, one of which is familiar to some of the children; and demonstrates meaning-making strategies. She weaves these and other activities—many of them suggested by the children's questions and comments—into a rich interaction about a simple story. As she reads a page about bears in pairs, for example, she first establishes a focus on meaning by asking the children to look at the illustration and call to mind what the story might be about. Then she points to the text as she reads.

Mrs. Poremba: I want you to look at the pictures and get some ideas. (pause) I want you to put your eyes right down here and I'll start reading (pointing to the text at the bottom of the page).

Mrs. Poremba reads, and the children laugh. Next, Mrs. Poremba responds to a child's question, capitalizing on the opportunity to expand their understandings about the meaning of the word *pair.*

Child: Pairs?

Mrs. Poremba: I wonder what it means—bears in pairs?

Jason: Two together make a pair.

Mrs. Poremba: Oh, there are two together. So this isn't the kind of *pear* that you buy at the store and eat, like a fruit. This is a different way to use the word *pair.* Jason said that a pair is when two things are together. Look at your shoes. Like a pair of socks.

Children: Pair of earrings . . . pair of shoelaces . . . eyes . . . ears . . . arms . . . pair of legs . . . pair of elbows!

Mrs. Poremba: So things that come in twos are pairs.

Still later, for a page about bears on chairs, Mrs. Poremba shifts to form and meaning-form links. She calls attention to the picture of bears on chairs and asks what the bears are doing. Then she takes a moment from the big book reading to demonstrate with her writing how written language works. Mrs. Poremba uses a small, erasable marker board that she keeps near her big book easel. In this case, she reads the page about bears on chairs, but stops before the word *on.*

Mrs. Poremba: What's this word (pointing)?

Several children respond at once with their guesses, including "Sitting in chairs," "Zero," and "No."

Mrs. Poremba: Does anyone know what O-N spells? . . . Let me show you.

Child: (still working on her own) On chairs.

Mrs. Poremba: (writing on the erasable board) Here is how you spell *no.* How do you spell it?—with *N* first and then—

Eric: Oh I get it! I get it. The *O* has to be on that side and the *N*'s on that side.

Mrs. Poremba: Yes when the *O* is on this side and the *N* is second, that's the word *on.*

Tara: It's like a pattern! (The children are used to finding patterns in the shapes on which the numbers of the calendar are written.)

Mrs. Poremba: It *is* kind of.

Children: (reading) On. On. On. On chairs! It's "On chairs"!

Mrs. Poremba then reads the page and comments, "Some of you have been writing *on* in your sign-in sheets."

Still later, when Mrs. Poremba points to the word *lair*, Tara says, "Just like the Blairs!" One of the class's favorite books is *Somebody and the Three Blairs* (Tolhurst, 1990), a parody of the Goldilocks and the three bears story.

Over the next several days, the children frequently reread *Bears, Bears Everywhere* together. They also read their own little-book versions of this book to one another and take them home to read to their families.

Often, children who at first say that they cannot read are willing to read a big book page after a group reading and discussion. They become enthusiastic about the big books and want to return to them again and again (Combs, 1987).

Shared reading in the examples from Mrs. Poremba's class was the vehicle for teaching and learning about all aspects of written language. For example, children learned about meaning making when Mrs. Poremba asked them to think about what a book or a page might be about from studying a book cover or page illustration. They learned about form when she asked them where to start reading a poem or where to find the title of a big book and when they worked together to reconstruct a poem from word cards. They taught one another about meaning-form links when they pointed out print-to-speech matches (e.g., Zack's, Alyssa's, Elise's, and Tara's finger-point reading). They learned about functions of written language, that it can provide information (e.g., "Author Unknown," "CTP Big Book") and entertain (e.g., a poem about bears in pairs, on chairs, in lairs, etc.).

It is important to keep in mind that shared reading is only one kind of reading aloud to children that takes place in Mrs. Poremba's classroom. Mrs. Poremba frequently reads aloud quality literature, including poems, stories, and informational books. The purposes of these readings are to promote children's enjoyment, to enrich children's vocabularies, to find out more about a topic of study (such as dinosaurs or recycling), and to extend children's experiences with literature. During these interactive read alouds, Mrs. Poremba focuses on meaning—responding to children's questions and comments and encouraging their predictions. Therefore, her attention to print in shared reading is balanced by her attention to meaning in a variety of other kinds of reading activities.

KINDERGARTEN EXPERIENCES WITH WRITING

Many of the activities and contexts we have already described include opportunities for kindergartners to experiment with writing. They write during the response activities that are part of shared reading and during applications in "What Can You Show Us?" They write at the writing center, computer center, and play center, and in a corner with a clipboard and before the class at the easel. In this section, we describe additional kindergarten writing activities: journal writing, the extended sign-in procedure, and shared writing.

Journal Writing

Kindergartners enjoy writing in **journals** both about self-selected topics and about topics suggested by their content study. Figure 8.4 presents a journal entry written by a kindergartner after he had played in a doctor dramatic-play-with-print center. Figure 8.5 presents Nathan's journal entry on the day Mrs. Poremba's class witnessed a chick's hatching.

Figure 8.4 *A Kindergartner's Journal Entry*

Figure 8.5 *Nathan's Journal Entry ("A chick just hatched!")*

Another teacher included journal writing in a unit about Pilgrims. As a part of the unit, the class "gathered around a small box and talked about what they would put in it to take to the New World where there would be no stores" (Fallon & Allen, 1994, p. 547). They acted out being Pilgrims and living on a cramped ship. Each day the teacher read aloud books about the *Mayflower,* and children wrote in journals as if they were traveling on the ship.

Kindergarten journals often become places where children dictate content information of personal interest. Marina dictated about a caterpillar that she brought to school on a stick. "A calipitter [*sic*] likes to climb on his stick. He's fuzzy. . . . And he gots short hair and its [*sic*] thick. I don't know how many legs he's got because he won't turn over on his back" (Fallon & Allen, 1994, p. 548). Journals are also places where teachers provide individual help with invented spellings (Freppon & Dahl, 1991). As teachers sit with children writing in journals, they help children listen for the big sounds in words and celebrate children's successes in inventing spellings.

The Extended Sign-In Procedure

A variation on kindergartners' daily journal writing is their writing more than their names as part of signing in at the beginning of their school day. We call this the **extended sign-in procedure.** At the beginning of this chapter, we described Mrs. Poremba's students' recording their answers to a question ("Can a dinosaur jump?") on a sign-in sheet. This was part of an attendance-taking routine in Mrs. Poremba's classroom. Each child goes to an assigned table where he or she shares a sign-in sheet with the three other children. By February, besides writing their names, students were recording their yes-or-no answers to a different question each day. By the end of the year, they wrote complete thoughts in answer to open-ended questions, for example, Ian's "win EHY HAT blue OFF" ("when the hat blew off") in answer to "What did you like at Blackberry Farm?" (Richgels, 1995, p. 250).

With another class, Mrs. Poremba's sign-in procedure evolved differently over the course of the school year. One morning in late September of the school year that followed the "Can a dinosaur jump?" episode, a few children wanted to write something other than their names on their sign-in sheets (there was no sign-in question this early in the year). They decided to copy words from the print in the classroom (e.g., labels on objects—*chair, desk, clock;* words on bulletin boards—*green, writing center, oval*). These children asked Mrs. Poremba for their own sign-in sheets (recall that up to now, sign-in sheets were shared by four children sitting at a table together). She provided new sheets for these children for their signing in and copying interesting words from the classroom. She celebrated this writing during a whole-class gathering, showing it to the rest of the class and congratulating the writers. Soon everyone wanted his or her own sign-in sheet.

Then one day there was a new Halloween bulletin board above the writing-center table. Several children wanted to sit at the writing center and copy onto their sign-in sheets the words labeling the Halloween pictures on the bulletin board, more children than could sit at the writing-center table. Several children pulled chairs up to make a second row of writers at the table. Mrs. Poremba gave these children clipboards for their sign-in sheets so that they, too, could write. Then everyone wanted a clipboard, and soon the entire class had clipboards and pencils and sign-in sheets, freeing them to wander around the room copying whatever print they found, not just the print on the new Halloween bulletin board. Figure 8.6 shows Meagan's sign-in from this day. She copied "Color Cats" and color words from a color-word bulletin board; "big blocks" from a label in the block center; "bat," "pumpkin," and "witch" from the Halloween bulletin board; and "Please," "Thank you!" and a smiley face from the sign-in sheet itself! She used dashes to mark spaces between some of the words she copied.

Figure 8.6 *Meagan's Writing the Room Sign-In Sheet*

This activity became known as **writing the room.** By midyear, Mrs. Poremba had added the sentence "Today is ______" and sometimes included a number identification activity on the sign-in sheets. As the year progressed, children used their clipboards and sign-in sheets to write down what was important to them in the morning's opening activities (calendar and weather report), to copy parts of a new poem displayed on chart paper on an easel in the large-group area, or to remember something special about the day, such as a classmate's birthday.

Children were free to complete the "Today is" sentence as they wished. For example, on March 15, Ian noted that "Today is 120," that is, it was the 120th day of school. The next day, Tara noted that "Today is Gym" (see Figure 8.7).

Shared Writing

Shared writing and a similar activity, **interactive writing,** are instructional activities designed to resemble shared reading (Fountas & Pinnell, 1996). Teacher and students compose a text together. Students suggest ideas, the teacher models writing processes, and the students participate in both the writing and the subsequent reading and rereading of the text. It is similar to writing in the **language experience approach** (Nelson & Linek, 1999; Stauffer, 1980; Van Allen & Van Allen, 1982), which also involves creation and subsequent learning from student-composed texts. Shared writing differs from language experience writing, however, in two ways. While language experience texts are usually accounts of class experiences, shared-writing texts are more varied. They may, for example, be lists, signs, letters, reminders, labels, poems, or extensions of favorite storybooks. While the language

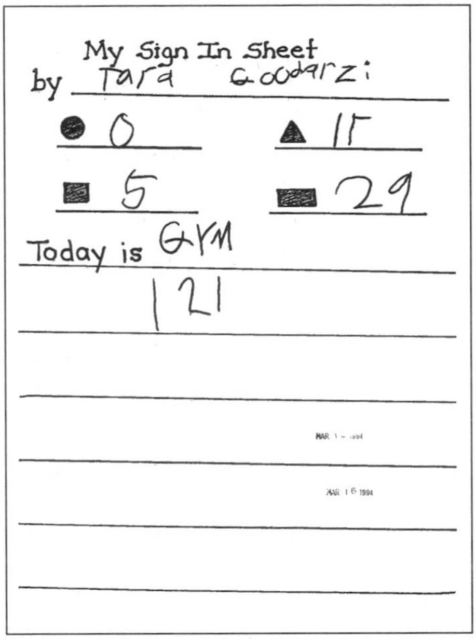

Figure 8.7 *Tara's Sign-In Sheet*

experience composing process is strictly limited to the teacher's acting as scribe for student dictation, shared writing involves greater interaction. This may take the form of the teacher's making connections (for example, between words in the text and other words children know, such as their names or words that appear in familiar classroom print), the students' contributing to the actual writing, and the teacher's using the writing process for related word study (for example, about beginning letters and sounds or about spelling patterns) as she writes the text one word at a time (Pinnell & Fountas, 1998). Shared-writing texts can be used for later shared reading.

Mrs. Bellanger and her class wrote the following shared-writing text about the human heart:

> We have a heart.
> Our heart is a muscle that pumps blood.
> It is as big as a fist.
> Animals have hearts, too.
> Hearts are usually found in the chest.

Then they read and reread it several times. Mrs. Bellanger placed it in the science center and invited children to read it to a friend during center time.

Mrs. Poremba's class used shared writing in an activity they called **Words for Today.** At the beginning of the year, as part of the class's opening-of-the-day routine, she wrote weather words the children suggested. She used this as an opportunity to model alphabet letter formation, letter identification, and spelling strategies. Usually children would repeat words from the classroom weather chart for Mrs. Poremba to write. By midyear, they often suggested weather words not on the weather chart (e.g., *foggy*) or even nonweather words (e.g., *Easter*). As Mrs. Poremba wrote these words, she would ask children to identify letters or hear big sounds in order to spell. In February, she changed the activity by giving one of the two daily helpers the option of writing the Words for Today. As children wrote, Mrs. Poremba would ask them to listen to the big sounds or to find the word somewhere in the room.

Zack's Words for Today writing on March 16 included the children's favorite weather word, *Brrrrr,* with an exclamation mark. When Ian suggested writing "totally sunny," Zack copied *sunny* from the weather chart, but at first did not want to attempt *totally.* Then he agreed to write just the first sound in *totally,* fitting a *T* before *sunny.* Last, Jeff suggested writing "damp," and Deborah helped Zack spell *damp* conventionally.

In Mrs. Poremba's classroom, shared writing in the form of Words for the Day influenced students' individual writing in the extended sign-in procedure. Figure 8.8 shows the back of Tara's March 15 sign-in sheet (the front of which is shown in Figure 8.7). She copied—with some modifications—Zack's Words for Today for that day.

Kindergarten teachers can use journal writing, extended sign-in writing, and shared writing to teach students about meaning making (for example, Tara's "Today is Gym" message), forms (for example, Meagan's concept of word, shown by the dashes she made between words she copied), meaning-form links (for example, Zack's *T* for "totally"), and functions of written language (for example, Nathan's recording of a significant class event, "A chick just hatched!"). As examples in this section show, writing opportunities are not limited to planned lessons. They arise during routine activities as well, such as weather chart work and Words for Today in Mrs. Poremba's classroom. Making use of such opportunities is one way to vary activity within a routine. In this way, a routine can provide the

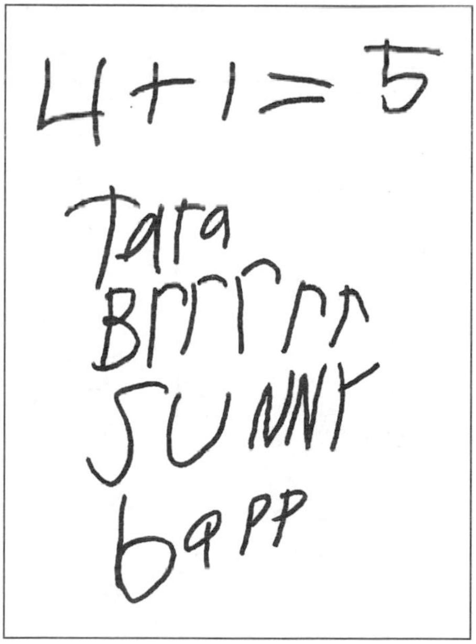

Figure 8.8 *The Back of Tara's Sign-In Sheet (see Figure 8.7 for the Front)*

structure and security that children often desire, while at the same time support their learning as teachers affirm existing understandings and provide scaffolding for next steps.

KINDERGARTEN EXPERIENCES WITH PLAY

Play is one of the most important activities in a kindergarten classroom. We described in Chapter 7 how one of the many benefits of play in preschool is its serving as a context for literacy learning. The same is true of play in kindergarten, and many of the methods for encouraging preschool literacy-related play are equally suitable for kindergarten. In the academic context of today's kindergartens, it is important for teachers to remember the benefits for their students of having plenty of space, materials, and time for free play. In this section, we describe some of the literacy-related uses of play in Mrs. Poremba's kindergarten.

Dramatic-Play-with-Print Centers

An example of play-related writing occurred when Deborah was taking orders at the **dramatic-play-with-print** pizza parlor. This was a popular play scenario for both boys and girls. Deborah chose it as a play activity for at least a small part of the free-choice time several times a week. Like most of her classmates, when taking a customer's order, she always wrote a line of mock cursive for each item in the customer's order. She took a pizza order from one of the authors of this book: seven lines of mock cursive for "extra large . . . thin and crispy . . . green olives . . . sausage . . . extra cheese . . . root beer . . . large." Later, however, when delivering the order, Deborah used a different writing strategy, one she had never before used during pizza parlor play. "Wait—you need your receipt," she said, and she used the numerals and symbols on the toy cash register to copy "¢25¢" and "$5" on the back of the paper she had used for writing the order (see Figure 8.9).

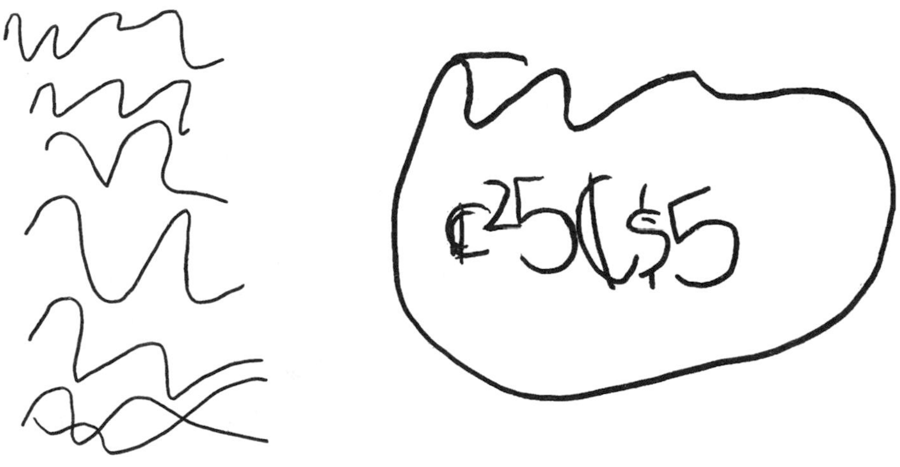

Figure 8.9 *Deborah's Pizza Parlor Writing ("Extra Large," "Thin and Crispy," "Green Olives," "Sausage," "Extra Cheese," "Root Beer," "Large" and a Receipt)*

Another time, Freddy, was similarly resourceful in finding a model for his writing in the pizza parlor. While waiting for some pizza business, he entertained himself by carefully and very legibly copying the brand name embossed on the metal clip of his clipboard. His writing is shown in Figure 8.10. The brand name on the clipboard that he was copying was STEMPCO COLEMAN; he wrote STEMPCO COVEMAN.

Sign making was another use of written language during play times. In December, Mrs. Poremba turned the block center into a dramatic-play-with-print shoe store. In response to a letter asking for help stocking the store, parents sent old shoes, slippers, and boots; shoehorns; and foot sizers. The children arranged the footwear on shelves and set up a checkout counter. They also wrote signs and their own paper money.

Frequently, children in Mrs. Poremba's room wanted to work on a play project for more than one day. When they asked Mrs. Poremba what they could do to be sure that what they had done was not disturbed in the meantime (especially by the afternoon kindergartners), Mrs. Poremba always suggested that they make a sign. In January, Ian taped such a sign to his half-finished Lego creation (see Figure 8.11). Ian does not yet always make a conventional *S*, but he does know that an apostrophe shows ownership. When asked the next day to tell "what you added to *Ian*," he replied, "Ian's."

Figure 8.12 shows another sign that several boys made in May to reserve a large dinosaur puzzle they had constructed on the floor. The sign tells others "No Stepping." As

Figure 8.10 *Freddy's Pizza Parlor Writing (A Pizza Order and Self-Scheduled Copying of a Brand Name, STEMPCO COLEMAN)*

Figure 8.11 *Ian's Sign*

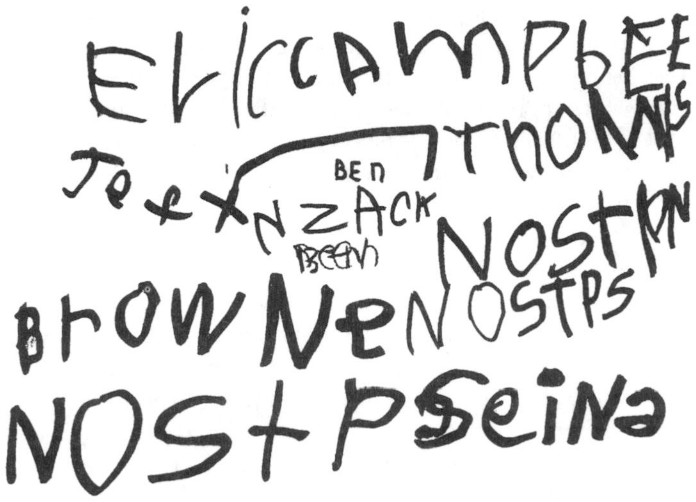

Figure 8.12 *Eric, Jeff, Zack, and Ben's "No Stepping" Sign*

they had been doing on their sign-in sheets at this time of the year, Jeff Browne included his last name and Eric Thomas Campbell included his middle and last names.

Similar playful explorations of written language forms and functions can occur in the computer center (Shilling, 1997). This is especially so when teachers model and make available to children such uses for the computer as sign making, greeting card making, and basic word processing.

Dramatizing Informational Books

Dramatizing information from nonfiction is a playful and powerful learning opportunity. After reading several informational books about bees, Mrs. Holcomb invited her kindergartners to play about being bees. "Now I would like you to pretend that you are bees looking for a flower. When I ring the bell, stop buzzing and land on a petal of a flower." After the teacher rang the bell, she said, "Suck up the nectar. All right, now brush some of the pollen to the back of your legs. . . . Now, you have the nectar in your honey stomach and the pollen on your back legs. . . . Fly home" (Putnam, 1991, p. 463).

Mrs. Poremba directed a similar play episode as part of her chick-hatching unit. Her students had read many informational books and posters about chick development and hatching. As the children anticipated their first chick's hatching, they applied what they had learned from their reading.

Mrs. Poremba: Let's pretend that we are a chick that's been in the egg twenty-one days. You are SO crowded, your legs and your wings and your head and your back and your beak are ALL crunched together. . . . Okay, the first thing you do is you SLOOOOOWLY move your head up and you're going to poke your air sack on the top of your egg to take that breath of your first air. Poke your air sack. Okay. Take your breath. Do you like that air?

Children:	Yes. Uh huh.
Mrs. Poremba:	But you know what? That took a lot of work. So now you're tired again. . . . Ohhhh. Now a little bit of a rest. Now we're going to take our head and get your egg tooth up, part of the end of your beak. And we're going to make our very first pip in the shell—and that's very hard work. Find your place to pip.
Children:	Pip, pip, pip. Peep, peep, peep.
Mrs. Poremba:	Did you get a pip in your shell?
Children:	Yeah, Yes.
Mrs. Poremba:	Go back to sleep. You are so tired. This is HARD work hatching. Okay, now let's look at our picture to see what we need to do next.

Play provides a rich context for extending children's understandings about written language. As children listen along with tapes in the listening center, they extend their understandings about stories. As they dramatize informational books, they show their understandings of the meanings of words such as *pollen, nectar, honey stomach, air sack, pip*, and *egg tooth*. Copying numbers, for example, copying *25* from a toy cash register, extends children's knowledge of written language forms. Using seven lines of mock cursive to write seven phrases in a pizza order allows children to test a meaning-form link hypothesis—that written language must relate to spoken language. Sign making is a functional activity—making a sign "No Stepping" means that children expect written language to be heeded.

ANOTHER LOOK: THE TEACHER'S ROLES

We have described kindergartners and their teachers as they participated in activities using reading and writing. The children had rich and numerous opportunities to learn about written language. In particular, Mrs. Poremba played at least six roles in supporting her kindergartners' language and literacy learning.

First, she *followed children's leads*. Mrs. Poremba invited children to tell what they knew as they read big books and sign-in questions. She said, "Tell us about that," demonstrating that children had something important to teach each other. Their information—what they knew about print—became part of each day's lessons. Mrs. Poremba also followed children's leads as she changed her sign-in procedures after noticing that children wanted to use the sheets for a new kind of writing—writing the room. She observed children as they talked and as they read and wrote. Each day she provided opportunities for children to show what they were learning about.

Second, Mrs. Poremba *planned routines that included functional reading and writing*. She used sign-in questions to foster reading for information and other beginning-of-the-day activities to orient children to their daily schedule and the weather. She expected that children would read and write as a part of these activities.

Third, Mrs. Poremba *modeled reading and writing strategies in ways that supported children's own reading and writing*. During shared reading, she demonstrated reading from print, knowing where to begin reading, and paying attention to titles as a clue for meaning. She pointed to words as she read and provided opportunities for children to practice pointing as they read. During shared writing, she modeled listening for the big sounds and finding words in the room, and she expected children to use these strategies when they wrote Words for Today.

Fourth, Mrs. Poremba *drew explicit attention to print.* She demonstrated by writing on a small, erasable board the differences between *no* and *on,* she elicited talk about print as she wrote the sign-in question, and she oriented children to print before and during shared reading by using the "What Can You Show Us?" activity.

Fifth, Mrs. Poremba *gradually shifted the responsibility for reading and writing to the children.* In the beginning of the year, children were expected to write only their names on their sign-in sheets. By the middle of the year, they wrote *yes* or *no* in answer to a sign-in question, or they might use their sign-ins as a personal journal-like record of the opening-of-the-day events. In the beginning of the year, Mrs. Poremba wrote the weather words, but by the middle of the year, she offered children the option of writing themselves. By the end of the year, the children were writing Words for Today.

Finally, Mrs. Poremba *planned individual and group activities involving reading and writing.* She planned shared reading activities, including special small-group- and individual-related activities, such as text reconstructions and pop-up books. She planned ways to make group learning more effective, including giving children a model for their text reconstructions.

Chapter Summary

Kindergartners are expected to recognize and begin to write alphabet letters, match spoken and written words, know rhyming words and beginning sounds in words, know sound–letter correspondences and use them in invented spellings, understand concepts of print, write their first and last names, begin to write some high-frequency words, and enjoy and participate in read alouds. Many of these expectations are in the area of meaning-form links, and their achievement depends on a related achievement—fully developed phonemic awareness. Kindergartners meet these expectations and continue to develop in all areas of written language acquisition when classrooms are filled with print, when teachers and children model reading and writing, and when children participate in functional and contextualized written language experiences.

Kindergartners' literacy learning is supported through classroom routines using print. Routines such as journal writing, "What Can You Show Us?," and the extended sign-in procedure encourage children's reading and writing and provide opportunities for teachers and children to talk about written language. Shared reading is a rich context for literacy learning; teachers orient children to print, read with children, and plan response activities. Shared reading is used with poems, songs, letters, stories, and informational texts presented on charts and in big books.

Shared writing is another context for language and literacy development in kindergarten. Teachers and students compose texts together. Students suggest ideas, teachers model writing processes, and the students participate in both the writing and the subsequent reading and rereading of the text. Finally, play is a critical component of the kindergarten curriculum. Children learn about written language in dramatic-play-with-print centers and during computer play.

Applying the Information

We suggest two activities for applying the information. First, make a list of the seven characteristics of literacy-rich classrooms from Chapter 6. Then reread this chapter and identify classroom activities appropriate for kindergartners that are examples of each of these seven characteristics. Discuss with your classmates why these activities fit the characteristics.

Second, make a list of all the literacy-learning activities described in this chapter, including the teacher activities of following children's leads, planning routines, modeling, focusing on print, transferring responsibility, and planning activities. List the group activities—writing the sign-in question, shared reading, text reconstruction and pocket-chart activities, and language experience—as well as individual activities—signing in, writing the room, Words for Today, using dramatic-play-with-print centers, bookmaking, keeping journals, finger-point reading, and sign making. For each of these activities, describe what children learn about written language meanings, forms, meaning-form links, or functions. For example, children who participate in text reconstruction activities with a pocket-chart text as a model are learning about written language forms as they match words by matching letters. Children who finger-point read a familiar poem are learning about meaning-form links as they adjust their pointing using what they know about sounds and letters.

Going Beyond the Text

Visit a kindergarten and observe several literacy activities. Take note of the interactions among the children and between the teacher and the children as they participate in literacy experiences. Make a list of the kinds of literacy materials and describe the classroom routines in which children read and write. Talk with the teacher about the school's academic expectations for kindergarten. Find out how the teacher meets those expectations. Compare these materials, interactions, and activities with those found in Mrs. Poremba's classroom.

References

ADAMS, M. J. (1990). *Beginning to read.* Cambridge: M.I.T. Press.

BALL, E. W., & BLACHMAN, B. A. (1991). Does phoneme segmentation training in kindergarten make a difference in early word recognition and developmental spelling? *Reading Research Quarterly, 26,* 46–66.

BORNSTEIN, H., SAULNIER, K. L., & HAMILTON, L. B. (Eds.). (1983). *The comprehensive signed English dictionary.* Washington, DC: Gallaudet University Press.

CHILDREN'S TELEVISION WORKSHOP. (1985). *Sign language ABC with Linda Bowe.* New York: Random House.

CLAY, M. M. (1985). *The early detection of reading difficulties* (3rd ed.). Portsmouth, NH: Heinemann.

COMBS, M. (1987). Modeling the reading process with enlarged texts. *The Reading Teacher, 40,* 422–426.

CONNELLY, L. (undated). *Bears, bears everywhere.* Cypress, CA: Creative Teaching Press.

CUNNINGHAM, P. (1998). Looking for patterns: Phonics activities that help children notice how words work. In C. Weaver (Ed.), *Practicing what we know: Informed reading instruction.* (pp. 87–110). Urbana, IL: National Council of Teachers of English.

ELKONIN, D. B. (1973). Reading in the U.S. S. R. In J. Downing (Ed.), *Comparative reading* (pp. 551–579). New York: Macmillan.

FALLON, I., & ALLEN, J. (1994). Where the deer and the cantaloupe play. *The Reading Teacher, 47,* 546–551.

FOUNTAS, I. C., & PINNELL, G. S. (1996). *Guided reading: Good first teaching for all children.* Portsmouth, NH: Heinemann.

FREPPON, P., & DAHL, K. (1991). Learning about phonics in a whole language classroom. *Language Arts, 68,* 190–197.

GRIFFITH, P. L., & OLSON, M. W. (1992). Phonemic awareness helps beginning readers break the code. *The Reading Teacher, 45,* 516–523.

HOLDAWAY, D. (1979). *The foundations of literacy.* New York: Ashton Scholastic.

INTERNATIONAL READING ASSOCIATION & NATIONAL ASSOCIATION FOR THE EDUCATION OF YOUNG CHILDREN. (1998). Learning to read and write: Developmentally appropriate practices for young children. *The Reading Teacher, 52,* 193–216.

LINDAMOOD, C. H., & LINDAMOOD, P. C. (1969). *Lindamood phoneme sequencing program for reading, spelling, and speech.* Austin, TX: Pro-Ed.

LUNDBERG, I., FROST, J., & PETERSEN, O. (1988). Effects of an extensive program for stimulating phonological awareness in preschool children. *Reading Research Quarterly, 23,* 263–284.

MARTINEZ, M., & TEALE, W. H. (1988). Reading in a kindergarten classroom library. *The Reading Teacher, 41,* 568–572.

MCGEE, L. M., & PURCELL-GATES, V. (1997). Conversations: So what's going on in research in emergent literacy? *Reading Research Quarterly, 32,* 310–327.

MCGUINNESS, C., & MCGUINNESS, G. (1998). *Reading reflex: The foolproof phonographix method for teaching your child to read.* New York: Free Press.

NELSON, O. G., & LINEK, W. M. (Eds.) (1999). *Practical applications of language experience: Looking back, looking forward.* Boston: Allyn and Bacon.

PINNELL, G. S., & FOUNTAS, I. C. (1998). *Word matters: Teaching phonics and spelling in the reading/writing classroom.* Portsmouth, NH: Heinemann.

PUTNAM, L. (1991). Dramatizing nonfiction with emerging readers. *Language Arts, 68,* 463–469.

RANKIN, L. (1991). *The handmade alphabet.* New York: Scholastic.

RASCHKA, C. (1992). *Charlie Parker played be bop.* New York: Orchard.

RICHGELS, D. J. (1995). A kindergarten sign-in procedure: A routine in support of written language learning. In K. A. Hinchman, D. J. Leu, & C. K. Kinzer (Eds.), *Perspectives on literacy research and practice, 44th yearbook of the National Reading Conference* (pp. 243–254). Chicago: National Reading Conference.

RICHGELS, D. J., POREMBA, K. J., & MCGEE, L. M. (1996). Kindergartners talk about print: Phonemic awareness in meaningful contexts. *The Reading Teacher, 49,* 632–642.

RIEKEHOF, L. L. (1978). *The joy of signing: The new illustrated guide for mastering sign language and the manual alphabet.* Springfield, MO: Gospel Publishing House.

SENDAK, M. (1991). *Chicken soup with rice: A book of months.* New York: HarperCollins.

SHARE, D. (1995). Phonological recoding and self-teaching: *Sine qua non* of reading acquisition. *Cognition, 55,* 151–218.

SHILLING, W. A. (1997). Young children using computers to make discoveries about written language. *Early Childhood Education Journal, 24,* 253–259.

STAUFFER, R. (1980). *The language experience approach to teaching reading* (2nd ed.). New York: Harper and Row.

TOLHURST, M. (1990). *Somebody and the three Blairs.* New York: Orchard.

TRACHTENBURG, P., & FERRUGGIA, A. (1989). Big books from little voices: Reaching high risk beginning readers. *The Reading Teacher, 42,* 284–289.

VAN ALLEN, R., & VAN ALLEN, C. (1982). *Language experience activities* (2nd ed.). Boston: Houghton Mifflin.

YOPP, H. K. (1992). Developing phonemic awareness in young children. *The Reading Teacher, 45,* 696–703.

Chapter 9

Supporting Literacy Learning in First Grade

Key Concepts

sight words
skills
strategies
whole to part to whole
instructional reading event
integrate the language arts
before, during, and after reading
basal reading series
scope and sequence of skills
decodable basals
controlled vocabulary basals
word identification
phonics
structural analysis
contextual analysis
vocabulary
sight vocabulary
comprehension
literal comprehension
inferential comprehension
critical comprehension
directed reading lessons
directed reading-thinking activity
predictable-text basals
literature-based basals
high-frequency words
Daily Oral Language (DOL)
words for the week
word wall
spelling poem
flashlight reading
vowel diagraphs
vowel dipthongs
partner reading
patterned writing
pocket-chart activity
take-home books
independent reading level
instructional reading level
guided reading approach
point of difficulty
teaching for strategies
leveled texts
dynamic ability groups
literacy centers
talk-through
interactive writing
word study
linking to the known
grand conversations
make-a-word activities
word sorts
journal writing
author's chair
process writing approach or writing workshop
minilessons
closed syllables
open syllables

WHAT'S NEW HERE?

The "what's new" in first grade is the expectation that by the end of the year all children will be reading and writing conventionally. They are expected to comprehend stories and informational text, learn the meanings of new words, learn a few hundred sight words, and use sound–letter relationships to identify unknown words. They are expected to learn the spellings of some words and to use sound–letter relationships and other strategies to spell words. They are expected to write a variety of kinds of compositions for a variety of purposes (to inform, to interact with others, to entertain).

But how do children get to these end points? Many children will begin first grade already reading and writing conventionally. The print-rich environment and literacy instruction provided for them in preschool and kindergarten were sufficient for them to make the transition from an experimenter to a conventional reader and writer. Children who begin first grade already reading and writing often make tremendous gains in reading during first grade. They often end their first grade year reading on a third grade level or above (Dahl, Scharer, Lawson, & Grogan, in press).

Other children will enter first grade as experimenters. They have sufficient knowledge about and experience with written language to make the transition to conventional reading and writing during first grade. For them, beginning to read and write conventionally will be relatively easy as they participate in instructional activities such as those we describe in this chapter (Snow, Burns, & Griffin, 1998). For other children, this transition will take careful attention from a highly knowledgeable teacher. Children who begin first grade with the knowledge and experiences of written language like that of novice readers and writers need carefully planned instruction in order to become conventional readers and writers by the time they are seven years old. We expect that most children will become early conventional readers and writers by age seven (IRA/ NAEYC, 1998).

Learning to Read Conventionally

We know a great deal about what children need to learn in order to begin reading conventionally (Adams, 1990; Juel, 1991). The hallmark of conventional reading is orchestrating all sources of information so attention is free to focus on meaning. Experienced conventional readers pay attention to print; they look at and read every word in a text. However, the print seems transparent; readers' attention is on the meaning they are constructing rather than on the print. Attention is free to focus on meaning when readers automatically and fluently recognize words, know their meanings, and chunk those meanings into phrases, sentences, and larger chunks. That is, readers recognize and access the meanings of words quickly (in less than a fraction of a second) "by sight" and chunk them together into phrases without consciously having to decode words or "sound them out." **Sight words** are words that readers recognize instantly.

Children do not begin acquiring sight words until several other foundational understandings are in place (Ehri & Sweet, 1991). Children begin learning sight words when they have (1) nearly complete alphabet knowledge (in fact, one predictor of early reading acquisition is how quickly a child can name alphabet letters), (2) some phonemic awareness (can at least generate rhyming words and detect words that have the same beginning and ending sounds), and (3) at least a rudimentary understanding of the alphabetic principle (often demonstrated first in early invented spellings). Without these foundational understandings in place, children will learn few if any words by sight.

The reason these three foundational understandings are critical to beginning conventional reading is in the way sight words are remembered—through letters and their relationships to spoken words and word parts. Much of sight word learning happens unconsciously, and many children acquire sight words without instruction. At first, readers unconsciously make mental connections between only a few letters of a word, such as the beginning and ending letters, and a word's pronunciation. As readers encounter the same word again and again during reading, the connections in memory between some of the word's letters and the spoken word and its meanings become stronger and stronger. Eventually, just a glance at the word triggers a match in memory between the letters, spoken word, and meaning. These words are sight words. A word becomes a sight word when the letter sequences in the word (at least some of the letter sequences) are firmly in a reader's memory, attached to the spoken word and meaning. Within less than a second a reader looks at the word, and the letters in the word trigger an association to the word's pronunciation and meaning. The pronunciation and meaning are available without conscious attention to the letters themselves.

For many readers, acquiring sight words happens unconsciously and easily. The meaning of sentences and predictability of many poems, stories, and informational text help children recognize words as they read before these words are firmly in memory as sight words. Over time, as children encounter the same words in these supportive contexts, they acquire many sight words that are firmly in place in memory. Children acquire sight words such as *the, he, is, was, me, they, us,* and *where* through repeated exposure. Gradually, they acquire more complex sight words, such as *fell, water, every, plant, trash, stuck, pans, clothes,* and *tomorrow.*

As most children acquire sight words, an amazing thing happens quite unconsciously. As children acquire more and more sight words, they go beyond just learning specific words. As they read more and more text, children automatically relate letter sequences in the words they encounter frequently with spoken word parts. Knowing the pronunciations of word parts allows children to decode very complicated words they have never before encountered. They can do so very quickly, seemingly without stopping to "sound out." For example, for older readers, the letters *con, tempt,* and *ible* in the word *contemptible* automatically trigger pronunciation of /con/, /tempt/, and /ibl/ even when they have never encountered the word *contemptible* in their reading before (see orthographic reading in Chapter 1).

Therefore, knowledge of letters and their associated sounds (phonics) is critical to sight word learning for two reasons. First, memory for words depends on knowing and attending to at least some letters in words. Second, children can use sound–letter knowledge to "sound out" unknown words in order to build and speed up the process of acquiring more sight words. Unknown words that must be decoded to reach a pronunciation, with repeated encounters, will then become sight words. Careful attention to a word's letters in sequence during the "sounding out" process, may actually speed sight word learning. Fewer encounters with a word may be necessary for acquiring the word as a sight word if children's first encounters with the word involve careful inspection and mapping many letters to the sounds in the word's pronunciation.

During early word encounters, word reading may require conscious attention to a word's letter sequences in order to figure out the word's pronunciation, but reading these words will take less attention in subsequent encounters. Thus, attention is freed for constructing meaning—and readers need all of their attention for this critical activity. Just knowing every word's meaning does not ensure that readers construct meaning for a whole passage.

This description of the processes involved in beginning to read words in ways that free attention for constructing meaning is simplistic. Most importantly, readers use many more strategies than merely decoding or using phonics to figure out unknown words. It is critical to keep in mind that the purpose of instruction in beginning reading and writing is not merely to develop sight words or strong decoding and spelling abilities (although these are important); it is to foster active readers and writers who have a wide variety of strategies, which they use to engage in deep thinking. Table 9.1 summarizes the wide variety of strategies and understandings that we expect children at the end of first grade to have acquired.

Table 9.1 *Reading and Writing Outcomes for First Grade*

By the end of first grade, children
Read and retell familiar narrative and informational text
Use strategies (predicting, rereading, imagining, questioning, commenting) for comprehension
Select to read and write for a variety of purposes
Have an awareness of a wide variety of literary elements found in narratives, informational texts, and poetry (character, setting, problem, event, sequence, lining, rhyming, repetition)
Write personal, narrative, informational, and poetic text
Have an interest in and strategies for learning meanings of vocabulary
Acquire sight words and spell words
Use a variety of strategies for decoding and spelling (including strategies that build from phonemic awareness, maintain fluency, detect and correct errors, solve problems with words using multiple sources of information, and link to current knowledge, including the use of consonants, short vowels, long vowels, and high-frequency phonograms)
Use punctuation and capitalization
Engage in independent reading and writing

Based on IRA/NAEYC (1998); Fountas & Pinnell, 1996; and Bear, Invernizzi, Templeton, & Johnston, 1996.

Balanced First Grade Reading and Writing Programs

First grade reading and writing instruction requires balancing many competing needs. Teachers must balance the need to provide continued opportunities for children's exploration of written language with instruction that moves children toward the levels of conventional achievement expected for all children in first grade. Teachers must balance instruction that is planned, systematic, and explicit, with opportunities for extended practice in which children read and write in meaningful activities. Teachers must balance the need for small-group instruction that is finely tuned to meet the needs of specific learners with the need for children to work with a wide variety of others.

Teachers must balance instruction that focuses on acquiring **skills** with instruction that supports children's learning of **strategies.** Skills are knowing about something, such as knowing that the letter *m* usually is associated with the sound /m/. Strategies are knowing how to accomplish something, such as elongating the sound usually associated with the letter *m* along with the sense of a sentence in order to decode or figure out an unknown word.

An important part of a balanced literacy program is providing instruction that focuses on learning words and strategies for decoding along with instruction that extends comprehension and deep thinking. Balanced strategy and skill instruction in extending vocabulary knowledge, comprehension, and decoding usually proceeds from **whole to part to whole** (Strickland, 1998b). That is, a skill or strategy is first demonstrated during reading or writing, such as in a shared reading or writing activity. For example, children may be reading a big book version of *Hats Hats Hats* (Morris, 1989). During shared reading, teachers draw attention to the word *hats* and emphasize the short sound associated with the letter *a*. Teachers then draw away from the shared reading or writing to teach a more focused lesson on the short sound associated with the letter *a* and a strategy for using this sound in reading and writing. Children might dictate words beginning with that sound while the teacher writes them on a small, dry erase board. Or children might select pictures of words that have and do not have the short sound associated with the letter *a*. Later, when children are working in other shared reading activities, they would practice using their knowledge of the /ă/ sound to decode other unfamiliar words.

The heart of reading instruction in first grade and beyond is what we call the **instructional reading event.** By this, we mean when children are reading on their own under the guidance of a teacher. Children in preschool and kindergarten are expected to engage in reading activities; they listen to their teacher reading aloud, participate in shared reading activities, and pretend read (see levels of emergent reading in Chapter 4) during independent reading times. In first grade, however, children are *expected* to read conventionally on their own. Teachers carefully craft instructional reading events so that children can read text on their own and at the same time extend their reading abilities. Over time children are also expected to get better at reading—to be able to read text with more difficult concepts and vocabulary. There are many ways that teachers prepare for instructional reading events. Early in first grade, shared reading provides a supportive instructional context. Shared reading can lead to partner reading or independent reading, in which teachers monitor progress in short conferences, daily or weekly. Children also can read as part of a small instructional group.

Much of what happens in first grade literacy instruction is preparing children for particular instructional reading events. One way of conceiving of reading instruction is to consider activities that will prepare children for reading, support them while they are reading, and extend their knowledge about reading and writing after reading. However, a balanced literacy program includes more than just reading; teachers **integrate the language arts**—drama, talking, writing, drawing, and other art activities—into **before, during, and after reading** events.

In this chapter, we describe three major approaches to reading and writing instruction in first grade. Most teachers in the United States use basal readers to teach reading (Hoffman et al., 1998). We describe three different kinds of basal readers and the assumptions guiding instruction in each of the three kinds of basals. We provide a rich description about one teacher who uses a basal as part of her reading program. Another approach to beginning reading is called the guided reading approach (Fountas & Pinnell, 1996). Again, we provide a description of this approach in use. Finally, many first grade teachers use components of the writing workshop approach to teach writing. We describe several teachers' use of the writing workshop. It is important to keep in mind that reading and writing occur throughout a first grader's day, and reading and writing are best taught when they are integrated. In the following portions of the chapter, observe how each teacher balances the variety of competing needs that we have described.

BASAL APPROACHES TO FIRST GRADE READING INSTRUCTION

Most teachers use at least parts of a basal reading series for reading instruction in first grade (Hoffman et al., 1998). The **basal reading series** is a published reading program with materials for kindergarten through the eighth grade, including a set of preprimers, primers, and first readers. These are anthologies of stories on increasingly difficult reading levels. Basal series also have a teacher's manual for each of the readers, and workbooks are available. The teacher's manual specifies a list of skills that are taught along with each reader (called the **scope and sequence of skills**).

Not all basal series are alike, and many basal series published after the early 1990s are markedly different than those published prior to that time. Basal series can be grouped into three broad categories depending on the major focus of instruction in first grade: decodable, controlled vocabulary, and predictable-text basals. The first category of basals we call **decodable basals** because the text in the readers is decodable. Most words adhere to phonics generalizations that have been taught in a particular sequence. For example, children are taught sounds related to particular vowels, and the decodable text they read in the basal reader includes many words with those vowel patterns. The rationale underlying decodable basals is that children need a strong foundation in understanding the alphabetic code and using it for reading.

Reading decodable texts can strengthen first graders' application of phonics skills and strategies while they are reading and may even extend their knowledge of phonics beyond the specific sound–letter relationships that are taught (Juel & Roper-Schneider, 1985). Unfortunately, we find a steady diet of decodable texts as they currently exist quite dull.

Another category of basals, **controlled vocabulary basals,** have been very popular prior to the early 1990s, and many teachers still rely on these basals for their instruction (Hoffman et al., 1998). In preprimer controlled vocabulary basals a small set of five to ten sight words is introduced in each story. Children are taught to read these sight words prior to reading the story. Then they read a story in which these words are repeated frequently. As children read each new story, new sight words are taught and the text becomes longer and more complex. From story to story, the sight words continue to be repeated so that children build an ever-increasing sight vocabulary. Phonics instruction is a component of controlled vocabulary basals, but the stories that children read do not necessarily have many words that include the generalizations that are taught.

Reading programs are organized around three major skill areas: word identification (decoding), vocabulary, and comprehension. **Word identification** skills include knowing how to sound out words by relating sounds to letters (**phonics**), recognizing and using prefixes and suffixes (**structural analysis**), and being able to use context or the surrounding words in a text to understand an unknown word in the text (**contextual analysis**). **Vocabulary** skills include being able to read a large store of words without having to sound them out (**sight vocabulary**) and learning meanings for vocabulary words. **Comprehension** is taught in terms of many skills for understanding and remembering what the author says (**literal comprehension**), inferring what the author implies but does not directly state (**inferential comprehension**), and using the author's ideas and determining whether or not they are relevant, biased, or logical (**critical comprehension**).

Controlled vocabulary basal programs are usually organized around directed reading lessons or activities. **Directed reading lessons** have three steps: preparation for reading, directed reading, and follow-up. The preparation phase involves helping children relate their background experiences and interests to the story they will be reading. Teachers introduce vocabulary words in oral discussion, followed by a presentation of a few of the words printed in sentences and in isolation. Word identification skills are often taught in this phase and applied to the new story vocabulary. In the directed reading phase, teachers ask questions to stimulate and guide children's silent reading of the story. The story is usually read in small segments, which are interspersed with questions and discussion. Silent reading is followed by reading aloud particular parts of the story, usually to provide answers to questions. The follow-up phase involves teaching skills that can be applied to further understanding or appreciating the story.

A frequently used alternative to the directed reading portion of the directed reading lesson is the **directed reading-thinking activity** (DRTA) (Stauffer, 1969). In DRTA lessons, the teacher reads the title and shows pictures to the children. The children make predictions about what will happen in the story, which the teacher may record on chart paper. Then the children read a short segment of the story to see which of their predictions are accurate and whether their predictions need adjusting. This three-step cycle (predict, read, prove) is repeated several times throughout the story (Davidson & Wilkerson, 1988).

A final category of basals (published since the early 1990s) we call **predictable-text basals.** These basals are generally part of a **literature-based basal** program; they gather existing words of children's literature instead of stories written specifically for basal readers, as is done in decodable and vocabulary-controlled basals. In first grade, the predictable-text basals include literature selections from predictable books and poems in which words and phrases are repeated in predictable sequences of events. In later grades, children read other kinds of literature selections.

Predictable-text basals recommend using shared reading techniques in first grade rather than the directed reading lesson typically recommended in controlled vocabulary basals (see Chapter 8 for descriptions of shared reading). In these basal programs, children reread predictable pattern stories with their teacher and with partners. They write in special journals and read and write in other response activities, such as retelling the story using storytelling props or writing a pattern story.

Through rereading predictable-text basals, children are expected to learn sight words and apply phonics generalizations in the context of reading. Even though these basals do not control vocabulary, they draw on the natural high frequency of words. That is, **high-frequency words** are words that occur frequently in text. Only one hundred words make up 50 percent of all the words found in almost any English-language text. Learning to read high-frequency words—such as *the, is, of, are, were, they, in, it,* and *has*—is a powerful tool for reading, because these words appear so often in stories, poems, and informational books.

Other words follow phonics patterns and are easily decoded using phonics. For example, the word *cat* is easily decoded because it follows the rule that the vowel sound is short in a word with one vowel between two consonants. However, predictable-text basals include many other content words in addition to high-frequency words and decodable words.

It is important to note that the recently published literature-based basals (including the predictable-text basals at the first grade level) are different from their earlier vocabulary-controlled counterparts in at least one critical way. Older basals were based on a skills-based philosophy. Children were taught a sequence of discrete skills (sight words, phonics, prediction, etc.), which were practiced both during reading and on work sheets focusing on a discrete skill. Newer literature-based basals are based on an integrated whole-part-whole philosophy. Children are taught to use a variety of strategies while they are reading and writing. Sight words are learned by reading, phonics is learned by applying phonics during reading, and comprehension strategies such as predicting are used during reading. Skills and strategies may be taught in isolation, but they are continually applied during reading and writing activities.

In the following section, we describe Mrs. Walker's first grade classroom. She uses a predictable basal as part of her literacy program. However, she uses a wide variety of other materials and activities to support her young readers and writers.

Reading in Mrs. Walker's First Grade

Mrs. Walker is a first grade teacher in a suburban public school. She is especially effective at meeting the needs of her thirty students. The following example is from November, when Mrs. Walker provided multiple reading and writing experiences, including daily oral language, word wall, reading aloud, shared reading, partner reading, reading extensions and follow-ups, and self-selected books.

Daily Oral Language

An important daily routine in Mrs. Walker's class is **Daily Oral Language (DOL)** (Vail & Papenfuss, 1982). It involves a three-line text that Mrs. Walker writes on the chalkboard and into which she has inserted errors in spelling, punctuation, and usage. Today's DOL text is

jimmy he CAN wach
the car jast lik his dad
what can you do

Mrs. Walker first asks children to read the text; then they determine whether the information in the text is true.

Mrs. Walker: Let's find out if that [sentence is] true first. Jimmy, can you wash the car like your dad? (Jimmy nods.) He can!

Jimmy: I can wash it better!

Then the children offer suggestions about how to correct the text.

Laura: (about CAN) You put all capitals. . . .

Mrs. Walker: There's no real reason to have all capitals here, although I'm still seeing a lot of capital letters in some of [your] journals. . . .

Kasey: We don't need the *he*.

Mrs. Walker: Okay, when we have that *he*, it's just like we said "Jimmy Jimmy," isn't it?

Robert suggests a period after *do*.

Mrs. Walker: Think about this—"What can *you* do?" (with question intonation and emphasis on *you*)

Child:	It's a question!
Mrs. Walker:	I'm asking you something, aren't I? I'm asking you what you can do. So does it need a period? What does it need, Robert?
Robert:	A question mark. . . .
Kara:	You need a *e* in *like.*
Mrs. Walker:	Is this how I spell *like?*
Children:	No! No!
Mrs. Walker:	L-I-K, actually if I were sounding it out, that sounds pretty good—/l/, /ī/—but if I wouldn't put the *e* on it, it would be /l/, /i/. Sometimes—
Child:	Like "Lick a stick!"
Mrs. Walker:	Sometimes we put an *e* on the end, and the *e* helps the other vowel say its name—/l/, /ī/. . . . Look at the word *just.* Now look real close at what I put—/j/-/a/-/ja/—I used the wrong vowel. Take a look at the vowels (points to short vowel posters at the side of the room). Vowels are special because every word has one.
Child:	I!
Child:	E!
Mrs. Walker:	Which one of those vowels do you think would make—listen—would make the /u/ sound?
Child:	I!
Child:	U!
Child:	E!
Mrs. Walker:	Like in what, A.J.?
A.J.:	U!
Mrs. Walker:	It would be the *U*—like in—
Child:	/u/, /u/.
Mrs. Walker:	—*fun tub* (These words are written on the short-*u* poster.)—hear the /u/ sound there?

Eventually, they find all the errors, and the text is now written correctly on the chalkboard.

Word Wall

After daily oral language, Mrs. Walker introduces six **words for the week.** These are words that the children will encounter during today's shared reading activity and that they will practice reading and spelling throughout the week. Later, these words can be added to a **word wall** (Cunningham, 1995; Wagstaff, 1997–1998), words that children are learning are displayed in alphabetical order on one wall of the classroom. Figure 9.1 presents an example of a word wall.

Aa	Bb	Cc	Dd	Ee	Ff	Gg	Hh
Aamir		Christopher	Daniel	Elizabeth		Gail	Hailey
a	be	come	do	eat	for	go	have
and	back	could	day			get	had
are	by	can't	down				

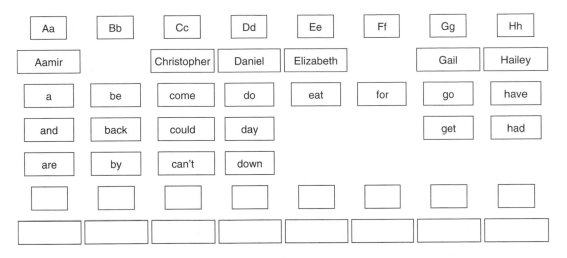

Figure 9.1 *Portion of a Word Wall*

To introduce these words, Mrs. Walker uses a poem placed in a pocket chart at the front of the room (McCracken & McCracken, 1986). The poem for her spelling lesson includes repetitions of the line "I can spell ______."

This week's new words are: *am, on, big, look, who,* and *can't.* Mrs. Walker places the first word, *am,* in one of the "I can spell ______" lines of the **spelling poem** in the pocket chart and helps children read the word. She emphasizes the known sound–letter correspondences.

During the week, the children practice reading the poem and reading and spelling the words. A favorite practice activity is **flashlight reading.** Mrs. Walker darkens the room and gives children turns shining a flashlight on words they know and reading them on the word wall.

Mrs. Walker uses the word wall daily for a variety of activities as part of her phonics and spelling instruction. For example, the children might use the words on the wall to find words with short-*a* and -*i* sounds. Other times, Mrs. Walker might add words to the wall when an occasion arises, such as when several children need the same high-frequency words (*they, where,* or *this*) in their writing. She may add words from social studies and science units, and later in the year, she may add words with suffixes such as *s, es,* and *ing.*

Later in the year, Mrs. Walker might use words from the word wall that have familiar phonograms to develop an analogy reading and writing strategy (Gaskins et al., 1997; Goswami & Bryant, 1990). That is, many first graders learn to spell words by spelling an unknown word that is like a word they already know how to spell. Similarly, children decode unfamiliar words by using words they do know how to read. To encourage children to use known words for reading and spelling, Mrs. Walker would use sentences to introduce familiar phonograms she wants the children to learn, such as teaching the children two long-*a* spelling patterns found in the words *sale* and *sail.* After reading a sentence that contains each of these words, the children discuss how the words sound alike and have the same long-*a* sound, but have different spellings and meanings. Mrs. Walker would help children write new words using the *ale* and *ail* phonograms (which she calls "word families"). She would demonstrate how to blend new consonants, consonant clusters, and consonant digraphs on to the word families to build words such as *male, mail, scale, trail,* and *shale.* She would make explicit the sounds of the onset consonants, clusters, and diagrams, and demonstrate blending them with the rimes *ail* and *ale.* Later, as children ask for spellings or encounter unknown words in their reading, Mrs. Walker would direct attention to similar word family words found on the word wall.

Mrs. Walker makes decisions about the nature of words to include on word walls, in her daily oral language activities, and for word family study based her knowledge of what the state and school system require first graders to know, the scope and sequence of skills taught in her basal, and from observations of children as they read and write. Figure 9.2 presents a general scope and sequence of phonics skills that children would be expected to learn in first through third grade.

Later in the morning, Mrs. Walker reads the picture book *Just Me and My Dad* (Mayer, 1977). As she reads, she talks about both the print and strategies for meaning making. She begins by calling attention to words in the title.

Figure 9.2 *Some Phonics and Spelling Generalizations K–3*

1. Each of the consonant letters corresponds to one sound, as in the words:

bag	hair	nest	toe
dog	jar	pipe	violin
fan	kite	queen	wig
	lamp	rug	box
	milk	sun	zebra

2. Consonant clusters are composed of two or three consonant sounds blended together (e.g., *bl, cr, dr, fl, gl, pr, sm, st, scr, str, thr, nt*)
3. The consonant digraphs correspond to the sounds in the words:

church	shoe	phone	thumb	whistle

4. The vowel letters take several sounds, such as:

long	***short***	***r-controlled***	***l-controlled***
ape	apple	her	hall
eagle	egg	sir	talk
ice	igloo	for	
oboe	octopus	fur	
unicorn	umbrella		
try			

5. Some consonants have more than one sound associated with them, as in the following:

   When the letter *g* is followed by the letters, *e, i,* or *y,* the *g* usually takes the soft sound, as in the letter *j* (*gym*). Otherwise, it takes the hard sound, as in the word *gum.*

   When the letter *c* is followed by the letters *e, i,* or *y,* the *c* usually takes the soft sound, as in the letter *s* (*cycle*). Otherwise, it takes the hard sound, as in the letter *k* (*cake*).

Figure 9.2 *(continued)*

6. **Vowel digraphs** are two or more vowel letters that together represent a single sound, as in the words:

say	seat	light	goal	blue	caught	boot	foot
sail	feet		stow	flew	awful		
weigh	field		hoe				
great							

7. **Vowel diphthongs** are vowel pairs that make a blended sound, as in the words:

oil	toy	mouse	cow

8. Some vowel digraphs and diphthongs have two sounds associated with them, as in the words:

cow	boot
blow	foot

9. When a word has the VCCV pattern, the vowel usually takes the long sound (*feet*).

10. Many phonograms illustrate the short, long, and other vowel patterns in VCV, VCVC, and VCCV words, such as in the words (this generalization may be utilized to teach vowel sounds and spelling patterns):

cat	bake	sail	loot	out
sat	make	mail	boot	shout
fat	take	tail	soot	scout

Mrs. Walker: This one has 1-2-3-4-5 words in the title. . . . Some of these words are in the morning sentences or in the morning graph question (pointing to the two texts still on the board from the opening routine). . . .

Kimberly: I know some of them.

Kimberly reads *My, Dad, Me,* and *and.*

Mrs. Walker: So the only one you don't know is the first one. "Blank me and my dad." J-U-S-T is in our morning sentence right here (pointing to the Daily Oral Language text)—remember that's the one I put the wrong vowel in?

Several children: Just!

Mrs. Walker calls on Nicholas, and he reads the whole title.

Mrs. Walker: What do you think this little boy and his dad are doing in this story?

Mrs. Walker points to the cover picture, which shows a Mercer Mayer creature and his dad fishing. She reminds the children of their responses to the morning question ("Have you ever gone fishing with your dad?") and suggests that they might have some ideas about what will happen in the story. She encourages children to use an important meaning-making strategy.

Mrs. Walker: What's a good question we could ask ourselves? Good readers always ask themselves a question before they start reading. What do you want to know about this book? What are you wondering about?

Child: I wonder where they go camping.

David: I wonder what kind of fish they are going to catch.

Mrs. Walker reads the story of the boy and his dad going camping. The story contains a pattern of events: The boy starts an activity (e.g., taking the dad for a canoe ride, cooking their fish), but it goes wrong (e.g., he launches the canoe too hard and it gets a hole in it, a bear steals their dinner), and the dad fixes it (e.g., takes them fishing, cooks eggs instead). The story is not limited to this pattern, however; other events occur (e.g., the dad takes a snapshot of the boy with the fish he caught). It is told with humor, some of which comes from its being told from the boy's perspective. For example, he says he gives his dad a big hug to make him feel better after they tell scary stories, but we know that the boy is the one who needs to feel better. The illustrations are Mercer Mayer's usual richly detailed, entertaining pictures. Mrs. Walker's students noticed and commented on the details (e.g., "There's always a spider on each page," "And a grasshopper!").

Shared Reading

Today's shared reading is carefully orchestrated with the graph question, the DOL sentences, and the story *Just Me and My Dad* in preparation for the children's reading of the first grade story *Just Like Daddy* (Asch, 1984). This simple pattern story about father and son bears who go fishing with their mother has been reproduced in the basal reader that Mrs. Walker uses. The pattern in *Just Like Daddy* is that the boy tells about performing a series of acts (yawning a big yawn when he gets up, having breakfast, getting dressed, picking a flower, baiting a hook) and each time adds the phrase "Just like Daddy." The twist that ends the story is that the boy catches a big fish "Just like Mommy" (Daddy is pictured with a much smaller fish).

The sentences in this story are shorter than those in *Just Me and My Dad;* the vocabulary is more regular; the pattern is more obvious; and the structure of the story is simpler (everything leads to the one joke of Mommy's big catch, in contrast to the multiple funny mishaps that befall the boy in *Just Me and My Dad*). There is an almost one-to-one correspondence between the illustrations and what the text tells. This story is typical of texts that provide the best kind of support for beginning readers.

Mrs. Walker combines the first two steps of shared reading (the teacher's reading and then the children's reading together) in order not to give away the joke at the end of the story. Instead of a big book, all the children have their own basal readers, which include this story. Mrs. Walker reads a page from her basal reader, and then the class rereads the same page together. They talk about the story and the illustrations as they go.

Partner Reading and Teacher Support

Next is **partner reading.** Mrs. Walker assigns each child a partner, and each pair has one book. The partners take turns: one reads while the other looks on and, as Mrs. Walker explains, "gets to be the teacher and help with any words they don't know."

Mark and Jacob are partners; they find a corner of the room, and Mark reads first. This text is easy for him; he reads fluently, with expression and no mistakes. Jacob follows Mark's reading with his eyes. When it is Jacob's turn, he works harder than Mark did, but with Mark's help he is able to finish the story with comprehension. He substitutes words that make sense in the story. He reads "jacket" for *coat,* "Mom" for *Mommy,* and "put on my worm on my hook" for *put a big worm on my hook.*

Most pairs of children read the story two or three times to each other and then begin working on reading extension activities that Mrs. Walker has planned (see the next section). However, some children may need Mrs. Walker's more explicit help (Turpie & Paratore, 1995). For these children, Mrs. Walker would gather a small group of children together for extra teaching and rereading of the story. Mrs. Walker would guide children's discussion of particular vocabulary words, support their use of phonics and other decoding strategies in reading portions of the story, and their rereading of the story several times. Then Mrs. Walker would prepare the children for writing a story extension: a summary, retelling, or pattern sentence. She would demonstrate elongating words and listening for big sounds (much like Mrs. Poremba in Chapter 8), rereading, using word spaces, and finding words in the classroom as composing strategies.

Reading Extensions

Mrs. Walker plans a variety of activities that extend children's reading interactions with *Just Like Daddy,* which she will use over the next few days. One extension activity is **patterned writing.** Each child makes his or her own "Just Like Daddy" or "Just Like Mommy" books, using the predictable pattern of the text to create their own sentences. Mrs. Walker types the phrase "Just like Daddy" (or "Mommy") and duplicates it so that each child has four pages of the pattern. She and the children discuss the things they like to do with their own moms and dads. Then the children write, using invented spelling, on their pattern paper and illustrate their pages. Two pages of Jacob's "Just Like Daddy and Mommy" pattern book are shown in Figure 9.3.

Another extension activity that Mrs. Walker might use is a **pocket-chart activity.** She would reproduce part of the text from *Just Like Daddy* on word cards and place them in a pocket chart. Children would take turns pointing to words and rereading the now familiar story. Mrs. Walker might remove several cards from the text and have children read the words without the support of the predictable text. They could confirm their reading by checking initial, middle, or final letters. Later, each child may be given a copy of the text printed on a paper with several words missing and small word cutouts located at the bottom. Children cut out the words and paste them in the blank spaces and then illustrate their texts.

Self-Selected Reading

As a balance to whole-group shared reading, Mrs. Walker makes sure that each child engages in daily independent reading at his or her reading level. One kind of self-selected reading she plans is what she calls **take-home books.** Each child has a basket of books that Mrs. Walker carefully selects to match with the child's current reading level. These are copies of poems, big books, and other little books suitable for children's independent reading. Each child's basket contains a dozen or more choices from which children select a

Figure 9.3 *Two Pages from Jacob's "Just Like Daddy and Mommy" Book ("I set the table. Just like Daddy," and "I rake leaves. Just like Mommy.")*

book to take home. Children practice reading these books at home and to each other or to another adult. For many children, the take-home books are predictable texts. Since many children who are struggling to make the transition to conventional reading often do not read on their own (Lysaker, 1997), Mrs. Walker's careful selection of books ensures that children practice reading appropriate text independently on a daily basis (Martinez, Roser, Worthy, Strecker, & Gough, 1997).

The take-home books play a critical role in Mrs. Walker's first grade literacy program. For many children the take-home books provide opportunities to practice reading and rereading books at their independent reading level. Books at children's **independent reading**

level are books that they can read with full comprehension and less than 5 percent errors in word recognition. In contrast to take-home books, Mrs. Walker selects books for partner reading that are at most children's **instructional reading level.** In order to be successful in reading these texts, children need much instructional support such as provided by Mrs. Walker's DOL, read aloud books, and shared reading. Reading books at the instructional level provides children with opportunities to encounter new words, discuss meaning, and try out reading strategies. In contrast, reading books at the independent level provides children the practice they need to consolidate sight words and develop fluency. **Fluency** is the ability to read with natural intonation. As children mature in reading, their reading rate increases along with their fluency. Even more important, reading books at an independent level is enjoyable, and children are naturally motivated to engage in reading for longer and longer time periods.

For some children in Mrs. Walker's class, the take-home books provide them with reading challenges. Reading *Just Like Daddy* was very easy for Mark during partner reading; he read it accurately and with full comprehension. In order to stretch his reading abilities, Mark needs more challenging texts. Mrs. Walker selects more difficult books for Mark's take-home reading.

The take-home books can be accompanied by a journal for parents to write their observations about the home reading (Morningstar, 1999). Teachers may write a letter to parents explaining the range of different reading behaviors and texts that are expected in first grade. The the teacher might invite parents to read along with their children and then listen to their children read. Parents are invited to make comments about the strategies their children seem to be using or points of discussion about a text's meaning. Parents who have used this journal are often surprised at the amount of growth children make in achieving success with new levels of text difficulty, strategy use, reading accuracy, and reading rate.

Mrs. Walker's Balanced Reading Program

It is important to note that Mrs. Walker has carefully constructed a balanced reading program. She provides many opportunities for children to extend strategies for comprehending and interpreting a wide variety of texts. She reads aloud in ways that engage children in predicting, confirming, and hypothesizing. Children extend their knowledge of vocabulary and understandings of stories, poems, and informational books that Mrs. Walker reads aloud and in shared in reading. Children also extend their strategic approaches to reading and writing during pattern writing and other extension activities. Mrs. Walker provides other opportunities for children to extend strategies for decoding and spelling through her word wall activities. She plans instruction that is systematic and intensive (Strickland, 1998a) based on the individual needs of children. Mrs. Walker also provides opportunities for extensive amounts of reading in shared reading, partner reading, and take-home books. Later we will describe Mrs. Walker's writing workshop, in which children have multiple opportunities for shared and independent writing.

GUIDED READING APPROACH TO FIRST GRADE READING

The **guided reading approach** (Fountas & Pinnell, 1996) to reading and writing instruction is based on strategies used in Reading Recovery (Clay, 1993), a specialized program for struggling first grade readers (Chapter 11 provides more information about the program), and components of the nonability, multileveled instructional program (Cunningham, Hall, & Defee, 1998), especially the use of word walls and word study.

Characteristics of Guided Reading

There are three critical characteristics of the instruction used in the guided reading approach. First, a major emphasis is placed on developing strategic readers as active problem solvers who are expected to take initiative in solving their own reading difficulties. Important teaching occurs at the **point of difficulty** (Askew & Fountas, 1998) while children are reading. Children are expected to work at difficult points in reading by monitoring and discovering new information for themselves. Children make new discoveries as they search for and use information in the text, check one source of information with another, and link to what they already know. **Teaching for strategies,** helping children develop strategies they use during reading and writing is an important focus of instruction in the guided reading approach.

A second critical component of the guided reading approach is using sets of **leveled texts** that begin with easy texts that are highly repetitive with few words. Gradually children read more difficult texts that include more words and more complex, literary and informational language. Reading Recovery uses over a dozen levels of text difficulty in the first grade. Fountas and Pinnell (1996) recommend using sixteen levels of text difficulty in first through third grade, and Gunning (1998) has identified thirteen levels of text difficulty from first through early second grade. Lists of texts at several levels of difficulty can be found in Fountas and Pinnell (1996) or Gunning (1998), and many school districts have developed their own lists of leveled texts. Many texts at the easiest levels of difficulty can be purchased through publishers such as Wright Group, Rigby, Sundance, or Scholastic. Table 9.2 presents a description of eight levels of text difficulty and example books for each level (based on Peterson, 1991; Gunning, 1998).

A final component of the guided reading program is small **dynamic ability groups** (Fountas & Pinnell, 1996). In dynamic ability grouping, a small number of children who have similar reading abilities are selected to read together. Texts are carefully selected to match the needs of the small group of readers. Teachers read twenty to thirty minutes with the small group of readers at least four times per week. However, many teachers meet twice daily with some small groups of children who are struggling to make progress. In the following section, we describe Mrs. Tran's first grade classroom and her use of the guided reading approach.

Guided Reading Instruction in Mrs. Tran's First Grade

Mrs. Tran teaches twenty first grade children in a large urban district. The majority of the children in her classroom have home languages that are not English; the classroom includes six different home languages. We describe six components of Mrs. Tran's instruction: **literacy centers, talk-through** as an introduction to children's guided reading, teaching for strategies while children are reading, **interactive writing,** teaching for comprehension, and **word study.** Mrs. Tran's literacy program also includes multiple daily read alouds, shared reading, independent reading, and writing workshop.

Table 9.2 *Levels of Text Difficulty*

LEVEL	DESCRIPTION	EXAMPLE
1. Picture or Phrase	Each page includes a single word or phrase with close relationship to illustrations.	*Colors* (Birningham) Crown *I Hunter* (Hutchins) Greenwillow *Count and See* (Hoban) Macmillan *Have You Seen My Cat?* (Carle) Scholastic
2. Sentence Pattern	Each page includes a repetitive sentence with some new content. From close to some relationship with illustration as difficulty increases. Number of different words in pattern increases with difficulty.	*I Went Walking* (Williams) Harcourt *Spots, Feathers, and Curly Tails* (Tafuri) Greenwillow *Things I Like* (Browne) Knopf *Five Little Ducks* (Raffi) Crown *Bears on Wheels* (Berenstain) Random House *It Looked Like Spilt Milk* (Shaw) Harper-Collins
3. Sight Word	Includes one sentence per page; most words are high frequency, but a few content words. Most words strongly related to illustrations. Up to thirty-five different words and may be one hundred words in text.	*Blue Bug Goes to School* (Poulet) Children's Press *All By Myself* (Mayer) Golden Books *Go Dog Go* (Eastman) Random House *Just Like Daddy* (Asch) Simon and Schuster *Pardon? Said the Giraffe* (West) HarperCollins *A Dark Dark Tale* (Brown) Dial *Cookie's Week* (Ward) Putnam *Marmalade's Nap* (Wheeler) Knopf
4. Easy Beginning	Text of 100 to 150 words, with many high-frequency words and some content words. Less repetition and more words per page. Up to fifty different words.	*The Carrot Seed* (Kraus) HarperCollins *One Monday Morning* (Shulevitz) Scribner *Peanut Butter and Jelly* (Wescott) Dutton *Sheep in a Jeep* (Shaw) Houghton Mifflin *Titch* (Hutchins) Macmillan *More Spaghetti I Say* (Gelman) Scholastic
5. Moderate Beginning	Text of 150 to 200 words, with more content words, but the majority are still high-frequency words.	*Are You My Mother?* (Eastman) Random House *Hattie and the Fox* (Fox) Harcourt *Henny Penny* (Galdone) Clarion *George Shrinks* (Joyce) HarperCollins *Where Are You Going Little Mouse?* (Kraus) Greenwillow *Hop on Pop* (Seuss) Random House

(continued)

Table 9.2 (continued)

LEVEL	DESCRIPTION	EXAMPLE
6. Difficult Beginning	Varied vocabulary, longer text, more detailed information and complex plots. Most vocabulary in reader's listening vocabulary.	*Mouse Soup* (Lobel) HarperCollins *Do Like Kyla* (Johnson) Orchard *Kiss for Little Bear* (Minarik) HarperCollins *More Tales of Amanda Pig* (Van Leeuwen) Dial *Elephant and the Bad Baby* (Vipont) Putnam *Clifford, the Big Red Dog* (Bridwell) Scholastic
7. Early Transitional	Some vocabulary not in reader's listening vocabulary. May have short chapters and some unfamiliar concepts.	*Henry and Mudge* (Rylant) Simon and Schuster *Frog and Toad Together* (Lobel) HarperCollins *Fox in Love* (Marshall) Dial *Three Little Pigs* (Galdone) Clarion *The Art Lesson* (dePaola) Putnam *Bear's Picnic* (Berenstain) Random House
8. Later	Vocabulary beyond reader's listening vocabulary, complex plots and unfamiliar concepts.	*Nate the Great* (Sharmat) Dell *Cam Jan and the Mystery of the Dinosaur* (Adler) Dell *The Chalk Box Kid* (Bulla) Random House

Based on B. Peterson (1991) and T. Gunning (1998).

Literacy Centers

In order to provide time for instruction of small guided reading groups, Mrs. Tran prepares several activities for children to work on independently, which she places in seven centers in her classroom. Mrs. Tran plans these activities carefully so they present a range of challenges to the variety of learners she has in her classroom. Mrs. Tran expects that the children will work together without teacher support in the centers, capitalizing on peer support for learning (MacGillivrary, 1994; Sipe, 1998). Figure 9.4 lists the materials found in Mrs. Tran's seven literacy centers and describes activities that are typical for each center. Mrs. Tran changes the materials and activities included in the centers weekly or bi-weekly. During September and early October, she demonstrates how to work in the centers, showing children how to find and replace materials and sustain their activity in a center for twenty minutes. She shares a classroom aide, who assists in supervising the children as they work in the centers for an hour three mornings a week, with three other first grade teachers in her building.

Mrs. Tran assigns four or five children with mixed abilities to a center group; each center group is assigned to three centers a day. The membership in the groups changes every month so that children work with a variety of others throughout the school year. Mrs. Tran's schedule includes a large block of uninterrupted time for reading instruction, during which the children spend one hour and twenty minutes in centers while Mrs. Tran

Figure 9.4 *Mrs. Tran's Literacy Centers*

Listening Center. Tape recorder, multiple headphones, and approximately one hundred audiotapes of children's literature, including commercially available tapes as well as tape recordings of parents of present and past students, the principal and other teachers, and other guests reading books aloud. Sentences from the informational book or storybook that is read aloud are placed on sentence strips. Children select a sentence after listening to the book and illustrate it.

Big and Little Book Center. Small easel with four or five recently read big books, small children's chair, pointer, and small tubs of books for each child in the classroom, with copies of five or six books or poems read during shared or guided reading. Children take turns being the teacher and pretending to direct a shared reading experience. They also reread poems and books from their book tubs.

Library Center. Cozy corner created by shelves with nearly 300 books, including books Mrs. Tran has recently read aloud, books included in a social studies or science unit, and books by favorite authors and illustrations. Children browse through books and use props to retell stories (during this week, the retelling props are spoon puppets for versions of *The Three Billy Goats Gruff* and transparency props for retelling *Where's Spot?* on an overhead projector, which sometimes is located in this center).

Writing Center. A large, round table with shelves stocked with a variety of writing tools and materials. This week, Mrs. Tran has included letter writing as a part of the writing center. She has posted several examples of letters children may use.

Letter and Word Center. An easel, a small table for writing, and shelves to hold letter and word games and puzzles. Mrs. Tran writes words on chart paper each day and places the paper on the easel for children to copy if they wish. This week, Mrs. Tran has written her name and invited children to write her name several times on the chart paper. This week, small clipboards are available for children to copy the names of other children in the class (located on sentences strips and clipped on a ring in the center). Children are also challenged to write ten words included on the word wall, using letter tiles.

Computer Center. A large table with two computers, word processing packages, reading and other games, and Internet access. This week, children are challenged to write a grocery list. Food ads from the newspaper and alphabet books with food are located at the computer center.

Specials Center. This center is for special activities that occur in the classroom. This week, three parents have volunteered to read aloud with children. Other specials include art projects, cooking activities, and science experiments.

teaches three guided reading groups. In early November, the children are divided into five groups, and Mrs. Tran reads with each group four or five times a week. A reading specialist works in Mrs. Tran's classroom four mornings a week, and she works with another guided reading group. The reading specialist returns to the class in the afternoon to conduct a final guided reading group lesson. Altogether, most children read with a teacher in a guided reading group once a day, but some children work with a teacher twice a day for three days a week.

Talk-Through to Introduce Guided Reading

The guided reading approach prepares children to read a particular text with the talk-through activity (Clay, 1991b; Fountas & Pinnell, 1996). Keep in mind that guided reading prepares children to read text on their own without teacher support during reading. Talk-through is intended to orient children to the text: to text meaning, repetitive patterns, particular words that might not be decodable, or practice the use of phonics and other strategies to identify unknown words and monitor meaning prior to reading. Talk-through can provide much support for children's reading, or minimal support. Teachers carefully gauge how much support to provide in talk-through, given their awareness of the reading abilities of the particular children and the level of challenge presented in the particular text.

In this lesson in early November, Mrs. Tran is working with six children who are beginning to read conventionally. Mrs. Tran carefully selects an instructional level text to use with this group and decides how much support to provide during talk-through. She considers what the children already can do. She knows that these children have acquired a few sight words and can track print at the word-by-word level in pattern sentence books by using some initial consonant sounds to monitor their finger-pointing. They know many consonant sound–letter associations, are beginning to learn vowel associations, use initial and sometimes final consonants in their invented spelling, and are developing a strong concept of written words. Mrs. Tran's goals for this group are to develop a larger store of high-frequency sight words, practice monitoring reading by using initial and final consonant cues to cross-check, and practice using the strategy of linking new with known.

After careful consideration, Mrs. Tran decides to use *Where's Spot?* (Hill, 1980) as an introduction to the guided reading text *Where's Tim?* (Cutting, 1996). *Where's Spot?* is familiar to the children, employs the same repetitive language pattern found in *Where's Tim?*, and includes many of the same positional words she intends children to learn (for example, the words *under* and *behind*). Further, Mrs. Tran plans to use the pattern in *Where's Spot?* during a writing process lesson within the next few weeks. Mrs. Tran reads through both books in order to make decisions about what to include in her talk-through activity.

Mrs. Tran knows that the words *no, he, the, is,* and *in,* which are found in the text of *Where's Tim?*, are familiar to these children. These words along with left-to-right pointing should anchor their reading. She will introduce the **linking to the known** strategy by having children try to figure out the word *Tim* in the title by using what they already know about short vowels. Later, she will work with the short-*i* vowel in further word study.

Before the talk-through, Mrs. Tran reads *Where's Spot?* to the children, asking questions and inviting children to make comments. She quickly rereads the story a second time. Then she introduces the guided reading book *Where's Tim?*, using the talk-through. Figure 9.5 presents her talk-through introduction to this text. Notice how she calls attention to the connection to the earlier book she read aloud; establishes the repetitive pattern; focuses on locating the words *under, bathroom,* and *behind;* has children figure out the surprise ending; and models the linking with the known strategy as they read the title. Following the talk-through, the six children read the book independently. They read quietly, but aloud, and Mrs. Tran listens to all the children as they read, noting children's tracking of print, cross-checking, and linking to the known strategy.

As children are reading aloud, Mrs. Tran observes and notes one or two teaching points she will make with the children during the next part of the lesson. She decides to refocus on the vowel sound in the word *Tim* and use a small, dry erase board to have children use the phonogram *im* to build more words such as *dim, him, rim,* and *slim.* Mrs. Tran has children reread portions of the entire text several times; she integrates teaching during the rereading. She prepares a printed version of the text without the picture cues which goes in

Figure 9.5 *Talk-Through for* Where's Tim? *(Cutting, 1996)*

T: We're going to start today by reading this book. (Several children make overlapping comments: "Where's Spot?" "I know that book." "I like that book.")

T: How many words are in the title?

c: Two.

T: Yes (points), one, two (reads and points to the words) *Where's Spot?*

(Mrs. Tran and children discuss the author and read the book together, stopping frequently to talk about the story. She reads the story twice and stresses the positional words, such as *under* and *behind.*)

T: Now, today for guided reading we are going to read this book (passes out copies of book for each child), and it is also a book about someone searching. This man is searching. He can't find someone. I wonder who he is searching for?

(Mrs. Tran and children make guesses about who the man might be searching for).

T: How many words in the title? Let's count them together. One, two. The title is *Where's* (pauses). Um, who are they searching for? Does anybody know anything that will help me figure out the name of the person this man is searching for?

c: It starts like Tamika.

T: Yes it starts with the sound (Mrs. Tran pauses and many children offer sounds, most of which are /t/. Mrs. Tran confirms the /t/ sound.)

T: Anything else that could help us? What about this vowel? Does anyone know anything that might help us? (Children offer a variety of vowel sounds, and Mrs. Tran helps the children blend /t/ /i/ /m/.)

T: Now let's look through the book. Find the title page. (Mrs. Tran observes as children locate the page.) Let's look and see where the man is searching for Tim.

(Children discuss each page and where the man is looking. Mrs. Tran stresses the positional words that will be read on each page, especially *under* and *behind.*)

T: (page 5) Where is the man looking on this page? (Some children suggest the bathtub.) Yes, he is looking in the room where we find the bathtub. He is looking in the *bathroom.* Put your finger on the word *bathroom.* (Mrs. Tran makes sure everyone is on the correct word.)

T: (page 8) There's Tim! Why he's *fast asleep,* isn't he? Who can find the word *fast.* How would you check if this word was *fast?* (Children discuss cross-checking the *f* and *t* sounds.) Ok. Now use your pointing fingers and read the book softly to yourself.

a special binder and is available in each child's independent reading tub. After rereading the illustrated text once or twice and participating in the instructional activity focusing on reading and spelling words with *im* phonogram, the children read the print-only version. Finally, children choose one or two stories from the binder that they have recently read during guided reading to reread.

Teaching for Strategies during Guided Reading

Keep in mind that a critical component of the guided reading approach is to foster active readers who solve by themselves the problems they encounter while reading. Teachers are aiming for readers who have self-extending reading strategies (Clay, 1991a). That is, eventually readers acquire a sufficient number of strategies that enable them to actually get better at reading with minimal teacher support. Rather than solve reading problems before reading by providing children with all the sight words they will need, teachers in the guided reading approach intentionally leave problems for children to solve on their own during the very first reading of a text. In this way, children must use strategies to solve their own reading difficulties (Askew & Fountas, 1998; Schwartz, 1997).

Mrs. Tran has already taught several strategies to this particular group of children and uses prompts to encourage children to employ these strategies while they are reading. Mrs. Tran demonstrates a strategy several times during talk-throughs and then uses prompts and comments to encourage and reinforce strategy use when children are at a point of difficulty in their reading. This group of children has some strategies firmly under control, such as moving left to right and matching word-for-word while reading. Mrs. Tran demonstrated "reading with her finger" and often praises children for carefully reading with their fingers during guided reading (Fountas & Pinnell, 1996). When children have difficulty, she prompts for this strategy by asking, "Are there enough words? Were there too many words? Try rereading it again."

These children sometimes use other strategies, such as cross-checking picture and meaning cues with initial consonants and noticing mismatches between words they attempt and the way they appear in print. Mrs. Tran demonstrated the strategy by reading text that makes sense but does not match the initial consonant and talking about how to cross check. When children have difficulty reading, she may provide several prompts for the strategy, such as asking, "Where's the tricky word? What did you notice? What letter did you expect at the beginning? Would ______ fit there?"

Children in this group are beginning to make more than one attempt at a word before asking for help. They are beginning to use the strategy of backing up and trying again. In this lesson, Mrs. Tran demonstrated a more complex strategy of linking to known information to figure out an unknown word during the talk-through. Later, she will use prompts such as, "Can you find something you know about here? Does is look like ______? Do you know a word like this? Do you know a word that starts with those letters? Do you know a word that ends with those letters? What do you know that might help?"

Other groups of children in Mrs. Tran's classroom are learning more sophisticated strategies, such as using decoding a new word by analogy (using a familiar phonogram to identify a new word, such as using *ham* to figure out *scram*) or decoding multisyllabic words by using several analogies (such as using *ex* and *fan* to figure out *Mexican*). Other strategies focus on expanding vocabulary knowledge, such as calling to mind related concepts for words that are only somewhat familiar. Still other strategies focus on meaning, such as inviting children to predict and confirm, pause and build a mental picture, assess whether a character's action is expected or unusual, and connect story events or characters to life experiences and acquaintances.

Interactive Writing

Mrs. Tran uses interactive writing as part of her guided reading program. She may use interactive writing as a part of following a guided reading lesson. Or she might use it prior to or after reading a particular text. Mrs. Tran has decided to use an interactive writing activity using the pattern found in *Where's Spot?* with another small group of children. Mrs. Tran is particularly concerned about these three children in her classroom because of their need to develop many foundational concepts. These children do not have a firm grasp on identifying and writing all alphabet letters and are just beginning to control the left-to-right print orientation. They need many experiences with rhyming words and words with similar beginning consonants.

This group has already heard Mrs. Tran read *Where's Spot?* several times. Mrs. Tran has made a pocket chart of the text from this book for shared reading experiences. The children have practiced using a pointer to reread the story from the pocket chart, pointing the words left to right. They have participated in many pocket-chart extensions, such as matching words on word cards to words on the pocket chart.

Now Mrs. Tran has decided they will use interactive writing to compose pattern writing. The children decide to compose a pattern story called *Where's Mrs. Tran?* For this lesson, the children will only write the title of the story together during the interactive lesson. Mrs. Tran guides the children by having them repeat the title (*Where's Mrs. Tran?*) and count the number of words. She writes three lines on chart paper from left to right, emphasizing that they will write the three words in the title across the paper on these lines.

Mrs. Tran reminds the children of the first word in the title that they will write. She tells the children they will use the strategy of finding the word and copying its spelling. She asks the children, "Where could we look? Where do we know to find this word?" Mrs. Tran recognizes that an important reading and writing strategy for children at this stage of reading and writing is to draw on resources such as familiar stories, poems, and charts to read and write words (Sipe, 1998). The children find the word *Where's* both on the book *Where's Spot?* and on their pocket chart. Then the children spell the word, saying its letters left to right. Mrs. Tran briefly discusses the apostrophe. She invites first one child and then another to come to the chart and write the first four letters in the word *Where's*. Mrs. Tran quickly writes the remaining letters on the chart as the children tell her the letters. She has children remember the second word in their title and again has children think of where they could find the word. They locate five different places in the classroom where Mrs. Tran's name is written. Again, they name the letters, and children are selected to write them on the chart. Figure 9.6 presents the interactive writing result of *Where's Mrs. Tran?*

Mrs. Tran uses interactive writing with all the groups in her classroom. Depending on what the children know, Mrs. Tran adjusts what she expects children to write, the amount of support she provides, and how much text will be written in one lesson. In some groups, children write sight words quickly and spend more time discussing how to write words with complex vowel spelling patterns or adding suffixes, such as consistent spelling of *ed* and *s*. In other groups, children focus on writing the beginning, middle, and final sounds in words.

Figure 9.6 *Interactive Writing of* Where's Mrs. Tran?

Teaching for Comprehension

The guided reading approach uses leveled texts, and many first graders begin reading picture and phrase– or sentence-level books, which are not difficult to understand. These books, of course, have meaning, but their meanings are obvious from the illustrations. Not much interpretation—going beyond the literal words of the text—is needed to enjoy and understand these texts. While children are having a heavy dose of these kinds of texts, they should also be engaged in comprehension activities from the teacher read alouds. Children should be encouraged to ask questions, make predictions, insert comments, and draw conclusions during teacher read alouds. Children may be part of small or large groups that have **grand conversations** about a book their teacher has read aloud (McGee, 1996). Grand conversations are directed by children's comments and questions rather than by a teacher's asking of questions. Teachers begin the conversation by asking, "What did you think?" or "Who has something to say about the book?" We have provided examples of children's comprehension work that emerges during a grand conversation.

However, first graders are also expected to move beyond reading easy books. They will read sight word–level, beginning-level, and transitional-level books that have more complex story structures and detailed information with unfamiliar vocabulary. Meaning in these books goes beyond what is illustrated, and children can be encouraged to interpret them beyond the literal level. Grand conversations about these books in guided reading activities support children's deep thinking. Similarly, there are many comprehension activities that extend children's understandings of what they have read. Children can retell stories or information in journals, act out stories or draw diagrams of information, or compose new endings for old favorites.

Word Study

Mrs. Tran uses twenty minutes daily to engage in word study with the entire class (Bear, Invernizzi, Templeton, & Johnston, 1996; Pinnell & Fountas, 1998). Word study involves looking carefully at how words are put together, learning sound–letter relationships useful for reading and writing words, and building new words from known words. Mrs. Tran also has a word wall and uses this wall daily as part of her word study program. Mrs. Tran began the year with **make-a-word activities** (Cunningham & Cunningham, 1992). She selected two familiar word families from phonograms that she knows are frequently found in words first graders encounter, such as *ack, ail, ain, amre, eat, est, ice, ide, ick, ock, oke, op, uck, ug,* and *ump.* (Figure 9.7 presents thirty-seven phonograms that are most frequently found in English spellings; Adams, 1990, pp. 321–322.) Each child is given a card with the phonogram written on it, several cards with individual consonants, and a folder that had been stapled to hold the cards. Mrs. Tran says, "I have the word *eat;* now what do we need to make the word *beat?* Who can show me?" She emphasizes the sound of the letter *b* by elongating it. The children use their letters and phonogram cards to spell words while Mrs. Tran or the other children pronounce them.

Mrs. Tran uses building word activities in her letter and word center. She writes several words on a sheet of writing paper and challenges children to write additional words when they are in the center. Figure 9.8 presents a word-building activity that Sindy completed in the letter and word center. She composed the words *bat, mat, rat, sat,* and *vat* using

Figure 9.7 *Thirty-Seven Phonograms That Are Most Frequently Found in English Spellings*

ack	ail	ain	ake	ale	ame	an
ank	ap	ash	at	ate	aw	ay
eat	ell	est	ice	ick	ide	ight
ill	in	ine	ing	ink	ip	ir
ock	oke	op	ore	or	uck	ug
ump	unk					

From Adams, 1990, pp. 321–322.

the pattern Mrs. Tran provided in her word *cat.* Then Sindy went on to build words from another pattern, one that Mrs. Tran did not suggest. She wrote *Mom* and *Tom.*

Mrs. Tran will increase the difficulty of making words by introducing consonant blends and digraphs. Later she will select a set of letters that can be used to spell single- and multisyllable words (Cunningham, Hall, & Defee, 1998; Gaskins et al., 1997). For example, children might have the letters *d, p, r, s, e,* and *i* and use these letters to spell a variety of words, including *is, rid, red, dip, ride, rise, rider, pride,* and finally, *spider* (Cunningham & Cunningham, 1992, p. 109).

Later in the year, Mrs. Tran will also introduce **word sorts** (Bear, Invernizzi, Templeton, & Johnston, 1996). Children will collect and sort words according to particular spelling patterns. For example, children may collect words that have the long-*a* sound in them over several days. All the words will be collected and placed on cards. Then children can sort the words to discover all the patterns used to spell long *a,* such as in the words *fade, rage, fail, raise, pale, paste,* and *straight.*

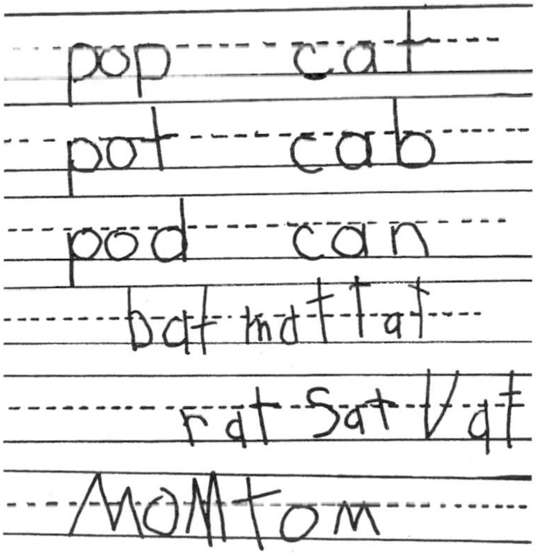

Figure 9.8 *Sindy's Word-Building Activity*

Mrs. Tran's Balanced Reading Program

Like Mrs. Walker, Mrs. Tran has crafted a balanced reading program that supports and extends the literacy learning of children who began first grade with a wide range of knowledge about literacy. Mrs. Tran uses multiple instructional contexts as a way to support children who might otherwise be at risk for literacy failure. For many children, she uses a mixture of shared reading and interactive writing to provide opportunities for children to gain foundational concepts about print, the alphabetic principle, and phonemic awareness. However, these children are also engaged in guided reading experiences in which they acquire sight words, develop strategies, and build vocabulary as they read text at increasing levels of difficulty. Mrs. Tran's word study extends children's reading and writing experiences through systematic examination of words. Finally, Mrs. Tran provides many opportunities for children to gain fluency by reading and rereading favorite books and poems. She carefully selects books for individual children, which she places in small tubs for each child in the room. Children read these materials at the beginning of every day and during some center activities. Mrs. Tran also provides time for children to browse through a variety of books, most of which will be beyond their reading level. She reads several books aloud daily and places these books in the library center.

WRITING INSTRUCTION IN FIRST GRADE

We have already shown ways that Mrs. Walker and Mrs. Tran capitalize on writing to strengthen reading instruction. Both teachers plan pattern writing experiences as ways to extend children's reading of predictable stories and poems. Mrs. Tran's classroom also includes a writing center where children engage in a variety of activities. In this section, we describe how these teachers use journal writing and writing workshop as an integral part of their literacy programs.

Journal Writing

Mrs. Walker introduced **journal writing** in late September. As a lead-in to this new activity, she and the children read a big book, *Cookie's Week* (Ward, 1988). This book tells, day-by-day, the misadventures of a kitty named Cookie. Mrs. Walker used this story to suggest that the children write in their journals about events in their daily lives. She also gave guidelines about her expectations for journal writing.

Mrs. Walker: I want one sentence—and a picture if you have time. Does Mrs. Walker think you can spell every word you want to write? No. But I do want you to try to write all the sounds you can.

Figure 9.9 presents Jacob's first journal writing. He included one sentence ("I like fishing") and an illustration.

One month later, Mrs. Walker changed her expectations for journal writing by inviting the children to write two sentences. She encouraged children to write longer entries in their journals by including two sentences in her DOL text. She also promoted more elaborate journal writing by helping the children to formulate ideas before they wrote.

Figure 9.9 Jacob's Journal Writing in September ("I like fishing.")

Mrs. Walker:	Could I have some ideas that are in your brains? What are you thinking about writing? Maybe we can help you with a second idea. . . .
A.J.:	Yesterday it was raining.
Zachary:	It got kind of dark.
A.J.:	It was really bad. It blew our pumpkins away.

Entries in the children's journals over the year provide evidence of the power of Mrs. Walker's approach. Figure 9.10 presents an entry from Jacob's journal written in the spring. This composition shows greater attention to words and greater knowledge of capitalization and punctuation than was found in his earlier writing (see Figure 9.9). It includes seven sentences and thirty-two words, of which ninteen are spelled conventionally. Jacob's invented spellings are fully phonemic or transitional spellings.

Each day, one group shares its journal writing with the class. Children in this group take turns sitting in the **author's chair** (a rocking chair at the front of the classroom) and reading their journal entries for that day (Graves & Hansen, 1982). The rest of the class is their audience. Mrs. Walker encourages audience members to ask questions that prompt the author to tell more (not yes-or-no questions).

Writing Workshop

Mrs. Walker uses journal writing as the beginning of an approach to writing called the **process writing approach or writing workshop** (Calkins, 1986; Graves, 1983). This approach focuses on helping children learn strategies for composing such as planning, revising, and sharing. Mrs. Walker introduces several strategies in her journal writing. She helps children plan for writing when she asks children to think about ideas they might write

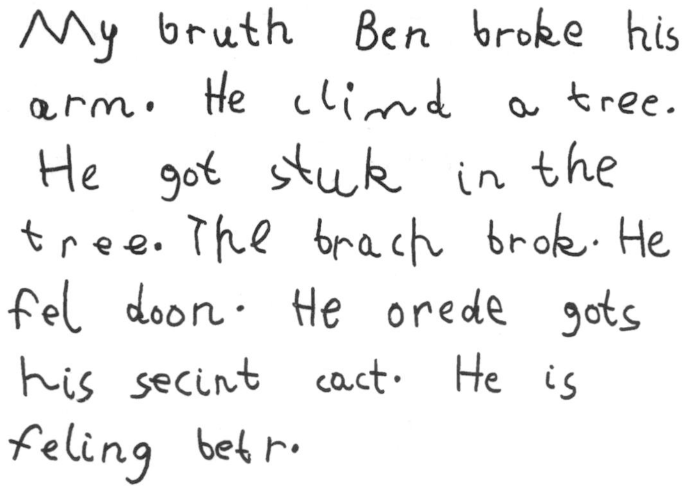
My bruth Ben broke his arm. He clind a tree. He got stuk in the tree. The brach brok. He fel doon. He orede gots his secint cact. He is feling betr.

Figure 9.10 Jacob's Journal Writing in the Spring

about and when she establishes the expectation that children should write two sentences. Mrs. Walker also provides a way for children to share their writing. Two or three children read entries from their journals in the author's chair every day. Having an audience who listens carefully to what a child has written provides that child with feedback about what was interesting about their writing. Questions posed by an audience help children learn how to revise by providing more details.

Minilessons are an important component of the writing workshop. **Minilessons** are short lessons in which teachers demonstrate a writing strategy that children might use. In the following section, we describe Mrs. Walker's minilessons for writing family stories.

Story Writing in Mrs. Walker's First Grade

In February, Mrs. Walker introduced story writing. She began by conducting a minilesson on collecting ideas for writing. She read *Earrings!* (Viorst, 1990), the story of a young girl's pleading with her parents to have her ears pierced. Then Mrs. Walker asked, "Where do you suppose Judith Viorst got the idea for this story?" The class speculated that the idea came from Judith Viorst's own life. Mrs. Walker then shared a picture book that she wrote, *Poppa's Coal Oil Story.* This story is her father's telling about an event in his childhood. Mrs. Walker tells her class how she got the idea for her book (from a favorite family story), planned her story, wrote several drafts, edited and typed her final draft, had a friend illustrate it, and bound it.

Mrs. Walker has several objectives for her students' story writing: "writ[ing] one idea per page—or maybe add some more about that idea"; being more careful about illustrations than in journal writing; and structuring stories with beginnings, middles, and ends. An example of her teaching with these objectives is a minilesson that began with her reading *My Cousin Katie* (Garland, 1989). This richly illustrated picture book tells about Katie's life on a farm. Each page contains one idea, sometimes with a sentence or two of elaboration. Its beginning middle-end structure coincides with one day on the farm, beginning at dawn ("Katie wakes up early") and ending at sunset ("The cows come home to sleep in the barn"). Mrs. Walker reads the story, and then she and the children talk about the beginning, middle, and end structure that she expects them to use in their writing.

During process writing time, the children plan and write stories in six-page stapled booklets; Mrs. Walker staples more pages in these books if needed. One day when we were visiting, Corey asked us to staple an additional page at the beginning of a book he was drafting. He explained that his story needed a beginning. Children share final versions by reading from the author's chair. They choose one story to be published in a special way. The text is typed and pasted into a hardbound, blank book. The student adds illustrations, Mrs. Walker adds a photograph and a note about the author, and the children share their published books at an authors' tea at the end of the school year. Figures 9.11 and 9.12 show two pages of a draft of Jacob's story, "I'm going to col sitee," and several pages of his published book, *When I Go to Coal City*

Informational Writing in Mrs. Duthie's First Grade

Mrs. Duthie teaches first grade in New York state and has written extensively on her experiences helping first graders read and write informational text (Duthie, 1996). She has discovered, like other teachers, that informational reading and writing is inspirational to all children, but especially to those children who naturally select this kind of text for their independent reading and writing (Casswell & Duke, 1998). Mrs. Duthie's classroom library has a special section for informational books, and she makes a special effort to read informational big books as part of shared reading experiences, as well as stories and poems. The class learns about as many informational book authors and illustrators as they do about authors and illustrators of stories and poems. Her children keep personal lists of the call numbers of books in the library for quick reference (informational books about cats are found under 636.8 and dinosaurs under 567.9!).

Figure 9.11 *Two Pages from Jacob's Draft for Story Writing ("I'm going to Coal City by Jacob P." and "We are going to fish at Coal City.")*

Figure 9.12 *Three Pages from Jacob's Published Book (last name masked)*

Mrs. Duthie uses minilessons to teach about information writing. First, she shares one or more informational books that have a special feature. Children talk about these special features and sometimes construct a group drawing or composition that includes the feature. For example, Mrs. Duthie showed *Oil Spill!* (Berger, 1994) to illustrate labeled drawings, *Jack's Garden* (Cole, 1995) to illustrate cutaway drawings, and *Water* (Asch, 1995) to illustrate cross-sectioned drawings.

As a part of minilessons about informational writing, children can learn how to put information into sets or groups, write about one part at a time, or lead with a question. They may discover and use captions, headings, tables of contents, and indexes. They may experiment with many different kinds of informational writing beyond that found in informational books. Figure 9.13 presents a first grader's want ad.

Want Ad

Cat wanted

I want a Siamese

cat by

Saturday. Be fluffy

and cute. Call

Will

739-6305

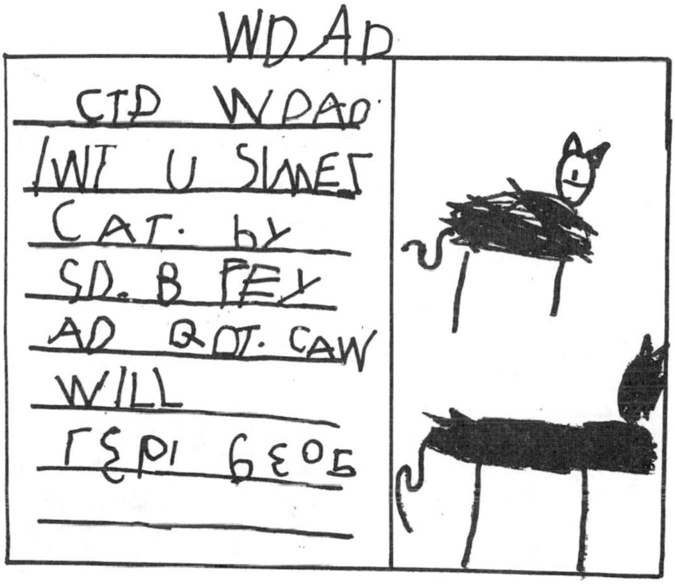

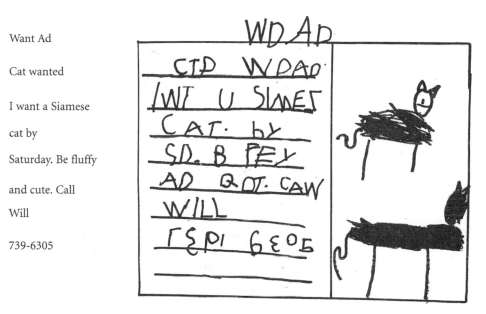

Figure 9.13 *A First Grader's Want Ad*

Poetry Writing in Mrs. Zickuhr's First Grade

Poetry reading and writing is an important part of literature enjoyment and literacy instruction in another first grade teacher's room. In Mrs. Zickuhr's room, children respond to poems through choral reading, collecting poems, drama, art, music, talking, and writing. Mrs. Zickuhr teaches several minilessons about poetry as a part of process writing. With one, she stresses the importance of feelings in writing and responding to poetry. She reads a poem about which she feels strongly, shares her feelings about it, and invites the students to respond in small groups. Another minilesson is about topic selection ("Poetry has to hit a person right in the heart or it won't work"). Another is about form. Mrs. Zickuhr suggests that after writing a draft, her young poets should think about structure: "Just like buildings have architecture—some are tall and thin, some are short and wide—poems also have to be built according to a design which works." She finds that first drafts often look proselike, so she has students read their poems aloud and add slashes for line breaks where they naturally pause. Another minilesson is about endings, that they can hold the rest of the poem together, can surprise the reader, make the reader think.

As inspiration, Mrs. Zickuhr reads poems that make use of sounds, such as the sound "vroom" found in the poem "The Go-Go Goons" from *Street Poems* (Froman, 1971). Children use these ideas in their own poetry compositions. Figure 9.14 shows a poem about motorcycles that Mike wrote, revised, edited, and published. Mike's poem shows attention to the sound words introduced in Mrs. Zickuhr's minilesson (see his use of the word *vrooming*). All published works in Mrs. Zickuhr's class bear the embossed seal of UKP, Unicorn Kids Press, a name they chose for their publishing company.

Motorcycle

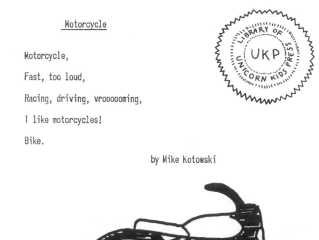

Motorcycle,
Fast, too loud,
Racing, driving, vroooooming,
I like motorcycles!
Bike.

by Mike Kotowski

Figure 9.14 *A First Grader's Poem*

Chapter Summary

First grade marks an important time in children's schooling. They are expected to begin "really" reading and writing; at the end of first grade, society expects children to have made great strides toward conventional reading and writing. We have shown that there are many ways in which this journey is taken.

We have described conventional reading as reading from print, but attending to meaning. Similarly, we could describe conventional writing as writing words, but attending to message. Acquiring knowledge about the alphabet, phonemic awareness, and print concepts forms a foundation for the later acquisition of sight words and strategies for identifying unknown words and extending understanding. This knowledge is built in a first grade reading program that balances skills and strategies and includes whole-part-whole instruction. We described three types of basals: decodable, vocabulary controlled, and predictable.

We described Mrs. Walker's first grade reading program, including her use of daily oral language, reading aloud, shared reading, reading extensions, take-home books, and word wall activities. Similarly, we described Mrs. Tran's first grade reading program, including her use of talk-through before guided reading, guided reading lessons, teaching for strategies, teaching for comprehension, and using interactive writing. Finally, we described a variety of writing activities, including using journal writing, the author's chair, and minilessons in composing stories, poems, and informational text.

Applying the Information

We suggest two applying-the-information activities. First, make a list of the seven characteristics of a literacy-rich classroom presented in Chapter 6. Then reread this chapter to locate an activity that is consistent with each of these characteristics. Discuss your examples with a classmate.

Make a list of all the literacy-learning activities described in this chapter. For each of these activities, describe what children learn about written language meanings, forms, meaning-form links, or functions.

Going Beyond the Text

Visit a first grade classroom and observe several literacy activities. Make a list of all the print and literacy materials in the classroom. Take note of the interactions among the children and between the children and the teacher during literacy activities. Talk with the teacher about his or her philosophy of beginning reading and writing. Compare these materials, activities, and philosophies with those of Mrs. Walker, Mrs. Zickuhr, and Mrs. Tran.

References

ADAMS, M. (1990). *Beginning to read: Thinking and learning about print.* Cambridge: MIT Press.

ASCH, F. (1984). *Just like Daddy.* New York: Simon & Schuster.

ASCH, F. (1995). *Water.* New York: Harcourt Brace.

ASKEW, B., & FOUNTAS, I. (1998). Building an early reading process: Active from the start! *The Reading Teacher, 52,* 126–134.

BEAR, D., INVERNIZZI, M., TEMPLETON, S., & JOHNSTON, F. (1996). *Words their way.* Saddle River, NJ: Prentice Hall.

BERGER, M. (1994). *Oil Spill!* New York: Harper Collins.

CALKINS, L. M. (1986). *The art of teaching writing.* Portsmouth, NH: Heinemann.

CASWELL, L., & DUKE, N. (1998). Non-narrative as a catalyst for literacy development. *Language Arts, 75,* 108–117.

CLAY, M. (1991a). *Becoming literate: The construction of inner control.* Portsmouth, NH: Heinemann.

CLAY, M. (1991b). Introducing a new storybook to young readers. *The Reading Teacher, 45,* 264–273.

CLAY, M. (1993). *Reading Recovery: A guidebook for teachers in training.* Portsmouth, NH: Heinemann.

COLE, H. (1995). *Jack's garden.* New York: Greenwillow.

CUNNINGHAM, P. (1995). *Phonics they use: Words for reading and writing* (2nd ed.) New York: HarperCollins.

CUNNINGHAM, P., & CUNNINGHAM, J. (1992). Making words: Enhancing the invented spelling-decoding connection. *The Reading Teacher, 46,* 106–115.

CUNNINGHAM, P., HALL, D., & DEFEE, M. (1998). Nonability-grouped, multilevel instruction: Eight years later. *The Reading Teacher, 51,* 652–664.

DAHL, K. L., SCHARER, P. L., LAWSON, L. L., & GROGAN, P. R. (in press). Phonics instruction and student achievement in whole language first grade classrooms. *Reading Reasearch Quarterly.*

DAVIDSON, J. L., & WILKERSON, B. C. (1988). *Directed reading-thinking activities.* Monroe, NY: Trillium.

DUTHIE, C. (1996). *True stories: Nonfiction literacy in the primary classroom.* York, ME: Stenhouse.

EHRI, L., & SWEET, J. (1991). Finger-point reading of memorized text: What enables beginners to process the print? *Reading Research Quarterly, 26,* 442–461.

FOUNTAS, I., & PINNELL, G. (1996). *Guided reading: Good first teaching for all children.* Portsmouth, NH: Heinemann.

FROMAN, R. (1971). *Street poems.* New York: McCall.

GARLAND, M. (1989). *My cousin Kate.* New York: HarperCollins.

GASKINS, I., EHRI, L., CRESS, C., O'HARA, C., DONNELLY, K. (1997). Procedures for word learning: Making discoveries about words. *The Reading Teacher, 50,* 312–327.

GOSWAMI, U., & BRYANT, P. (1990). *Phonological skills and learning to read.* Hillsdale, NJ: Erlbaum.

GRAVES, D. H. (1983). *Writing: Teachers and children at work.* Portsmouth, NH: Heinemann.

GRAVES, D., & HANSEN, J. (1982). The author's chair. *Language Arts, 60,* 176–183.

GUNNING, T. (1998). *Best books for beginning readers.* Boston: Allyn and Bacon.

HILL, E. (1980). *Where's Spot?* New York: Putnam.

HOFFMAN, J., MCCARTHEY, S., ELLIOTT, B., et al. (1998). The literature-based basals in first-grade classrooms: Savior, satan, or same-old, same-old? *Reading Research Quarterly, 33,* 168–197.

INTERNATIONAL READING ASSOCIATION (IRA) AND THE NATIONAL ASSOCIATION FOR THE EDUCATION OF YOUNG CHILDREN (NAEYC). (1998). Learning to read and write: Developmentally appropriate practices for young children. *The Reading Teacher, 52,* 193–216.

JUEL, C. (1991). Beginning reading. In R. Barr, M. Kamil, P. Mosenthal, & P. Pearson (Eds.), *Handbook of reading research* (Vol. 2, pp. 759–788). New York: Longman.

JUEL, C., & ROPER-SCHNEIDER, D. (1985). The influence of basal readers on first grade reading. *Reading Research Quarterly, 20,* 134–152.

LYSAKER, J. (1997). Learning to read from self-selected texts: The book choices of six first graders. In C. Kinzer, K. Hinchman, & D. Leu (Eds.), *Inquiries in literacy theory and practice* (pp. 273–282). Chicago: National Reading Conference.

MACGILLIVRARY, L. (1994). Tacit shared understanding of a first-grade writing community. *Journal of Literacy Research, 26,* 245–266.

MARTINEZ, M., ROSER, N., WORTHY, J., STRECKER, S., & GOUGH, P. (1997). Classroom libraries and children's book selection: Redefining "access" in self-selected reading. In C. Kinzer, K. Hinchman, & D. Leu (Eds.), *Inquiries in literacy theory and practice* (pp. 265–271). Chicago: National Reading Conference.

MAYER, M. (1977). *Just me and my dad.* Racine, WI: Golden Books.

MCCRACKEN, R. A., & MCCRACKEN, M. J. (1986). *Stories, songs, and poetry to teach reading and writing: Literacy through language.* Chicago: American Library Association.

MCGEE, L. (1996). Response-centered talk: Windows on children's thinking. In L. Gambrell & J. Almasi (Eds.), *Lively discussions: Fostering engaged reading* (pp. 194–207). Newark, DE: International Reading Association.

MORNINGSTAR, J. (1999). Home response journals: Parents as informed contributors in the understanding of their children's literacy development. *The Reading Teacher, 52,* 690–697.

MORRIS, A. (1989). *Hats Hats Hats.* New York: Lothrop, Lee & Shepard.

PETERSON, B. (1991). Selecting books for beginning readers. In D. E. DeFord, C. Lyns, & G. Pinnell (Eds.), *Bridges to literacy: Learning from Reading Recovery* (pp. 111–138). Portsmouth, NH: Heinemann.

PINNELL, G., & FOUNTAS, I. (1998). *Word matters.* Portsmouth, NH: Heinemann.

SCHWARTZ, R. (1997). Self-monitoring in beginning reading. *The Reading Teacher, 51,* 40–48.

SIPE, L. (1998). Transitions to the conventional: An examination of a first grader's composing process. *Journal of Literacy Research, 30,* 357–388.

SNOW, C., BURNS, S., & GRIFFIN, P. (1998). *Preventing reading difficulties in young children.* Washington, DC: National Academy Press.

STAUFFER, R. G. (1969). *Directing reading maturity as a cognitive process.* New York: Harper and Row.

STRICKLAND, D. (1998a). *Teaching phonics today: A primer for educators.* Newark, DE: International Reading Association.

STRICKLAND, D. (1998b). What's basic in beginning reading? Finding common ground. *Educational Leadership, 56,* 6–10.

TURPIE, J., & PARATORE, J. (1995). Using repeated reading to promote reading success in a heterogeneously grouped first grade. In K. Hinchman, D. Leu, & C. Kinzer (Eds.), *Perspective on literacy research and practice* (pp. 255–264). Chicago: National Reading Conference.

VAIL, N. J., & PAPENFUSS, J. F. (1982). *Daily oral language.* Racine, WI: D.O.L. Publications.

VIORST, J. (1990). *Earrings!* New York: Atheneum.

WAGSTAFF, J. (1997–1998). Building practical knowledge of sound–letter correspondences: A beginner's word wall and beyond. *The Reading Teacher, 51,* 298–304.

WARD, C. (1988). *Cookie's week.* New York: Putnam.

Chapter 10

Supporting Literacy Learning Beyond First Grade

Key Concepts

social construction of meaning
rehearsing
collecting
drafting
revising
editing
publishing
minilesson
status of the class
writing block
conference groups
legibility
reading workshop
reading block
response journals
reading conferences
core literature approach
core literature book or text set
literature discussions
book clubs
literature circles
literature discussion
story retelling
interactive storytelling
readers' theater
well-developed stories
character cluster
herringbone
circle stories
word clusters
list, group, and label
literary opposites
question-making activity
"long questions"
multiple-character perspective
choral reading
call and response
solo and chorus arrangement
two or more parts
music, movement, and sound effects
poem-a-day routine
poetry festival
think aloud
content units
idea circles
recording grid
content-specific vocabulary
homophones
homographs
word hunts
closed syllables
open syllables
divide and compare/contrast
spelling cycle
word pool
spelling challenge

WHAT'S NEW HERE?

In grades beyond first grade there are explicit outcomes for all subject areas. A second or third grade teacher is helped in planning for those outcomes by a new level of student competence in reading and writing. As a part of children's new competence, they are given greater responsibility. The teacher's role remains one of flexibility and careful attention to individual students' needs.

Increasing Expectations for Traditional Skills and Child-Centered Classrooms

In the primary grades and beyond, children are held accountable for mastering an ever-increasing number of academic skills in all subject areas. They are expected to apply sophisticated word identification strategies, including using spelling patterns and knowledge of familiar word parts, such as prefixes and suffixes. They are expected to attend to the meanings of words and to learn thousands of words by sight. They are expected to comprehend a variety of literary genres at increasingly more interpretive levels. They are expected to know literary elements found in stories and to use these elements in their own compositions. Children are expected to learn several spelling strategies, including using a dictionary, and to learn the conventional spellings of hundreds of words. Finally, they are expected to read and write compositions of increasing complexity, especially informational texts.

Child-centeredness does not have to end in the primary grades. Student choice continues to be an essential component in the reading and writing program. As we will demonstrate, second and third grade teachers continue to weave opportunities for children's own active exploration of reading and writing with instruction that is directed at helping children achieve the school's expectations for second and third grade literacy achievement.

New Competence

An important aspect of the context beyond first grade is that a class as a whole usually has achieved a critical mass of literacy competence. Teachers can rely on this competence to allow a degree of subject-matter integration and student independence that is impossible in the earlier grades. Even in second or third grade, not all students are fully conventional readers and writers, but a large enough proportion of them are so that all students can work together with increasing independence on tasks that require literacy competence. All can function in the sort of heterogeneous cooperative-learning groups, whose strategies for problem solving and content learning include reading and writing.

Activities like these have a characteristic that we can call **social construction of meaning** (Wells & Chang-Wells, 1992). They involve both a social component and a process of revision. In social construction of meaning, children work together to create an understanding, by which we mean that they interact with others in order to construct compositions and understand literature. This creative process, whether for composing or comprehending, always involves more than one pass at a text; it usually involves several rounds of remaking a message.

A piece of writing is sometimes only part of what results from social construction of meaning. Continued growth in oral language competence is an important part of this broader concept of literacy as well.

A Balanced Reading and Writing Program

The balancing act of teachers in second grade and beyond continues with many of the same struggles faced by first grade teachers. Perhaps the biggest struggle to achieve balance in the second grade and beyond is meeting the very diverse needs of children. Some children will begin second grade reading and writing far above grade-level expectations. They are capable of reading complex picture storybooks, informational books and easy chapter books independently. These children will improve their reading and writing with small amounts of teacher guidance.

Other children will end first grade reading at the difficult beginning-reading text level. They may or may not yet be reading books at the transitional level (see Table 9.2 for levels of text difficulty), which is considered second grade text–level material. However, these children will have in place many literacy skills and strategies. They are solidly on their way, but will need continued teacher support and extended practice to move into and beyond the transitional text levels.

Some children will not yet have accomplished what we expect in first grade. In fact, there is so much to be learned in first grade that many, many children do not reach the goals that many school systems have set for these young children. They may be reading only at the moderate or early beginning text level or below. They will need considerable teacher support and extensive amounts of practice in texts at their instructional level to enhance their early literacy skills and strategies. For a time, these children will continue to benefit from a guided reading program in which teachers direct instruction to the specific needs of a small group of children.

Teaching for strategies within the context of rich reading and writing experiences with narrative, poetic, and informational text is another component of balancing the literacy program in second and third grade. During second and third grade, children consolidate and extend beyond beginning reading and writing by expanding their power as independent readers and writers. Children develop flexible strategies for decoding and spelling words, acquiring new vocabulary meanings, comprehending and composing a variety of texts, and engaging in deep thinking about text.

Teachers must balance the amount of time used for instruction, guided practice, and independent reading and writing. Teachers continue to provide direct instruction in reading and writing strategies during instructional lessons. They also provide children with opportunities for guided practice using strategies in reading and writing activities. However, strategy development is only a part of competent reading and writing. Competent readers and writers are motivated and knowledgeable about a variety of text genres (Dowhower, 1999; Guthrie & McCann, 1997). Therefore, strategy instruction is embedded in rich conversations about literature in which children identify and assess their own strategy use while they jointly construct meaning. Teacher-directed instruction is balanced with child-initiated discoveries and self-assessment (Dowhower, 1999).

We describe five components of a balanced literacy program: using reading and writing workshop, reading and writing stories as a part of a core reading program, reading and writing information in content units, reading and writing poetry, and learning strategies and conventions. As we will show, teachers continue to provide instruction focusing on decoding and spelling, vocabulary development, oral language development, and deep thinking about text in extensive and meaningful reading and writing activities.

USING WRITING AND READING WORKSHOP

Children in the second grade and beyond benefit from their kindergarten and first grade writing experiences using the beginnings of a process approach to writing. In second and third grade, children continue using writing processes as they develop greater writing sophistication.

Writing Workshop

As we showed in Chapter 9, first graders use at least three writing processes: planning, revising, and sharing. Some first grade teachers introduce children to all five writing processes in their writing workshop. That is, most descriptions of writing processes (e.g., Murray, 1987) describe five writing processes: planning or rehearsing, drafting, revising, editing, and sharing or publishing. However, it is misleading to think of these processes as occurring linearly or sequentially; rather, they are interactive, and they often occur simultaneously (Graves, 1983).

One writing process is called **rehearsing** (Calkins, 1986) or **collecting** (Murray, 1987). This process includes a writer's search for a topic, identification of audience and purpose, and collection of ideas about which to write. Many young children draw pictures as planning for writing. Other children plan by talking to a friend or to their teacher, by writing a list of ideas, by role-playing an experience, by listening to or reading literature, or by simply thinking. The purpose of rehearsing and planning is to generate ideas and formulate plans for writing.

Another writing process is called **drafting** (Calkins, 1986). In this process children commit their ideas to paper. Drafting for young children may consist of as much talking and drawing as it does writing. First drafts of conventional readers and writers can be short, sometimes consisting of only a few words. More accomplished readers and writers write longer first drafts and more consciously consider the necessity of writing details.

A third writing process is **revising;** it consists of children's rethinking what they have written. In revising, children reread their drafts; add or delete words, phrases, or sentences; and move sentences. The focus of these activities is the content of the writing. In another writing process, **editing,** children focus on misspellings and errors in capitalization, punctuation, and usage. Children gradually learn to edit their own writing. The last writing process, **publishing,** consists of sharing writing with an audience.

Many teachers use the author's chair for informal classroom sharing as one way of publishing. Other ways of sharing children's published writing include having a "Share Fair" once a month, in which child-authors read to their parents or to other classrooms of children, write letters to members of the community, construct birthday cards to authors and illustrators, publish a class newspaper or literary magazine, bind books for a nursing home or children's ward of the hospital, and send compositions to children's magazines that publish children's writing (Temple, Nathan, Burris, & Temple, 1988).

Writing Workshop Format

Most teachers use a routine format for their writing workshop that includes the following:

- (Five to ten minutes) **Minilesson** on a writing or illustrating technique; literary elements; features of informational text; organizational patterns such as sequence or compare and contrast; rehearsal strategies for gathering and organizing information; revision strategies; or editing strategies
- (Three to four minutes) **Status of the class** (Atwell, 1987), in which each child very briefly states what he or she will do during workshop
- (Twenty to thirty minutes) **Writing block,** in which children write while the teacher conducts large and small group conferences
- (Five to ten minutes) Whole-group share by one or two children who read their compositions and lead discussion (from Duthie, 1996, p. 56)

Minilessons and Conference Groups

Minilessons are short whole-class lessons in which teachers demonstrate particular writing strategies, patterns that can be used in writing, or a special feature of text (Calkins, 1986). Throughout this chapter we present many ideas for minilessons related to writing narratives, poetry, and informational books.

Conference groups serve as collaborative learning groups. Writers' conference groups can be used to provide additional time and support for small groups of children to try out various strategies introduced in minilessons. They can also be used to teach children knowledge related to literary and written language conventions, such as letter writing, using similes or metaphors, and sequencing of events, as well as proper use of capital letters, periods, commas, quotation marks, and even colons.

Figure 10.1 presents an editing checklist that would be useful for second graders. To develop such a list, teachers plan a minilesson focusing on just one editing skill, such as listening for sentences. The teacher demonstrates this strategy using her own writing. Later, in a writers' conference group, children practice the strategy using a selected piece of their own writing. Then the teacher adds the strategy to a class list of editing strategies. The list grows longer as children learn more and more strategies. Often teachers will ask children to come to a writers' conference group and bring a draft of their writing with the editing checklist completed for that composition.

Computers

Classrooms beyond the first grade usually include at least one microcomputer. We suggest using computer time for word processing, exploring graphics, and conducting Internet projects.

Students can do some of their writing on computers, using a word-processing program, but it is not practical for them to do all their writing that way. Most students can do much of their planning and drafting with paper and pencil, rather than with a word processor. They are adept at making revisions with cross-outs, arrows, and brackets and cut-and-paste (see Figure 10.2). Then students can sign up for word processor time to do final drafts, to run spelling checks, to add graphics, and to print final copies of their pieces for publication in the classroom. They appreciate the ease of making changes with the word processor and the clean look of their computer-printed final copies.

Figure 10.1 *An Editing Checklist*

- ☐ I have reread my writing to a writing partner.
- ☐ I have listened for sentences.
- ☐ I have a capital letter at the beginning of each sentence.
- ☐ I have a period, question mark, or exclamation mark at the end of each sentence.
- ☐ I have a capital letter for every time I used the word *I*.
- ☐ I have a capital letter for every person's name.
- ☐ I have checked spellings of the word wall words.

Figure 10.2 *Carrie's Writing in Writing Workshop (A Rough Draft and One Page from the Published Story)*

Some students never use the word processor because they do not like waiting for a sign-up time or because they lack keyboard skills. Either they are quite satisfied with their handwritten products—many of which are very neatly produced—or they can get a classmate or teammate to type their pieces for them.

Handwriting

Handwriting is an important part of composing. When children labor over remembering how letters are formed, not to mention over listening to the sounds they hear in each word, their compositions suffer. The best ideas disappear when children focus on pencil and paper instead of on the content of what they are writing.

Instruction in handwriting should focus on **legibility** rather than on imitation of examples; it should provide children with language with which to talk about their handwriting and letters, and it should be connected with publishing children's writing.

There are four aspects of legibility that young writers need to learn. First, letters should conform to expected formations as defined by the writing program. Expected formations, especially of capital letters, differ from one handwriting program to another. Zaner-Bloser, a publisher of writing programs, is famous for its "ball and stick" manuscript letter formations (Barbe, Wasylyk, Hackney, & Braun, 1984). The D'Nealian handwriting program is known for slanted manuscript letters that are formed with a continuous stroke producing more curved lines (Thurber, 1981). Making expected letter formations does not always mean using the strokes suggested in a handwriting program. Children who begin making the letter *e* by writing it from bottom to top will probably not develop an unbreakable bad habit.

The second aspect of legibility is that letters should be of uniform size, proportion, and alignment. Third, letters and words should be evenly spaced. Fourth, letters should have a consistent slant.

The time to be concerned about legible handwriting is when writing is for an audience. Just prior to binding children's writing into a hardbound book is an opportune time for handwriting instruction.

Reading Workshop

Reading workshop is an approach to reading instruction that uses a format similar to that of writing workshop. It is an alternative to the guided reading approach for children who have achieved reading competence at approximately the first grade level or beyond (such as the Difficult Beginning level of text difficulty described in Table 9.2). Instruction during reading workshop does not take place in small group lessons guided by the teachers, and not all children read the same text. Instead, children select their own reading texts, and instruction takes place in a variety of places including during teacher read alouds and conferences. Reading workshop includes five components (Hansen, 1987; Reutzel & Cooter, 1991):

- Teacher reads aloud to children and conducts a minilesson demonstrating a reading strategy.
- Teacher holds a status-of-the-class discussion in which each child states the text(s) he or she will read or what will be accomplished on a response project.
- Children read during a twenty- to thirty-minute **reading block;** they may also work on a response project.
- Teacher holds conferences with individuals and small groups of children.
- Two or three children share from a book they are reading or present a response project.

Teachers begin readers' workshop by reading aloud to students. Through read alouds, teachers demonstrate reading strategies by talking aloud sometimes as they read (for example, stopping to imagine a scene in a story or to comment on connections among ideas in an informational book). In minilessons teachers may demonstrate reading strategies; provide information about authors, illustrators, styles of illustration, genres, or literary conventions; model response activities, including ways of writing in a response journal; and provide information about record keeping, such as how to record in a log the titles and authors of books read during readers' workshop. Students read independently for extended periods of time as a major part of the readers' workshop. The purpose of the reading block is to develop reading fluency, to create interest in reading, and to enhance children's reading ability.

Students respond to the literature they are reading in a variety of ways.

An important weekly response activity is writing in **response journals.** Children are encouraged to reveal parts of the book that are memorable, surprising, or unusual, or to describe related personal experiences or connections thay made to another book or poem (Barone, 1990; Dekker, 1991; Kelly & Farnan, 1991). Students are usually not required to write an entry in their response journal for every book they read, but may be required to write responses two or three times a week. Other response activities include writing a letter to the teacher or a classmate about a book they have read (Atwell, 1987).

While children are reading and responding to books during reading block, teachers hold **reading conferences** with students about the books they are reading. During these conferences, teachers talk with students about their books, listen to students read, and discuss response-journal entries and other response projects. Teachers use conferences to teach strategies and make assessments of students' progress and needs. As a last part of readers' workshop, students share their response projects and talk about books they are reading. Small groups of students act as audiences for response activities such as dramatizations and readers' theater productions.

Some teachers organize their reading workshop around studies of authors, illustrators, or genres (Duthie, 1996). Teachers gather books written by a particular author or illustrator for children to read during reading block. They teach minilessons of the author's or illustrator's style and provide information about the author's or illustrator's life. Teachers balance authors and illustrators of narrative, poetry, and informational books in their units.

READING AND WRITING NARRATIVES

Children expand their reading power as they read works by a variety of authors and illustrators, and read texts in a variety of genres we associate with narratives or stories. Narrative genres include realism (including historical fiction, mysteries, and sports stories), traditional literature (including folktales, fairytales, myths, and legends), and fantasy. As teachers guide children's reading and writing of narratives, children expand their strategies for reading, extend their vocabularies, and develop awareness of literary elements associated with narrative genres. Teachers provide direct instruction in strategies for reading narrative text and about the special literary elements that can be enjoyed in a variety of narrative genres. However, the goal is beyond a comprehension approach; reading narratives does not merely involve finding the meaning set in the page—uncovering the one, true meaning of a literary work. Instead, teachers expect "multiple meanings that stem from children's interactions with texts. Meaning is created, negotiated, and challenged, and most important, personally compelling" (Wolf, Carey, & Mieras, 1996).

Core Literature Approach

One way to organize instruction about narratives is to use the **core literature approach.** With this approach, a class or a small group of students reads a common literature selection (Zarillo, 1989). The core literature approach is very similar to the guided reading approach for readers who have achieved approximately first grade level competence. Depending on the teacher's goals and the children's instructional needs, children may read their core literature text without the teacher's guidance. Or, children may be guided by the teacher as they read the selection. The following are elements of the core literature approach:

- Children or teachers select a **core literature book or text set** (text sets are five to ten books around a topic or theme).
- Teachers model comprehension strategies, teach literary elements, provide examples of what to talk about during book discussions, and teach lessons on various response activities in whole-group lessons.
- Children read the core literature book or text sets with or without teacher guidance.
- Children participate in **literature discussions** with or without the teacher.
- Children participate in response activities.
- Teachers hold conferences with individual and small groups of children, focusing on extending children's responses; assessing, modeling, and guiding comprehension

strategy use; and expanding strategies for indentifying vocabulary meanings and reading unknown words.

Teachers may form three to five related **book clubs** (Goatley, Brock, & Raphel, 1995) or **literature circles** (Short, 1992) in a classroom. Each group reads its own core literature book or text set. To start a book club, the teacher provides multiple copies of a book, previews it for the class, and then signs up a club of children who are interested in that book. Children read assigned portions of the book with or without teacher guidance and then have a literature discussion. Teachers often participate in the literature discussion groups, providing alternative interpretive perspectives and challenging children to think more critically. Teachers and children may describe strategies used during reading. However, children may also have very productive literature discussions without the involvement of the teacher (Kauffman, Short, Crawford, Kahn, & Kaser, 1996)

Literature Discussions

A critical component of the core literature approach is **literature discussion** (Almasi, 1995), or grand conversation (McGee, 1995). Small groups of children gather with or without a teacher to talk about a book they have read. The expectation is that children will talk about things they thought were important, issues of concern, or things they do not understand. Literature discussions are not dominated by teacher questions (Scharer, 1996). Instead, conversation is shared between the teacher and children. Literature discussions can be initiated by having children identify topics or "seeds" that they would like to talk about at length (Villaume, Wordon, Williams, Hopkins, & Rosenblatt, 1994), or teachers can generate a list of possible discussion questions from which children select a few for discussion. Literature discussion questions include the following (Vogt, 1996, pp. 188–189):

- What does the author do to begin the story? Suppose the beginning were changed. How would the story be changed?
- What kind of person is the main character? Did he or she change in the story? How? What caused the change?
- Where does the story take place? If it took place somewhere else or at another time, how would the story be changed?
- In what ways are the characters and events like those you know or have seen?

Response Activities

There are many ways to respond to literature, including writing a retelling of a book, constructing simple props for a dramatic retelling, or experimenting with the medium used by an illustrator, such as learning to use scratchboard (found in Brian Pinkney's illustrations) or collage (found in Leo Lionni's illustrations). There are many other ideas for response activities throughout this chapter. Teachers establish guidelines on how often children are expected to respond to books to determine a balance between extended periods of time for reading and time for response activities.

Expanding Comprehension and Interpretation

A major component of instruction in second grade and beyond is helping children comprehend and interpret narratives with increasingly complex language and literary plot structures. Teachers support children's expanding comprehension abilities by planning activities in which children practice retelling stories and examine literary elements such as characterization and plot.

Story Retelling

Story retelling is a complex activity and a proven strategy for improving children's comprehension and fluency (Gambrell, Pfeiffer, & Wilson, 1985). Children must recall the main characters and critical events in a story in the order in which they appeared and with sufficient detail so that someone not familiar with the story will get the gist from the retelling. They naturally use the story's rich vocabulary and complex sentence structure as they retell the story thereby expanding their own language and vocabulary. Teachers can guide retelling in small groups by having children retell a story with teacher prompts. As the group recalls events in the story, teachers can encourage children to evaluate whether certain events are critical and should be included in a retelling and prompt children to include language from the story.

Retelling activities are enlivened with simple handmade props (see Chapter 6 for a description of several story retelling props). Teachers can demonstrate storytellings with props.

They begin with stories that are familiar and contain repeated dialogue and repeated action. Next, students will become storytellers themselves. Folktales are often well suited for this

To help children become storytellers, teachers may use interactive storytelling. **Interactive storytelling** involves the teacher's beginning a story, but inviting children to add dialogue or make up new episodes. Stories with repetitive episodes and dialogue are especially appropriate for this kind of storytelling. "By making storytelling an interactive event we can help children feel comfortable enough in storytelling to be confident of their own emergent narrative ability, to take risks, to elaborate, to invent, to explore, and thereby to grow" (Trousdale, 1990, p. 173). This is a prescription for children's growth not only as storytellers, but also as story writers and comprehenders of their world.

Having children write retellings is another effective comprehension stretcher. Teachers may introduce written retellings by having children write on each page of a little book an event that occurred in the beginning, middle, and end of the story (Tompkins, 1998). Eventually, children expand their retellings, as shown in the retelling of *There's an Owl in the Shower* (George, 1995) found in Figure 10.3.

Readers' theater is a special kind of retelling in which children read lines from a special script that reproduces a story. It adds a dimension of drama much like that of story retelling with props. **Readers' theater** is a simply staged form of dramatization in which players read their lines rather than memorize them (Shanklin & Rhodes, 1989; Sloyer, 1982; Trousdale & Harris, 1993; Wolf, 1993). Players usually sit on stools but may stand in groups. There are few props and only the simplest of costumes. To begin readers' theater, teachers can write their own script from a simple story or informational text. They demonstrate how dialogue from stories is translated into dialogue in script form and how narrative in text is

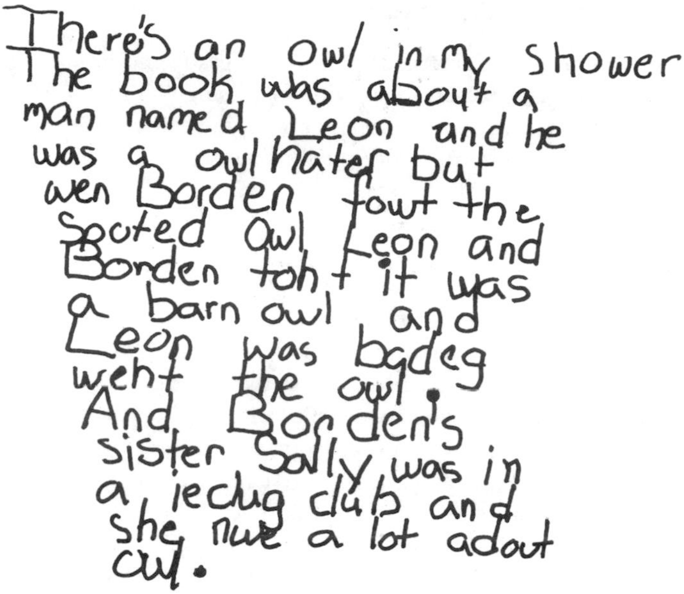

Figure 10.3 *An Expanded Retelling of* There's an Owl in the Shower *(George, 1995)*

translated into a narrator's words in a script. Eventually, students compose their own readers' theater scripts from a picture or informational book they have selected. Because children need not memorize lines, they are free to work on interpretation as they read the script aloud, they feel less anxiety, and, overall, there is less emphasis on the performance than in traditional drama.

The Judge: An Untrue Tale (Zemach, 1969) was a second grade class's choice for its first readers' theater (Trousdale & Harris, 1993). Next the class worked from a teacher-scripted version of *Leo the Late Bloomer* (Kraus, 1971) and a published readers' theater adaptation of *Where the Wild Things Are* (Sendak, 1963). Each child had a speaking part in one of the plays, and the class presented all three plays at their annual young authors' tea for parents.

In the readers' theater, rehearsals begin with the teacher's gathering the whole class so that all groups report progress. The children ask questions and make suggestions for solutions to problems in play making and playacting. Then the groups disperse to different parts of the room for rehearsals as the teacher circulates among them.

Once children (or the teacher) have composed a readers' theater script, teachers read it aloud during rehearsal. Then players experiment with reading the script by varying their voices and rate of speaking. The teacher assists students who are having difficulty (Hoyt, 1992). Even the least able readers can participate in readers' theater. They are helped by the repeated reading of the scripts that occurs as a natural part of rehearsal. In fact, rereading is another proven comprehension booster and fluency enhancer (Dowhower, 1987).

Nonverbal contributions are as important as spoken parts. For example, "[t]he child who played 'the horrible thing' in *The Judge* had no lines but simply suddenly appeared at the end of the story affecting a misshapen form under his white sheet; he crossed to the unbelieving judge and enveloped him in the folds of the sheet" (Trousdale & Harris, 1993, p. 203).

Readers' theater works just as well using nonfiction books as an alternative to content-area textbooks. It "gives the words on the page a voice, and the students in the classroom an active role in internalizing and interpreting new knowledge" (Young & Vardell, 1993, p. 405).

Discovering Literary Elements and Structures

Children in second grade and beyond develop an awareness of a variety of literary elements and structures found in narratives. In fact, there are so many literary elements and structures, we will only be able to touch on a few in this chapter (see Sipe, 1998). We focus on developing children's awareness of character and plot, and helping children notice structural elements.

At least one or two characters in quality stories are **well developed;** they have several character traits. Character traits must be inferred; they are revealed through a character's actions, words, and thoughts and by other characters' reactions. Learning to infer character traits is a critical literary strategy. Teachers may introduce the idea of character traits by reading a story with a strong character, such as Sylvester in *Sylvester and the Magic Pebble* (Steig, 1969). Teachers may think aloud as they read, commenting on certain character traits they have inferred as they read aloud. For instance, a teacher may note that Sylvester is generous; when he finds the magic pebble, he plans to let all his family and friends have a wish. Then children can be invited to infer a character trait and justify the reasons for their inference.

Teachers may demonstrate creating a **character cluster** as a visual representation of a character's many traits. A cluster for Sylvester's character traits might include the traits generous, naive, resigned, brave, and more mature. Teachers and children would discuss the meanings of these traits (notice the opportunities to expand vocabulary in this activity!) and find examples from the illustrations and text that support each trait. Eventually, children compose their own character clusters.

For example, Figure 10.4 presents a character cluster written by third graders for the main character, the boy, in *The Polar Express* (Van Allsburg, 1985). These children noticed

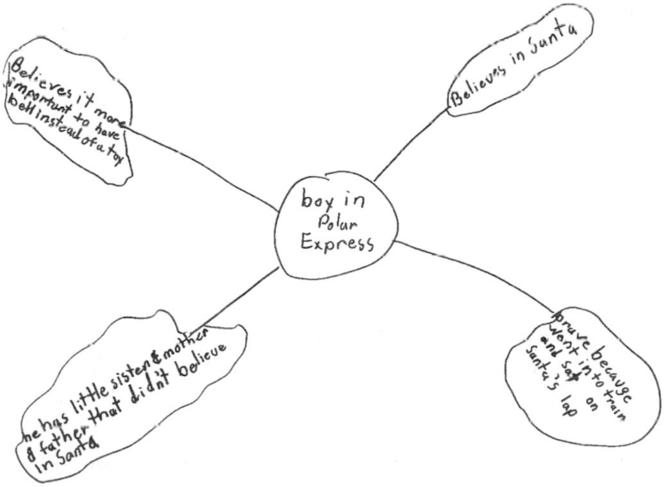

Figure 10.4 *A Character Cluster for* The Polar Express *(Van Allsburg, 1985)*

the boy's altruism (although they did not have the sophisticated vocabulary to label this concept) when they said, "[I]t was more important to have the bell instead of a toy." They also clearly identified the boy as a believer and as brave, two character traits strongly implied in the text. They were able to find two details from the text as support for one character trait (the boy was brave "because he went on the train" and "he sat on Santa's lap").

Again, the value of constructing character clusters lies in the quality talk generated about stories. As children work together to make hypotheses about characters' traits, they challenge one another to find supporting details. This kind of talk allows children to move back and forth between the literal information provided in the text and inferential ideas that they construct.

Clusters and other visual diagrams can be used to develop a strong sense of plot sequence. Children can construct beginning, middle, and end clusters in which they write several events from the plot for each node in the cluster. Figure 10.5 presents another visual diagram, called a **herringbone,** for the sequence of events in *The Polar Express* (Van Allsburg, 1985). This third grader began at the top of her diagram with the first event in the plot, and moved across left to right and down the herringbone pattern to retell the plot sequence.

Discovering the way authors organize their stories around recognizable structures improves comprehension and writing (Dowhower, 1999; Dressell, 1990). For example, one literary structure is the home-away-home pattern found in many familiar stories. Sylvester in *Sylvester and the Magic Pebble* leaves home one Saturday morning, finds a magic pebble, but meets a lion. He panics and turns himself into a rock, which he remains through the summer, fall, and winter. In the spring, his mother and father are picnicking on the very rock that is Sylvester. With a stroke of luck, Sylvester manages to become himself again. He returns to his home wiser, having gained an understanding that family is more important than having the ability to make wishes. These stories are also called **circle stories** because of the round structure created by the home-away-home movement of the character.

Children are fascinated to discover the home-away-home structure and other organizing structures in stories. One second grade class used reading workshop to focus on mysteries. They made a class chart of all the elements found in mysteries, such as clues, scary characters, scary events, and scary settings. They used their list of elements found in mysteries to plan events in a mystery. Figure 10.6 on page 290 presents a planning cluster in which Sarah identified characters, settings, and clues for her Campout Mystery.

Expanding Vocabulary

Teachers of second grade and beyond are concerned with expanding children's vocabularies. We have already shown that comprehension activities such as retelling and creating character clusters provide many opportunities to discuss vocabulary meanings. However, in the second grade and beyond, children encounter an increasing number of words in reading that are not included in their listening vocabularies. They need independent strategies for learning the meanings of these new words. Teachers must plan frequent activities that draw attention to words and their meanings.

One activity that helps children focus on word meanings is constructing word clusters. **Word clusters** are visual displays of knowledge related to a word (Pearson & Johnson, 1978). A word is placed in the center of a circle, and around the circle, information related

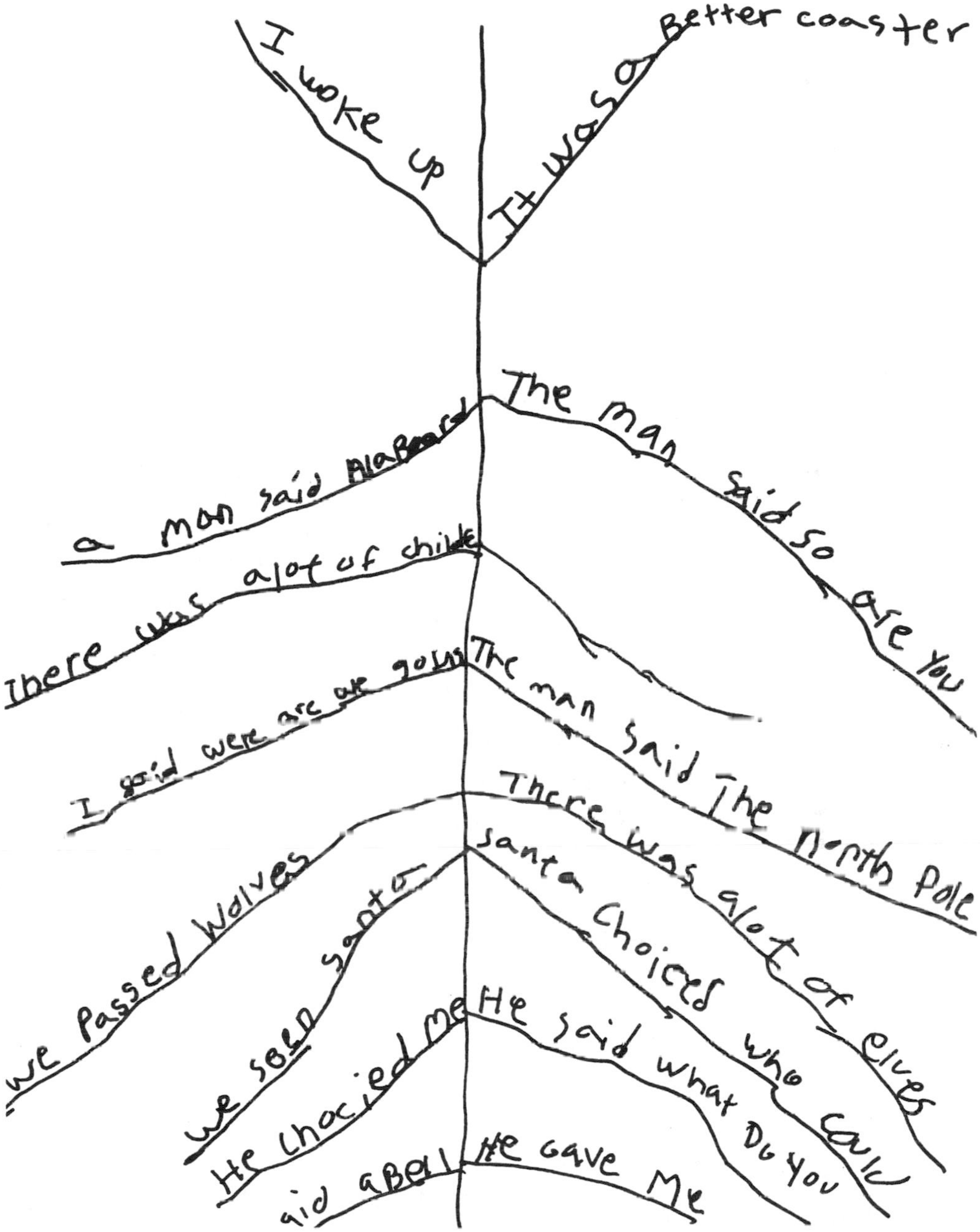

Figure 10.5 *A Herringbone Diagram for* The Polar Express *(Van Allsburg, 1985)*

to the word is written. Figure 10.7 presents a word cluster for the word *polar* written by a third grader before and after reading *The Polar Express* (Van Allsburg, 1985). First, Fran wrote about *polar* that "it's a train" and "it's big and black," reflecting her knowledge of the

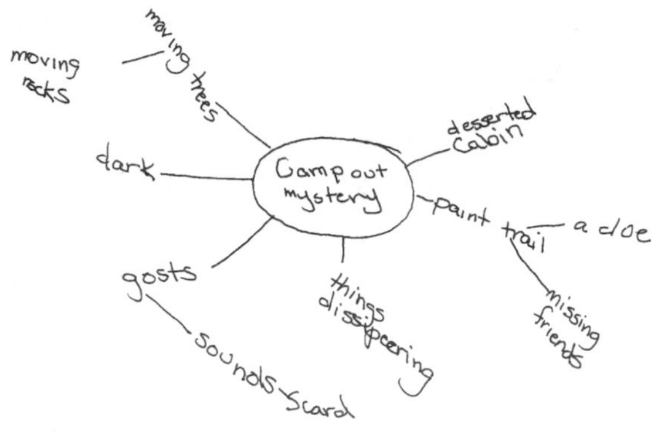

Figure 10.6 *Sarah's Cluster for the Camp-Out Mystery*

story but little awareness of the meaning of the word *polar.* After reading the story and discussing how *polar* was used in the story (to describe the polar ice cap and the polar sky), Fran became more aware of the word's meaning. However, when she spontaneously said, "Hey, polar bear! It's like a *polar* bear. They must live at the North Pole," she finally made the connection between the word *polar* and its referent *North Pole.*

Group construction of word clusters before and after reading is more useful than having individual students write their own clusters. Groups of students can pool their knowledge to come to a richer understanding of words. They notice clues in the text that allow readers to construct understandings of word meanings. Fran's knowledge about the word *polar* expanded as she paid attention to clues provided in the story text. Teachers can use

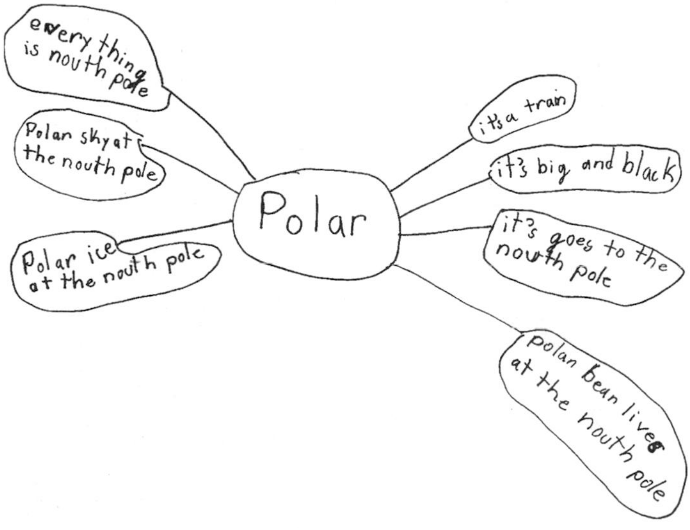

Figure 10.7 *A Word Cluster for the Word* Polar

think alouds to demonstrate strategies they use to gather ideas about a word's meaning. Or, children can describe how they uncover word meaning clues.

Another vocabulary expanding activity is **list, group, and label** (Tompkins & McGee, 1993) using words displayed on a word wall. Children gather words from a story they are reading and add them to a special word wall. As children gather words, teachers and children discuss the words and their meanings in and out of the context of the story. Children are encouraged to use words from the word wall in their literature journals and other response activities. Then they use the words in a list, group, and label activity.

A group of third graders reading *Keep the Lights Burning, Abbie* (Roop & Roop, 1985) gathered several vocabulary words from the story into a list and constructed a *Keep the Lights Burning, Abbie* word wall. The word wall included the words *Puffin, medicine, lighthouse, trimmed, wicks, towers, pecked, scraped, waded, henhouse, dangerous, weather, whitecaps, steered, ruffled, Hope, Patience,* and *Charity.* Next, small groups of children selected three to five words from the word wall to form a group. Then they described how the words were alike (the label portion of the activity). They wrote the words on a transparency along with the label for their group of words. Then, using the overhead projector, they shared their group of words and title with the whole class. One group of children grouped the words *scraped, waded, trimmed, pecked,* and *steered* with the title "things you can do." Another group of children grouped *pecked, ruffled,* and *henhouse* with the title "words related to hens," while a third group of children gathered *weather, whitecaps,* and *dangerous* with the title "words related to a storm."

Fostering Deep Thinking

Effective reading and writing programs make extensive use of children's literature. Quality literature is so critical because it calls for deep thinking. Literature invites multiple interpretations, via which readers go beyond the literal to make varied and personal connections with literature. Literature discussions or grand conversations are one way of fostering deep thinking.

Another way of encouraging the deep thinking that results in multiple interpretations is to use the idea of **literary opposites** (Temple, 1991), that literature has characters and events that are opposites. A story will have a greedy character and one that is more generous, events that happen at night contrasted with events that occur in the daytime, or strong girls who rescue weak men. Finding opposites often leads children deeper into stories (Temple, 1991).

A third grade class used literary opposites to explore character traits and themes in *Rumpelstiltskin* (Zelinsky, 1986). They noticed that the miller and his daughter were poor, the king was rich, but the miller's daughter became rich when she was queen. They thought Rumpelstiltskin, the miller, and the king were greedy, but thought the miller's daughter was generous and giving. They noted that the miller's daughter and the king were tall and beautiful and handsome; Rumpelstiltskin was small and ugly. They noted that, at night, the miller's daughter was with Rumpelstiltskin, and during the day, she was with the king.

After listing these and many other opposites in the story, their teacher initiated a **question-making activity** (Commeyras & Sumner, 1995). In this activity, children construct questions that will lead to long discussions about literature. The teacher modeled asking questions that could be easily answered and did not generate much talk versus questions that generated many different ideas and opinions. Good questions are those that have no single correct answer, create many different ideas, and take a long time to discuss. This class called these kinds of questions **"long questions."**

The teacher invited children to suggest long questions to use for talking about *Rumpelstiltskin.* The children posed the following questions with the teacher's guidance:

> If the miller was poor, why did he give a daughter to the king?
>
> What kind of father was he to lie to the king in a way that might harm the daughter?
>
> Why would the daughter fall in love with a king who demanded she spin gold or be killed?
>
> Why are the king and Rumpelstiltskin so alike in character, but not looks? Did the miller's daughter think about this?

Children selected one of the long questions that they wanted to talk about, and the class broke into small groups to discuss their question. After the small-group discussion, they shared parts of their conversation with the whole class. As a part of this whole-group sharing, some children offered a thematic observation that, "out of desperation we sometimes do not tell the truth and make promises we never intend to keep." Children described how this theme was played out in the story and in their own lives.

A similar activity which requires children to take multiple perspectives on a story is the **multiple-character perspective** approach. Here, teachers select books that have characters who are in conflict, such as Nyasha and Manyara in *Mufaro's Beautiful Daughters* (Steptoe, 1987). Children discuss the story from first one character's, and then the other character's perspectives, focusing especially on the character's conflicting goals, motivations, intentions, and actions. Differing themes which emerge from discussions of the differing goals, motivations, intentions, and actions of characters can be critically compared and contrasted (Shanahan & Shanahan, 1997).

Teaching for Strategies

The spirited discussions that arise from using literary opposites, long questions, and multiple-character perspectives provide teachers with opportunities to help children reflect on critical thinking strategies that they use during these activities (Shanahan & Shanahan, 1997). As children construct arguments, they recall details from the text and illustrations, make inferences, draw conclusions, and make intertextual connections between stories and life and story to story. As children use these strategies, teachers can comment on their use, encouraging other children to draw on these strategies.

Children should already have acquired some comprehension strategies during first grade. They are likely to be familiar with predicting and rereading. However, in the second grade and beyond children need many comprehension strategies that they can apply to a variety of different reading contexts. The most powerful reading strategies are summarizing (creating a gist of what has been read), constructing a mental picture, relating what a reader knows to relevant portions of the text, and applying knowledge of text structures (such as knowledge of story grammar and literary elements described in this chapter and Chapters 2 and 5) (Pressley & Harris, 1990). Helping students learn to use strategies such as these is a critical part of a reading instructional program.

One framework for strategy instruction is to use the before, during, and after reading lesson design (Dowhower, 1999). Before reading, teachers select a text that lends itself to a particular strategy. For example, "The New Girl at School" (Delton, 1986) is a story about a girl moving to a new home and finding new friends. Because its theme is reflected in the changing feelings of the girl, the story lends itself to using the strategy of relating what a reader knows (in this case, what a reader knows about being in a new situation) to relevant portions of the text. Before reading, children can be invited to discuss feelings they might have if they were to move and leave all their friends behind. They might predict what they would do in the new situation and what might happen to them. Then the text can be read in several segments carefully selected to focus on changing feelings. Each time children read, they discuss how the character is feeling and how it is alike or different from feelings they have had in similar situations. After reading the entire story, children describe how the strategy of using what you already know helped them better understand the story.

Children should have ample opportunities to use one strategy before teachers introduce another. They should be encouraged to describe ways that they use the strategy in their own independent reading. Teachers can construct a bulletin board with examples of specific ways children use the strategies being taught (Dowhower, 1999).

Children also need to learn strategies for reading unfamiliar words in their independent reading. As teachers respond to children's reading miscues, they can demonstrate independent word-reading strategies. The best response to miscues is to wait and see if the child notices the miscue and makes attempts to self-correct. If students do not notice the miscue and, particularly, when it changes meaning, teachers can ask, "Does _______ make sense to you?" rereading the sentence with the child's miscue. If children stop and hesitate, trying to decode the word, teachers can suggest that children read the remainder of the sentence. Often children will self-correct on rereading. If children are still stuck, teachers can provide brief help by covering up most of the word to focus on troubling spots or by inviting children to think of something they know that will help them. Teachers should avoid using more than one strategy. Instead they should make a note of the difficulty and resolve to teach a more directed lesson later (see the word study later in this chapter). Teachers can provide the word and have children reread the sentence to regain meaning. Children can use this strategy on their own. They should ask, "Does this make sense?", take a shot at reading the word, reread the sentence, make another guess if needed, and reread again (D. M. Murray, personal communication, 1998).

READING AND WRITING POETRY

Poetry is an important literary genre that all too often is neglected in the elementary school (Denman, 1988). However, teachers have discovered that poetry "not only [is] accessible to primary children, [but] can be *the* genre that excites children and motivates them to read and write" (Duthie & Zimet, 1992, p. 14).

Enjoying Poetry

Choral reading is ideal for demonstrating the joy of poetry and providing opportunities to develop reading fluency (Trousdale & Harris, 1993). Poetry is meant to be read aloud again and again. First, teachers read a poem aloud, perhaps displaying the poem on an overhead projector. Children are invited to respond to the poem by discussing interesting words, phrases, and events in the poem. A copy of the poem is distributed to the children, and the teacher rereads the poem again. Children are invited to reread favorite lines or phrases, using different voices, such as loud or soft, fast or slow, for effect. Finally, the teacher guides the children in a choral reading, in which the children read the poem aloud.

Choral reading uses several different reading methods that make it a unique experience (Trousdale & Harris, 1993). One method of choral reading is to use **call and response.** Here, a leader reads a line or two of the poem and the remainder of the group rereads the line or lines as a response. Another method of choral reading is to use a **solo and chorus arrangement.** One child or the teacher may read particular lines of the poem and the remainder of the children read other particular lines. This arrangement is good to use with poems with repeating refrains. Another way to arrange choral reading is to use **two or more parts.** Two groups of children may alternate reading every other line of the poem, or several groups of children may read specific stanzas of the poem, and all the children may read the concluding stanza. A combination of approaches is also effective. A group of children could read the first stanza, two groups of children could read the next stanza, and so on.

Choral reading is enriched by **music, movement, and sound effects** (Trousdale & Harris, 1993). Children can use their hands to create a variety of sounds, including snapping, clapping, brushing, and tapping. Children decide how the sounds can be used to enhance the poem's effect and include them in their choral readings. Sound effects also can be created by having children repeat a phrase in rhythm to the reading of the poem. The nursery rhyme "Pease Porridge Hot, Pease Porridge Cold" is enlivened when one group of children adds the refrain "cold, cold, cold" for a first choral reading and then another group of children chants the refrain "hot, hot, hot" for a second reading. As the children chant their refrains, they can use voicing and body movements to demonstrate coldness or hotness. As first the "cold" group of children and then the "hot" group of children quietly chant their refrain, the other children choral read the poem, keeping to the rhythm created by the chanted refrain.

Choral reading provides for more than enjoyment; it offers meaningful rereading opportunities that extend fluent reading (Dowhower, 1987). First, teachers read the poem, modeling fluency and effective voice techniques. The children and teacher decide on several possible ways to choral read the poem, using multiple voices, sounds, or refrains. The children divide into small groups to make a final decision on how they will choral read the poem. Children reread the poem several times to practice their choral reading technique as the teacher circulates and provides suggestions. When children are fluent, they present their choral reading of the poem to the entire class.

Establishing a **poem-a-day routine** is another way to create interest in poetry (Durham, 1997). Teachers read at least one poem at either the beginning or the end of the day as a regular and daily routine. Children can be invited to select poems for the day. Teachers can establish a special shelf in the classroom library for poetry books or have a decorated box in which ten to fifteen poetry books are kept. Children can fill out a poetry request form with their name, the poem's title, the book title, and the page number (Durham, 1997). Teachers can use the request forms to select poems for reading aloud. Children may ask to read their own poem for the day. Reading poems daily prepares children for more concentrated study of poems.

Poetic Elements

Writing workshop is an excellent place to begin a poetry unit or to prepare for a **poetry festival** in which children present to their parents or other classrooms of children their favorite poems and poems they have written (Durham, 1997). During minilessons in a poetry-writing workshop, children can learn that not all poems have rhyme, but many do. They can learn effective sound elements, such as repetition, alliteration (repeating beginning sounds), rhyme, and assonance (repeating vowel sounds). They can learn about using invented words, focusing on a single image, and saying common things in uncommon ways. Finally, children can learn about lining, shape, and special uses of punctuation, capitalization, and spaces (Duthie & Zimet, 1992).

Teachers share several poems that include one of the poetic elements. They invite children first to respond to the poems, and then to discover and talk about the highlighted element. Together the teacher and children discuss the impact of using the poetic element in the poem. For example, children notice that indentations in the poem's lines make the shape of stair steps in the poem "Descent" (Merriam, 1989, p. 36) and different-length lines and special indenting create the shape of a wiggly snake in "The Serpent's Hiss" (Merriam, 1989, p. 48). A third grader composed the poem "Tree House," making use of line length and indenting to create a tree-shaped poem appropriate to the topic of his poem.

Tree house
Just you and me house
Kick up your feet house
Tree house
Free
House

READING AND WRITING INFORMATIONAL TEXT

Like poetry, informational text is often neglected in the primary reading and writing program (Duke, 1998), but just as some children find their way into reading and writing through poetry, other children find their way into reading and writing through informational books. Fortunately, in the last few years publishers have made informational books for young readers a priority. There are now many informational books with appropriate text difficulty levels for primary children.

Comprehension of Informational Books

Reading informational books should be part of guided reading, core reading, or reading workshop. A combination of reading and writing workshop is effective in expanding children's knowledge of the special features of informational text (Duthie, 1996). We recommend that teachers share one or two informational books during each minilesson. The books they select will have one or more special features of informational books (see Chapter 9 for a description of some of these features). Teachers may focus on one or two of these features and how the features provide supporting information related to the content of the book. Over time, as teachers read more and more informational books, showing more and more features, children will develop a sophisticated understanding of the variety of ways in which information is presented in them.

During reading workshop conferences or guided reading, teachers guide children's viewing of illustrations and reading of tables of contents, indexes, and text for a variety of purposes. Careful reading of informational text includes making explicit how the information is organized in a text. Some authors use sequence, such as found in how-to books; other authors use narrative; and still others ask and answer questions. Children should think through text slowly and carefully, using a **think aloud** procedure (Loxterman, Beck, & McKeown, 1994). Children read a sentence or two and then explain the information in their own words. They describe how the information they just read was connected to what was just previously read and make predictions about upcoming information.

Content Units

Reading and writing informational texts is an important part of content-area learning. Children need to learn how to search for specific information, evaluate whether information is relevant for their topic or question, and integrate and summarize information across several texts. **Content units** involving the study of particular topics in social studies and science, using hands-on experiences, a variety of informational texts, and reading and writing activities, increase children's reading and writing abilities as well as their understanding of scientific and social concepts (Morrow, Pressley, Smith, & Smith, 1997). Units can be organized into four phases: (1) observe and personalize, (2) search and retrieve, (3) comprehend and integrate, and (4) communicate to others (Guthrie et al., 1996).

Observe and Personalize

During the observe and personalize phase, children observe objects and events from the natural world. For example, in a unit on birds, children can observe a variety of birds in zoos or museums. They can examine different kinds of bird nests, feathers, and bird bones. They can observe and record behavior at a bird feeder. Observations are extended by browsing through informational books that provide facts and present drawings related to the observations. Using both observations and informational resources, children can make drawings of feathers and bird features such as different kinds of claws and beaks, and they can construct bird nests (Guthrie et al., 1996). As children gain more knowledge of birds, they generate questions that they might use for later searches. Teachers gather questions on large charts posted in the room. Questions are added, deleted, and revised as children continue observing in the natural world and in information resources.

Search and Retrieve

In the search and retrieve phase of the unit, children participate in **idea circles** (Guthrie & McCann, 1996), in which they extend their concept knowledge. They learn and practice locating sources that will provide information on a specific topic or question. For example, children who are studying garden flowers would participate in an initial discussion about flowers. As the children share information, the teacher would write headings related to the different kinds of information that children share. For example, a teacher would write the following headings: height, spread, color, foliage, and fragrance. As a part of the discussion, the teacher would take opportunities to expand children's vocabulary. He might introducing the words *fragrance* and *foliage* as children talk about a flower's *smell* or the different kinds of *flowers* and *leaves* (Wray & Lewis, 1996, p. 64). Later these headings would be used in an activity in which children search for and select information about flowers from informational texts.

Then the teacher and children would gather a variety of resource books, including children's information books, adult information books, and pamphlets about gardening. The teacher would prepare a **recording grid** with the headings he had gathered during the class discussion. Over several days, each child would fill in the recording grid with information about one or two flowers of their choice. To begin the work, the class would brainstorm a list of flowers, which the teacher would record on a chart. Then the teacher would demonstrate searching through informational texts to find information about a particular flower. He would show the children how to find the name of the flower in an index or table of contents.

Children would begin their search by locating one or two books that have information about the flower they have selected to study. Then the teacher would demonstrate selecting and retrieving information about the flower from one of the books found in the search phase. The teacher would demonstrate locating the page with information related to the flower and reading aloud the information found there. He would think aloud about the information in the text and whether it describes the flower's color, height, fragrance, trailing, or size. He would demonstrate how to put the information in his own words and write it on the recording grid. Then children work in idea circles, helping one another with finding, selecting, and retrieving information until their recording grids are completed.

It is important to keep in mind that the goal of idea circles is to gather a wide variety of information that will build conceptual knowledge about a science or social studies topic. Children who are searching for information about a particular flower and using the reporting grid are doing more than merely locating facts about one flower. The children's collaborative work allows them to learn strategies for locating, comprehending, and recording information. Further, over time, as children begin to notice patterns and relationships, their concepts about flowers and their growth and care will expand.

Comprehend, Integrate, and Communicate

In the comprehend and integrate phase of the unit, children work on more complex questions, often questions they generate for themselves. For example, third graders were answering the questions, "What are the body parts of your bird, and how do these body parts help this bird to survive?" (Guthrie et al., 1996, p. 326). Children selected birds of choice, located information about body parts, and wrote explanations for how the body parts allowed the bird to adapt to its environment through breeding, feeding, and protecting itself. Here, children needed to read carefully in order to detect critical information relevant to the question, integrate information across different texts, and find meanings of specialized vocabulary they were encountering. Children capitalized on knowing how to read graphs, diagrams, and other illustrations. They learned how to break up the question into parts, gather information, and then put the parts back together. In the final phase, children communicated their information in reports, group-authored books, charts, and informational stories.

Writing Informational Texts

Minilessons in reading workshop can spill into writing workshop, in which children are challenged to include the special informational book features in their writing. However, there are a variety of other kinds of informational writing opportunities that extend children's learning. Figure 10.8 presents an entry from a second grader's science log. His class was studying frogs, and each child had a guppy to observe daily. Mark included six facts that he observed about the guppy on this particular day.

Learning to write letters is an expected outcome in the primary grades, and teachers can use this opportunity to have children write to authors or illustrators. Teachers should keep in mind that popular authors get thousands of letters a year to which they cannot possibly write responses. Therefore, children should select less well known authors, authors of informational books, or new authors who are just beginning to publish (Phelan, 1994). In addition, teachers need to find out whether authors or illustrators are still alive before helping children write letters to them!

Before writing to an author (or illustrator), children should read as many of the author's works as possible, as well as information about the author's life. Librarians can help teachers locate biographical information about the author to share with children. Once children have read the author's works and information about the author, they should determine what they admire about the author's works. Because a popular author cannot respond to a whole classroom of children's questions, children should invite the author, for example, to sign a handmade bookmark. Teachers should gather all of the letters in one envelope and include a stamped, self-addressed envelope for the author to use if he or she wishes to return a letter to the class on a signed bookmark. Authors and illustrators do not provide their addresses in their books, so teachers will need to find the address of their publishing company, which will forward letters.

A simple alternative to writing to authors is to visit their web sites. Many authors and illustrators have exciting web sites and sometimes engage in e-mail discussions. Figure 10.9 presents the addresses of several authors' and illustrators' web sites.

Figure 10.8 *An Entry from a Second Grader's Science Log*

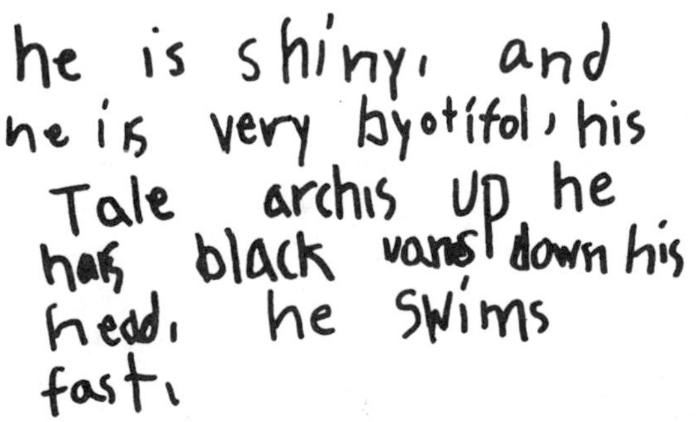

He is shiny, and he is very beautiful. his Tail archs up he has black vanes down his head. he swims fast.

Figure 10.9 *Web Sites of Authors and Illustrators*

Ted Arnold:	http://www.geocities.com/~teddarnold/
Judy Blume:	http://www.judyblume.com/
Jan Brett:	http://www.janbrett.com/
Eric Carle:	http://www.eric-carle.com/
Nancy Carlson:	http://www.nancycarlson.com/
Beverly Cleary:	http://www.teleport.com/~krp/cleary.html
Tomie de Paola:	http://www.bingley.com/
Leo and Dianne Dillon:	http://www.best.com/~libros/dillon/
Mem Fox:	http://www.memfox.net/
William Joyce:	http://www.harperchildrens.com/williamjoyce/
Ezra Jack Keats:	http://www.lib.usm.edu/~degrum/keats/main.html
Kathryn Lasky:	http://www.xensei.com/users/newfilm/homelsk.htm
Cynthia Rylant:	http://www.rylant.com/
Allen Say:	http://www.eduplace.com/rdg/author/say/index.html
Seymour Simon:	http://www.pipeline.com/~simonsi/
Janet Stevens:	http://www.janetstevens.com/
Chris Van Allsburg:	http://www.eduplace.com/rdg/author/cva/index.html
Audry Wood:	http://www.AudryWood.com/

Teachers are beginning to utilize the special features of computer word-processing and graphics programs to help children compose unique kinds of text. For example, a third grade teacher combined learning about computer graphics with newspaper writing. Children read and analyzed newspapers to discover their special features. At the same time, they explored a graphics and word-processing program on the computer. Figure 10.10 presents a page of two children's newspapers about the Oklahoma City bombing. In their multimedia composition they used a drawing to create the bomb, graphics to create a picture, and word processing to write their text.

Content-Specific Vocabulary

Informational texts have much **content-specific vocabulary,** words that have specific scientific meanings and that do not appear in everyday conversation (Leu & Kinzer, 1999). Informational books intentionally introduce scientific terms which are used to explain phenomena. For example, *Bald Eagle* (Morrison, 1998) provides definitions and illustrations of *nestling, prenatal down, natal down, egg tooth, eye shield, fledgling, thermal soaring, kettle, eyrie,* and *embryo.* Most informational books provide more than one source of information about content-specific vocabulary. Definitions are embedded in text, provided in glossaries, and illustrated in diagrams and drawings.

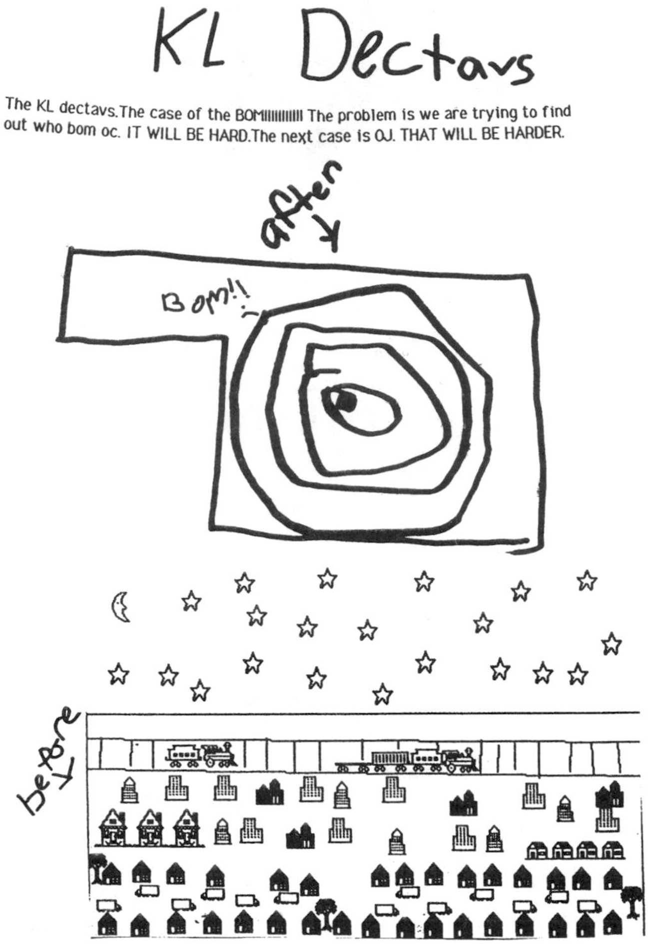

Figure 10.10 *A Page from Two Children's Newspapers about the Oklahoma City Bombing*

Teachers can demonstrate strategies such as using multiple sources to find and cross-check definitions of content-specific vocabulary. Children can be encouraged to demonstrate other strategies for locating information about content-specific vocabulary. Figure 10.11 presents a third grader's labeled drawing of a spider, which demonstrates his awareness of the content-specific words *abdomen,* and *spinnerets.*

LEARNING CONVENTIONS

There are a variety of written language conventions that second and third graders are expected to know. They learn about punctuation, capitalization, and grammar; and they develop more sophisticated strategies for decoding and spelling unfamiliar words. Children practice handwriting, study spelling patterns, and acquire an ever larger vocabulary of

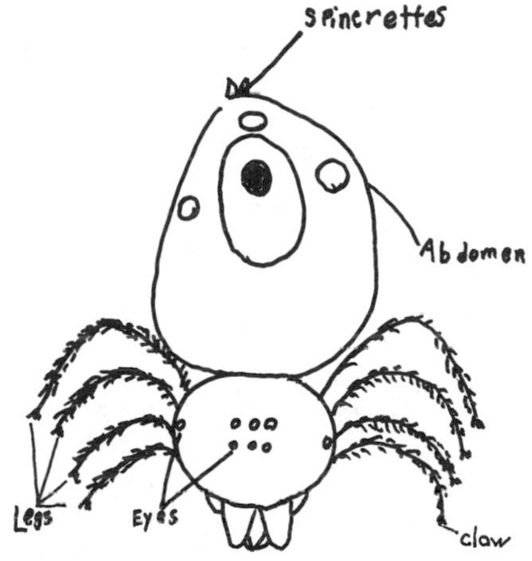

Figure 10.11 *A Third Grader's Labeled Drawing of a Spider*

words they spell conventionally. We have already described teaching many of these conventions earlier in the chapter. We described teaching capitalization, punctuation, grammar, and handwriting as part of the writing process. This is because the most powerful way to teach conventions is at the point of need. The time to teach how to use commas is when children need to use commas in their writing. Here, we discuss using word study for expanding decoding and spelling and teaching spelling in a weekly spelling program.

Word Study

Word study continues to be an important component of the reading and writing program in second and third grade. Word study should develop children's concepts about the orthographic structures of words and help them to use those structures to decode and spell multisyllabic words. Children in second and third grade are generally at a variety of levels of decoding and spelling understanding (Bear, Invernizzi, Templeton, & Johnston, 1996). Therefore, word study activities should be geared to those levels of understanding.

Most second and third grade spellers benefit from activities focusing on the variety of long-vowel and other vowel spellings. Knowing how to change word spellings when adding suffixes is also a critical skill acquired at this time. For example, children learn that words having a CVC pattern require doubling the final consonant before adding the suffix, as with *hop* and *hopping.* Also important is learning to differentiate the appropriate spellings of homophones and homographs. **Homophones** are words that sound alike but are not spelled alike, as in *bear* and *bare.* **Homographs** are words that are spelled alike but do not sound alike, such in the words *bow* (weapon used to shoot arrows) and *bow* (to bend from the waist). Again word sorts are appropriate. For example, children can sort words that take *s* or *es* or *ies* as their plural spellings (Fresch & Wheaton, 1997). Other activities include **word hunts,** in which children search for words with specific patterns in books, magazines, and newspapers.

A critical part of word study is learning strategies for decoding multisyllabic words, which are increasingly encountered in second and third grade reading. Eventually, children learn that when two consonants are between two vowels, the syllable is usually divided between the consonants (such an in *win dow*). The first syllable in these words is called a **closed syllable,** and the vowel usually has the short sound. In contrast, when one consonant is between two vowels, the syllable is usually divided between the first vowel and the consonant (such as in the word *fla vor*). The first syllable in these words is called an **open syllable,** and the vowel usually has the long sound. When a word ends with a consonant followed by *le,* the syllable is usually divided before the consonant (such as in the word *bu gle*). Even if the *le* is preceded by two consonants, the syllable is usually divided before the consonant preceding the *le* (such as in the word *bat tle*).

The most effective strategy for decoding multisyllable words is to **divide and compare/contrast** (Gaskins, Gaskins, & Gaskins, 1991). This is an extension of the analogy strategy described in Chapter 9. Children first divide the word into syllables and then think of a similar word for each syllable.

Spelling Programs

Spelling is an important part of the literacy program beyond first grade. Children need to learn to spell many words to use in their writing, to become aware of alternative spelling patterns, and to develop strategies for spelling unknown words (Wilde, 1992). We describe here a spelling program for second and third grades that has five features:

1. A large number of words that children are expected to learn to spell come from the children's needs, for example, from their own writing and reading, from current and upcoming content-area units, and from current events.

2. There is a balance between individualization and whole-class work. Students work with spelling lists that include personal words, which only they are expected to learn, and words that the whole class is expected to learn.

3. There is a balance between words that follow generalizations (e.g., *sight* words) and high-frequency words that do not follow generalizations (e.g., *said*). The teacher may have a master list of high-frequency words and generalizations that children will encounter at some point in the year.

4. There is a routine in the teaching and learning of spelling, including some routine way to begin a spelling unit and a routine way to bring closure to that unit.

5. Children are involved in identifying words to learn and in discovering spelling generalizations or rules.

With these features in mind, we suggest a program using a three- or four-week **spelling cycle.** For each spelling cycle unit, children generate a large pool of words with which they will work for three or four weeks. During this time, children are expected to be able to read these words and to know their meanings. Each week, small groups of children select a short list of words from the word pool for spelling. Each student learns to spell these words and two or three other words of personal interest or need. Each week for the three or four weeks of the spelling unit, children continue to generate a new spelling list from the word pool.

At the start of each spelling unit, the teacher and the children generate a **word pool** of seventy to eighty words from content units, high-frequency words, words that follow spelling patterns, words whose spellings children have requested during writing workshop, words collected from personal reading, or words that children find interesting. Children keep their own lists of words.

In some activities, the whole class works with words from the word pool for understanding, not for spelling. For example, children may categorize the words or make word clusters, resulting in adding related words to the word pool. In other activities, the class works together to discover spelling rules or devices to help remember spellings. Children may divide the pool into words that follow spelling generalizations, words that do not follow spelling generalizations (most high-frequency words do not), proper nouns, long words, and short words. Word groupings should highlight features of the words that will aid in learning to spell them.

Small groups of children choose twelve to fifteen words from the word pool to create a list of words to study and learn to spell for the first week. Each child is expected to add one or two personal challenge words to the group list that are unique to that child.

The children learn the words from their group's list. They test each other on Friday. Then groups generate new lists for the next week, still using the pool of seventy to eighty words that began the unit. The cycle continues through several weeks. Three or four weeks seem long enough to make good use of the original pool of words, but not so long that it gets boring.

To review and expand on words that children have already learned to spell, and as a break from the spelling cycle, the teacher may want to provide a **spelling challenge** from time to time before starting a new spelling cycle unit. Figure 10.12 shows an example of a spelling challenge activity.

Figure 10.12 *A Spelling Challenge Test Activity*

Spelling Challenge

This week's spelling challenge words are:

fight	eight	caught
night	height	though
light	straight	cough
slight	thought	rough
tight	through	ghost

Most of these words have a silent *gh*, but in the last three words, the *gh* sounds like a hard *g* or an *f*.

I challenge you to find more words with a silent *gh* and a *gh* that sounds like an *f* or a hard *g*. Think about it. Pay attention to words while you read. Start keeping a list. Compare lists with your classmates. Can you know anything for sure about where a *gh* will be silent or where it will sound like an *f*—or at least where it *won't* sound like an *f*?!

There will be a special challenge test on Friday with words not from this list.

Chapter Summary

Second grade and third grade are an exciting time for children and their teachers. The great strides that students make toward becoming fully competent readers and writers present teachers with great challenges, opportunities, and satisfactions.

In writing workshop, children use five writing processes: rehearsing, drafting, revising, editing, and sharing. Teachers model a variety of writing strategies for each of these processes in minilessons and provide guided practice in conference groups. Similarly, teachers demonstrate reading strategies in minilessons during reading workshop. Children read extensively and respond to books they have read.

The core literature approach involves small groups of children reading and discussing a book together. Teachers extend children's understanding of narratives by inviting retellings and helping children discover literary elements by using activities such as constructing character clusters and herringbones. They extend children's vocabulary knowledge with activities such as list, group, and labels. Choral reading allows children to enjoy poetry and provides opportunities for the rereading that is so important for comprehension and fluency development. Teachers extend children's understanding of poems in writer's workshop by calling attention to poetic elements. Teachers continue to help children develop flexible and powerful comprehension strategies.

Children read and write informational texts in content units in science and social studies. They learn organizational patterns found in expository text. As part of idea circles, children locate, retrieve, and comprehend informational text. They pay particular attention to the content-specific vocabulary they encounter in informational books and learn strategies for independent vocabulary learning. Word study continues in second grade and beyond, extending children's abilities to spell and decode multisyllabic words. A program for learning the spellings of words is also critical.

Applying the Information

We suggest two activities for applying the information. Make a list of the seven characteristics of a literacy-rich classroom presented in Chapter 6. Then reread this chapter to locate one activity from those presented that is consistent with each of these characteristics. Discuss your examples with a classmate.

Next, make a list of all the literacy learning activities described in this chapter. For each of these activities, describe what children learn about written language meanings, forms, meaning-form links, or functions.

Going Beyond the Text

Visit a second or third grade classroom and observe several literacy activities. Write a list of all the print and literacy materials in the classroom. Take note of the classroom layout and the interactions among the children and between the children and the teacher during literacy activities. Talk with the teacher about his or her philosophy of literacy instruction. Compare these materials, activities, and philosophies with those presented in this chapter.

References

ALMASI, J. (1995). The nature of fourth graders' sociocognitive conflicts in peer-led and teacher-led discussions of literature. *Reading Research Quarterly, 30,* 314–351.

ATWELL, N. (1987). *In the middle.* Portsmouth, NH: Heinemann.

BARBE, W. B., WASYLYK, T. M., HACKNEY, C. S., & BRAUN, L. A. (1984). *Zaner-Bloser creative growth in handwriting (Grades K–8).* Columbus, OH: Zaner-Bloser.

BARONE, D. (1990). The written responses of young children: Beyond comprehension to story understanding. *The New Advocate, 3,* 49–56.

BEAR, D., INVERNIZZI, M., TEMPLETON, S., & JOHNSTON, F. (1996). *Words their way.* Saddle River, NJ: Prentice Hall.

CALKINS, L. M. (1986). *The art of teaching writing.* Portsmouth, NH: Heinemann.

COMMEYRAS, M., & SUMNER, G. (1995). *Questions children want to discuss about literature: What teachers and students learned in a second grade classroom* (NRRC Reading Research Rep. No. 47). Athens: University of Georgia and University of Maryland, National Reading Research Center.

DEKKER, M. (1991). Books, reading, and response: A teacher researcher tells a story. *The New Advocate, 4,* 37–46.

DELTON, J. (1986). The new girl at school. In W. Durr (Ed.), *Adventures* (pp. 12–20). Boston: Houghton Mifflin.

DENMAN, G. (1988). *When you've made it on your own . . . teaching poetry to young people.* Portsmouth, NH: Heinemann.

DOWHOWER, S. (1987). Effects of repeated reading on second grade transitional readers' fluency and comprehension. *Reading Research Quarterly, 22,* 389–406.

DOWHOWER, S. (1999). Supporting a strategic stance in the classroom: A comprehension framework for helping teachers help students to be strategic. *The Reading Teacher, 52,* 672–688.

DRESSEL, J. H. (1990). The effects of listening to and discussing different qualities of children's literature on the narrative writing of fifth graders. *Research in the Teaching of English, 24,* 397–414.

DUKE, N. (1998, December). 3.6 minutes per day: The scarcity of informational texts in first grade. Paper presented at the annual meeting of the National Reading Conference, Austin, TX.

DURHAM, J. (1997). On time and poetry. *The Reading Teacher, 51,* 76–79.

DUTHIE, C. (1996). *True stories: Nonfiction literacy in the primary classroom.* York, ME: Stenhouse.

DUTHIE, C., & ZIMET, E. (1992). "Poetry is like directions for your imagination!" *The Reading Teacher, 46,* 14–24.

FRESCH, M., & WHEATON, A. (1997). Sort, search, and discover: Spelling in the child-centered classroom. *The Reading Teacher, 51,* 20–31.

GAMBRELL, L., PFEIFFER, W., & WILSON, R. (1985). The effects of retelling upon reading comprehension and recall of text information. *Journal of Educational Research, 78,* 216–220.

GASKINS, R., GASKINS, J. & GASKINS, I. (1991). A decoding program for poor readers—and the rest of the class, too! *Language Arts, 68,* 213–225.

GEORGE, J. (1995). *There's an owl in the shower.* New York: HarperCollins.

GOATLEY, V. J., BROCK, C. H., & RAPHAEL, T. E. (1995). Diverse learners participating in regular education "Book Clubs." *Reading Research Quarterly, 30,* 352–380.

GRAVES, D. H. (1983). *Writing: Teachers and children at work.* Exeter, NH: Heinemann.

GUTHRIE, J., & MCCANN, N. (1996). Idea circles: Peer collaborations for conceptual learning. In L. Gambrell & J. Almasi (Eds.), *Lively discussions! Fostering engaged reading* (pp. 87–105). Newark, DE: International Reading Association.

GUTHRIE, J., VAN METER, P., MCCANN, A., WIGFIELD, A., BENNETT, L., POUNDSTONE, C., RICE, M., FAIBISCH, F., HUNT, B., & MITCHELL, A. (1996). Growth of literacy engagement: Changes in motivations and strategies during concept oriented reading instruction. *Reading Research Quarterly, 31,* 306–332.

HANSEN, J. (1987). *When writers read.* Portsmouth, NH: Heinemann.

HOYT, L. (1992). Many ways of knowing: Using drama, oral interactions, and the visual arts to enhance reading comprehension. *The Reading Teacher, 45,* 580–584.

IRA/NAEYC (1998). Learning to read and write: Developmentally appropriate practices for young children. *Young Children, 53,* 30–46.

KAUFFMAN, G., SHORT, K., CRAWFORD, K., KAHN, L., & KASER, S. (1996). Examining the roles of teachers and students in literature circles across classroom contexts. In D. Leu, C. Kinzer, & K. Hinchman, (Eds.), *Literacies for the 21st century: Research and practice* (pp. 372–384). Chicago: National Reading Conference.

KELLY, P. R., & FARNAN, N. (1991). Promoting critical thinking through response logs: A reader-response approach with fourth graders. In J. Zutell & S. McCormick (Eds.), *Learner factors/teacher factors: Issues in literacy research and instruction* (pp. 227–284.). Chicago: The National Reading Conference.

KRAUS, R. (1971). *Leo the late bloomer.* New York: Crowell.

LEU, D., & KINZER, C. (1999). *Effective literacy instruction* (4th Ed.). Columbus, OH: Merrill.

LOXTERMAN, J., BECK, I., & MCKEOWN, M. (1994). The effects of thinking aloud during reading on students' comprehension of more or less coherent text. *Reading Research Quarterly, 29,* 353–366.

MARTIN, B. JR. (1972). *Sounds of laughter.* New York: Holt, Rinehart and Winston.

MCGEE, L. (1995). Talking about books with young children. In N. Roser & M. Martinez (Eds.), *Book talk and beyond* (pp. 105–115). Newark, DE: International Reading Association.

MERRIAM, E. (1989). *Chortles.* New York: Morrow.

MORRISON, G. (1998). *Bald eagle.* Boston: Houghton Mifflin.

MORROW, L., PRESSLEY, M., SMITH, J., & SMITH, M. (1997). The effect of a literature-based program integrated into literacy and science instruction with children from diverse backgrounds. *Reading Research Quarterly, 32,* 54–76.

MURRY, D. M. (1987). *Write to learn* (2nd ed.). New York: Holt, Rinehart and Winston.

PEARSON, P., & JOHNSON, D. (1978). *Teaching reading comprehension.* New York: Holt.

PHELAN, C. (1994). Writing to writers. *Book Links, 5,* 46–49.

PRESSLEY, M., & HARRIS, K. (1990). What we really know about strategy instruction. *Educational Leadership, 48,* 31–34.

RAPHAEL, T., & MCMAHON, S. (1994). Book Club: An alternative framework for reading instruction. *The Reading Teacher, 48,* 102–116.

REUTZEL, D., & COOTER, R. JR. (1991). Organizing for effective instruction: The reading workshop. *The Reading Teacher, 44,* 548–554.

ROOP, P., & ROOP, C. (1985). *Keep the lights burning, Abbie.* Minneapolis: Carolrhoda.

SCHARER, P. (1996). "Are we supposed to be asking questions?": Moving from teacher-directed to student-directed book discussions. In D. Leu, C. Kinzer, & K. Hinchman (Eds.), *Literacies for the 21st century: Research and practice* (pp. 420–429). Chicago, IL: National Reading Conference.

SENDAK, M. (1963). *Where the wild things are.* New York: Harper and Row.

SHANAHAN, T., & SHANAHAN, S. (1997). Character perspective charting: Helping children to develop a more complete conception of a story. *The Reading Teacher, 50,* 668–677.

SHANKLIN, N. L., & RHODES, L. K. (1990). Comprehension instruction as sharing and extending. *The Reading Teacher, 42,* 496–500.

SHORT, K. (1992). Intertextuality: Searching for patterns that connect. In D. J. Leu & C. K. Kinzer (Eds.), *Literacy research, theory, and practice: Views from many perspectives.* Chicago: National Reading Conference.

SIPE, L. (1998). Learning the language of picturebooks. *Journal of Children's Literature, 24,* 66–75.

SLOYER, S. (1982). *Readers' theatre: Story dramatization in the classroom.* Urbana, IL: National Council of Teachers of English.

STEIG, W. (1969). *Sylvester and the magic pebble.* New York: Simon and Schuster.

STEPTOE, J. (1985). *Mufaro's beautiful daughters.* Boston: Houghton Mifflin.

TEMPLE, C. (1991). Seven readings of a folktale: Literary theory in the classroom. *The New Advocate, 4,* 25–35.

TEMPLE, C., NATHAN, R., BURRIS, N., & TEMPLE, F. (1988). *The beginnings of writing* (2nd ed.). Boston: Allyn and Bacon.

THURBER, D. N. (1981). *D'Nealian handwriting (Grades K–8).* Glenview, IL: Scott, Foresman.

TOMPKINS, G. (1998). *Language Arts: Content and Teaching Strategies* (4th ed.). Columbus, OH: Merrill.

TOMPKINS, G., & MCGEE, L. (1993). *Teaching reading with literature: From case studies to action plans.* Columbus, OH: Merrill.

TROUSDALE, A. (1990). Interactive storytelling: Scaffolding children's early narratives. *Language Arts, 67,* 164–173.

TROUSDALE, A., & HARRIS, V. (1993). Missing links in literary response: Group interpretation of literature. *Children's Literature in Education, 24,* 195–207.

VAN ALLSBURG, C. (1985). *The polar express.* Boston: Houghton Mifflin.

VILLAUME, S., WORDON, T., WILLIAMS, S., HOPKINS, L., & ROSENBLATT, C. (1994). Five teachers in search of a discussion. *The Reading Teacher, 47,* 480–487.

VOGT, M. (1996). Creating a response-centered curriculum with literature discusssion groups. In L. Gambrell & J. Almasi (Eds.), *Lively discussions!: Fostering engaged reading* (pp. 181–193). Newark, DE: International Reading Association.

WELLS, G., & CHANG-WELLS, G. L. (1992). *Constructing knowledge together: Classrooms as centers of inquiry and literacy.* Portsmouth, NH: Heinemann.

WILDE, S. (1992). *You kan red this! Spelling and punctuation for whole language classrooms, K–6.* Portsmouth, NH: Heinemann.

WOLF, S. A. (1993). What's in a name? Labels and literacy in readers' theatre. *The Reading Teacher, 46,* 540–545.

WOLF, S., CAREY, A., & MIERAS, E. (1996). "What is this literachurch stuff anyway?" Preservice teachers' growth in understanding children's literary response. *Reading Research Quarterly, 31,* 130–157.

WRAY, D., & LEWIS, M. "But bonsai trees don't grow in baskets": Young children's talk during authentic inquiries. In L. Gambrell & J. Almasi (Eds.), *Lively discussions! Fostering engaged reading* (pp. 63–72). Newark, DE: International Reading Association.

YOUNG, T., & VARDELL, S. (1993). Weaving readers' theatre and nonfiction into the curriculum. *The Reading Teacher, 46,* 396–406.

ZARRILLO, J. (1989). Teachers' interpretation of literature-based reading. *The Reading Teacher, 43,* 22–28.

ZELINSKY, P. O. (1986). *Rumpelstiltskin.* New York: Dutton.

ZEMACH, H. (1969). *The judge: An untrue tale.* New York: Farrar, Straus and Giroux.

Chapter 11

Diverse Learners

Key Concepts

at-risk learners
Reading Recovery
children with special needs
individulaized educational plan (IEP)
repeated reading
diverse cultural backgrounds
ethnicity
social class
cultural discontinuity
culturally responsive instruction
participation structures
constructivist models of instruction
scaffolding
balance of rights
experience-text-relationship approach
diverse language backgrounds
mainstream dialect
nonmainstream dialects
English-as-a-second-language learners
additive approaches
subtractive approaches
shared language
character clues
extended discourse

LEARNERS AT RISK

Teachers are concerned with supporting all children's literacy growth, and most children do succeed in becoming reflective, motivated readers and writers with thoughtful instruction. That is, all children are unique and they approach literacy tasks with their own special styles and unique knowledge. Yet most children develop a range of expected knowledge within a reasonable time frame when they are given adequate opportunities and instruction. For young children, this time frame and range of expected knowledge is wide and allows for much individual variation. However, teachers also recognize that some children seem to struggle to acquire literacy even within literacy-rich classrooms and with a wide variety of instructional experiences. We call these children **at-risk learners.** At-risk learners need teachers who are especially observant and adept at modifying instructional techniques. Effective teachers are aware of the variety of special literacy-intervention programs that have been successfully used to accelerate the literacy learning of at-risk learners.

Using Observations to Modify Instruction

At-risk learners are more likely to experience school failure if their teachers do not use observations to modify instruction to better fit their needs. For example, a kindergarten teacher noticed that two children in her class had a great deal of difficulty listening to stories read aloud. Most children in her class were interested in the stories and informational books that she read aloud in whole-class gatherings. The children eagerly responded to questions and made thoughtful comments during short grand conversations. They sat still and watched the illustrations intently as she read the text. However, these two children were obvious exceptions to this general pattern of behavior. John and Pedro seemed to be behavior problems at storytime. They often brought small toys to play with, rolled around on the rug, and disrupted the group by attempting to talk with other children while the teacher was reading.

The teacher realized that both boys needed experiences with books. John had had few experiences with storybook reading prior to coming to school, and Pedro could benefit from more interaction with books to support his learning English as a second language. She hypothesized that the boys' behavior during storytime reflected John's lack of experience interacting with books and Pedro's problems understanding English. She decided to read with just Pedro and John for a few minutes every day. Both boys listened more intently in this small group, and the teacher was able to select books that were more engaging for them. However, she could not coax either boy to contribute much in discussions about the books she read; they used one or two words to answer her questions. The teacher decided to include other children in the group, who could model talking about books. She carefully selected two children who were sensitive to Pedro's attempts to communicate in English. Now the small-group discussions were more lively, and gradually both John's and Pedro's responses became longer and more complex.

As this teacher discovered, most at-risk children learn better in small-group settings than in whole-class gatherings (Kameenui, 1993). This setting provides more opportunities for children's active participation and allows teachers to provide explicit instruction targeted to children's needs. At-risk learners need immediate interventions, instruction that moves them quickly toward successful reading and writing behaviors and understandings, and more frequent opportunities to engage in reading and writing activities.

Teachers who support at-risk learners are sensitive to children's responses to instructional settings and techniques. They make hypotheses about the difficulties that children experience and plan modifications in their instruction to overcome these difficulties. They are patient and understanding of children's unwillingness to take risks and fear of failure (Allen & Carr, 1989). They are watchful for small signs of success, and help children celebrate their new accomplishments.

Literacy-Intervention Programs for At-Risk Learners

Researchers have developed several intervention programs designed to ensure the success of young at-risk learners (Hiebert & Taylor, 1994). Teachers who are aware of these programs may be able to adapt some of their procedures to support at-risk learners in the regular classroom. The best-known literacy-intervention program for at-risk learners is Reading Recovery, a literacy program designed by Marie Clay in New Zealand (Clay, 1985) and implemented widely in the United States.

Reading Recovery

Reading Recovery is targeted at first graders who are experiencing difficulty learning to read, who are identified early, and who receive daily one-on-one instruction fine-tuned to match their instructional needs. Instruction is intended to accelerate their learning so that on leaving the program (generally after twelve to fifteen weeks), children achieve at the average reading level of the other children in first grade and continue adequate reading improvement without special instruction.

Reading Recovery teachers provide daily thirty-minute lessons in which children read, write, and analyze language. The materials used in the lesson and the way in which teachers respond to children during the lesson are highly dependent on daily observation of children's reading and writing strategies. The materials are organized from easier to more difficult according to repetition and language patterns. Easier texts have fewer words, more repetition, and spoken language patterns. More difficult texts have more words, less repetition, and literary language (Peterson, 1991). Children are taught to use several reading strategies, including using the meaning (does that make sense?), language patterns (does that sound right?), and orthographics (do you expect to see that letter?). Each lesson has five components: reading familiar stories, taking a running record, working with letters, writing a message or story, and reading a new book (Pinnell, Fried, & Estice, 1990). Reading Recovery has survived a good deal of controversy (e.g., Barnes, 1996–1997a, 1996–1997b; Browne, Fitts, McLaughlin, McNamara, & Williams, 1996–1997) and even has inspired change in more traditional reading remediation programs (Spiegel, 1995).

Reading Recovery Lessons

Reading Recovery lessons begin with reading a familiar book. Familiar books are books read in previous lessons. Sometimes teachers select a particular book for instructional purposes, and sometimes children select familiar books for rereading. Familiar books provide children with opportunities to read fluently and practice using a variety of reading strategies.

Each day the teacher takes a running record of the child's independent reading of a book that was read for the first time during the previous lesson. Running records are used to gauge reading level and to reveal children's reading strategies (see Chapter 12 for a discussion of running records). The results of running records are used, in part, to make decisions about the next lesson.

Working with letters is an optional component of the Reading Recovery lesson. In this portion of the lesson, children work with magnetic letters on a magnetic board. They may use the letters to write words or to engage in word analysis.

Children write a message or story every day. The message may be related to a book the child has read or to a school event. The message is relatively short (only one or two sentences), but the writing may extend over several days. The child composes the message and then writes it word for word with the teacher's assistance as needed. All words are spelled conventionally, but the teacher uses every opportunity to call attention to sound–letter information or spelling patterns. The child predicts letters, analyzes sounds, and practices writing correctly spelled words. Immediately after the message is composed, the teacher writes it on a sentence strip and cuts it apart. The child reassembles the message and reads it. The sentence is taken back to the classroom to share with the teacher and other children.

An important part of each Reading Recovery lesson is reading a new book. The teacher thoughtfully selects a book that will push the child's abilities forward, yet still be accessible. The teacher introduces the book by having the child look at and talk about the illustrations. The teacher may interject several vocabulary words during the discussion and may have the child locate the words in the text before reading (Clay, 1991). After the teacher has helped the child become familiar with the plot, the important ideas, and some of the language of the text, the child reads the book with the teacher's assistance when needed. As the child reads, the teacher draws attention to the child's successful use of strategies and gently nudges the child to use different strategies and strategies in combination. Children are taught to use more than one reading strategy to cross-check their reading.

Among the strengths of Reading Recovery are that it uses one-on-one instruction and that it includes intensive but contextualized word study. Words are studied using sound–letter correspondences and spelling patterns, but the words are taken from context in a story or dictated sentence and then returned to that context. Juel (1996) described another one-on-one tutoring program with these same strengths. University students who were poor readers tutored poor first grade readers one-on-one. Four word study activities especially contributed to the first graders' reading improvement: reading texts with many repeated words and words with the same spelling patterns, direct instruction about sound–letter correspondences within words, many tutor-scaffolded interactions involving word identification and word spelling, and the tutors' modeling aloud their processes of identifying and spelling unknown words. Juel emphasizes the personal and contextualized nature of these activities: "Part of what appears to make one-on-one tutuoring successful is that all of these 4 forms of word activities can be personalized, *delivered at the right moment,* and repeated as frequently as needed for an individual child to understand, internalize, and recall" (p. 288, emphasis added). It is significant that both the tutors' and the first graders' reading improved. Other cross-age tutoring programs have also been beneficial for all parties (e.g., Caserta-Henry, 1996; Invernizzi, Juel, & Rosemary, 1996–1997).

Although Reading Recovery is more successful when delivered one-on-one than when delivered in small groups (Pinnell, Lyons, Deford, Bryk, & Seltzer, 1994), it does incorporate many features that we recommend for all children. For example, children read and write every day, and instruction is embedded within reading and writing activities. Teachers can implement a variety of other Reading Recovery principles and procedures for use in the regular classroom. They can regularly assess children's learning. Taking stock of each child's reading and writing abilities several times during the school year highlights successes, identifies potential problems, and signals the need for instructional modifications. Teachers can provide many opportunities for children to reread favorite books. Finally, teachers can encourage children to discuss their use of reading strategies and teach children to use several strategies to cross-check their reading.

Other Tutorial Programs

Wasik and Slavin (1993) reviewed research about five one-on-one tutorial programs: Reading Recovery, Success for All (Madden, Slavin, Karweit, & Livermon, 1987), Prevention of Learning Disabilities (Silver & Hagin, 1979), the Wallach Tutoring Program (Wallach & Wallach, 1976), and Programmed Tutorial Reading (Elson, Barber, Engle, & Kampwerth, 1965). They provide helpful descriptions of the programs and compilations of findings from sixteen studies that evaluated the programs. Results showed that the programs are effective compared with traditional methods.

Wasik and Slavin point out that Reading Recovery and Success for All are designed on the bases of comprehensive models of reading and as such provide more complete instructional interventions than programs with designs that are based on limited notions of reading. The more complete interventions "appear to have larger impacts than programs that address only a few components of the reading process" (p. 196).

At-Risk Revisited

Our definition of at-risk learners focuses on children who have difficulties learning in a literacy-rich classroom with many opportunities to read and write. Other definitions of at-risk learners include children from backgrounds with historically high drop-out rates and low achievement levels: children with special needs, children from low socioeconomic or minority backgrounds, and English-as-a-second-language learners.

Many children who have special needs, have diverse cultural backgrounds, and speak English as a second language are at-risk learners. Of course, not all of these children are at-risk learners, but there are many reasons to give special attention to these diverse learners. The remainder of this chapter describes issues related to supporting the literacy learning of children with special needs, from diverse cultural backgrounds, and from diverse language backgrounds.

SPECIAL-NEEDS LEARNERS

Children with special needs include children with challenging social and emotional behaviors, pronounced differences in learning styles or rates, or deficits in hearing, vision, or mobility (Truax & Kretschmer, 1993). Despite being singled out as having special learning difficulties, most special-needs children develop literacy knowledge in patterns that are similar to those found in all children's literacy understandings. For example, one researcher examined the literacy development of young children who were prenatally exposed to the drug crack or cocaine (Barone, 1993). The children were asked to reread a favorite storybook, write a story, and spell words once a month over a year. During this time, the children's emergent readings became more advanced and their writing evidenced more sophisticated concepts about written language. In a similar study, profoundly deaf preschoolers with delayed receptive language were found to have understandings of written language that were developmentally appropriate (Williams, 1994).

Therefore, we could conclude that the most effective way to support special-needs children's literacy learning is similar to the way in which we support all children's learning. Many special education professionals recommend the use of holistic, integrated approaches to reading and writing instruction similar to the activities and approaches proposed in the preceding chapters (Cousin, Weekley, & Gerard, 1993; Truax & Kretschmer, 1993).

Supporting Special-Needs Children's Literacy

Many educators argue that *all children* acquire literacy when they pursue topics of personal interest, interact with others who share similar interests, and make connections between known and new information. Of course, children with special needs "may vary from their age peers, making connections in their own time and in their own ways; but the steps in the learning process" are similar (Truax & Kretschmer, 1993, pp. 593–594). Effective teachers carefully observe children, including special-needs children, and make adjustments in activities and instruction to meet their needs. Adapting instruction to serve special-needs learners often means careful observation of children as they participate in reading and writing activities in order to make modifications that will allow all learners to take small risks and reap large rewards (Salvage & Brazee, 1991).

The early childhood classroom is an especially supportive environment for young children with developmental or learning differences. Here, children select activities that promote growth in all areas and levels of development. Because teachers spend less time in whole-group instruction and more time with small groups and individual children, accommodating instruction for the special-needs child is usually not difficult.

Children with developmental or learning differences in elementary school are placed in regular classrooms when special education teachers feel they can benefit from instruction and activities planned for non-special-needs children. With some adjustments, children with special needs can benefit from instruction along with other children in the regular classroom.

All special-needs children from the age of three who have identified developmental or learning differences have an **individualized educational plan (IEP)** developed by a team of specialists and the child's parents. Teachers should ask for a copy of the plan and quickly become familiar with it so that they can prepare activities to help the child achieve the goals outlined in the IEP.

Modifying Instruction for Children with Developmental Delays

One of the most effective techniques for supporting the literacy learning of children with developmental delays is to provide instruction that is compatible with the child's developmental level, rather than with the child's age. A second effective technique is to provide social experiences that involve interacting with other children on similar social developmental levels, rather than with children of similar ages. Many of the techniques that we have described for younger novice readers and writers or experimenters with reading and writing are appropriate for older children with developmental delays.

More formal techniques for teaching children with developmental delays to read and write are similar to techniques that support all children's learning to read and write (Dixon, 1987; Sindelar, 1987). Special educators suggest that if children are to become effective readers, they need to read whole texts (not isolated words); however, children with developmental delays may need more practice and may take a longer time than other children. There are several ways for teachers to help children read whole texts and give them the extra practice they need to become good readers. Teachers can read stories first as children follow the text. The method of **repeated reading** provides practice with whole texts (Dowhower, 1989; O'Shea & O'Shea, 1987). In this method, children repeatedly read stories (or parts of stories) that are about fifty or one hundred words in length until they can read the selection with only three to six errors. Children begin the repeated readings only when they understand the story.

Modifying Instruction for Children with Emotional, Learning, and Language Disabilities

The writing process is an effective approach in helping emotionally and learning-disabled children successfully communicate their feelings (D'Alessandro, 1987). Daily writing encourages children by implying that they have something meaningful to communicate. A process approach to writing deemphasizes spelling and mechanics, which can be significant stumbling blocks for special-needs children. By focusing on ideas, the writing process supports these children's self-esteem.

As the children brainstorm ideas, teachers can record their ideas on a chart. Then teachers can help the children cluster their ideas into groups. Teachers can demonstrate how to use the cluster by writing a group-collaborated composition that in turn may also be used in reading instruction. During revision, teachers need to be especially careful, because too much revision can frustrate the child into discarding a good composition. The most effective motivation for revision occurs when children discover that they have difficulty reading their own compositions as they present their work in the author's chair (D'Alessandro, 1987).

There are many ways in which teachers can help special-needs children become more actively involved in reading and writing. Two ways in which children are active during reading are by making predictions about what they are going to read and by drawing conclusions about what they have already read (Norris, 1988). Pattern books are effective for supporting active reading and writing of learning-disabled children. These books have predictable sequences that make it easier for children to draw inferences as they predict what will happen next.

Avoiding Reductionist Teaching

Opponents of integrated, holistic approaches to literacy learning argue that children learn better when instruction is systematic and explicit (Dolman, 1992; Shapiro, 1992). Because of the tendency of many special-needs children to be easily distracted from completing tasks, teachers have been encouraged to break tasks into smaller or easier-to-complete components and to use tasks that are highly structured. One activity that might seem to make learning to write letters easier is to have children copy only three letters several times. Although learning-disabled children might learn to form the three letters from this activity, they will not learn how letters operate within the written language system, which is much more important than merely learning to form a few letters. We recommend that teachers rarely use drills on isolated written language tasks with any child, and especially with children who may have trouble figuring out the complexities of reading and writing.

LEARNERS FROM DIVERSE CULTURAL BACKGROUNDS

Children from **diverse cultural backgrounds** may be distinguished by their ethnicity, social class, or language (Au, 1993). **Ethnicity** is determined by the racial, linguistic, cultural, or religious ties of one's national heritage, and most children from diverse cultural backgrounds are included in groups we call African American, Hispanic American, Asian American, or Native American, although people usually identify their ethnicity more precisely with a country of family origin, for example, Puerto Rican, Haitian, or Vietnamese. **Social class** is related to socioeconomic level as reflected in parents' occupations and family income. Children from diverse cultural backgrounds may speak a nonmainstream dialect of English or a language other than English (we discuss the influence of diverse language backgrounds in the next section of this chapter).

Cultural Influences on Learning

Some cultural groups have different ways of helping children learn. In some Native American communities, children are expected to learn by observing adults as they perform tasks; this implies that little verbal interaction takes place. Children who expect to learn from watching adults may not learn well in writing centers, in which teachers expect children to learn by talking with each other as they write. In other communities, children learn cooperatively with other children; the emphasis is on developing a group understanding and performance rather than on individual achievement. Children from these communities may have difficulty in reading groups, in which teachers expect only one child at a time to answer a question.

Culture also influences how children are socialized into being readers and writers. That is, all cultural groups share attitudes and beliefs about the uses and values of literacy and have preferred literacy practices. In general, children from mainstream backgrounds are socialized to use language and literacy within a tradition that places a large responsibility on the primary caregiver, usually the mother (Faltis, 1993). Mainstream mothers often talk with babies from birth and share books with their young children, asking questions that call for labels and clarifications. They include their children in dinner-table talk that supports their recounting of their daily activities or telling stories (see Chapter 2).

In contrast, Mexican American families recently immigrated to the United States often distribute caregiving among family members and close friends (Heath, 1986). In general, children are expected to observe adults' actions and conversation. In a working-class African American community, children observe parents and other adults as they read aloud and talk together about the meaning of texts (Heath, 1983).

There is considerable variation among families in the ways in which they socialize their young children into language and literacy use. However, we do have evidence of distinctive methods used by particular cultural groups to socialize children to become readers and writers. In mainstream cultural groups, children are expected to share in the construction of meaning with a parent during storybook reading and to construct stories on their own. Children from Mexican and African American backgrounds are less likely to be included in storybook reading experiences and are more likely to learn by observing rather than by participating in language activities.

Differences between mainstream and other cultural groups in how they socialize their children into language and literacy use provide an example of **cultural discontinuity** (Au, 1993). Cultural discontinuity means that there may be a mismatch between the literacy culture of the home and that of the school (which usually represents mainstream practices and values). Children who experience a cultural discontinuity are more likely to have learning difficulties in school. This is one possible explanation for the difference in achievement between children from mainstream and from other cultural backgrounds.

If teachers are to support the literacy learning of children from diverse cultural backgrounds, they need to be sensitive to the possibilities of cultural discontinuities as well as knowledgeable of how to change the classroom to better fit the learning of all children (Gee, 1990). Instruction that supports all children's learning and capitalizes on their cultural ways of learning is called culturally responsive instruction (Au, 1993).

Culturally Responsive Instruction

Culturally responsive instruction is instruction that is "consistent with the values of students' own cultures and aimed at improving academic learning" (Au, 1993, p. 13). We describe three examples of culturally responsive instruction. In these examples, teachers develop instructional strategies that are compatible with the learning styles of their children and at the same time help their children learn to operate more successfully with the learning styles usually associated with schools. This kind of instruction is called *culturally responsive.* The first example of instruction is from Au and Kawakami's (1985) description of the Kamehameha Early Education Project (KEEP); the second is from Heath's (1982) description of a project examining children's questions and talk conducted in schools in a southeastern city; and the third example presents learning in school and in the community at the Warm Springs Indian Reservation (Philips, 1972).

KEEP: The Talk Story Lesson

Teachers in a special school in Honolulu for children of Polynesian Hawaiian ancestry studied carefully the kinds of interactions or talk used by Hawaiian children. They researched talk in the community and talk in the classroom. These teachers discovered that their Hawaiian children engaged in interactions resembling "talk stories." In talk stories, many speakers participate together, jointly speaking—often at the same time—to create a narrative. There are few times in a talk story when only one child is speaking. Leaders in talk stories are skillful in involving other children, rather than in carrying the conversation alone. This way of interaction is not compatible with interaction that teachers traditionally expect during reading instruction.

Once teachers recognized that children who "spoke out" during reading group time were not being disruptive, they began to consider ways of using this type of interaction to foster reading growth. They decided that they would plan the questions they asked, but allow children freedom in the way they answered questions. They allowed more than one child to respond at a time. The teachers tape-recorded reading lessons to examine whether allowing children to talk in what seemed to be a disruptive manner helped children to learn better. They found that 80 percent of the children's responses in "talk story" reading lessons focused on the story. In contrast, only 43 percent of the children's responses in a traditional lesson focused on the story (Au & Kawakami, 1985).

Questioning at School

An important way that children learn and demonstrate their learning is by answering questions. As teachers, we assume that the kinds of questions we ask make sense to children. Heath (1982) discovered that children from different communities in nearby towns and cities in the southeast were exposed to different kinds of questions from their earliest language experiences. In one community, the kinds of questions toddlers and preschoolers were familiar with were not the kinds of questions that were later used by their teachers. In another community, toddlers and preschoolers were exposed to questions much like those their teachers would use later in elementary school. When children from these two different communities began attending elementary school together, differences in their achievement were noted. When faced with unfamiliar school-like questions, some children seemed unable to learn and were considered less able than other children.

Teachers in these schools were concerned with helping their children achieve success. They worked closely with Heath to identify ways to help their students, especially the less successful ones, to learn more effectively (Heath, 1982). First, the teachers tape-recorded the kinds of questions they asked in their classrooms and compared them with the kinds of questions children were exposed to in their communities. They discovered that the questions they used in the classroom were requests for labels (for example, "What is that?" about an object in an illustration), were veiled attempts to control or direct behavior ("Is someone not following the rules?" which really means, "Someone had better sit down and be quiet"), or were requests for displays of book-related knowledge or skill ("Where should I begin reading?"). Many of their children seldom heard such questions in their communities. At home children were asked questions that were like analogies ("What is that like?"), questions that started stories ("What happened to Maggie's dog yesterday?"), and questions that accused them of wrongdoing ("What's that all over your face?") (Heath, 1982, p. 116).

Once teachers realized that their questions were not the kind their students were accustomed to answering, they began planning ways to use different kinds of questions in their instruction. They prepared social studies units based on pictures taken in the children's communities. Teachers asked questions that did not require children to label or name objects in the pictures; rather, they asked questions such as "What is going on here?" and "What is this like?" that were similar to the questions children were familiar with. Only later did teachers ask naming and labeling questions. When the teachers tape-recorded the lessons, the children enjoyed listening to the questions and their answers. The tape also provided children with valuable practice in listening to new kinds of questions and their answers.

Learning on the Warm Springs Reservation

The final example of culturally sensitive instruction comes from a study of Native American children's learning in school and in their community (Philips, 1972). On the Warm Springs Indian Reservation, Native American adults work together to solve problems. Leadership is assumed by many adults who have special skills or knowledge, rather than by an appointed leader, and adults choose whom they follow. Adults participate in group activities only when they feel they will be successful, and they participate at the level at which they feel comfortable. Children are observers in community meetings, but are often included in conversation.

These cultural ways of interacting are very different from the behaviors usually expected in school. In school, teachers expect children to follow their directions, to speak when asked a question, and to participate willingly in classroom activities. In contrast, Native American children expect to choose their own leader and make decisions about whether to participate in an activity. It is not surprising that Native American children do not volunteer to answer questions and often refuse to speak when called on in whole-class discussions.

One reason for the lack of participation by Native American children in whole-class recitation activities in school is that the **participation structures** in classrooms and in the community differ. Participation structures include the different rules for speaking, listening, and turn taking. Native American children are uncomfortable in the participation structures of whole-class recitations and discussions used frequently in school. They are more comfortable in the participation structures of small groups in which children initiate and direct their own activities. These participation structures have patterns of interaction more like those that the children have observed in their community.

Culturally Sensitive Instruction: A Summary

These three projects demonstrate how teachers can alter their ways of instruction and help children develop new ways of interacting in the classroom. First, teachers researched not only their children's community, but also their own way of teaching. They were willing to make changes in how they conducted lessons in order to support their students' learning. Second, teachers sought methods of helping their children make the transition from community ways of learning to school ways of learning. Teachers not only helped children learn, but also helped children learn how to learn in school. Tape-recording lessons, visiting community activities, and talking to parents can provide all teachers with valuable information about developing culturally sensitive learning activities for their children.

Culturally Sensitive Instruction in Multicultural Settings

Many classes, especially in urban settings, comprise children from several different cultural backgrounds. For example, a classroom might include Hispanic American children from different Spanish-speaking countries, African American children, and Vietnamese children. In these situations, developing culturally sensitive instruction cannot be a matter of merely matching instruction with cultural features. Instead, teachers employ instructional approaches that are successful with most of the children, and at the same time provide extra support for those children who are struggling. They are willing to depart from familiar approaches to instruction and to experiment with different ways of learning and teaching (Au, 1993). Teachers craft culturally sensitive instruction when they invite collaboration from families and the community, use interactional styles of instruction, strive for a balance of rights, and seek culturally relevant content (Au, 1993; Cummins, 1986).

Community Collaboration

Involving parents from diverse cultural backgrounds in educational activities is an important part of teachers' responsibilities. In mainstream cultures, most parents acknowledge the importance of their involvement in school activities. Mainstream parents are likely to participate in school activities by helping their children with homework, participating in fund-raising activities, attending school functions, such as open houses or music performances, attending parent–teacher conferences, and accompanying children on field trips.

Parents from nonmainstream cultures are also concerned about their children's education (Flores, Cousin, & Díaz, 1991). However, their perceptions about their involvement in schools may differ from the school's expectations. For example, many recently immigrated Mexican American families teach their children to be respectful of elders and to be accountable for their actions. However, they rarely work with their children on homework or other school activities. This may be because they assume that the school is responsible for educational matters.

Teachers using culturally sensitive instruction assume that all parents are interested in their children's success in school. They initiate contact with parents early in the school year through telephone calls, notes, and a weekly newsletter to parents. Inviting parents or other family members to school to share a family story is another way of initiating contacts with parents. Teachers communicate with parents often about the progress of their children's learning and provide concrete suggestions about how parents can help their children. Research has shown that nonmainstream parents are effective in supporting their children's learning at home (Goldenberg, 1989).

Instruction through Interaction

Children from diverse cultural backgrounds learn best when instruction involves children in constructing their own meaning, when higher level thinking strategies are stressed, and when students set their own goals for learning (Cummins, 1986). This style of instruction is consistent with the instruction that we have recommended throughout this book and is called **constructivist models of instruction.** The essential ingredient of constructivist approaches is that children actively construct understandings. At first, children construct understandings with the support of others. The support that teachers provide for children's learning is sometimes called **scaffolding** (Cazden, 1988). The child accomplishes as much of the task as possible, and the adult scaffolds, or assists (see Chapter 1 for a discussion of the zone of proximal development). The constructivist model recognizes that learning begins with what children already know. Children's understandings about concepts are the beginning point of all learning experiences. In this way, children's experiences become a central part of the classroom.

Examples of interactive or constructivist models of instruction in literacy learning include using grand conversations to build understandings about literature, using writing workshop and the author's chair to support children's writing development, and using small, cooperative groups to learn new concepts, vocabulary, and spellings. In each of these teaching approaches, the children and teacher jointly identify topics of interest about which to talk and write, children's talk is acknowledged as an important avenue for encouraging critical thinking, and children learn to value the insights of their classmates.

Balance of Rights

The concept of balance of rights is similar to an interactive style of teaching in which both the children and the teacher have input into what is learned. **Balance of rights** recognizes that in a classroom there are three dimensions of control over who gets to speak, what topic is discussed, and with whom children speak (Au & Mason, 1981). In mainstream classrooms with conventional recitation lessons or discussion-participant structures, teachers control which children speak, what they speak about, and to whom they speak (usually the teacher). Achieving a balance of rights means allowing children choices about one or more of the three dimensions of interactions (Au & Mason, 1981).

For example, in grand conversations, teachers and children together choose topics of discussion. Children talk about events or characters of interest to them, but the teacher also poses one or two interpretive questions. Children may speak without raising their hands, but the teacher helps quiet children hold the floor or facilitates turn taking when many children want to speak at once. The children listen carefully to one another and react to each other's comments, and teachers encourage such interactions by asking such questions as, "Jane, did you want to comment on what Jeff just said?"

An example of a lesson in which teachers and children share a balance of control is the **experience-text-relationship approach** to guiding reading lessons (Au, 1979). In this approach to reading stories, poems, or informational books, teachers first select a major theme that will help the children understand the text as a whole. They decide how the theme might be related to their children's background experiences (the *experience* phase of the lesson). For example, a second grade teacher guided some of her students in reading *Annie and the Old One* (Miles, 1971). In this story, a young Navajo girl does not wish her grandmother to die. Her grandmother helps Annie see that she must return to Mother Earth and complete the cycle of life. The teacher decided that the children needed to understand the natural cycle of life and death in order to understand the story. She began the lesson by inviting children to talk about their own grandparents and what it was like to lose a grandparent (Au, 1993).

In the second part of the experience-text-relationship approach, teachers guide children as they read the text (the *text* phase of the lesson). Teachers may divide the text into segments and have grand conversations about each segment. In this part of the lesson, it is crucial for teachers to help children grasp the main theme identified in the experience phase of the lesson. For example, the second grade teacher used considerable prompting and questioning to ensure that the children understood that Annie was trying to keep her grandmother from dying and that the grandmother was trying to help Annie see why she must go to Mother Earth (Au, 1993).

In the last phase of the experience-text-relationship approach, children relate their experiences to what they learned from reading (the *relationship* phase of the lesson). In this part of the approach, children discuss the theme of the text and relate it to their own experiences discussed prior to reading. The second graders recalled their own feelings when they lost a grandparent and compared them with Annie's feelings in the story.

Culturally Relevant Content

Children who perceive that what they are learning affirms their cultural heritage are more likely to become engaged in learning (Ferdman, 1990). Teachers can draw on three sources to provide culturally relevant content in the classroom: multicultural literature that is culturally authentic, children's experiences, and community resources.

Multicultural literature. Multicultural literature is literature that incorporates people of diverse cultural backgrounds, including African Americans, Hispanic Americans, Asian Americans, Native Americans, and people from other cultures (see Chapter 6). Culturally authentic multicultural literature is usually written by members of a particular culture and accurately reflects the values and beliefs of that culture.

Children from diverse backgrounds need access to literature that includes characters from those backgrounds. Seeing children like themselves in literature increases children's self-esteem and enlightens others about the worth of different cultural backgrounds. All children need experiences with culturally authentic literature about a variety of different cultural backgrounds.

Teachers must carefully choose the literature they share with children so that the literature does not distort children's concepts about others. Aoki, an Asian American, reported a childhood incident that illustrates this point (Aoki, 1981). She remembered when her teacher read the story *The Five Chinese Brothers* (Bishop & Wiese, 1938) to her class. (While this book is often considered a classic, it portrays Asians as stereotyped characters.) As her teacher showed the illustrations, a few children darted quick glances at her. Aoki began to sink down in her chair. She recalled that other children taunted her by pulling their eyes so that they slanted. This incident makes a point about helping diverse learners, and all children, to develop more positive attitudes and self-esteem—diverse learners need to feel welcome and safe in their classrooms, and they need to believe in their own worth and abilities.

Children's literature offers many opportunities to explore both language differences and cultural heritages with children. There are many literature selections about different cultural groups and heritages that present nonstereotyped characters. As teachers read these selections to children, they can help children explore common heritages, customs, and human qualities. If Aoki's teacher had been sensitive to stereotypical portrayals in children's books, she might have instead shared *Umbrella* (Yashima, 1958). Then the children would have learned to identify with the little girl in the story. Their teacher could have asked them to describe their common experiences.

Using multicultural literature in the classroom should entail more than merely highlighting the heroes or holidays of a culture or reading works of culturally authentic literature (Rasinski & Padak, 1990) as teachers help children see issues from multiple cultural perspectives. The Appendix presents a list of multicultural literature including folk literature, poetry, fantasy, and realistic fiction that reflect the culture of African Americans, Asian Americans, Hispanic Americans, and Native Americans.

Children's experiences. Children's experiences provide an important starting point for many kinds of literacy activities. For example, having children write about their experiences is a critical component of process writing and the writing workshop approach (see Chapters 9 and 10). Children identify topics of interest about which they wish to write, and teachers help them shape their writing by teaching minilessons, guiding writers' groups in which children revise and edit their compositions, and offering opportunities for sharing through the author's chair or other kinds of publishing.

Having children talk about events and people in their experiences is a base for guided reading lessons, especially using the experience-text-relationship approach. Teachers identify broad themes related to what children will read and then invite children to talk about their experiences related to these themes.

Community resources. The community can provide many rich resources for the classroom. Inviting local storytellers into the classroom is especially useful when teachers have difficulty locating children's literature representative of a child's cultural heritage. For example, a first grade teacher had a few children in her classroom from Cape Verde, an island off the African coast. When she failed to locate literature that included children from this cultural background, she turned to the community liaison in her school for help and learned that the neighborhood included many families from Cape Verde. The community liaison helped the teacher locate a storyteller from the neighborhood, who came to class and shared several stories from Cape Verde. After the storyteller's visit, the children retold two stories, which the teacher recorded in big book format. The children illustrated the big books, and these books became class favorites.

Culturally sensitive instruction is inclusive—it invites participation from children, parents, and the community. It recognizes the value of cultural heritage and children's experiences. It uses children's knowledge as a beginning point for instruction.

CHILDREN FROM DIVERSE LANGUAGE BACKGROUNDS

An increasing number of children in school are from **diverse language backgrounds.** They speak a nonmainstream dialect of English or a language other than English in their homes.

Learners Who Speak Nonmainstream Dialects of English

The way we speak English varies according to our social class, gender, occupation, locale, and ethnic background. Variations of a language are called *dialects.* All dialects of a language are understandable by all speakers of a language, but they are sufficiently different from one another to be distinctive (Bryen, 1982). Many speakers from New York City, for example, have what speakers from other parts of the country consider a dialect, but New Yorkers are easily understood by English speakers from San Francisco, Atlanta, or any other location in the United States.

Dialects are distinguished by differences in pronunciation, word choice, grammatical structure, and communicative style or usage. For example, the words *park* and *car* are pronounced *pahk* and *cah* in Boston or New York and *pawk* and *caw* in New Orleans (Barnitz, 1980). A sandwich on a long roll is called a *hoagie* in Philadelphia and a *Po Boy* in parts of Louisiana. Some people say they must be home by *quarter til 5,* while others say they must be there by *quarter of 5.*

Nonmainstream and Mainstream Dialects

There is no one variety or dialect of English that is the standard or **mainstream dialect.** This is a difficult concept to accept. As speakers, we are capable of, and unconsciously make, judgments regarding other people's use of language. When we consider their language use to be standard or nonstandard, we are not applying any consistent criteria. Many speakers would label, "I ain't parkin' no car," as **nonmainstream** (or nonstandard) **dialect.** When asked why, they usually say that it violates rules of grammar. Yet they may consider the sentence "None of the cars were parked" to be standard even though it violates a rule of grammar: the use of a singular subject (*none*) with a plural verb (*were*). In other words, although the word *standard* implies otherwise, there are no objective criteria for determining whether a dialect is standard. All speakers have a range of language patterns that they use depending on situation and audience.

Dialects considered nonmainstream. There are many dialects frequently considered nonstandard or nonmainstream by large segments of the population, especially by teachers and other educated groups. Some of these dialects are tied to locale, and others are tied to social class (Labov, 1966). Even though there is not just one African American dialect, many researchers (e.g., Smitherman, 1977) have described a dialect referred to as Black English or as African American Vernacular English. Many African Americans do not use Black English, and many of the features of Black English are found not only in so-called standard English, but also in many other dialects. Nevertheless, an important court case, *King Elementary School Students* vs. *The Ann Arbor, Michigan, School District Board* highlighted the need to recognize children's dialects, and in particular the dialect known as Black English, as an important consideration in children's education (Smitherman, 1977). The court ruled that teachers need to be familiar with children's home language, and to become more sensitive to their special needs.

We will not be able to explore different dialects in detail here. Nevertheless, there are two facts related to dialects that early childhood educators need to know. First, all language systems, including dialects considered nonstandard or nonmainstream, are rule-bound, and the rules describing both nonstandard and standard dialects are often similar. Rule-bound means that the features of the language can be described. Linguists' rules are *descriptive* rather than *prescriptive.* They do not tell speakers what to do and they do not explain why speakers do what they do; they do allow us to predict what speakers of a given dialect will say under certain conditions. For example, many speakers of dialects considered nonstandard pronounce the word *left* as *lef;* that is, they simplify the word by deleting the final consonant sound of the letter *t* (Bryen, 1982). However, when the word *left* precedes a word beginning with a consonant, as in "She left *T*om all her money," even speakers of dialects considered standard do not pronounce its final consonant (*t*) sound. Some Black English–speaking communities have emphasized the linguistic equality of all dialects and thus the linguistic legitimacy of Black English by renaming it Ebonics (Lippi-Green, 1997).

Second, some features of dialects are more stigmatizing than others (Wolfram, 1970). Listeners use just some features of language to label a speaker's dialect. One such feature of a dialect considered by many to be nonstandard is the absence of the copula (a form of the verb *to be*), as in "He good to me." This feature of the dialect is more likely to be used as a labeling criterion than another feature of the same dialect, such as embedding of direct questions, as in "I wonder, did the package come?"

Nonmainstream dialects and attitudes. We not only make subjective judgments about whether speakers have standard or nonstandard speech patterns, but we also make other kinds of judgments based on our assessment of their language. Sometimes people unconsciously think that speakers of a different dialect might not be very intelligent or may have a low social status. Such judgments are especially harmful when teachers make them about children (Gee, 1996). Children who speak dialects that their teachers consider nonstandard are more likely to be identified as having cognitive lags, needing language therapy, and needing special remedial reading and writing instruction (Bartoli, 1986). They are more likely to be placed in lower ability groups for instruction and to receive lower achievement scores than are their peers. This is an injustice. We must understand why it occurs so that we will not perpetuate it.

There are three reasons that children who speak dialects considered nonstandard are more likely to be included in remedial or lower ability groups. The first reason is related to the unconscious practice of using language patterns to judge the worth of a whole person. Teachers are not exempt from the phenomenon of unconsciously deciding on a person's intellectual capacity by virtue of his or her speech. The second reason is that tests that assess reading and writing do not use these students' dialect. The third reason is that teachers may spend more time helping these students acquire standard or mainstream English than they do helping them learn to read and write.

Literacy Instruction for Children with Nonmainstream Dialects

One of the most hotly debated topics in language education is whether, how, and when children should be taught to speak what is considered standard English. Because language is so closely interwoven with a person's sense of identity and self-worth, using language in a different way can be threatening. However, it is hard to counter the argument that people who speak so-called standard English have more access to educational and economic opportunities.

Teaching children to speak English that is considered standard in their region. Most experts agree that preschoolers should be encouraged to communicate, whether their language is perceived as standard or as nonstandard (Genishi & Dyson, 1984). Teachers need to be more concerned with what children have to say than with how they say it. The practice of requiring children to speak in complete sentences or to "say it right" is not recommended. As all children get older and as they hear a greater variety of language models, they naturally begin to include in their speech more forms considered standard by most people in their region (Padak, 1981). Reading aloud to young children provides a model of written English, which is actually different from any spoken dialect, yet is often the standard against which people compare their so-called standard dialects (Feitelson, Goldstein, Iraqi, & Share, 1993).

Children in elementary school should have opportunities to use language in many different situations. Role-playing activities can provide children with opportunities to use a variety of language patterns. For example, they may practice interviewing a community leader, a minister, and a senior citizen as preparation for data gathering in a social studies unit. Children in elementary school are capable of discussing how different kinds of language are appropriate in different situations.

Children's literature provides rich models for language growth. Children enjoy hearing and saying many kinds of language found in literature. There are many fine examples of literature in which a dialect considered nonstandard contributes to the authenticity and enjoyment of the story. These selections can be used to demonstrate the variety and richness of language. As children explore language variety through literature, they can also explore language that most consider standard (Cullinan, Jaggar, & Strickland, 1974). Children naturally use the language of literature as they retell stories, role-play story actions, and write stories of their own.

Teaching reading and writing. No special techniques are necessary to introduce written language to preschoolers who speak with a dialect considered nonstandard. All children, whether in preschool or in elementary school, learn about reading and writing when written language is presented in meaningful activities.

In more formal reading and writing programs in the elementary school, teachers need to be knowledgeable of how children's dialects are reflected in their reading and writing. For example, children who speak with a dialect considered nonstandard will use that language as they read aloud—they may translate the text into their own speech patterns. Similarly, they may use their language as a basis for writing—what children write may reflect their oral language patterns. Teachers of children who speak with a dialect considered nonstandard should recognize that children translate text into their own oral language patterns. As children read the text, they may translate it into their spoken language. These translations from text language to spoken language are expected based on what we know about dialects considered nonstandard (Bryen, 1982). Teachers who are sensitive to children's language recognize dialect translations as positive indications that children comprehend as they read.

Children's dialects are reflected in what and how they write. Figure 11.1 presents a story written by a boy whose dialect is considered nonstandard by many (Meier & Cazden, 1982, p. 507). Even when we are sensitive to Darryl's dialect, we know that he has several problems with writing. His story lacks the details that make writing vivid, although it is certainly startling. He has many misspelled words (over a fourth of the text), and most of the sentences are ineffective. Although teachers do not need to know a great deal about dialects to see Darryl's weaknesses, they may need this knowledge to see his strengths (Meier & Cazden, 1982). For example, Darryl's use of *in* for both the words *in* and *and* may reflect that he says the word *and* like the word *in*. Similarly, the deletion of the letters *ed* on some of his past tense verbs reflects that the pronunciation rules of his dialect include simplification of past tense verbs (that is, dropping the pronunciation of the final sounds /t/, /əd/, or /d/).

There are many more important strengths to this story that reflect what all children learn, and specifically, what Darryl is learning, about good stories. His story has a beginning, complications, and an ending all centered on a single character, Eddie Mcdevitt. Darryl's story also contains features of a "trickster tale" (Smitherman, 1977). This is a special kind of story told by African Americans that usually involves an African American male who triumphs over adversaries through cunning and unusual feats (Meier & Cazden, 1982). Although he lacks a head or a body, Eddie lives on at the end of the tale. Teachers who are sensitive to children's language recognize what children bring to writing and are in a better position to build on children's strengths. Writing may be the most effective way to help children gain control over language considered standard.

Dialects and dictation. Although many teachers are sensitive to their children's language and they view *oral* language diversity as valid, they wonder what to do when writing down children's dictations. Should teachers translate children's speech into standard text or should they write what children say? Figures 11.2 and 11.3 present a kindergartner's dictated story and a first grader's dictated retelling of *There's Something in My Attic* (Mayer, 1988). These child-authored texts include some language that many consider nonstandard.

Figure 11.1 *Darryl's Story: "The Spooky Halloween Night"*

The Spooky Halloween Night

One there was a mummy named Eddie Mcdevitt he was so dume at he dump his head in the can in then he chod his head off and then he went and to his house and then he went outside and chod his arm off then the cops came and chase him away and then he tuck some lade and kidl here in then she came alive and chod his bode off and then his spirt comed in kill everybody.

Figure 11.2 *Natasha's Story*

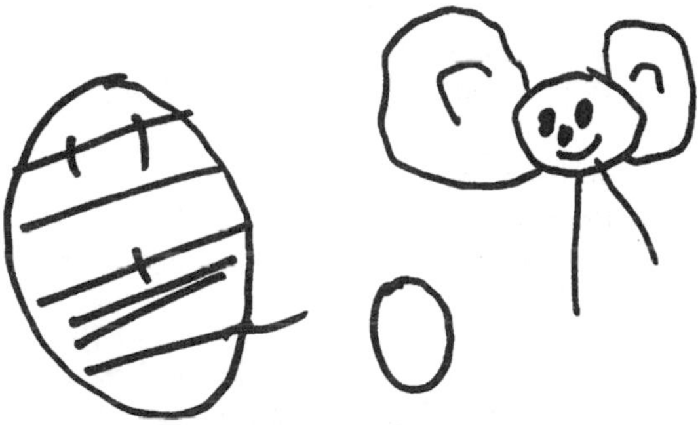

They was hiding eggs in the grass.
When they went to bed the Easter Bunny come.

Figure 11.3 *Latosha's Retelling*

There was a little girl.
She had a dream about a ghost.
She got off the bed and her dad put her back in the bed.
He say, "Go to sleep."
She got off her bed and went upstairs to her attic.
The little girl tooks a rope and catch the ghost.

Many teachers are concerned that parents will object to such a text, since it is not regarded as standard English. They wonder if children's reading of such texts will somehow be harmful.

There are at least three arguments for writing what children dictate, although words should be spelled conventionally and not as children pronounce them (Jaggar, 1974). First, the main reason for writing down children's dictations, such as stories about their art work, is so that children can realize that what they say is what is written. Children whose dictations are not written as they are dictated may not discover this concept. Second, one of children's most valuable reading strategies is their understanding of what language is like. Therefore, teachers will want to write what children say in dictations so that children can use this strategy as a method of reading. Finally, writing what a child says demonstrates acceptance of the child; it suggests that teachers find children's ideas important and that they recognize the validity of children's expressions.

One method of helping children build bridges from the oral language patterns they use in dictations to patterns found in written texts is to use more than one language story for some dictation experiences (Gillet & Gentry, 1983). In some dictation exercises, the teacher might prepare an experience story that is similar to the children's dictated story, but in language considered standard. Figure 11.4 presents a language story dictated by six-year-olds that includes some language considered nonstandard. Figure 11.4 also presents a story

Figure 11.4 *"The Holiday Memory Book"*

Children's Dictated Story

The Christmas Tree and Hanukkah Candles

We put seven ball on the Christmas tree.
We puts some lights on the Christmas tree.
We put a lot of candy cane on the Christmas tree.
We lighted candles for Hanukkah.

Teacher's Story

Holiday Celebrations

We celebrated Christmas and Hanukkah. We decorated a Christmas tree. First, we put lights on the tree. Then we put balls and candy canes on the tree. Last, we lit Hanukkah candles. We enjoyed our celebration of Christmas and Hanukkah.

written by their teacher. This story includes many of the same words used in the children's dictation. The teacher and children read and reread both stories many times. Teachers need to use this technique with care so that the children's stories are as valued as their teacher's stories.

Learners Who Speak English as a Second Language

Children whose home language is not English are **English-as-a-second-language learners** and may speak English fluently, a little, or not at all. Their entry into preschool or elementary school may be the first time they are expected to speak English, or they may have had many opportunities to speak English prior to their school experiences. One of the first concerns that teachers voice is how to teach children, especially children who speak little English, to speak and to understand English.

Teaching Spoken English

The easiest way to learn to speak English is to participate in meaningful activities (Genishi & Dyson, 1984). The structure provided by familiar objects and activities supports children's language learning. To be effective, the objects must be real and the children must use them in real activities. Just as many toddlers first learn familiar phrases or words associated with repeated activities (called "routines"), so do English-as-a-second-language learners first learn familiar phrases and words in English (Urzua, 1980). Many children learn to say "Night night," "go to sleep," and "read books" because these routine phrases are repeated daily as they participate in the activity of getting ready for bed. Preschool English-as-a-second-language learners can learn the same phrases as they interact with their teacher and other children in their play with dolls, blankets, beds, and books in the housekeeping center. Many dramatic-play activities, such as grocery shopping, visiting the dentist, and taking a trip to McDonald's, provide rich language-learning experiences. Teachers can join in play and provide models of language. At first, many English-as-a-second-language learners will be silent in their play as they internalize the sounds of English and discover the actions of routines. They may switch between using English and using their home language (this practice should not be forbidden; Lara, 1989).

Even in elementary school, props and dramatic play can be used as a bridge to English. All children enjoy a pretend trip to McDonald's that includes such props as bags, hamburger containers, drink cups, and hats for the employees. As part of the McDonald's play, children will learn the English words *hamburgers, French fries, Coke, milk, ketchup, salt,* and *money.* They might learn routine phrases such as "Welcome to McDonald's," "May I take your order, please?" "I'd like a hamburger," or "Give me a Coke." Pictures of familiar activities can also be used to increase English-as-a-second-language learners' oral language proficiency (Moustafa & Penrose, 1985).

Teaching Reading and Writing

Children need not be proficient speakers of English in order to begin reading and writing in English (Abramson, Seda, & Johnson, 1990). In fact, reading and writing instruction supports learning spoken English. Effective strategies for literacy instruction in English include using additive approaches, developing comprehensive input, using shared language, and providing opportunities for extended discourse.

Additive approaches. **Additive approaches** build on children's home language and culture (Cummins, 1986) and are in contrast with **subtractive approaches,** which replace children's home language and culture with English and mainstream values. The best approaches to supporting the literacy learning of English-as-a-second-language learners are those in the children's home language. But in many classrooms this approach is not possible. Sometimes children speak many different languages, and at other times, parents request that children receive instruction in English.

All teachers can take an additive approach to their literacy instruction when they allow students to use their home language in some reading and writing activities. For example, a third grade teacher who had several Spanish-speaking children in her class introduced the characters and events in *Mirandy and Brother Wind* (McKissack, 1988) by using simple props to act out important parts of the story. As part of her introduction, the teacher used descriptive phrases from the story and illustrated the meaning of these phrases through her dramatic portrayal of the characters in action. Then the children divided into pairs to read the story. Next the children gathered together to have a grand conversation about the story. As part of the conversation, the teacher shared many responses in which she used several of the vocabulary words from the story. These portions of the lesson were all conducted in English. Finally, the class broke into small groups to act out portions of the story, and several children planned their dramatic reenactments in Spanish. Although most groups presented their dramas to the class using English, one group used Spanish in its enactment.

Using a class or school postal system provides another example of how teachers can support children's use of home language in literacy activities. Children can help make mailboxes and establish a routine for delivering and receiving mail. Teachers can encourage children to write to them, to each other, to school personnel, and to famous people (including favorite children's authors). Writing letters and notes can become part of free-time activities, or it can become part of more formal reading and writing lessons. Teachers who have used this system have found that English-as-a-second-language learners begin writing in their home language. This practice should be encouraged as a way for children to continue their literacy growth in their home language. Teachers in areas where a majority of children come from families whose first language is not English will welcome this opportunity to demonstrate the value of being literate not only in English, but also in other languages. This cross-cultural literacy can be reinforced by including materials written in languages other than English in the classroom, sending notes home to parents in both the language of the home and English, and posting signs and labels in both the predominant language and English (Ortiz & Engelbrecht, 1986).

Gradually, English-as-a-second-language learners begin to write their notes and letters in English to communicate with children who write in English (Greene, 1985). English-as-a-second-language learners may find letter and note writing especially motivating because the emphasis is placed on communicating meaning to friends, rather than on correct conventions. Writing may be a particularly meaningful bridge to literacy in English (Urzua, 1987).

Instruction can also be additive when written language and spoken language are used as mutually supportive systems (Fitzgerald, 1993). For example, teachers can reinforce their spoken questions by writing the questions as well. Before having children read to find answers, teachers write two or three questions on the chalkboard. As children read, they can refer to the written questions as a guide for their reading (Gersten & Jiménez, 1994).

Another way in which spoken and written language support reading is through the use of the language experience approach. Dialogues that emerge from activities such as a pretend trip to McDonald's provide material for reading and writing (Feeley, 1983). After participating in dramatic play about a visit to McDonald's, children can learn to read and write many words found on the environmental print at McDonald's and associated with going to a McDonald's restaurant, such as *McDonald's, restrooms, men, women,* and *push* (Hudelson & Barrera, 1985). The teacher can prepare a story about the children's activities, incorporating English words and phrases used as part of the McDonald's play experience. Children can also dictate or write about their experiences (Moustafa & Penrose, 1985). Photos of the children taken during the activity provide useful supports for reading these stories or writing about the experience (Sinatra, 1981). These language stories can be used to help children develop sight words or practice decoding skills. Figure 11.5 presents a story dictated by an English-as-a-second-language learner in second grade after he made Play Doh.

Figure 11.5 *English-as-Second-Language Learner's Dictation*

Lim Makes Play Doh

I can use two cup flour.
I put one cup salt.
I am mix with spoon.
I am measure with water and flour.
I put spice in bucket.
I put two tablespoon oil in bucket.
We put color in bucket.

In addition to language-experience materials, English-as-a-second-language learners need frequent and early experiences with children's literature both to read and as a support for their writing (Hough, Nurss, & Enright, 1986). Pattern books are particularly effective as first reading materials for all children, including English-as-a-second-language learners. Pattern books are especially useful in developing English-as-a-second-language learners' sense of syntax as well as giving them experience with new vocabulary. Chapter 9 describes how pattern books can be used to encourage children's reading and writing. Wordless picture books are also useful to stimulate dictation and writing.

Finally, additive approaches invite participation from parents and the community. Teachers make every effort to communicate with parents despite language differences. School systems provide community liaisons—people who know the different school communities and are native speakers of the languages spoken in the various communities. English-as-a-second-language and bilingual teachers are also useful resources and may be able to locate bilingual parent volunteers to help communicate with parents or to work in classrooms. Teachers make sure that all notes and newsletters sent to parents are written in the home language. They check with community liaisons or school volunteers to find ways of showing respect to parents during parent–teacher conferences or telephone conversations. They invite parents or other community members to school to share family stories or traditions, to read books related to their culture, or to demonstrate special skills.

Shared language. Effective teachers of English-as-a-second-language learners realize that students can be easily overwhelmed by too many changing instructional techniques. These children need repeated use of familiar instructional routines and activities using shared language. **Shared language** refers to vocabulary that is used repetitively when talking about a reading or writing task (Gersten & Jiménez, 1994). For instance, one teacher who taught many children with limited knowledge of English repeatedly used a few familiar words when talking about literature. She taught her children the components of a *story grammar* (see Chapter 2 for a description of a story grammar and its components), and her students understood the English words *character, goal, obstacle, outcome,* and *theme.* The students knew how to look for **character clues** because the teacher frequently asked questions such as, "What kind of character is he? What are the clues?" (Gersten & Jiménez, 1994) and modeled answer-finding techniques.

Another teacher taught students the vocabulary needed to conduct writers' conferences with partners. Using whole-class minilessons, the teacher taught children to talk about " 'favorite part,' 'part you didn't understand,' 'part you'd like to know more about,' and 'part you might like to work on' " (Blake, 1992, p. 606). Through modeling, the teacher showed children the kinds of language that he expected them to use and the kinds of information that he expected them to talk about in a writer's conference.

These teachers focused on teaching their children how to participate in highly successful activities. They did not use many different strategies, but instead used only a few strategies routinely. As children gained confidence using these strategies, these teachers gradually added other instructional strategies.

Extended discourse. Mastering English and becoming competent readers and writers of English is possible only when students use English for a variety of purposes in situations that are not anxiety producing (Faltis, 1993). That is, children need opportunities for

extended discourse, or talking and writing extensively in a variety of settings (with a variety of partners, including the teacher, in small groups, and in whole-class gatherings). Teachers can encourage extended discourse by acknowledging children's input to lessons and by providing models of more complete English-language structure, as in the following example (Gersten & Jiménez, 1994, p. 445).

Teacher: What does he hope will happen when he shoots the arrow?

Child: The rain (gestures like rain falling).

Teacher: Right, the rain will fall down.

Another way to engage students in extended discourse is to elaborate on vocabulary meanings. It is crucial for English-as-a-second-language learners to grasp the meanings of core vocabulary in stories. Engaging children in talk about vocabulary words and their meanings helps teachers confirm that the children understand vocabulary meanings and provides opportunities for extended discourse. For example, in one story that a teacher was reading aloud, a character was eavesdropping. The teacher stopped reading, told the children the meaning of the word *eavesdropping,* and then invited children to demonstrate what the word meant. Several children acted out eavesdropping and talked about their experiences with eavesdropping. Another teacher stopped reading to talk about the meaning of the word *pierced* by relating the word to the pierced ears of many of the girls in the classroom and by piercing a piece of paper with scissors. These teachers often wrote key words on the chalkboard as they talked about their meanings and encouraged children to use the words as they talked and wrote about stories (Gersten & Jiménez, 1994).

A kindergarten teacher provided opportunities for extended discourse that use repeated readings of a favorite book, storytelling with flannel-board props, and emergent reading of the favorite book (Carger, 1993). First, the teacher read aloud an engaging picture book that appealed to young Hispanic children. After each reading, the teacher invited individual children to reread the story using the pictures in the picture storybook as prompts (for emergent readings). The teacher accepted the children's attempts at reading using their limited English. Then the teacher reread the story and retold the story in Spanish, using flannel-board props. She invited the children to retell the story once again in English, this time using the flannel-board props.

Issues Related to Teaching Children from Diverse Backgrounds

The models of instruction that we and others (Au, 1993) have proposed for supporting children from diverse backgrounds are called by many names, including constructivist, interactional, socio-psycholinguistic, process oriented, and holistic. They share the underlying principles that learning is more effective when learners actively construct understandings for themselves rather than passively repeat what teachers tell them, when teachers stress processes rather than adultlike products, and when learners engage in meaningful activities that involve reading and writing rather than practice skills in isolation.

However, it is important to keep in mind that children from diverse backgrounds also need instruction that ensures their academic success. "If students from diverse backgrounds are to have access to opportunities in the mainstream culture, schools must acquaint them with the rules and codes of the culture of power, such as the grammar of standard English" (Au, 1993, p. 51). Many children from diverse backgrounds will benefit from explicit teaching of the conventions of writing. One educator put it this way: "Unless one has the leisure of a lifetime of 'immersion' to learn them, explicit presentation [of the rules of the culture of power] makes learning immeasurably easier" (Delpit, 1988, p. 283).

Explicit teaching, however, does not mean that teachers necessarily need to resort to traditional drills and recitation. Instead, teachers can provide explicit teaching within the context of reading and writing activities, as is done during the writing phase of Reading Recovery lessons, during minilessons in the writing workshop approach, or through guided reading lessons. All teachers must strike a balance between allowing children to construct their own understandings and providing direct, explicit instruction (Spiegel, 1992). All good instruction includes both opportunities to explore and explicit teaching.

Careful observation and assessment of learners is the key to making thoughtful decisions about when to step back and allow children time and space to develop their own understandings and when to step in and direct children's learning. This may be particularly true for children for whom English is a second language. For these children, for example, merely inviting them to read books of their choice or to write about topics of personal interest may not be enough to support their literacy growth (Peréz, 1994; Reyes, 1991). Teachers may find that they need to model how to find an appropriate book and teach strategies for decoding unfamiliar print. Teachers know that teaching children conventional punctuation, standard grammar, and print-oriented reading strategies is part of reading and writing instruction for all children. Observant teachers recognize when children could benefit from explicit teaching and when children need opportunities to construct their own understandings.

Chapter Summary

At-risk learners are children who are especially at risk for school failure. At-risk learners include children who struggle to acquire literacy concepts despite quality classroom support. Teachers use observations to modify their instruction for at-risk learners and may adapt techniques from Reading Recovery. Reading Recovery, a special intervention program for first graders, engages children in daily reading, writing, and language analysis. It focuses on teaching independent reading strategies.

Children who may be at-risk learners may also include those with special needs, from diverse cultural backgrounds, and from diverse language backgrounds. As with other at-risk learners, observant teachers adapt instructional activities to meet the needs of special learners without resorting to reductionist methods of instruction.

Teachers recognize that culture influences the way in which children learn and how they interact with each other and with adults. For example, children of Hawaiian ancestry are familiar with interaction styles in which more than one speaker talks at a time; children from some African American communities are not exposed to known-answer questions often used by teachers; and children from one Native American culture are more familiar with talking in small informal groups than in whole-class recitation. Once teachers recognize the ways in which culture affects how children learn and interact, they are on the way to crafting culturally sensitive instruction. Culturally sensitive instruction is characterized by interactive instruction, a balance of rights, and culturally relevant content. Culturally relevant content includes multicultural literature, resources from the community, and children's own experiences.

Children who speak a nonmainstream or nonstandard dialect of English may be the victims of teachers' unconscious judgments about their academic potential. To counter this possibility, teachers understand that all dialects, including nonmainstream dialects, reflect an underlying logic and structure. They help children feel comfortable and accepted when using their dialect to communicate while they help children to expand their language use to include the dialect that is considered standard in their region.

Children who speak English as a second language learn spoken English at the same time that they learn to read and write in English. Teachers support this process when they use additive approaches, shared language, and extended discourse. All teachers of diverse learners must strive for a balance between supporting children as they construct their own understandings and providing explicit instruction.

Applying the Information

Julia Felix is a first-year teacher in a large urban school that serves children from a variety of cultural and language backgrounds. This year she will be teaching third grade (or, you may assume that she will be teaching kindergarten). She opens her class list and reads the following names (X = ESL Student) (Faltis, 1993, p. 5).

1.	Brown, Leon	
2.	Cavenaugh, Kimberly	
3.	Cui, Xiancoung	X
4.	Cohen, Daniel	
5.	Evans, Lisa	
6.	Fernandez, Maria Eugenia	X
7.	Freeman, Jeffrey	
8.	Garcia, Aucencio	X
9.	Gomez, Concepcion	X
10.	Hamilton, Jessica	
11.	Mason, Tyrone	
12.	O'Leary, Sean	
13.	Pak, Kyung	X
14.	Petruzzella, Gina	
15.	Quinn, Frank	
16.	Rosen, Chatty	
17.	Rojas, Guadalupe	X
18.	Sandoval, Kathy	
19.	Tran, Do Thi	X
20.	Vasquez, Jimmy	X
21.	Williamson, Amy	
22.	York, Leonard	
23.	Zbikowski, Antonin	

Julie thinks to herself, "I especially want the ESL students to fully join in my class" (Faltis, 1993, p. 6). How will Julie accomplish this task? What suggestions can you make about her room arrangement, the materials she will need, and the modifications she can be expected to make in instruction? Suppose that Julie decides to teach a unit about animals. Make suggestions for materials that she can include in the unit, and plan at least one lesson that will meet the needs of the English-as-a-second-language learners in her class.

Going Beyond the Text

Visit a preschool or elementary school that has special-needs children. Observe the children in their classroom as they interact with the other children and during literacy activities. Take note of ways in which the special-needs children are similar to and different from the other children. If possible, talk to a teacher about supporting the literacy learning of special-needs children. Take at least one reading and one writing activity that you can share with a special-needs child. For example, take a children's book and literature props for the child to retell the story; plan a hands-on experience, such as popping corn, that will stimulate writing; or prepare a special book that you can give to the child for his or her own journal. Carefully observe the child's language and behaviors during these literacy activities. Be ready to discuss what this child knows about literacy.

References

ABRAMSON, S., SEDA, I., & JOHNSON, C. (1990). Literacy development in a multilingual kindergarten classroom. *Childhood Education, 67,* 68–72.

ALLEN, J., & CARR, E. (1989). Collaborative learning among kindergarten writers: James learns how to learn at school. In J. Allen & J. Mason (Eds.), *Risk Makers, risk takers, risk breakers: Reducing the risks for young literacy learners* (pp. 30–47). Portsmouth, NH: Heinemann.

AOKI, E. (1981). "Are you Chinese? Or are you just a mixed-up kid?" Using Asian American children's literature. *The Reading Teacher, 34,* 382–385.

AU, K. (1979). Using the experience-text-relationship method with minority children. *The Reading Teacher, 32,* 677–679.

AU, K. (1993). *Literacy instruction in multicultural settings.* New York: Harcourt Brace Jovanovich.

AU, K. H., & KAWAKAMI, A. J. (1985). Research currents: Talk story and learning to read. *Language Arts, 62,* 406–411.

AU, K., & MASON, J. (1981). Social organizational factors in learning to read: The balance of rights hypothesis. *Reading Research Quarterly, 17,* 115–152.

BARNES, B. L. (1996–1997a). But teacher you went right on: A perspective on Reading Recovery. *The Reading Teacher, 50,* 284–292.

BARNES, B. L. (1996–1997b). Response to Browne, Fitts, McLaughlin, McNamara, and Williams. *The Reading Teacher, 50,* 302–303.

BARNITZ, J. G. (1980). Black English and other dialects: Sociolinguistic implications for reading instruction. *The Reading Teacher, 33,* 779–786.

BARONE, D. (1993). Wednesday's child: Literacy development of children prenatally exposed to crack or cocaine. *Research in the Teaching of English, 27,* 7–45.

BARTOLI, J. S. (1986). Is it really English for everyone? *Language Arts, 63,* 12–22.

BISHOP, C. H., & WIESE, K. (1938). *The five Chinese brothers.* New York: Coward, McCann and Geoghegan.

BLAKE, B. (1992). Talk in non-native and native English speakers' peer writing conferences: What's the difference? *Language Arts, 69,* 604–610.

BROWNE, A., FITTS, M., MCLAUGHLIN, B., MCNAMARA, M. J., & WILLIAMS, J. (1996–1997). Teaching and learning in Reading Recovery: Response to "But teacher you went right on." *The Reading Teacher, 50,* 294–300.

BRYEN, D. (1982). *Inquiries into child language.* Boston: Allyn and Bacon.

CARGER, C. (1993). Louie comes to life: Pretend reading with second language emergent readers. *Language Arts, 70,* 542–547.

CASERTA-HENRY, C. (1996). Reading buddies: A first-grade intervention program. *The Reading Teacher, 49,* 500–503.

CAZDEN, C. (1988). *Classroom discourse.* Portsmouth, NH: Heinemann.

CLAY, M. (1985). *The early detection of reading difficulties* (3rd ed.). Portsmouth, NH: Heinemann.

CLAY, M. (1991). Introducing a new storybook to young readers. *The Reading Teacher, 45,* 264–273.

COUSIN, P., WEEKLEY, T., & GERARD, J. (1993). The functional uses of language and literacy by students with severe language and learning problems. *Language Arts, 70,* 548–556.

CULLINAN, B. E., JAGGAR, A. M., & STRICKLAND, D. S. (1974). Oral language expansion in the primary grades. In B. E. Cullinan (Ed.), *Black dialects and reading* (pp. 43–54). Urbana, IL: National Council of Teachers of English.

CUMMINS, J. (1986). Empowering minority students: A framework for intervention. *Harvard Educational Review, 56,* 18–36.

D'ALESSANDRO, M. E. (1987). "The ones who always get the blame": Emotionally handicapped children writing. *Language Arts, 64,* 516–522.

DELPIT, L. (1988). The silenced dialogue: Power and pedagogy in educating other people's children. *Harvard Educational Review, 58,* 280–298.

DIXON, R. (1987). Strategies for vocabulary instruction. *Teaching Exceptional Children, 19,* 61–63.

DOLMAN, D. (1992). Some concerns about using whole language approaches with deaf children. *American Annals of the Deaf, 137,* 278–282.

DOWHOWER, S. L. (1989). Repeated reading: Research into practice. *The Reading Teacher, 42,* 502–507.

ELLSON, D. G., BARBER, L., ENGLE, T. L., & KAMPWERTH, L. (1965). Programmed tutoring: A teaching aid and a research tool. *Reading Research Quarterly, 1,* 77–127.

FALTIS, C. (1993). *Joinfostering: Adapting teaching strategies for the multilingual classroom.* New York: Merrill/Macmillan.

FEELEY, J. T. (1983). Help for the reading teacher: Dealing with the Limited English Proficient (LEP) child in the elementary classroom. *The Reading Teacher, 36,* 650–655.

FEITELSON, D., GOLDSTEIN, Z., IRAQI, J., & SHARE, D. (1993). Effects of listening to story reading on aspects of literacy acquisition in a diglossic situation. *Reading Research Quarterly, 28,* 70–79.

FERDMAN, B. (1990). Literacy and cultural identity. *Harvard Educational Review, 60,* 181–204.

FITZGERALD, J. (1993). Literacy and students who are learning English as a second language. *The Reading Teacher, 46,* 638–647.

FLORES, B., COUSIN, P., & DÍAZ, E. (1991). Transforming deficit myths about learning, language, and culture. *Language Arts, 68,* 369–379.

GEE, J. P. (1996). *Social linguistics and literacies: Ideology in discourses* (2nd ed.). Bristol, PA: Taylor & Francis.

GEE, J. (1990). *Social linguistics and literacies: Ideology in discourses.* London: The Falmer Press.

GENISHI, C., & DYSON, A. H. (1984). *Language assessment in the early years.* Norwood, NJ: Ablex.

GERSTEN, R., & JIMÉNEZ, R. (1994). A delicate balance: Enhancing literature instruction for students of English as a second language. *The Reading Teacher, 47,* 438–449.

GILLET, J. W., & GENTRY, J. R. (1983). Bridges between nonstandard and standard English with extensions of dictated stories. *The Reading Teacher, 36,* 360–364.

GOLDENBERG, C. (1989). Making success a more common occurrence for children at risk for failure: Lessons from Hispanic first graders learning to read. In J. Allen & J. Mason (Eds.), *Risk makers, risk takers, risk breakers: Reducing the risks for young literacy learners* (pp. 48–79). Portsmouth, NH: Heinemann.

GREENE, J. E. (1985). Children's writing in an elementary school postal system. In M. Farr (Ed.), *Advances in writing research. (Vol. 1,* pp. 201–296). Norwood, NJ: Ablex.

HEATH, S. B. (1982). Questioning at home and at school: A comparative study. In G. Spindler (Ed.), *Doing the ethnography of schooling: Educational anthropology in action* (pp. 102–131). New York: Holt, Rinehart and Winston.

HEATH, S. (1983). *Ways with words: Language, life, and work in communities and classrooms.* New York: Cambridge University Press.

HEATH, S. (1986). Sociocultural context of language development. In California State Department of Education (Ed.), *Beyond language: Social and cultural factors in school language minority students* (pp. 143–186). Los Angeles: California State University.

HIEBERT, E., & TAYLOR, B. (Eds.). (1994). *Getting reading right from the start: Effective early literacy interventions.* Boston: Allyn and Bacon.

HOUGH, R. A., NURSS, J. R., & ENRIGHT, D. S. (1986). Story reading with limited English speaking children in the regular classroom. *The Reading Teacher, 39,* 510–514.

HUDELSON, S., & BARRERA, R. (1985). Bilingual/second-language learners and reading. In L. W. Searfoss & J. E. Readence, *Helping children learn to read* (pp. 370–392). Englewood Cliffs, NJ: Prentice-Hall.

INVERNIZZI, M., JUEL, C., & ROSEMARY, C. A. (1996–1997). A community tutorial that works. *The Reading Teacher, 50,* 304–311.

JAGGAR, A. M. (1974). Beginning reading: Let's make it a language experience for Black English speakers. In B. E. Cullinan (Ed.), *Black dialects and reading* (pp. 87–98). Urbana, IL: National Council of Teachers of English.

JUEL, C. (1996). What makes literacy tutoring effective? *Reading Research Quarterly, 31,* 268–289.

KAMEENUI, E. (1993). Diverse learners and the tyranny of time: Don't fix blame; fix the leaky roof. *The Reading Teacher, 46,* 376–383.

LABOV, W. A. (1966). *The social stratification of English in New York City.* Washington, DC: Center for Applied Linguistics.

LARA, S. G. M. (1989). Reading placement for code switchers. *The Reading Teacher, 42,* 278–282.

LIPPI-GREEN, R. (1997). What we talk about when we talk about Ebonics: Why definitions matter. *Black Scholar, 27,* 7–11.

MADDEN, N. A., SLAVIN, R. E., KARWEIT, N. L., & LIVERMON, B. (1987). *Success for all: Teacher's manual for reading.* Baltimore: Johns Hopkins University, Center for Research on Elementary and Middle Schools.

MAYER, M. (1988). *There's something in my attic.* New York: Dial.

MCKISSACK, P. (1988). *Mirandy and Brother Wind.* New York: Knopf.

MEIER, T. R., & CAZDEN, C. B. (1982). Research update: A focus on oral language and writing from a multicultural perspective. *Language Arts, 59,* 504–512.

MILES, M. (1971). *Annie and the old one.* Boston: Little, Brown.

MOUSTAFA, M., & PENROSE, J. (1985). Comprehensible input PLUS, the language experience approach: Reading instruction for limited English speaking students. *The Reading Teacher, 38,* 640–647.

NORRIS, J. A. (1988). Using communication strategies to enhance reading acquisition. *The Reading Teacher, 41,* 668–673.

ORTIZ, L., & ENGELBRECHT, G. (1986). Partners in biliteracy: The school and the community. *Language Arts, 63,* 458–465.

O'SHEA, L., & O'SHEA, D. (1987). Using repeated reading. *Teaching Exceptional Children, 20,* 26–29.

PADAK, N. D. (1981). The language and educational needs of children who speak Black English. *The Reading Teacher, 35,* 144–151.

PÉREZ, B. (1994). Spanish literacy development: A descriptive study of four bilingual whole-language classrooms. *Journal of Reading Behavior, 26,* 75–94.

PETERSON, B. (1991). Selecting books for beginning readers. In D. DeFord, C. Lyons, & G. Pinnell (Eds.), *Bridges to literacy: Learning from Reading Recovery* (pp. 119–147). Portsmouth, NH: Heinemann.

PHILIPS, S. (1972). Participant structures and communicative competence: Warm Springs children in community and classroom. In C. Cazden, V. John, & D. Hyumes (Eds.), *Functions of language in the classroom.* New York: Teachers College Press.

PINNELL, G., FRIED, M., & ESTICE, R. (1990). Reading recovery: Learning how to make a difference. *The Reading Teacher, 43,* 282–295.

PINNELL, G. S., LYONS, C. A., DEFORD, D. E., BRYK, A. S., & SELTZER, M. (1994). Comparing instructional models for literacy education of high-risk first graders. *Reading Research Quarterly, 29,* 8–39.

RASINSKI, T., & PADAK, N. (1990). Multicultural learning through children's literature. *Language Arts, 67,* 576–580.

REYES, M. (1991). A process approach to literacy instruction for Spanish-speaking students: In search of a best fit. In E. Hiebert (Ed.), *Literacy for a diverse society: Perspectives, practices, and policies* (pp. 157–171). New York: Teachers College Press.

SALVAGE, G., & BRAZEE, P. (1991). Risk taking, bit by bit. *Language Arts, 68,* 356–366.

SHAPIRO, H. (1992). Debatable issues underlying whole-language philosophy: A speech-language pathologist's perception. *Language, Speech, and Hearing Services in Schools, 23,* 308–311.

SILVER, A. A., & HAGIN, R. A. (1979). *Prevention of learning disabilities.* (Submission to Joint Dissemination Review Panel). Washington, DC: U.S. Department of Education.

SINATRA, R. (1981). Using visuals to help the second language learner. *The Reading Teacher, 34,* 539–546.

SINDELAR, P. T. (1987). Increasing reading fluency. *Teaching Exceptional Children, 19,* 59–60.

SMITHERMAN, G. (1977). *Talkin and testifying: The language of Black America.* Boston: Houghton Mifflin.

SPIEGEL, D. (1992). Blending whole language and systematic direct instruction. *The Reading Teacher, 46,* 38–44.

SPIEGEL, D. L. (1995). A comparison of traditional remedial programs and Reading Recovery: Guidelines for success for all programs. *The Reading Teacher, 49,* 86–96.

TRUAX, R., & KRETSCHMER, R. (1993). Focus on research: Finding new voices in the process of meeting the needs of all children. *Language Arts, 70,* 592–601.

URZUA, C. (1987). "You stopped too soon": Second language children composing and revising. *TESOL Quarterly, 21,* 279–304.

WALLACH, M. A., & WALLACH, L. (1976). *Teaching all children to read.* Chicago: University of Chicago Press.

WASIK, B. A., & SLAVIN, R. E. (1993). Preventing early reading failure with one-to-one tutoring: A review of five programs. *Reading Research Quarterly, 28,* 178–200.

WILLIAMS, C. (1994). The language and literacy worlds of three profoundly deaf preschool children. *Reading Research Quarterly, 29,* 124–155.

WOLFRAM, W. A. (1970). Nature of nonstandard dialect divergence. *Elementary English, 41,* 739–748.

YASHIMA, T. (1958). *Umbrella.* New York: Viking.

Chapter 12

Assessment

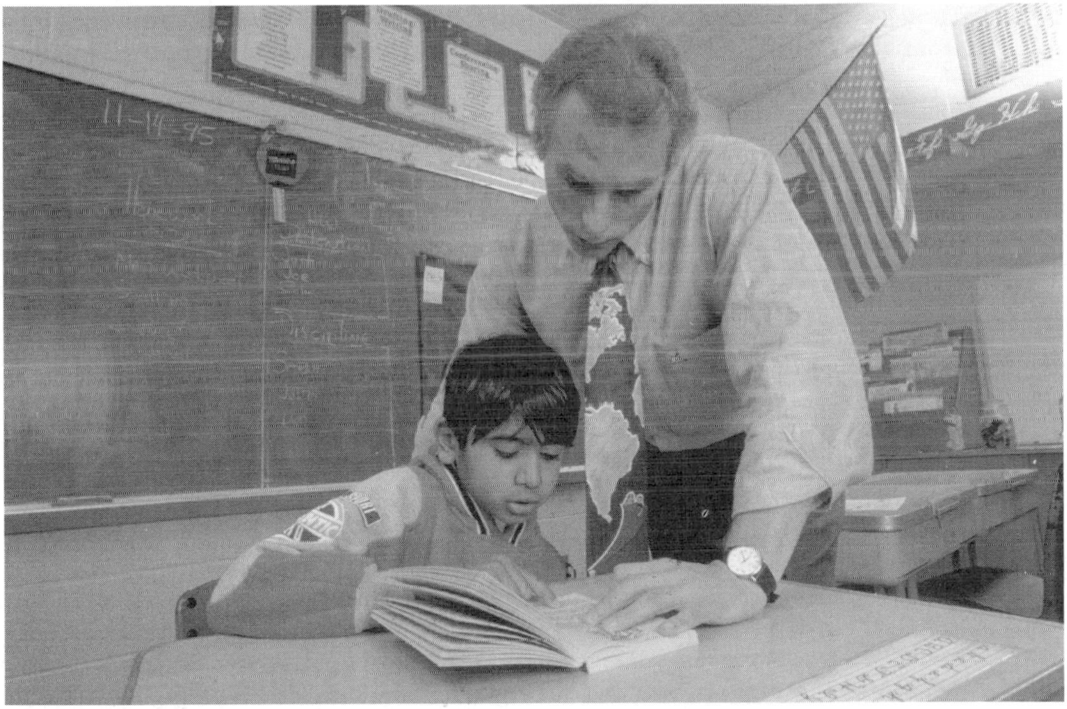

Key Concepts

observation notebook
caption
classroom assessment
portfolio
portfolio assessment
anecdotal notes
checklists
work samples
assessment planning guide
alphabet recognition task
concepts-about-print task
emergent reading checklist
running record
accuracy rate
miscue analysis
word recognition analysis
retellings
retelling checklist
story retelling analysis sheet
informational text analysis
response-to-literature checklist
portfolio conferences
portfolio summaries

A DAY IN KINDERGARTEN

The following is a story of a day in a kindergarten classroom that is similar to several classrooms that we have observed. Ms. Orlando and her children are studying travel in a combined literature and content unit. As a part of this unit, Ms. Orlando has read many stories about characters who travel away from their homes (including books with a circle structure) and poems about traveling (including imaginary travel of the mind). The children have learned different methods of transportation and are examining ways in which seeds travel.

A Day in Ms. Orlando's Classroom

Ms. Orlando's half-day kindergarten class is divided into four blocks: whole-class gathering, center time, snack and recess or a special class, and storytime.

Whole-Group Gathering

The children are gathered on the rug as the teacher reads Kovalski's (1987) version of *The Wheels on the Bus.* Two other versions of this story are displayed in the classroom library center. Ms. Orlando holds up the book and says, "I'm going to read a new version of *The Wheels on the Bus.* This one is written and illustrated by Maryanne Kovalski. It begins differently from the other 'Wheels on the Bus' stories that we have read before. Listen carefully to find out how this version is different. When I come to the part of the story that you know, join right in and read with me." Then she begins reading, and after several pages all the children are reciting the familiar story along with her.

After reading the story, Ms. Orlando and the children talk about how this story is different from the other two versions they read.

Finally, Ms. Orlando says, "Let's sing our version of the song." She flips over some charts on the chart stand until she finds the chart for "The Wheels on the Bus" song. The children dictated the words to this song earlier in the week. Ms. Orlando says, "Husalina, you can be pointer first." Husalina comes to the front of the group and takes a long pointer. The children sing the song as Husalina points across the lines of the text (she matches most of the words the children sing to the printed words). Then another child is selected to be pointer, and the class sings the song again.

Next Ms. Orlando introduces a new story. She says, "Our new story today is about another character who leaves home and travels to many different places. But instead of reading the story to you, I am going to tell it. The title of the story is *The Runaway Bunny,* and it was written by Margaret Wise Brown (1942)." Ms. Orlando hangs a copy of the front cover of the book on the classroom story clothesline as she reads the title (see clothesline props in Chapter 6). Then she says, "Who would like to guess where this little bunny might run away to?" Many of the children make guesses. Then, using the clothesline props, Ms. Orlando tells the story.

After telling the story, Ms. Orlando begins a grand conversation by saying, "What did you think about the story?" The children spend several minutes sharing their personal responses. Then Ms. Orlando says, "Little Bunny sure did become a lot of things in this. You might want to draw a picture in the art center about Little Bunny and his mother and all the different things they became. Let's write a list of all the things Little Bunny turned into, and I'll put the list in the art center to remind you what you might want to draw."

Ms. Orlando uses the interactive writing technique with the children to write the list of things Little Bunny turns into. One child offers, "Little Bunny turned into a flower." Ms. Orlando asks the children to tell her which letters she will need. She says, "Flower. FFFFFlower. Everyone say out loud what letter I need to begin spelling the word *flower.*" Many of the children say "F," some children offer other letters, and a few children are silent. Ms. Orlando confirms, "Yes. *F.* FFF." She calls on Rayshawn, who comes to the chart and writes the letter *f.* Ms. Orlando writes the remainder of the word. She and the children complete the chart, with different children writing each initial letter.

Center Time: Ms. Orlando Teaches a Minilesson and Observes Children

The children select centers, and Ms. Orlando circulates among the children helping them find materials and making sure that everyone has settled into an activity. (Figure 12.1 presents a description of the activities available in the centers in Ms. Orlando's classroom.) Then she calls five children over to the worktable (a table at which she frequently conducts small-group lessons) for a minilesson on phonemic awareness and spelling. She has a collection of environmental print objects and small toys that the children have brought to school in the past two weeks. The objects include toys or print objects that begin with the letters *T, R, V,* or *L,* including a box of rice, a toy rabbit, a scrap of rug, a bottle of Tums, a box of Tide, a toy train, a box of Vicks cough drops, a bunch of violets, a plush lion, and a box of lima beans. Each of the children has a metal pizza pan and several magnetic letters.

To begin a familiar game, Ms. Orlando holds up an object and emphasizes its beginning sound. She says, "Rrrrice. Now let's listen to the first sound at the beginning of rrrice." She models saying /r/ and several children select the letter *r* and put it on their pizza pans. After spelling several more words, Ms. Orlando says, "Today we are going to change

Figure 12.1 *Ms. Orlando's Centers*

Blocks:	sets of large and small blocks, several toy trucks, several toy cars, road maps, toy road signs, clipboards with paper and pencils (on which children pretend to keep track of mileage)
Art:	assorted art materials (including a variety of papers, crayons, markers, collage materials, scissors, and glue) and materials for making a visor, including paper plates and a pattern (for cutting the plate into a visor shape), elastic, and hole punchers (to punch a hole for the elastic)
Travel—Dramatic Play:	dress-up clothes, including purses and wallets; checkbook, play credit cards, play airline and bus tickets; materials for going to the beach, such as empty bottles of suntan lotion, towels, sunglasses, sand bucket and shovel; travel brochures and other materials, such as maps, blank postcards, paper, markers; materials for an ice-cream stand, including play money, cups, spoons, order pads, and a cash register
Library:	quality collection of literature; retelling props for "Henny Penny" and "The Gingerbread Man"; display of "Wheels on the Bus" books; display of books featuring ways to travel and toy boats, airplanes, trucks, motorcycles, and cars that the children collected; special tub of books, labeled "Traveling Characters," which includes four books each in a plastic bag with an audiotape for the listening center
Letter and Word Center:	two pieces of chart paper on which Ms. Orlando has printed the letters *T* and *R* in upper- and lowercase letters and markers (children write on the charts practicing letter formations); magazines, scissors, glue, and paper (children cut letters and pictures out of magazines and glue them on the paper); a collection of environmental print items and toys with beginning sounds of /t/, /r/, /v/, and /l/, which the children have gathered, and four grocery store sacks labeled with those letters; picture dictionaries; names of all the children in the class, and other words, such as the days of the week, months of the year, colors, and numbers
Math:	assorted manipulatives and math materials for sorting and counting; toy coins; directions for playing a game with the coins (money madness)
Discovery:	a display of different kinds of seeds the children have collected; several books about seeds and how seeds travel; magnifying glass; directions for an experiment exploring how far a piece of paper can travel when it is shaped like an acorn and when it is shaped like a maple seed, string for measuring, and paper for drawing and writing the results
Writing:	assorted writing materials and tools, blank postcards, paper, envelopes, a variety of stamps (which children use as postage stamps), picture dictionaries, photo album of children in the class with their pictures, first and last names, directory of children's addresses, telephone book, maps

this game a little bit. We are going to spell the beginning and ending of words. Like this (she holds up the toy rabbit). First I listen to the beginning of the word. Rrrrabbit. I hear an *r*." (She puts the letter *r* on her pizza pan.) "Now I have to listen for the ending. Rabbit /t/ /t/. I hear a *t*." (She puts the letter *t* after the letter *r* on her pizza pan.) "Now I've spelled *rabbit* with two letters, one for the beginning and one for the ending. Now let's try one together."

Ms. Orlando and the children spell several more words. Then Ms. Orlando says, "I want everyone to visit the writing center today or tomorrow. When you are writing, think about using beginning and ending letters." Then the five children choose centers for the remainder of center time; three of the children begin writing at the writing center.

Ms. Orlando picks up a clipboard on which she has placed six pieces of sticky notepaper with five children's names written at the top of each paper (one extra, blank notepaper is included). Ms. Orlando observes five or six children nearly every day. At the beginning of the year, she divided her twenty-two children into two groups of five and two groups of six children. Then she assigned each group of children to a day of the week. The first group of children are observed on Monday, the second group on Tuesday, and so on. One day a week she does not observe children, but uses the day for more small-group instruction, guests, films, cooking, or other special activities.

Ms. Orlando circulates among the children in the centers. She decides to watch Ishmail as he works in the letter and word center. She observes as he dumps out the bag of *R* and *T* objects that the class has gathered and separates them into two piles. He says "ro-bot," and places the toy in the *R* bag. He says "rrr-ice," and places it in the *R* bag. He says "t-t-tums," and places it in the *T* bag. He says "tr-ain," and places it in the *T* bag. Ms. Orlando writes her observations on one of the sticky notes as shown in Figure 12.2.

Then Ms. Orlando observes Jasmine as she reads the "Wheels on the Bus" chart. Jasmine says the words to the song aloud as she points with the pointer. She does not correctly match the words she says to the printed words, but at the end of each line she adjusts her pointing so that she begins a new line saying the correct word for that line.

Ms. Orlando observes Rayshawn looking at books in the block center. He has gathered several of the toy trucks in the center and is trying to match the trucks in the center to the trucks in the books' illustrations. In the library center, Ms. Orlando observes Husalina retell "Henny Penny" using the story clothesline. Husalina includes every event in the story, recalls the characters' names correctly, and repeats the dialogue, "Wanna come? Yes. Tell king sky's falled." Ms. Orlando then observes Cecelia playing in the travel dramatic-play center with Josephine and Barbara. All three girls pretend to write a letter home to their mothers. Ms. Orlando observes their writing and then asks Cecelia to read her letter. Cecelia reads, "Dear Mom, I'm having fun. Cecelia."

Last, Ms. Orlando invites Rayshawn to read the "Wheels on the Bus" chart with her; she is aware that he rarely chooses to reread the classroom charts or retell stories in the library center. Rayshawn points to the text from left to right and across the lines as he recites the words to the song. Ms. Orlando notes that he has memorized the words to the song, but is not matching the words he says with the words in the text. The notes that Ms. Orlando wrote about her observations of these children are also included in Figure 12.2.

Storytime

As center time comes to an end, Ms. Orlando helps the children put away their center activities and get ready for snack and outdoor recess. After recess, she reads a big book version of *Rosie's Walk* (Hutchins, 1968). As she reads, she pauses to invite children to make predictions about what will happen next. She notes that Jasmine, Tuong, and Ishmail catch on to the repetitive pattern and make accurate predictions of the story. After reading, the children share responses.

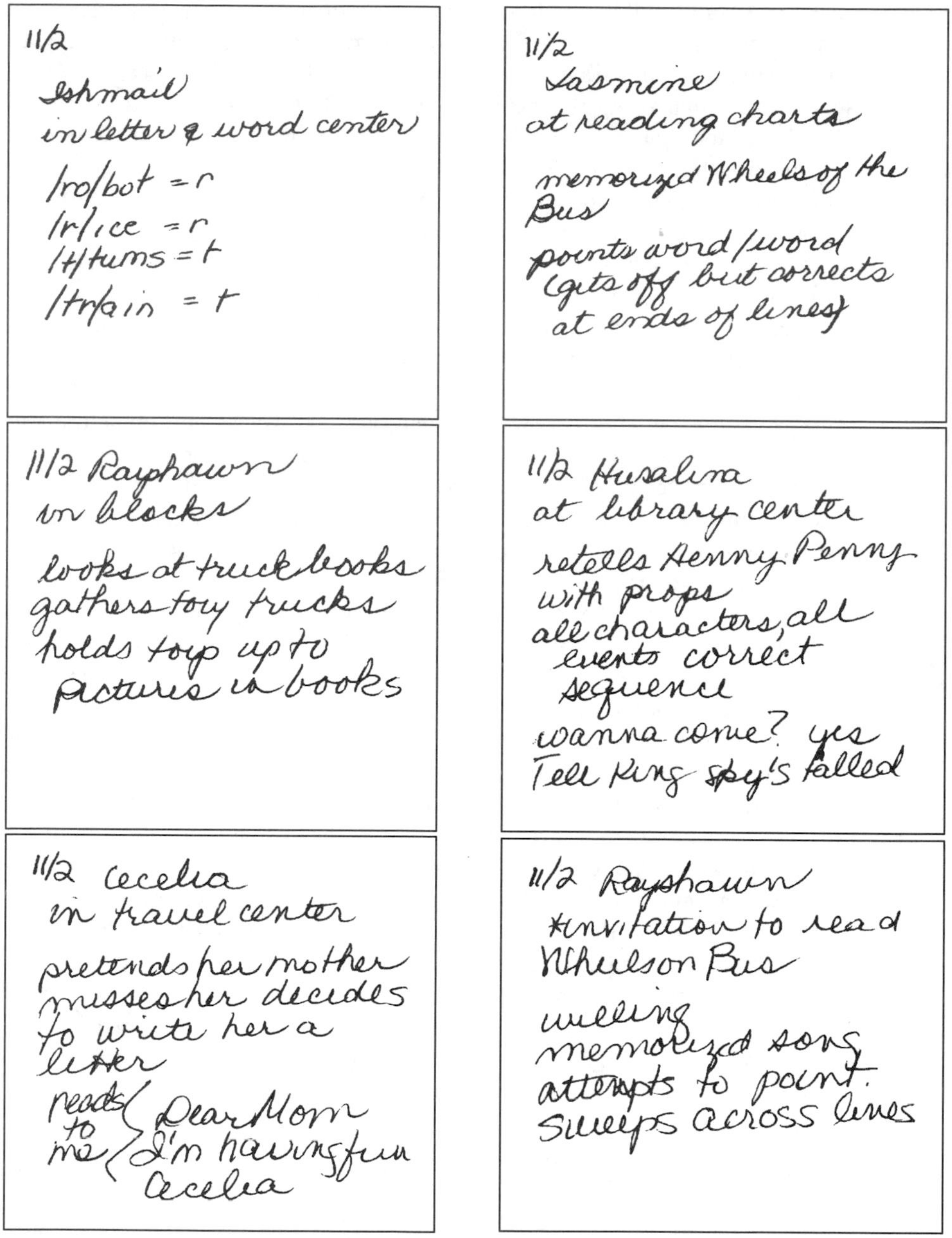

Figure 12.2 *Ms. Orlando's Anecdotal Notes*

Ms. Orlando Reflects and Plans

After the children are dismissed, Ms. Orlando takes time to organize her observations and make plans for instruction. First she takes the sticky notes off the clipboard and puts each note in her **observation notebook.** This notebook is divided into sections, one for each child in the classroom. As she places the sticky notes in the notebook, she reflects on what the observations show about each child's understanding about reading or writing. She writes her analysis beside the sticky note in the observation notebook. Figure 12.3 presents Ms. Orlando's analyses of her observations of the children. Finally, Ms. Orlando takes a few minutes to write notes in the observation notebook about the accurate predictions that Jasmine, Tuong, and Ishmail made during reading.

Ms. Orlando decides to put Cecelia's letter, which she collected from the travel dramatic-play center, in Cecelia's portfolio. Each child has a large folder in which Ms. Orlando keeps examples of that child's work. Sometimes children select activities to include in their portfolios. Ms. Orlando also keeps in their portfolios information about children's performance on special assessment tasks. She talks with the children about the contents of their portfolios at the end of each unit and shares the portfolios with parents every twelve weeks. Ms. Orlando quickly writes a caption for Cecelia's letter and clips it to the letter. The **caption** includes the date and Ms. Orlando's analysis of what the letter reveals about Cecelia's understanding about writing. Figure 12.4 shows Cecelia's letter and Ms. Orlando's caption.

Then Ms. Orlando thinks back on the day's activities and her observations. She decides that she needs to teach a small-group lesson with Jasmine, Rayshawn, and a few other children on finger-point reading of memorized stories. She plans to teach a minilesson on monitoring finger-point reading and plans to include a pocket-chart activity for the "Wheels on the Bus" song.

CLASSROOM ASSESSMENT

Classroom assessment is a critical component of effective teaching; teachers use information from their assessments of children's learning to guide instructional decisions and inform parents about their children's progress in literacy acquisition. Many teachers, like Ms. Orlando, gather information from their classroom assessments of children into portfolios. A **portfolio** is a collection of samples of a child's writing and reading. It also includes

Figure 12.3 *Analysis of Anecdotal Notes*

Ishmail:	Ishmail segments words between syllables and onset and rimes. He knows the sounds associated with *T* and *R*. He is making the transition from phonological to phonemic awareness.
Jasmine:	Jasmine knows that print is read left to right. She is developing print-to-speech match at the level of lines of text.
Rayshawn:	(at block center) Rayshawn uses reading to find information. He willingly looks at books of personal interest.
Rayshawn:	(reading chart) Rayshawn memorizes familiar text and knows print is read from left to right.
Cecelia:	Cecelia writes to communicate with the others.
Husalina:	Chooses to retell stories. Accurate recall of characters and events. English is developing in repeated dialogue.

Figure 12.4 Cecelia's Letter and Caption

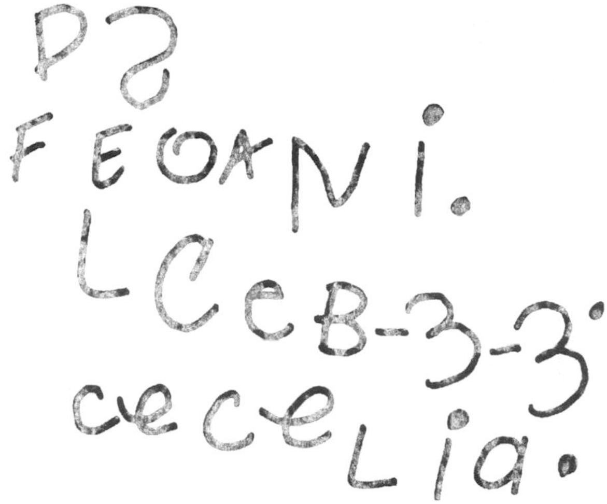

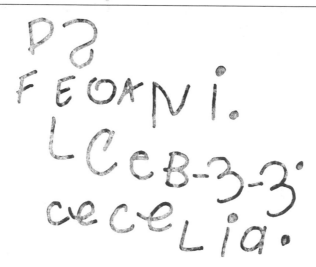

Caption: 11/2 Cecelia is using emerging letter form. Her signature is in the appropriate location for letters. She shows awareness of linearity, hyphens, and periods. Her meaning is appropriate for the situation (pretending her mother misses her) and includes language used in a letter. She uses conventional alphabet letter forms (with one reversal). She relies on contextual dependency.

Text: Dear Mom,
I'm having fun.
Cecelia

teachers' observational notes or checklists documenting the child's behaviors during reading or writing. A type of classroom assessment, **portfolio assessment** is a collection and analysis of information from several different sources, including anecdotal notes, checklists, interviews, samples of children's work, and performance on special literacy tasks. Portfolio assessment is (1) multidimensional, (2) reflective, (3) systematic, and (4) collaborative (Harp, 1991; Tierney, Carter, & Desai, 1991).

Portfolio Assessment Is Multidimensional

Portfolios are collections from a variety of sources of information, such as anecdotal notes, checklists, work samples, and special literacy tasks (Valencia, 1990). **Anecdotal notes** are objective recordings of what teachers observe children doing and are free from interpretation or inference (Rhodes & Nathenson-Mejia, 1992). They may focus on what children are reading and writing, children's comments about their reading and writing, aspects of text to which children attend, or strategies that children use. For example, Ms. Orlando noted Jasmine's strategy of self-correcting her pointing to words in the text at the end of each line, Ishmail's attention to smaller-than-word parts, and Husalina's use of language (see Figure 12.2).

Checklists are another source of information included in portfolios. They are prepared lists of behaviors or concepts that are used to guide observation. Some checklists are designed to document children's use of reading or writing processes. For example, teachers might use a checklist to observe children's use of writing processes during writing workshop. Other checklists are designed help children document their reading and writing.

Work samples are samples of children's reading and writing activities collected from ongoing classroom experiences. Work samples might include compositions, grocery lists written in a grocery store dramatic-play center, pages from journals, stories or reports, copies of improvised structure stories that children compose collaboratively, or copies of children's signatures from sign-in sheets. These samples reflect the diversity of children's classroom literacy experiences. Ms. Orlando collected a work sample when she kept a copy of Cecelia's letter.

Portfolio Assessment Is Reflective

Teachers' and children's analyses of children's current understandings about written language and progress in literacy acquisition are an important part of portfolio assessment. Ms. Orlando took time after she wrote anecdotal notes to reflect on the behaviors she observed and what those behaviors revealed about children's knowledge. For example, she recognized that Ishmail's talk at the letter and word center reflected his level of phonemic awareness (he could segment some words at syllable boundaries and segment the onset in others). She wrote her analysis for each observation in her observation notebook.

Children's reflections are also a part of portfolios. Part of children's reflections include choosing which work samples to add to a portfolio. Ms. Orlando's children selected work samples to add to their portfolios at the end of every theme unit. Children may decide to select works that are

- Best works
- Most interesting works
- Works that demonstrate learning
- Works that demonstrate variety
- Easy and difficult work

Portfolio Assessment Is Systematic

Information in portfolios is collected systematically and regularly. At the beginning of the year, teachers consider their instructional goals and make decisions about the kinds of assessments that they will use to provide evidence of children's progress toward each of the instructional goals (Winograd, Paris, & Bridge, 1991). Instructional goals reflect the expectations of the particular grade level as dictated by district or state curriculum guides as well as teachers' understandings about children's literacy acquisition. Once teachers have identified their instructional goals, they prepare an **assessment planning guide** (Tierney, Carter, & Desai, 1991). This guide lists the instructional goals and outlines some instructional activities designed to meet the goals as well as assessments to capture information about children's learning related to the goals.

Figure 12.5 presents Ms. Orlando's kindergarten assessment planning guide. This figure shows that Ms. Orlando's instructional plan includes goals for children's growing knowledge about written language meanings, forms, functions, and meaning-form links. Her plan shows that each goal is extended through a variety of instructional activities. Similarly, Ms. Orlando intends to use several assessments to capture information about children's progress in each goal.

Ms. Orlando took considerable time stating her instructional goals so that her goals would be challenging to all the children in her classroom, regardless of the level of their entering knowledge. Therefore, she did not state her goals in terms of levels of achievement, but rather in terms of growth.

Figure 12.5 *Assessment Planning Guide*

GOALS	ACTIVITIES	ASSESSMENT
Meanings:		
1. children demonstrate increased understanding of books read aloud	grand conversations retellings KWL	response checklist retelling checklist
2. children demonstrate increased use of meaning strategies (predicting, recalling, sequencing)	grand conversations retellings	anecdotal notes response checklist
Forms:		
3. children increase in complexity of written language forms	writing center theme activities	work samples anecdotal notes alphabet task
4. children increase in complexity of story forms used in compositions	writing center improvised structure stories sharing	work samples
Meaning-Form Links:		
5. children demonstrate increased emergent reading	independent reading chart and big books pocket charts	anecdotal notes emergent reading checklist
6. children demonstrate increased understanding of alphabetic principles, including knowledge of alphabet letters, letter sounds, and phonemic awareness	writing center chart and big books word and letter center	anecdotal notes emergent reading checklist work samples invented spelling task
Functions:		
7. children use reading and writing for a variety of purposes	drama centers theme activities (invitations, etc.)	anecdotal notes work samples
8. children choose to read and write	center activities independent reading	anecdotal notes work samples

Teachers and children gather information for portfolios continuously throughout the school year. Teachers may plan to make a particular assessment each week; Ms. Orlando set up a plan whereby she observed each child in her classroom at least once a week. Other assessments might be planned at the end of each grading period or theme unit.

Portfolio Assessment Is Collaborative

Self-evaluation is a critical component of portfolio assessment (Farr & Tone, 1994). Children play an important role in assessing their own learning and setting their own goals for learning. They help select information to be included in their portfolios, and they reflect on what the information in the portfolio reveals about them as learners. Some teachers include children in parent–teacher conferences in which portfolios are shared with parents. Children show the contents of their portfolios to their parents and discuss with them what the contents show about their learning progress.

ASSESSMENT TOOLS

There are a variety of assessment tools that teachers may use to assess children's literacy knowledge. These include observations, alphabet recognition tasks, concepts-about-print tasks, emergent reading checklists, phonemic awareness assessments, running records, retellings, analyses of grand conversations and journals, and analyses of compositions.

Observations

Observation is one of the most important classroom assessment tools. As teachers observe children interacting with other children and using reading and writing in functional ways, children's concepts about written language meanings, forms, meaning-form links, and functions are revealed. Teachers capture this information for portfolios by writing anecdotal notes about their observations. Teachers usually choose to write an anecdotal note when they observe an event that reflects a child's current level of understanding about written language or a new level of understanding. For example, Ms. Orlando recognized that her observation of Rayshawn's reading books in the block center was a reflection of his current level of interaction with books. She knew that Rayshawn rarely visited the library center or willingly retold books using the many props available in the classroom. Therefore, Ms. Orlando decided to write an anecdotal note of this behavior.

An important part of observation is reflection. That is, teachers not only note behaviors, but also consider what those behaviors mean. Teachers capture the behavior in their anecdotal notes, which are objective recordings of behaviors. Then they write an analysis that identifies children's concepts. Ms. Orlando's anecdotal notes are good examples of objective reportings of behavior (see Figure 12.2), and her analyses identify children's literacy knowledge (see Figure 12.3).

Analysis of anecdotal notes depends on the teacher's awareness of children's knowledge. For example, suppose that a first grade teacher is concerned about a child's inability to select and sustain interest in a book for independent reading. The teacher observes that the child selects three different books in five minutes and does no more than look quickly through the books at the illustrations. Figure 12.6 presents the teacher's anecdotal note and

Figure 12.6 *Anecdotal Notes Showing Development*

Note 10/15

10/15 Barbara
sits near bookcase
pulls books out at
random, flips through
looking at pictures,
spends 4 minutes
then leaves center

Analysis 10/15

Barbara willingly participates in independent reading. She browses through books looking at pictures. (needs support in selecting books and strategies for sustaining interest)

Note 2/7

2/7 Barbara
searches for &
retells Hop on
Pop
sustains retelling
for over 10
minutes

Analysis 2/7

Barbara enjoys reading books to others. She is comfortable reading books she has memorized and spends long periods of time rereading these books. She selects these books for independent reading. Note progress from unable to sustain interest in books to sustains interest for prolonged periods of time from 10/15.

analysis of this behavior. Several months later, the teacher may observe the same child spending more than fifteen minutes reading *Hop on Pop* (Seuss, 1963) with a friend in the library center. The teacher writes an anecdotal note about this event because the teacher knows that it documents significant growth in the child's ability and willingness to sustain interest in reading. Figure 12.6 also shows the teacher's anecdotal note about this new behavior and analysis of the child's progress.

Teachers frequently read over their anecdotal notes about children to assess any patterns of growth. Ms. Orlando reads through her anecdotal notes every two to three weeks. Whenever her anecdotal notes indicate a change in a child's learning, she notes this change in the child's observation record.

Alphabet Recognition Task

To assess children's knowledge of alphabet letter names, teachers can prepare an **alphabet recognition task.** They write (or type) all the uppercase and lowercase alphabet letters in random order on a sheet of paper or on index cards. Children are asked to name the letters, and teachers record the letters that children fail to identify. Preschool and kindergarten teachers are particularly interested in recognizing children's progress in identifying letters correctly.

Concepts-about-Print Task

The **concepts-about-print task** is designed to assess children's understanding of familiar words used to talk about books, awareness of directionality in how print is read, and understanding of the conventions of written language (Clay, 1985). Teachers can construct their own concepts-about-print test. They select an unfamiliar picture book and ask children to point to the front and back of the book, to the beginning and ending of the story, and to the top and bottom of a page. They have children point to where to start reading (upper left), where to go next (across to the right), and then where to read next (return sweep to the next line of text). Using a big book, teachers can have child locate one word, the first and last letter in a word, a period, and a capital letter.

Phonemic Awareness Assessment

Children's invented spelling provides one indication of their level of phonemic awareness. Children who invent spellings with at least one letter that has a reasonable relationship with a sound in a spoken word have at least a beginning level of phonemic awareness. They are able to hear a phoneme and represent it with a letter. A more systematic assessment of phonemic awareness includes finding out whether children hear rhyming words, hear words with the same initial and final sound, and segment a word into individual phonemes. Teachers can construct phonemic awareness measures by collecting pictures of rhyming words, words with the same initial consonants, and words with the same final sounds and having children detect matches (for descriptions of phonological and phonemic awareness assessments, see Adams, Foorman, Lundberg, & Beeler, 1998; Swank, Meier, Invernizzi, & Juel, 1997; Yopp, 1995).

Emergent Reading Checklist

An **emergent reading checklist** is a list of behaviors that signals children's movement toward more conventional reading. Figure 12.7 shows an emergent reading checklist that can be used to document young children's growth from emergent to conventional reading (adapted from Tompkins & McGee, 1993, p. 358). Teachers use the checklist as they observe children reading independently, with partners, and in small groups. They observe children several times throughout the school year, using the checklist to document changes in children's reading abilities. Teachers may use the information from emergent reading checklists to plan instruction.

Running Record

A **running record** is used to analyze children's reading; it provides information about reading level and children's use of cueing systems during reading. A running record includes several steps. First, teachers listen to children read and record children's miscues or errors. Then, they analyze the running record using a miscue analysis. Teachers may also analyze the miscues to determine children's knowledge of word recognition strategies. As an optional part of a running record, children may retell the story or informational book after reading, and then teachers analyze the retelling.

Taking a Running Record

The first step of a running record is to obtain a record of the child's reading—the running record. To begin, teachers select texts of at least one hundred words at a variety of difficulty levels. These texts can be selected from basal readers or from commercial materials and have

Figure 12.7 *Emergent Reading Checklist*

Child's Name ______________________________ Date ________

Emergent Reading

_____ reading related to pictures but not text

_____ reading closely matched to text but not coordinated with pages of text

_____ reading closely matched to text and coordinated with pages of text

_____ reading exact match to text and pages of text

Directionality (pointing while reading)

_____ sweeps across text (uncoordinated)

_____ sweeps from left to right across lines of text (continuous and coordinated sweep across lines of text)

_____ sweeps from left to right across text pointing to words

Speech-to-Print Match

_____ points to words and assigns segment of speech

_____ points to a word in text and assigns a spoken word

_____ tracks print correctly (points to a word in text and assigns correct spoken word)

Word Identification

_____ matches words

_____ tracks print to identify words

_____ identifies words in text without tracking

_____ identifies words out of text

_____ learns new words from reading

Cue Systems

_____ uses memory to read text

_____ uses pictures and memory to read text

_____ uses tracking, memory, and pictures to monitor reading

_____ uses sound–letter relationships to monitor reading

_____ uses tracking, memory, pictures, and sound–letter relationships to monitor reading

an indication of difficulty level (see, for example, materials published by The Wright Group). Reading Recovery also has a list of books at several levels of difficulty (Peterson, 1991, pp. 139–147).

Next, children read several of the texts, and the teacher records the kinds of miscues they make as they read. Figure 12.8 presents a running record of Charlie's reading "The Three Little Pigs." This figure indicates words that Charlie omitted—crossed out in text; words that he inserted—added above the text; words that he substituted—written over the text; and

Figure 12.8 *Running Record for "The Three Little Pigs"*

TEXT: The Three Little Pigs

Once upon a time there were three pigs. Mother pig sent the three little pigs out to make their way in the world. The first pig made a house of straw. The second pig made a house of sticks. The third pig made a house of bricks. A wolf came to the first pig's house and said, "I'll huff and puff and blow your house down." The wolf blew the house down and the little pig ran away fast. The wolf came to the second pig's house and said, "I'll huff and puff and blow your house down." The wolf blew the house down but the little pig ran away faster. The wolf came to the third pig's house and said, "I'll huff and puff and blow your house down." He blew and blew but could not blow down the house. He tried to sneak down the chimney but the pig put a big pot of water on the fire. The wolf came down the chimney and burned his tail. He ran away the fastest of all.

EXAMPLES:

child matches text	✓
child substitutes	child / text
child omits	• / text
child inserts	child / •
child repeats	⌊text
child self-corrects	SC
teacher prompts	T

RUNNING RECORD

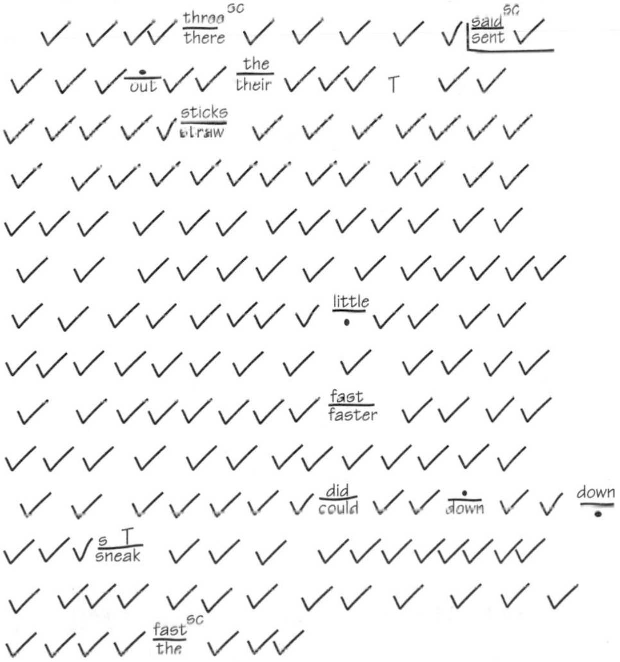

words that he self-corrected—marked with "SC." The figure also shows the teacher's running record, which captures Charlie's omissions, insertions, substitutions, and self-corrections (see the directions included in the figure).

Teachers then determine the child's **accuracy rate,** percentage of words read correctly, by counting the total number of miscues not including miscues that were self-corrected. The total number of miscues is subtracted from the total number of words in the passage to find the number of words read correctly. Finally, the number of words read correctly is divided by the total number of words in the passage. For example, Charlie read the "The Three Little Pigs" passage with 14 miscues including 3 self-corrected miscues for a total of 11 miscues. This number (11) is subtracted from the total number of words in the passage (181) to determine the number of words read correctly (170). The number of words read correctly is divided by the total number of words to reach the percentage of words read correctly—the accuracy rate. The accuracy rate for Charlie's reading of "The Three Little Pigs" is 93 percent. The accuracy rate is used to determine whether the text is on the independent, instructional, or frustrational reading level. According to Clay (1985, p. 17), independent level texts should be read with 95–100 percent accuracy and instructional texts should be read with 90–94 percent accuracy. Texts that are read with less than 90 percent accuracy are at the frustration level. Charlie's accuracy rate indicates that the passage "The Three Little Pigs" is at his instructional level.

Miscue Analysis

A **miscue analysis** provides information about children's use of semantic (meaning), syntactic (language), and graphophonic cueing systems (Goodman & Burke, 1972). To assist in a miscue analysis, teachers construct a miscue analysis chart. Figure 12.9 displays the miscue analysis for Charlie's reading of "The Three Little Pigs." First, the teacher analyzes all substitutions to determine whether they are semantically acceptable (miscue has a

Figure 12.9 *Miscue Analysis Chart for "The Three Little Pigs"*

CHILD/TEXT	SEMANTICALLY ACCEPTABLE	SYNTACTICALLY ACCEPTABLE	GRAPHOPHONICALLY SAME AS			SELF-CORRECTS	COMMENTS
			B	M	E		
three/there			✓			✓	*
said/sent			✓			✓	*
the/their		✓	✓				
sticks/straw		✓	✓				
fast/faster		✓	✓	✓			
did/could		✓			✓		
fast/the						✓	*
s/sneak			✓				
	0/8	4/8	6/8	1/8	1/8	3/8	

* sentence makes sense up to point of miscue

similar meaning as the text word), syntactically acceptable (miscue is syntactically acceptable in the sentence), or graphophonically acceptable (miscue matches the text word at the beginning, middle, or end). The teacher also records whether the miscue was self-corrected.

According to the miscue analysis presented in Figure 12.9 none of Charlie's miscues were semantically acceptable, but Charlie self-corrected three miscues. In addition, all his miscues up to the point of the error made sense. Over half of his miscues were syntactically acceptable. All the miscues except two had the same beginning letters as the text word. According to this analysis, Charlie attends especially to beginning letters, but also to meaning. His miscues make sense and are often syntactically acceptable.

Word Recognition Analysis

Children's miscues in running records provide excellent resources for determining their knowledge of word recognition cues, including phonics (knowledge of sound–letter relationships) and structural analysis (knowledge of prefixes, suffixes, and familiar word parts). Teachers examine children's miscues for knowledge of

- Consonants
- Consonant clusters (*br, gl, st,* etc.)
- Consonant digraphs (*sh, ch, th, ph, wh,* and *ng*)
- Short vowels (m*a*d, etc.)
- Silent *e* long vowels (m*a*d*e*, etc.)
- Vowel combinations (m*ai*l, p*ay*, m*ea*t, t*oy*, etc.)
- Prefixes
- Suffixes
- Familiar word parts (*le* in *bottle*, etc.)

A third grade teacher recorded the following miscues in Raymond's running record.

Text	**Child**
street	stairs
strutting	starting
mournful	m
deserted	distant
abruptly	ab
mysterious	mysteries

In a **word recognition analysis** of Raymond's miscues, his teacher noted that Raymond consistently used beginning consonants but frequently omitted the *r* in the *str* consonant cluster and had difficulty decoding multisyllabic words (all the miscues were words of more than one syllable, except for *ceased*). However, Raymond is aware of some prefixes and familiar word parts (for example, he correctly read the *ab* prefix).

Retellings

Retellings are tasks in which children read and then retell a text. To retell, children recall everything they can remember from the story or informational text either orally or in writing. Retellings reflect children's understanding of text; but of course, retellings also reflect children's memory and their level of spoken or written language competence. Retellings usually assess children's recall of the literal facts of a story. Running records always include a retelling as a measure of comprehension. Other texts may also be used for retelling.

To assess retellings, teachers prepare a retelling checklist that includes all the important information from a story or informational text. Figure 12.10 is a **retelling checklist** for assessing children's retelling of *Fly Away Home* (Bunting, 1991). As a child retells the story, the teacher checks off each event included in the child's retelling. After the child finishes retelling, the teacher may use several prompts to see whether the child has understood more about the story than he or she recalled at first. Depending on the parts of the story that were not recalled, teachers ask, "Do you remember any other characters?" "Where (when) did the story take place?" "What was (the main character's) problem?" "How did (the main character) solve the problem?" "Can you remember anything else that happened in the story?" "How did the story end?" Children's original retelling is called *unprompted recall,* and their responses to these questions is called *prompted recall.* The *retelling score* is the percentage of total ideas (prompted and unprompted) recalled.

To make retelling checklists, teachers select short stories of 100 to 300 words, read the stories carefully, and make a list of the important events. Retelling checklists can be constructed for informational texts as well. In this case, teachers make a list of all main ideas and supporting details or examples.

In addition to measuring the quantity of ideas recalled (retelling score), teachers can examine the quality of retelling. To do so usually requires that teachers tape-record retellings or gather written retellings. Teachers examine whether children include the major literary elements of stories in expected order or whether children remember the main ideas and supporting details in the organizational pattern used by the author. Figure 12.11 pre-

Figure 12.10 *Retelling Checklist for* Fly Away Home *(Bunting, 1991)*

Unprompted	Prompted	
______	______	1. Boy and dad live in airport.
______	______	2. They have no home.
______	______	3. They are careful they don't get caught.
______	______	4. The important thing is not to get noticed.
______	______	5. Boy and Dad don't get noticed.
______	______	6. The boy and his dad sleep in different parts of the airport.
______	______	7. One day a bird got caught inside the terminal.
______	______	8. After a few days the bird flew out the door.
______	______	9. The dad works on weekends as a janitor.
______	______	10. The boy stays with the Medinas.
______	______	11. He returns luggage carts for tips.
______	______	12. Dad looks for an apartment but can't find one.
______	______	13. The boy is sad he lives in the airport.
______	______	14. The boy knows he will be free of the airport like the bird.

Figure 12.11 *Story Retelling Analysis Sheet*

Setting

_____ States introduction (1 point)
_____ States place or time (1 point)
_____ Names main character (1 point)
_____ Names other characters (1 point)

Problem

_____ Names or implies problem (1 point)

Plot

_____ Recalls most major events (2 points)
_____ Recalls some major events (1 point)

Resolution

_____ Recalls climax (1 point)
_____ Recalls ending (1 point)

Sequence

_____ Recalls story in sequence (2 points)
_____ Recalls story with some sequence (1 point)

Theme (1 point)

_____

Total score (possible 12 points)

_____

Adapted from L. M. Morrow, "Using Story Retelling to Develop Comprehension," in K. Muth (Ed.), *Children's Comprehension of Text: Research into Practice*, p. 187.

sents a **story retelling analysis sheet,** which teachers can use to analyze the quality of retellings of stories (Morrow, 1989). Figure 12.12 presents an **informational text analysis** sheet (Cooper, 1993).

To analyze retellings along with running records, children read the text aloud and teachers take a running record. Then children retell the text so that teachers can assess their understanding of the text. The running record provides evidence of the level of text that children can read fluently and of the kinds of reading strategies they employ. Retellings provide evidence of children's comprehension.

Grand Conversations and Response Journals

Children construct meaning beyond the literal level. One way of assessing their comprehension beyond the literal level is to examine their responses to literature in grand conversations and response journals. As children participate in grand conversations or write in response journals, they recall events, evaluate the text globally, make inferences or evaluations of characters and events, identify with a character, state themes, relate personal experiences, make connections to other literature, and comment on or evaluate literary structures or languages (McGee, 1992; Sipe, in press). Children also make predictions, hypothesize about outcomes or reasons for actions, and ask questions or identify confusing

Figure 12.12 *Informational Text Retelling Analysis*

Introduction

_____ Identifies topic (1 point)

_____ Gives purposes or focus (1 point)

Main Ideas

_____ Identifies main ideas
(3 points most major ideas identified)
(2 points some major ideas identified)
(1 point a few major ideas identified)

Supporting Details

_____ Provides supporting details for main ideas
(3 points if supporting details for most main ideas are provided)
(2 points if supporting details for some main ideas are provided)
(1 point if some supporting details are identified)

Relationships

_____ Makes explicit the relationship between ideas (for example, stating that the fire *caused* many people to lose their homes)
(2 points if many relationships are stated)
(1 point if some relationships are stated)

Organization

_____ Recalls information in a sequence similar to text
(2 points for well-organized recall)
(1 point for somewhat organized recall)

Total score (12 points possible)

_____

parts of the text. These responses indicate children's personal involvement with the story or informational text and their ability to construct inferential, evaluative, and interpretive understandings. Figure 12.13 presents five first graders' grand conversation about *Hey, Al* (Yorinks, 1986), which illustrates the variety of different responses that teachers can expect in grand conversations (see also Figure 5.3 in Chapter 5).

Figure 12.14 on page 361 presents a **response-to-literature checklist,** which can be used to analyze children's responses in grand conversations and response journals. To use the response checklist, teachers audiotape or videotape grand conversations or collect entries from children's response journals. They review their recordings and focus on the contributions of one child at a time. They complete a checklist for each child participating in the grand conversation and note the levels of understanding reflected in children's responses.

The response-to-literature checklist in Figure 12.14 includes the teacher's analysis of Annie's participation in the grand conversation presented in Figure 12.13. The checklist shows that Annie recalled story events, responded to a symbol, made inferences, and used illustrations to support her responses. Her responses ranged from the first level to the fourth level.

Figure 12.13 *Grand Conversation about* Hey, Al *(Yorinks, 1986)*

Teacher (T):	What did you think of the story?
Chris:	I like the part when he turns into a bird. The dog and Eddie.
Ryan:	Hey! Eddie's the dog. I like the part when he's laying down in the water, and the birds bring him food and stuff and he's wearing the old hat that he used to have and I like the dog, too.
Annie:	I like the part when they were going back to their own house and Eddie fell into the ocean.
T:	Why did you like that part?
Annie:	Because it was gonna be okay.
T:	Did you know that for sure?
John:	No, no.
Chris:	Yeah, because if they were on earth they wouldn't be birds.
Annie:	I like the part when they got home and they painted everything yellow so everything would be okay. Al's dog came back so Al wouldn't be afraid that he didn't have a dog anymore.
Alice:	I liked the part when he was a janitor but then he said, there's no—like when he was gonna go up there, and he was gonna change his mind, but he didn't.
Ryan:	I like the part when the bird comes to say, "Hey, Al," and he jumps when he's shaving his face and the bird came and says, "Al, Al," and he jumped and said, "Who's that?" and the razor came out of his hand.
John:	Yeah, it was funny.
Alice:	I liked those birds with all those big, big legs.
Annie:	I like the part when they were going up there and Al lost his luggage. Hey! Look at that! Look at that hand! (Annie points to illustration in which a bird has a human hand)
T:	Oh, where?
Annie:	He's turning back.
T:	Look what Annie's found.
John:	He was a person.
Annie:	All of them were persons.
Ryan:	They were all persons?
Annie:	People! All of these were people! Look at his hands.
John:	I know. That's what I said.
Chris:	If they all stay there, they'll all be birds.
Annie:	Oh, look. How can he be changed back?
Alice:	I could tell he was an old man because look at his skin.
Annie:	I think all the animals were humans before they came out there because one of these animals was the real one and they turn real people into
John:	animals.

(continued)

Figure 12.13 *(continued)*

Ryan: Yeah, birds and they have to go back but they don't know how to get back because some of them don't have wings.

Eric: I like the bird there with the hand in the cage with the funny mouth.

John: I liked the part when he fell in that place up in the air.

Annie: In the water.

John: No. When he fell in the place in the sky. When the bird was dropping him down into the place.

T: Well, what do you think Al found out at the island?

Annie: I think he would be better as a janitor instead of up there. He learned never talk to strangers.

Ryan: If he stayed up there, he would really be a bird and we don't know if he could change back again and his whole body would be a bird.

John: He loves his home.

T: How do you know?

John: Because he was happy to be back and the dog came back and they painted it.

Annie: They painted it yellow like the place. He was happy at the end.

Chris: Yeah, and he got a new shirt like it wasn't the shirt from, like he was a janitor again, but he's got a nicer shirt and he looks happy.

Alice: Eddie is smiling. Yeah. The story has a happy ending.

Compositions

Teachers and children select compositions to include in portfolios. These compositions may be written during writing workshop and may be highly polished stories that have gone through several drafts, or they may be informal compositions written at a writing center. Compositions can be written, dictated, or presented orally. Teachers analyze compositions for children's understanding of written forms, meanings, and spellings.

Analysis of Form

Young children's compositions can be examined for the following forms.

- Mock cursive (indicates awareness of linearity)
- Mock alphabet letters (indicates awareness of letter features)
- Conventional alphabet letters (indicates knowledge of alphabet formations)
- Copied words (indicates awareness of words in environment)

Figure 12.14 *Response-to-Literature Checklist*

Name Annie Date 4/16

Title Hey, Al

Other Children in Group Chris, Ryan, John, Alice, Eric

Product (What child said or wrote)	**Comments**
Level 1: Recall and global evaluation	
✓ recalls story events and characters	Eddie fell ocean
makes global evaluations	
recalls text language	
✓ notes details in illustrations	notes hand
Level 2: Connections	
identifies with character	
relates personal stories	
relates personal feelings	
connects to other literature	
Level 3: Inferences and evaluations	birds are people
✓✓ makes inferences about characters' motivations, feelings, traits	Al doesn't have to be afraid doesn't have dog
makes evaluations of characters' actions, traits, motivations, feelings	
✓ makes inferences about events	gonna be ok
makes evaluations of events	
makes inferences about language meaning	
Level 4: Intrepretation at the Story Level	
✓ states theme related to the story	better off janitor
✓ interprets literary elements (symbol, etc.)	yellow/happy
interprets author's use of literary structures	(symbol?)
Level 5: Intrepretation at the Abstract and Personal Level	
✓ states theme at abstract level	don't talk to strangers
states theme at personal level	
interprets story as rejection of society	
Processes: Child's participation in group interactions	
✓ asks questions	how can be turned back?
✓ makes hypotheses	one person "real one"
acknowledges comments of others	
✓ contributes ideas to argument	
asks for clarifying or supporting evidence	
✓ uses appropriate turn-taking procedures	
	high level participation

- Spelled words such as the child's name or other learned words such as *mom, dad,* and *love* (indicates learned spellings)
- Conventions (such as capitalization and punctuation)
- Invented spelling

In addition, teachers note whether children's writing shows awareness of linearity (for example, writing mock letters from left to right in lines) or spacing (for example, leaving spaces between strings of conventional letters as if writing words). Young children frequently circle words, place periods between words, or separate words with dashes. These unconventional strategies indicate that children are experimenting with word boundaries.

Older children's compositions can be analyzed for their knowledge of conventions, such as capital letters and punctuation. Teachers note all examples of children's use of these conventions and keep a list of all conventions the children use correctly. For example, a teacher may note that a child capitalizes the beginnings of sentences, the word *I,* the name of the local town, and the name of the school; consistently uses a period or question mark at the end of a sentence; uses apostrophes in the contractions *don't* and *I've;* and uses a comma after the greeting in a letter.

Story form. Teachers take special note of children's control over story form. Chapter 5 described the literary elements found in the story form (see Table 5.1), which include

- Setting, which identifies time, place, and weather
- Characters, who are revealed through their thoughts, actions, appearance, and dialogue
- Plot, which includes a problem, episodes, climax, and resolution—episodes consist of actions toward solving the problem and outcomes
- Point of view, which reveals who tells the story
- Mood
- Theme

Teachers may use their knowledge of literary elements to analyze children's compositions (written, dictated, or told).

Figure 12.15 presents a story composition dictated by five-year-old Kristen to her kindergarten teacher. The composition contains sixteen pages and a title page. As Kristen's kindergarten teacher analyzed the form of Kristen's story, she noted that Kristen had included three characters: a little girl, a cat, and baby cats. These characters were developed through the illustrations (which showed what the characters looked like), a few revelations of the cat's thoughts (she wanted to go home and she was happy), the girl's and cat's actions, and dialogue.

Kristen's story incorporates three plot episodes (rescuing the cat, the cat's birthday, and taking the baby cats to live in the woods). The first episode, about rescuing the cat, has a fully developed plot. It includes a problem (the cat was caught in a trap), actions toward solving the problem (the girl pulled and pulled, and pushed and pushed on the trap), a climax (the cat was almost out), and an outcome (the cat was out). The other episodes are descriptions of actions, and all the episodes are loosely connected through common characters.

Figure 12.15 *"The Girl with the Cat and the Babies"*

Title:	The Girl with the Cat and the Babies
page 1	The little girl took her cat for a walk.
page 2	She got caught in a trap.
page 3	The little girl came.
page 4	And she pulled, and she pulled, and she pushed, and she pushed on the trap.
page 5	She opened the cage and the cat was almost out.
page 6	The little cat was out. She was happy.
page 7	The cat was purring because the little girl was rubbing her.
page 8	The little girl was taking her home.
page 9	The sun was coming down.
page 10	Tomorrow was the cat's birthday. She was happy because she was going to have a party.
page 11	It was the cat's birthday and the people were fixing it up because they were awake.
page 12	One day the cat was knocking on the little girl's door because she had four babies on her birthday.
page 13	The cat asked, "Can I go out in the woods with my babies to live?"
page 14	Far, far away they went. She waved good-bye and so did the babies.
page 15	The cat built five houses.
page 16	They were all ready to go to sleep.

Kristen relied on having the cats go to sleep to resolve the story. The story is told in the third person, with the cat's thoughts revealed. The mood of the story is pleasant except for when the cat is caught in the trap. Kristen's story shows her ability to manipulate all the literary elements of a story form except for theme.

Expository text form. Teachers also analyze the form of children's informational writing. At the simplest level, children's expositions consist of labels (see Chapter 5). They may be one-word, phrase, or sentence labels identifying objects, people, or events. At the next level, children's expository texts are organized into lists, in which the ideas included in the text are related to a single topic. At the third level, children's expositions consist of ordered paragraphs, which include at least three ideas on a single topic related to one another through cause–effect, compare–contrast, problem–solution, or sequence. At the highest level, children's expositions are ordered expositions that include ideas divided into two or more related topics, with ideas within each topic related to each other.

As teachers analyze children's compositions, they use their knowledge of these four levels of text forms to describe children's expository text forms. First, they determine whether the composition consists of labeling or whether children have included a main topic. Then, teachers determine whether the ideas are consistently related to the main topic and whether they are related to one another.

Meaning

In analyzing the meanings in children's compositions, teachers consider the characters, events, settings, or information in relation to children's own experiences and to literature. They analyze the ideas included in compositions for consistency, believability, and unity. They examine children's use of dialogue, literary word order, or literary language such as alliteration, rhyme, repetition, simile, or imagery.

In the story presented in Figure 12.15, Kristen included a familiar character (she has a cat). Many of the actions of the story are from Kristen's own life—her cat often follows her on walks, she likes to rub her cat until he purrs, her birthday was less than a month away, she often explores the woods around her house, and she wishes that her cat could have babies.

Kristen also incorporated three examples of literary language in her composition. She used repetition of words and actions, including actions similar to those in the familiar folktale *The Enormous Turnip* (Parkinson, 1986) (And she pulled, and she pulled, and she pushed, and she pushed on the trap). She also used literary word order (Far, far away they went) and dialogue (Then the cat asked, "Can I go out in the woods with my babies to live?").

Spelling

Teachers assess children's spelling development by analyzing the spellings in their compositions. To do this, teachers can make a chart with six columns: non-spelling, early invented spelling, purely phonetic spelling, early orthographic spelling, and later orthographic and meaning-based, and conventional spelling. They analyze all the spellings in a composition by writing each word in its appropriate column. For example, suppose that a child wrote the following sentence using invented and conventional spellings: *The kat ran doun the steet but the man cawt him.*

The teacher would include the words *the, ran, but,* and *him* under conventional spellings; the words *doun, cawt,* and *steet* under early orthographic spellings; and the word *kat* under purely phonetic spellings. Over time, teachers expect more of children's spellings to fall into higher levels of invented spelling. (For a description of a developmental spelling assessment, see Bear, Invernizzi, Templeton, & Johnston, 1996).

USING PORTFOLIOS

Portfolios serve several functions in the classroom. They are used to make instructional decisions, help children reflect on what they have been learning, and share with parents information about their children's literacy growth (Hansen, 1996; Porter & Cleland, 1995). For portfolios to be useful, they must be manageable and up-to-date. Most importantly, portfolios help teachers reflect on their own practice (Bergeron, Wermuth, & Hammar, 1997; Kieffer & Faust, 1994)

Using Portfolios to Make Instructional Decisions

We have stressed that teachers' observations and analyses focus on what children *can* do (Neuman & Roskos, 1993). Ms. Orlando's notes and analyses were positive statements about what children had learned or currently knew. Making instructional decisions means that teachers look beyond what children can do and consider the next steps in learning. For example, Ms. Orlando noticed that Jasmine could correct her finger-point reading at the end of each line of text and that Rayshawn attempted to point to text while he recited a familiar song. These are positive statements that identify what children can do. But Ms. Orlando is also sensitive to the next step in the children's learning. She knows that eventually the children need to be able to match the text word for word. With this objective in mind, she made plans to provide instruction to nudge children in this direction.

Kristen's kindergarten teacher was careful to include positive comments about Kristen's story "The Girl with the Cat and the Babies." However, she was also aware of problems with Kristen's composition. The three episodes were only loosely connected, the reasons for the character's actions were not obvious, and the story did not have a real ending. Because Kristen is a kindergartner, the teacher may not plan any instruction. After all, this is a fairly sophisticated story for a five-year-old. But suppose that this composition had been written by a third grader. In this case, the teacher might plan minilessons on tightly focusing the ideas in stories or writing effective story endings. Teachers always keep in mind the next step in learning and consider whether they need to plan instruction to help children take that next step.

Using Portfolios to Support Children's Reflections

One way to encourage children to reflect on their learning is to hold portfolio conferences. **Portfolio conferences** provide opportunities for children to select pieces to include in their portfolios and to reflect on their learning (Bauer & Garcia, 1997). Ms. Orlando holds short portfolio conferences at the end of each of her theme units (which usually last from four to six weeks). She gathers small groups of children and helps them select work samples to include in their portfolios. Children talk about reasons for selecting samples to add to a portfolio (most interesting story, best writing, favorite poem, and so on). Then Ms. Orlando helps the children prepare a caption for each piece they select. The caption includes the reasons for selecting the sample and reflections on what the child can do as a reader and writer. Ms. Orlando also shares any anecdotal notes, checklists, or samples that she has collected during the unit.

At the end of each grading period (every nine weeks) Ms. Orlando has the children review their entire portfolio, select works to stay in the portfolio, and prepare a statement about what the portfolio shows about their literacy growth (Courtney & Abodeeb, 1999). After the conferences, Ms. Orlando prepares **portfolio summaries,** which summarize the children's literacy growth and achievement toward the literacy goals. To prepare the summaries, she reviews all her anecdotal notes and checklists, children's work samples, and children's performances on any literacy tasks that she has administered. She carefully reads through the children's captions and summaries and her analyses, looking for patterns of growth. The portfolio summary is an important step in preparing to share the portfolio with parents.

Using Portfolios to Inform Parents

Portfolios provide teachers with an excellent resource for sharing information about children's learning with parents. To prepare to share with parents, teachers consider information that parents will find useful and make a list of a few of each child's key new understandings. Then they select eight to ten work samples, anecdotal notes, or checklists to illustrate each child's learning. Finally, teachers think about one or two areas in which the child needs further practice or instruction.

Teachers can begin parent conferences by inviting parents to share what they have observed their child doing at home and to discuss any concerns they may have. Then, teachers describe the child's learning and share the selected examples, highlighting what the child says about his or her learning. Teachers are careful to share with parents positive experiences that show what the child is learning. Teachers may then want to highlight one or two areas in which they plan to work with the child in the future, and they may have suggestions for possible home activities.

Children may be involved in the parent conferences. If so, teachers help children prepare for the conferences by having them identify two or three things that they have learned and find evidence of this learning in their work samples. During the conferences, children share what they have learned. Teachers extend the conferences by sharing their analyses with both parents and children. The conferences might end with having the children formulate one or two goals for future learning.

Keeping Portfolios Manageable

Teachers' time is limited, and collecting and analyzing assessment information is time-consuming. Teachers need to make manageable plans and then make a commitment to follow those plans. For example, Ms. Orlando takes fifteen minutes four days a week to observe her children. She writes anecdotal notes as she observes in the classroom and analyzes those notes the same day. She realizes that collecting notes on children over time is extremely valuable in helping her to know individual children. She is careful to plan her observations so that she observes behaviors related to each of her instructional goals (see Figure 12.5). She uses an emergent reading checklist with each child three times a year—at the beginning of the year, after the second grading period, and at the end of the year. She collects compositions from each child about once a month and analyzes the samples on the day she collects them. She is especially careful to analyze children's invented spellings in the compositions. Finally, she administers a retelling task twice a year—at the end of the first and third grading periods.

Ms. Orlando has found this plan to be workable. During the first month of school, she concentrates on getting the children used to centers, administering the emergent reading checklist, and collecting samples of children's compositions. During the second month of school, she begins her weekly observations of each child and begins collecting a variety of work samples. She continues to observe children and gather work samples, and she selects one composition for each child per month of the school year. In the middle of the third month (the end of the first grading period), Ms. Orlando collects a retelling and phonemic awareness assessment from each child and prepares portfolio summaries. At the end of the second grading period, Ms. Orlando completes another emergent reading checklist for each child and again prepares portfolio summaries. At the end of the third grading period, she collects a second phonemic awareness assessment and retelling. Near the end of the year, she completes the last emergent reading checklist and writes portfolio summaries.

Ms. Orlando finds that her assessments are time-consuming—especially completing the retelling, phonemic awareness assessment, emergent reading checklists, and writing the portfolio summaries. However, she believes that the information provided by these activities is worth the time. All teachers must make decisions about how much time they have to devote to assessment and which assessments will provide them with the information they need. Teachers cannot use all the assessments described in this chapter—they would do nothing but assess! Nevertheless, teachers are responsible for documenting children's growth as readers and writers. Their assessments reflect their commitment to a quality, child-centered program that supports the literacy learning of all children.

Chapter Summary

Teachers are responsible for supporting children's literacy learning, and assessing children's learning is an important part of that process. Classroom assessment relies on teachers' observations and analyses of children's work. Portfolio assessment is a systematic form of classroom assessment based on an assessment planning guide. Portfolios are multidimensional, systematic, reflective, collaborative, and concerned with process and product. Portfolios may include anecdotal notes, checklists, work samples, and performances from special literacy tasks, such as running records. Portfolios also include children's and teachers' reflections in the form of analyses, captions, and summaries.

Teachers assess children's knowledge of written language meanings, forms, meaning-form links, and functions. Teachers analyze retellings, grand conversations, response journals, and compositions to reveal information about children's meaning making. They administer alphabet recognition tasks and concept-about-print tasks and analyze children's compositions for understandings of written language forms. Emergent reading checklists, phonemic awareness assessments, miscue analyses, word recognition analyses, and analysis of spellings in compositions provide evidence of meaning-form link knowledge. Finally, observations of children's reading and writing document their understandings of the functions of written language.

Portfolios are used to make instructional decisions, encourage children's reflections on their own learning, and share information about children's learning with parents. Assessments must be kept manageable by planning a reasonable time frame for collecting assessment information, selecting only a few most informative assessments, and collecting information on a systematic basis.

Applying the Information

We provide samples from Katie's third grade reading and writing portfolio. Katie selected a letter that she wrote to her grandmother and included the first two drafts as well as a copy of the final draft of the letter in her portfolio. Figure 12.16 presents Katie's drafts of her letter. Write a caption for the letter, analyzing Katie's knowledge of written language meanings, forms, meaning-form links, and functions.

Jonathan is a five-year-old beginning kindergarten. His teacher has observed him four times over the first two months of school. For three of the observations, she also collected work samples of his writing. Figure 12.17 presents Jonathan's work samples and his teacher's anecdotal notes about her observations. Write an analysis for the anecdotal note and captions for the compositions. Then write a portfolio summary that describes what Jonathan knows about written language meanings, forms, meaning-form links, and functions.

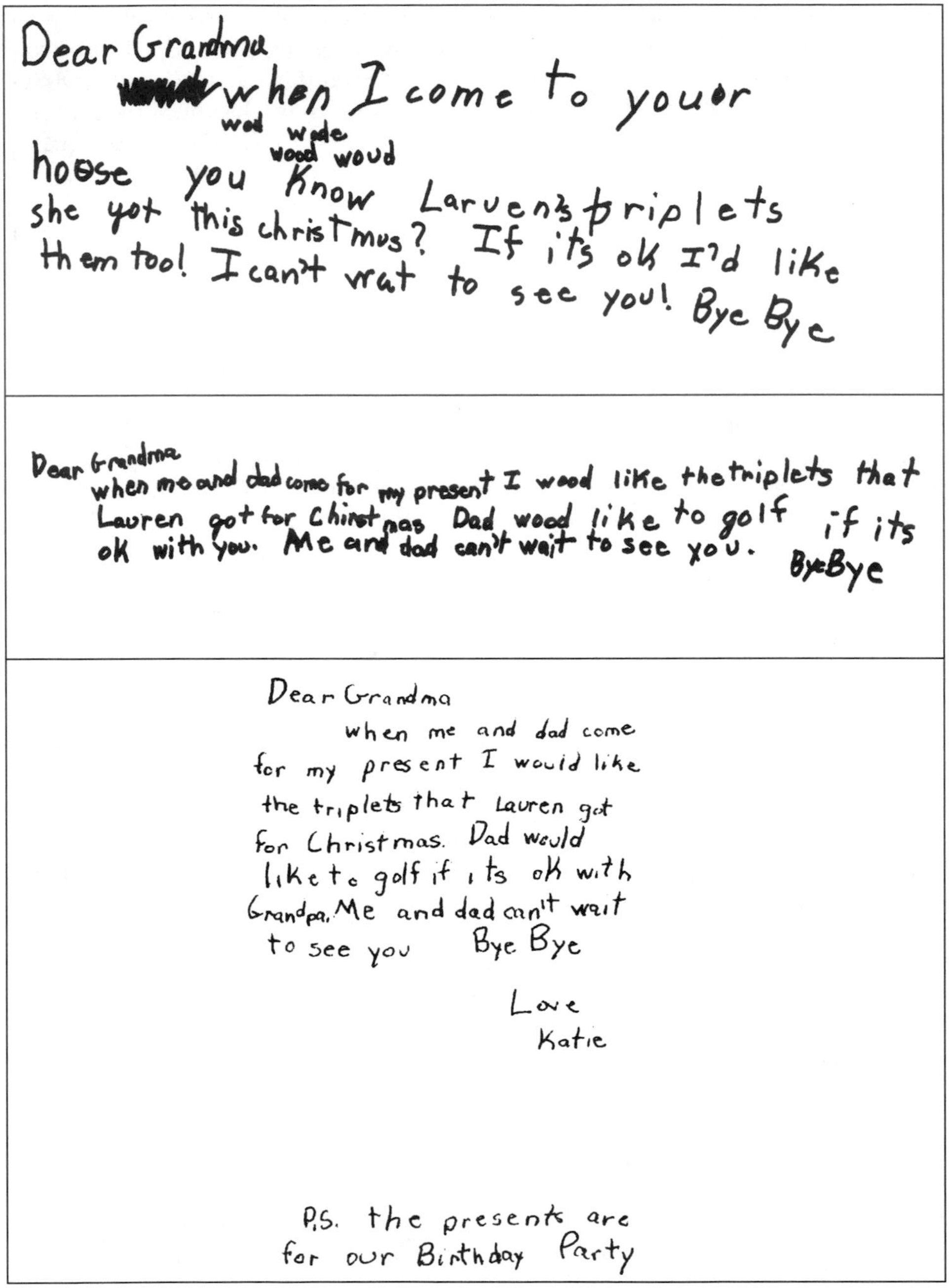

Dear Grandma
[redacted] when I come to youor
wod wode wood woud
hoose you Know Larven's triplets
she got this christmus? If it's ok I'd like
them too! I can't wat to see you! Bye Bye

first draft

Dear Grandma
when me and dad come for my present I wood like the triplets that
Lauren got for Chirstmas Dad wood like to golf if its
ok with you. Me and dad can't wait to see you. ByeBye

second draft

Dear Grandma
when me and dad come
for my present I would like
the triplets that Lauren got
for Christmas. Dad would
like to golf if its ok with
Grandpa. Me and dad can't wait
to see you Bye Bye

Love
Katie

P.S. the presents are
for our Birthday Party

final draft

Figure 12.16 *Katie's Letter*

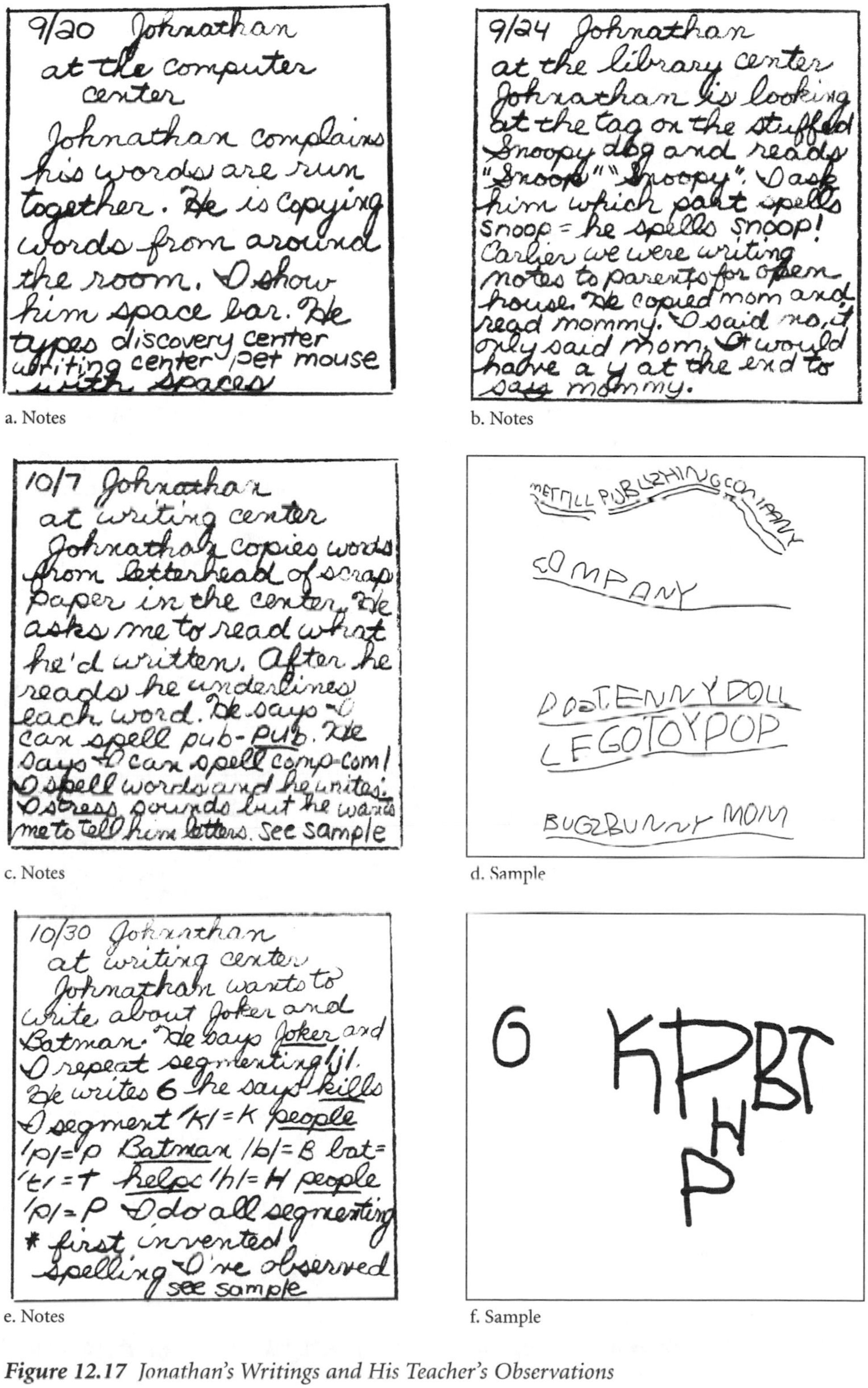

9/20 Johnathan
at the computer center
Johnathan complains his words are run together. He is copying words from around the room. I show him space bar. He types discovery center writing center pet mouse with spaces
9/24 Johnathan
at the library center
Johnathan is looking at the tag on the stuffed Snoopy dog and reads "Snoop" "Snoopy". I ask him which part spells snoop = he spells snoop! Earlier we were writing notes to parents for open house. He copied mom and read mommy. I said no, it only said mom. It would have a y at the end to say mommy.
10/7 Johnathan
at writing center
Johnathan copies words from letterhead of scrap paper in the center. He asks me to read what he'd written. After he reads he underlines each word. He says I can spell pub-PUB. He says I can spell comp-com! I spell words and he writes. I stress sounds but he wants me to tell him letters. See sample
COMPANY
LEGOTOYPOP
BUGZBUNNY MOM
10/30 Johnathan
at writing center
Johnathan wants to write about Joker and Batman. He says Joker and I repeat segmenting /j/. He writes G he says kills I segment /k/ = K people /p/ = P Batman /b/ = B bat = /t/ = T helps /h/ = H people /p/ = P I do all segmenting
* first invented spelling I've observed
see sample
G KPBT
H
P

a. Notes

b. Notes

c. Notes

d. Sample

e. Notes

f. Sample

Figure 12.17 *Jonathan's Writings and His Teacher's Observations*

Going Beyond the Text

Interview a teacher who uses portfolio assessment about his or her classroom assessments. Find out what the teacher expects to collect in the portfolios, how he or she analyzes the information, and how he or she shares the information with parents. Examine the contents of several of the children's portfolios. Talk with children about the contents of their portfolios. Compare the results of your interview with Ms. Orlando's portfolio assessment plans and procedures.

References

ADAMS, M. J., FOORMAN, B. R., LUNDBERG, I., & BEELER, T. (1998). *Phonemic awareness in young children: A classroom curriculum.* Baltimore: Paul H. Brookes.

BAUER, E., & GARCIA, G. (1997). Blurring the lines between assessment and instruction: A case study of a low-income student in the lowest reading group. In C. Kinzer, K. Hinchman, & D. Leu (Eds.), *Inquiries in literacy theory and practice* (pp. 166–176). Chicago: National Reading Conference.

BEAR, D. R., INVERNIZZI, M., TEMPLETON, S., & JOHNSTON, F. (1996). *Words their way: Word study for phonics, vocabulary, and spelling instruction.* Columbus, OH: Merrill.

BERGERON, B., WERMUTH, S., & HAMMAR, R. (1997). Initiating portfolios through shared learning: Three perspectives. *The Reading Teacher, 50,* 552–561.

BROWN, M. (1942). *The runaway bunny.* New York: Harper and Row.

BUNTING, E. (1991). *Fly away home.* New York: Clarion.

CLAY, M. (1985). *The early detection of reading difficulties* (3rd ed.). Portsmouth, NH: Heinemann.

COOPER, J. (1993). *Literacy: Helping children construct meaning* (2nd ed.). Boston: Houghton Mifflin.

COURTNEY, A., & ABODEEB, T. (1999). Diagnostic reflective portfolios. *The Reading Teacher, 52,* 708–714.

FARR, R., & TONE, B. (1994). *Portfolio and performance assessment: Helping students evaluate their progress as readers and writers.* New York: Harcourt Brace.

GOODMAN, Y., & BURKE, C. (1972). *The reading miscue inventory.* New York: Macmillan.

HANSEN, J. (1996). Evaluation: The center of writing instruction. *The Reading Teacher, 50,* 188–195.

HARP, B. (Ed.). (1991). Assessment and evaluation in whole language programs. Norwood, MA: Christopher–Gordon.

HUTCHINS, P. (1968). *Rosie's walk.* New York: Scholastic.

KIEFFER, R. D., & FAUST, M. A. (1994). Portfolio process and teacher change: Elementary, middle, and secondary teachers reflect on their initial experiences with portfolio evaluation. In C. K. Kinzer & D. J. Leu (Eds.), *Multidimensional aspects of literacy research, theory, and practice* (pp. 82–88). Chicago: National Reading Conference.

KOVALSKI, M. (1987). *The wheels on the bus.* Boston: Little, Brown.

MCGEE, L. (1992). An exploration of meaning construction in first graders' grand conversations. In C. Kinzer & D. Leu (Eds.), *Literacy research, theory, and practice: Views from many perspectives* (pp. 177–186). Chicago: National Reading Conference.

MORROW, L. (1989). Using story retelling to develop comprehension. In D. Muth (Ed.), *Children's comprehension of text: Research into practice* (pp. 37–58). Newark, DE: International Reading Association.

NEUMAN, S., & ROSKOS, K. (1993). *Language and literacy learning in the early years: An integrated approach.* New York: Harcourt Brace Jovanovich.

PARKINSON, K. (1986). *The enormous turnip.* Niles, IL: Albert Whitman.

PETERSON, B. (1991). Selecting books for beginning readers. In D. DeFord, C. Lyons, & G. Pinnell (Eds.), *Bridges to literacy: Learning from Reading Recovery* (pp. 119–147). Portsmouth, NH: Heinemann.

PORTER, C., & CLELAND, J. (1995). *The portfolio as a learning strategy.* Portsmouth, NH: Heinemann.

RHODES, L., & NATHENSON-MEJIA, S. (1992). Anecdotal records: A powerful tool for ongoing literacy assessment. *The Reading Teacher, 45,* 502–509.

SEUSS, DR. (1963). *Hop on pop.* New York: Random House.

SIPE, L. (in press). The construction of literary understanding by first and second graders in oral response to picture storybook readalouds. *Reading Research Quarterly.*

SWANK, L., MEIER, J., INVERNIZZI, M., & JUEL, C. (1997). *PALS 1: Phonological awareness & literacy screening, teacher's manual.* Charlottesville, VA: The Rector and The Board of Visitors of the University of Virginia.

TIERNEY, R., CARTER, M., & DESAI, L. (1991). *Portfolio assessment in the reading writing classroom.* Norwood, MA: Christopher–Gordon.

TOMPKINS, G., & MCGEE, L. (1993). *Teaching reading with literature: Case studies to action plans.* New York: Merrill/Macmillan.

VALENCIA, S. (1990). A portfolio approach to classroom reading assessment: The whys, whats and hows. *The Reading Teacher, 43,* 338–440.

WINOGRAD, P., PARIS, S., & BRIDGE, C. (1991). Improving the assessment of literacy. *The Reading Teacher, 45,* 108–116.

YOPP, H. (1995). Read-aloud books for developing phonemic awareness: An annotated bibliography. *The Reading Teacher, 48,* 538–542.

YORINKS, A. (1986). *Hey, Al.* New York: Farrar, Straus and Giroux.

Appendix

Children's Literature

BOOKS FOR VERY YOUNG CHILDREN

AHLBERG, J., & AHLBERG, A. (1979). *Each pair each plum.* New York: Viking.

BERENSTAIN, J., & BERENSTAIN, S. (1971). *Bears in the night.* New York: Random House.

BROWN, M. (1942). *The runaway bunny.* New York: Harper.

BROWN, M. (1947). *Goodnight moon.* New York: Harper.

BURNINGHAM, J. (1971). *Mr. Grumpy's outing.* New York: Holt.

CANIZARES, S., & CHANKO, P. (1998). *Water.* New York: Scholastic.

*CARROLL, R. (1932). *What Whiskers did.* New York: Walck.

*CARROLL, R. (1970). *The Christmas kitten.* New York: Walck.

CAULEY, L. (1982). *The three little kittens.* New York: Putnam.

CHORAO, K. (1977). *The baby's lap book.* New York: Dutton.

CLIFTON, L. (1977). *Amifika.* New York: E.P. Dutton.

CREWS, D. (1978). *Freight train.* New York: Greenwillow.

DE PAOLA, T. (1985). *Tomie de Paola's Mother Goose.* New York: Putnam.

EASTMAN, P. D. (1960). *Are you my mother?* New York: Random House.

FLETCHER, N. (1993). *See how they grow: Penguin.* New York: Dorling Kindersly.

FREEMAN, D. (1968). *Corduroy.* New York: Viking.

GALDONE, P. (1973). *The little red hen.* New York: Scholastic.

GALDONE, P. (1973). *The three bears.* New York: Scholastic.

GALDONE, P. (1985). *Cat goes fiddle-i-fee.* New York: Clarion.

GALDONE, P. (1986). *Three little kittens.* New York: Clarion.

HILL, E. (1982). *The nursery rhyme peek-a-book.* New York: Price/Stern/Sloan.

HILL, E. (1989). *Where's Spot?* New York: Putnam.

HUGHES, S. (1985). *Bathwater's hot.* New York: Lothrop, Lee and Shepard.

HUTCHINS, P. (1971). *Rosie's walk.* New York: Macmillan.

*KEATS, E. (1974). *Kitten for a day.* Danbury, CT: Franklin Watts.

KUSKIN, K. (1959). *Which horse is William?* New York: Harper and Row.

LESLIE, A. (1997). *Let's look inside the red car.* Cambridge, MA: Candlewick.

LEWIS, K. (1991). *Emma's lamb.* Cambridge, MA: Candlewick.

LEWIS, K. (1996). *One summer day.* Cambridge, MA: Candlewick.

LEWIS, K. (1997). *Friends.* Cambridge, MA: Candlewick.

MARSHALL, J. (1979). *James Marshall's Mother Goose.* New York: Farrar.

MORRIS, A. (1990). *On the go.* New York: Lothrop, Lee and Shepard.

*ORMEROD, J. (1981). *Sunshine.* New York: Puffin.

*Wordless books

*OXENBURY, H. (1982). *Good night, good morning.* New York: Dial.
RICE, E. (1981). *Benny bakes a cake.* New York: Greenwillow.
SLOBODKINA, E. (1947). *Caps for sale.* New York: Addison.
TOLSTOY, A. (1968). *The great big enormous turnip.* Danbury, CT: Franklin Watts.
WRIGHT, B. F. (Illustrator). (1916). *The real Mother Goose.* New York: Rand McNally.

ALPHABET BOOKS

ANNO, M. (1976). *Anno's alphabet.* New York: Crowell.
ARCHAMBAULT, J., & MARTIN, B. (1989). *Chicka chicka boom boom.* New York: Scholastic.
BASKIN, L. (1972). *Hosie's alphabet.* New York: Viking Press.
BRUNA, D. (1967). *B is for bear.* New York: Macmillan.
BURNINGHAM, J. (1964). *John Burningham's ABC.* London: Johnathan Cape.
EHLERT, L. (1989). *Eating the alphabet.* New York: Harcourt Brace Jovanovich.
EICHENBERG, F. (1952). *Ape in cape.* San Diego, CA: Harcourt Brace Jovanovich.
ELTING, M., & FOLSOM, M. (1980). *Q is for duck.* New York: Clarion.
HOBAN, T. (1987). *26 letters and 99 cents.* New York: Greenwillow.
HOLTZ, L. T. (1997). *Alphabet book.* New York: DK Publishing.
IPCAR, D. (1964). *I love an anteater with an A.* New York: Knopf.
ISADORA, R. (1983). *City seen from A to Z.* New York: Greenwillow.
JOHNSON, S. T. (1995). *Alphabet city.* New York: Penguin.
KELLOGG, S. (1987). *Aster Aardvark's alphabet adventures.* New York: Morrow.
LIONNI, L. (1985). *Letters to talk about.* New York: Pantheon.
LOBEL, A. (1981). *On Market Street.* New York: Greenwillow.
MCCURDY, M. (1998). *The sailor's alphabet.* Boston: Houghton Mifflin.
MCMILLAN, B. (1986). *Counting wildflowers.* New York: Lothrop.
SCHNUR, S. (1997). *Autumn: An alphabet acrostic.* New York: Houghton Mifflin.
SEUSS, DR. (THEODORE GEISEL). (1963). *Dr. Seuss's ABC.* New York: Random House.
SHANNON, G. (1996). *Tomorrow's alphabet.* New York: Greenwillow.
TUDOR, T. (1954). *A is for Annabelle.* New York: Walck.
WILDSMITH, B. (1963). *Brian Wildsmith's ABC.* Danbury, CT: Franklin Watts.

WORDLESS PICTURE BOOKS

BAKER, J. (1991). *Window.* New York: Greenwillow.
DAY, A. (1985). *Good dog, Carl.* New York: Scholastic.
DE PAOLA, T. (1978). *Pancakes for breakfast.* San Diego: Harcourt Brace Jovanovich.
GOODALL, J. (1988). *Little red riding hood.* New York: McElderry Books.
HOBAN, T. (1972). *Push-pull, empty-full.* New York: Macmillan
HOBAN, T. (1980). *Take another look.* New York: Greenwillow.
HOBAN, T. (1988). *Look! Look! Look!* New York: Greenwillow.
MAYER, M. (1974). *Frog goes to dinner.* New York: Dial.
MAYER, M. (1977). *Oops.* New York: Dial.
MCCULLY, E. (1984). *Picnic.* New York: Harper and Row.
MCCULLY, E. (1985). *First snow.* New York: Harper and Row.
MCCULLY, E. (1987). *School.* New York: Harper and Row.
MCCULLY, E. (1988). *New Baby.* New York: Harper and Row.
ROHMANN, E. (1994). *Time flies.* New York: Crown.
SPIER, P. (1982). *Peter Spier's rain.* New York: Doubleday.
TURKLE, B. (1976). *Deep in the forest.* New York: Dutton.
WEISNER, D. (1991). *Tuesday.* New York: Clarion.
WINTER, P. (1976). *The bear and the fly.* New York: Crown.

PREDICTABLE BOOKS

BURNINGHAM, J. (1978). *Would you rather . . . ?* New York: Crowell.

CARLE, E. (1977). *The grouchy ladybug.* New York: Crowell.

CARTER, D. A. (1991). *In a dark, dark wood.* New York: Simon and Schuster.

CHARLIP, R. (1964). *Fortunately.* New York: Parents.

DUNBAR, J. (1998). *Baby bird.* Cambridge, MA: Candlewick.

ETS, M. (1973). *Elephant in the well.* New York: Viking.

FLACK, M. (1932). *Ask Mr. Bear.* New York: Bradbury.

FOX, M. (1987). *Hattie and the fox.* New York: Bradbury.

GALDONE, P. (1968). *Henny Penny.* New York: Scholastic.

HUTCHINS, P. (1982). *Goodnight, owl!* New York: Macmillan.

KAVALSKI, M. (1987). *The wheels on the bus.* Boston: Little, Brown.

KEATS, E. (1971). *Over in the meadow.* New York: Scholastic.

KENT, J. (1971). *The fat cat.* New York: Scholastic.

KRAUS, R. (1970). *Whose mouse are you?* New York: Collier.

LEXAU, J. (1969). *Crocodile and hen.* New York: Harper and Row.

MARTIN, B., JR. (1983). *Brown bear, brown bear.* New York: Henry Holt.

MARTIN, B. (1991). *Polar bear, polar bear, what do you hear?* New York: Scholastic.

ROOT, P. (1998). *One duck stuck.* Cambridge, MA: Candlewick.

SCHNEIDER, R. M. (1995). *Add it, dip it, fix it.* Boston: Houghton Mifflin.

SENDAK, M. (1962). *Chicken soup with rice.* New York: Harper and Row.

SMITH, M., & ZIEFERT, H. (1989). *In a scary old house.* New York: Penguin.

SWEET, M. (1992). *Fiddle-i-fee.* Boston: Little, Brown.

TAFURI, N. (1984). *Have you seen my duckling?* New York: Greenwillow.

TRESSELT, A. (1964). *The mitten.* New York: Lothrop, Lee, and Shepard.

WEISS, N. (1989). *Where does the brown bear go?* New York: Trumpet Club.

WESTCOTT, N. B. (1987). *Peanut butter and jelly.* New York: Trumpet Club.

WILLIAMS, L. (1986). *The little old lady who wasn't afraid of anything.* New York: Harper and Row.

WOOD, A. (1982). *Quick as a cricket.* Singapore: Child's Play (International).

ZEMACH, M. (1965). *The teeny tiny woman.* New York: Scholastic.

ZIEFERT, H. (1998). *Who walks on this halloween night?* New York: Little Simon.

LANGUAGE PLAY BOOKS

AHLBERG, J., & AHLBERG, A. (1978). *Each peach pear plum.* New York: Scholastic.

BENJAMIN, A. (1987). *Rat-a-tat, pitter pat.* New York: Harper.

CARLSTROM, N. W. (1987). *Wild wild sunflower child Anna.* New York: Macmillan.

DEMMING, A. G. (1994). *Who is tapping at my window?* Puffin.

EDWARDS, P. M. (1996). *Some smug slug.* New York: Harper-Collins.

EHLERT, L. *A pair of socks.* New York: Scholastic.

KOCH, M. (1991). *Hoot howl hiss.* New York: Greenwillow.

KOMAIKO, L. (1987). *Annie Bananie.* New York: Harper and Row.

LECOURT, N. (1991). *Abracadabra to zigzag.* New York: Lothrop, Lee and Shepard.

LENSKI, L. (1987). *Sing a song of people.* Boston: Little, Brown.

LESTER, H. (1995). *Listen, buddy.* Boston: Houghton Mifflin.

MAHY, M. (1987). *17 Kings and 42 elephants.* New York: Dial.

MARTIN, B. (1991). *The happy hippopotami.* New York: Harcourt.

MARZOLLO, J. (1997). *I'm a caterpillar.* New York: Scholastic.

MELSER, J. (1998). *One, one, is the sun.* Wright.

MOST, B. (1996). *Cock a doodle moo.* Harcourt Brace.

NOLL, S. (1987). *Jiggle wiggle prance.* New York: Greenwillow.

PAPARONE, P. (1995). *Five little ducks.* New York: Scholastic.

PERKINS, A. (1969). *Hand, hand, fingers, thumb.* New York: Random House.
RASCHKA, C. (1992). *Charlie Parker played be bop.* New York: Orchard.
REDDIX, V. (1992). *Millie and the mud hole.* New York: Lothrop, Lee and Shepard.
SEUSS, DR. (THEODORE GEISEL) (1957). *The cat in the hat.* New York: Random House.
SEUSS, DR. (THEODORE GEISEL) (1963). *Hop on pop.* New York: Random House.
SILVERSTIEN, S. (1964). *A giraffe and a half.* New York: Harper and Row.
SONNEBORN, R. A. (1974). *Someone is eating the sun.* New York: Random House.
THOMAS, P. (1990). *The one and only, super-duper, golly-whopper, Jim-dandy, really-handy, clock-tock-stopper.* New York: Lothrop, Lee and Shepard.
TRINCA, R., & ARGENT, K. (1987). *One wooly wombat.* Brooklyn, NY: Kane/Miller.
WATSON, C. (1971). *Father Fox's penny-rhymes.* New York: Scholastic.
WELLS, R. (1973). *Noisy Nora.* New York: Dial.
WILDSMITH, B. (1986). *Goat's trail.* New York: Knopf.
WOOD, A. (1987). *Heckedy Peg.* New York: Harcourt Brace Jovanovich.

MULTICULTURAL BOOKS

BAYLOR, B. (1986). *Hawk, I'm your brother.* New York: Scribner's.
BRUCHAC, J. (1985). *Iroquois stories: Heroes and heroines, monsters and magic.* Freedom, CA: The Crossing Press.
BRUCHAC, J., & LONGDON, J. (1992). *Thirteen moons on turtle's back: A Native American year of moons.* New York: Philomel.
BRYAN, A. (1977). *The dancing granny.* New York: Atheneum.
BRYAN, A. (1986). *Lion and the ostrich chick and other African folk tales.* New York: Atheneum.
BUNTING, E. (1998). *So far from the sea.* New York: Clarion.
CAINES, J. (1982). *Just us women.* New York: Harper and Row.
CHOI, S. (1993). *Hal Moni and the picnic.* Boston: Houghton Mifflin.
CLIFTON, L. (1970). *Some of the days of Everett Anderson.* New York: Holt, Rinehart and Winston.
CONNOLLY, J. (1985). *Why the possum's tail is bare and other North American Indian nature tales.* Owings Mills, MD: Stemmer House.
COUTANT, H., & VO-DINH. (1974). *First snow.* New York: Knopf.
CREWS, D. (1991). *Big Mama's.* New York: Greenwillow.
CRUZ MARTINEZ, A. (1991). *The woman who out-shone the sun/La mujer que brillaba aun mas que el sol.* San Francisco: Children's Book Press.
DELACRE, L. (1989). *Arroz con leche: Popular songs and rhymes from Latin America.* New York: Scholastic.
DELACRE, L. (1990). *Las Navidades: Popular Christmas songs from Latin America.* New York: Scholastic.
DORROS, A. (1991). *Abuela.* New York: Dutton.
DORROS, A. (1991). *Abuela.* New York: Puffin.
ERDOES, R. (1976). *The sound of flutes and other Indian legends.* New York: Pantheon.
GARCIA, R. (1987). *My Aunt Otilia's spirits.* San Francisco: Children's Book Press.
GARZA, C. (1990). *Family pictures.* San Francisco: Children's Book Press.
GIOVANNI, N. (1985). *Spin a soft black song.* New York: HarperCollins.
GOBLE, P. (1989). *Iktomi and the berries.* New York: Orchard.
GOBLE, P. (1992). *Crow chief: A Plains Indian story.* New York: Orchard.
GREENE, B. (1974). *Philip Hall likes me. I reckon maybe.* New York: Dial.
GREENFIELD, E. (1975). *Me and Nessie.* New York: Crowell.
GREENFIELD, E. (1978). *Honey, I love.* New York: Harper and Row.
GREENFIELD, E. (1988). *Grandpa's face.* New York: Philomel.
GREENFIELD, E. (1988). *Nathaniel talking.* New York: Black Butterfly Children's Books.
HAMILTON, V. (1985). *The people could fly.* New York: Knopf.
HAMILTON, V. (1992). *Drylongso.* New York: Harcourt Brace Jovanovich.
HAVILL, J. (1989). *Jamaica tag-along.* Boston: Houghton Mifflin.
HOWARD, E. (1991). *Aunt Flossie's hats (and crab cakes later).* Boston: Houghton Mifflin.
JOHNSON, A. (1989). *Tell me a story, Mama.* New York: Orchard.
JOHNSON, A. (1990). *Do like Kyla.* New York: Orchard.
MARTINEZ, E., & SOTO, G. (1993). *Too many tamales.* New York: Putnam.
MATHIS, S. (1975). *The hundred penny box.* New York: Viking.

MCKISSACK, P. (1986). *Flossie and the fox.* New York: Dial.
MCKISSACK, P. (1989). *Nettie Jo's friends.* New York: Knopf.
MOLLELL, T. M. (1995). *Big boy.* New York: Clarion.
ORTIZ, S. (1988). *The people shall continue.* San Francisco: Children's Book Press.
PENA, S. (1987). *Kikiriki: Stories and poems in English and Spanish for children.* Houston: Arte Publico Press.
PRICE, L. (1990). *Aida.* New York: Harcourt Brace Jovanovich.
ROHMER, H., & ANCHONDO, M. (1988). *How we came to the fifth world: Como vinimos al quinto mundo.* San Franscisco: Children's Book Press.
SAY, A. (1982). *The bicycle man.* Boston: Houghton Mifflin.
SAY, A. (1988). *The lost lake.* Boston: Houghton Mifflin.
SAY, A. (1990). *El Chino.* Boston: Houghton Mifflin.
SAY, A. (1991). *Tree of cranes.* Boston: Houghton Mifflin.
SAY, A. (1993). *Grandfather's journey.* Boston: Houghton Mifflin.
SAY, A. (1997). *Allison.* Boston: Houghton Mifflin.
SNEEVE, V. (1989). *Dancing teepees: Poems of American Indian youth.* New York: Holiday House.
SOTO, G. (1993). *Too many tamales.* New York: Putnam.
STEPTOE, J. (1969). *Stevie.* New York: Harper and Row.
STEPTOE, J. (1987). *Mufaro's beautiful daughters.* New York: Lothrop, Lee and Shepard.
STRETE, C. (1990). *Big thunder magic.* New York: Greenwillow.
TAFOLLA, C. (1987). *Patchwork colcha: A children's collection.* Flagstaff, AZ: Creative Educational Enterprises.
TAKESHITA, F. (1988). *The park bench.* New York: Kane/Miller.
WRIGHT, C. (1994). *Jumping the broom.* New York: Holiday House.
YASHIMA, R. (1958). *Umbrella.* New York: Viking.
YOUNG, E. (1989). *Lon po po.* New York: Putnam.
ZHENSUN, A., & LOW, A. (1991). *A young painter.* New York: Scholastic.

Author Index

Abrahamson, R., 146
Abramson, S., 64, 329
Adams, M., 27, 75, 130, 152, 178, 211, 241, 264
Allen, J., 227, 228, 310
Allington, R., 161
Almasi, J., 284
Altwerger, B., 42, 59
Anbar, A., 66
Anderson, R., 152, 153
Aoki, E., 321
Applebee, A., 45
Arno, E., 158
Arnold, T., 299
Asch, F., 252, 270
Ash, G., 148, 149, 150
Askew, B., 256, 262
Atwell, N., 279, 282
Au, K., 156, 315, 316, 317, 319, 320, 321, 332, 333

Baghban, M., 58, 63, 65, 179
Bailey, C., 187
Ball, E., 218
Barbe, W., 281
Barber, L., 312
Barnes, B., 311
Barnhart, J., 103
Barnitz, J., 323
Barone, D., 153, 282, 313
Barr, R., 161
Barrera, R., 330
Bartoli, J., 324
Battle, J., 152
Baumann, J., 161
Beals, D., 47
Bear, D., 129, 133, 243, 264, 265, 301, 364
Beardsley, L., 191
Beck, I., 296
Beers, J., 101
Berenstain, J., 50, 51, 93, 104
Berenstain, S., 50, 51, 93, 104
Berger, M., 270
Berghoff, B., 161
Bishop, C., 321
Bishop, R., 157
Bissex, G., 89, 118
Blachman, B., 101, 218
Blake, B., 331
Blume, J., 145, 299
Bornstein, H., 214
Botvin, G., 45
Braun, L., 281
Brazee, P., 313
Brett, J., 299
Bridge, C., 146, 347
Brock, C., 284
Brown, A., 114
Brown, M., 33, 49, 158, 193
Brown, R., 192
Browne, A., 311
Brownell, C., 18
Bruce, B., 148
Bruner, J., 34, 61, 127
De Brunhoff, L., 33
Bryant, P., 178, 249
Bryen, D., 323, 324, 326
Bryk, A., 312
Bunting, E., 144
Burke, C., 7, 58, 73, 89, 192
Burnie, D., 147
Burns, M., 46
Burns, S., 142, 241
Burris, N., 89, 279

Calkins, L., 118, 160, 267, 279, 280
Canizares, S., 146
Carey, A., 283
Carger, C., 332
Carle, E., 70, 193, 299
Carlson, N., 299
Carr, E., 310
Carr, J., 146
Carter, M., 346, 347
Casbergue, R., 46, 123
Caserta-Henry, C., 312
Caswell, L., 269
Cauley, L., 145, 158
Cazden, C., 320, 326
Chall, J., 98, 117
Chaney, C., 180
Chang-Wells, G., 277
Chanko, P., 146
Chomsky, C., 101, 144
Clay, M., 17, 18, 71, 104, 161, 255, 259, 262, 310, 311
Cleary, B., 144, 299

Cleland, J., 364
Cliatt, M., 153
Cochran-Smith, M., 14, 61, 77
Cole, H., 270
Cole, J., 146
Colt, J., 161
Combs, M., 185, 226
Commeyras, M., 291
Conlon, A., 44
Connelly, L., 223, 224
Cook-Gumperz, J., 16
Cooter, R., 282
Cousin, P., 313, 319
Cox, B., 95
Crawford, K., 284
Cullinan, B., 325
Cummins, J., 319, 320, 329
Cunningham, A., 16
Cunningham, J., 264, 265
Cunningham, P., 182, 216, 217, 248, 256, 264, 265
Cutting, 260, 261

Dahl, K., 99, 160, 228, 241
D'Allesandro, M., 314, 315
Davidson, J., 246
de Paola, T., 146, 299
de Regniers, B., 146
Defee, M., 256, 265
DeFord, D., 73, 160, 312
Dekker, M., 156, 282
Delpit, L., 333
Delton, J., 293
Denman, G., 293
Desai, L., 346, 347
DeTemple, J., 47
Dewey, J., 157
Diaz, E., 319
Dickinson, D., 39, 44, 61, 63, 152, 162
Diehl-Faxon, J., 42
Dillon, D., 299
Dillon, L., 299
Dixon, R., 314
Doake, D., 34
Dockstader-Anderson, K., 42
Dole, J., 160
Dolman, D., 315
Dorsey-Gaines, C., 34, 38, 48, 76
Dowhower, S., 278, 286, 288, 293, 294
Downing, J., 21
Dreeben, R., 161
Dressel, J., 144, 288
Drozdal, J., 18
Duffy, G., 160
Duffy-Hester, A., 22
Duke, N., 68, 70, 269, 295
Durham, J., 294, 295
Duthie, C., 269, 279, 283, 293, 295
Dyson, A., 22, 59, 65, 72, 325, 328

Eberhardt, N., 101
Edelsky, C., 89, 121
Edwards, N., 101
Edwards, P., 48
Eeds, M., 144, 153
Egawa, K., 161
Ehlert, L., 147
Ehri, L., 25, 26, 98, 103, 130, 241
Eimas, P., 74
Elkonen, D., 218
Ellson, D., 312
Engelbrecht, G., 330
Engle, T., 312
Enright, D., 331
Estice, R., 311

Fallon, I., 227, 228
Faltis, C., 316, 331, 334
Fang, Z., 95
Farnan, N., 282
Fayden, T., 185
Feeley, J., 330
Feitelson, D., 144, 152, 325
Ferdman, B., 156, 321
Ferreiro, E., 7, 65, 68, 72
Ferruggia, A., 223
Fielding, L., 153
Fitts, M., 311
Fitzgerald, J., 330
Five, C., 153
Fletcher, J., 160
Fletcher, N., 127
Flores, B., 319
Foorman, B., 160
Fountas, I., 161, 229, 230, 243, 244, 255, 256, 259, 262, 264
Fox, C., 183
Fox, M., 299
Fractor, J., 144, 149

Francis, D., 160
Freeman, D., 33
Freppon, P., 99, 114, 228
Fresch, M., 301
Fried, M., 311
Friedberg, J., 49
Frith, U., 27
Froman, R., 271
Frost, J., 218

Galdone, P., 49, 69, 145, 146, 158
Gambrell, L., 142, 285
Gardner, H., 38
Garland, M., 269
Gaskins, I., 249, 265, 302
Gaskins, J., 302
Gaskins, R., 302
Gee, J., 316, 324
Geller, L., 75
Genishi, C., 160, 325, 328
Gentry, J., 101, 102, 129, 327
George, J., 285, 286
Gerard, J., 313
Gersten, R., 330, 331, 332
Gibson, E., 17
Gibson, J., 17
Gillet, J., 327
Glazer, J., 153, 155
Glenn, C., 45
Goatley, V., 284
Goldenberg, C., 320
Goldstein, Z., 144, 152, 325
Golenbock, P., 146
Goodman, K., 98
Goodman, Y., 58, 59, 65, 104, 160
Gopnick, A., 5
Goss, J., 193
Goswami, U., 178, 249
Gough, P., 254
Graves, D., 160, 267
Greene, J., 330
Griffin, P., 142, 241
Griffith, P., 218
Grimm, J., 145
Grimm, W., 145
Grogan, P., 99, 160, 241
Gundlach, R., 76
Gunning, T., 256, 258
Guthrie, J., 278, 296, 297

Hackney, C., 281
Hagin, R., 312
Hall, D., 256, 265
Halliday, M., 13, 14, 15, 35
Hamilton, L., 214
Hansen, J., 267, 282
Hao, Z., 162
Harris, K., 293
Harris, V., 285, 286, 293, 294
Harste, J., 7., 58, 73, 89, 192, 193
Hays, J., 68, 70
He, W., 162
Head, M., 125
Heald-Taylor, G., 185
Heath, S., 47, 48, 69, 77, 125, 156, 316, 317, 318
Hellard, S., 40
Henderson, E., 101
Hepler, S., 49
Hest, A., 145
Hickman, J., 49, 144, 155
Hiebert, E., 59, 66, 152, 161, 310
Hildreth, G., 66, 67
Hill, E., 40, 260
Hilliker, J., 85
Hipple, M., 155
Hoffman, J., 152, 244, 245
Holdaway, D., 184, 220
Hopkins, L., 284
Hopmann, M., 18
Hough, R., 70, 331
Howe, D., 145
Howe, J., 145
Howker, J., 146
Hoyt, L., 286
Huck, C., 49
Hudelson, S., 330
Hughes, M., 157
Hulme, C., 22
Hutchins, P., 115
Hyman, T., 145

Invernizzi, M., 129, 133, 243, 264, 265, 301, 312, 351, 364
Iraqi, J., 325
Ivey, G., 161

Jacob, E., 76
Jaggar, A., 325, 327
Jiménez, R., 330, 331, 332

Johnson, C., 64, 329
Johnson, D., 288
Johnson, N., 45
Johnston, F., 129, 133, 243, 264, 265, 301, 364
Jordan, H., 159
Joyce, W., 299
Juel, C., 25, 26, 241, 245, 312, 351
Jukes, M., 145
Jusczyk, P., 74

Kahn, L., 284
Kamberelis, G., 26
Kameenui, E., 310
Kamii, C., 160
Kampwerth, L., 312
Karweit, N., 312
Kaser, S., 284
Kauffman, G., 284
Kawakami, A., 317
Keats, E., 299
Keegan, M., 158
Kellogg, R., 38
Kelly, P., 153, 282
Kiefer, B., 184
King, M., 70
Kintisch, L., 155
Kinzer, C., 115, 299
Kita, B., 144, 152
Kovalski, M., 340
Kraus, R., 286
Kretschmer, R., 313
Kunhardt, D., 32

Labbo, L., 148, 149, 150, 151, 152
Labov, W., 323
Laminack, L., 60
Lancaster, W., 101
Lanford, C., 63
Langer, J., 123
Lara, S., 329
Lasky, K., 146, 299
Lass, B., 38, 65, 66, 179
Lavine, L., 17
Lawson, L., 99, 160, 241
Leaf, M., 42
Lehr, S., 116
Leondar, B., 45
Lester, H., 127
Leu, D., 115, 299
Lewis, M., 297
Lindamood, C., 212
Lindamood, P., 212
Linek, W., 229
Linfors, J., 160
Lionni, L., 284
Lippi-Green, R., 324
Lipson, M., 157
Livermon, B., 312
Lomax, R., 66, 125
Loxterman, J., 296
Lukens, R., 119
Lundberg, I., 218
Lynch-Brown, C., 144
Lyons, C., 112, 160, 312
Lysaker, J., 254

MacGillivray, L., 258
MacLachlan, P., 144
Madden, N., 312
Maddern, E., 145
Mandler, L., 45
Many, J., 115
Mareck-Zeman, M., 191
Martin, B., 112
Martinez, M., 63, 144, 149, 223, 254
Mason, J., 320
Matthews, K., 85
Mayer, M., 61, 62, 250, 251, 252, 326
McCann, N., 278, 296
McCarrier, A., 160
McCartney, K., 44
McConaghy, J., 183
McCormick, S., 160
McCracken, M., 249
McCracken, R., 249
McDermott, G., 145
McGee, L., 44, 66, 115, 116, 125, 158, 162, 184, 185, 186, 212, 213, 264, 284, 291, 351, 352, 357, 360, 361
McGill-Franzen, A., 63, 141
McGuinness, C., 212
McGuinness, G., 212
McIntyre, E., 99, 161
McKenzie, M., 70
McKeown, M., 296
McKissack, P., 329
McLane, J., 76
McLaughlin, B., 311
McNamara, M., 311
McNamee, G., 76

Mehta, P., 160
Meier, J., 351
Meier, T., 326
Meltzoff, A., 5
Merriam, E., 295
Michaels, S., 148
Mieras, E., 283
Miles, M., 321
Moffett, J., 117, 127
Mollel, T., 145
Moore, E., 146
Morgan, A., 66, 77
Morningstar, J., 255
Morris, A., 243
Morris, D., 98, 101, 102
Morrison, G., 299
Morrow, L., 142, 144, 148, 149, 152, 197, 296, 357
Moss, T., 158
Moustafa, M., 329, 330
Murray, B., 151, 152
Murray, D., 279, 293
Muth, K., 357
Myers, D., 146

Nathan, R., 89, 279
Nathenson-Mejia, S., 346
Nation, K., 22
Naylor, A., 144
Nelson, K., 44
Nelson, L., 101
Nelson, O., 229
Neuman, S., 196, 197, 364
Newkirk, T., 122, 123, 125, 126
Ninio, A., 34, 35, 43, 61
Norris, J., 315
Nurss, J., 70, 331
Nussbaum, N., 160

Oldfather, P., 142
Oliver, P., 21
Olson, M., 218
Ormerod, J., 146
Ortiz, L., 330
O'Shea, D., 314
O'Shea, L., 314
Osser, H., 17
Otto, B., 95

Padak, N., 322, 325
Paley, V., 196, 198–199
Pallotta, J., 147
Papenfuss, J., 247
Pappas, C., 70, 71
Paratore, J., 253
Paris, S., 114, 347
Parkinson, K., 158, 364
Paul, R., 101
Pearson, D., 160
Pearson, P., 288
Pease-Alvarez, L., 48
Peet, B., 146
Penrose, J., 329, 330
Peréz, B., 333
Peters, C., 157
Petersen, O., 218
Peterson, B., 256, 258, 311, 352
Pettegrew, B., 70
Pfeiffer, W., 285
Phelan, C., 298
Philips, S., 317, 318
Phillips, M., 151, 152
Piaget, J., 1-3
Pick, A., 17, 18
Pienkowski, J., 193
Pinkney, B., 284
Pinnell, G., 160, 161, 229, 230, 243, 244, 255, 256, 259, 262, 264, 311, 312
Place, Q., 160
Poremba, K., 208-236, 253
Porter, C., 364
Prelutsky, J., 146
Pressley, M., 161, 293, 296
Purcell-Gates, V., 12, 39, 46, 48, 77, 212
Putnam, L., 234

Rand, M., 197
Randazzo, M., 160
Rankin, L., 214
Raphael, T., 284
Raschka, C., 179, 217
Rasinski, T., 322
Read, C., 101
Reutzel, D., 282
Reyes, M., 333
Rhodes, L., 285, 346
Richgels, D., 66, 101, 104, 181, 195, 199, 200, 212, 213, 228
Riekehof, L., 214
Ringgold, F., 145

Robbins, C., 130
Roberts, B., 88
Roehler, L., 160
Roof, B., 147
Roop, C., 291
Roop, P., 291
Roper-Schneider, D., 245
Rosemary, C., 312
Rosenblatt, C., 284
Rosenblatt, L., 115
Roser, N., 152, 254
Roskos, K., 196, 197, 364
Ross, R., 153
Roth, H., 32
Routman, R., 157
Rowe, D., 16, 148, 197
Rubin, H., 101
Rylant, C., 299

Salvage, G., 313
Saulnier, K., 214
Sawyer, R., 158
Say, A., 144, 146, 299
Scharer, P., 99, 160, 241, 284
Schatschneider, C., 160
Schickedanz, J., 49, 197
Schieffelin, B., 77
Schwartz, R., 262
Scollon, R., 12
Scollon, S., 12
Scott, F., 76
Scott, J., 152
Seda, I., 64, 329
Seltzer, M., 312
Sendak, M., 144, 153, 213, 286
Seuss, Dr., 33, 179, 182, 350
Shanahan, S., 292
Shanahan, T., 292
Shanklin, N., 285
Shapiro, H., 315
Share, D., 178, 211, 325
Shaw, J., 153
Shilling, W., 234
Short, K., 284
Sierra, J., 145
Silver, A., 312
Simon, S., 299
Sinatra, R., 330
Sindelar, P., 313
Sipe, L., 258, 263, 287, 357
Siqueland, E., 74
Slavin, R., 162, 312
Sloyer, S., 285
Smith, J., 296
Smith, M., 44, 61, 63, 152, 296
Smitherman, G., 323, 324, 326
Smolkin, L., 44
Snow, C., 7, 34, 35, 43, 47, 61, 142, 241
Sowers, S., 101
Spiegel, D., 311, 333
Stahl, A., 22
Stahl, S., 22
Stanovich, K., 16
Stauffer, R., 229, 246
Steig, W., 144, 287
Stein, N., 45
Steptoe, J., 145, 158, 292
Stevens, J., 299
Strecker, S., 254
Strickland, D., 243, 255, 325
Stubbs, M., 14
Sulzby, E., 18, 25, 26, 45, 59, 70, 72, 91, 95, 96, 97, 98, 99
Sumner, G., 291
Sutton-Smith, B., 45
Swank, L., 351
Sweet, J., 98, 241

Tabors, P., 39, 44
Tangel, D., 101
Taylor, B., 310
Taylor, D., 12, 34, 38, 48, 76
Teale, W., 63, 144, 149, 223
Teberosky, A., 7, 72
Temple, C., 89, 144, 279, 291
Temple, F., 89, 279
Templeton, S., 21, 129, 133, 180, 243, 264, 265, 301, 364
Thorndyke, P., 45
Thurber, D., 281
Tierney, R., 346, 347
Timberlake, P., 101
Tolhurst, M., 226
Tomlinson, C., 144
Tompkins, G., 116, 158, 184, 185, 186, 285, 291, 351, 352, 360, 361
Trachtenberg, P., 223
Treiman, R., 178
Trousdale, A., 285, 286, 293, 294
Truax, R., 313

Tunnell, M., 146
Turkle, B., 46, 146
Turner, A., 145
Turner, J., 114
Turpie, J., 253

Unze, M., 18
Urzua, C., 328, 330

Vail, N., 247
Valencia, S., 157, 346
Van Allen, C., 229
Van Allen, R., 229
Van Allsburg, C., 147, 287, 288, 289, 299
Vardell, S., 287
Vars, G., 157
Vigorito, J., 74
Villaume, S., 284
Viorst, J., 193, 268
Vogt, M., 284
Voss, M., 69
Vukelich, C., 101
Vuong, L., 145
Vygotsky, L., 1, 3, 5, 39, 160

Wagstaff, J., 248
Wallach, L., 312
Wallach, M., 312
Ward, C., 112, 266
Wasik, B., 114, 312
Wason-Ellam, L., 193
Wasylyk, T., 281
Watson, C., 147
Watson-Gregeo, K., 148
Weekley, T., 313
Weinstein, C., 144, 148, 149, 152
Wells, D., 144, 153
Wells, G., 39, 44, 277
Wheaton, A., 301
White, M., 146
Whitehurst, G., 39
Wiese, K., 321
Wilde, S., 101, 128, 302
Wildsmith, B., 70, 71
Wilkerson, B., 246
Wilkes, A., 174
Wilkinson, I., 152
Williams, C., 313
Williams, J., 311
Williams, S., 284
Wilson, P., 153
Wilson, R., 285
Winograd, P., 347
Wisniewski, D., 145
Wixson, K., 157
Wolf, D., 15
Wolf, S., 69, 283, 285
Wolfram, W., 324
Wood, A., 299
Wood, D., 70
Woodruff, M., 144, 149
Woodward, V., 7, 58, 73, 89, 192
Wordon, T., 284
Worthy, J., 254
Wray, D., 297
Wright, B., 32

Xiong, B., 155

Yaden, D., 21, 44, 87, 180
Yashima, T., 322
Yokota, J., 144
Yopp, H., 218, 351
Yorinks, A., 116, 156, 358, 359
Young, T., 287

Zarillo, J., 157, 283
Zelinsky, P., 291
Zemach, H., 286
Zimet, E., 293, 295
Zukowski, A., 178

Subject Index

Academic agenda, 205–206
Accuracy rate, 354
Action, learning through, 3–4
Additive approaches, to ESL teaching, 329–331
Affrication, 101
African American Vernacular English, 323
African Americans, learning environment for, 316, 319
All-about stories, 118
Alliteration, 93
Alphabet
  experimenters' discovery of, 85
  letters of, 17–18, 65–66
Alphabet books, 146, 374
Alphabet recognition task, 350
Alphabetic reading, 25–26, 95, 211
Alphabetic writing, 25–26
Analogy
  decoding by, 130
  reading and writing strategy, 249–250
Anecdotal notes, 346, 350
Applications, defined, 213
Articulation, manner of, 100
Ascribing intentionality, 38
Assessment, 160
  classroom, 345
  planning guide for, 347–348
  of portfolios, 346–349
  tools for, 346–347, 349–364
At-risk learners
  defined, 309, 313
  issues related to teaching, 332–333
  literacy intervention programs for, 310–312
  observation of, 309–310
Audiovisual materials, 147
Author's chair, 267
Autobiographies, 146

Balance of rights, 320
Basal reading series, 244–245
Basals
  controlled vocabulary, 245–247
  decodable, 245
  literature-based, 246
  predictable-text, 246
Beginners
  defined, 25
  distinguished from novices, 56
  child care and, 48–50
  home influences on, 39–48
  lessons learned from, 32–39
  preschool and, 48–50
Big and little book center, 259
Big books, 144, 185–186
  shared reading with, 223–226
Biographies, 146
Birthday charts, 220
Black English, 323
Book clubs, 162, 284
Bookhandling skills, 34
Books
  alphabet, 374
  attitudes toward, 34
  beginning readers, 144
  chapter, 144
  first storybooks, 49–50
  informational, 70, 146, 234–235
  language play, 375–376
  meaning and, 35
  multicultural, 157, 321–322, 376–377
  picture, 144, 146–147
  predictable, 146, 375
  take-home, 256, 259–261
  for very young children, 373–374
  word play, 179
  wordless, 46, 146, 374
Booksharing, 40–46, 183–184
  guidelines for, 18
  meaning making in, 43–44
  routines in, 34

Calendar routine, 180
Call and response, 294
Causal relationships, 69
Chapter books, 144
Character, of story, 120
Character cluster, 287–288
Checklists, 347
Child care, and literacy, 48–50
Child-centered classroom, 276–277
Choral reading, 221
  enhancement with music, movement, and sound effects, 294
  types of, 293–294

Circle stories, 288
Classroom
  assessment in, 345–349
  child-centered, 276–277
  computers in, 280–281
  literacy-rich, 142–143
  literature in, 144–148
  physical arrangement of, 148–152, 164–165
Classroom print, 219
Classroom routines, 152–156
Climax, of story, 120
Closed syllables, 302
Clothesline props, 153, 155, 189
Cognitive engagement, levels of, 63
Communication, intention of, 59
Community
  involvement in instruction, 319–320
  as resource, 322
Composition
  analysis of, 360, 362–364
  by copying, 93
  by dictation, 92
  by spelling, 94
Comprehension
  expanding, 285–291
  teaching for, 256, 264
  skills in, 133, 134, 245
Computer center, 148, 149–152, 259
  software for, 152
Computers, classroom use of, 280
Concept of story, 44–46
Concept of word, 21, 87–89, 118
Concept-about-story activities, 184
Concepts, 2
  of print, 184–186
  related, 3
Concepts-about-print task, 350–351
Conference groups, 280
Confirmation, in reading, 114
Conflict, of story, 120
Consistency, defined, 122
Constructivism, 320
Content units, organizing, 296–298
Content-specific vocabulary, 299–300
Context bound, vs. print bound, 95
Contextual analysis, 245
Contextual dependency, 71–72
Contextualization clues, 16
Contextualized written language, 60
Continuum of literacy development, 48–49
Controlled vocabulary basals, 245–247
Conventional readers and writers, 26
  examples of, 112–113
  forms mastery by, 117–128, 135
  identifying, 111–112
  instruction for, 241–242
  meaning making by, 114–117, 135
  and meaning-form links, 128–133, 135
  and writing functions, 133, 135
Cooperative reading groups, 162
Core literature approach, 283–284
Critical comprehension, 245
Cue systems, 114
Cultural discontinuity, 316
Cultural relevance, 321
Cultural sensitivity, 156–158
Culturally authentic literature, 157
Culturally diverse children, 313
Culturally relevant topics, 156
Culturally responsive instruction, 316–319
  in multicultural settings, 319–322
Culture, literacy experiences embedded in, 49
Curriculum
  culturally sensitive and integrated, 156–158
  defined, 156
Cursive, mock, 91

Daily Oral Language (DOL), 247–248
Decodable basals, 245
Decoding
  by analogy, 130
  whole to part to whole, 243
Decontextualized language, 44
Demonstrations, by students, 212–213
Developmental delays, and literacy learning, 314
Developmentally appropriate practice, 48, 140–142
Dialogue markers, 97–98
Dictation, 92
  dialect and, 326–328
  English as a second language and, 330
Dictionaries, 147
Digraphs, vowel, 251
Diphthongs, vowel, 251
Direct instruction, 212–218
Directed reading lessons, 245–246
Directed reading-thinking activity (DRTA), 246
Discovery strategies, 128

Diverse cultural background, and literacy learning, 315–322
Diverse language backgrounds, 323
dialect, 323–328
English as a second language, 328–332
Divide and compare/contrast strategy, 302
Drafting, defined, 279
Dramatic-play-with-print centers, 196–197, 232–234
Drawing
attitudes toward, 37–38
characteristics of, 38
and meaning-form links, 72–74
symbolic value of, 39
Drawing materials, and literacy development, 35–36
Drawing routines, 38
Dynamic ability groups, 256

Early invented spelling, 102
Early orthographic spelling, 129–130, 130–131
Ebonics, 324
Editing
checklist for, 280
defined, 279
Elkonin boxes, 204
Emergent reading, 70
checklist for, 351, 352
Emotional disabilities, and literacy learning, 314–315
Engagement, levels of, 63
English as a second language, 313
and instruction in spoken English, 328–329
and reading and writing in English, 329–332
Environmental print, 46–47, 59–60
Environmental print puzzles, 176
Episodes, 120
Ethnicity, 315
Evaluative meaning, 63
Experience-text-relationship approach to guided reading, 320–321
Experimenters
attitude of, 8
defined, 26
examples of, 86–87
forms experimentation by, 87–94, 106
identifying, 84–86
and meaning-form links, 94–104, 106
meaning-making by, 87, 106
and written language, 104–105, 106
Explicit focus on print, 204–205
Expositions
defined, 122
types of, 123–127
Expository writing, 123–127
combined with narrative, 127–128
form of, 363
structure of, 122–123
Extended discourse, 331–332
Extended sign-in procedure, 228–229, 231

Fables, 145
Fantasy, 145
Features, 2
Fiction, types of, 145
Finger-point reading, 98
First grade, 240–241
balanced reading and writing programs in, 243–244
reading in, 241–243
reading instruction in, 244–266
writing instruction in, 266–272
First storybooks, 49–50
Fix-up strategies, 114
Flannel board props, 154
Flashlight reading, 249
Fluency, defined, 255
Folktales, 145
Form, 16–21, 24
analysis of, 360, 362–363
conventional readers and, 117–128, 135
experimenters and, 87–94, 106
links with meaning. *See* Meaning-form links
novices and, 65–71, 79
Functions of language, 13–15, 24
beginners and, 51
conventional readers and, 133, 135
experimenters and, 104, 106
novices and, 75–77, 79

Grand conversations, 264, 357–360
Graphemes, 17
Grapho-phonic relationships, 22
Graphs, 176
Guided reading, 162
experience-text-relationship approach to, 320–321
talk-through and, 259–261
teaching for strategies in, 261–262

Guided reading approach, 255–266
  characteristics of, 256

Handwriting, 281
Herringbone, 288, 289
Heuristic language, 14
Hierarchical relationships, 122
High-frequency words, 246
Hispanic Americans, learning environment for, 316, 319
Historical fiction, 145
Home, and literacy development, 39–48
Homogeneous reading abilities, 161
Homographs, 301
Homophones, 301

"I can hear" activities, 179
"I can read" bags, 176
Idea circles, 296
Identity of sound, 101
Imaginative language, 14
Independent reading 155, 162
Independent reading level, 254–255
Independent writing, 155, 163
Individualized educational plan (IEP), 314
Infants, and schemas, 3–4
Inferential comprehension, 245
Inferential meaning, 63
Informational books, 146
  classroom dramatization of, 234–235
  organization of, 70
Informational text analysis sheet, 357, 358
Informational writing, 269–270
  comprehension of, 295–296
  reading, 296–297
  writing, 298–299
Informative language, 14
Informed refusal, 91
Instruction
  balanced, 277–278
  community collaboration in, 319–320, 322
  constructivist models of, 320
  culturally responsive, 316–319
  direct, 212–218
  framework for, 161–163
  through interaction, 320
  portfolios and, 364–365
  variety of, 160
Instructional reading event, 244
Instructional reading level, 255
Instrumental language, 14
Integrated content units, 158
Integration
  of curriculum, 157
  of language arts, 157
Intentionality, ascribing, 38
Interactional language, 14
Interactive read alouds, 187, 189–190
Interactive storytelling, 285
Interactive writing, 163, 229, 256, 262–263
Interpretation
  defined, 114–115
  of literature, 291–292
Invented spelling, 89, 211
  stages of, 101

Journal, 226–228, 231
  in first grade, 266–267
  response, 156, 282, 357

Kid watching, 160
Kindergarten
  literacy in, 204–205
  phonemic awareness in, 211–218
  play in, 232–235
  reading in, 208–211, 219–226
  research in, 209
  sample day in, 340–345
  setting for, 206–207
  teacher's role in, 205–206, 235–236
  writing in, 208–211, 226–232
King Elementary School case, 323–323
Knowledge(s)
  comprehending, integrating, and communicating, 297
  creation of, 4
  observing and personalizing, 296
  repertoire of, 59
  searching and retrieving, 296–297

Label exposition, 123
Language
  decontextualized, 44
  functions of, 13–15
  home and, 47–48
  integrated arts of, 157
  literary, 16
  meaning in, 15–16
  oral interactions, 47
Language arts, integration of, 244

Language development, 9–27
  Piagetian view of, 7
  schemas and, 2–4
  social context of, 4–5
  Vygotskian view of, 7–9
Language disabilities, and literacy learning, 314–315
Language experience approach, 229–230
Language interactions
  at home, 47–48
  oral, 47
Language play books, 375–376
Later orthographic spelling, 129, 131–132
Learning
  cultural and social context of, 12–13, 316
  language and, 4–6
  questioning and, 317–318
  schemas and, 2–4
  social basis for, 4–5
Learning disabilities, and literacy learning, 314–315
Left-to-right organization, 19
Legends, 145
Legibility, 281
Letter and word center, 259
Letter game, 172
Letter name strategy, 101
Letter strings, 63
Letterlike forms, 63, 65
Letters
  concept of, 65
  features of, 65
  relationship to sounds, 99–104
  stringing together, 91
Leveled texts, 256, 257–258
Library center, 148–149, 150, 259
Linearity, 19
Linguistically diverse children, 323–324
  literacy instruction for, 325–332
Linking to the known, 260
Listening center, 259
List
  group, and label activity, 291
  making, 193
Literacy
  first-person experiences and, 322
  materials for, 49–50
  preschool, 172–173
  routines for, 152–156
Literacy centers, 256, 258–259
Literacy development
  child care and, 48–50
  continuum of, 48–49
  culture and, 49
  early, 32–39
  early book experiences and, 33–35
  home influences on, 39–48
  in nursery school, 48–50
  Piagetian view of, 7
  Vygotskian view of, 7–9
Literacy experiences, embedded in culture, 49
Literacy knowledges, repertoire of, 59
Literacy learning
  English as a second language and, 328–332
  nonmainstream dialect and, 323–328
  variation in, 141–142
Literacy materials, 143–148
Literacy-rich classroom, 142–143
  assessment in, 160
  audiovisual materials in, 147
  curriculum for, 156–158
  instructional framework for, 161–163
  literature in, 144–148
  physical arrangement of, 148–152, 164–165
  reference material in, 147–148
  routines in, 152–156
Literal comprehension, 245
Literal meaning, 61
Literary awareness, 183
Literary language, 16
Literary opposites, 291
Literary prop boxes, 190
Literary syntax, 87
Literature
  alphabet books, 374
  books for very young children, 373–374
  chapter books, 144
  comprehension of, 285–291
  culturally authentic, 157
  discussions of, 283, 284
  first storybooks, 49–50
  genres of, 144–147
  informational, 70, 146, 234–235
  interpretation of, 291–292
  language play books, 375–376
  multicultural, 157, 321–322, 376–377
  predictable books, 146, 375
  response to, 155–156, 284
  traditional, 145
  wordless books, 46, 146, 374
Literature circles, 162, 284

Literature theme units, 158
Literature-based basals, 246
Logographic reading and writing, 24–25
Long questions, 292

Magazines, children's, 148
Main idea-detail exposition, 123–125
Mainstream dialect, defined, 323
Make-a-word activities, 264
Meaning, 15–16, 24
  analysis of, 364
  books and, 35
  conventional readers and writers and, 114–117
  of environmental print, 59–60
  evaluative, 63
  experimenters and, 87, 106
  inferential, 63
  literal, 61
  novices and, 61–65
  social construction of, 277
Meaning-based spelling, 129, 132–133
Meaning-form links, 12, 21–24
  contextual dependency and, 71–72
  by conventional readers, 128–133, 135
  by experimenters, 94–104, 106
  through letter and scribble strings, 22–23
  by matching print and speech, 23–24
  by novices, 72–75, 79
Meaning-making strategies, 43–44
  of experimenters, 87, 106
  of novices, 61–65, 79
Metacognitive awareness, 114
Metalinguistic awareness, 21, 87, 180
Mexican Americans, learning environment for, 316, 319
Minilessons, 268, 279, 282
Miscue analysis, 354–355
Mock cursive, 91
Mock letters, 17–18, 66
Monitoring, as strategy for reading, 114
Mood, of story, 120, 121
Morphemes, 15, 118
Motor schemes, 38
Multicultural literature, 157, 321–322, 376–377
Multiple-character perspective, 292
Myths, 145

Name displays, 180
Naming actions, 46
Naming game, 34
Narrative, 121–122
  combined with exposition, 127–128
  comprehension and interpretation of, 285–293
  core literature approach to, 283–284
  elements of, 120–121
Native Americans, learning environment for, 318
Non-spelling, 101–102
Nonimmediate events, 47
Nonmainstream dialect, 323
  attitudes toward, 324
  and literacy instruction, 325–328
  types of, 323–324
Novices
  defined, 25
  distinguished from beginners, 56
  examples of, 57–59
  and forms of writing, 65–71, 79
  identified, 56–57
  meaning making by, 61–65, 79
  and meaning-form links, 71–75, 79
  and writing, 75–77, 79
Nursery school, and literacy, 48–50

Object props, 153
Observation, as assessment tool, 349–350
Observation notebook, 345
Onset, defined, 103, 178
Open syllables, 302
Opposites, literary, 291
Ordered expositions, 126–127
Ordered paragraphs, 126
Ordered relationships, 122
Orthographic reading and writing, 27, 130
Orthographic spelling, 129–132
Orthographics, 22

Paragraphs, ordered, 126
Participation structures, 318
Partner reading, 162, 252–253
Pattern stories, 192
Patterned writing, 193, 253
Performance strategies, 128
Personal language, 14
Phonemes, 21–22, 75–76
  defined, 100
  deletion of, 215
  segmenting of, 182, 215
Phonemic awareness, 22, 75, 100
  assessment of, 351
  direct instruction of, 212

in kindergarten, 211
in preschool, 178–183
Phonetic cue reading, 103–104
Phonics, 22, 75, 85, 134, 245
generalizations for, 250–251
Phonograms, 22, 130
frequency of, 265
Phonological awareness, 22, 75
Phonological knowledge, 22
Phonology, 13, 24
Piagetian theory of learning, 2–4
on literacy development, 7
Picture books, 144
genres of, 146–147
Pictures, as symbols, 34–35
Play, 175–177
dramatic-play-with-print centers, 196–197, 232–234
dramatizing informational books, 234–235
storytelling and, 198–199
text and toy sets, 197–198
Plot, 120
Pocket charts, 182
Pocket-chart activity, 253
Poem, spelling, 249
Poem-a-day, 294
Poetry
defined, 146
elements of, 295
enhancement with music, movement, and sound effects, 294
enjoying, 293–295
writing of, 271–272
Poetry festival, establishing, 295
Point of difficulty, 256
Point of view, of story, 120
Pointer reading, 222–223
Polysyllabic words, 131
Portfolio
assessment of, 346–349
defined, 345
to guide reflection, 365
to inform parents, 365–366
and instructional decisions, 364–365
managing, 366–367
Portfolio conferences, 365
Portfolio summaries, 365
Pragmatics, 13, 24
Predictable books, 146, 375
Predictable-text basals, 246
Prediction, 114
Preparation
for phonemic awareness, 212
preschool and, 178–186
Preschool
books in, 186–190
literacy in, 172–173
play in, 175–177, 196–199
preparatory role of, 178–186
setting for, 173–175
teacher's role in, 177–178, 199–200
writing in, 190–196
writing center in, 191–192
Pretend readings, 70
Prevention of Learning Disabilities, 312
Previewing, defined, 212
Print, tracking, 95
Prior knowledge, drawing on, 128
Process writing approach, 267
Props, for storytelling, 152, 153–155
Publishing, defined, 279
Puppets, 154
Purely phonetic spelling, 102

Question-making activity, 291
Questions, characteristics of, 291–292

Reader's theater, 285–287
Reading
aloud, 153–155, 161–162, 187–190
alphabetic, 25–26, 95, 211
basal approach to, 244–255
before, during, and after events, 244
choral, 221, 293–294
conventional, 26
dialect and, 325–326
directed, 245–246
emergent, 70, 95, 351
by English as a second language students, 329–332
finger-point, 98
flashlight, 249
guided, 162, 209–211, 259–262, 320–321
guided reading approach to, 255–266
independent, 155, 162
logographic, 24–25
meaning making in, 114–116
monitoring as strategy for, 114
of new words, 216
by novices, 56

Reading *(cont.)*
orthographic, 27, 130
parallel, 97
partner, 162, 252–253
phonetic cue, 103–104
pointer, 222–223
precision in, 98
preschool experiences with, 186–190
pretend, 70
repeated, 314
self-selected, 253–255
shared, 162, 186–189, 220–226, 252
SSR, 155
by word, 241–242
Reading block, defined, 282
Reading conferences, 282
Reading level
independent, 254–255
instructional, 255
Reading Recovery, 310–311
lessons of, 311–312
Reading workshops, 162
aspects of, 282–283
Realistic fiction, 145
Recording grid, 297
Reductionism, pitfall of, 315
Reference materials, 147
Refusal, informed, 91
Regulatory language, 14
Rehearsing, defined, 279
Related concepts, 3
Repeated reading, 314
Repertoire of literacy knowledges, 59
Representational drawings, 39
Research, kindergarten-style, 209
Response journal, 156, 282, 357
Response-to-literature activities, 155–156
Response-to-literature checklist, 358, 361
Retelling, 356
checklist for, 356–357
Revising, defined, 279
Rhymes, making, 181–183
Rime, defined, 103, 179
Romancing, 38
"Rounding Up the Rhymes," 182, 216–218
Running record, 351
taking, 351–354

Say-it-and-move-it activities, 218
Scaffolding, 5–6, 320
Scale of emergent readings, 95
Schemas, 2–3
infants and, 3–4
and learning, 3
Scope and sequence of skills, 245
Scribbles, writinglike, 63
Segmenting, of phonemes, 182, 215
Semantics, 13, 24
Sentences, features of, 19
Sequence, 69
Setting, 119, 120
Shared language approach, to ESL teaching, 331
Shared reading, 162, 186–189, 252
with big books, 223–226
steps in, 220–223
Shared writing, 163, 190–191, 192–193, 229–232
Sight vocabulary, 245
Sight words, 99, 241–242
Sign concept, 71
Sign-in, 192, 208–209
extended, 228–229, 231
Signatures, 66–68
concepts about, 68
Signs, making, 233–234
Skills
scope and sequence of, 245
and strategies, 243
Social class, 315
Social construction of meaning, 277
Solo and chorus poetry reading, 294
Sound, identity of, 101
Sound-letter relationships, 21, 99–104
Sounding literate, 95–98
Special-needs children
defined, 313
literacy for, 313–314
modifying instruction for, 314–315
Specials center, 259
Specials schedule, 219–220
Speech, written language-like, 97
Spelling
analysis of, 364
composition by, 94
generalizations for, 250–251
invented, 89, 211
programs to teach, 302–303
stages of invented, 101
strategies for, 128–133
Spelling challenge, 303
Spelling cycle, 302–303

Spelling patterns, 216
Spelling poem, 249
Spoken English, teaching, 325, 328–329
Spoken language
functions in, 13–15
phonological system in, 21–22
semantics in, 15–16
strategies for using, 15
syntax in, 17
Stanzas, inventing, 217
Status of the class, defined, 279
Stories
all-about, 118
circle, 288
classroom use of, 153–155
concept of, 44–46, 69, 184–186
form of, 118–122, 362–363
literary elements in, 119–121
retelling of, 285
well-developed, 287
writing of, 193–195, 268–269
Story extensions, 192
Story grammars, 45
Story retelling analysis sheet, 357
Story-as-a-whole, 69
Storybook reading styles, 63
Storybooks, first, 49–50
Storytelling, interactive, 285
Storytelling and playing, 198–199
Storytelling props, 152, 153–155
Strategies, and skills, 243
Structural analysis, 245
Style, of story, 120, 121
Subtractive approaches, to ESL teaching, 329
Success for All, 312
Summarization, 114
Sustained silent reading (SSR), 155
Symbols
defined, 115
pictures as, 34–35
Syntax, 13, 17, 24
literary, 87

Tabula rasa, 3
Take-home books, 253–255
Talk-throughs, 256, 259–261
Teaching for comprehension, 256, 264
Teaching for strategies, 256, 261–262, 278, 292–293
Text and toy sets, 197–198
Text features, 68
Text forms, 68
Texts
experimenters' use of, 89–94
formats of, 19–20
leveled, 256
reconstruction of, 222
Theme
defined, 115
of story, 120, 121
Thinking aloud, 296
Top-to-bottom organization, 19
Tracking, of print, 95
Traditional literature, 145
Transaction, defined, 115

Vietnamese Americans, learning environment for, 319
Visual dictionaries, 147
Visualization, 114
Vocabulary
content-specific, 299–300
word clusters and, 288–291
Vocabulary knowledge, 133, 134
Vocabulary skills, 245
Voice-to-print match, 98
Vowels, 216
digraphs and diphthongs of, 251
Vygotskian theory of learning, 4–6
on literacy development, 7–9

Wallach Tutoring Program, 312
"What Can You Show Us" activity, 212
Whole to part to whole decoding, 243
Word(s)
concept of, 21, 87–89, 118
features of, 18–19
high-frequency, 246
identification of, 245
for the week, 248
Word boundaries, 89
Word clusters, 288–291
Word families, 128–129
Word frames, 214–215
Word hunts, 301
Word identification, 133, 134
Word play books, 179
Word pool, 303
Word recognition analysis, 355
Word sorts, 265

Word study, 256, 264–265
  aspects of, 301–303
Word wall, 248–252
Wordless picture books, 46, 146, 374
Words for Today, 230
Work samples, 347
Writers, novice, 56
Writing
  alphabetic, 25–26
  breaking into print, 85
  concepts about, 184–186
  contextualized, 60
  conventional, 26
  dialect and, 325–326
  by English as a second language students, 329–332
  expository, 123–128
  hybrid forms of, 127–128
  independent, 155, 163
  informational, 269–270
  interactive, 163, 229, 256, 262–263
  language forms, 65–71
  logographic, 24–25
  matching to spoken language, 72, 86
  meaning making in, 116–117
  and meaning-form links, 72–74
  narrative, 118–122
  of new words, 216
  by novices, 75–77
  orthographic, 27, 130
  patterned, 193, 253
  poetry, 271–272
  preschool, 56–59
  processes of, 279
  referential dimension of, 117
  shared, 163, 190–191, 192–193, 229–232
  story, 118–122, 193–195, 268–269
  word-by-word understanding of, 86
Writing block, defined, 279
Writing center, 148, 149, 259
  materials for, 151
Writing materials, and literacy development, 35–36
Writing the room, 229
Writing routines, 38
Writing workshop, 163, 267–268
  aspects of, 278–281
  format of, 279
Writinglike scribbles, 63
Written language
  attitudes toward, 37–38
  characteristics of, 38
  children's concepts about, 9–13
  conventions about, 300–303
  forms in, 17–21
  functional and contextualized experiences with, 212
  functions in, 13–15
  meaning in, 16
  meaning-form links in, 22–24
  metalinguistic awareness of, 21
  strategies for using, 15
Written language talk, 195–196
Written language-like talk, 97

Zone of proximal development, 5–6